Rick Steves'
GERMANY
AUSTRIA &
SWITZERLAND
2004

GERMANY, AUSTRIA & SWITZERLAND

══A24══	Freeway/Motorway
	Major Roads
	Major Rail Line
✈	Airport
St. Goar	Recommended Location*
Bebra	Just passing through**
■	Ruin, Museum, Other Point of Interest
🏰	Castle/Monument/Palace

* Black locations are places of interest to tourists, sized by importance.

** Gray locations are not places of interest to tourists and are sized by population.

0 km	50	100 km

0 miles	50 miles

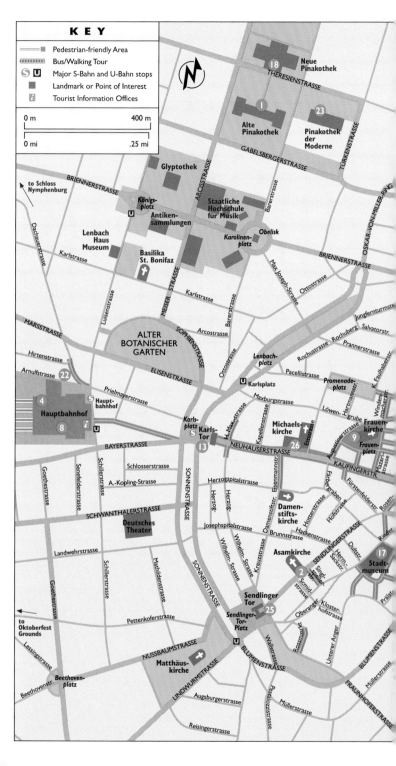

KEY

- Pedestrian-friendly Area
- Bus/Walking Tour
- **S** **U** Major S-Bahn and U-Bahn stops
- Landmark or Point of Interest
- *i* Tourist Information Offices

0 m   400 m

0 mi   .25 mi

THERESIENSTRASSE

18 Neue Pinakothek

1 Alte Pinakothek

23 Pinakothek der Moderne

TÜRKENSTRASSE

GABELSBERGERSTRASSE

Glyptothek

BRIENNERSTRASSE

Königsplatz

Antikensammlungen

ARCOSSTRASSE

Staatliche Hochschule für Musik

Barerstrasse

OSKAR-VON-MILLER-RING

Lenbach Haus Museum

Basilika St. Bonifaz

Karolinenplatz

Obelisk

to Schloss Nymphenburg

MEISER STRASSE

Karlstrasse

BRIENNERSTRASSE

Dachauerstrasse

Luisenstrasse

SOPHIENSTRASSE

Karlstrasse

Arcosstrasse

Barerstrasse

Max Joseph-Strasse

Ottostrasse

MARSSTRASSE

ALTER BOTANISCHER GARTEN

Jungfernturmstr.

Hirtenstrasse

ELISENSTRASSE

Lenbachplatz

Rochusstrasse

Rochusberg

Salvatorstr.

Prannerstrasse

Arnulfstrasse

22

Prielmayerstrasse

Pacellistrasse

Promenadeplatz

K. Faulhaberstr.

Hartmannstr.

4 Hauptbahnhof

S Hauptbahnhof

8 *i* **U**

U Karlsplatz

Maxburgstrasse

Löwen-grube

Windenmacherstr.

Frauenkirche

9 Frauenplatz

BAYERSTRASSE

Karlsplatz

Karls-Tor

S

13

Karls-Tor

NEUHAUSERSTRASSE

H.-Mack-Strasse

Kapellenstrasse

Michaelskirche

26

Ettstrasse

Augustinerstrasse

Fürstenfelderstr.

KAUFINGERSTR

Rosen-

Nazar-

KAUFINGERSTR.

Schlosserstrasse

A.-Kopling-Strasse

Herzogspitalstrasse

Eisenmannstr.

Färbergraben

Hofstatt

Goethestrasse

Senefelderstrasse

Schillerstrasse

SCHWANTHALERSTRASSE

SONNENSTRASSE

Herzog-

Herzog-

Josephspitalstrasse

Damenstiftstr.

Kreuzstrasse

Damenstiftskirche

Hotterstr.

Hackenstrasse

Brunnstrasse

Fürstenfelderstr.

Deutsches Theater

Landwehrstrasse

Mathildenstrasse

Wilhelm-Strasse

Asamkirche

2

SENDLINGERSTRASSE

Hermstr.

Dultstr.

Stadt-museum

17

to Oktoberfest Grounds

Goethestrasse

Schillerstrasse

Pettenkoferstrasse

SONNENSTRASSE

Sendlinger Tor

25

Sendlinger-Tor-Platz

Sendl-Straße

Sckmid-strasse

Rossmarkt

Oberanger

Kloster-hofstrasse

Unterer Anger

Prälat-

BLUMENSTRASSE

FRAUNHOFERSTRASSE

Lessingstrasse

Beethovenstr.

Beethovenplatz

U

NUSSBAUMSTRASSE

Matthäuskirche

LINDWURMSTRASSE

Augsburgerstrasse

BLUMENSTRASSE

Wallstrasse

Müllerstrasse

Pestalozzistrasse

Reisingerstrasse

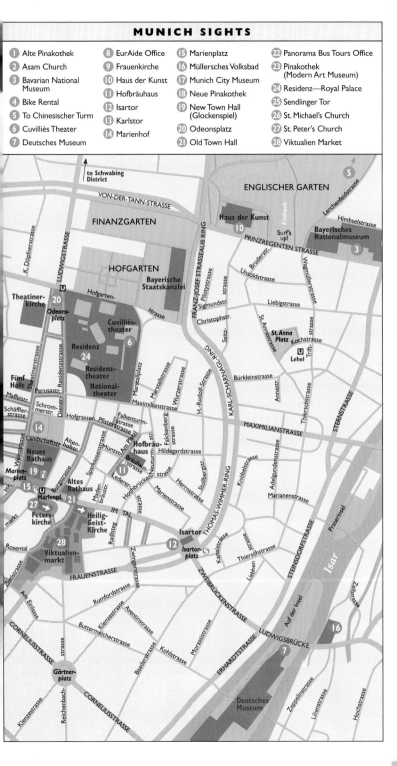

MUNICH SIGHTS

1. Alte Pinakothek
2. Asam Church
3. Bavarian National Museum
4. Bike Rental
5. To Chinesischer Turm
6. Cuvilliés Theater
7. Deutsches Museum
8. EurAide Office
9. Frauenkirche
10. Haus der Kunst
11. Hofbräuhaus
12. Isartor
13. Karlstor
14. Marienhof
15. Marienplatz
16. Müllersches Volksbad
17. Munich City Museum
18. Neue Pinakothek
19. New Town Hall (Glockenspiel)
20. Odeonsplatz
21. Old Town Hall
22. Panorama Bus Tours Office
23. Pinakothek (Modern Art Museum)
24. Residenz—Royal Palace
25. Sendlinger Tor
26. St. Michael's Church
27. St. Peter's Church
28. Viktualien Market

BERLIN SIGHTS

1. Alexanderplatz
2. Bahnhof Zoo Station & EurAide
3. Bebelplatz
4. Berlin Cathedral
5. Berlin Philharmonic
6. Brandenburg Gate
7. Erotic Art Museum
8. Europa Center
9. Gemäldegalerie (Painting Gallery)
10. Gendarmenmarkt
11. German History Museum
12. German Resistance Memorial
13. Hackesche Höfe (Courtyard Shops)
14. Haus am Checkpoint Charlie Museum
15. Jewish Museum Berlin
16. KaDeWe Department Store
17. Kaiser Wilhelm Memorial Church
18. Käthe Kollwitz Museum
19. Lehrter Station
20. Museum of Arts and Crafts
21. Music Instruments Museum
22. Natural History Museum
23. Neue Wache Memorial
24. New National Gallery (Modern Art)
25. New Synagogue
26. Old National Gallery
27. Palace of the Republic
28. Pariser Platz
29. Pergamon Museum
30. Potsdamer Platz
31. Reichstag
32. Savignyplatz (Hotels)
33. Siegessäule Column
34. Topography of Terror
35. TV Tower
36. Zoo

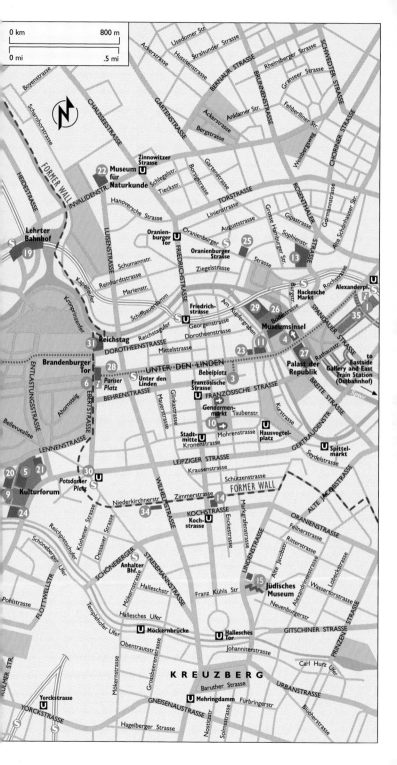

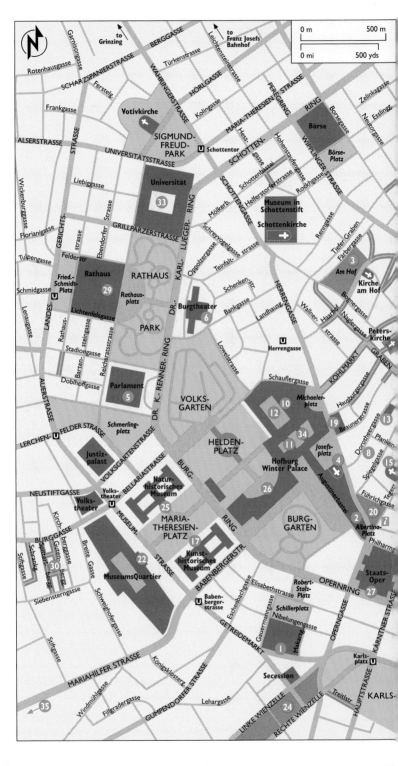

VIENNA SIGHTS

1. Academy of Fine Arts
2. Albertina Museum
3. Am Hof Square
4. Augustinian Church
5. Austrian Parliament
6. Burgtheater
7. Cathedral Museum
8. Dorotheum Auction
9. Haus der Musik
10. Hofburg Imperial Apartments
11. Hofburg Treasury
12. In der Burg Square
13. Jewish Museum
14. Judenplatz Memorial and Museum
15. Kaisergruft
16. To KunstHausWien & Hundertwasserhaus
17. Kunsthistorisches Museum
18. Kursalon
19. Lipizzaner Museum
20. Monument Against War and Fascism
21. Museum of Applied Arts
22. MuseumsQuartier
23. Musikverein
24. Nasch Market
25. Natural History Museum
26. New Palace
27. Opera
28. To Prater Park/ Ferris Wheel & Danube Hydrofoils
29. Rathaus (City Hall)
30. Spittelberg Quarter
31. St. Stephan's Cathedral
32. Stephansplatz
33. University
34. Vienna Boys' Choir Chapel
35. To Westbahnhof and Mariahilfer Strasse Hotels and Schönbrunn Palace
36. Wien Ticket Pavilion

Rick Steves'
GERMANY
AUSTRIA &
SWITZERLAND
2004

AVALON
TRAVEL

For a list of Rick Steves' guidebooks, see page 10.

Avalon Travel Publishing
1400 65th Street, Suite 250
Emeryville, CA 94608
Avalon Travel Publishing is a division of Avalon Publishing Group.

Printed in the USA by Worzalla. First printing December 2003.
Distributed by Publishers Group West.

ISBN 1-56691-526-0
ISSN 1085-7222

For the latest on Rick's lectures, guidebooks, tours, and public television series, contact Europe Through the Back Door, Box 2009, Edmonds, WA 98020, 425/771-8303, fax 425/771-0833, www.ricksteves.com, rick@ricksteves.com.

Thanks to my hardworking team at Europe Through the Back Door, and most of all to my wife, Anne, for her support.

Europe Through the Back Door Managing Editor: Risa Laib
Europe Through the Back Door Editor: Cameron Hewitt
Avalon Travel Publishing Editor and Series Manager: Laura Mazer
Copy Editor: Kate McKinley
Research Assistance: Cameron Hewitt, Kristen Kusnic, Susana Minich
Production & Typesetting: PDBD
Cover Design: Kari Gim, Laura Mazer
Interior Design: Jane Musser, Amber Pirker, Laura Mazer
Maps & Graphics: David C. Hoerlein, Rhonda Pelikan, Zoey Platt, Mike Morgenfeld
Front Matter Color Photos: p. i, © Rick Steves; p. viii, Schloss Linderhof, Bavaria © Andrew Wakeford/Getty Images/Photodisc Green; p. ix, Alphorn Music Celebration, Munich, Germany © Bachmann/PHOTOPHILE; p. xii, Hallstatt, Austria © 2003 Digital Vision
Cover Photo: Front: © Alan and Sandy Carey/Getty Images/Photodisc Green; Back: © Dominic Bonucelli
Avalon Travel Publishing Graphics Coordinator: Susan Snyder

CONTENTS

Top Destinations in Germany, Austria, and Switzerland

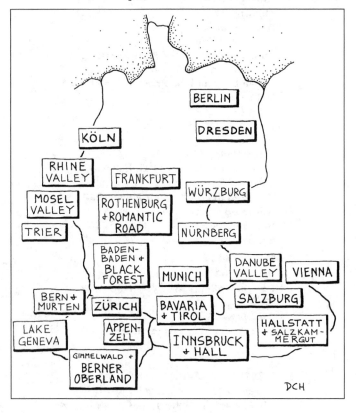

INTRODUCTION

This book breaks Germany, Austria, and Switzerland into their top big-city, small-town, and rural destinations. It then gives you all the information and opinions necessary to wring the maximum value out of your limited time and money in each of these destinations. If you plan a month or less in this region, this lean and mean little book is all you need.

Experiencing this region's culture, people, and natural wonders economically and hassle-free has been my goal for 25 years of traveling, tour guiding, and travel writing. With this book, I pass on to you the lessons I've learned, updated (in mid-2003) for 2004.

Rick Steves' Germany, Austria & Switzerland is your friendly Franconian, your German in a jam, a tour guide in your pocket. The book includes a balance of cities and villages, mountaintop hikes and forgotten Roman ruins, sleepy river cruises and sky-high gondola rides. It covers the predictable biggies while mixing in a healthy dose of Back Door intimacy.

Along with visiting Rhine castles, Mozart's house, and the Vienna Opera, you'll ride a thrilling Austrian mountain luge, soak in a Black Forest mineral spa, share a beer with Bavarian monks, and ramble through traffic-free Swiss alpine towns. I've been selective, including only the most exciting sights. For example, it's redundant to visit both the Matterhorn and the Jungfrau. I take you up and around the better of the two (the Jungfrau).

The best is, of course, only my opinion. But after more than two busy decades of travel writing, lecturing, and tour guiding, I've developed a sixth sense for what stokes the traveler's wanderlust. Just thinking about the places featured in this book makes me want to slap dance and yodel.

This Information Is Accurate and Up-to-Date

This book is updated every year. Most publishers of guidebooks that cover a country from top to bottom can afford an update only every two or three years (and, even then, it's often by letter). Since this book is selective, covering only the top destinations in Germany, Austria, and Switzerland, I am able to update it personally each year. Even with an annual update, things change. But if you're traveling with the current edition of this book, I guarantee you're using the most up-to-date information available (for the latest, see www.ricksteves.com/update). Also at our Web site, check our Graffiti Wall (select "Rick Steves' guidebooks," then "Germany, Austria & Switzerland") for a huge, valuable list of reports and experiences—good and bad—from fellow travelers.

Use this year's edition. You'd be crazy to save a few bucks by traveling on old information. If you're packing an old book, you'll understand the gravity of your mistake...in Europe. Your trip costs about $10 per waking hour. Your time is valuable. This guidebook saves lots of time.

Planning Your Trip

This book is organized by destination. Each destination is covered as a mini-vacation on its own, filled with exciting sights and homey, affordable places to stay. In each chapter, you'll find:

Planning Your Time, a suggested schedule with thoughts on how best to use your limited time.

Orientation, including tourist information, city transportation, and an easy-to-read map designed to make the text clear and your arrival smooth.

Sights with ratings: ▲▲▲—Worth getting up early and skipping breakfast for; **▲▲**—Worth getting up early for; **▲**—Worth seeing if it's convenient; No rating—Worth knowing about.

Sleeping and Eating, with addresses and phone numbers of my favorite budget hotels and restaurants.

Transportation Connections, including train information and route tips for drivers, with recommended roadside attractions along the way.

The **appendix** is a traveler's tool kit, with a climate chart, telephone tips, rail routes, and German survival phrases.

Browse through this book, choose your favorite destinations, and link them together. Then have a great trip! You won't waste time on mediocre sights because, unlike other guidebook authors, I cover only the best. Since lousy, expensive hotels are a major financial pitfall, I've worked hard to assemble the best accommodations values for each stop. You'll travel like a temporary local, getting the absolute most out of every mile, minute, and dollar. As you travel the route I know and love, I'm happy you'll be meeting some of my favorite Europeans.

Trip Costs

Five components make up your trip cost: airfare, surface transportation, room and board, sightseeing/entertainment, and shopping/miscellany.

Airfare: Don't try to sort through the mess. Get and use a good travel agent. A basic round-trip flight from the United States to Frankfurt should cost $600–1,000 (even cheaper in winter), depending on where you fly from and when. Always consider saving time and money in Europe by flying "open jaw" (flying into one city and out of another).

Surface Transportation: For a three-week whirlwind trip of all my recommended destinations, allow $650 per person for public transportation (train pass and buses) or $600 per person (based on 2 people sharing the car) for a three-week car rental, parking, gas, and insurance. Car rental is cheapest when reserved from the United States. Train passes are normally available only outside of Europe. You may save money by simply buying tickets as you go (see "Transportation," page 13).

Room and Board: You can thrive in this region on $70 a day per person for room and board. A $70-a-day budget per person allows $10 for lunch, $15 for dinner, and $45 for lodging (based on 2 people splitting the cost of a $90 double room that includes breakfast). That's doable. Students and tightwads do it on $40 a day ($20 per bed, $20 for meals and snacks). But budget sleeping and eating require the skills and information covered later in this chapter (and in much more depth in my book *Rick Steves' Europe Through the Back Door*).

Sightseeing and Entertainment: In big cities, figure $5–10 per major sight, $3 for minor ones, and $30–40 for bus tours and splurge experiences (for example, concert tickets, alpine lifts, conducting the beer-hall band). An overall average of $20 a day works for most. Don't skimp here. After all, this category directly powers most of the experiences all the other expenses are designed to make possible.

Shopping and Miscellany: Figure $1 per postcard and $2 per coffee, beer, and ice-cream cone. Shopping can vary in cost from nearly nothing to a small fortune. Good budget travelers find that this category has little to do with assembling a trip full of lifelong and wonderful memories.

Exchange Rates

I've priced things throughout this book in local currencies. Germany and Austria have adopted the euro currency. Switzerland, which isn't a member of the European Union, has retained its traditional currency, the Swiss franc.

---

1 euro (€) = about $1.10.
1 Swiss franc (SF) = about 70 cents, and 1.40 SF = about $1.

One euro is broken down into 100 cents. You'll find coins ranging from one cent to two euros, and bills from five euros to 500 euros. To convert prices in euros to dollars, add 10 percent: €20 = about $22, €45 = about $50.

One Swiss franc is broken down into 100 *Rappen* (or *centimes*, in French Switzerland). To roughly convert prices from Swiss francs into dollars, subtract one-third (for example, 60 SF = about $40—actually, $42). Although Switzerland hasn't officially adopted the euro, the majority of Swiss hotels, restaurants, and shops (especially in touristy areas) accept smaller euro bills. Most businesses will not take euro coins or larger bills, and you'll usually get bad rates (and your change in Swiss francs). Many coin-op phone booths even accept euros (marked with a big yellow €). If you're just passing through the country, never fear: Your euros will work. But if you're staying awhile, get some Swiss francs...they're prettier, anyway.

So, that €65 German cuckoo clock is about $72, the 15-SF Swiss lunch is about $10, and the €90 taxi ride through Vienna is...uh-oh.

Prices, Times, and Discounts

The prices in this book, as well as the hours and telephone numbers, are accurate as of mid-2003. But Europe is always changing, and I know you'll understand that this, like any other guidebook, starts to yellow even before it's printed.

In Europe—and throughout this book—you'll be using the 24-hour clock. After 12:00 noon, keep going—13:00, 14:00, and so on. For anything over 12, subtract 12 and add p.m. (14:00 is 2:00 p.m.).

While discounts for sightseeing and transportation are not listed in this book, youths (under 18) and students (only with International Student Identity Card) often get discounts—but only by asking.

Sightseeing Priorities

Depending on the length of your trip, here are my recommended priorities.

3 days:	Munich, Bavaria, Salzburg
5 days, add:	Romantic Road, Rhine castles
7 days, add:	Rothenburg, slow down
10 days, add:	Berner Oberland (Swiss Alps)
14 days, add:	Vienna, Hallstatt
17 days, add:	Bern, Danube Valley, Tirol (Reutte)
21 days, add:	West Switzerland, Baden-Baden, Mosel Valley, Köln
24 days, add:	Berlin, Appenzell
30 days, add:	Black Forest, Nürnberg, Dresden

(The map on page 6 and the 3-week itinerary on pages 6–7 include everything in the top 30 days except Berlin, Dresden, and Nürnberg.)

When to Go

The "tourist season" runs roughly from May through September.

Summer has its advantages: best weather, snow-free alpine trails, very long days (light until after 21:00), and the busiest schedule of tourist fun.

In spring and fall—May, June, September, and early October—travelers enjoy fewer crowds, milder weather, plenty of harvest and wine festivals, and the ability to grab a room almost whenever and wherever they like.

Winter travelers find concert seasons in full swing, with absolutely no tourist crowds, but some accommodations and sights are either closed or run on a limited schedule. Confirm your sightseeing plans locally, especially when traveling off-season. The weather can be cold and dreary, and nighttime will draw the shades on your sightseeing before dinnertime. You may find the climate chart in the appendix helpful. Pack warm clothing for the Alps no matter when you go.

Red Tape

Currently, Americans need only a passport, but no visa or shots, to travel in Europe. Even as borders fade, when you change countries, you must still change telephone cards, postage stamps, and *Unterhosen.*

Watt's up? If you're bringing electrical gear, you'll need a two-prong adapter plug (sold cheap at travel stores like mine, www.ricksteves .com) and a converter. Travel appliances often have convenient, built-in converters; look for a voltage switch marked 120V (U.S.) and 240V (Europe).

Banking

Bring your ATM, credit, or debit card, along with several hundred dollars in cash as a backup. Traveler's checks are a waste of time and money.

The best and easiest way to get the local currency is to use the omnipresent bank machines (always open, low fees, quick processing); you'll need a PIN code (numbers only, no letters) to use with your Visa or MasterCard. Some ATM bank cards will work at some banks, though Visa and MasterCard are more reliable. Before you go, verify with your bank that your card will work overseas—and let them know you'll be using the card on your trip so they won't question sudden international activity on your account. Bring two cards; demagnetization seems to be a common problem. The word for cash machine in German is *Bankomat.*

If you bring traveler's checks, note that regular banks have the best rates for cashing checks, but many German banks charge €2.50 per check, so rather than cashing five $100 checks, cash one $500 check. For a large exchange, it pays to compare rates and fees. Post offices (business hours) and train stations (long hours) usually change money if you can't get to a bank.

GERMANY, AUSTRIA, AND SWITZERLAND: BEST THREE-WEEK TRIP

Note: Although this itinerary is designed to be done by car, it works by train with minor modifications. For the best three weeks traveling by train, sleep in Füssen rather than Reutte, sleep on the train from Vienna to the Swiss Alps (skipping Hall and Appenzell), skip French Switzerland, skip the Black Forest, and add two days in Berlin, connecting it by night trains.

Just like at home, credit (or debit) cards work easily at larger hotels, restaurants, and shops, but smaller businesses prefer payment in local currency.

Germany: Banks are generally open Monday through Friday from 8:00 to 12:00 and 14:00 to 16:00.

Austria: Bank hours are roughly Monday through Friday from 8:00 to 15:00 and until 17:30 on Thursday. Austrian banks charge exorbitant commissions to cash traveler's checks (about $8). Bring plastic. As a backup, you could carry American Express checks and cash them at

Day	Plan	Sleep in
1	Arrive in Frankfurt	Rothenburg
2	Rothenburg	Rothenburg
3	Romantic Road to the Tirol	Reutte
4	Bavaria and castles	Reutte
5	Reutte to Munich	Munich
6	Munich	Munich
7	Salzburg	Salzburg
8	Salzkammergut Lake District	Hallstatt
9	Mauthausen, Danube to Vienna	Vienna
10	Vienna	Vienna
11	Vienna to the Tirol	Hall
12	Tirol to Swiss Appenzell	Ebenalp
13	Appenzell to Berner Oberland	Gimmelwald
14	Free day in the Alps, hike	Gimmelwald
15	Bern, west to Murten	Murten
16	Lake Geneva and French Switzerland	Murten
17	Murten to Black Forest	Staufen
18	Black Forest	Baden-Baden
19	Baden-Baden, relax, soak	Baden-Baden
20	Drive to the Rhine, castles	Bacharach
21	The Mosel Valley, Burg Eltz	Bacharach or Beilstein
22	Köln and Frankfurt, night train to Berlin, or fly home	

American Express offices (no commission).

Switzerland: Bank hours are typically Monday through Friday from 8:00 to 17:00.

VAT Refunds and Customs Regulations

VAT Refunds: Wrapped into the purchase price of your souvenirs is a Value Added Tax (VAT): 13.8 percent in Germany, 16.7 percent in Austria, and 7 percent in Switzerland. If you make a purchase of more than a certain amount (€25 in Germany, €75 in Austria, and 400 SF in Switzerland) at a store that participates in the VAT refund scheme, you're entitled to get most of that tax back. Personally, I've never felt that VAT refunds are worth the hassle, but if you do, here's the scoop.

If you're lucky, the merchant will subtract the tax when you make your purchase (this is more likely to occur if the store ships the goods to your home). Otherwise, you'll need to do all this:

Get the paperwork. Have the merchant completely fill out the necessary refund document, called a "cheque." You'll have to present your passport at the store.

Have your cheque(s) stamped at the border at your last stop in the country (or as you leave the European Union, if you bought the goods in Germany or Austria) by the customs agent who deals with VAT refunds. It's best to keep your purchases in your carry-on for viewing, but if they're too large or dangerous (such as knives) to carry on, then track down the proper customs agent to inspect them before you check your bag. You're not supposed to use your purchased goods before you leave. If you show up at customs wearing your new lederhosen, officials might look the other way—or deny you a refund.

To collect your refund, you'll need to return your stamped documents to the retailer or its representative. Many merchants work with services such as Global Refund or Cashback that have offices at major airports, ports, or border crossings. These services, which extract a 4 percent fee, can refund your money immediately in your currency of choice or credit your card (within 2 billing cycles). If you have to deal directly with the retailer, mail the store your stamped documents and then wait. It could take months.

Customs Regulations: You can take home $800 in souvenirs per person duty-free. The next $1,000 is taxed at a flat 3 percent. After that, you pay the individual item's duty rate. You can also bring in duty-free a liter of alcohol (slightly more than a standard-size bottle of wine), a carton of cigarettes, and up to 100 cigars. To check customs rules and duty rates, visit www.customs.gov.

Language Barrier

German is the predominant language in Germany and Austria (though each region has slightly different dialects). Most Swiss speak singsongy *Schwyzerdütsch* (Swiss German) around the house, but in schools and at work, they speak and write in the same standard German used in Germany and Austria (called "High" German, or *Hochdeutsch*—though many Swiss prefer to call it *Schriftdeutsch,* or written German).

Most Germans, Austrians, and Swiss in larger towns and the tourist trade speak at least some English. Still, you'll get more smiles by using the German pleasantries. In smaller, nontouristy towns, German is more common. See the "Survival Phrases" near the end of this book (excerpted from *Rick Steves' German Phrase Book*).

German—like English, Dutch, Swedish, and Norwegian—is a

Germanic language, making it easier on most American ears than Romance languages (such as Italian and French). German is pronounced just as it's spelled. There are a few potentially confusing vowel combinations: *ie* is pronounced "ee" (as in *hier* and *Bier,* the German words for "here" and "beer"); *ei* is pronounced "aye" (as in *nein* and *Stein,* the German words for "no" and "stone"), and *eu* is pronounced "oy" (as in *treu* and *Deutsch,* the German words for "true" and "German"). The umlaut over a vowel *(ä, ö, ü)* makes that vowel rounder (purse your lips when you say it). The letter *Eszett (ß)* you'll see in Germany and Austria (but not used by the Swiss) represents *ss.* Written German always capitalizes all nouns.

Give it your best shot. The locals will appreciate your efforts.

Travel Smart

Your trip is like a complex play—easier to follow and really appreciate on a second viewing. While no one does the same trip twice to gain that advantage, reading this book in its entirety before your trip accomplishes much the same thing.

Reread entire chapters as you travel, and visit local tourist information offices. Upon arrival in a new town, lay the groundwork for a smooth departure. Buy a phone card and use it for reservations and confirmations. Enjoy the hospitality of the Germanic people. Ask questions. Most locals are eager to point you in their idea of the right direction. Wear your money belt, pack along a pocket-size notebook to organize your thoughts, and practice the virtue of simplicity. Those who expect to travel smart, do. Plan ahead for banking, laundry, postal chores, and picnics. To maximize rootedness, minimize one-night stands. Mix intense and relaxed periods. Every trip (and every traveler) needs at least a few slack days. Pace yourself. Assume you will return.

As you read through this book, note special days (festivals, colorful market days, and days when sights are closed). Saturday morning feels like any bustling weekday morning, but at lunchtime, many shops close down through Sunday. Sundays have pros and cons, as they do for travelers in the United States (special events, limited hours, shops and banks closed, limited public transportation, no rush hours). Popular places are even more popular on weekends. Many sights are closed on Monday.

Tourist Information

The tourist information office is your best first stop in any new city. Try to arrive, or at least telephone, before it closes. In this book, I'll refer to a tourist information office as a TI. Throughout Germany, Austria, and Switzerland, you'll find TIs are usually well organized and have English-speaking staff.

As national budgets tighten, many TIs have been privatized. This means they become sales agents for big tours and hotels, and their "information" becomes unavoidably colored. While TIs are eager to book you a room, you should use their room-finding service only as a last resort. TIs can as easily book you a bad room as a good one—they are not allowed to promote one place over another. Go direct, using the listings in this book.

Tourist Offices, U.S. Addresses

Each country's national tourist office in the United States is a wealth of information. Before your trip, get the free general information packet and request any specifics you want (such as regional and city maps and festival schedules).

German National Tourist Office: 122 E. 42nd Street, 52nd floor, New York, NY 10168, tel. 212/661-7200, fax 212/661-7174, www.visits-to-germany.com, gntony@aol.com. Maps, Rhine schedules, castles, biking, and city and regional information.

Austrian Tourist Office: Box 1142, New York, NY 10108-1142, tel. 212/944-6880, fax 212/730-4568, www.austria-tourism.com, info@oewnyc.com. Ask for their "Vacation Kit" with map. Fine hikes and city information.

Switzerland Tourism: For questions and brochures call 877/794-8037. Comprehensive "Welcome to the Best of Switzerland" brochure, great maps, and hiking material. Or contact 608 Fifth Ave., New York, NY 10020, fax 212/262-6116, www.myswitzerland.com, info.usa @switzerland.com.

Rick Steves' Books, Videos, and DVDs

Rick Steves' Europe Through the Back Door 2004 gives you budget travel tips on minimizing jet lag, packing light, planning your itinerary, traveling by car or train, finding budget beds, avoiding rip-offs, using mobile phones, hurdling the language barrier, staying healthy, using your bidet, and lots more. The book also includes chapters on 38 of my favorite "Back Doors."

Rick Steves' Country Guides are a series of nine annually updated guidebooks—including this book—covering Great Britain, Ireland, France, Italy, Spain/Portugal, Scandinavia, the Best of Europe, and—new for 2004—the Best of Eastern Europe.

My **City and Regional Guides** include a brand-new Provence & the French Riviera guidebook, along with Paris, Venice, Florence, London, and Amsterdam, Bruges & Brussels. These practical, annually updated guides offer in-depth coverage of the sights, hotels, restaurants, and nightlife in these grand cities and regions, plus illustrated tours of their great museums.

Rick Steves' Easy Access Europe (working title), new for 2004, is written for travelers with limited mobility. This book offers our latest tips and information on the best places to see, eat, and sleep in London, Paris, Bruges, Amsterdam, and the Rhine River—tailored for slow walkers and wheelchair users.

Rick Steves' Europe 101: History and Art for the Traveler (with Gene Openshaw) gives you the story of Europe's people, history, and art. Written for smart people who were sleeping in their history and art classes before they knew they were going to Europe, *101* really helps Europe's sights come alive.

Rick Steves' Mona Winks (with Gene Openshaw) gives you fun, easy-to-follow, self-guided tours of Europe's top 25 museums and cultural sites, covering all the biggies in London, Paris, Madrid, Amsterdam, Venice, Florence, and Rome.

The *Rick Steves' German Phrase Book* is a fun, practical tool for independent budget travelers. This handy book has everything you'll need while traveling in Germany, Austria, and Switzerland, including a menu decoder, conversational starters for connecting with locals, and an easy-to-follow telephone template for making hotel reservations.

My new public television series, *Rick Steves' Europe,* keeps churning out shows. Of 82 episodes (from the new series and from *Travels in Europe with Rick Steves*), 15 half-hour shows are on Germany, Austria, and Switzerland. These air nationally on public television and the Travel Channel. They're also available in information-packed home videos and DVDs (order online at www.ricksteves.com or call us at 425/771-8303 for our free newsletter/catalog).

Rick Steves' Postcards from Europe, my autobiographical book, packs 25 years of travel anecdotes and insights into the ultimate 2,000-mile European adventure. Through my guidebooks, I share my favorite European discoveries with you. *Postcards*—much of which is set in Germany and Switzerland—introduces you to my favorite European friends.

All of my books are published by Avalon Travel Publishing (www.travelmatters.com).

Other Guidebooks

You may want some supplemental information if you'll be traveling beyond my recommended destinations. When you consider the improvements they'll make in your $3,000 vacation, $25 or $35 for extra maps and books is money well spent. Especially for several people traveling by car, the weight and expense are negligible.

Students, backpackers, and those interested in the night scene should consider either the hip Rough Guides (British researchers, more insightful but not updated annually) or the Let's Go guides (by Harvard students, more accommodations listings than Rough Guides, updated annually). Lonely Planet's Germany, Austria, and Switzerland guides are well researched and mature (but not updated annually). The popular, skinny, green Michelin Guides to Germany, Austria, and Switzerland are excellent, especially if you're driving. They're known for their city and sightseeing maps, dry but concise and helpful information on all major sights, and good cultural and historical background. English editions are sold locally at gas stations and tourist shops.

More Recommended Reading and Movies

For information on Germany, Austria, and Switzerland past and present, consider these books and films:

Non-Fiction: *Germany and the Germans* (by John Ardagh), *La Place de la Concorde Suisse* (by John McPhee, about Switzerland, in English), *A Tramp Abroad* (by Mark Twain), *The Story of the Trapp Family Singers* (Maria von Trapp), *Inside the Third Reich* (Albert Speer), *Germany: A New History* (H. Schulze), *Culture Shock! Germany* (Richard Lord), and *Of German Ways* (Lavern Rippley).

Fiction: *Stones from the River* and *Floating in My Mother's Palm* (both by Ursula Hegi), *The Reader* (Bernard Schlink), *1632* (Eric Flint), *Summer at Gaglow* (Esther Freud), *Airs Above the Ground* (Mary Stewart), *The Tin Drum* (Günter Grass), *All Quiet on the Western Front* (Erich Maria Remarque), *Address Unknown* (Kathrine Kressman Taylor), *Berlin Noir* (Philip Kerr), *Saints and Villains* (Denise Giardina), *The Silent Angel* (Heinrich Böll), *Buddenbrooks* and *The Magic Mountain* (both by Thomas Mann), and *Narcissus and Goldmund* (Herman Hesse).

Flicks: *The Third Man; The Sound of Music; Before Sunrise; Amadeus; Immortal Beloved; Schindler's List; Heidi; The White Rose; Swing Kids; Das Boot; The Tin Drum; Cabaret; Marriage of Maria Braun; Triumph of the Will; Run, Lola, Run; Mephisto; Wings of Desire;* and *Far Away, So Close!*

Maps

The maps in this book, drawn by Dave Hoerlein, are concise and simple. Dave, who is well traveled in Germany, Austria, and Switzerland, has designed the maps to help you locate recommended places and get to the tourist offices, where you can pick up a more in-depth map (usually free) of the city or region. For an overall map of Europe, consider my Rick Steves' Europe Planning Map—geared to travelers' needs, with sightseeing destinations listed prominently (order online at www .ricksteves.com or call 425/771-8303 for free newsletter/catalog).

European bookstores, especially in touristy areas, have good selections of maps. For drivers, I'd recommend a 1:200,000- or 1:300,000-scale map for each country. Train travelers usually manage fine with the freebies they get with the train pass and from the local tourist offices.

Tours of Germany, Austria, and Switzerland

Travel agents can tell you about all the mainstream tours, but they won't tell you about ours. At Europe Through the Back Door, we offer 16-day tours of Germany, Austria, and Switzerland that feature most of the all-

Major Train Lines

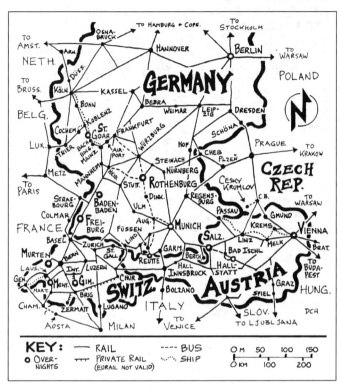

KEY:
— RAIL	---- BUS	
o OVER-NIGHTS	⊤⊤⊤ PRIVATE RAIL (EURAIL NOT VALID)	⋯⋯ SHIP

0 M 50 100 150
0 KM 100 200

stars covered in this book. This tour comes in two versions: fully guided (26–28 people on a big, roomy bus with a great guide) and the cheaper Bus Plus version, supplying bus transportation and hotels (28 people with an enthusiastic escort, ideal for families and independent travelers). For more information, call 425/771-8303 or visit www.ricksteves.com.

Transportation
By Car or Train?
The train is best for single travelers, those who'll be spending more time in big cities, and those who don't want to drive in Europe. While a car gives you the ultimate in mobility and freedom, enables you to search for hotels more easily, and carries your bags for you, the train zips you effortlessly from city to city, usually dropping you in the center and near the tourist office. Cars are great in the countryside but a worthless headache in places like Munich, Berlin, and Vienna.

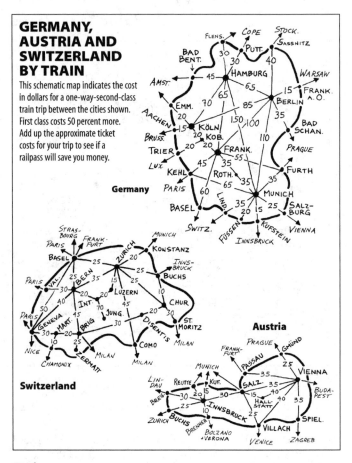

GERMANY, AUSTRIA AND SWITZERLAND BY TRAIN

This schematic map indicates the cost in dollars for a one-way-second-class train trip between the cities shown. First class costs 50 percent more. Add up the approximate ticket costs for your trip to see if a railpass will save you money.

Trains

Trains are generally slick, speedy, and punctual, with synchronized connections. They cover cities well, but some frustrating schedules make a few out-of-the-way recommendations (such as the concentration camp at Mauthausen) not worth the time and trouble for the less determined. For timetables, visit http://bahn.hafas.de/english.html. At most train stations, attendants will print out a step-by-step itinerary for you, free of charge. (Major German stations also have handy Service Points offering general help to travelers.) Each country has a train info number you can dial from anywhere in the country: Germany—tel. 01805-996-633 (ask for an English-speaking operator), Austria—tel. 051717 (wait through long German recording for operator), and Switzerland—toll tel. 0900-300-3004.

Prices listed are for 2003. My free *Rick Steves' Guide to European Railpasses* has the details. To get the railpass guide or an order form, call us at 425/771-8303 or visit www.ricksteves.com/rail.

GERMAN FLEXIPASS

	1st class individual	1st class twin	2nd class individual	2nd class twin	2nd class youth
4 days in a month	$260	$195	$180	$135	$142
5 days in a month	294	220.50	202	151.50	156
6 days in a month	326	244.50	226	169.50	166
7 days in a month	358	268.50	248	186	180
8 days in a month	392	294	270	202.50	192
9 days in a month	424	318	292	219	204
10 days in a month	458	343.50	316	237	216

"Twin" pass prices are per person for 2 traveling together. Third person pays full fare. Covers Rhine & Mosel boats, Salzburg and Basel (border towns), 60% off Romantic Road bus ride. Kids 6-11 half of full fare.

AUSTRIAN FLEXIPASS

	1st class	2nd class
Any 3 days out of 15 days	$158	$107
Add-on days (max 5)	20	15

Kids 6-11 half adult fare, under 4: free.

SWISS PASS AND SWISS FLEXIPASS

	1st class Individual	1st class Saver	1st class Youth	2nd class Individual	2nd class Saver	2nd class Youth
4 consec. days	$245	$208	$184	$160	$136	$120
8 consec. days	340	289	255	225	192	169
15 consec. days	410	349	308	270	230	203
22 consec. days	475	404	357	315	268	237
1 month	535	455	402	350	298	263
Any 3 days in 1 mo. flexi	234	198	N/A	156	132	N/A
Any 4 days in 1 mo. flexi	276	234	N/A	184	156	N/A
Any 5 days in 1 mo. flexi	318	270	N/A	212	180	N/A
Any 6 days in 1 mo. flexi	360	306	N/A	240	204	N/A
Any 8 days in 1 mo. flexi	424	360	N/A	282	240	N/A

Saverpass prices are per person for 2 or more traveling together. Covers all trains, boats and buses with 25% off high mountain rides. Kids under 16 free with parent.

The most economical railpass for a focused tour of this region is the Eurail Selectpass, which gives you up to 10 travel days (within a two-month period) in three, four, or five adjacent countries—including Germany, Austria, Switzerland, and other Western European countries. Another possibility is a 17-country Eurailpass (cost-effective only if you're doing a whirlwind trip of Europe). These passes are available in a Saverpass version, which gives a 15 percent discount to two or more companions traveling together.

SELECTPASSES

This pass covers travel in three adjacent countries.

	1st cl Selectpass	1st cl Saverpass	2nd cl Youthpass
5 days in 2 months	$356	$304	$249
6 days in 2 months	394	336	276
8 days in 2 months	470	400	329
10 days in 2 months	542	460	379

Please see www.ricksteves.com/rail for four- and five-country options.
Saverpass prices are per person for 2 or more people traveling together.
Prices subject to change.

Eurailpass/Selectpass diagram key:
Every **Eurailpass** includes travel in every country shown at right. A **Selectpass** can be designed to connect a "chain" of any three, four or five countries in this diagram linked by direct lines. (Examples that qualify: Norway-Sweden-Germany; Spain-France-Italy; Austria-Italy-Greece.) "Benelux" is considered one country.

EURAILPASSES

	1st class Eurailpass	1st class Saverpass	2nd class Youthpass*
10 days in 2 months flexi	$694	$592	$488
15 days in 2 months flexi	914	778	642
15 consecutive days	588	498	414
21 consecutive days	762	648	534
1 month consec. days	946	804	664
2 months consec. days	1338	1138	938
3 months consec. days	1654	1408	1160

These passes cover all 17 Eurail countries. Saverpass prices are per person for 2 or more traveling together. Youth = under 26. Kids 4-11 pay half adult or Saver fare.

SELECTPASS DRIVE

Any 3 days of rail travel + 2 days of Hertz or Avis car rental in 2 months within 3 adjoining countries.

Car Category	First Class	Extra car day
Economy	$291	$49
Compact	305	64
Intermediate	315	75
Small Automatic	331	95

Extra rail day $39 (max. 7). Price shown is per person for 2 traveling together. Third and fourth persons sharing car get a 3-day out of 2-month railpass for approx. $246 (kids 4-11: $123). A fourth or fifth country ads about $35 to these prices. For more info, call your travel agent or Rail Europe at 800/438-7245.

Each country has its own individual train passes that offer good value for trips limited to one country. But patchworking several second-class country passes together (for example, a 10-day-in-a-month German railpass, a 3-days-in-15 Austrian pass, and an 8-day Swiss pass) is only about $100 less than a 21-day Eurailpass that covers first-class travel in 17 countries ($740). You can purchase railpasses from your travel agent or Europe Through the Back Door; find our free Railpass Guide at www.ricksteves.com.

Eurailers (including Select and single-country passholders) should know what extras are included with their pass; for example, free travel on any German buses marked "Bahn" (run by the train company); free travel on city S-Bahn systems; free or discounted boats on the Rhine, Mosel, and Danube Rivers and on Swiss lakes; and a 60 percent discount on the Romantic Road bus tour. Flexipass holders should note that discounted trips don't use up a day of a Flexipass, but bonus (free) trips do. The "used" flexipass day can also cover your train travel on that day (but if you're not planning to travel more that day, it makes sense to pay for, say, a short boat ride rather than use up a day of your pass for it).

Those traveling in the Swiss Alps can use their Eurailpass or Eurail Selectpass to get discounts (but not free passage) on many private trains and lifts in the mountains. If you want to focus on Switzerland (where many scenic rides are not covered by Eurail or Eurail Selectpasses), consider a Swiss Pass or the various Alps passes sold at Swiss train stations. The Swiss Junior Card allows children under 16 to travel free with their parents (20 SF per child at Swiss stations, or free with Swiss train passes when requested with purchase in the United States). For more information on the Swiss rail system, see page 448.

If you decide to buy train tickets as you go, look into local specials. Germany offers several different point-to-point discounts (which can all be combined): If **two to five people** travel together on one ticket, the first person pays the regular price, and the rest pay half of that price. **Kids under 14** travel free with parents or grandparents. With **Plan & Save discounts,** you save 25 percent by buying a round-trip ticket at least three days in advance (or 50 percent with a Saturday night stay and other restrictions). Seats available at each fare level are limited.

If your plans change, refunds are available on any of these German tickets up to one day ahead (less a €15–30 penalty). If you miss your train, you can use the value of your ticket toward the cost of a new ticket (€50 or more). Fares are shown on the map on page 15 or at http://bahn.hafas.de/english.html (for discount info, click "Int. Guests").

Off-peak specials in Germany include a wild *Schönes Wochenende* ticket for €28; it gives groups of up to five people unlimited second-class travel on non-express trains all day Saturday or Sunday. *Länder-Tickets* are a similar deal (€21 for up to 5 people after 9:00 on weekdays on local trains within a single region, such as Bavaria).

Those staying longer in Germany can get additional discounts for a full year by purchasing one of several Bahn Cards (starting at €50).

While Eurailers over 26 automatically travel first class, people of any age buying individual tickets or single-country passes should remember that traveling in second class provides the same transportation for 33 percent less.

Hundreds of local train stations rent bikes for about $5 a day, and sometimes have easy "pick up here and drop off there" plans. For mixing train and bike travel, ask at stations for information booklets.

Car Rental

It's cheaper to arrange your car rental in advance in the United States than in Europe. You'll want a weekly rate with unlimited mileage. For three weeks or longer, leasing is cheaper because it saves you money on taxes and insurance. Comparison-shop through your agent. DER, a German company, often has the best rates (800/782-2424, www .dertravel.com).

Expect to pay about $600 per person (based on 2 people sharing the car) for a small economy car for three weeks with unlimited mileage, including gas, parking, and insurance. I normally rent a small, inexpensive model like a Ford Fiesta. For a bigger, roomier, more powerful but inexpensive car, move up to a Ford Escort or VW Polo. If you drop your car off early or keep it longer, you'll be credited or charged at a fair, prorated price.

For peace of mind, I splurge for the CDW insurance (about $10–15 a day), which covers virtually the full value of the car (minus a small deductible) in case of an accident. A few "gold" credit cards include CDW if you rent the car using that card; quiz your credit-card company on the worst-case scenario. Travel Guard sells CDW insurance for $7 a day (800/826-1300, www.travelguard.com). With the luxury of CDW, you'll enjoy the autobahn knowing you can bring back the car in a shambles and just say, "S-s-s-sorry."

For driving in Switzerland, your driver's license is all you need. For Austria and Germany, you're strongly advised to get an international driver's license (at your local AAA office—$10 plus 2 passport-type photos).

Driving

Every long drive between my recommended destinations is via the autobahn (super freeway), and nearly every scenic backcountry drive is paved and comfortable.

Austria and Switzerland charge drivers who use their roads. In Austria, you'll need a *Vignette* sticker for your rental car (buy at the border crossing, big gas stations near borders, or a rental car agency)—

AND LEARN THESE ROAD SIGNS

Speed Limit (km/hr)

Yield

No Passing

End of No Passing Zone

One Way

Intersection

Main Road

Freeway

Danger

No Entry

No Entry for Cars

All Vehicles Prohibited

Parking

No Parking

Customs

Peace

€8 for one week or €22 for two months. (Dipping into the country on regular roads—such as around Reutte in Tirol—requires no special payment.) To use the autobahn in Switzerland, you'll pay a one-time 40 SF fee (at the border, a gas station, or a rental agency).

Learn the universal road signs (explained in charts in most road atlases and at service stations). Seat belts are required, and two beers under those belts are enough to land you in jail.

Use good local maps and study them before each drive. Learn which exits you need to look out for, which major cities you'll travel toward, where the ruined castles lurk, and so on.

To get to the center of a city, follow signs for *Zentrum* or *Stadtmitte*. Ring roads go around a city. For parking, you can pick up

Driving: Distance and Time

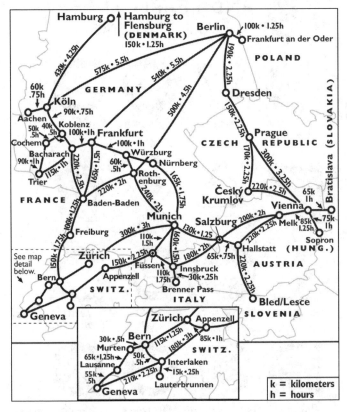

the "cardboard clock" (*Parkscheibe*, available free at gas stations, police stations, and *Tabak* shops) and display your arrival time on the dashboard so parking attendants can see you've been there less than the posted maximum stay (blue lines indicate 90-minute zones on Austrian streets).

In Europe, the shortest distance between any two points is the autobahn. Signs directing you to the autobahn are green in Austria and Switzerland, blue in Germany. To understand the complex but super-efficient autobahn (no speed limit, toll-free), look for the *Autobahn Service* booklet at any autobahn rest stop (free, lists all stops, services, road symbols, and more). Learn the signs: *Dreieck* (literally, "three corners") means a "Y" in the road; *Autobahnkreuz* is an intersection. Exits are spaced about every 20 miles and often have a gas station (*bleifrei* means unleaded), a restaurant, a mini-market, and sometimes a tourist information desk. Exits and intersections refer to the next major or the nearest small town. Study the map and anticipate which town names to look out for. Know what you're looking for—miss it, and you're long autobahn-gone. When navigating, you'll see *nord, süd, ost, west,* or *mitte.*

Autobahns generally have no speed limit, but you will commonly see a recommended speed posted. While no one gets a ticket for ignoring this recommendation, exceeding this speed means your car insurance no longer covers you in the event of an accident. Don't cruise in the passing lane; stay right. In fast-driving Germany, the backed-up line caused by an insensitive slow driver is called an *Autoschlange,* or "car snake." What's the difference between a car snake and a real snake? According to locals, "on a real snake, the ass is in the back."

Get used to metric. A liter is about a quart, four to a gallon; a kilometer is 0.6 of a mile. Convert kilometers to miles by cutting them in half and adding back 10 percent of the original (120 km: 60 + 12 = 72 miles).

Telephones, Mail, and E-mail

Smart travelers learn the phone system and use it daily to reserve or reconfirm rooms, get tourist information, or phone home. Many European phone booths take cards, but not coins.

Phone Cards: There are two kinds of phone cards: official phone cards that you insert into the phone (which can only be used from phone booths), and long-distance scratch-off PIN cards that can be used from virtually any phone (you dial a toll-free number and enter your PIN code). Both kinds of card work only in the country where you bought them (for example, a Swiss phone card works when you're making calls in Switzerland, but is worthless in Austria).

You can buy insertable phone cards from post offices, newsstands, or tobacco shops. Insert the card into the phone, make your call, and the value is deducted from your card. These are a good deal for calling within Europe, but can make calling home to the United States expensive (at least 50 cents per minute). One exception is in Switzerland, where a call home to the United States costs just seven cents a minute, plus a 35-cent connection charge.

PIN cards, which have a scratch-off personal identification number, allow you to call home at the rate of about a dime a minute. To use a PIN card, dial the toll-free access number listed on the card; then, at the prompt, enter your personal identification number (also listed on card) and dial the number you want to call. If the prompts are in German, experiment—dial your code, followed by the pound sign (#), then the number, then pound again, and so on—until it works. These are sold throughout Germany and Austria—mostly in big or touristy cities—at newsstands, exchange bureaus, souvenir shops, and minimarts; look for shop-window fliers that advertise long-distance rates. (PIN cards are unnecessary in Switzerland, where calling with an insertable phone card is about as cheap; see above.) There are many different brands. Ask for a "cheap international telephone card" *(billige internationelle Telefonkarte)*. Ask the vendor which brand is cheapest for calling the United States. Buy a lower denomination in case the card is a dud.

These PIN cards are such a good deal that the irritated German phone company is making them less cost-effective. In Germany, the cards are only cheap if you use them from a fixed line, like a hotel-room phone. From a pay phone, you'll get far fewer minutes for your money (for example, 10 minutes instead of 100 on a €5 card). No such pay phone problem exists in Austria (at least, not yet).

If you use coins to make your calls, have a bunch handy. Or look for a metered phone ("talk now, pay later") in the bigger post offices. Avoid using hotel-room phones for anything other than local calls and PIN-card calls.

Dialing Direct: You'll save money by dialing direct rather than going through an operator. You just need to learn to break the codes. For a list of **international access codes and country codes**, see the appendix.

When calling long distance within Germany or Austria, first dial the area code (which starts with 0), then dial the local number. For example, Munich's area code is 089, so if the number of one of my recommended Munich hotels were 264-043, to call the hotel within Munich, you'd dial 264-043. To call it from Frankfurt, you'd dial 089/264-043. When dialing internationally, dial the international access code (of the country you're calling from), the country code (of the country you're calling to), the area code (without the initial 0), and the local number. For example, to call the Munich hotel from home, you'd dial 011 (the international access code for the U.S. and Canada), 49 (Germany's country code), 89 (Munich's area code *without* the initial 0), and 264-043. Note that when you make an international call to either Germany or Austria, you must drop the initial 0 of the area code.

Switzerland has dropped area codes in favor of a direct-dial phone system, so you'll always dial what used to be the area code—whether you're calling across the street or across the country. For instance, to call a recommended Swiss hotel in Gimmelwald, you'd dial the same number (tel. 033-855-1658) whether you're calling from the Gimmelwald gondola station or from Zürich. If calling the Swiss hotel from outside the country, dial the international access code (011 from U.S. or Canada; 00 from Europe), Switzerland's country code (41), and then the local number *without* its initial 0 (33-855-1658). Note that when you call internationally to Switzerland, you must drop the initial 0 of the telephone number.

To call my office from Europe, I dial 00 (Europe's international access code), 1 (U.S. country code), 425 (Edmonds' area code), and 771-8303. European time is six/nine hours ahead of the East/West Coast of the United States.

Don't be surprised if local phone numbers in Germany and Austria have different numbers of digits within the same city or even the same hotel (for example, a hotel can have a 6-digit phone number and an 8-digit fax number).

U.S. Calling Card Services: Since direct-dialing rates have dropped, calling cards (offered by AT&T, MCI, and Sprint) are no longer the good value they used to be. In fact, they are a rip-off. You're likely pay $3 for the first minute with a $4 connection fee; if you get an answering machine, it'll cost you $7 to say, "Sorry I missed you." Now it's much cheaper to make your international calls using a phone card purchased in Europe.

Mobile Phones: Many travelers now buy cheap mobile phones in Europe to make both local and international calls. (Typical American mobile phones don't work in Europe, and those that do work have horrendous per-minute costs.) For about $75, you can get a phone with $20 worth of calls that will work only in the country where you purchased it. (You can buy more time at newsstands or mobile phone shops.) For about $100, you can get an "unlocked" phone that will work in most countries once you pick up the necessary chip per country (about $20). If you're interested, stop by any European shop that sells mobile phones (you'll see prominent store-window displays). Depending on your trip and budget, ask for a phone that works only in that country or one that can be used throughout Europe. If you're on a budget, skip mobile phones and use PIN cards instead.

Mail: To arrange for mail delivery, reserve a few hotels along your route in advance and give their addresses to friends, or use American Express Company's mail services (free for AmEx cardholders and for a minimal fee to others). Allow 10 days for a letter to arrive. Phoning and e-mailing are so easy that I've dispensed with mail stops altogether.

If you need to mail items home (be warned, it's expensive), you can buy boxes and tape at most post offices. But in Austria, buy sturdy boxes anywhere except the post office, which sells poorly designed boxes that get mangled in the package-sorting machinery.

E-mail: More and more hoteliers have e-mail addresses and Web sites (listed in this book). Note that mom-and-pop pensions, which can get deluged by e-mail, are not always able to respond immediately to an e-mail you've sent.

Internet cafés are available at just about every destination in this book, giving you reasonably inexpensive and easy Internet access. Your hotelier can direct you to the nearest place. Many hotels even have Internet terminals in their lobbies for guests.

Sleeping

In the interest of smart use of your time, I favor hotels and restaurants handy to your sightseeing activities. Rather than list hotels scattered throughout a city, I describe two or three favorite neighborhoods and recommend the best accommodations values in each, from $10 bunks to plush $200 doubles.

While accommodations in Germany, Austria, and Switzerland are fairly expensive, they are normally very comfortable and come with breakfast. Plan on spending $70–120 per hotel double in big cities, and $40–70 in towns and in private homes. Swiss beds are 25 percent more expensive than those in Austria and Germany.

A triple is much cheaper than a double and a single. While hotel singles are most expensive, private accommodations *(Zimmer)* have a flat per-person rate. Hostels and dorms always charge per person. Especially in private homes, where the boss changes the sheets, people staying several nights are most desirable. One-night stays are sometimes charged extra.

In recommending hotels, I favor small, family-run places that are central, inexpensive, quiet, clean, safe, friendly, English speaking, and not listed in other guidebooks. I also like local character and simple facilities that don't cater to American "needs." Obviously, a place meeting every criterion is rare, and all of my recommendations fall short of perfection—sometimes miserably. But I've listed the best values for each price category, given the above criteria. The very best values are family-run places with showers down the hall and no elevator.

Any room without a bathroom has access to a bathroom in the corridor (free unless otherwise noted). All rooms have a sink. For environmental reasons, towels are often replaced in hotels only when you leave them on the floor. In cheaper places, they aren't replaced at all, so hang them up to dry and reuse.

Unless I note otherwise, the cost of a room includes a breakfast (sometimes continental, but usually buffet). The price is usually posted in the room. Before accepting, confirm your understanding of the complete price. I appreciate feedback on your hotel experiences.

Making Reservations

It's possible to travel at any time of year without reservations, but given the high stakes, erratic accommodations values, and the quality of the gems I've found for this book, I'd highly recommend calling for rooms at least several days in advance as you travel (and book well in advance for festivals, such as Munich's Oktoberfest). If tourist crowds are minimal, you might make a habit of calling between 9:00 and 10:00 on the day you plan to arrive, when the hotel knows who'll be checking out and just which rooms will be available. I've taken great pains to list telephone numbers with long-distance instructions (see "Dialing Direct," above). Use the telephone and the convenient telephone cards. Most hotels

SLEEP CODE

To give maximum information in a minimum of space, I use these codes to describe accommodations listed in this book. Prices listed are per room, not per person. When a range of prices is listed for a room, the price fluctuates with room size or season.

S = Single room (or price for 1 person in a double).
D = Double or Twin. Double beds are usually big enough for non-romantic couples.
T = Triple (often a double bed with a single bed moved in).
Q = Quad (an extra child's bed is usually cheaper).
b = Private bathroom with toilet and shower or tub.
s = Private shower or tub only (the toilet is down the hall).
no CC = Does not accept credit cards; pay in local cash.
SE = Speaks English.
NSE = Does not speak English. Used only when it's unlikely you'll encounter English-speaking staff.

According to this code, a couple staying at a "Db-€90" hotel would pay a total of 90 euros (about $100) for a double room with a private bathroom. The hotel accepts credit cards or cash in payment; you can assume a hotel takes credit cards unless you see "no CC" in the listing.

I've divided the rooms into three categories, based on the price for a standard double room with bath:

$$$ **Higher Priced**
$$ **Moderately Priced**
$ **Lower Priced**

listed are accustomed to English-only speakers. A hotel receptionist will trust you and hold a room until 16:00 without a deposit, though some will ask for a credit-card number. Honor (or cancel by phone) your reservations. Long distance is cheap and easy from public phone booths. Trusting people to show up is a hugely stressful issue and a financial risk for B&B owners. Don't let these people down—I promised you'd call and cancel if for some reason you can't show up. Don't needlessly confirm rooms through the tourist offices; they'll take a commission.

If you know exactly which dates you need and really want a particular place, reserve a room long before you leave home. To reserve from home, call, e-mail, or fax the hotel. E-mail is free, phone and fax costs are reasonable, and simple English is usually fine. To fax, use the form in the appendix (e-mailers can find it online at www.ricksteves.com/reservation). If you're writing, add the ZIP code and confirm the need and method for a deposit. A two-night stay in August would be "2 nights, 16/8/04 to 18/8/04" (Europeans write the date day/month/year, and European hotel jargon uses your day of departure). Hotels often require one night's deposit to hold a room. Usually a credit-card number and expiration date will be accepted as the deposit. If that's the case, you can pay with your card or cash when you arrive; if you don't show up, you'll be billed for one night. Reconfirm your reservations a day or two in advance for safety. Ask about the hotel's cancellation policy when you reserve—sometimes you have to cancel as much as two weeks ahead to avoid being charged.

Camping and Hosteling

Campers can manage with Let's Go listings and help from the local TI (ask for a regional camping listing). Your hometown travel bookstore also has guidebooks on camping in Europe. You'll find campgrounds just about everywhere you need them. Look for *Campingplatz* signs. You'll meet lots of Europeans—camping is a popular, middle-class-family way to go. Campgrounds are cheap ($6–10 per person), friendly, safe, more central and convenient than rustic, and rarely full.

Hostelers can take advantage of the wonderful network of hostels. Follow signs marked *Jugendherberge* (with triangles) or with the logo showing a tree next to a house. Generally, travelers without a membership card ($25 per year, sold at hostels in most U.S. cities or online at www.hiayh.org, U.S. tel. 202/783-6161) are admitted for an extra $5.

Hostels are open to members of all ages (except in Bavaria, where a maximum age of 26 is strictly enforced). They usually cost $10–20 per night (cheaper for those under 27, plus $4 sheet rental if you don't have your own) and serve good, cheap meals and/or provide kitchen facilities. If you plan to stay in hostels, bring your own sheet. While many hostels have a few doubles or family rooms available upon request for a little extra money, plan on gender-segregated dorms with 4–20 beds per room. Hostels can be idyllic and peaceful, but school groups can raise the rafters. School groups are most common on summer weekends and on school-year weekdays. I like small hostels best. While many hostels may say over the telephone that they're full, most hold a few beds for people who drop in, or they can direct you to budget accommodations nearby.

Eating

Germanic cuisine is heavy and hearty. Though it's tasty, it can get monotonous if you fall into the schnitzel or *Wurst*-and-potatoes rut. Be adventurous. My German phrase book has a handy menu decoder that works well for most travelers, but galloping gluttons will prefer the

TIPS ON TIPPING

Tipping in Europe isn't as automatic and generous as it is in the United States—but for special service, tips are appreciated, if not expected. As in the United States, the proper amount depends on your resources, tipping philosophy, and the circumstance, but some general guidelines apply.

Restaurants: Tipping is an issue only at restaurants that have waiters and waitresses. If you order your food at a counter, don't tip.

At German and Austrian restaurants that have a wait staff, service is included, although it's common to round up the bill after a good meal (usually 5–10 percent; so, for an €18.50 meal, pay €20). Rather than leaving coins on the table, Germans usually pay with paper, saying how much they'd like the bill to be (for example, for an €8.10 meal, give a €20 bill and say "*Neun Euro*"—9 euros—to get €11 change). In Switzerland, tipping is optional, though appreciated (up to 5 percent is enough).

Taxis: To tip the cabbie, round up. For a typical ride, round up to the next euro on the fare (to pay a €13 fare, give €14); for a long ride, to the nearest 10 (for a €75 fare, give €80). If the cabbie hauls your bags and zips you to the airport to help you catch your flight, you might want to toss in a little more. But if you feel like you're being driven in circles or otherwise ripped off, skip the tip.

Special services: Tour guides at public sites sometimes hold out their hands for tips after they give their spiel; if I've already paid for the tour, I don't tip extra, though some tourists do give a euro or two, particularly for a job well done. I don't tip at hotels, but if you do, give the porter a euro for carrying bags and leave a couple of euros in your room at the end of your stay for the maid if the room was kept clean. In general, if someone in the service industry does a super job for you, a tip of a couple of euros is appropriate . . . but not required.

When in doubt, ask: If you're not sure whether (or how much) to tip for a service, ask your hotelier or the TI; they'll fill you in on how it's done on their turf.

meatier *Marling German Menu Master.* Each region has its specialties, which, though not cheap, are often good values.

There are many kinds of restaurants. Hotels often serve fine food. A *Gaststätte* is a simple, less-expensive restaurant. For smaller portions, order from the *kleine Hunger* (small hunger) section of the menu.

Ethnic restaurants provide a welcome break from Germanic fare. Foreign cuisine is either the legacy of a crumbled empire (Hungarian and Bohemian, from which Austria gets its goulash and dumplings) or a new arrival to feed the many hungry-but-poor guest workers. Italian, Turkish, and Greek food are good values.

The cheapest meals are found in department-store cafeterias, *Schnell-Imbiss* (fast-food) stands, university cafeterias *(Mensas),* and hostels. For a quick, cheap bite, have a deli make you a *Wurstsemmel,* a meat sandwich.

Most restaurants tack a menu onto their door for browsers and have an English menu inside. Only a rude waiter will rush you. Good service is relaxed (slow to an American). In Germany and Austria, you might be charged for bread you've eaten from the basket on the table; have the waiter take it away if you don't want it. To wish others "Happy eating!" offer a cheery *"Guten Appetit!"* When you want the bill, ask for *"Die Rechnung, bitte."*

For most visitors, the rich pastries, wine, and beer provide the fondest memories of Germanic cuisine. The wine (85 percent white) is particularly good from the Mosel, Rhine, Danube, eastern Austria, and southwestern Switzerland areas. Order wine by the *Viertel* (quarter liter, or 8 oz.) or *Achtel* (eighth liter, or 4 oz.). You can say, *"Ein Viertel Weisswein* (white wine), *bitte* (please)." Order it *süss* (sweet), *halbe trocken* (medium), or *trocken* (dry). *Rotwein* is red wine and *Sekt* is German champagne. Menus list drink size by the tenth of a liter, or deciliter (dl).

The Germans enjoy a tremendous variety of great beer. The average German, who drinks 40 gallons of beer a year, knows that *dunkles* is dark, *helles* is light, *Flaschenbier* is bottled, and *vom Fass* is on tap. *Pils* is barley-based, *Weize* is wheat-based, and *Malzbier* is the malt beer that children learn with. *Radler* is half beer and half lemon-lime soda. When you order beer, ask for *ein Halbe* for a half-liter (not always available) or *eine Mass* for a whole liter (about a quart). Tap water—which many waiters aren't eager to bring you—is *Leitungswasser* or *Wasser vom Fass.* They would rather you buy *Mineralwasser (mit/ohne Gas,* with/without carbonation).

Back Door Manners

While updating this book, I heard over and over again that my readers are considerate and fun to have as guests. Thank you for traveling as temporary locals who are sensitive to the culture. It's fun to follow you in my travels.

Send Me a Postcard, Drop Me a Line

If you enjoy a successful trip with the help of this book and would like to share your discoveries, please fill out the survey at the end of this book and send it to Europe Through the Back Door, Box 2009, Edmonds, Washington 98020. I personally read and value all feedback. Thanks in advance—it helps a lot.

For our latest information, visit our Web site: www.ricksteves.com. To check for any updates for this book, look into www.ricksteves.com /update. My e-mail address is rick@ricksteves.com. Anyone can request a free issue of our Back Door quarterly newsletter.

Judging from the happy postcards I receive from travelers, it's safe to assume you'll enjoy a great, affordable vacation—with the finesse of an independent, experienced traveler.

Thanks, and happy travels—*gute Reise!*

BACK DOOR TRAVEL PHILOSOPHY
by Rick Steves, author of *Europe Through the Back Door*

Travel is intensified living—maximum thrills per minute and one of the last great sources of legal adventure. Travel is freedom. It's recess, and we need it.

Experiencing the real Europe requires catching it by surprise, going casual..."through the Back Door."

Affording travel is a matter of priorities. (Make do with the old car.) You can travel—simply, safely, and comfortably—anywhere in Europe for $80 a day plus transportation costs. In many ways, spending more money only builds a thicker wall between you and what you came to see. Europe is a cultural carnival, and, time after time, you'll find that its best acts are free and the best seats are the cheap ones.

A tight budget forces you to travel close to the ground, meeting and communicating with the people, not relying on service with a purchased smile. Never sacrifice sleep, nutrition, safety, or cleanliness in the name of budget. Simply enjoy the local-style alternatives to expensive hotels and restaurants.

Extroverts have more fun. If your trip is low on magic moments, kick yourself and make things happen. If you don't enjoy a place, maybe you don't know enough about it. Seek the truth. Recognize tourist traps. Give a culture the benefit of your open mind. See things as different, but not better or worse. Any culture has much to share.

Of course, travel, like the world, is a series of hills and valleys. Be fanatically positive and militantly optimistic. If something's not to your liking, change your liking. Travel is addictive. It can make you a happier American, as well as a citizen of the world. Our Earth is home to six billion equally important people. It's humbling to travel and find that people don't envy Americans. They like us, but with all due respect, they wouldn't trade passports.

Globe-trotting destroys ethnocentricity. It helps you understand and appreciate different cultures. Travel changes people. It broadens perspectives and teaches new ways to measure quality of life. Many travelers toss aside their hometown blinders. Their prized souvenirs are the strands of different cultures they decide to knit into their own character. The world is a cultural yarn shop. And Back Door travelers are weaving the ultimate tapestry.

Come on, join in!

GERMANY

(Deutschland)

- Germany is 136,000 square miles (a little smaller than Montana).
- Population is 83 million (about 570 per square mile, declining slowly).
- 1 euro (€) = about $1.10.

Deutschland is energetic, efficient, and organized, and it is Europe's muscle man—both economically and wherever people line up (Germans have a reputation for pushing ahead). Its bustling cities hold 85 percent of its people, and average earnings are among the highest on earth. Ninety-seven percent of the workers get one-month paid vacations, and, during the other 11 months, they create a gross national product that's about one-third of the United States' and growing. Germany has risen from the ashes of World War II to become the world's fifth-largest industrial power, ranking fourth in steel output and nuclear power and third in

automobile production. Germany shines culturally, beating out all but two countries in production of books, Nobel laureates, and professors.

Though its East-West division lasted about 40 years, historically Germany has been divided between north and south. Northern Germany was barbarian, is Protestant, and assaults life aggressively, while Southern Germany was Roman, is Catholic, and enjoys a more relaxed tempo of life. The American image of Germany is beer-and-pretzel Bavaria (probably because that was "our" sector after the war). This historic North-South division is less pronounced these days as Germany becomes a more mobile society. The big chore facing Germany today is integrating the wilted economy of what was East Germany into the powerhouse economy of the West. This monumental task has given the West higher taxes (and second thoughts).

Germany's tourist route today—Rhine, Romantic Road, Bavaria—was yesterday's trade route, connecting its most prosperous medieval cities. Germany as a nation is just 130 years old. In 1850, there were 35 independent countries in what is now Germany. In medieval times there were 350, each with its own weights, measures, coinage, king, and lottery.

Germans eat lunch and dinner about when we do. Order house specials whenever possible. Pork, fish, and venison are good, and don't miss the bratwurst and sauerkraut. Potatoes are the standard vegetable, but *Spargel* (giant white asparagus) is a must in season. The bread and pretzels in the basket on your table often cost extra. When I need a break from pork, I order the *Salatteller*. Great beers and white wines abound. Go with whatever beer is on tap.

Gummi bears are local gumdrops with a cult following (beware of imitations—you must see the word *Gummi*), and Nutella is a chocolate-hazelnut spread that may change your life.

GERMAN HISTORY

There was no Germany before 1871, but the cultural heritage of the German-speaking people (of modern-day Germany and Austria) stretches back 2,000 years.

Romans (A.D. 1–500)

German history begins in A.D. 9, when Romans troops are ambushed and driven back by the German chief Arminius. For the next 250 years, the Rhine and Danube rivers marked the border between civilized Roman Europe (to the southwest) and "barbarian" German lands (northeast). While the rest of Europe's future would be Roman, Christian, and Latin, Germany would follow its own pagan, *Deutsch*-speaking path.

Rome finally fell to the German chief Theodoric (Dietrich, A.D. 476), and the Germanic Franks controlled northern Europe, ruling a mixed population of Romanized Christians and tree-worshipping Germans. Gradually, the pagans traded their gods Thor and Freia (of "Thor's-day" and "Frei-day") for Jesus and Mary.

Charlemagne and the Franks (A.D. 500–1000)

For Christmas in A.D. 800, the pope gave Charlemagne the title of Holy Roman Emperor. Charlemagne, the king of the Franks, was the first of many German kings to be called *Kaiser* (Caesar) over the next thousand years. Allied with the pope, Charlemagne ruled an empire that included Germany, Austria, France, the Low Countries, and northern Italy.

Charlemagne (*Karl der Grosse,* or Charles the Great, ruled 768–814) stood a head taller than his subjects, and his foot became a standard measurement. The stuff of legend, Charles the Great had five wives and four concubines, producing descendants with names like Charles the Bald, Louis the Pious, and Henry the Quarrelsome. After Charlemagne died of pneumonia (814), his united empire did not pass directly to his oldest son but was divided into (what would become) Germany, France, and the lands in between (Treaty of Verdun, 843).

The Holy Roman Empire (1000–1500)

Medieval Germany was not a unified country but a chaotic patchwork of some 350 small, quarreling dukedoms with nominal loyalty to the German Emperor. The title of Holy Roman Emperor was pretty bogus, implying that the German king ruled the same huge European empire as the ancient Romans. In fact, he was Holy because he was blessed by the Church, Roman to recall ancient grandeur, and the figurehead Emperor of only a scattered kingdom.

WHY WE CALL DEUTSCHLAND "GERMANY"

Our English name "Germany" comes from the Latin *Germania,* the name of one of the "barbarian" tribes. The French and Spanish call it *Allemagne* and *Alemania* after the Alemanni tribe. Italians call the country *Germania,* but the German language is known as *tedesco,* after another Germanic tribe.

To Germans, their country is *Deutschland,* a name used for at least 1,200 years. It probably derives from *deutsch*—which is what 8th-century folks called the common language that developed in the east half of the Frankish empire. *Alles klar?*

Germany's emperors had less hands-on power than other kings around Europe. Because of the inheritance custom, they couldn't pass the crown father to son. Instead, emperors were elected by nobles and archbishops. This gave nobles great power, and the peasants huddled close to their local noble's castle, for protection from attack by the noble next door. There were no empire-wide taxes and no national capital.

When Emperor Henry IV (ruled 1056–1106) tried to assert his power by appointing bishops, he was slapped down by the nobles, and forced to repent to the pope by standing barefoot in the Alpine snow for three days at Canossa (north Italy, 1077).

Emperor Frederick I Barbarossa (1152–1190), blue-eyed and red-bearded (hence *barba rossa*), gained an international reputation as a valiant knight, gentleman, bon vivant, and lover of poetry and women. Still, his great victories were away in Italy and Asia (on the Third Crusade, where he drowned in a river), while back home real power was wielded by nobles.

This was the era of Germany's troubadors *(Meistersingers)*, who traveled from castle to castle singing love songs *(Minnesang)* and telling the epic tales of chivalrous knights (Tristan and Isolde, Parzival, and the Nibelungen) that would later inspire German nationalism and Wagnerian operas.

While France, England, and Spain were centralizing power around a single ruling family to create modern nation-states, Germany remained a decentralized, backward, feudal battleground.

Medieval Growth

Nevertheless, Germany was located at the center of Europe, and trading towns prospered. Several northern towns (especially Hamburg and Lübeck) banded together into the Hanseatic League, promoting open trade around the Baltic Sea. To curry favor at election time, emperors granted powers and priviliges to certain towns, designated Free Imperial Cities. Some towns, such as Köln, Mainz, Dresden, and Trier, held higher status than many nobles, as hosts of one of the seven Electors of the emperor.

Textiles, mining, and the colonizing of eastern lands made Germany an economic powerhouse with a thriving middle class. In towns, middle-class folks (burghers), not the local aristocrats, began running things. Around 1450, Johann Gutenberg of Mainz invented moveable type for printing, an invention that would allow the export of a new commodity—ideas.

Religious Struggles and the Thirty Years' War (1500–1700)

Martin Luther—German monk, fiery orator, and religious whistle-blower—sparked a century of European wars by speaking out against the Catholic Church.

Luther (1483–1546) lived a turbulent life. In early adulthood, the newly ordained priest suffered a severe personal crisis of faith, weighed down by his own feelings of unworthiness. He devoured the Bible, searching for an answer, finally deciding that he could be saved from sin not by his good deeds but by faith in God alone. As this concept of unearned grace sank in, Luther later said, "I felt myself to have been born again."

Coincidentally, just as Luther was raising these issues, a monk rode into town on papal business—selling forgiveness through indulgences. It was clear to Luther that the Christian Church based in Rome had grown corrupt, worldly, and out of touch with people's needs.

In 1517, Luther nailed a list of 95 items for debate on a church door in Wittenburg. He openly protested against church corruption and was excommunicated. Defying both the pope and the emperor, he lived on the run as an outlaw. He still found time to translate the New Testament from Latin to modern German, write hymns such as "A Mighty Fortress," spar with the humanist Erasmus, and father six children with an ex-nun.

Luther's protests ("Protestantism") threw Germany into a century of turmoil, as each local prince took sides between Catholics and Protestants. In the 1525 Peasant Revolt, peasants attacked their feudal masters with hoes and pitchforks, fighting for more food, political say-so, and respect. The revolt was brutally put down.

The German Emperor, Charles V (r. 1519–1556) sided with the pope. Charles was the most powerful man in Europe, having inherited an empire that included Germany and Austria, plus the Low Countries, much of Italy, Spain, and Spain's New World possessions. But many local German nobles took the opportunity to go Protestant—some for religious reasons, but also to seize Church assets and powers.

The 1555 Peace of Augsburg allowed each local noble to decide the religion of his realm. In general, the northern lands became Protestant, while the south (Bavaria, Austria) remained Catholic.

Unresolved religious and political differences eventually expanded into the Thirty Years' War (1618–1648). This Europe-wide war fought mainly on German soil involved Denmark, Sweden, France, and Bohemia (in the modern-day Czech Republic), among others. It was one of history's bloodiest wars, fueled by religious extremism and political opportunism, and fought by armies of brutal mercenaries who worked on commission, paid in loot and pillage.

By war's end (Treaty of Westphalia, 1648), a third of all Germans had died, France was the rising European power, and the Holy Roman Empire was a medieval mess of scattered, feudal states. In 1689, France's Louis XIV swept down the Rhine, gutting and leveling its once-great castles, and Germany ceased to be a major player in European politics.

Austria and Prussia (1700s)

The German-speaking lands now consisted of three "Germanies": Austria in the south, Prussia in the north, and the rest in between.

Prussia—originally colonized by celibate ex-Crusaders called Teutonic Knights—was forged into a unified state by two strong kings. Frederick I (the "King Sergeant," r. 1701–1713) built a modern state around a highly disciplined army, a centralized government, and national pride. His grandson, Frederick II "The Great" (r. 1740–1786), added French culture and worldliness, preparing militaristic Prussia to enter the world stage. A well-read, flute-playing lover of the arts and liberal ideals, Frederick also ruled with an iron fist—the very model of the "enlightened despot."

Meanwhile, Austria thrived under the laid-back rule of the Hapsburg family. Hapsburgs gained power in Europe by marrying it. They acquired the Netherlands, Spain, Bohemia, and Hungary that way—a strategy that didn't work so well for Marie-Antoinette, who married the king of France.

The Germanic lands in the 1700s became a cultural powerhouse, producing musicians (Bach, Haydn, Mozart, Beethoven), writers (Goethe, Schiller), and thinkers (Kant, Leibniz). But politically, feudal Germany was no match for the modern powers.

After the French Revolution (1789), Napoleon swept through Germany with his armies, deposing feudal lords, confiscating Church lands, and forcing the emperor to hand over his crown (1806). After a thousand years, the Holy Roman Empire (or *Reich*) was dead.

German Unification (1800s)

Napoleon's invasion helped unify the German-speaking peoples by rallying them against a common foreign enemy. After Napoleon's defeat, the Congress of Vienna (1815), presided over by the Austrian Prince Metternich, realigned Europe's borders. "Germany" consisted of three Germanic nations—Prussia in the north, Austria in the south, and the German Confederation, a loose collection of small states in between. The idea of unifying these three into one began to grow, and by mid-century most German-speaking people favored forming a modern nation-state. The only question was whether the Confederation would be under Prussian or Austrian dominance.

Economically, Germany was becoming increasingly modern, with railroads (1835), a unified trade organization (1834), mechanical engineering prowess, and factories booming on a surplus of labor.

Energetic Prussia took the lead in unifying the country. Otto von Bismarck (served 1862–1890), the strong minister of Prussia's weak king, used cunning politics to engineer a unified Germany under Prussian dominance. First he started a war with Austria, ensuring that any united Germany would be under Prussian control. (Austria-

Hungary became a separate country.) Next, Bismarck provoked a war with France (Franco-Prussian War, 1870–1871). This united Prussia and the German Confederation against their common enemy, France.

Fueled by hysterical patriotism, German armies swept through France and, in the Hall of Mirrors at Versailles, crowned Prussia's Wilhelm I as Emperor *(Kaiser)* of a new German Empire uniting Prussia and the German Confederation (but excluding Austria). This Second Reich (1871–1918) featured elements of democracy (an elected *Reichstag*, or parliament) offset by a strong military and an emperor with veto powers.

A united and resurgent Germany was suddenly flexing its muscles in European politics. With strong industry, war spoils, overseas colonies, and a large disciplined military, it sought its rightful "place in the sun." *Volk* art flourished (Wagner's operas, Nietzche's essays), fueled by nationalist fervor, reviving medieval German myths and Nordic gods. The rest of Europe saw Germany's rapid rise and began arming themselves to the teeth.

World War I and Hitler's Rise (1914–1939)

When Austria's heir to the throne was assassinated in 1914, all of Europe took sides as the political squabble quickly escalated into World War I. Germany and Austria-Hungary attacked British and French troops in France, but were stalled at the Battle of the Marne. Both sides dug defensive trenches, then settled in for four years of bloodshed, boredom, mud, machine-gun fire, disease, and mustard gas.

Finally, at 11:00 in the morning of November 11, 1918, fighting ceased. Germany surrendered, signing the Treaty of Versailles in the Hall of Mirrors at Versailles. The war cost the defeated German nation 1.7 million men, precious territory, colonies, their military rights, reparations money, and national pride.

A new democratic government called the Weimar Republic (1919) dutifully abided by the Treaty of Versailles and tried to maintain order among Germany's many divided political parties. But the country was in ruins, the economy a shambles, and the war's victors demanded heavy reparations. Communists rioted in the streets, fascists plotted coups, and a loaf of bread cost a billion inflated marks. War vets grumbled in their beer about how their leaders had sold them out. All Germans, regardless of their political affiliations, were fervently united in their apathy toward the new democracy. When the worldwide depression of 1929 hit Germany with brutal force, the nation was desperate for a strong leader with answers.

Adolf Hitler (1889–1945) was a disgruntled vet who had spent the post–World War I years homeless, wandering the streets of Vienna with sketchpad in hand, hoping to become an artist. In Munich, he joined other disaffected Germans to form the National Socialist (Nazi) party.

GERMANY DURING WORLD WAR II
(1939–1945)

1939: Soldiers singing "Muss ich denn, Muss ich denn" ("I must leave my happy home") march off to war. On September 1, Germany invades Poland, sparking World War II. Germany, Italy, and Japan (the Axis) would eventually square off against the Allies—Britain, France, the United States, and the Soviet Union.

1940: The Nazi *Blitzkrieg* (lightning war) quickly sweeps through Denmark, Norway, the Low Countries, France, Yugoslavia, and Greece. With fellow fascists ruling Italy (Mussolini), Spain (Franco), and Portugal (Salazar), all of the Continent is now dominated by fascists, creating a "fortress Europe."

1941: Hitler invades his former ally, the U.S.S.R. Bombastic victory parades in Berlin celebrate the triumph of the Aryan race over the lesser peoples of the world.

1942: Allied bombs begin falling on German cities. In the fall and winter, German families receive death notices from the horrific Battle of Stalingrad. On the worst days, 50,000 men died. (America lost 58,000 total in Vietnam.) Back home, Nazi officials begin their plan for the "final solution to the Jewish problem"—systematic execution of Europe's Jews in specially built death camps.

In stirring speeches, Hitler promised to restore Germany to its rightful glory, blaming the country's current problems on Communists, foreigners, and Jews. After an unsuccessful coup attempt (the Beer Hall Putsch in Munich, 1923), Hitler was sent to jail, where he wrote an influential book of his political ideas, called *Mein Kampf* (My Struggle).

By 1930, the Nazis—now wearing power suits and working within the system—had become a formidable political party in Germany's democracy. They won 38 percent of the seats in the *Reichstag* in 1932, and Hitler was appointed Chancellor (1933). Two months later, the *Reichstag* building mysteriously burned to the ground—an apparent act of terrorism with a September 11–size impact—and a terrified Germany gave Chancellor Hitler sweeping powers to preserve national security.

Hitler wasted no time in using this Enabling Act to jail opponents, terrorize the citizenry, and organize every aspect of German life under

1943: Germany has to fight a two-front war: against tenacious Soviets on the chilly Eastern Front, and against Brits and Yanks advancing north through Italy on the Western Front. Germany's industrial output tries desperately to keep up with the Allies'. The average German suffers through shortages, rationing, and frequent trips to the bomb shelter.

1944: Hitler's no-surrender policy is increasingly unpopular, and he narrowly survives being assassinated by a bomb planted in an office. After the Allies reach France on D-Day, Germany counterattacks with a last-gasp offensive (the Battle of the Bulge) that slows but does not stop the Allies.

1945: Soviet soldiers approach Berlin from the east, and Americans and Brits from the west. Adolf Hitler commits suicide, and families lock up their daughters to protect them from rapacious Soviet soldiers. When Germany finally surrenders on May 8, the country is in ruins, occupied by several foreign powers, divided into occupation zones, and viewed by the world as an immoral monster.

In the war's aftermath, many German citizens learn for the first time of the mass killings and atrocities committed by their leaders.

the watchful eye of the Nazi party. Plumbers' unions, choral societies, school teachers, church pastors, movie-makers, and artists all had to account to a Nazi party official about how their work furthered the Third Reich.

For the next decade, an all-powerful Hitler proceeded to revive Germany's economy, building the autobahns and rebuilding the military. Defying the Treaty of Versailles and world opinion, Hitler occupied the Saar region (1935) and the Rhineland (1936), annexed Austria and the Sudetenland (1938), and invaded Czechoslovakia (March 1939). The rest of Europe finally reached its appeasement limit.

Two Germanies (1945–1990)

The Allies divided occupied Germany into two halves, split down the middle by an 855-mile border—Winston Churchill called it an "Iron

Curtain." By 1949, Germany was officially two separate countries. West Germany (the Federal Republic of Germany) was democratic and capitalist, allied with the powerful United States. East Germany (the German Democratic Republic) was a socialist state under Soviet control. The former capital, Berlin—sitting in East German territory—was itself split into two parts, allowing a tiny pocket of Western life in the Soviet-controlled East. Armed guards prevented Germans from crossing the border to see their cousins on the other side.

In 1948, Soviet troops blockaded West Berlin. The Allies responded by airlifting food and supplies into the stranded city, forcing the Soviets to back off. In 1961, the Soviets erected a 12-foot-high concrete wall through the heart of Berlin. The Berlin Wall—built at the height of the Cold War between the U.S. and the U.S.S.R.—was designed to prevent the westward flow of East German citizens, and it came to symbolize divided Germany.

In West Germany, Chancellor Konrad Adenauer (who had suffered imprisonment under the Nazis), tried to restore Germany's good name, paying war reparations and joining international organizations of nations. Thanks to U.S. aid from the Marshall Plan, West Germany was rebuilt, democracy was established, and its "economic miracle" quickly exceeded pre-war levels. Adenauer was succeeded in 1969 by the U.S.-friendly Willy Brandt.

East Germany was ruled with an iron fist by Walter Ulbricht (who had been exiled by the Nazis). In 1953, demonstrations and protests against the government were brutally put down by Soviet—not German—troops. Erich Honecker (having endured a decade of Nazi imprisonment), succeeded Ulbrich as ruler of the East in 1971. Honecker was a kinder, gentler tyrant.

Throughout the 1970s and 1980s, both the United States and the Soviet Union used divided Germany as a military base. West Germans debated whether U.S. missiles aimed at the Soviets should be placed in their country. Economically, the West just got stronger while the East stagnated.

On November 9, 1989, East Germany unexpectedly opened the Berlin Wall. Astonished Germans from both sides climbed the Wall, hugged each other, shared bottles of beer, sang songs, and chiseled off souvenirs. Negotiations and elections immediately began to reunite the two Germanies. October 3, 1990, was proclaimed German Unification Day, with Berlin as the capital (1991).

Germany Today (1990–2004)

Differences between *Ossis* (former East Germans) and *Wessis* remain, but they're diminishing as the two economies find equilibrium. Germany is again an economic and political powerhouse in Europe, politically stable, and peaceful. After a decade of a center-right government (under

Chancellor Helmut Kohl), the country is currently led by the center-left Chancellor Gerhard Schroeder. Germany is fully integrated into the international community as a member of the European Union—an organization whose chief aim was to avoid future wars with an aggressive Germany by embracing it in the economic web of Europe.

MUNICH
(München)

Munich, Germany's most livable and "yuppie" city, is also one of its most historic, artistic, and entertaining. It's big and growing, with a population of more than 1.3 million. Until 1871, it was the capital of an independent Bavaria. Its imperial palaces, jewels, and grand boulevards constantly remind visitors that this was once a political and cultural powerhouse. And its recently bombed-out feeling reminds us that 75 years ago it provided a springboard for Nazism, and nearly 60 years ago it lost a war.

Orient yourself in Munich's old center with its colorful pedestrian mall. Immerse yourself in Munich's art and history—crown jewels, Baroque theater, Wittelsbach palaces, great paintings, and beautiful parks. Munich evenings are best spent in frothy beer halls, with their oompah, bunny-hopping, and belching Bavarian atmosphere. Pry big pretzels from buxom, no-nonsense beer maids.

ORIENTATION

(area code: 089)
The tourist's Munich is circled by a ring road (site of the old town wall) marked by four old gates: Karlstor (near the train station, known as the *Hauptbahnhof*), Sendlinger Tor, Isartor (near the river), and Odeonsplatz (no surviving gate, near the palace). Marienplatz marks the city's center. A great pedestrian-only zone (Kaufingerstrasse and Neuhauserstrasse) cuts this circle in half, running nearly from Karlstor and the train station through Marienplatz to Isartor. Orient yourself along this east–west axis. Ninety percent of the sights and hotels I recommend are within a 20-minute walk of Marienplatz and each other.

Planning Your Time

Munich is worth two days, including a half-day side-trip to Dachau. If necessary, its essence can be captured in a day (walk the center, tour a palace and a museum, and enjoy a beer-filled evening). Those without a car and in a hurry can do King Ludwig's castles (covered in the Bavaria and Tirol chapter) as a day trip from Munich by tour. Even Salzburg (2 hrs by train) can be a handy day trip from Munich.

Tourist Information

Munich has two helpful TIs. One is in front of the train station (with your back to the tracks, walk through the central hall, step outside and turn right; Mon–Sat 9:00–20:00, Sun 10:00–18:00, sometimes less Nov–March, tel. 089/233-0300). The other TI is on the main square, Marienplatz (Mon–Fri 10:00–20:00, Sat 10:00–16:00, closed Sun, some-times open later on summer Saturdays, www.muenchen-tourist.de). Pick up brochures and a city map (€0.30, often free in hotel lobbies) and con-firm your sightseeing plans. Consider the *Monats-programm* (€1.55, German-language list of sights and events calendar) and the free twice-monthly magazine *In München* (in German, lists all movies and enter-tainment in town, available at TI or any big cinema until supply runs out). The TI also sells Panorama city and castle tour tickets (no discount on castle tickets; purchase at EurAide or Panorama office for discount, see below). The TI can book you a room (you'll pay a down payment of about 15 percent, then pay the rest at the hotel), but you'll get a better value with my recommended hotels—contact them directly.

The **München Welcome Card,** sold by the TI, covers transporta-tion plus small discounts on minor sights (€6.50/1 day, €15.50/3 days). For most visitors, the transportation-only tickets are a better deal (see "Getting around Munich," below). If the line at the TI is bad, go to EurAide.

EurAide: The industrious, eager-to-help EurAide office in the train station is a godsend for Eurailers and budget travelers (June–Sept daily 7:45–12:45 & 14:00–18:00; Oct–May Mon–Fri 8:00–12:00 & 13:00–16:00, closed Sat–Sun; room 3 at track 11; tel. 089/593-889, fax 089/550-3965, www.euraide.com, see www.euraide.de/ricksteves for Romantic Road bus and Rhine cruise schedules, euraide @compuserve.com).

EurAide helps 600 visitors per day in the summer; do your home-work and have a list of questions ready. Mornings are busiest. Alan Wissenberg and his EurAide staff know your train-travel and accom-modations questions and have answers in clear American English. The German rail company pays them to help you design your best train travels. They make train reservations and sell train tickets, *couchettes,* and sleepers for the same price as the station ticket windows. EurAide can help locate rooms for a €3 fee. They offer a €1 city map and a free, information-packed newsletter. They sell Panorama city and castle tour tickets (castle tour discounted with railpass or ISIC student card). EurAide also sells a Prague Excursion train pass, convenient for Prague-bound Eurailers—good for train travel from any Czech border station to Prague and back to any border station within seven days (first class-€50, second class-€40, youth second class-€35; also through their U.S. office: tel. 941/480-1555, fax 941/480-1522). Every Wednesday in June and July, EurAide offers a Two Castle tour of Neuschwanstein and Linderhof that includes Wieskirche (frustrating without a car, see "Sights—Near Munich," page 66).

Arrival in Munich

By Train: Munich's train station is a sight in itself—one of those places that can turn an accountant into a vagabond. For a quick orientation in the station, use the big wall **maps** (as you leave the tracks, on the left wall of central hall) that show the train station, Munich, and Bavaria. For a quick rest stop, the Burger King's toilets (upstairs, free) are as pleasant and accessible as its hamburgers. More toilets are downstairs near track 26 (clean, but €1.10). Check out the bright and modern complex of **restaurants** and shops opposite track 14. The **k presse + buch** (across from track 23) is great for English-language books, papers, and magazines, including *Munich Found* (informative English-speaking residents' monthly, €3). You'll also find two **TIs** (the city TI and EurAide, see "Tourist Information" above) and **lockers** (€2, tracks 18, 26, and 31). **Car rental agencies** are up the steps opposite track 21 (Mon–Fri 7:00–21:00, Sat–Sun 9:00–17:00). A **pharmacy** is out the front door to the right, next to the TI (Mon–Fri 8:00–18:30, Sat 8:00–14:00, closed Sun, tel. 089/594-119). A quiet, non-smoking waiting room for train ticket/passholders is across from track 24 and up the escalator. You'll find a **Romantic Road Bus** office near track 36 (Deutsche Touring; see "Transportation Connections," page 80).

The U-Bahn, S-Bahn, and buses connect the station to the rest of the city (though many hotels listed in this book are within walking distance of the station). If you're looking for the train station and you're lost in the maze of underground corridors at the Hauptbahnhof U- and S-Bahn stations, follow the signs for DB (DeutscheBahn) to reach the train station.

By Plane: There are two good ways to connect the airport and downtown Munich: Take an easy 40-minute ride on subway S-8 (runs every 20 min between airport and Marienplatz, €8 or free with a validated and dated railpass—but it uses up a day of a Flexipass), or take the Lufthansa airport bus to—or from—the train station (€10, 3/hr, 45 min, buy tickets on bus; buses line up near taxi stands facing Arnulfstrasse, exit station near track 26). Airport info: tel. 089/97500, www.munich-airport.de.

Getting around Munich

Much of Munich is walkable. To reach sights away from the city center, use the fine tram, bus, and subway systems. Taxis are honest and professional, but expensive and generally unnecessary (except perhaps to avoid the time-consuming trip to Nymphenburg).

By Public Transit: Subways are called U-Bahns or S-Bahns (actually an underground-while-in-the-city commuter railway). Subway lines are numbered (for example, S-3 or U-5). Eurailpasses are good on the S-Bahn, but it will use up a day of a Flexipass.

Regular tickets cost €2 and are good for two hours of changes in one direction. For the shortest rides (1 or 2 stops), buy the €1 ticket (*Kurzstrecke*). The €4.60 all-day pass is a great deal. The Partner Daily Ticket (for €8) is valid all day for up to five adults and a dog (2 kids count as 1 adult, so 2 adults, 6 kids, and a dog can travel with this ticket). One-day single and partner tickets are valid until 6:00 the following morning. For longer stays, consider a Three-Day Ticket (€11 for 1 person, €18.50 partner ticket for the gang; valid until 6:00 the fourth morning).

Tickets are available from easy-to-use ticket machines (which take bills and coins), subway booths, and TIs. The entire system (bus/tram/subway) works on the same tickets. You must punch your own ticket in the machine on board (stamping it with the date and time). Plainclothes ticket-checkers enforce this honor system, rewarding freeloaders with stiff €40 fines. For more information, call 089/4142-4344 or see www.mvv-muenchen.de.

Important: All S-Bahn lines connect the Hauptbahnhof (main station) with Marienplatz (main square). If you want to use the S-Bahn and you're either at the station or Marienplatz, follow signs to the S-Bahn (U is not for you), and concern yourself only with the direction (Hauptbahnhof/Pasing or Marienplatz)—in German, *Richtung.*

By Bike: Munich—level and compact, with plenty of bike paths—feels good on two wheels. Bikes can be rented quickly and easily at the train station from **Radius Tours** (May–mid-Oct daily 10:00–18:00, closed mid-Oct–April, city bikes-€3/hr, €14/day, €17/24 hrs, €25/48 hrs, mountain bikes 20 percent more; for security they'll take a €50 deposit, credit-card imprint, or passport; in front of track 32, tel. 089/596-113, www.munichwalks.com). Radius also offers Dachau tours (see "Sights—Near Munich," below) and dispenses all the necessary tourist information (city map, bike routes).

Helpful Hints

Monday Tips: Most Munich sights (including Dachau) are closed on Monday. If you're in Munich on Monday, here are some suggestions: Visit the Deutsches Museum, Residenz, Neue Pinakothek, Nymphenburg Palace, or churches; take a walking tour or bus tour;

climb high for city views; stroll the pedestrian streets; have lunch at the Viktualien Markt (see "Eating," page 76); rent a bike for a spin through Englischer Garten; take a day trip to Salzburg or Ludwig's castles; or, if Oktoberfest is on, join the celebration.

Useful Phone Numbers: Pharmacy (at train station next to TI)—tel. 089/594-119; EurAide train info—tel. 089/593-889; American Express travel agency—tel. 089/2280-1465 (Mon–Fri 9:00–18:00, Sat 9:30–12:30, closed Sun, Promenade Platz 6); taxi—tel. 089/21610.

Internet Access: There's plenty of online access in Munich; easyInternetcafé dominates the scene, with great rates and an ideal location (daily 24 hrs, 500 terminals, opposite main entrance of station at Bahnhofplatz 1).

Laundry: A handy self-service *Waschcenter* is a 10-minute walk from the train station at Paul-Heyse-Strasse 21 (€6.50/15 lbs, €11/25 lbs, daily 7:00–23:00, English instructions, tel. 089/531-311, near the intersection with Landwehrstrasse).

Car Rental: Allround Car Rental has reasonable rates (around €40/day including insurance, Boschetsrieder Strasse 12, U-3: Obersendling, tel. 089/723-8383, www.allroundrent.de). Several car-rental agencies are located upstairs at the train station (Mon–Fri 7:00–21:00, Sat–Sun 9:00–17:00, opposite track 21).

Driver: Johann Fayoumi is reliable and speaks English (€50/hr, mobile 0174-183-8473, johannfayoumi@compuserve.de).

Bikes and Pedestrians: Signs painted on the sidewalk or blue-and-white street signs show which side of the sidewalk is designated for pedestrians and which is for cyclists. The strip of sidewalk closest to the street is usually reserved for cyclists. Wandering pedestrians may hear the ding-ding of a cyclist's bell, alerting them to move off the bike path.

TOURS OF MUNICH:
BY FOOT, BIKE, AND BUS

Walking Tours—Original Munich Walks offers two city walking tours: an introduction to the old town (€10, April–Oct daily at 10:00, 2.5 hrs, no tours Nov–March) and "Hitler and the Third Reich" (€10, April–Oct daily at 15:00, 3 hrs, no tours Nov–March). Contact Original Munich Walks to confirm the schedule (tel. 089/5502-9374, www.munichwalks.com, info@munichwalks.com). Both tours depart from the EurAide office (track 11) in the train station. There's no need to register—just show up. They also run a Dachau Memorial tour (see "Sights—Near Munich," page 66).

Local Guides—Three good local guides are Renate Suerbaum (€100/2 hrs, €120/3 hrs, tel. 089/283-374), Monika Hank (€100/2 hrs, €120/3 hrs, tel. 089/311-4819), and Georg Reichlmayr (€120/3 hrs, tel. 08131/86800, mobile 0170-341-6384, info@muenchen-stadtfuehrung.de). They helped me with much of the historical information in this chapter.

Bike Tours—Mike's Bike Tours, popular with the college crowd, are four-hour frat parties on wheels. The tours are slow-paced and the guides are better comedians than historians, but you do ride through the English Garden (€22, tips encouraged, 60-min break in Chinese Tower beer garden, daily March–Oct, 2/day mid-April–May and Aug, 3/day June–July, no need to reserve, bikes provided, meet under tower of Old Town Hall; for schedule, tel. 089/651-4275, mobile 0172-852-0660, www.mikesbiketours.com, or pick up brochure at TI).

City Bus Tour—Panorama Tours offers many itineraries, including

Munich Center

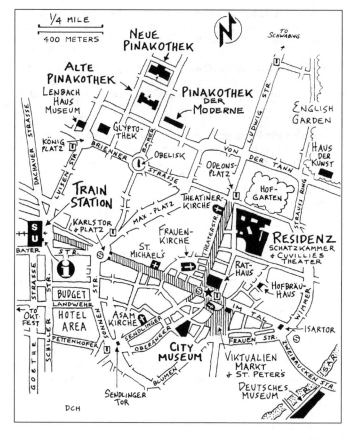

MUNICH AT A GLANCE

▲▲▲**Deutsches Museum** Germany's version of our Smithsonian Institution, with 10 miles of exhibits on science and technology. **Hours:** Daily 9:00–17:00.

▲▲**Marienplatz** Munich's main square, at the heart of a lively pedestrian zone, watched over by the New Town Hall (and its Glockenspiel show). **Hours:** Always open.

▲▲**Residenz** The elegant family palace of the Wittelsbachs, awash with Bavarian opulence. **Hours:** April–mid-Oct daily 9:00–18:00, mid-Oct–March daily 10:00-16:00.

▲▲**Residenz Schatzkammer** The Wittelsbachs' treasury, showing off a thousand years of crowns and royal knickknacks. **Hours:** April–mid-Oct daily 9:00–18:00, mid-Oct–March daily 10:00-16:00.

▲▲**Nymphenburg Palace** The Wittelsbachs' impressive summer palace, three miles from downtown, featuring a hunting lodge, coach museum, and fine royal porcelain collection. **Hours:** April–mid-Oct daily 9:00–18:00, mid-Oct–March daily 10:00–16:00.

▲▲**Alte Pinakothek** Bavaria's best painting gallery, with a wonderful collection of European masters from the 14th-19th centuries. **Hours:** Tue–Sun 10:00–17:00, Tue and Thu until 20:00, closed Mon.

▲**Neue Pinakothek** The Alte's hip twin sister, with paintings from 1800-1920. **Hours:** Wed–Thu 10:00-20:00, Fri-Mon 10:00–17:00, closed Tue.

one-hour orientation bus tours (departs from Hertie store across the street from front of train station). To take the orientation tour, call to confirm the departure time and place, then just show up and pay the driver (€11, daily, on the hour 10:00–16:00, April–Oct also 11:30 & 17:00, guide speaks German and English, exit station near track 26 and cross street to Arnulfstrasse 8, 3 doors left of big Eden-Hotel Wolff, tel. 089/5502-8995, www.autobusoberbayern.de). Tickets are also sold at EurAide and the TI. If you brought your AAA card to Europe with you, show it to get a €1 discount on the tour.

▲**Pinakothek der Moderne** The new modern art museum near the Alte and Neue Pinakotheks—with a building as interesting as the art. **Hours:** Tue-Sun 10:00-17:00, Thu-Fri until 20:00, closed Mon.

▲**Munich City Museum** The history of the city in five floors. **Hours:** Tue–Sun 10:00–18:00, closed Mon.

▲**English Garden** The largest city park on the Continent, packed with locals, tourists, surfers, and nude sunbathers. **Hours:** Always open.

▲**Olympic Grounds** The stadium and sports complex from Munich's 1972 Olympic stadium, now a lush park with a view tower and swimming pool. **Hours:** Grounds always open; tower daily 9:00–24:00, pool daily 7:00–23:30.

BMW Museum The BMW headquarters, with a car museum and factory tours. **Hours:** Museum daily 9:00–17:00, tours by appointment only.

Haus der Kunst Once Hitler's former temple of Nazi art, now hosts various modern art exhibitions. **Hours:** Daily 10:00–22:00.

Bavarian National Museum Collection of artifacts celebrating the culture of Germany's biggest state. **Hours:** Tue–Sun 10:00–17:00, Thu until 20:00.

Viktualien Markt Munich's "small-town" open-air market, perfect for a quick snack or meal. **Hours:** Mon-Sat, food stalls open until late.

SIGHTS

Central Munich
▲▲**Marienplatz and the Pedestrian Zone**—Riding the escalator out of the subway into sunlit Marienplatz (Mary's Square) gives you a fine first look at the glory of Munich: great buildings bombed flat and rebuilt, outdoor cafés, and people bustling and lingering like the birds and breeze with which they share this square. Notice the ornate facades of the gray, pointy Old Town Hall (Altes Rathaus) and the neo-Gothic New Town Hall (Neues Rathaus) with its famous *Glockenspiel.*

The **New Town Hall,** built from 1867 until 1906, dominates the square. Munich was a very royal city. Notice the politics of the statuary. The 40 statues—though sculpted only in 1900—decorate the city hall not with civic leaders, but with royals and blue-blooded nobility. Because this building survived the bombs and had a central location, it served as the U.S. military headquarters in 1945.

The New Town Hall is famous for its *Glockenspiel*—only 100 years old—which "jousts" daily at 11:00 and 12:00 all year (also at 17:00 May–Oct). The *spiel* recreates a royal wedding from the 16th century: The duke and his bride watch the action as the Bavarians (in white and blue) forever beat their enemies. Below, the coopers—famous for being the first to dance in the streets after a deadly plague lifted—do their popular jig.

Marienplatz is marked by a 1636 statue of the Virgin Mary, built here as a rallying point for the struggle against the Protestants. The cherubs are fighting against the four great biblical enemies of civilization: war, hunger, disease, and the wrong faith. The "wrong faith" is represented by the serpent (a.k.a. Martin Luther).

The **Old Town Hall** (right side of square as you face New Town Hall) was completely destroyed by WWII bombs and later rebuilt. Ludwig IV, an early Wittelsbach who was Holy Roman Emperor (back in the 14th century), stands in the center of the facade. He donated this great square to the people. On the bell tower, find the city seal with its monk and towers. Munich flourished because, in its early days, all salt trade had to stop here on Marienplatz.

Walking under the New Town Hall tower (past the TI), you enter a quiet courtyard (with a restaurant). Continue behind the building into **Marienhof**—a vast, peaceful, grassy square—medieval Munich's Jewish quarter, eyed by developers for years. Locals have decided to keep this space as a breather in Munich's otherwise intense core. Marienhof is a wonderful place to relax.

Back at Marienplatz, the **pedestrian mall** (Kaufingerstrasse and Neuhauserstrasse) leads you through a great shopping area, past carnivals of street entertainers and good old-fashioned slicers and dicers, the twin-towering Frauenkirche (built in 1470, rebuilt after World War II), and several fountains, to Karlstor and the train station. As one of Europe's first pedestrian zones, the mall enraged shopkeepers when it was built in 1972 for the Olympics. Today, it is "Munich's living room." Nine thousand shoppers pass through it each hour. The shopkeepers are happy...and merchants nearby are begging for their streets to become traffic-free. Imagine this street in hometown USA.

Three Churches near Marienplatz—In the pedestrian zone around Marienplatz, there are three noteworthy churches: St. Michael's, the Frauenkirche, and St. Peter's. To locate these churches: As you face the New Town Hall, St. Michael's is a few blocks down the pedestrian street

MUNICH BOMBED

As World War II drew to a close, it was clear that Munich would be destroyed. Hitler did not allow the evacuation of much of the town's portable art treasures and heritage, because a mass emptying of churches and civil buildings would have caused hysteria and been a statement of no confidence. While museums were closed (and therefore could be systematically emptied over the war years), public buildings were not. Rather than save the treasures, the Nazis photographed everything. What the bombs didn't get was destroyed by 10 years of rain and freezing winters. The first priority after the war was to get roofs over the ruined buildings. Only now, nearly 60 years after the last bombs fell, are the restorations—based on those Nazi photographs—finally being wrapped up.

Shortly after World War II, German cities established commissions to debate how they'd rebuild their cities: restoring the old towns or bulldozing and going modern. While Frankfurt voted to bulldoze (hence its Manhattan feel today), Munich voted—by a close margin—to rebuild its old town. Buildings cannot exceed the height of the church spires. Today, Munich has no real shopping malls. Consequently, its downtown is vital, filled with people who come to shop.

to your left; the Frauenkirche is the big twin-domed church at 10 o'clock; and St. Peter's is over your right shoulder.

St. Michael's Church, while one of the first great Renaissance buildings north of the Alps, has a brilliantly Baroque interior. Notice the interesting photos of the bombed-out city center near the entrance. The crypt contains 40 stark royal tombs, including the tomb of King Ludwig II, the "mad" king still loved by romantics (church entry free, daily 8:00–19:30; crypt-€2, Mon–Fri 9:30–16:30, Sat 9:30–14:30, closed Sun, less off-season).

The twin onion domes of the 500-year-old **Frauenkirche** (Church of Our Lady) are the symbol of the city. While much of the church was destroyed in World War II, the towers survived and the rest has been gloriously rebuilt. It was built in Gothic style, but money problems meant the domes weren't added until Renaissance times. Late Gothic buildings in Munich were generally brick—made locally, cheaper and faster than stone. This church was constructed in a remarkable 20 years. It's built on the grave of Ludwig IV (who died in 1348). His big, black, ornate tomb (now in the back) was originally in front at the high altar.

Standing in the back of the nave, notice how your eyes go to the only source of light—the altar...Christ...and Ludwig. Those Wittelsbachs—always trying to be associated with God. In fact, this alliance was instilled in people through the prayers they were forced to recite: "Virgin Mary, mother of our duke, please protect us."

You can ascend the tower for the city's highest public viewpoint, at 280 feet (€3, 86 steps, then elevator, April–Oct Mon–Sat 10:00–17:00, closed Sun and Nov–March).

St. Peter's Church, the oldest in town, overlooks Marienplatz. It's built on the hill where Munich's original monastic inhabitants probably settled. Outside, notice the old tombstones plastered onto the wall—a reminder that in the Napoleonic age, the cemeteries surrounding most city churches were (for hygienic and practical space reasons) dug up and moved. Inside, notice photos of the WWII bomb damage (on pillar closest to entrance). Then look at the marvelously restored altar and ceiling frescoes—possible with the help of Nazi catalog photos (see "Munich Bombed," page 51).

Munich has more relics than any city outside of Rome. For more than a hundred years, it was the pope's bastion against the rising tide of Protestantism in Northern Europe during the Reformation. Favors done in the defense of Catholicism earned the Wittelsbachs neat relic treats. For instance, check out the tomb of Mundita (second side chapel on left as you enter). She's a second-century martyr whose remains were given to Munich by Rome as thanks and a vivid reminder that those who die for the cause of the Roman Church go directly to Heaven without waiting for Judgment Day.

It's a long climb to the top of the spire (306 steps, no elevator)—much of it with two-way traffic on a one-lane staircase—but the view is dynamite (€1.50, Mon–Sat 9:00–19:00, Sun 10:00–19:00, off-season until 18:00). Try to be two flights from the top when the bells ring at the top of the hour, and then, when your friends back home ask you about your trip, you'll say, "What?"

▲▲City Views—Downtown Munich's three best city viewpoints are from the tops of: 1) St. Peter's Church (stairs only, described above); 2) Frauenkirche (stairs plus elevator, also described above); and 3) the New Town Hall (€2, elevator from under Marienplatz Glockenspiel, Mon–Fri 9:00–19:00, Sat–Sun 10:00–19:00).

Viktualien Markt—Early in the morning, you can still feel small-town Munich here—long a favorite with locals for fresh produce and good service (closed Sun). The most expensive real estate in town could never really support such a market, but the town charges only a percentage of the gross income, enabling these old-time shops to carry on (and keeping fast food chains out).

The huge maypole is a tradition. Fifteenth-century town market squares posted a maypole decorated with various symbols to explain which crafts and merchants were doing business in the market. Munich's maypole shows the city's six great brews and the crafts and festivities associated with brewing. (You can't have a kegger without coopers— find the merry barrel-makers.)

Munich's breweries each take turns here—notice the beer counter. A sign *(Heute im Ausschank)*, which changes every day or two, announces which of the six Munich beers is being served. Here, unlike at other beer gardens, you can order half a liter (for shoppers who want to have a quick sip and then keep on going).

The Viktualien Markt is an ideal place for a light meal (see "Eating—On or near Marienplatz," page 79).

Alois Dallmayr Delicatessen—When the king called out for dinner, he called Alois Dallmayr. As you enter, read the black plaque with the royal seal by the door: *Königlich Bayerischer Hof-Lieferant*—deliverer for the king of Bavaria and his court. This place became famous for its exotic and luxurious food items—tropical fruits, seafood, chocolates, fine wines, and coffee. Catering to royal and aristocratic tastes (and budgets), it's still the choice of Munich's old rich. Today, it's most famous for its coffee, dispensed from fine hand-painted Nymphenburg porcelain jugs (Mon–Wed 9:30–19:00, Thu–Fri 9:30–20:00, Sat 9:00–16:00, closed Sun, Dienerstrasse 14, behind New Town Hall).

▲Munich City Museum (Münchner Stadtmuseum)—The Munich city museum has five floors of exhibits. The ground floor contains an exhibit tracing the development of National Socialism. The first floor focuses on life in Munich through the centuries (including World War II), illustrated with paintings, photos, and models. The second floor hosts special exhibits (often more interesting than the permanent ones). The third floor features historic carnivals and puppets, and the fourth floor displays musical instruments from around the world (€2.50, €4 includes special exhibits, €4 family ticket includes only permanent exhibits, free on Sun, Tue–Sun 10:00–18:00, closed Mon, no English descriptions, no crowds, bored and playful guards, 3 blocks off Marienplatz at St. Jakob's Platz 1, tel. 089/2332-2370, www.stadtmuseum-online.de).

Across the street from the musuem entrance, they're building a new home for Munich's Jewish Museum (due to be finished in 2005, www.juedisches-museum.muenchen.de).

Rococo Churches—Near the Stadtmuseum, the private church of the Asam brothers **(Asamkirche)** is a gooey, drippy, Baroque-concentrate masterpiece by Bavaria's top two rococonuts. A few blocks away, the small **Damenstift Church** has a sculptural rendition of the Last Supper so real, you feel you're not alone (at intersection of Altheimer Ecke and Damenstiftstrasse, a block south of the pedestrian street).

Munich's Cluster of Art Museums (Pinakotheks)

This powerful cluster of museums (Alte, Neue, and Moderne Pina-kotheks) displays art spanning from the 14th century to modern times. The three museums sit around a grassy square just northeast of Königsplatz. They're a 10-minute walk from the nearest U-Bahn stops (listed below), but handy tram #27 whisks you right there from Karlsplatz (near the train station). The museums are free on Sunday. On other days, you can get a €12 combo-ticket that covers all three museums, which saves you money if you visit the modern art museum and at least one other. Each museum has an audioguide included in the price of entry, but on free Sundays, audioguides cost €4 apiece.

▲▲Alte Pinakothek—Bavaria's best painting gallery is newly renovated to show off a great collection of European masterpieces from the 14th to 19th centuries. You'll see paintings from the North (Germany, Holland, Belgium) and the South (mainly Italy). In general, as the Middle Ages came to an end, the Northern countries became capitalistic, democra-tic, and Protestant, while Southern countries (including Bavaria) remained more feudal, aristocratic, and Catholic. Since art reflects the society that produced it, we'll see two distinct styles.

Begin with the Northern Renaissance room, highlighting the art of Hieronymus Bosch, Lucas Cranach, and Grünewald. At Dürer's monumental *Four Apostles*, notice that the faces aren't those of ideal-ized Roman statues, but of real men with very human weaknesses. (John, left, seems to be brooding about his receding hairline.) These apostles by Dürer, as well as his Christ-like *Self-portrait in Fur Coat*, are symbols of a brand-new religion—Protestantism. For more on Dürer, see page 259.

Walk through the Italian Renaissance galleries and visit with the superstars—Giotto, Raphael, da Vinci, and Botticelli—until you get to the Rubens room. Peter Paul Rubens' art embodies the fleshy, emo-tional, Baroque style of Catholic countries, including his hometown of Flanders (Belgium). Examine *Hélène Fourment* and *Pastoral Scene* and decide for yourself—are the paintings gaudy or genius? Cool off with some calm still lifes, like Delff's dead ducks, and end up in frilly rococo-land, the province of wealthy aristocrats like Boucher's *Madame de Pompadour* (€5, free on Sun, Tue–Sun 10:00–17:00, Tue and Thu until 20:00, closed Mon, last entry 30 min before closing, free audioguide but no other English descriptions, €1.50 English booklet, €2 deposit for obligatory lockers, no flash photos, U-2 or U-8: Königsplatz, Barer Strasse 27, tel. 089/2380-5216, www.alte-pinakothek.de).

▲Neue Pinakothek—The Alte Pinakothek's hip sister is a twin build-ing across the square, showing off paintings from 1800 to 1920: Romanticism, realism, Impressionism, *Jugendstil*, Monet, Renoir, van Gogh, Goya, and Klimt (€5, free on Sun, Wed–Thu 10:00–20:00, Fri–Mon 10:00–17:00, closed Tue, €1.50 English booklet, classy café in basement, U-2 or U-8: Theresienstrasse, Barer Strasse 29 but enter on Theresienstrasse, tel. 089/2380-5195, www.neue-pinakothek.de).

▲**Pinakothek der Moderne**—This brand-new museum picks up where the other two leave off, covering the 20th century. It brags that it's six museums in one: four permanent displays (art, design, architecture, and works on paper) and two temporary exhibition halls. The permanent collections boast no greatest hits, but you'll find several lesser works by Picasso, Dalí, Miró, Magritte, Beckmann, Max Ernst, and abstract artists. The big, white, high-ceilinged building itself is worth a look. Even if you don't pay to visit the exhibits, step into the free entrance hall to see the sky-high atrium and the colorful blob-column descending the staircase (€9, combo-ticket for €3 more gets you into the other two Pinakotheks, free on Sun, Tue–Sun 10:00–17:00, Thu–Fri until 20:00, closed Mon, U-4 or U-5: Odeonsplatz, Barer Strasse 40, tel. 089/2380-5360, www.pinakothek-der-moderne.de).

Near the English Garden
▲**English Garden (Englischer Garten)**—Munich's "Central Park," the largest on the Continent, was laid out in 1789 by an American. Up to 300,000 locals commune with nature here on a sunny summer day. The park stretches three miles from the center, past the university, to the trendy and bohemian Schwabing quarter. For the best quick visit, follow the river from the surfers (under the bridge just past Haus der Kunst) downstream into the garden. Just beyond the hilltop temple, you'll find the big Chinese-pagoda beer garden. A rewarding respite from the city, the park is especially fun on a bike under the summer sun (bike rental at train station; unfortunately, there are no bike rental places near the park). Caution: While local law requires sun worshipers to wear clothes

GREEN MUNICH

Although the capital of a very conservative part of Germany, Munich has long been a liberal stronghold. For 13 years, the city council has been controlled by a Social Democrat/Green Party coalition. The city policies are pedestrian-friendly—you'll find most of the town center closed to normal traffic, with plenty of bike lanes and green spaces. Talking softly and hearing birds rather than motors, it's easy to forget you're in the center of a big city. On summer Mondays, the peace and quiet makes way for "blade Monday"—when streets in the center are closed to cars and as many as 30,000 in-line skaters swarm around town in a giant rolling party.

on the tram, this park is sprinkled with buck-naked sunbathers—quite a spectacle to most Americans (they're the ones riding their bikes into the river and trees).

Haus der Kunst—Built by Hitler as a temple of Nazi art, this bold and fascist building is now an impressive shell for various temporary art exhibits. Ironically, the art displayed in Hitler's "house of art" is the kind that annoyed the Führer most—modern (€7 per exhibit, combo-ticket for €10 if there are 2 exhibits, daily 10:00–22:00, at south end of Englischer Garten, tram #17 or bus #53 to Nationalmuseum/Haus der Kunst, Prinzregentenstrasse 1, tel. 089/211-270, www.hausderkunst.de). Just beyond the Haus der Kunst, where Prinzregentenstrasse crosses the Eisbach canal, you can watch locals actually surfing in the rapids created as the small river tumbles underground.

Bavarian National Museum (Bayerisches Nationalmuseum)—This is an interesting collection of Riemenschneider carvings, manger scenes, traditional living rooms, and old Bavarian houses (€3, free on Sun, Tue–Sun 10:00–17:00, Thu until 20:00, closed Mon, tram #17 or bus #53 to Nationalmuseum/Haus der Kunst, Prinzregentenstrasse 3, tel. 089/211-2401, www.bayerisches-nationalmuseum.de).

Near Deutsches Museum

▲▲▲**Deutsches Museum**—Germany's answer to our Smithsonian Institution, the Deutsches Museum traces the evolution of science and technology. With 10 miles of exhibits from astronomy to zymurgy, even those on roller skates will need to be selective. I have a good time wandering through well-described rooms of historic bikes, cars (Benz's first car...a 3-wheeler from the 1880s), trains, airplanes (Hitler's flying bomb from 1944), spaceships, mining, the harnessing of wind and water power, hydraulics, musical instruments, printing, chemistry, computers, astronomy, clocks...it's the Louvre of science and technology.

Most sections are well-described in English. The much-vaunted high-voltage demonstrations (3/day, 15 min, all in German) show the noisy creation of a five-foot bolt of lightning—not that exciting. There's also a state-of-the-art planetarium—in German (museum entry-€7.50, daily 9:00–17:00, worthwhile €4 English guidebook, self-service cafeteria; S-Bahn to Isartor, then walk 300 yards over the river, following signs; tel. 089/21791, www.deutsches-museum.de). Save this for a Monday, when virtually all of Munich's other museums are closed.

In 2003, the Deutsches Museum celebrated its 100th anniversary by opening a new annex across town called the **Verkehrszentrum** (Transportation Center), showing off all aspects of transport, from old big-wheeled bikes to sleek ICE super-trains. This branch museum is in a recently renovated turn-of-the-century conference hall near the Oktoberfest grounds, a.k.a. Theresienwiese (€2.50, daily 9:00–17:00,

Thu until 20:00, Theresienhöhe 14a, U-4 or U-5: Theresienwiese, tel. 089/2179-529).

Imax Theater—Adjacent to the Deutsches Museum, big-screen movies play hourly in regular format and 3-D (€8.50, Sun–Thu 11:00–22:00, Fri–Sat until 23:00, 12 different movies/day, call on weekends for reservations, Museumsinsel 1, tel. 089/2112-5180, www.fdt.de).

▲**Müllersches Volksbad**—This elegant *Jugendstil* (1901) public swimming pool, with steam baths and saunas, is just across the river from the Deutsches Museum (€3, daily 7:30–23:00, big pool closes Mon at 17:00, towels-€1.50, lockers-€5 deposit, no swimsuit rental, café, Rosenheimerstrasse 1, tel. 089/2361-3434).

Residenz

For a long hike through rebuilt corridors of gilded imperial Bavarian grandeur, tour the family palace of the Wittelsbachs, who ruled Bavaria for more than 700 years. This enormous palace, rated ▲▲, evolved from the 14th through the 19th centuries—as you'll see on the charts near the entrance.

Cost, Hours, Location: €5, combo-ticket for Residenz and treasury-€8.50, April–mid-Oct daily 9:00–18:00, mid-Oct–March daily 10:00–16:00, last entry 30 min before closing, 3 blocks north of Marienplatz, enter on Max-Joseph Platz or on Residenzstrasse.

Information: There are no English descriptions, but a free audioguide is planned for 2004. A €10 English book is also available. Tel. 089/290-671.

Touring the Residenz: While impressive, the Residenz can be confusing for visitors. Since it's so big, different sections are open in the mornings and in the afternoons (after 13:30 in summer, 12:30 in winter). Follow the *Führungslinie* signs and the self-guided tour below, which is designed to coincide with the afternoon route (a little more interesting than the morning), though due to ongoing renovations, either tour route can change without notice.

To help you find the highlights, I have numbered the rooms as they appear on the official map (free at entry), though be warned the rooms themselves aren't numbered. Between this important stuff, you'll wander through endless halls and throne rooms.

Shell Grotto (Room 6, actually outside, ground floor): This artificial grotto was an exercise in man controlling nature—a celebration of humanism. Renaissance humanism was a big deal when this was built in the 1550s. Imagine the ambience here during that time, with Mercury—the pre-Christian god of trade and business—overseeing the action, and red wine spurting from the mermaid's breasts and dripping from Medusa's head in the courtyard. The strange structure is made from Bavarian freshwater shells. This palace was demolished by WWII bombs. After the war, people had no money to contribute to the reconstruction—but they could gather shells. All the shells you see here were donated by small-town Bavarians as the grotto was rebuilt according to Nazi photos (see "Munich Bombed," page 51).

Antiquarium (Room 7, ground floor): In the mid-16th century, Europe's royal families (such as the Wittelsbachs) collected and displayed busts of emperors—implying a connection between themselves and the ancient Roman rulers. Given the huge demand for these classical statues in the courts of Europe, many of the "ancient busts" are fakes cranked out by crooked Romans. Still, a third of the statuary you see here is original. This was, and still is, a festival banquet hall. Two hundred dignitaries can dine here, surrounded by allegories of the goodness of just rule on the ceiling. Notice the small paintings around the room—these survived the bombs because they were painted in arches. Of great historic interest, these paintings show 120 Bavarian villages as they looked in 1550. Even today, when a Bavarian historian wants a record of how his village once looked, he comes here. Notice the town of Dachau in 1550 (above the door on the right as you leave). Just outside, photos show WWII bomb damage.

Gallery of the Wittelsbach Family (Room 4, ground floor): This room is from the 1740s (about 200 years younger than the Antiquarium). All official guests had to pass through here to meet the duke. The family tree in the center is labeled "genealogy of an imperial family." A big Wittelsbach/Hapsburg rivalry was worked out through 500 years of marriages and wars—when weddings failed to sort out a problem, they had a war. Opposite the tree are portraits of Charlemagne and Ludwig IV, each a Holy Roman Emperor and each wearing the same crown (now in Vienna). Ludwig IV was the first Wittelsbach HRE—an honor used for centuries to substantiate the family's claim to power. You are surrounded by a scrapbook covering 738 years of the Wittelsbach family.

Allied bombs took their toll on this hall. Above, the central ceiling painting is restored, but since there were no photos of the other two ceiling paintings, those spots remain empty. On the walls, notice how each painting was hastily cut out of its frame. Museums were closed in 1939 and would gradually be evacuated in anticipation of bombings. But public buildings like this palace could not prepare for the worst. Only in 1944, when bombs were imminent, was the hasty order given to slice each portrait out of its frame and hide them all away.

Nymphenburg Porcelain (Room 5, ground floor): In the 18th century, a royal family's status was bolstered by an in-house porcelain works (like Meissen for Dresden). The Wittelsbach family had their own Nymphenburg porcelain made for the palace. Notice how the mirrors give the effect of infinite pedestals with porcelain vases.

Reliquary (Room 95, upper floor, likely closed in the morning): Meet St. John the Baptist and his mother, Elizabeth (#47 and #48). The case in the center contains skeletons of three babies from the slaughter of the innocents in Bethlehem (when Herod, in an attempt to kill the baby Jesus, ordered all sons of a certain age killed).

Chapel (ground-floor Room 89, but also viewable from upper-floor room 96, likely closed in the morning): Dedicated to Mary, this late-Renaissance/early-Baroque gem was the site of Mad King Ludwig's funeral after his mysterious murder—or suicide—in 1886. (He's buried in St. Michael's church, see above.) While Ludwig was not popular in the political world, he was beloved by his people, and the funeral drew huge crowds. Mad King Ludwig's grandfather (Ludwig I) was married here in 1810. After the wedding ceremony, carriages rolled his guests to a rollicking reception, which turned out to be such a hit that it became an annual tradition—Oktoberfest.

Private Chapel of Maximilian I (Room 98, upper floor, likely closed in the morning): Maximilian I, the dominant Bavarian figure in the Thirty Years' War, built one of the most precious rooms in the palace. The miniature pipe organ (from around 1600) still works. The room is sumptuous, from the gold leaf and the fancy hinges to the stucco marble. (Stucco marble is fake marble—a mix of stucco, applied and polished. Designers liked it because it was less expensive than real marble and the color could be controlled.) Note the post-Renaissance perspective tricks decorating the walls; they were popular in the 17th century.

Precious Rooms (Rooms 55–62, upper floor): The Wittelsbachs were always trying to keep up with the Hapsburgs, and this long string of ceremonial rooms was all for show. The decor and furniture are rococo. The family art collection, now in the Alte Pinakothek, once decorated these walls. The bedroom (Room 60) was the official sleeping room, where the duke would get up and go to bed publicly, à la Louis XIV.

Red Room (Room 62, upper floor): The ultimate room is at the end of the corridor—the coral red room from 1740. (Coral red was *the* most royal of colors.) Imagine visiting the duke and having him take you here to ogle at miniature copies of the most famous paintings of the day, painted with one-haired brushes. (While these are copies, the originals will soon be on public display at Nymphenburg.) Notice the fun effect of the mirrors around you—the corner mirrors make things go forever and ever.

Halls of the Nibelungen (Room 75–80, ground floor): As you leave, the last few rooms are the Halls of the Nibelungen. The mythological scenes here were the basis of Wagner's *Der Ring des Nibelungen*. Wagner and Mad King Ludwig II (of Neuschwanstein fame) were friends and spent time hanging out here (c. 1864). These very images could well have inspired Wagner to write his *Ring* and Ludwig to build his "fairy-tale castle."

▲▲**Schatzkammer**—This treasury, next door to the Residenz, shows off a thousand years of Wittelsbach crowns and knickknacks (€5, includes audioguide, combo-ticket for Residenz and treasury-€8.50, same ticket window and hours as Residenz). Vienna's palace and jewels are better, but this is Bavaria's best, with fine 13th- and 14th-century crowns and delicately carved ivory and glass. A long clockwise circle through the eight rooms takes you chronologically through a thousand years of royal treasure. (It's a one-way system—getting lost is not an option.)

The oldest jewels in the first room are 200 years older than Munich itself. Many of these came from various prince-bishop collections when they were secularized (and their realms came under the rule of the Bavarian king from Munich) in the Napoleonic era (c. 1800). The tiny mobile altar allowed a Carolingian king to pack light in 890—and still have a little Mass while on the road.

In Room 3, study the reliquary with St. George killing the dragon—sparkling with more than 2,000 precious stones (#58). Get up close—you can almost hear the dragon hissing. It was made to contain the relics of St. George, who never existed (Pope John Paul II recently declared him nothing more than a legend). If you could lift the miniscule visor, you'd see that the carved ivory face of St. George is actually the Wittelsbach duke (the dragon represents the evil forces of Protestantism).

In the next room (#4), notice the vividly carved ivory crucifixes from 1630 (#157 and #158, on the right). These incredibly realistic sculptures were done by local artist Georg Petel, who was a friend of Peter Paul Rubens (whose painting of Christ on the cross—which you'll see across town in the Alte Pinakothek—is Petel's obvious inspiration). Look at the flesh of Jesus' wrist pulling around the nails.

Continue into the next room (#5). The freestanding glass case (#245) holds the never-used royal crowns of Bavaria. Napoleon ended the Holy Roman Empire and let the Wittelsbach family rule as kings of Bavaria. As a sign of friendship, this royal coronation gear was made in Paris by the same shop that made Napoleon's crown. But before the actual coronation, Bavaria joined in an all-Europe get-rid-of-Napoleon alliance, and suddenly these were too French to be used.

Attached to the Residenz is the Cuvilliés Theater (currently closed for renovation), dazzling enough to send you back to the days of divine monarchs. Even when the theater is open for visitors, you see only the sumptuous interior; there is no real exhibit.

To get to the Hofgarten (see below), face the Residenz entrance, then go left around the Residenz one long block to the palace's original entryway (flanked by the second set of lions—rub their noses for good luck) and enter the complex. After the first arch, bear left across the courtyard and cut through the entry to the Egyptian collection to reach the...

Hofgarten and Odeonsplatz—The elegant people's state garden (Hofgarten) is a delight on a sunny afternoon. The "Renaissance" temple centerpiece has great acoustics (and usually has a musician performing for tips from lazy listeners). The lane leads to a building housing the

Greater Munich

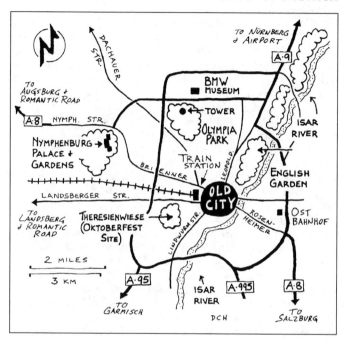

government of Bavaria and the Bavarian war memorial, which honors the fallen *heroes* of World War I, but only the *fallen* of World War II. The venerable old **Café Tambosi**—with a Viennese elegance inside and a relaxing garden setting outside—is a good antidote to all the beer halls (daily 8:00–1:00, Odeonsplatz 18, tel. 089/298-322).

The nearby Odeonsplatz is a part of the grand Munich vision. Studying your map, you'll see that this loggia (honoring Bavarian generals) is modeled in the Florence Renaissance style; the Greek-inspired museum quarter is one way, and in the distance (at the end of Ludwig Strasse) is the Roman-inspired triumphal arch. The church on Odeonsplatz contains nearly all the Wittelsbach tombs.

Nymphenburg Palace Complex

Nymphenburg Palace and the surrounding one-square-mile park are good for a royal stroll or bike ride. Here you'll find a pair of palaces, the Royal Stables Museum, and playful extras such as a bathhouse, pagoda, and artificial ruins.

Cost, Hours, and Information: €7.50 for everything, less for individual parts; all sights: April–mid-Oct daily 9:00–18:00, mid-Oct–March

daily 10:00–16:00; park: daily 6:00–dusk; tel. 089/179-080, www
.schloesser.bayern.de.

Getting to Nymphenburg: The palace is three miles northwest of
central Munich. Getting there from the center is easy, if time-consuming: Take tram #17 from Karlstor (20 min to palace) or the train station
(15 min to palace) to the Schloss Nymphenburg stop. From the bridge
by the tram stop, you'll see the palace, but you'll have to walk another 10
minutes to get there.

▲▲**Nymphenburg Palace**—In 1662, after 10 years of trying, the
Bavarian ruler Ferdinand Maria and his wife, Henriette Adelaide of
Savoy, finally had a son—Max Emanuel. In gratitude for a male heir,
Ferdinand gave this land to his Italian wife, who proceeded to build
an Italian-style Baroque palace. Their son expanded the palace to
today's size. For 200 years, this was the Wittelsbach family's summer
escape from Munich. (They still refer to themselves as princes and
live in one wing of the palace.) If "Wow!" is your first impression,
that's intentional.

Your visit is limited to 16 rooms on one floor—the Great Hall
(where you start), the King's Wing (to the right), and the Queen's Wing
(on the left). The €2.50 audioguide is informative and easy to use, but
the €6 English guidebook does little to make the palace meaningful. For
most visitors, the following self-guided tour is all you'll need:

The **Great Hall** in the middle was the dining hall. One of the
grandest rococo rooms in Bavaria, it was decorated by Zimmermann (of
Wieskirche fame) and Cuvilliés around 1760. The painting on the ceiling shows Olympian gods keeping the peace (the ruler's duty).

The **King's Wing** (right of entrance) has walls filled with
Wittelsbach portraits and stories. In the second room straight ahead,
notice the painting showing the huge palace grounds, with Munich (and
the twin onion domes of the Frauenkirche) three miles in the distance.
Imagine the logistics when the royal family—with their entourage of
200—decided to move out to the summer palace. The Wittelsbachs
were high rollers because, from 1624 until 1806, a Wittelsbach was one
of seven Electors of the Holy Roman Emperor. In 1806, Napoleon
ended that institution and made the Wittelsbachs kings. (Note: For simplicity, I've referred to the Wittelsbachs as kings and queens, even
though before 1806, these rulers were technically Electors.)

The **Queen's Wing** (left of entrance): Enter the first room, then
head to the right to find the very red room. You'll see the founding
couple, Henriette Adelaide and Ferdinand Maria (after the Counter-
Reformation, Bavarian men were named Maria—but his high heels and
leggings were another story altogether). The inlaid table was a wedding
present. The real pay-off—this palace—didn't come until Henriette
(who was 14 when married) got pregnant. The green room is the ceremonial bedroom. The painting to the right of the bed shows Max

Emanuel as a kid in a double portrait with his older sister. Both are dressed in the latest French fashions.

King Ludwig's Gallery of Beauties, near the end of the long hall in the Queen's Wing, is decorated with portraits of 36 beautiful women—all of them painted by Joseph Stieler from 1827 to 1850. King Ludwig I was a consummate girl-watcher who prided himself on the ability to appreciate beauty regardless of social rank. He would pick the prettiest women from the general public and invite them to the palace for a portrait. The women range in status from royal princesses to a humble cobbler's daughter...but Ludwig seemed to prefer brunettes. The portraits reflect the Biedermeier-style Romanticism of the day. If only these creaking floors could talk. Something about the place feels highly sexed, in a Prince Charles kind of way.

The next rooms are decorated in the neoclassical style of the Napoleonic era. At the rope, see the room where Ludwig II was born (August 25, 1845). Royal births were carefully witnessed. The mirror allowed for a better view. While Ludwig's death was shrouded in mystery, his birth was well-documented.

Amalienburg Palace—Three hundred yards from the palace, hiding in the park (ahead and to the left as you go through to back of palace), you'll find one of the finest rococo buildings in all of Europe. In 1734, Elector Karl Albrecht had this hunting lodge built for his wife, Maria Amalia—another rococo jewel designed by Cuvilliés and decorated by Zimmermann. Above the pink-and-white grand entryway, notice Diana, goddess of the chase, flanked by busts of satyrs. Look for the perch atop the roof where the queen would do her shooting. Behind a wall in the garden, dogs would scare non-flying pheasants. When they jumped up in the air above the wall, the sporting queen—as if shooting skeet—would pick them off.

Tourists enter this tiny getaway through the back door. The first room has doghouses under gun cupboards. Next, in the fine yellow-and-silver bedroom, see Vulcan forging arrows for amorous cupids at the foot of the bed. The bed is flanked by portraits of Karl Albrecht and Maria Amalia—decked out in hunting attire. She liked her dogs. The door under the portrait leads to stairs to the rooftop pheasant-shooting perch.

The mini–Hall of Mirrors is a blue-and-silver commotion of rococo nymphs designed by Cuvilliés in the mid-1700s. Cuvilliés, short and hunchbacked, showed a unique talent for art and was sent to Paris to study. In the next room, paintings show court festivities, formal hunting parties, and no-contest kills (where the animal is put at an impossible disadvantage—like shooting fish in a barrel). Finally, the kitchen is decorated with Chinese picnics on blue Dutch tiles.

Royal Stables Museum (Marstallmuseum)—This huge garage is lined with gilded Cinderella coaches. The highlight is just inside the entrance: the 1742 Karl Albrecht coronation coach. Because Karl Albrecht was an

Near Munich

emperor, this coach has eight horses. Kings only get six.

Wandering through the collection, you can trace the evolution of 300 years of coaches—getting lighter and with better suspension as they were harnessed to faster horses. The carousel for the royal kids made development of dexterity fun—lop off noses and heads and toss balls through the snake. The glass case is filled with accessories.

In the room after the carousel, find the painting on the right of Ludwig II on his sleigh at night. In his later years, Mad King Ludwig was a Michael Jackson-type recluse, who stayed away from the public eye and only went out at night. (At his nearby Linderhof Palace, he actually had a hydraulic-powered dining table that would rise from the kitchen below, completely set for the meal—so he wouldn't be seen by his servants.) In the next room, you'll find Ludwig's actual sleighs. Next to them is the coach designed for his wedding, but it was never used. Ludwig's over-the-top coaches were Baroque. But this was 1870. The coaches—like the king—were in the wrong century. Notice the photos (c. 1865, in the glass case) of Ludwig with the Romantic composer Richard Wagner.

Dachau

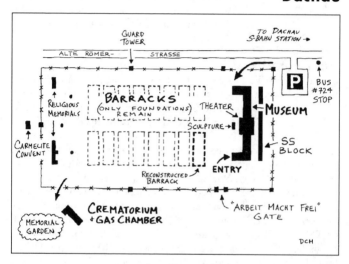

Ludwig cried on the day Wagner was married. Hmmm.

Across the passage from the museum entrance, the second hall is filled with coaches for everyday use. Upstairs is a collection of **Nymphenburg porcelain** (described by an English loaner booklet at the entrance). Historically, royal families such as the Wittelsbachs liked to have their own porcelain plants to make fit-for-a-king plates, vases, and so on. The Nymphenburg palace porcelain works is still in operation. Ludwig II ordered the masterpieces of his royal collection (now at the Alte Pinakothek) to be copied in porcelain for safekeeping into the distant future. Take a close look—these are exquisite.

Near the Olympic Grounds

▲**Olympic Grounds (Olympiapark München)**—Munich's great 1972 Olympic stadium and sports complex is now a lush park. It offers a tower with a commanding but so-high-it's-boring view from 820 feet (Olympiaturm, €3, daily 9:00–24:00, last trip 23:30, tel. 089/3067-2750); an excellent swimming pool (Olympia-Schwimmhalle, €3, daily 7:00–23:30, last entry 22:00, tel. 089/3067-2290); a good look at the center's striking "cobweb" style of architecture; and plenty of sun, grass, and picnic potential. Take U-3 to Olympia-Zentrum direct from Marienplatz (www.olympiapark-muenchen.de).

BMW Museum—The BMW headquarters, located in a striking building across the street from the Olympic Grounds, offers a museum popular with car buffs—but disappointing to others (the Deutshes Museum has a much better old-car exhibit; BMW Museum-€3, daily 9:00–17:00, last entry at 16:00, 1-hr audioguide-€2, U-3: Olympia-Zentrum, tel. 089/3822-5652). BMW fans should call several weeks in advance for factory tours (free, 2.5 hrs, by appointment, books up fast July–Aug, same tel. as above).

Near Munich

Castle Tours—Two of Mad King Ludwig's castles, Neuschwanstein and Linderhof, are a great day trip by tour. Without a tour, only Neuschwanstein is easy (2 hrs by train to Füssen, then 10-min bus ride to Neuschwanstein). For info on Ludwig's castles, see the Bavaria and Tirol chapter.

Panorama Tours offers rushed all-day bus tours of the two castles that include 30 minutes in Oberammergau (€41, castle admissions-€15 extra, daily April–Oct, Nov–March most days but not Mon, tickets also at EurAide office and TI, discounts for railpass and ISIC holders except when purchased at TI, Panorama office next to train station, exit station near track 26, Arnulfstrasse 8, 3 doors left of Eden-Hotel Wolff, tel. 089/5490-7560, www.autobusoberbayern.de). In summer, it's wise to purchase tickets a day ahead. Tours meet at 8:10 and depart at 8:30 from the Neptune fountain on Elisenstrasse near the botanical gardens (10-min walk from station). From the station, take Luisenstrasse, then turn right on Elisenstrasse.

On Wednesdays in June and July, EurAide operates an all-day train/bus Neuschwanstein–Linderhof–Wieskirche day tour (€40, €34 with railpass, castle admissions–€15 extra, departs at 7:30 from the EurAide office and beats most groups to avoid the long line, tel. 089/593-889).

Berchtesgaden—This resort, near Hitler's Eagle's Nest getaway, is easier as a day trip from Salzburg (just 12 miles away). See page 407 in the Salzburg chapter for more information.

▲**Andechs Monastery**—Where can you find a fine Baroque church in a rural Bavarian setting at a monastery that serves hearty food and perhaps the best beer in Germany, in a carnival atmosphere full of partying locals? At the Andechs Monastery, which crouches quietly with a big smile between two lakes just south of Munich. Come ready to eat tender chunks of pork, huge pretzels, spiraled white radishes, savory sauerkraut, and Andecher monk-made beer that would almost make celibacy tolerable. Everything is served in medieval portions; two people can split a meal. The great picnic center offers first-class views and second-class prices (beer garden open daily 10:00–23:00, last meal order 20:00, church until 18:00, tel. 08152/3760). To reach Andechs from Munich without a car, take the S-5 train to Herrsching, then catch a Rauner shuttle bus (€3 round-trip, hourly but not coordinated with S-Bahn). Consider sharing a €12 taxi from Herrsching or walk three miles. Don't miss a stroll up to the church, where you can sit peacefully and ponder the striking contrasts a trip through Germany offers....

▲▲**Dachau Concentration Camp Memorial (KZ-Gedenkstätte Dachau)**—Dachau was the first Nazi concentration camp (1933). Today, it's the most accessible camp for travelers and an effective voice from our recent but grisly past, pleading "Never again." A visit here is a valuable experience and, when approached thoughtfully, well worth the trouble. After this most powerful sightseeing experience, many people gain more respect for history and the dangers of not keeping tabs on their government. You'll likely see lots of students here, as all German schoolchildren are required to visit a concentration camp. It's interesting to think that a generation or two ago, people greeted each other with a robust *Sieg Heil!* Today, almost no Germans know the lyrics of their national anthem, and German flags are a rarity.

In the 1930s, the camp was outside the town, surrounded by a mile-wide restricted area. A huge training center stood next to the camp. While a relatively few 32,000 victims died in Dachau between 1933 and 1945 (in comparison, over a million were killed at Auschwitz in Poland), the camp is notorious because the people who ran the entire concentration camp system were trained here. Given the strict top-down Nazi management style, it's safe to assume that most of the demonic innovations for Hitler's mass killing originated here. This was a work camp, where inmates were used for slave labor. It was also a departure point for shipments of people destined for gas chambers in the east—where most of the mass murder took place (conveniently distant—far out of view of the German public).

Few realize that Dachau actually housed people longer *after* the war than during the war. After liberation, the fences were taken down, but numerous survivors who had nowhere else to go stayed. The camp was also used as a prison for camp officials convicted in the Dachau trials. And later, the camp was used for refugees from Eastern Europe. Until the 1960s, it was like a small town, with a cinema, shops, and so on.

A visit to the Dachau memorial consists of the museum, the bunker behind the museum, the restored barracks, and a pensive walk across the huge but now-empty camp to the shrines and crematorium at the far end. Upon arrival, pick up the mini-guide (€0.50), consider the excellent €2 booklet, and note when the next documentary film in English will be shown (20 min, normally shown at 11:30, 14:00, and 15:30, verify times on board as you enter museum). The memorial camp is free (Tue–Sun 9:00–17:00, last entry 30 min before closing, closed Mon, www.cc-memorial-site-dachau.org). For maximum understanding, rent the €2.50 audioguide, consider the English guided walk (daily in summer at 13:30, 2 hrs, donation requested, call 08131/669-970 or ask at door to confirm), or take a tour from Munich (see below).

The museum—which tries valiantly to personalize the plight of the victims—is thoughtfully described in English. Computer tap screens let you watch early newsreels. The theater shows a powerful documentary movie (see above for times).

The bunker was for "special prisoners," such as big-name politicians and failed Hitler assassins. It contains an exhibit on the notorious SS. (It's behind the theater; direct access after movie lets out, otherwise walk around museum past *Arbeit macht frei* sign.)

The most famous image of Dachau is the iron gate with the taunting slogan *Arbeit macht frei* (Work makes you free). Future plans call for visitors to enter here, through the camp's original entrance.

The big square between the museum and the reconstructed barracks was used for roll call. Twice a day, the entire camp population assembled here. They'd stand at attention until all were accounted for. If someone was missing (more likely dead than escaped), everyone would have to stand—often through the night—until the person was located.

Beyond the two reconstructed barracks (one is open to the public, where you can rent an audioguide), a long walk takes you past the foundations of the other barracks to four places of meditation and worship (Jewish, Catholic, Protestant, and Russian Orthodox). Beyond that is a Carmelite Convent.

To the left of the shrines, a memorial garden surrounds the camp crematorium. Look at the smokestack. You're standing on ground nourished by the ashes of those who died at Dachau.

While the Dachau gas chamber is like those at all other concentration camps, this one was never used.

Dachau is a 45-minute trip from downtown Munich: Take S-2 (direction: Petershausen) to Dachau, then from the station catch bus #724 or #726, Dachau-Ost, to KZ-Gedenkstätte (the camp). The two-zone €9 ticket covers the entire trip (both ways); with a railpass, just pay for the bus (€1 each way). Drivers follow Dachauerstrasse from downtown Munich to Dachau-Ost. Then follow the KZ-Gedenkstätte signs.

The town of Dachau is more pleasant than its unfortunate image (TI tel. 08131/75286). With 40,000 residents, located midway between Munich and its airport, it's now a high-priced and in-demand place to live.

Radius Tours, in front of track 32 in the Munich train station, offers hassle-free and thoughtful tours of the Dachau camp from Munich (€18 including the €9 cost of public transportation, April–Oct Tue–Sun at 9:20 & 13:00, also at 11:20 May–Aug, Nov–March Tue–Sun at 12:00, no Mon tours, allow 5 hrs round-trip, tel. 089/5502-9374, www.munichwalks.com).

SHOPPING

Shoppers will want to stroll from Marienplatz down **Theaterinstrasse.** On your left is **Fünf Höfe**—named for its five courtyards and filled with

Munich Hotels near the Train Station

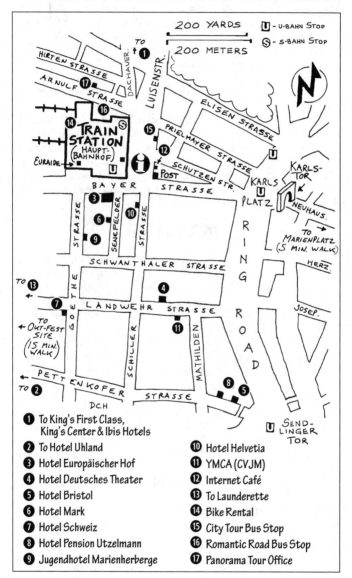

1 To King's First Class, King's Center & Ibis Hotels
2 To Hotel Uhland
3 Hotel Europäischer Hof
4 Hotel Deutsches Theater
5 Hotel Bristol
6 Hotel Mark
7 Hotel Schweiz
8 Hotel Pension Utzelmann
9 Jugendhotel Marienherberge
10 Hotel Helvetia
11 YMCA (CVJM)
12 Internet Café
13 To Launderette
14 Bike Rental
15 City Tour Bus Stop
16 Romantic Road Bus Stop
17 Panorama Tour Office

Germany's top shops (open until 20:00)—and the **Kunsthalle,** a big bank-sponsored art center with excellent temporary exhibits and impressive events (€7, half-price Mon, daily 10:00–20:00, tel. 089/224-412, www.hypo-kunsthalle.de). Note how its Swiss architects (who are also designing Munich's new grand soccer stadium for the 2006 World Cup) play with light and color. If you're not a shopper, wander through the Kunsthalle to appreciate the architecture. Across Theaterinstrasse at #30, the world-famous **Escada** is the home of Germany's premier fashion store.

For more top shops, stroll **Maximilian Strasse.** Ludwig made the grand but very impersonal Ludwig Strasse. As a reaction to this unpopular street by this unpopular king, his son Maximilian built a street designed for the people and for shopping. It leads from the National Theater over the Isar to the Bavarian Parliament (which you can see from the theater end). Birkenstocks are 40 percent cheaper in Munich than in the United States.

OKTOBERFEST

When King Ludwig I had his marriage reception in 1810, it was such a success that they made it an annual bash. These days, the Oktoberfest lasts 16 days (Sept 18–Oct 3 in 2004), ending on the first full weekend in October. It starts with an opening parade of more than 6,000 participants and fills eight huge beer tents with about 6,000 people each. A million gallons of beer later, they roast the last ox.

It's best to reserve a room early, but if you arrive in the morning (except Fri or Sat) and haven't called ahead, the TI can normally help. The Theresienwiese fairground (south of the train station), known as the "Wies'n," erupts in a frenzy of rides, dancing, and strangers strolling arm-in-arm down rows of picnic tables while the beer god stirs tons of beer, pretzels, and *Wurst* in a bubbling cauldron of fun. The three-loops roller coaster must be the wildest on earth (best before the beer-drinking). During the fair, the city functions even better than normal. It's a good time to sightsee, even if beer-hall rowdiness isn't your cup of tea.

SLEEPING

Near the Train Station
Budget hotels (€70–95 doubles, no elevator, shower down the hall) cluster in the area immediately south of the station. It feels seedy after dark (erotic cinemas, barnacles with lingerie tongues, men with moustaches in the shadows), but it's dangerous only for those in search of trouble. Still, I've listed places in more polite neighborhoods, generally a 5- or 10-minute walk from the station and handy to the center. They usually include a buffet breakfast.

$$$ **King's Hotel First Class,** a fancy 90-room business-class hotel, is a good, elegant splurge on weekends. You'll get a lobby with chandeliers and carved wooden ceilings, rooms with canopy beds, a sauna, and a well-polished staff (Sb-€140, Db-€170, Tb-€230, Fri–Sun special: Db-€105 except during fairs, 25 percent more during conventions and Oktoberfest, non-smoking rooms, air-con, elevator, cheap Internet access, parking-€13/day, 500 yards north of station at Dachauer Strasse 13, tel. 089/551-870, fax 089/5518-7300, www.kingshotels.com, 1stclass@kingshotels.com).

$$$ **King's Center Hotel,** a little less plush than its sister hotel (above), still has great rooms. It sits a half-block closer to the station, with 90 canopy-bed rooms, elegant public spaces, modern bathrooms,

SLEEP CODE

(€1 = about $1.10, country code: 49, area code: 089)
Sleep Code: **S** = Single, **D** = Double/Twin, **T** = Triple, **Q** = Quad, **b** = bathroom, **s** = shower only, **no CC** = Credit Cards not accepted, **SE** = Speaks English, **NSE** = No English, ***** = French hotel rating system (0–4 stars). Unless otherwise noted, credit cards are accepted.

To help you sort easily through these listings, I've divided the rooms into three categories based on the price for a standard double room with bath:

$$$ **Higher Priced**—Most rooms €90 or more.
$$ **Moderately Priced**—Most rooms between €60-90.
$ **Lower Priced**—Most rooms €60 or less.

There are no cheap beds in Munich. Youth hostels strictly enforce their 26-year-old age limit, and side-tripping in is a bad value. But there are plenty of decent, moderately priced rooms. I've listed places in two neighborhoods: within a few blocks of the central train station (Hauptbahnhof) and in the old center. Many of these places have complicated, slippery pricing schemes. I've listed the normal non-convention, non-festival prices. There are major conventions about 30 nights a year—prices increase from 20 percent to as much as 300 percent during Oktoberfest (Sept 18–Oct 3 in 2004; reserve well in advance). Prices can also go up slightly for smaller conventions. On the other hand, during slow times, you may be able to do better than the rates listed here—always ask.

and professional service (Sb-€93, Db-€115, Tb-€145, these special prices promised through 2004 for readers of this book, ask about Fri–Sun special: Sb/Db-€75, 30 percent more during conventions and Oktoberfest, breakfast-€12 extra but readers of this book get free breakfasts for 2-night stays, non-smoking rooms, elevator, cheap Internet access, from station walk north on Dachauer Strasse, take second left onto Marsstrasse, walk 200 yards to Marsstrasse 15, tel. 089/515-530, fax 089/5155-3300, www.kingshotels.com, center@kingshotels.com).

$$$ Hotel Uhland, a stately mansion in a safe-feeling residential neighborhood near the Theresienwiese Oktoberfest grounds, is a worthwhile splurge. Each one of its 31 rooms is different (normal non-convention rates: Sb-€68–72, Db-€80–95, Tb-€115; big discounts for booking online: Sb-€56–66, Db-€70–87, Tb-€107; non-smoking floor, elevator, cheap Internet access, free loaner bikes, free parking, bus #58 from station to Georg-Hirth-Platz or 15-min walk from station, walk up Goethestrasse and turn right on Pettenkoferstrasse, cross Georg-Hirth-Platz to Uhlandstrasse and find #1, tel. 089/543-350, fax 089/5433-5250, www.hotel-uhland.de, info@hotel-uhland.de).

$$$ Hotel Europäischer Hof is a huge, impersonal business hotel with 158 fine rooms. They have four categories of rooms, ranging from moderately expensive to outrageous: tourist (WC and shower down the hall), standard, comfort, and business class (sky-high official rates, but actual rates are usually closer to S-€40, Sb-€80, D-€50, Db-€92, 10 percent discount on prevailing rate if you reserve ahead and mention this book, further discount if you pay cash, no discounts during conventions and Oktoberfest weekends, non-smoking rooms, family rooms, elevator, free Internet access, Bayerstrasse 31, tel. 089/551-510, fax 089/5515-1222, www.heh.de, info@heh.de).

$$ Hotel Deutsches Theater is a brass-and-marble-filled place with 28 tight, modern, three-star rooms. Hardworking manager Johannas promises these special cash-only rates for readers of this book (Sb-€59, Db-€79, Tb-€89, more during fairs, non-smoking floor, pricier suites, elevator, Landwehrstrasse 18, tel. 089/545-8525, fax 089/5458-5261, www.hoteldeutschestheater.de, info@hoteldeutschestheater.de).

$$ Hotel Bristol has 57 similarly comfortable rooms and is also managed by Johannas, who offers the same special cash-only rates with this book (Sb-€59, Db-€79, Tb-€89, non-smoking rooms, elevator, hearty buffet breakfast on terrace, 1 metro stop from station, U-1 or U-2: Sendlinger Tor, Pettenkoferstrasse 2, tel. 089/595-151, fax 089/5482-2299, www.bristol-muc.com).

$$ Hotel Herzog is worth considering if you're having trouble finding a room, even though it's a bit farther from the center than my other listings (but handy to the U-Bahn). It's also run by Johannas, with 80 newly renovated rooms and the same cash-only prices with this book (Sb-€59, Db-€79, Tb-€89, non-smoking rooms, elevator, U-3 or U-6:

Munich Center Hotels & Restaurants

U = U-BAHN STOP   **S** = S-BAHN STOP

1. Pension Seibel
2. Pensions Lindner & Stadt Munich
3. Hotel Münchner Kindl
4. Hofbräuhaus
5. Weisses Bräuhaus
6. To Augustiner Beer Garden
7. Jodlerwirt Pub
8. Restaurants Nürnberger Bratwurst Glöckl & Andechser am Dom
9. Restaurant Altes Hackerhaus
10. Restaurant Spatenhaus
11. To Chinesischer Turm Biergarten & Seehaus
12. Heilig Geist Stuberl Pub
13. Restaurant Suppenküche
14. Glockenspiel Café
15. Alois Dallmayr Deli
16. Buxs Self-Service Vegetarian Restaurant
17. Forum Speisecafé
18. Prinz Myshkin Vegetarian Restaurant
19. Riva Pizzeria

Goetheplatz, Häberlstrasse 9, tel. 089/5999-3901, fax 089/5999-3996, www.hotel-herzog.de, info@hotel-herzog.de).

$$ Hotel Schweiz is simple outside and decent inside, with 57 new-feeling rooms and a good breakfast (Sb-€70, Db-€90, Tb-€110, soft prices with demand, non-smoking rooms, elevator, free Internet access, from the station walk 2 blocks down Goethestrasse to #26, tel. 089/543-6960, fax 089/5436-9696, www.hotel-schweiz.de, info@hotel -schweiz.de).

$$ Hotel Mark, run by Hotel Europäischer Hof (see above) and just around the corner from it, has a large, bright lobby, dim hallways, and 95 plain, cheaper rooms (high official rates, but normal rates usually around S-€35, basic Sb-€75, D-€50, basic Db-€88, newly renovated and non-smoking "basic plus" rooms cost 10 percent more, 10 percent discount on prevailing rate if you reserve ahead and mention this book, no discounts during conventions and Oktoberfest weekends, prices are squishy soft, their Web site often lists the biggest discounts, request quiet rooms in back facing courtyard, elevator, free Internet access, Senefelderstrasse 12, tel. 089/559-820, fax 089/5598-2333, www.hotel -mark.de, mark@heh.de).

$$ Hotel Ibis is a big, plain, efficient chain hotel offering 202 simple but comfortable little industrial-strength staterooms for a good price to local businesspeople on a tight per diem (Sb-€72, Db-€84, convention/Oktoberfest rate: Sb-€99, Db-€111; breakfast €9 per person extra, non-smoking rooms, air-con, elevator, Dachauer Strasse 21, tel. 089/551-930, fax 089/5519-3102, www.ibishotel.com, h1450@accor -hotels.com).

$$ Hotel Pension Utzelmann feels less cozy because of its huge rooms—especially the curiously cheap room #6—but they're lacy and richly furnished. It's in a pleasant neighborhood just a 10-minute walk from the station and a block off Sendlinger (S-€30–40, Ss-€50, Sb-€70, D-€55, Ds-€70, Db-€80, T-€85, Ts-€95, Tb-€110, more expensive during conventions and Oktoberfest, 1 metro stop from station, U-1 or U-2: Sendlinger Tor, Pettenkoferstrasse 6, enter through iron gate, tel. 089/594-889, fax 089/596-228, hotel-utzelmann@t-online.de, Frau Schlee).

$ Hotel Helvetia, with 44 rooms, is a family-run, well-maintained, on-the-ball backpacker's favorite (S-€30–39, D-€40–59, Ds-€50–69, T-€55–75, Q-€80–95, 20 percent more during Oktoberfest, ask for quiet side, free Internet access, elevator, laundry-€6/load, Schillerstrasse 6, tel. 089/590-6850, fax 089/5906-8570, www.hotel-helvetia.de, info@hotel -helvetia.de, courteous Pasha and Changiz SE).

$ Jugendhotel Marienherberge, for young women only, is clean and pleasant and has the best cheap beds in town (20 rooms, S-€30, €25/bed in D and T, €22/bed in 6-bed rooms, prices higher for those over 25, no CC, non-smoking, elevator, laundry machines, office open 8:00–24:00, harmless sex shop next door, a block from station at Goethestrasse 9, tel. 089/555-805, fax 089/5502-8260, invia-marienherberge@t-online.de).

$ CVJM (YMCA), open to all ages and sexes, has 85 beds in modern rooms (S-€32–37, D-€54, T-€75, €25/bed in a shared triple, those over 26 pay about 10 percent more, cheaper for 3 nights or more and in winter, €10/night more during Oktoberfest, free showers, includes breakfast, elevator, 24:30 curfew, Landwehrstrasse 13, tel. 089/552-1410, fax 089/550-4282, www.cvjm-muenchen.org).

In the Old Center

$$ Pension Seibel, two blocks off Marienplatz in a fun neighborhood, is central and cozy, run by friendly Kirstin and her trusty assistant, Ludwig, who both speak excellent English. This place is a great value given the location, but some readers have complained about cleanliness and street noise; request a quiet room in the back (S-€35–49, Sb-€45–65, D-€59–69, Db-€66–87, Tb-€77–99, these prices are promised through 2004 during non-fair periods if you show this book and pay cash, family apartment for up to 5 people-€36 each, tries to be non-smoking, good breakfast in small breakfast room, Reichenbachstrasse 8, tel. 089/231-9180, fax 089/267-803, www.seibel-hotels-munich.de, pension.seibel@t-online.de). Tram #17 takes you directly to the station and to Nymphenburg Palace. Kirstin's family runs the fine but inconveniently located **Hotel Seibel** (same prices, tel. 089/540-1420), a 15-minute walk behind the station overlooking the Oktoberfest fairgrounds.

$$ Pension Lindner is clean, quiet, and modern, with 10 pastel-bouquet rooms, mediocre plumbing, and—at times—indifferent service (S-€39, D-€64, Ds-€75, Db-€85, more during conventions and Oktoberfest, reception and breakfast in café below, elevator, Dultstrasse 1; from the train station, take U-2 one stop to Sendlinger Tor, then walk along Sendlinger Strasse toward the center and turn right on Dultstrasse; tel. 089/263-413, fax 089/268-760, www.pension-lindner.com, info@pension-lindner.com, Marion and Arzu SE).

$$ Hotel Münchner Kindl is a jolly place with 16 decent but over-priced rooms above a friendly local bar (S-€52, Ss-€66, Sb-€77, D-€72, Ds-€82, Db-€92, Tb-€107, Qb-€120, these prices through 2004 with this book, same rates 365 days a year, non-smoking rooms, night noises travel up central courtyard, a 15-min walk from station, or take the S-Bahn 1 stop to Karlstor, walk along main pedestrian street toward Marienplatz, turn right onto Eisenmann Strasse, go 2 blocks to Damenstiftstrasse 16, tel. 089/264-349, fax 089/264-526, www.hotel-muenchner-kindl.de, reservierung@hotel-muenchner-kindl.de, Renate Dittert SE).

$ The quirky **Pension Stadt Munich** (1 floor below Pension Lindner, above), isn't as homey, but it's OK if the Lindner is full (4 Ds-€60, no CC, a tad smoky, Dultstrasse 1, tel. 089/263-417, fax 089/267-548, Frau

Meiler is there in the morning, otherwise you must call and she'll come). From the station, take U-2 one stop to Sendlinger Tor. Walk along Sendlinger Strasse toward the center and turn right on Dultstrasse.

$ Munich's **youth hostels** charge €16 in 4- to 8-bed dorms and €21 in doubles (including breakfast and sheets) and strictly limit admission to YH members who are under 27. **Burg Schwaneck Hostel** is a renovated castle (23:30 curfew, 30 min from city center—take the S-7 to Pullach and then follow signs to Burgweg 4, tel. 089/7448-6670, fax 089/7448-6680, www.jugendherberge-burgschwaneck.de).

$ Munich's **International Youth Camp Kapuzinerhölzl** (a.k.a. "The Tent") offers 400 places on the wooden floor of a huge circus tent. You'll get a mattress (€8.50) or bed (€11), blankets, showers, lockers, washing machines, bike rental, Internet access, and breakfast. It can be a fun (but noisy) experience—kind of a cross between a slumber party and Woodstock. There's a cool table-tennis-and-Frisbee atmosphere throughout the day and no curfew at night (June–Aug only, no check-in 10:30–16:30, confirm first at TI that it's open, then catch tram #17 from train station to Botanischer Garten, direction Amalienburgstrasse, and follow the crowd down Franz-Schrankstrasse, tel. 089/175-090, fax 089/141-4300 www.the-tent.com, see-you@the-tent.de).

EATING

Munich cuisine is best seasoned with beer. You have two basic choices: beer halls like the Hofbräuhaus, where you'll find music and tourists, or the mellower beer gardens, where you'll find the Germans. Though Munich has more Michelin-star restaurants than any other German city, I'm here for the beer-garden fun. But when the *Wurst* and kraut get to be too much for you, consider one of the trendy spots south of Marienplatz.

In beer halls, beer gardens, or at the Viktualien Markt, try the most typical meal in town: *Weisswurst* (white sausage) with *süss* (sweet) *Senf* (mustard), a salty *Brezel* (pretzel), and *Weissbier*. Also unique and memorable is a *Stecherlfisch*—local fish on a stick (great with a pretzel and a big beer).

Beer Halls *(Bräuhäuser)* and Beer Gardens *(Biergarten)*

In Munich's beer halls and beer gardens, meals are inexpensive, white radishes are salted and cut in delicate spirals, and surly beer maids pull mustard packets from their cleavage.

Beer gardens go back to the days when monks brewed their beer and were allowed to sell it directly to the thirsty public. They stored their beer in cellars under courtyards kept cool by the shade of bushy chestnut trees. Eventually, tables were set up, and these convivial eateries evolved. The tradition (complete with chestnut trees) survives, and any real beer garden will keep a few tables (identified by not having a tablecloth) available for customers who only buy beer and bring in their own food.

Huge liter beers (called *ein Mass* in German, or *ein* pitcher in English) cost about €6. You can order your beer *helles* (light but not "lite," which is what you'll get if you say "*ein* beer"), *dunkles* (dark), or *Radler* (half lemon-lime soda, half beer). Beer gardens have a deposit system for their big glass steins: pay €1 extra and take the mug to the return man for your refund, or leave it on the table and lose your money. When you visit the WC, look for the vomitoriums.

Many beer halls have a cafeteria system. Eating outside is favored by the *Föhn* (warm winds that come over the Alps from Italy), which gives this part of Germany 30 more days of sunshine than the North—and sometimes even an Italian ambience. (Many locals attribute their ever-more-common outdoor dining to global warming.)

Beer halls take care of their regular customers. You'll notice many *Stammtische* (tables reserved for regulars and small groups such as the Happy Saturday club). They have a long tradition of being places of grassroots action—where the community activates. The Hofbräuhaus was the first place Hitler talked to a big crowd.

The **Hofbräuhaus** is the world's most famous—and grotesquely touristy—beer hall (read beer hall primer above, daily 9:00–24:00, music during lunch and dinner, Platzl 6, 5-min walk from Marienplatz, tel. 089/290-1360, www.hofbraeuhaus.de). Even if you don't eat here, check it out; it's fun to see 200 Japanese people drinking beer in a German beer hall...across from a Hard Rock Café. Germans go for the entertainment—to sing "Country Roads," see how Texas girls party, and watch salaried professionals from Tokyo chug beer. The music-every-night atmosphere is thick, and the fat, shiny-leather bands even get church mice to stand up and conduct three-quarter time with bread-sticks. My favorite light meal: €6.10 for a *paar Schweinswurst mit Kraut* (pork sausages with sauerkraut). The Hofbräuhaus hosts a gimmicky folk evening upstairs in the *Festsaal* nightly from 19:00 to 22:30. You can drop by anytime and eat their €20 buffet, or pay €5 and just order a drink. Walk up the stairs to the left of the entrance just to see the historic old Hofbräuhaus photos and prints.

Weisses Bräuhaus is more local and features good food and the region's fizzy wheat beer (€5–14, daily 9:00–24:00, Tal 7, between Marienplatz and Isartor, 2 blocks from Hofbräuhaus, tel. 089/290-1380). Hitler met with fellow fascists here in 1920, when his Nazi party had yet to ferment.

Augustiner Beer Garden is a sprawling haven for well-established local beer-lovers on a balmy evening (daily 10:00–24:00, food until 22:00, across from train tracks, 3 loooong blocks from station, away from the center at Arnulfstrasse 52, tram #17, taxis always waiting at the gate). For a true under-the-leaves beer garden packed with locals, this is very good.

The tiny **Jodlerwirt** is a woodsy, smart-alecky, yodeling kind of pub. The food is great, and the ambience is as Bavarian as you'll find. Avoid the basic ground-floor bar and climb the stairs into the action (Mon–Sat 19:00–3:00, closed Sun, food until 23:00, accordion act nightly from 20:30, Altenhofstrasse 4, between Hofbräuhaus and Marienplatz, tel. 089/221-249). Good food, lots of belly laughs...completely incomprehensible to the average tourist.

For a classier, fiercely Bavarian evening stewed in antlers, eat under a tree or inside at the **Nürnberger Bratwurst Glöckl am Dom** (famous with tourists, dark, medieval, cozy-feeling, with wenches or under the trees, €5–15 dinners, daily 9:30–24:00, Frauenplatz 9, at the rear of the twin-domed Frauenkirche, tel. 089/291-9450).

The trendier **Andechser am Dom,** on the same breezy square, serves Andechs beer and great food to appreciative locals. Locals say their dark beer is the best in town (ask for *dunkles*), but I love the light *(helles)*. The *Gourmetteller* is a great sampler of their specialties (€5–15, daily 10:00–24:00, Weinstrasse 7, reserve during peak times, tel. 089/298-481).

Locals enjoy the **Altes Hackerhaus** for traditional *Bayerischer* fare with a dressier feel. It offers a small courtyard and a fun forest of characteristic nooks festooned with old-time paintings and posters (daily 9:00–24:00, €15–25 meals, *Wurst* dishes €5–10, Sendlinger Strasse 14, tel. 089/260-5026).

Spatenhaus is the opera-goers' beer garden, serving more elegant Bavarian fare in a classier but still woodsy, traditional setting since 1896. Or eat outside, on the square facing the opera and palace (€20, daily 9:30–24:00, on Max-Joseph Platz opposite opera, Residenzstrasse 12, tel. 089/290-7060).

For outdoor atmosphere and a cheap meal, spend an evening at the Englischer Garten's **Chinesischer Turm** (Chinese pagoda) **Biergarten.** You're welcome to B.Y.O. food and grab a table or buy from the picnic stall *(Brotzeit)* right there. Don't bother to phone ahead—they have 6,000 seats. This is a fine place for a *Stecherlfisch,* sold for €9 at a separate kiosk (daily, long hours in good weather, usually live music, tel. 089/3838-7327, www.chinaturm.de).

Seehaus im Englishchen Garten is famous among Müncheners for its idyllic lakeside setting and excellent Mediterranean and traditional cooking. It's dressy and a bit snobbish, and understandably filled with locals who fit the same description. Choose from classy indoor or lakeside seating (daily 10:00–24:00, €20 meals, a fine 15-min hike into Englischer Garten—located on all the city maps, or tram #44 or taxi to the doorstep, Kleinhesselohe 3, tel. 089/3816-130).

Seehaus Beer Garden, adjacent to the fancy Seehaus restaurant, is a cheaper, more casual beer garden with all the normal *Wurst,* kraut, pretzels, and fine beer at typical prices. What makes this place special:

You're buried in Englischer Garten, enjoying the fine lakeside setting (daily, long hours from 11:00 when the weather's fine).

Heilig Geist Stuberl is a smoky, *Fasching*-all-year pub filled with all-day alcoholics aggressively inviting you in. Walk by and see what I mean (spirits listed on the door, Heiliggeiststrasse, just off the Viktualien Markt, see below).

Nontouristy Beer Halls Away from the Center

Wirthaus in der Au, near the Deutsches Museum, is a delightful place with friendly staff serving extremely traditional Bavarian cuisine to a young, local crowd (Mon–Fri 17:00–24:00, Sat–Sun 10:00–24:00, not very smoky, reservations a must, tram #18 or walk 10 min from Isartor S-Bahn, near Munich's English-language cinema, 2 blocks south of Deutsches Museum at Lilienstrasse 51, tel. 089/448-1400).

Unions-Bräu Haidhausen is a straightforward beer hall serving straightforward locals quality food with excellent Löwenbräu beer. Their coasters are decorated with a Jackie Onassis lookalike riding a keg—great souvenirs (Mon–Sat 10:00–24:00, Sun 10:00–16:00, immediately at Max-Weber-Platz U-Bahn station, Einsteinstrasse 42, tel. 089/477-677).

On or near Marienplatz

The **Viktualien Markt beer garden** taps you into about the best budget eating in town (closed Sun, see also "Sights—Central Munich," page 49). Countless stalls surround the beer garden and sell *Wurst*, sandwiches, produce, and so on. This B.Y.O.F. tradition goes back to the days when monks served beer, but not food. To picnic, choose a table without a tablecloth. This is a good place to grab a typical Munich *Weisswurst* and some beer. **Suppenküche** (soup kitchen) is fine for a small, cozy, sit-down lunch (€4 soup meals, go straight into market 50 yards from the intersection of Frauenstrasse and Reichenbachstrasse, green shop with black-and-white awning).

▲**Glockenspiel Café** is a good place for a coffee or a meal with a view down on the Marienplatz action (Mon–Sat 10:00–24:00, Sun 10:00–19:00, ride elevator from Rosenstrasse entrance, opposite Glockenspiel at Marienplatz 28, tel. 089/264-256).

The crown in **Alois Dallmayr**'s emblem indicates that the royal family assembled its picnics at this historic and expensive delicatessen (described in "Sights—Central Munich," above, Mon–Wed 9:30–19:00, Thu–Fri until 20:00, Sat 9:00–16:00, closed Sun, Dienerstrasse 14, behind New Town Hall). An elegant but pricey café serves light meals on the ground floor. Explore this dieter's purgatory and put together a royal picnic to munch in the nearby Hofgarten.

To save money, browse at Dallmayr's but buy in the basement **supermarkets** of the Kaufhof stores across Marienplatz or at Karlsplatz (Mon–Fri 9:30–20:00, Sat 9:30–16:00, closed Sun).

Trendy Non–Beer Hall Eateries
South of Marienplatz

The area south of Marienplatz is becoming a kind of Soho, with lots of trendy shops, wine bars, and classy bistros. Tucked in here are some handy, healthy, and quick places for lunch, as well as some fine old traditional restaurants.

Buxs Self-Service Vegetarian Restaurant is a fast, healthy, handy cafeteria. You'll find exactly what you want—as long as it's vegetarian. Fill a plate with your choice of soups, salads, and hot dishes, then pay by weight (€10 per typical plate, non-smoking, Mon–Fri 11:00–18:45, Sat 11:00–15:00, closed Sun, at bottom end of Viktualien Markt at Frauenstrasse 9, tel. 089/291-9550).

Forum Speisecafé, a young and dressy place without a hint of tourism, features international cuisine. It's famous for its creative breakfasts, served all day long, and for its weekly theme specials posted outside on the chalkboard (Sun–Thu 8:00–24:00, Fri–Sat 8:00–3:00, €6 lunches 11:30–14:30, €10 plates, smoky interior or breezy outdoor seating, corner of Corneliusstrasse and Müllerstrasse, tel. 089/268-818).

Prinz Myshkin is everybody's favorite dressy vegetarian place in the old center. You'll find an appetizing and creative selection of €10 plates. The decor is mod and the clientele is entirely local (daily 11:30–23:30, non-smoking section doesn't quite work, Hackenstrasse 2, tel. 089/265-596).

Riva Pizzeria has a wood-burning oven and lots of good-looking Italian cooks and waiters. This is the best place for an Italian alternative to all the pork and kraut (fresh, homemade-quality pizza, pasta, and salads, crowded indoor or pleasant streetside dining, Mon–Sat 8:00–24:00, Sun 11:00–24:00, a block toward Marienplatz from Isartor at Tal 44, tel. 089/220-240).

TRANSPORTATION CONNECTIONS

Munich is a super transportation hub (one reason it was the target of so many WWII bombs). Train info: tel. 01805/996-633.

By train to: Füssen (hrly, 2 hrs; for a Neuschwanstein Castle day trip, depart at 6:50 and arrive at 9:00 with transfer in Buchloe; or go direct at 8:51 and arrive at 10:57—confirm times at station), **Berlin** (hrly, 7 hrs), **Würzburg** (4/hr, 4 hrs, 1 change), **Nürnberg** (hrly, 1.75 hrs), **Frankfurt** (hrly, 4 hrs, 1 change), **Salzburg** (hrly, 2 hrs), **Vienna** (hrly, 5 hrs, 1 change), **Venice** (3/day, 8 hrs, changes), **Paris** (4/day, 9 hrs, changes), **Prague** (3/day, 7 hrs, 1 change—see "EurAide," above, for a Prague Excursion pass to supplement your railpass), and just about every other point in Western Europe. Munich is three hours from **Reutte,** Austria (every 2 hrs, 3 hrs, 1 change). Night trains run daily to Berlin, Vienna, Venice, Florence, Rome, Paris, Amsterdam, Brussels,

Copenhagen, and Prague (at least 7 hours to each city).

Romantic Road Bus: From Munich, the Romantic Road bus travels north to Dinkelsbühl and Rothenburg (and with a change, on to Würzburg and Frankfurt; daily April–Oct). To buy tickets in Munich, visit the Deutsche Touring office near track 36 in the Hauptbahnhof (Mon–Fri 9:00–18:00, Sat 9:00–12:30, closed Sun, Arnulfstrasse 3, tel. 089/5458-7011).

BAVARIA AND TIROL

Two hours south of Munich, between Germany's Bavaria and Austria's Tirol, is a timeless land of fairy-tale castles, painted buildings shared by cows and farmers, and locals who still yodel when they're happy.

In Germany's Bavaria, tour Mad King Ludwig's ornate Neuschwanstein Castle, Europe's most spectacular. Stop by the Wieskirche, a textbook example of Bavarian rococo bursting with curly curlicues, and browse through Oberammergau, Germany's woodcarving capital and home of the famous Passion play.

In Austria's Tirol, hike to the ruined Ehrenberg castle, scream down a ski slope on an oversized skateboard, and then catch your breath for an evening of yodeling and slap dancing.

In this chapter, I'll cover Bavaria first, then Tirol. Austria's Tirol is easier and cheaper than touristy Bavaria. My favorite home base for exploring Bavaria's castles is actually in Austria, in the town of Reutte. Füssen, in Germany, is a handier home base for train travelers.

Planning Your Time

While Germans and Austrians vacation here for a week or two at a time, the typical speedy American traveler will find two days' worth of sight-seeing. With a car and more time, you could enjoy three or four days, but the basic visit ranges anywhere from a long day trip from Munich to a three-night, two-day visit. If the weather's good and you're not going to Switzerland, be sure to ride a lift to an alpine peak.

By Car: A good schedule for a one-day circular drive from Reutte is 7:30-Breakfast, 8:00-Depart hotel, 8:30-Arrive at Neuschwanstein to pick up tickets for two castles (which you reserved by telephone several days earlier), 9:00-Tour Hohenschwangau, 11:00-Tour Neuschwanstein, 13:00-Drive to the Wieskirche (20-min stop) and on to Linderhof, 14:30-Tour Linderhof, 16:30-Drive along scenic Plansee back into Austria, 17:30-Back at hotel, 19:00-Dinner at hotel and per-

Highlights of Bavaria and Tirol

haps a folk evening (or the Ludwig II musical). In peak season, you might arrive later at Linderhof to avoid the crowds. The next morning, you could stroll through Reutte, hike to the Ehrenberg ruins, and ride the luge on your way to Innsbruck, Munich, Switzerland, Venice, or wherever.

By Public Transportation: Train travelers can use Füssen as a base and bus or bike the three miles to Neuschwanstein. Reutte is connected by bus with Füssen (except Sun; taxi €28 one-way). If you're based in Reutte, you can bike to the Ehrenberg ruins (just outside Reutte) and to Neuschwanstein Castle/Tegelberg luge (90 min). A one-way taxi from Reutte to Neuschwanstein costs about €32. Or, if you stay at the recommended Gutshof zum Schluxen hotel, you can hike through the woods to Neuschwanstein (60 min).

Getting around Bavaria and Tirol

By Car: This region is ideal by car. All the sights are within an easy 60-mile loop from Reutte or Füssen. Even if you're doing the rest of your trip by train, consider renting a car for the day here (as cheap as €50/day; see "Car Rental," page 86).

By Public Transportation: It can be frustrating. Local bus service in the region is spotty for sightseeing. If you're rushed and without wheels, Reutte, the Wieskirche, Linderhof, and the luge rides are probably not worth the trouble, but the Tegelberg luge near Neuschwanstein is within walking distance of the castle.

Füssen (with a 2-hr train ride to/from Munich every hour, some with a transfer in Buchloe) is three miles from Neuschwanstein Castle with easy bus and bike connections (see "Getting to the Castles from Füssen or Reutte," page 90). Reutte is a 30-minute bus ride from Füssen (Mon–Fri 6/day, Sat 2/day, none Sun, €3.20; taxis from Reutte to the castles are €32 one-way; to Füssen, €28).

Buses also run from Füssen to Oberammergau (4–5/day, less off-season, 1.5 hr, some with transfer in Echelsbacher Brücke; bus often marked Garmisch, confirm with driver that bus will stop in Oberammergau). From Munich, visiting Oberammergau directly by train is easier (hrly, 1.75 hrs, change in Murnau) than going to Füssen to catch the bus.

Füssen to Linderhof by public transportation will burn most of a valuable sightseeing day; you'll spend more time on the bus (or waiting for it) than you will at the castle. Skip Linderhof—or rent a car for the day. If you must go, take an early bus to Oberammergau, which has direct bus connections to Linderhof (4/day in summer, less off-season, 30 min).

Confirm all bus schedules in Füssen by checking the big board at the bus stop across from the train station, buying a bus timetable (€0.30) at the TI or train station, or calling 08362/939-0505. For longer-distance bus trips (such as to Garmisch or Linderhof), you'll save money if you by a *Tagesticket* (day pass).

By Tour: If you're interested only in Bavarian castles, consider an all-day organized bus tour of the Bavarian biggies as a side trip from Munich (see Munich chapter).

By Bike: This is great biking country. Shops in or near train stations rent bikes for €8–15 per day. The ride from Reutte to Neuschwanstein and the Tegelberg luge (90 min) is great for those with the time and energy.

By Thumb: Hitchhiking, always risky, is a slow-but-possible way to connect the public transportation gaps.

Füssen

Füssen has been a strategic stop since ancient times. Its main street sits on the Via Claudia Augusta, which crossed the Alps (over Brenner Pass) in Roman times. The town was the southern terminus of a medieval trade route now known among modern tourists as the "Romantic Road." Dramatically situated under a renovated castle on the lively Lech River, Füssen just celebrated its 700th birthday.

Unfortunately, Füssen is overrun by tourists in the summer. Traffic can be exasperating. Apart from Füssen's cobbled and arcaded town center, there's little real sightseeing here. The striking-from-a-distance **castle** houses a boring picture gallery. The mediocre **city museum** in the monastery below the castle exhibits lifestyles of 200 years ago and the story of the monastery, and offers displays on the development of the violin, for which Füssen is famous (€2.50, €3 includes castle gallery, April–Oct Tue–Sun 10:00–17:00, closed Mon, Nov–March Tue–Sun 13:00–16:00, closed Mon, English descriptions, tel. 08362/903-145).

Füssen's newest attraction, the **Model Railroad Museum** (Modelleisenbahn-Museum ZeitscHieneN), is small and overpriced but interesting, featuring model trains of all types—including, probably, the one you rode to town. The collection, gathered over a lifetime by brothers Ulf and Falk Haase, was donated by their mom to the town under the condition that this museum would be built (€4.50, Tue–Sun 10:00–18:00, closed Mon, Kemptener Strasse 7, tel. 08362/929-678).

Halfway between Füssen and the border (as you drive, or a woodsy walk from the town) is the **Lechfall,** a thunderous waterfall (with a handy WC).

ORIENTATION

(area code: 08362)

Füssen's train station is a few blocks from the TI, the town center (a cobbled shopping mall), and all my hotel listings (see "Sleeping in Füssen," below). If necessary, the TI can help you find a room (June–mid-Sept Mon–Sat 8:30–18:30, Sun 10:00–12:00, less off-season, 3 blocks down Bahnhofstrasse from station, tel. 08362/93850, fax 08362/938-520, www.fuessen.de). After hours, the little self-service info pavilion (7:00–24:30) near the front of the TI features an automated room-finding service.

Arrival in Füssen: Exit left as you leave the train station (lockers available) and walk a few straight blocks to the center of town and the TI. To get to Neuschwanstein or Reutte, catch a bus from in front of the station.

Bike Rental: Rent from friendly Christian at Preisschranke next to the train station (€8/24 hrs, May–Sept Mon–Sat 9:00–20:00, Oct–April Mon–Fri 10:00–18:00, Sat 10:00-15:00, closed Sun, tel. 08362/921-544; if Christian is not there during opening hours, call his mobile: 0178-374-0219). Rad Zacherl has a bigger selection but less convenient location (€8/24 hrs, mountain bikes-€15/24 hrs, passport number for deposit, May–Sept Mon–Fri 9:00–18:00, Sat 9:00–13:00, closed Sun, Oct–April Mon–Fri 9:00–12:00 & 14:00–18:00, Sat 9:00–13:00, closed Sun, 1.25 miles out of town at Kemptener Strasse 119, tel. 08362/3292, www.rad-zacherl.de).

Car Rental: Peter Schlichtling (€50/24 hrs, includes insurance, Kemptener Strasse 26, tel. 08362/922-122, www.schlichtling.de) is cheaper and more central than Hertz (Füssenerstrasse 112, tel. 08362/986-580).

Laundry: Pfronter Reinigung Wäscherei does full-service wash and dry in three hours (€11/load, Mon–Fri 9:00–12:00 & 14:00–17:00, Sat 10:00–12:30, closed Wed afternoon and Sun, in parking lot of Hotel Hirsch, 2 blocks past TI on the way out of town, Sebastianstrasse 3, tel. 08362/4529).

Internet: Try Videoland (€2/30 min, €3/hr, Mon–Sat 16:00–22:00, Sun 16:00–20:00, Luitpoldstrasse 11, tel. 08362/38300).

SIGHTS

Neuschwanstein and Hohenschwangau Castles

The most popular tourist destination in Bavaria is the "King's Castles" *(Königsschlösser)*. With fairy-tale turrets in a fairy-tale alpine setting built by a fairy-tale king, they are understandably popular. The well-organized visitor can have a great four-hour visit. Others will just stand in line and perhaps not even see the castles. The key: Phone ahead for a reservation (details below) or arrive by 8:00 (you'll have time to see both castles, consider fun options nearby—mountain lift, luge course, Füssen town—and get out by early afternoon). Off-season (Oct–June), you have a little more flexibility—but it's still a good idea to get an early start (try to arrive by 9:00).

▲▲▲**Neuschwanstein Castle**—Imagine Mad King Ludwig as a boy, climbing the hills above his dad's castle, Hohenschwangau (see below), dreaming up the ultimate fairy-tale castle. He had the power to make his dream concrete and stucco. Neuschwanstein was designed by a painter first...then an architect. It looks medieval, but it's only about as old as the Eiffel Tower. It feels like something you'd see at a home show for 19th-century royalty. Built from 1869 to 1886, it's the epitome of the Romanticism popular in 19th-century Europe. Construction stopped with Ludwig's death (only a third of the interior was finished), and within six weeks, tourists were paying to go through it.

"MAD" KING LUDWIG

Ludwig II (a.k.a. "Mad" King Ludwig), a tragic figure, ruled Bavaria for 23 years until his death in 1886 at the age of 41. Politically, his reality was to "rule" either as a pawn of Prussia or a pawn of Austria. Rather than deal with politics in Bavaria's capital, Munich, Ludwig frittered away most of his time at his family's hunting palace, Hohenschwangau. He spent much of his adult life constructing his fanciful Neuschwanstein Castle— like a kid builds a tree house—on a neighboring hill upon the scant ruins of a medieval castle. Although Ludwig spent 17 years building Neuschwanstein, he lived in it only 172 days. Ludwig was a true Romantic living in a Romantic age. His best friends were artists, poets, and composers such as Richard Wagner. His palaces are wallpapered with misty medieval themes—especially those from Wagnerian operas. Eventually he was declared mentally unfit to rule Bavaria and taken away from Neuschwanstein. Two days after this eviction, Ludwig was found dead in a lake. To this day, people debate whether the king was murdered or committed suicide.

Today, guides herd groups of 60 through the castle, giving an interesting—if rushed—30-minute tour. You'll go up and down more than 300 steps, through lavish Wagnerian dream rooms, a royal state-of-the-19th-century-art kitchen, the king's gilded-lily bedroom, and his extravagant throne room. You'll visit 15 rooms with their original furnishings and fanciful wall paintings. After the tour, you'll see a room lined with fascinating drawings (described in English) of the castle plans, construction, and drawings from 1883 of Falkenstein—a whimsical, over-the-top, never-built castle that makes Neuschwanstein look stubby. Falkenstein occupied Ludwig's fantasies the year he died. Following the tour, a 20-minute slide show (alternating German and English) plays continuously. If English is on, pop in. If not, it's not worth waiting for.

Mary's Bridge (Marienbrücke)—Before or after the Neuschwanstein tour, climb up to Mary's Bridge to marvel at Ludwig's castle, just as Ludwig did. This bridge was quite an engineering accomplishment 100 years ago. From the bridge, the frisky can hike even higher to the "Beware—Danger of Death" signs and an even more glorious castle view. (Access to the bridge is closed in bad winter weather, but many travelers walk around the barriers to get there—at their own risk, of course.) For the most interesting descent from Neuschwanstein (15 min longer and extremely slippery when wet), follow signs to the Pöllat Gorge.

Neuschwanstein and Hohenschwangau

NOTE: MAP NOT TO SCALE
BORDER TO ALPSEE PARKING = 3 MI. DRIVE
ALPSEE PARKING TO NEUSCH. = 30 MIN. WALK

❶ Beim "Landhannes" Rooms
❷ Alpenhotel Meier
❸ Sonnenhof Rooms

▲▲**Hohenschwangau Castle**—Standing quietly below Neuschwanstein, the big yellow Hohenschwangau Castle was Ludwig's boyhood home. Originally built in the 12th century, it was ruined by Napoleon. Ludwig's father, Maximilian, rebuilt it, and you'll see it as it looked in 1836. It's more lived-in and historic, and excellent 30-minute tours actually give a better glimpse of Ludwig's life than the more-visited and famous Neuschwanstein Castle tour.

Cost and Hours: Each castle costs €8, a *Königsticket* for both castles costs €15, and children under 18 are admitted free (castles open April–Sept daily from 9:00 with last tour departing at 18:00, Oct–March daily from 10:00 with last tour at 16:00).

Getting Tickets for the Castles: Every tour bus in Bavaria converges on Neuschwanstein, and tourists flush in each morning from

Munich. A handy reservation system (see below) sorts out the chaos for smart travelers. Tickets come with admission times. (Miss this time and you don't get in.) To tour both castles, you must do Hohenschwangau first (logical, since this gives a better introduction to Ludwig's short life). You'll get two tour times: Hohenschwangau and then, two hours later, Neuschwanstein.

If you arrive late and without a reservation, you'll spend two hours in the ticket line and may find all tours for the day booked. A **ticket center** for both Neuschwanstein and Hohenschwangau is located at street level between the two castles, a few blocks from the TI toward the Alpsee (April–Sept daily 7:30–18:00, Oct–March daily 8:30–16:00, last tickets sold for Neuschwanstein 60 min before closing, for Hohenschwangau 30 min before closing). First tours start around 9:00. Arrive by 8:00 and you'll likely be touring by 9:00. Warning: During the summer, tickets for English tours can run out by 16:00.

It's best to reserve ahead in peak season (July–Sept, especially Aug). You can make reservations a minimum of 24 hours in advance by contacting the ticket office by phone (tel. 08362/930-830) or e-mail (info@ticket-center-hohenschwangau.de), or booking online (www .ticket-center-hohenschwangau.de). Tickets reserved in advance cost €1.60 extra (per person, per castle), and ticket holders must be at the ticket office well before the appointed entry time (30 min for Hohenschwangau, 60 min for Neuschwanstein, allowing time to make your way up to the castle). Remember that many of the businesses are owned by the old royal family, so they encourage you to space the two tours longer than necessary in hopes that you'll spend a little more money. Insist on the tightest schedule—with no lunchtime—if you don't want too much down time.

Services: The helpful TI, bus stop, ATM, and telephones cluster around the main intersection (TI open April–June daily 9:00–17:00, July–Sept daily 9:00–18:00, Oct–March daily 9:00–16:00, tel. 08362/ 819-840, www.schwangau.de).

The "village" at the foot of Europe's Disney castle feeds off the droves of hungry, shop-happy tourists. The Bräustüberl cafeteria serves the cheapest grub (often with live folk music). The Alpsee is ideal for a picnic, but there are no grocery shops in the area. Your best bet is getting food to go from one of the many bratwurst stands (between the ticket center and TI) for a lazy lunch at the lakeside park or in one of the old-fashioned rowboats (rented by the hour in summer).

Getting to the Castles: From the ticket booth, Hohenschwangau is an easy 10-minute climb. Neuschwanstein is a steep 30-minute hike. To minimize hiking to Neuschwanstein, you can take a shuttle bus (from in front of Hotel Lisl, just above ticket office and to the left) or horse-drawn carriage (from in front of Hotel Müller, just above ticket office and to the right), but neither gets you to the castle doorstep. The frequent shuttle buses drop you off at Mary's Bridge, leaving you a steep 10-minute downhill walk from the castle—be sure to see the view from Mary's Bridge before hiking down to the castle (€1.80 up; €2.60 round-trip not worth it since you have to hike up to bus stop for return trip). Carriages (€5 up, €2.50 down) are slower than walking and they stop below Neuschwanstein, leaving you a five-minute uphill hike. Note: If it's less than an hour until your Neuschwanstein tour time, you'll need to hike—even at a brisk pace, it still takes 30 minutes. For a lazy, varied, and economical plan, ride the bus to Mary's Bridge for the view, hike down to the castle, and then catch the carriage from there back down.

Getting to the Castles from Füssen or Reutte: If arriving by **car,** note that road signs in the region refer to the sight as *Königsschlösser,* not Neuschwanstein. There's plenty of parking (all lots-€4). Get there early, and you'll park where you like. Lot E—past the ticket center and next to the lake—is my favorite.

From **Füssen,** those without cars can catch the roughly hourly **bus** (€1.50 one-way, €3 round-trip, 10 min, note times carefully on the meager schedule, catch bus at train station), take a **taxi** (€8.50 one-way), or ride a rental **bike** (3 miles).

From **Reutte,** take the bus to Füssen (Mon–Fri 6/day, Sat 2/day, none Sun, €3.20, 30 min), then hop a city bus to the castle.

For a Romantic twist, hike or mountain-bike from the trailhead at the recommended hotel **Gutshof zum Schluxen** in Pinswang (see "Sleeping—Near Reutte," page 107). When the dirt road forks at the top of the hill, go right (downhill), cross the Austria–Germany border (marked by a sign and deserted hut), and follow the narrow paved road to the castles. It's a 60- to 90-minute hike or a great circular bike trip (allow 30 min; cyclists can return to Schluxen from the castles on a different 30-min bike route via Füssen).

Near Neuschwanstein Castle

▲**Tegelberg Gondola**—Just north of Neuschwanstein is a fun play zone around the mighty Tegelberg gondola. Hang gliders circle like vultures. Their pilots jump from the top of the Tegelberg Gondola. For €15, you can ride the lift to the 5,500-foot summit and back down (May–Oct daily 9:00–17:00, Dec–April daily 9:00–16:30, closed Nov, frequency depends on demand, last lift goes up 10 min before closing time, in bad weather call first to confirm, tel. 08362/98360). On a clear day you get great views of the Alps and Bavaria and the vicarious thrill of watching hang gliders and parasailors leap into airborne ecstasy. Weather permitting, scores of adventurous Germans line up and leap from the launch ramp at the top of the lift. With one leaving every two or three minutes, it's great spec-tating. Thrill seekers with exceptional social skills may talk themselves into a tandem ride with a parasailor. From the top of Tegelberg, it's a steep 2.5-hour hike down to Ludwig's castle. Avoid the treacherous trail directly below the gondola. At the base of the gondola, you'll find a playground, a cheery eatery, and a very good luge ride (below).

▲**Tegelberg Luge**—Next to the lift is a luge course. A luge is like a bobsled on wheels (for more details, see "Sights—Near Reutte," page 104). This stainless-steel track is heated, so it's often dry and open when drizzly weather shuts down the concrete luges. It's not as scenic as Bichlbach and Biberwier (see below), but it's handy (€2.50/ride, 6-ride sharable card-€10, July–Sept daily 9:00–18:00, otherwise same hours as gondola, in winter sometimes opens later due to wet track, in bad weather call first to confirm, tel. 08362/98360). A funky cable system pulls riders (in their sleds) to the top without a ski lift.

▲**Ludwig II Musical**—A spectacular opera/musical based on the Romantic life and troubled times of Ludwig plays in a grand lakeside theater. While billed as a musical, *Ludwig II: Longing for Paradise* felt like opera to me—with an orchestra in the pit, creative stage sets, fine singing, wonderful acoustics, and an easy-to-follow story line about Ludwig abandoning the normal, guy-thing rush of political power to pal around with his muses (3 vampy women dressed in purple). It's Bismarck the realistic politician on one side versus Wagner the Romantic composer on the other, as art triumphs (and Ludwig disappears into the lake).

The music is wonderful and the show's a hit with Germans. It's clearly top classical quality, but the superscripts in English are tough to read and tickets are pricey. The state-of-the-art theater is romantically set on a lake (Forgensee) with a view of floodlit Neuschwanstein in the distance (€50–105 per seat, nightly all year Tue–Sun 19:30 plus a matinee Sat–Sun at 14:30, no shows Mon, 3 hrs including intermission, plenty of chances to eat a good light meal, parking-€3, about 1 mile north of Füssen—follow signs for Musical, book in advance, for tickets call 01805/583-944, www.ludwigmusical.com). It's possible to book directly at the TI in Füssen. If you're staying in Füssen, catch the shuttle bus that conveniently runs to and from the play.

More Sights in Bavaria

These are listed in driving order from Füssen.

▲▲**Wies Church (Wieskirche)**—Germany's greatest rococo-style church, this "church in the meadow" is newly restored and looking as brilliant as the day it floated down from heaven. Overripe with decoration but bright and bursting with beauty, this church is a divine droplet, a curly curlicue, the final flowering of the Baroque movement (donation requested, summer daily 8:00–19:00, winter daily 8:00–17:00, parking-€1, tel. 08862/932-930, www.wieskirche.de).

This pilgrimage church is built around the much-venerated statue of a scourged (or whipped) Christ, which supposedly wept in 1738. The carving—too graphic to be accepted by that generation's church—was the focus of worship in a peasant's barn. Miraculously, it wept—empathizing with all those who suffer. Pilgrims came from all around. A tiny and humble chapel was built to house the statue in 1739. (You can see it where the lane to the church leaves the parking lot.) Bigger and bigger crowds came. Two of Bavaria's top rococo architects, the Zimmermann brothers, were commissioned to build the Wieskirche that stands here today.

Follow the theological sweep from the altar to the ceiling: Jesus whipped, chained, and then killed (notice the pelican above the altar—recalling a pre-Christian story of a bird that opened its breast to feed its young with its own blood); the painting of a baby Jesus posed as if on the cross; the sacrificial lamb; and finally, high on the ceiling, the resurrected Christ before the Last Judgment. This is the most positive depiction of the Last Judgment around. Jesus, rather than sitting on the throne to judge, rides high on a rainbow—a symbol of forgiveness—giving any sinner the feeling that there is still time to repent, and there's plenty of mercy on hand. In the back, above the pipe organ, notice the empty throne—waiting for Judgment Day—and the closed door to paradise.

Above the entrances to both side aisles are murky glass cases with 18th-century handkerchiefs. People wept, came here, were healed, and no longer needed their hankies. Walk up either aisle flanking the high altar to see votives—requests and thanks to God (for happy, healthy babies, and so on). Notice how the kneelers are positioned so that worshipers can meditate on scenes of biblical miracles painted high on the ceiling and visible through the ornate tunnel frames. A priest here once told me that faith, architecture, light, and music all combine to create the harmony of the Wieskirche.

Two paintings flank the door at the rear of the church. One shows the ceremonial parade in 1749 when the white-clad monks of Steingaden carried the carved statue of Christ from the tiny church to its new big one. The second painting, from 1757, is a votive from one of the Zimmermann brothers, the artists and architects who built this church. He is giving thanks for the successful construction of the new church.

The Wieskirche is 30 minutes north of Neuschwanstein. The northbound Romantic Road bus tour stops here for 15 minutes. You can take a bus from Füssen to the Wieskirche, but you'll spend more time waiting for the bus back than you will seeing the church. By car, head north from Füssen, turn right at Steingaden, and follow the signs. Take a commune-with-nature-and-smell-the-farm detour back through the meadow to the car park.

If you can't visit Wieskirche, visit one of the other churches that came out of the same heavenly spray can: Oberammergau's church, Munich's Asam Church, Würzburg's Residenz Chapel, the splendid Ettal Monastery (free and near Oberammergau) and, on a lesser scale, Füssen's cathedral.

If you're driving from Wieskirche to Oberammergau, you'll cross the Echelsbacher Bridge, which arches 230 feet over the Pöllat Gorge. Thoughtful drivers let their passengers walk across (for the views) and meet them at the other side. Any kayakers? Notice the painting of the traditional village woodcarver (who used to walk from town to town with his art on his back) on the first big house on the Oberammergau side, a shop called Almdorf Ammertal. It has a huge selection of over-priced carvings and commission-hungry tour guides.

▲Oberammergau—The Shirley Temple of Bavarian villages, exploited to the hilt by the tourist trade, Oberammergau wears way too much makeup. If you're passing through anyway, it's worth a wander among the half-timbered *Lüftlmalerei* houses frescoed (in a style popular throughout the town in the 18th century) with Bible scenes and famous fairy-tale characters. Browse through woodcarvers' shops—small art galleries filled with very expensive whittled works. The beautifully frescoed Pilat's House on Ludwig-Thomas-Strasse is a living workshop full of woodcarvers and painters in action (free, May–Oct, Dec, and Feb Mon–Fri 13:00–18:00, closed Sat-Sun; closed Nov, Jan, and March–April). Or see folk art at the town's Heimatmuseum (Tue–Sun 14:00–18:00, closed Mon; TI Mon–Fri 8:30–18:00, Sat 8:30-12:00, closed Sun, tel. 08822/92310, www.oberammergau.de).

Oberammergau Church: Visit the church, a poor cousin of the one at Wies. This church looks richer than it is. Put your hand on the "marble" columns. If they warm up, they're fakes—"stucco marble." Wander through the graveyard. Ponder the deaths that two wars dealt Germany. Behind the church are the photos of three Schneller brothers, all killed within two years in World War II.

Passion Play: Still making good on a deal the townspeople struck with God when they were spared devastation by the Black Plague several centuries ago, once each decade Oberammergau presents its Passion play. For 100 summer days in a row, the town performs an all-day dramatic story of Christ's crucifixion (in 2000, 5,000 people attended per day). Until the next performance in 2010, you'll have to settle for reading the book, seeing Nicodemus tool around town in his VW, or browsing through the theater's exhibition hall (€2.50, German tours daily 10:00–17:00, tel. 08822/945-8833 or 08822/32278). English speakers get little respect here, with only two theater tours a day scheduled (often at 11:00 and 14:00). They may do others if you pay the €25 or gather 10 needy English speakers.

Sleeping in Oberammergau: $ Hotel Bayerischer Löwe is central, with a good restaurant and 18 comfortable rooms (Db-€56, no CC, Dedlerstrasse 2, tel. 08822/1365, fax 08822/882, www.bayerischerloewe .com, gasthof.loewe@freenet.de, family Reinhofer). $ Gasthof zur Rose is a big, central, family-run place with 21 rooms (Sb-€33, Db-€56, Tb-€71, Qb-€82, Dedlerstrasse 9, tel. 08822/4706, fax 08822/6753, gasthof-rose@t-online.de). **$ Frau Magold's** three bright and spacious rooms are twice as nice as the cheap hotel rooms for much less money (Db-€37–43, no CC, immediately behind Gasthof Zur Rose at Kleppergasse 1, tel. & fax 08822/4340, NSE). **$ Frau Maderspacher** rents three cozy, old-time rooms in her very characteristic 160-year-old home (D-€30, no CC, July–Sept only, a block past Gasthof zur Rose at Daisenbergerstrasse 11, tel. 08822/3978, NSE). Oberammergau's modern **$ youth hostel** is on the river a short walk from the center (€13 beds, tel. 08822/4114, fax 08822/1695).

Getting to Oberammergau: From Füssen to Oberammergau, four to five buses run daily (fewer in winter, 1.5 hrs). Trains run from Munich to Oberammergau (hrly, 1.75 hrs, change in Murnau). Drivers entering the town from the north should cross the bridge, take the second right, and park in the free lot a block beyond the TI. Leaving town, head out past the church and turn toward Ettal on Road 23. You're 20 miles from Reutte via the scenic Plansee. If heading to Munich, Road 23 takes you to the autobahn, which gets you there in less than an hour.

▲▲**Linderhof Castle**—This homiest of Mad King Ludwig's castles is small and comfortably exquisite—good enough for a minor god. Set in the woods 15 minutes from Oberammergau and surrounded by fountains and sculpted, Italian-style gardens, it's the only palace I've toured that actually had me feeling envious. Don't miss the grotto, which is located outside and uphill from the palace; 15-minute tours are included with the palace ticket (€6, April–Sept daily 9:00–18:00, Oct–March daily 10:00–16:00, parking-€2, fountains often erupt on the hour, English tours every 30 min or when 15 gather—sparse off-season, so you may have to wait, tel. 08822/92030). Plan for lots of walking and a two-hour stop to fully enjoy this royal park. Pay at the entrance and get an admission time. Visit outlying sights in the garden to pass any wait time. The outside of the palace is undergoing a long-term renovation, with lots of scaffolding. But the interior, freshly refurbished, is glorious. Without a car, getting to (and home from) Linderhof is a huge headache—skip it (but diehards can find details in "Getting around Bavaria and Tirol," above).

▲▲**Zugspitze**—The tallest point in Germany is a border crossing. Lifts from Austria and Germany travel to the 10,000-foot summit of the Zugspitze. You can straddle the border between two great nations while enjoying an incredible view. Restaurants, shops, and telescopes await you at the summit.

On the German side, the 75-minute trip from Garmisch costs €43 round-trip; family discounts are available (buy a combo-ticket for cogwheel train to Eibsee and cable-car ride to summit, drivers can park for free at cable-car station at Eibsee, tel. 08821/7970). Allow plenty of time for afternoon descents: If bad weather hits in the late afternoon, cable cars can be delayed at the summit, causing tourists to miss their train from Eibsee back to Garmisch. Hikers enjoy the easy 6-mile walk around the lovely Eibsee (German side, 5 min downhill from cable car *Seilbahn*).

On the Austrian side, from the less-crowded Talstation Obermoos above the village of Erwald, the tram zips you to the top in 10 minutes (€31 round-trip, cash only, goes every 20 min, late May–Oct daily 8:40–16:40, tel. in Austria 05673/2309, www.zugspitze.com).

The German ascent from Garmisch is easier for those without a car, but buses do connect the Erwald train station and the Austrian lift nearly every hour.

SLEEPING

Füssen

Though I prefer sleeping in Reutte (see "Sleeping" in Tirol, page 105), convenient Füssen is just three miles from Ludwig's castles and offers a cobbled, riverside retreat. It's very touristy, but it has plenty of rooms. All recommended places are within a few blocks of the train station and the town center. Parking is easy at the station.

$$$ **Hotel Kurcafé** is deluxe, with 30 spacious rooms and all of the amenities. The standard rooms are comfortable, and the newer, bigger rooms have elegant touches and fun decor—like canopy drapes and cherubic frescoes over the bed (Sb-€82, standard Db-€99, bigger Db-€113–139 depending on size, Tb-€123, Qb-€139, 4-person suite-€159, €10 more for weekends and holidays, cheaper off-season, non-smoking rooms, elevator, parking-€5/day, on tiny traffic circle a block in front of station at Bahnhofstrasse 4, tel. 08362/930-180, fax 08362/930-1850, www.kurcafe.com, info@kurcafe.com, Schöll family).

$$$ **Hotel Hirsch** is a big, romantic, old tour-class hotel with 53 rooms on the main street in the center of town. Their standard rooms are fine, and their theme rooms are a fun splurge (Sb-€56–82, standard Db-€87–133, theme Db-€118–162, prices depend on room size and demand, cheaper Nov–March and during slow times, only the expensive theme rooms are non-smoking, family rooms, elevator, free parking, Kaiser-Maximilian Platz 7, tel. 08362/93980, fax 08362/939-877, www.hotelhirsch.de, info@hotelhirsch.de).

$$$ **Hotel Sonne,** in the heart of town, rents 32 mod, institutional, yet comfy rooms (Sb-€85, Db-€105, Tb-€129, cheaper Oct–mid-June, non-smoking rooms, elevator, free parking, kitty-corner from TI at Reichenstrasse 37, tel. 08362/9080, fax 08362/908-100, www.hotel-sonne.de, info@hotel-sonne.de).

$$ **Altstadthotel zum Hechten** offers all the modern comforts in a friendly, traditional shell right under Füssen Castle in the old-town pedestrian zone (35 rooms, S-€30, Sb-€45, D-€60, Db-€75–80, Tb-

SLEEP CODE

(€1 = about $1.10, country code: 49, area code: 08362)

Sleep Code: **S** = Single, **D** = Double/Twin, **T** = Triple, **Q** = Quad, **b** = bathroom, **s** = shower only, **no CC** = Credit Cards not accepted, **SE** = English spoken, **NSE** = No English spoken. Unless otherwise noted, credit cards are accepted, English is spoken, and breakfast is included.

To help you sort easily through these listings, I've divided the rooms into three categories, based on the price for a standard double room with bath:

$$$ **Higher Priced**—Most rooms €85 or more.
$$ **Moderately Priced**—Most rooms between €55–85.
$ **Lower Priced**—Most rooms €55 or less.

Prices listed are for one-night stays. Most places give about 10 percent off for two-night stays—always request this discount. Competition is fierce, and off-season prices are soft. High season is mid-June through September. Rooms are generally about 12 percent less in shoulder season and much cheaper in off-season.

€100, Qb-€112, free parking, cheaper off-season and for longer stays, non-smoking rooms, fun mini–bowling alley in basement, nearby church bells ring hourly at night; from TI, walk down pedestrian street, take second right to Ritterstrasse 6, tel. 08362/91600, fax 08362/916-099, www.hotel-hechten.com, hotel.hechten@t-online.de, Pfeiffer and Tramp families).

$$ Suzanne's B&B is run by a plain-spoken, no-nonsense American woman who strikes some travelers as brusque. Suzanne runs a tight ship, offering lots of local travel advice, backyard-fresh eggs, local cheese, a children's yard, laundry (€20/load), and bright, woody, spacious rooms (Db-€80, Tb-€115, Qb-€145, Db suite-€100, Tb suite-€140, Qb suite-€160, attic special: €70 for 2, €100 for 3, €120 for 4; another room holds up to 6—ask for details, no CC, non-smoking, exit station right and backtrack 2 blocks along tracks, cross tracks at Venetianerwinkel to #3, tel. 08362/38485, fax 08362/921-396, www.suzannes.de, svorbrugg @t-online.de). Her kid-friendly loft has very low ceilings (you'll crouch), a private bathroom (you'll crouch), and up to six beds.

$$ Hotel Bräustüberl has 16 decent rooms at fair rates attached to a gruff, musty, old beer hall–type place. Don't expect much service (S-€25,

Füssen

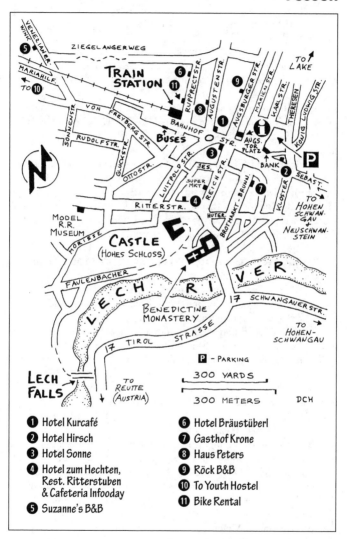

1 Hotel Kurcafé
2 Hotel Hirsch
3 Hotel Sonne
4 Hotel zum Hechten, Rest. Ritterstuben & Cafeteria Infooday
5 Suzanne's B&B
6 Hotel Bräustüberl
7 Gasthof Krone
8 Haus Peters
9 Röck B&B
10 To Youth Hostel
11 Bike Rental

Sb-€47, D-€50, Db-€64–74, no CC, Rupprechtstrasse 5, a block from station, tel. 08362/7843, fax 08362/923-951, brauereigasthof-fuessen @t-online.de).

$ **Gasthof Krone,** a rare bit of pre-glitz Füssen in the pedestrian zone, has dumpy halls and stairs and big, time-warp rooms at good prices (S-€28, D/Ds-€52, extra bed-€29, €3 more per person for 1-night stays, reception in restaurant, from TI head down pedestrian street, take first left to Schrannengasse 17, tel. 08362/7824, fax 08362/37505, www.krone-fuessen.de).

$ **Haus Peters** is comfy, smoke-free, and friendly. But Frau Peters takes reservations only a short time in advance and shuts down in May, July, and when she's out of town (4 rooms, Ds/Db-€50, Tb-€60, no CC, Augustenstrasse 5 1/2, tel. 08362/7171).

$ **Wilhelm and Elisabeth Röck,** a sweet old couple, rent out two rooms in their home a block from the TI (D-€51, Db-€52, no CC, non-smoking, Augsburgerstrasse 7, tel. 08362/6353, just enough English spoken).

$ **Füssen Youth Hostel,** a fine, German-run place, welcomes travelers under 27 (€15-dorm beds in 2- to 6-bed rooms, D-€36, €3 more for non-members, includes breakfast and sheets, non-smoking, laundry-€3.50/load, dinner-€5, office open 7:00–12:00 & 17:00–23:00, from station backtrack 10 min along tracks, Mariahilferstrasse 5, tel. 08362/7754, fax 08362/2770, jhfuessen@djh-bayern.de).

Hohenschwangau, near Neuschwanstein Castle

Inexpensive farmhouse *Zimmer* (B&Bs) abound in the Bavarian countryside around Neuschwanstein, offering drivers a decent value. Look for *Zimmer Frei* signs ("room free," or vacancy). The going rate is about €50–65 for a double, including breakfast.

$$ **Beim "Landhannes"** is a hundred-year-old working dairy farm run by Johann and Traudl Mayr. They rent six creaky, well-antlered rooms and keep flowers on the balconies, big bells in the halls, and cows in the yard (Sb-€30, Ds-€50, Db-€60, 10 percent discount for 2 nights, no CC, poorly signed in the village of Horn on the Füssen side of Schwangau, look for the farm 100 yards in front of Hotel Kleiner König, Am Lechrain 22, tel. 08362/8349, fax 08362/819-646, www.landhannes.de, mayr@landhannes.de).

$$ **Sonnenhof** is a big, woody, old house with four spacious, traditionally decorated rooms and a cheery garden. It's a 15-minute walk through the fields to the castles (S-€20, D-€45, Db-€55, no CC, at Pension Schwansee on the Füssen–Neuschwanstein road, follow the small lane 100 yards to Sonnenweg 11, tel. 08362/8420, Frau Görlich SE).

$$ **Alpenhotel Meier** is a small, family-run hotel with 15 rooms in a bucolic setting within walking distance of the castles, just beyond the lower parking lot (Sb-€46, Db-€77, plus €1.20 tourist tax per person, 5 percent discount with cash and this book, non-smoking rooms, all rooms have porches or balconies, family rooms, sauna, easy parking, just before tennis courts at Schwangauerstrasse 37, tel. 08362/81152, fax 08362/987-028, www.alpenhotel-allgaeu.de, alpenhotelmeier@web.de, Frau Meier SE).

EATING

Füssen

Füssen's old town and main pedestrian drag are lined with a variety of eateries. Three good places cluster on Ritterstrasse, just under the castle, off the top of the main street:

Rritterstuben offers reasonable and delicious fish, salads, veggie plates, and a fun kids' menu (Tue–Sun 11:30–14:30 & 17:30–23:00, closed Mon, Ritterstrasse 4, tel. 08362/7759). Demure, English-speaking Gabi serves while her husband cooks.

Zum Hechten Restaurant serves hearty, traditional Bavarian fare and specializes in pike *(Hecht)* pulled from the Lech River (€8–12 meals, Thu–Tue 11:30–14:30 & 17:30–21:00, closed Wed, Ritterstrasse 6).

Infooday is a clever and modern self-service eatery that sells its hot meals and salad bar by weight and offers English newspapers (filling salad-€3, meals-€5, Mon–Fri 10:30–18:30, Sat 10:30–14:30, closed Sun, Ritterstrasse 6).

Hotel Kurcafé's fine restaurant, right on Füssen's main traffic circle, has good and reasonable weekly specials, plus a tempting bakery (daily 11:30–14:30 & 17:30–22:00, choose between a traditional dining room and a pastel "winter garden," live Bavarian zither music most Fri–Sat during dinner, tel. 08362/930-180).

TRANSPORTATION CONNECTIONS

To: Neuschwanstein (hrly buses, 10 min, €1.50 one-way, €3 round-trip; taxis cost €8.50 one-way), **Reutte** (by bus, Mon–Fri 6/day, Sat 2/day, none Sun, 30 min, €3.20 one-way; taxis cost €28 one-way), **Munich** (hrly trains, 2 hrs, some change in Buchloe). Train info: tel. 01805-996-633.

Romantic Road Buses: The northbound Romantic Road bus departs Füssen at 8:00; the southbound bus arrives at Füssen at 20:15 (bus stops at train station). Railpasses get you a 60 percent discount on the Romantic Road bus (and the ride does not use up a day of a Flexipass). For more information, see the Rothenburg chapter.

Reutte, Austria

(€1 = about $1.10)

Reutte (ROY-teh, with a rolled "r"), a relaxed town of 5,700, is located 20 minutes across the border from Füssen. It's far from the international tourist crowd, but popular with Germans and Austrians for its climate. Doctors recommend its "grade 1" air. Reutte's one claim to fame with Americans: As Nazi Germany was falling in 1945, Hitler's top rocket scientist, Werner von Braun, joined the Americans (rather than the Russians) in Reutte. You could say the American space program began here.

Reutte isn't featured in any other American guidebook. While its generous sidewalks are filled with smart boutiques and lazy coffeehouses, its charms are subtle. It was never rich or important. Its castle is ruined, its buildings have painted-on "carvings," its churches are full, its men yodel for each other on birthdays, and lately, its energy is spent soaking its Austrian and German guests in *Gemütlichkeit*. Most guests stay for a week, so the town's attractions are more time-consuming than thrilling. If the weather's good, hike to the mysterious Ehrenberg ruins, ride the luge, or rent a bike. For a slap-dancing bang, enjoy a Tirolean folk evening. For accommodations, see Tirol's "Sleeping" section, page 105.

ORIENTATION

(area code: 05672)

Tourist Information: Reutte's TI is a block in front of the train station (Mon–Fri 8:00–12:00 & 14:00–17:00, Sat 8:30–12:00, closed Sun, tel. 05672/62336 or, from Germany, 00-43-5672/62336, www .reuttetourism.at). Go over your sightseeing plans, ask about a folk evening, pick up city and biking maps and the *Sommerprogramm* events schedule (German only), and ask about discounts with the hotel guest cards. Their "Information" booklet has a good self-guided town walk.

Bike Rental: In the center, the Heinz Glätzle shop rents out good bikes (city and mountain bikes-€15/day, kids' bikes-€7.50/day, inside toy store at Obermarkt 61, Mon–Fri 8:15–12:00 & 14:00–18:00, Sat 8:15–12:00, closed Sun, tel. 05672/62752). Several recommended hotels loan or rent bikes to guests. Most of the sights described in this chapter make good biking destinations. Ask about the bike path (*Radwanderweg*) along the Lech River.

Laundry: Don't ask the TI about a launderette. Unless you can infiltrate the local campground, Hotel Maximilian, or Gutshof zum Schluxen (see "Sleeping—Ehenbichl, near Reutte," page 107), the town has none.

SIGHTS

Ehrenberg Castle Ensemble (Festungsensemble Ehrenberg)

Just a mile outside of Reutte are the brooding ruins of four castles that once made up the largest fort in Tirol (built for defense against he Bavarians). Today, these castles are gradually being turned into a European Castle Museum, showing off 500 years of military architecture in one swoop (due to be completed in 2007, www.ehrenberg.at). The

Reutte

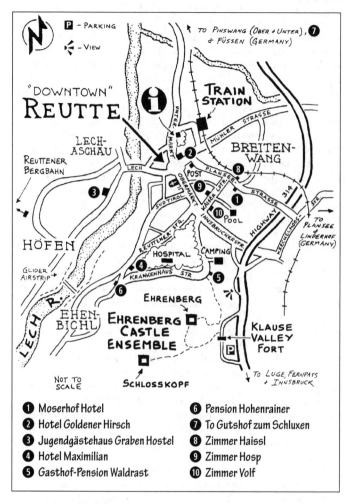

P – PARKING
– VIEW

TO PINSWANG (OBER & UNTER), 7
& FÜSSEN (GERMANY)

"DOWNTOWN"
REUTTE

TRAIN STATION

LECH-ASCHAU

BREITEN-WANG

REUTTENER BERGBAHN

MÜHLER STRASSE

UNTER MARKT

POST

PLANSEE STRASSE

OBERMARKT

SÜD TIROL

2

8

9

1

10 POOL

REUTTENER STR.

INNSBRUCKERSTR.

HOFEN

HOSPITAL

CAMPING

GLIDER AIRSTRIP

KRANKENHAUS STR

4

6

5

314

TO PLANSEE & LINDERHOF (GERMANY)

EHRENBERG

EHEN-BICHL

EHRENBERG CASTLE ENSEMBLE

KLAUSE VALLEY FORT

LECH R.

NOT TO SCALE

SCHLOSSKOPF

P

TO LUGE, FERNPASS & INNSBRUCK

1 Moserhof Hotel
2 Hotel Goldener Hirsch
3 Jugendgästehaus Graben Hostel
4 Hotel Maximilian
5 Gasthof-Pension Waldrast

6 Pension Hohenrainer
7 To Gutshof zum Schluxen
8 Zimmer Haissl
9 Zimmer Hosp
10 Zimmer Volf

European Union is helping fund the project because it promotes the heritage of a multinational region—Tirol—rather than a country (the EU's vision is for a zone of regions rather than nations).

Three of the castles cluster together; the fourth (Fort Claudia) is across the valley, though all four used to be connected by walls. The first three—the easiest and most interesting to visit—are described below, from lowest to highest. New signage throughout the castle complex will help you find your way and explain some background on the region's history, geology, geography, culture, flora, and fauna.

Getting to the Castle Ensemble: The Klause, Ehrenberg, and Schlosskopf castles are on the road to Lermoos and Innsbruck. These are a pleasant walk or a short bike ride from Reutte; bikers can use the *Radwanderweg* along the Lech River (the TI has a good map).

▲**Klause Valley Fort**—At the parking lot at the base of the ruin-topped hill, you'll find the recently modernized remains of a Gothic fortification. It was located on the medieval salt road (which used to be the ancient Roman road, Via Claudia). Beginning in the 14th century, this fort controlled traffic and levied tolls on all that passed through this strategic valley. Today it houses a new 60-minute **sound-and-light show** (*son et lumière*) about the castles (€10). You'll sit inside the shell of the old castle while the 2,000-year history of this valley's fortresses is projected on the old stone walls and modern screens around you. By early 2005, this will also be the home to an extensive museum about the "castle ensemble." If you're hungry, drop by the nearby café/guest house, Gasthof Klause (closed Wed), which offers a German-language flier and a wall painting of the intact castle.

▲▲**Ehrenberg Ruins**—Ehrenberg, a 13th-century rock pile, provides a great contrast to King Ludwig's "modern" castles and a super opportunity to let your imagination off its leash. Hike up 20 minutes from the parking lot for a great view from your own private ruins. Facing the hill from the parking lot, find the gravelly road at the Klaus sign. Follow the road to the saddle between the two hills. From the saddle, notice how the castle stands high on the horizon. This is Ehrenberg (which means "mountain of honor"), the first of the four ensemble castles, built in 1296. Thirteenth-century castles were designed to stand boastfully tall. With the advent of gunpowder, castles dug in. Notice the **ramparts** around you. They are from the 18th century. Approaching Ehrenberg castle, look for the small door to the left. It's the night entrance (tight and awkward, therefore safer against a surprise invasion). While hiking up the hill, you go through two doors. Castles allowed step-by-step retreat, giving defenders time to regroup and fight back against invading forces.

Before making the final and steepest ascent, follow the path around to the right to a big, grassy courtyard with commanding views and a fat, newly restored **turret.** This stored gunpowder and held a big cannon that enjoyed a clear view of the valley below. In medieval times, all the trees approaching the castle were cleared to keep an unobstructed view.

Look out over the valley. The pointy spire marks **Breitenwang,** which was a stop on the ancient Via Claudia. In A.D. 46, there was a Roman camp there. In 1489, after the Reutte bridge crossed the Lech River, Reutte (marked by the onion-domed church) was made a market town and eclipsed Breitenwang in importance. Any gliders circling? They launch from just over the river in Höfen (see "Flying and Gliding," page 103).

For centuries, this castle was the seat of government—ruling an area called the "judgment of Ehrenberg" (roughly the same as today's "district of Reutte"). When the emperor came by, he stayed here. In 1604, the ruler moved downtown into more comfortable quarters and the castle was no longer a palace.

Climb the steep hill to the top of the castle. Take the high ground. There was no water supply here, just kegs of wine, beer, and a cistern to collect rain.

Ehrenberg repelled 16,000 Swedish soldiers in the defense of Catholicism in 1632. Ehrenberg saw three or four other battles, but its end was not glorious. In the 1780s, a local businessman bought the castle in order to sell off its parts. Later, when vagabonds moved in, the roof was removed to make squatting miserable. With the roof gone, deterioration quickened, leaving this evocative shell and a whiff of history.

▲**Schlosskopf**—If you have energy left after conquering Ehrenberg, hike up to the mighty Schlosskopf (literally "castle head"). When the Bavarians captured Ehrenberg in 1703, the Tiroleans climbed up to the bluff above it to rain cannonballs down on their former fortress. In 1740, a mighty new castle—designed to defend against modern artillery—was built on this same sky-high strategic location. By 2001, the castle was completely overgrown with trees—you couldn't see it from Reutte. But today the trees are shaved away, and the castle has been excavated. Beginning in 2005, the Castle Ensemble project will reconstruct the original equipment used to build this fortress (such as wooden cranes)—and then use those same means to restore parts of it. By 2007, Schlosskopf will be partially rebuilt, and the 18th-century construction equipment will retire and become part of the exhibit.

Reutte

Folk Museum (Heimatmuseum)—Reutte's Heimatmuseum, offering a quick look at the local folk culture and the story of the castles, is more cute than impressive. Ask to borrow the packet of information in English (€2, May–Oct Tue–Sun 10:00–17:00, closed Mon and Nov–April, in the bright green building on Untermarkt, around corner from Hotel Goldener Hirsch, tel. 05672/72304).

▲▲**Tirolean Folk Evening**—Ask the TI or your hotel if there's a Tirolean folk evening scheduled. Usually on Thursdays in the summer (July–mid-Sept), Reutte or a nearby town puts on an evening of yodeling, slap dancing, and Tirolean frolic worth the €8–10 and short drive. Off-season, you'll have to do your own yodeling. There are also weekly folk concerts in the park (July–Aug only, ask at TI). For listings of these and other local events, pick up a copy of the German-only *Sommerprogramm* schedule at the TI.

▲**Flying and Gliding**—For a major thrill on a sunny day, drop by the tiny airport in Höfen across the river, and fly. A small single-prop plane can buzz the Zugspitze and Ludwig's castles and give you a bird's-eye peek at Reutte's Ehrenberg ruins (2 people for 30 min-€110, 1 hr-€220, tel. 05672/62827, phone rarely answered, and then not in English, so your best bet is to show up at Höfen airport on good-weather afternoons). Or, for something more angelic, how about *Segelfliegen*? For €36, you get 30 minutes in a glider for two (you and the pilot). Just watching the towrope launch the graceful glider like a giant, slow-motion rubber-band gun is exhilarating (May–mid-Sept 12:00–19:00, in good but breezy weather only, find someone in the know at the "Thermic Ranch," tel. 05672/71550 or 05672/64010, or mobile 0676/711-0100).

Swimming—Plunge into Reutte's Olympic-size Alpenbad swimming pool to cool off after your castle hikes (€6, June–mid-Sept daily 10:00–21:00, mid-Nov–May Tue–Sun 14:00–21:00, closed Mon and mid-Sept–mid-Nov; indoor/outdoor pools, big water slide, mini-golf, playground on-site, 5 min on foot from Reutte center, head out Obermarkt and turn left on Kaiser Lothar Strasse, tel. 05672/62666).

Reuttener Bergbahn—This mountain lift swoops you high above the treeline to a starting point for several hikes and an alpine flower park with special paths leading you past countless local varieties (€9 one-way, €13 round-trip, flowers best in late July, lift usually mid-May–Oct daily 9:00–11:50 & 13:00–17:00, tel. 05672/62420, www.reuttener
-seilbahnen.at).

Near Reutte

▲▲**The Luge** *(Sommerrodelbahn)*—Near Lermoos, on the road from Reutte to Innsbruck, you'll find two exciting luge courses, or *Sommerrodelbahn*. To try one of Europe's great €6 thrills, take the lift up, grab a sled-like go-cart, and luge down. The concrete course banks on the corners, and even a novice can go very, very fast. Most are cautious on their first run, speed demons on their second...and bruised and bloody on their third. A woman once showed me her journal illustrated with her husband's dried five-inch-long luge scab. He disobeyed the only essential rule of luging: Keep both hands on your stick. To avoid getting into a bumper-to-bumper traffic jam, let the person in front of you get way ahead before you start. No one emerges from the course without a windblown hairdo and a smile-creased face. Both places charge the same price (€6 per run, 5- and 10-trip discount cards) and shut down at the least hint of rain (call ahead to make sure they're open; you're more likely to get luge info in English if you call the TIs, listed below). If you're without a car, these are not worth the trouble (consider the luge near Neuschwanstein instead—see "Tegelberg Luge," page 91).

The short and steep luge: Bichlbach, the first course (330-foot drop, over a 2,600-foot course), is four miles beyond Reutte's castle ruins. Look for a chairlift on the right, and exit on the tiny road at the Almkopfbahn Rosthof sign (June–Sept daily 10:00–17:00, sometimes opens in spring and fall—especially weekends—depending on weather, call first, tel. 05674/5350, or contact the local TI at tel. 05674/5354).

The longest luge: The Biberwier *Sommerrodelbahn* is a better luge and, at 4,250 feet, the longest in Austria (15 min farther from Reutte than Bichlbach, just past Lermoos in Biberwier—the first exit after a long tunnel). The only drawbacks are its short season and hours (open late-May–June Sat–Sun 9:00–16:30 only, closed Mon–Fri, July–Sept daily 9:00–16:30, call first, tel. 05673/2323 or 05673/2111, TI tel. 05673/2922).

▲**Fallerschein**—Easy for drivers and a special treat for those who may have been Kit Carson in a previous life, this extremely remote log-cabin village is a 4,000-foot-high, flower-speckled world of serene slopes and cowbells. Thunderstorms roll down the valley like it's God's bowling alley, but the pint-size church on the high ground, blissfully simple in a land of Baroque, seems to promise that this huddle of houses will survive, and the river and breeze will just keep flowing. The couples sitting on benches are mostly Austrian vacationers who've rented cabins here. Many of them, appreciating the remoteness of Fallerschein, are having affairs.

Getting to Fallerschein: The village, at the end of the 1.25-mile Berwang Road, is near Namlos and about 45 minutes southwest of Reutte. You'll find a car park at the end of the road, leaving you with a two-mile walk down a drivable but technically closed one-lane road.

SLEEPING

Reutte is a mellow Füssen with fewer crowds and easygoing locals with a contagious love of life. Come here for a good dose of Austrian ambience and lower prices. Those with a car should make their home base here; those without should consider it. (To call Reutte from Germany, dial 00-43-5672, then the local number.) You'll drive across the border without stopping. Reutte is popular with Austrians and Germans, who come here year after year for one- or two-week vacations. The hotels are big, elegant, and full of comfy, carved furnishings and creative ways to spend lots of time in one spot. They take great pride in their restaurants, and the owners send their children away to hotel management schools. All include a great breakfast, but few accept credit cards. Most places give about a 5 percent discount for stays of two nights or longer.

SLEEP CODE

(€1 = about $1.10, country code: 43, area code: 05672)

Sleep Code: **S** = Single, **D** = Double/Twin, **T** = Triple, **Q** = Quad, **b** = bathroom, **s** = shower only, **no CC** = Credit Cards not accepted, **SE** = Speaks English, **NSE** = No English, * = French hotel rating system (0–4 stars). Unless otherwise noted, credit cards are accepted.

To help you sort easily through these listings, I've divided the rooms into three categories, based on the price for a standard double room with bath:

$$$ **Higher Priced**—Most rooms €80 or more.
$$ **Moderately Priced**—Most rooms €50–80.
$ **Lower Priced**—Most rooms €50 or less.

Reutte

$$$ Moserhof Hotel is a plush Tirolean splurge with 30 new-feeling rooms and polished service and facilities, including an elegant dining room (Sb-€47, Db-€84, extra bed-€35, these special prices only if you reserve ahead and ask for Rick Steves rates, almost all rooms have balconies, free parking, elevator, Internet access-€3/hr; from downtown Reutte, follow signs to village Breitenwang, it's just after church at Planseestrasse 44, tel. 05672/62020, fax 05672/620-2040, www.hotel-moserhof.at, info@hotel-moserhof.at, Hosp family).

$$ Hotel Goldener Hirsch, located in the center of Reutte just two blocks from the station, is a grand old hotel renovated with Tirolean *Jugendstil* flair. It boasts 56 rooms and one lonely set of antlers (Sb-€56, Db-€80, Tb-€110, Qb-€124–131, 2-night discounts, family rooms, elevator, quality food in their restaurant, tel. 05672/62508, fax 05672/625-087, www.goldener-hirsch.at, info@goldener-hirsch.at, Monika, Helmut, and daughters Vanessa and Nina all SE).

$ The homey **Jugendgästehaus Graben** hostel has two to six beds per room and includes breakfast and sheets. Frau Reyman and her son Rudy keep the place traditional, clean, and friendly, and serve a great €6.50 dinner for guests only. This is a super value. If you've never hostelled and are curious (and have a car or don't mind a bus ride), try it. They accept non-members of any age (dorm bed-€19, Db-€45, no CC, non-smoking rooms, Internet access, laundry service, no curfew, less than 2 miles from Reutte, bus connection to Neuschwanstein via Reutte; from downtown Reutte, cross bridge and follow main road left along river, or take the bus—1 bus/hr until 19:30, ask for Graben stop, no

buses Sun; Graben 1, tel. 05672/626-440, fax 05672/626-444, www
.hoefen.at, jgh-hoefen@tirol.com).

Ehenbichl, near Reutte

The next two listings are a couple miles upriver from Reutte in the village of Ehenbichl, under the Ehrenberg ruins. From central Reutte, go
south on Obermarkt and turn right on Reuttenerstrasse, following signs
to Ehenbichl.

$$ Hotel Maximilian is a great value. It includes free bicycles,
table tennis, a children's playroom, and the friendly service of the Koch
family. Daughter Gabi speaks flawless English. The Kochs host many
special events, and their hotel has lots of wonderful extras such as a
sauna, a masseuse, and a beauty salon (Sb-€35–40, Db-€70–80, family
deals, fast Internet access, laundry service-€7/load even for non-guests,
good restaurant, tel. 05672/62585, fax 05672/625-8554, www
.maxihotel.com, maxhotel@netway.at). They rent cars to guests only
(1 VW Golf, 1 VW van, book in advance).

$$ Gasthof-Pension Waldrast, separating a forest and a meadow,
is run by the farming Huter family and their huge, friendly dog, Bari.
The place feels hauntingly quiet and has no restaurant, but it does offer
10 nice rooms with sitting areas and castle-view balconies (Sb-€30, Db-
€51–55, Tb-€66, Qb-€88, 10 percent discount with this book and 2
nights, no CC, non-smoking, less than 1 mile from Reutte, just off main
drag toward Innsbruck, past campground and under castle ruins on
Ehrenbergstrasse, tel. & fax 05672/62443, www.waldrasttirol.com,
info@waldrasttirol.com).

$ Pension Hohenrainer is a big, no-frills alternative to Hotel
Maximilian—a quiet, good value with 12 modern rooms and some
castle-view balconies (Sb-€23–28, Db-€41–50, cheaper for longer stays,
free Internet access, follow signs up the road behind Hotel Maximilian
into village of Ehenbichl, tel. 05672/62544 or 05672/63262, fax
05672/62052, www.hohenrainer.at, hohenrainer@aon.at).

Pinswang

The village of Pinswang is closer to Füssen (and Ludwig's castles), but
still in Austria.

$$$ Gutshof zum Schluxen, run by helpful Hermann, gets the
Remote Old Hotel in an Idyllic Setting award. This family-friendly
working farm offers modern rustic elegance draped in goose down and
pastels, and a chance to pet a rabbit and feed the deer. Its picturesque
meadow setting will turn you into a dandelion picker, and its proximity
to Neuschwanstein will turn you into a hiker. King Ludwig II himself is
said to have slept here (Sb-€41, Db-€82, extra person-€22, 10 percent
discount for 4 nights or more, Internet access, self-service laundry, free
pickup from Reutte and Füssen, good restaurant, fun bar, mountain bike

rental, between Reutte and Füssen in village of Pinswang, tel. 05677/
8903, fax 05677/890-323, www.schluxen.com, welcome@schluxen.com).

Private Homes in Breitenwang, near Reutte

The Reutte TI has a list of 50 private homes that rent out generally good
rooms *(Zimmer)* with facilities down the hall, pleasant communal living
rooms, and breakfast. Most charge €15 per person per night and speak
little or no English. Reservations are nearly impossible for one- or two-
night stays, but short stops are welcome if you just drop in and fill available gaps. Most *Zimmer* charge around €1.50 extra for heat in winter
(worth it). The TI can always find you a room when you arrive.

Right next door to Reutte is the older and quieter village of
Breitenwang. It has all the best *Zimmer,* the recommended Moserhof
Hotel (above), and a bakery (a 20-min walk from Reutte train station—
at post office roundabout, follow Planseestrasse past onion dome to
pointy straight dome; unmarked Kaiser Lothar Strasse is first right past
this church).

The following *Zimmer* (all reasonably priced, rated $) are comfort-
able and quiet, have few stairs, and are within two blocks of the
Breitenwang church steeple: **Helene Haissl** (the best of the bunch, D-
€30, 2-night discounts, no CC, children's loft room available, beautiful
troll-filled garden, free bikes, laundry service, across from big Alpenhotel
Ernberg at Planseestrasse 63, tel. 05672/67913); **Walter and Emilie
Hosp** (3 rooms in a modern house, D-€40, D-€36 for 2 nights or
more, extra person-€15, no CC, Kaiser Lothar Strasse 29, tel. 05672/
65377); and **Irene and Rudolf Volf** (3 rooms closer to Reutte's main
drag, D-€40, D-€30 for 2 nights, no CC, Kaiser Lothar Strasse 2, tel.
05672/65066).

EATING

The hotels here take great pride in serving local cuisine at reasonable
prices to their guests and the public. Rather than go to a cheap restaurant, try a hotel. Most offer €8–14 dinners from 18:00 to 21:00 and are
closed one night a week. Reutte itself has plenty of inviting eateries—
traditional, ethnic, fast food, grocery stores, and delis.

TRANSPORTATION CONNECTIONS

By train to: Innsbruck (7/day, 2.5 hrs, change in Garmisch and sometimes also in Mittenwald), **Munich** (hrly, 2.5–3 hrs, change in
Garmisch, Pfronten-Steinach, or Kempten), **Garmisch** (every 2 hrs, 1 hr).

By bus to: Füssen (Mon–Fri 6/day, Sat 2/day, none Sun, 30 min,
€3.20, buses depart from in front of the train station, pay driver). Taxis
cost €28 one-way.

By car into Reutte from Germany: Skip the north *(Nord)* exit and take the south *(Süd)* exit into town. While Austria requires a toll sticker for driving on its highways (€8/10 days, buy at the border, gas stations, car rental agencies, or *Tabak* shops), those just dipping into Tirol from Bavaria do not need one.

BADEN-BADEN AND THE BLACK FOREST

Combine Edenism and hedonism as you explore this most romantic of German forests and dip into its mineral spas. The Black Forest, or *Schwarzwald* in German, is a range of hills stretching 100 miles north–south along the French border from Karlsruhe to Switzerland. Its highest peak is the 4,900-foot Feldberg. Because of its thick forests, people called it black.

Until the last century, the Schwarzwald was cut off from the German mainstream. The poor farmland drove medieval locals to become foresters, glass blowers, and clock makers. Strong traditions continue to be woven through the thick dialects and thatched roofs. On any Sunday, you will find Germans in traditional costumes coloring the Black Forest on *Volksmärsche* (group hikes—open to anyone; for a listing, visit www.ava.org/clubs/germany).

Popular with German holiday-goers and those looking for some serious R&R, the Black Forest offers clean air, cuckoo clocks, cherry cakes, cheery villages, and countless hiking possibilities.

The area's two biggest tourist traps are the tiny Titisee (a lake not quite as big as its tourist parking lot) and Triberg, a small town filled with cuckoo-clock shops. In spite of the crowds, the drives are scenic, the hiking is *wunderbar,* and the attractions listed below are well worth a visit. The two major (and very different) towns are Baden-Baden in the north and Freiburg in the south. Freiburg may be the Black Forest's capital, but Baden-Baden is Germany's grandest 19th-century spa resort. Stroll through its elegant streets and casino. Soak in its famous baths.

Planning Your Time

Save a day and two nights for Baden-Baden. Tour Freiburg, but sleep in charming and overlooked Staufen. By train, Freiburg and Baden-Baden are easy, as is a short foray into the forest from either. With more time, do the small-town forest medley between the two. With a car, I'd do

The Black Forest

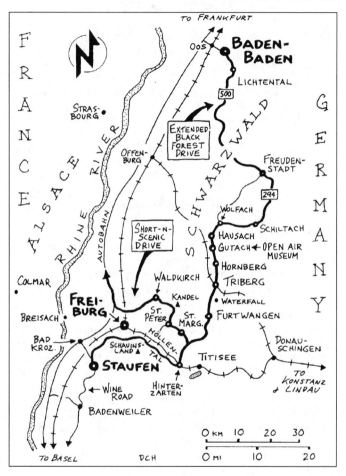

the whole cuckoo thing: a night in Staufen, a busy day touring north, and two nights and a relaxing day in Baden-Baden.

A blitz day from Murten or Interlaken (Switzerland) would go like this: 8:30-Depart, 11:00-Staufen (stroll town, change money, buy picnic), 12:30-Scenic drive to Furtwangen with a scenic picnic along the way, 14:30-Tour clock museum, 15:30-Drive to Gutach, 16:30-Tour open-air folk museum, 18:00-Drive to Baden-Baden, 20:00-Arrive in Baden-Baden. With an overnight in Staufen, you could spend the morning in Freiburg and arrive in Baden-Baden in time for a visit to the spa (last entry 19:00).

Baden-Baden

Of all the high-class resort towns I've seen, Baden-Baden is the easiest to enjoy in jeans with a picnic. The town makes a great first stop in Germany, especially for honeymooners (1.5-hr direct train ride from Frankfurt's airport).

Baden-Baden was the playground of Europe's high-rolling elite 150 years ago. Royalty and aristocracy would come from all corners to take the *Kur*—a soak in the curative (or at least they feel that way) mineral waters—and enjoy the world's top casino.

Today, the lush town of Baden-Baden (pop. 55,000) attracts a middle-class crowd consisting of tourists in search of a lower pulse, and Germans enjoying the fruits of their generous health-care system.

ORIENTATION

(area code: 07221)

Baden-Baden is made for strolling with a poodle. The train station is in a suburb called Baden-Oos, three miles from the center but easily connected with the center by bus. Except for the station and a couple of hotels on the opposite side of town, everything that matters is clustered within a 10-minute walk between the baths and the casino.

Tourist Information: Baden-Baden's TI is in the ornate Trinkhalle building. Pick up the free monthly events program, *Baden-Baden Aktuell*, with a fine-print map. If you don't like squinting, buy the larger *zu Fuss* map (€1). The TI has enough recommended walks and organized excursions to keep the most energetic vacationer happy. If you're headed into the countryside, consider the good €1 Outline Map and the €5 Black Forest guidebook (Mon–Sat 10:00–17:00, Sun 14:00–17:00, WC-€0.50, tel. 07221/275-200, www.baden-baden.de). The TI shares space with a café (see "Eating," page 121) and an agency that sells tickets to performances in town (theater, opera, orchestra, and musicals). Another TI is on the B-500 autobahn exit at Schwartzwaldstrasse 52 (Mon–Sat 9:00–18:00, Sun 9:00–13:00).

Arrival in Baden-Baden: Walk out of the train station (€1–2 lockers at platform 1) and catch bus #201 (€1.90) in front of the kiosks on your right. Get off in about 15 minutes at the Leopoldplatz stop, usually also announced as *Stadtmitte* (center of town). Allow €15 for a taxi from the train station to the center. If you arrive at Baden-Baden's airport, catch #205 to Leopoldplatz in the city center (€2.40, hrly, runs 6:00–19:00).

Helpful Hints

Internet Access: Check your e-mail at the town library (€2/hr, best to reserve a day or two ahead, usage limited to 2 hrs/week, check in at library's info desk, Tue–Wed and Fri 10:00–18:00, Thu 13:00–18:00, Sat 10:00–13:00, closed Sun–Mon, look for Stadt-Bibliothek kitty-corner from post office/Wagener shopping center, Langestrasse 43, tel. 07221/932-260).

Laundry: Try SB-Waschcenter (€7/load, Mon–Sat 7:30–21:00, closed Sun, uphill then down the alley at Scheibenstrasse 14, tel. 07221/24819).

Bike Rental: You can rent cheap bikes at the Kurhaus Garage under the casino (€1/2 hrs, €2.50/6 hrs, €5/12 hrs, half-price with *Kurkarte* discount card from your hotel, rental daily 8:00–18:00, return until 20:00, enter garage through casino and find main payment window near where cars exit, or easier, take the stairs on Kaiserallee behind concert hall, tel. 07221/277-203).

Train Info: The DB Reisebüro on Goetheplatz can help you with train tickets and schedules, saving a trip back out to the station (Mon–Fri 9:00–18:00, Sat 10:00–14:00, closed Sun).

Getting around Baden-Baden

Only one bus matters. Bus #201 runs straight through Baden-Baden, connecting its Oos train station, town center, and the east end of town (every 10 min until 19:00, then about every 20 min until 1:00; buy tickets from driver: €1.90 per person, or the €4.80 24-hr pass good for 2 adults or a family with 2 kids under age 15). Tickets are valid for 90 minutes, but only in one direction. With bus #201, you don't need to mess with downtown parking.

SIGHTS

▲▲**Casino and Kurhaus**—The impressive building called the *Kurhaus* is wrapped around a grand casino. Built in the 1850s in wannabe-French style, it was declared "the most beautiful casino" by Marlene Dietrich. Inspired by the Palace of Versailles, it's filled with rooms honoring French royalty who never set foot in the place. But many other French did. Gambling was illegal in 19th-century France...just over the border. The casino is licensed on the condition that it pay about 90 percent of its earnings in taxes to fund state-sponsored social programs and public works. It earns $35 million a year and is the toast of Baden-Baden—or at least its bread and butter. The staff of 300 is paid by tips from happy gamblers.

You can visit the casino on a tour (when it's closed to gamblers, see below), or you can drop by after 14:00 to gamble or just observe. (This is no problem—a third of the visitors only observe.) The place is most interesting in action; you can people-watch under chandeliers. The scene is more subdued than at an American casino; anyone showing emotion is a tourist. Lean against a gilded statue and listen to the graceful reshuffling of personal fortunes. Do some imaginary gambling or buy a few

Baden-Baden

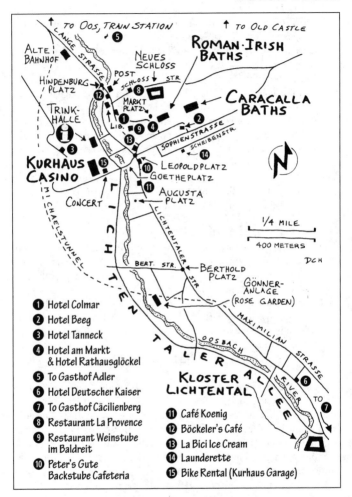

Hotels and Restaurants:

1. Hotel Colmar
2. Hotel Beeg
3. Hotel Tanneck
4. Hotel am Markt & Hotel Rathausglöckel
5. To Gasthof Adler
6. Hotel Deutscher Kaiser
7. To Gasthof Cäcilienberg
8. Restaurant La Provence
9. Restaurant Weinstube im Baldreit
10. Peter's Gute Backstube Cafeteria
11. Café Koenig
12. Böckeler's Café
13. La Bici Ice Cream
14. Launderette
15. Bike Rental (Kurhaus Garage)

chips at the window near the entrance (an ATM is nearby). The casino is open for gambling daily from 14:00 to 2:00 in the morning (Fri–Sat to 3:00, €3 entry, €1.50 entry with *Kurkarte* discount card from your hotel, €5 minimum bet, €10,000 maximum bet, no blue jeans or tennis shoes, tie and coat required and can be rented for €11 with an €11 deposit, passport absolutely required, under 21 not admitted, liveliest after dinner and later, pick up English history and game rules as you enter, tel. 07221/21060, www.casino-baden-baden.de). Lower rollers and budget travelers can try their luck at the casino's €0.50 slot machines *(Automatenspiel)* downstairs (€1 entry fee or included in €3 casino admission, same hours, no dress code).

Casino Tour: The casino gives 30-minute German-language tours every morning from 9:30 to 12:15 (€4, 2/hr, from 10:00 off-season, last departure at 11:45, call a few days ahead to request an English tour, tel. 07221/21060, otherwise organize English speakers in the group and lobby for information; or just pick up the paltry English brochure). Even peasants in T-shirts, shorts, and sandals are welcome on tours.

Town Orientation: From the steps of the casino, stand between big white columns #2 and #3 and survey the surroundings (left to right): Find the ruined castle near the top of the hill, the rock-climbing cliffs next, the new castle (top of town) next to the salmon spire of the Catholic church (the famous baths are just behind that), the Merkur peak (marked by tower, 2,000 feet above sea level), and the bandstand in the *Kurhaus* garden. The Baden-Baden orchestra plays here most days (free, usually at 16:00).

Trinkhalle: Beyond the colonnade on your left is the old *Trinkhalle*—a 300-foot-long entrance hall decorated with nymphs and romantic legends (explained by a €9 English book sold inside) and the home of the TI, a café, and ticket agency.

▲▲**Strolling Lichtentaler Allee**—Bestow a royal title on yourself and promenade down the famous Lichtentaler Allee, a pleasant, picnic-perfect, 1.5 mile-long lane. You'll stroll through a park along the babbling, brick-lined Oos River, past old mansions and under hardy oaks and exotic trees (street lit until 22:00), to the historic Lichtentaler Abbey (a Cistercian convent founded in 1245). At the elitist tennis courts, cross the bridge into the free art-nouveau rose garden (*Gönneranlage*, 100 labeled kinds of roses, great lounge chairs, best in early summer). Either walk the whole length round-trip, or take city bus #201 one way (runs between downtown and Klosterplatz, near the abbey). Many bridges cross the river, making it easy to shortcut to bus #201 anytime. Biking is another option (see "Bike Rental," page 113), but you'll have to stay on the road in the bike lane, since the footpath is only for pedestrians.

Russian Baden-Baden—Many Russians, including Dostoyevsky and Tolstoy, flocked to Baden-Baden after the czars banned gambling in their motherland. Many lost their fortunes, borrowed a pistol, and did themselves in on the "Alley of Sighs" (Seufzerallee, past the baths just off Sophienstrasse/Vincentistrasse). You'll find a Russian church—and cemetery—just south of the center (€0.70, daily 10:00–18:00, closed Dec–Jan, near *Gönneranlage* rose garden across river from Lichtentaler Allee).

▲**Mini–Black Forest Walks**—Baden-Baden is at the northern end of the Black Forest. If you're not going south but want a taste of Germany's favorite woods, consider one of several hikes from town.

The best hike starts from the old town past the *Neues Schloss* (new castle) to the *Altes Schloss* (ruined old castle), which crowns a hill above town, past cliffs tinseled with rock climbers and on to Ebersteinburg, a village with a ruined castle (allow 90 min one-way; only on Sun can you catch bus #215 back into town at 13:36 or 16:36).

For another good hike, take the bus to Rote Lache, then hike two hours downhill via Scherrhof to the Geroldsauer Waterfall. Walk along the waterfall and stream into nearby Geroldsau to catch the bus back to Baden-Baden (get details at TI).

For less work and more views, consider riding the cogwheel Merkur Bergbahn to the 2,000-foot summit of Merkur (€4 round-trip, daily 10:00–22:00, closed Jan–Feb; take bus #204 from Augustaplatz or #205 from Leopoldsplatz to the end of the line and catch the funicular, tel. 07221/277-631). You can also hike down, following the trails to Lichtentaler Abbey and then along Lichtentaler Allee into town.

The Baths

Baden-Baden's two much-loved but very different baths stand side by side in a park at the top of the old town. The Roman-Irish Bath is traditional, stately, indoors, not very social, and extremely relaxing...just you, the past, and your body. The perky, fun, and modern Baths of Caracalla are half the price, indoor and outdoor, and more social. Caracalla is better in the sunshine. Roman-Irish is fine anytime. Most visitors do both.

In each case, your admission ticket works like a subway token—you need it to get out. If you overstay your allotted time, you pay extra. Save 10–15 percent by buying tickets from your hotel. You can relax while your valuables are stowed in very secure lockers. Both baths share a huge underground Bäder-Garage, which is free (for 2 hrs) only if you validate your parking ticket before leaving either bath.

▲▲▲**Roman-Irish Bath (Friedrichsbad)**—The highlight of most visits to Baden-Baden is a sober two-hour ritual called the Roman-Irish Bath. Friedrichsbad pampered the rich and famous in its elegant surroundings when it opened 120 years ago. Today, this steamy world of marble, brass columns, tropical tiles, herons, lily pads, and graceful nudity welcomes gawky tourists as well as locals. For €29, you get up to three hours and the works (€21 without the 8-min massage).

Read this carefully before stepping out naked: In your changing cabin, load all your possessions onto the fancy hanger (hang it in locker across the way, slip card into lock, strap key around wrist). As you enter (in the "crème" room), check your weight on the digital kilo scale. Do this again as you leave. You will have lost a kilo...all in sweat. The complex routine is written (in English) on the walls with recommended time—simply follow the room numbers from 1 to 15.

Take a shower; grab a towel and put on plastic slippers before hitting the warm-air bath for 15 minutes and the hot-air bath for five minutes; shower again; if you paid extra, take the soap-brush massage—rough, slippery, and finished with a spank; play Gumby in the shower; lounge under sunbeams in one of several thermal steam baths; glide like a swan under a divine dome in a royal pool (one of three "mixed" pools); don't skip the cold plunge; dry in warmed towels; and lie cocooned, clean, and thinking prenatal thoughts on a bed for 30 minutes in the mellow, yellow, silent room. You don't appreciate how clean you are after this experience until you put your dirty socks back on. (Bring clean ones.)

All you need is money. You'll get a key, locker, and towel. Hair dryers are available (Mon–Sat 9:00–22:00, Sun 12:00–20:00, last admission 3 hrs before closing if you're getting a massage, 2 hrs before otherwise; men and women together Tue, Wed, Fri–Sun, women separate Mon and Thu; Römerplatz 1, tel. 07221/275-920, www.carasana.de).

About the dress code: It's always nude. Men and women use parallel and nearly identical facilities. During "mixed" times, men and women share only three pools in the center. On Mondays and Thursdays, two of the shared pools are reserved for women only, but the biggest pool is still used by both sexes.

Afterward, before going downstairs, browse through the Roman artifacts in the Renaissance Hall, sip just a little of the terrible but "magic" hot water *(Thermalwasser)* from the elegant fountain, and stroll down the broad royal stairway, feeling, as they say, five years younger—or at least 2.2 pounds lighter.

▲▲**Caracalla Therme**—For a more modern experience, spend a few hours at the Baths of Caracalla (daily 8:00–22:00, last entry at 20:00, tel. 07221/275-940, www.carasana.de), a huge palace of water, steam, and relaxed people (professional daycare available).

Bring a towel (or pay €5 plus a €5 deposit to rent one) and swimsuit (shorts are OK for men). Buy a card (€12/2 hrs, €14/3 hrs, €16/4 hrs, 10 2-hr entries for repeat visits or a group cost €105) and put the card in the locker to get a key. Change clothes, strap the key around your wrist, and go play. Your key gets you into another poolside locker if you want money for a tan or a drink. The Caracalla Therme is an indoor/outdoor wonderland of steamy pools, waterfalls, neck showers, Jacuzzis, hot springs, cold pools, lounge chairs, exercise instructors (extra fee), saunas, a cafeteria, and a bar. After taking a few laps around the fake river, you can join some kinky Germans for water spankings (you may have to wait a few minutes to grab a vacant waterfall). Then join the gang in the central cauldron. The steamy "inhalation" room seems like purgatory's waiting room, with misty minimal visibility, filled with strange, silently aging bodies.

The spiral staircase leads to a naked world of saunas, tanning lights, cold plunges, and sunbathing. There are three eucalyptus-scented saunas of varying temperatures: 80, 90, and 95 degrees. Follow the instructions on the wall. Towels are required, not for modesty but to separate your body from the wood bench. The highlight is the Arctic bucket in the shower room. Pull the chain. Only rarely will you feel so good. And you can do this over and over. As you leave, take a look at the Roman bath that Emperor Caracalla soaked in to conquer his rheumatism nearly 2,000 years ago (free, in the underground Bäder-Garage between the two spas).

SLEEPING

In the Center

$$$ Hotel Colmar, run with a personal touch by the Özcan family, offers 26 pastel-elegant rooms, some with balconies (Sb-€75–82, Db-€95, 2-room apartment Db-€110, extra bed-€28, prices guaranteed through 2004 with this book, non-smoking rooms, elevator, parking-€8/day, Lange Strasse 34, tel. 07221/93890, fax 07221/938-950, www.hotel-colmar.de, info@hotel-colmar.de).

$$$ Hotel Beeg rents 15 attractive and comfortable rooms, run from a delectable pastry shop/café on the ground floor. It's wonderfully located on a little square in a pedestrian zone, facing the baths (Sb-€80, Db-€100, balcony-€10 extra, apartment Tb-€150, elevator, reception in café, on Römerplatz at Gernsbacher Strasse 44, tel. 07221/36760, fax 07221/367-610, hccbeeg@t-online.de, Herr Beeg SE).

$$$ Hotel Tanneck is a funky, rambling, late-19th-century place where Persian rugs clash with flowery wallpaper. Perched on a hill behind the casino, it was once a sanitarium for the rich and aimless. Its 17 spacious rooms are now presided over by commonsense den mother Heidi (S-€31, Sb-€70–75, Ds-€80, Db-€85–100, Tb-€112–118, Qb-€138, Quint/b-€159, baby crib-€8, ground-floor rooms, family rooms, several balconies—my favorites face the south, 7-min walk from casino, Werderstrasse 14, tel. 07221/23035, fax 07221/38327, www.hotel-tanneck.com, info@hotel-tanneck.com).

$$ Hotel am Markt is a warm, 25-room, family-run hotel with all the comforts a commoner could want in a peaceful, central, nearly traffic-free location, two cobbled blocks from the baths (S-€30–32, Sb-€42–47, D-€58–62, Db-€73–80, Tb-€90, extra bed-€15, Marktplatz 18, tel. 07221/27040, fax 07221/270-444, www.hotel-am-markt-baden.de, info@hotel-am-markt-baden.de, Herr und Frau Bogner-Schindler and Frau Jung all SE). For romantics, the church bells blast charmingly through each room every quarter hour from 6:15 until 22:00; for others, they're a nuisance. Otherwise, quiet rules. The ambience and the clientele make killing time on their small terrace a joy. To reach the hotel from Leopoldsplatz, locate McDonald's where Langestrasse hits the square. Walk three minutes up Langestrasse (4 sets of stairs, past

SLEEP CODE

(€1 = about $1.10, country code: 49, area code: 07221)
Sleep Code: **S** = Single, **D** = Double/Twin, **T** = Triple, **Q** = Quad, **b** = bathroom, **s** = shower only, **no CC** = Credit Cards not accepted, **SE** = Speaks English, **NSE** = No English. Unless otherwise noted, credit cards are accepted, English is spoken, and breakfast is included.

To help you sort easily through these listings, I've divided the rooms into three categories based on the price for a standard double room with bath:

$$$ **Higher Priced**—Most rooms €90 or more.
$$ **Moderately Priced**—Most rooms between €70–90.
$ **Lower Priced**—Most rooms €70 or less.

The TI can nearly always find you a room—but don't use the TI for places listed here, or you'll pay more. Go direct! The only tight times are during the horse races (May 15–23 and Aug 27–Sept 5 in 2004). If you arrive at Baden-Baden's Oos station, you can stay near the station (see below). But I'd hop on bus #201, which goes to the center of town (and most of the recommended hotels), then follows the river (and Lichtentaler Allee) to the Abbey (and more hotels). Hotel am Markt, clearly the best value, is worth calling in advance.

All hotels and pensions are required to extract an additional €2.80 per-person, per-night "spa tax." This comes with a "guest card" *(Kurkarte)*, offering small discounts on tourist admissions around town (including casino entry and bike rental).

stone giant) to the red-spired church on Marktplatz. By car, follow signs for *Therme* until you reach Sophienstrasse, then look for little green hotel signs leading you up the hill.

$$ **Hotel Rathausglöckel,** around the corner and below the Hotel am Markt at Steinstrasse 7, is a 16th-century guest house with six cozy rooms and steep stairs (Sb-€60, Db-€60–80, third person-€20, 2-room apartment with kitchen-€80–150, church bells every 15 min 6:15–22:00, parking-€6/day, tel. 07221/90610, fax 07221/906-161, www.rathausgloeckel.de, info@rathausgloeckel.de, kind Michael Rothe SE). To reach the hotel on foot, follow the directions for Hotel am Markt, above, but turn right at the top of the stairs.

Away from the Center

The following two listings are southeast of the center, across the Oosbach River from Lichtentaler Allee (for either hotel, take bus #201 from station, passing through center, to the stop noted).

$ **Deutscher Kaiser,** with spacious old rooms, is a big, traditional guesthouse run by Frau Peter, who enjoys taking care of my readers. Herr Peter cooks fine local-style meals (€7–15) in the hotel restaurant. It's right on the bus #201 line (Eckerlestrasse stop, 20 min from train station) or a 25-minute stroll from the city center down polite Lichtentaler Allee—cross the river at the green Restaurant Deutscher Kaiser sign, then turn right (S-€33, Sb-€46–49, D-€46–49, Db-€59–67, discounts on their Web site, non-smoking rooms, Internet access, free and easy parking, Hauptstrasse 35, tel. 07221/72152, fax 07221/72154, www.hoteldk.de, info@hoteldk.de). Drivers: From the autobahn, skip the town center by following Congress signs into Michaelstunnel. Take the tunnel's first exit, then another right at the end of the exit (direction Lichental). Outside, the hotel is about a half-mile down on the left. From the Black Forest, follow *Zentrum* signs. Ten yards after Aral gas station, turn left down the small road to Hauptstrasse.

$ **Gasthof Cäcilienberg** is farther out, but still on the bus line at the end of Lichtentaler Allee (Brahmsplatz stop). It's a good fallback if the other recommended hotels are full (9 rooms, S-€35, Sb-€41, D-€45, Db-€52, no CC, closed Nov, sits above a restaurant, Geroldsauer Strasse 2, tel. 07221/72297, fax 07221/70459, a little English spoken).

Near the Station

Baden-Baden's train station is in Baden-Oos, three miles from the center (see "Orientation," page 112).

$$ **Gasthof Adler,** near the train station, is clean, simple, friendly, and on a very busy intersection; ask for *ruhige Seite,* the quiet side (S-€33, Ss-€36, Sb-€45, D-€59, Ds-€64, Db-€69–79, non-smoking rooms, Kermit-green bathrooms; veer right from station, walk 3 blocks passing post office to stoplight, hotel is on left corner, Ooser Hauptstrasse 1, tel. 07221/61858 or 07221/61811, fax 07221/17145, Herr and Frau Troger S a little E). Bus #201 stops across the street.

$ **Werner Dietz Hostel,** between the station and the center, has the cheapest beds in town (€18/bed in 4- to 6-bed dorms, €3 less for 2 nights or more, €2.50 more if you're over 26, non-members pay €3.10 extra, S/D rooms €5 extra per person, includes sheets and breakfast, no CC, 23:30 curfew, Hardbergstrasse 34, bus #201 from station or downtown to Grosse Dollenstrasse—announced as *Jugendherberge,* about 7 stops from station, 5 from downtown; it's a steep, well-marked, 10-min climb from there, tel. 07221/52223, fax 07221/60012, jh-baden-baden@t -online.de). They give discount coupons (€3–6.50) for both city baths and serve inexpensive meals. Drivers: After the freeway to Baden-Baden ends, turn left at the first light and follow the signs. Wind your way uphill to the big, modern hostel next to the public swimming pool.

EATING

Hotel Rathausglöckel's restaurant, personal and homey, has long had a good reputation and great food. In the 16th century, prisoners were granted a last meal here before being executed. Eat here if it's the last thing you do (€8–15, Thu–Sun 11:30–14:00 & 18:00–21:30, Wed 18:00–21:30, closed Mon–Tue, reservations smart in winter, Steinstrasse 7, tel. 07221/90610, Michael SE).

The recommended hotel **Deutscher Kaiser** serves a fine dinner (make it part of your evening Lichtentaler Allee stroll, Wed–Mon 12:00–14:00 & 18:15–21:00, closed Tue, tel. 07221/72152).

La Provence, with a romantic setting, an eclectic menu, and good food, is popular, especially on weekends (€10–20, Mon–Fri 17:00–11:00, Sat–Sun 12:00–24:00, reservations smart, from Marktplatz hike up to Schloss Strasse 20, tel. 07221/216-515).

At **Weinstube im Baldreit,** for meals or just a glass of wine, choose between their terrace courtyard or cozy cellar (€8–14 meals, Tue–Sun from 17:00, closed Mon, Küferstrasse 3, from Langestrasse walk up Büttenstrasse, it's just past the stairs on your left, tel. 07221/23136).

Commoners pile their plates high at **Peter's Gute Backstube ("am Leo"),** a fun self-service place offering salads, pasta, fish, omelettes, and pastries. The lively staff dons lederhosen for Oktoberfest, Hawaiian shirts in sunny weather, and striped shirts for the horse races (€5, Mon–Fri 6:30–19:00, Sat 6:30–18:00, Sun 8:00–19:00, free coffee and tea refills, on Leopoldsplatz at Sophienstrasse 4, tel. 07221/392-817).

If you want to spend too much for an elegant 19th-century cup of coffee, **Café Koenig** is the place (daily 9:00–18:30, fine shady patio, look for sign with squiggly script, just before Augustaplatz at Lichtentaler Strasse 12, tel. 07221/23573).

In der Trinkhalle, another swanky coffee joint, has comfy leather sofas, international newspapers and magazines, and a casino-view terrace (daily 10:00–2:00, next to TI in *Trinkhalle* building at Kaiserallee 3, tel. 07221/302-905).

For a slice of Black Forest cake, try Café Koenig (see above) or **Böckeler's Café** (Mon–Sat 8:00–18:30, Sun 9:30–18:00, Langestrasse 40-42, tel. 07221/949-594).

For good gelato or fancy ice-cream desserts, stop by **La Bici,** just off Leopoldplatz. Servers call their mystery-flavor blue ice cream an "experiment" (Lang Strasse 1, next to McDonald's).

TRANSPORTATION CONNECTIONS

By train to: Freiburg (hrly, 45 min, sometimes with a change in Offenburg), **Triberg** (hrly, 60 min), **Heidelberg** (hrly, 60 min, catch Castle Road bus to Rothenburg), **Munich** (hrly, 4 hrs, some direct but most with 1–2 changes), **Frankfurt** (2/hr, 1.5 hrs, most with a change in Mannheim or Karlsruhe), **Frankfurt Airport** (every 2 hrs direct, 1.5 hrs, or hrly with a change in Karlsruhe, 1.5 hrs), **Koblenz** (hrly, 2.5 hrs with a change), **Mainz am Rhine** (hrly, 2 hrs, some direct but most with 1 change), **Strasbourg** (9/day, 90 min, sometimes with a change in Appenweier), **Bern** (hrly, 3.5 hrs, change in Basel). Train info: tel. 01805-996-633.

Freiburg

Freiburg (FRY-burg) is worth a quick look, if for nothing else than to appreciate its thriving center and very human scale. Bikers and hikers seem to outnumber cars, and trams run everywhere. This "sunniest town in Germany," with 30,000 students, feels like the university town that it is. Freiburg, bombed nearly flat in 1944, skillfully put itself back together. It feels cozy, almost Austrian; in fact, it was Hapsburg territory for 500 years. This "capital" of the Schwarzwald, exuding an "I could live here" appeal, is surrounded by lush forests and filled with environmentally aware people so dedicated to solar power that they host an annual Intersolar trade fair (June 24–26 in 2004).

Marvel at the number of pedestrian-only streets. Freiburg's trademark is its system of *Bächle*, tiny streams running down each street. These go back to the Middle Ages (serving as fire protection, cattle refreshment, and a constantly flushing disposal system). A sunny day turns any kid-at-heart into a puddle-stomper. Enjoy the ice cream and street-singing ambience of the cathedral square, which has a great produce and craft market (Mon–Sat 7:30–13:00, biggest Wed and Sat).

ORIENTATION

(area code: 0761)

Tourist Information: Freiburg's busy but helpful TI sells three unnecessary city guidebooks: The €4 guide has tons of practical information, the €4.20 city guide with photos has the most information on sights, and the €6.55 book is geared toward student types, with lots of bar and nightlife suggestions. Persistently ask for the free city map (or €0.50 will buy you better map—without the hassle). The TI also offers a room-booking service (€2.55 per booking for Freiburg and Black Forest area), German-English **walking tours** (€6, 2 hrs, Mon and Fri at 14:30,

Wed–Thu, Sat, and sometimes Sun at 10:30), and lots of information on the Black Forest region (including a €5 book; TI open May–Oct Mon–Fri 9:30–20:00, Sat 9:30–17:00, Sun 10:00–12:00, Nov–April Mon–Fri 9:30–18:00, Sat 9:30–14:00, Sun 10:00–12:00, hotel availability board in front, free WC around corner, tel. 0761/388-1880, www.freiburg.de).

Arrival in Freiburg: Walk out of the bustling train station (€2 lockers, WC–€0.80, bus station next door to the right), cross the street, and head straight up Eisenbahnstrasse, the tree-lined boulevard (passing the post office). Within three blocks, you'll take an underpass under a busy road; as you emerge, the TI is immediately on your left and the town center is dead ahead.

Helpful Hints

Internet: Get online at the Pingwing Internet Café (€4/hr, or €3/hr after 18:00, Mon–Fri 10:00–20:00, Sat 10:00–18:00, closed Sun, Niemensstrasse 3, close to Martinstor, tel. 0761/409-8732).

Bike Rental: Try Mobile near the station (€7.50/6 hrs, €10/24 hrs, €50 cash and passport for deposit, daily 5:00–24:00, includes helmet and lock; from bus station, cross tram bridge to round building and walk downstairs, tel. 0761/292-7998).

SIGHTS

▲**Cathedral (Münster)**—This impressive church, completed in 1513, took more than three centuries to build, ranging in style from late Romanesque to lighter, brighter Gothic. It was virtually the only building in town to survive WWII bombs. The lacy tower *(Münster-turm),* considered by many the most beautiful around, is as tall as the church is long...and not worth the 329-step ascent (€1.50, Mon–Sat 9:30–17:00, Sun 13:00–17:00). From this lofty perch, watchmen used to scan the town for fires. While you could count the 123 representations of Mary throughout the church, most gawk at the "mooning" gargoyle and wait for rain. Browse the market in the square. The ornate Historisches Kaufhaus, across from the church, was a trading center in the 16th century.

Augustiner Museum—This offers a good look at Black Forest art and culture through the ages. Highlights are downstairs: a close-up look at some of the Münster's original medieval stained glass and statuary (€2, €4 family card, Tue–Sun 10:00–17:00, closed Mon, 2 blocks south of cathedral in big yellow building on Augustinerplatz, tel. 0761/201-2531).

Schlossberg (Castle Hill)—Schlossberg towers over the east end of Freiburg's old town. It was named Castle Hill because a 17th-century fort once stood here, built by the French to control the citizens of Freiburg during a period of French occupation. Schlossberg today is popular for its views over the city. Though the old fort is long gone, a new modern lookout tower (100 feet high) stands where the French Fort d'Aigle (eagle tower) once stood.

To get to the top of Schlossberg, you can hike or take an elevator from Schwabentor, the half-timbered tower at the east end of the old town. From the tower, look for the footbridge on Oberlinden street. Cross the bridge and hike up 10 minutes (to the left), or continue straight through the tunnel to the elevator *(Aufzug)*. At the top of the elevator and trail, you'll come to the restaurant Greiffenegg Schlössle (see "Eating in Freiburg," below). From there, walk another seven minutes up to the viewpoint. To continue 20 more minutes to the Fort d'Aigle lookout tower from the viewpoint, walk the level path to the left (with your back to the benches), then veer right uphill at the big white cross (look for small silver signs pointing through forest).

Schauinsland—Freiburg's own mountain, while little more than an oversized hill, is nine miles southeast of the center. This viewpoint, which won't wow Americans from Colorado, offers the handiest panorama view of the Schwarzwald for those without wheels. A gondola system, one of Germany's oldest, was designed for Freiburgers relying on public transportation (€10.20 round-trip, May–Oct daily 9:00–18:00, Nov–April daily 9:30–17:00, catch tram #4 from town center or from tram bridge over the tracks at train station to the end, then take bus #21 seven stops to Talstation stop for gondola, tel. 0761/292-930, www.bergwelt-schauinsland.de). At the 4,000-foot summit, you'll find a view restaurant, pleasant circular walks, and the Schniederli Hof, a 1592 farmhouse museum. A tower on a nearby peak offers an even more commanding Black Forest view.

SLEEPING

(€1 = about $1.10, country code: 49, area code: 0761)
Though I prefer nights in sleepy Staufen (see below), many will enjoy a night in lively Freiburg. Prices include breakfast, and English is spoken. Hotel Alleehaus offers the most value for your money.

In the Town Center
Hotels in central Freiburg are convenient but overpriced.

$$$ **Hotel Barbara,** near the train station, has 21 fine and bright rooms (Sb-€69–79, Db-€92–109, extra bed-€20, prices €10 higher during fairs, nearby parking garage-€9/day, on quiet street 2 min from station, head toward TI but turn left at post office to Poststrasse 4, tel. 0761/296-250, fax 0761/26688, www.hotel-barbara.de, mail@hotel -barbara.de, friendly Herr Wahl SE).

$$$ **City Hotel** is business-class sterile with 42 clean, modern

rooms. It's just off the main shopping street, a five-minute walk from the TI (Sb-€76–79, Db-€98–109, third person-€25, elevator, parking-€8/day, Weberstrasse 3, tel. 0761/388-070, fax 0761/388-0765, www .cityhotelfreiburg.de, city.hotel.freiburg@t-online.de).

$$$ **Markgräfler Hof** is overpriced, but the rooms are clean with modern comforts, and the location is good. This place works if you can't get in anywhere else (Sb-€82–98, Db-€100–135, Gerberau 22, tel. 0761/32540, fax 0761/296-4949, www.markgraeflerhof.de, info @markgraeflerhof.de).

Outside the Town Center

These listings are a much better value, a 15-minute walk or easy bus or tram ride from the station but still handy to the center.

$$ **Hotel Alleehaus** is tops. Located on the edge of the center on a quiet, leafy street in a big house that feels like home, its 19 rooms are thoughtfully decorated, comfy, and warmly run by Bernd, Claudia, and their team (S-€46, Sb-€50–64, small Db-€67, small twin Db-€72, larger Db-€87, suite Db-€98, Tb-€94–118, Qb-€138, reception closed 19:30–6:00, call by 18:00 if arriving later than 19:30, parking-€7/day, good buffet breakfast, non-smoking rooms, Marienstrasse 7, tram #4 from station to Holzmarkt, near intersection with Wallstrasse, tel. 0761/387-600, fax 0761/387-6099, www.hotel-alleehaus.de, wohlfuehlen @hotel-alleehaus.de).

$$ **Hotel am Stadtgarten** is on the opposite side of town (10-min walk from TI) with 37 comfortable rooms—some new and all heavy on beige (Sb-€57–63, Db-€72, Tb-€96, Qb-€118, Quint/b-€148, tram #5 from station 3 stops to Bernhardstrasse 5, at intersection with Karlstrasse, usually free parking nearby or pay €7/day, tel. 0761/282-9002, fax 0761/282-9022, www.hotel-am-stadtgarten.com, kindly run by Paul who SE and loves taking care of his American guests).

$ **Black Forest Hostel** has 105 of the cheapest beds in town. Run by friendly Tania, with a young, bohemian attitude, it's bare-bones simple (€12–20/person in 3- to 20-bed rooms, S-€27, D-€22, no CC, non-smoking, lockers, Internet access, self-service kitchen, laundry facilities, 24-hour reception, no curfew, Kartäuserstrasse 33, 20-min walk from station or tram #1 direction Littenweiler, get off at Oberlinden stop, tel. 0761/881-7870, fax 0761/881-7895, www.blackforest-hostel.de, backpacker@blackforest-hostel.de).

$ **Freiburg Youth Hostel** is a big, modern option on the east edge of town (€19 per bed including sheets and breakfast, €3 less for 2 nights or more, "seniors" over 26 pay €3 extra, non-members pay €3.10 extra, 2:00 curfew, Kartäuserstrasse 151, tram #1 direction Littenweiler to Römerhof stop, then 10-min walk, tel. 0761/67656, fax 0761/60367).

EATING

Freiburg has plenty of dining options. I've listed a few good places in the town center, and a couple atop the scenic Schlossberg.

In the Town Center
Kleiner Meyerhof, around the corner from the TI, offers regional specialties, a good salad bar, dessert buffet, and reasonable prices (daily 10:00–24:00, Rathausgasse 27, tel. 0761/26941).

Hausbrauerei Feierling brews its own beer and serves fine meals. On warm summer evenings, their *Biergarten* across the street offers cool, leafy shade and a lively atmosphere (€5–12, daily 11:00–24:00, Gerberau 46, tel. 0761/243-480).

Vegetarians enjoy **Caruso's** large portions and fair prices (Mon–Sat 10:00–2:00, closed Sun, Kaiser Joseph Strasse 258 near Martinstor, tel. 0761/31000).

Freiburg's Schlossberg
To get to these scenic restaurants, see Schlossberg under "Sights," page 123.

Greiffenegg Schlössle offers rooftop views over Freiburg, but the meals are expensive and worth it only if you can get a table on the terrace in good weather (daily 11:00–24:00, meals start at €20, Schlossbergring 3, reservations smart, tel. 0761/32728).

The **Biergarten Kastaniengarten** is self-service, offering budget travelers a few peek-a-boo views just above the Greiffenegg Schlössle (€5–8, daily 11:00–24:00). Cheaper yet, consider a picnic at the Schlossberg viewpoint.

TRANSPORTATION CONNECTIONS

Freiburg in Breisgau (Brsg)
By train to: Staufen (hrly, 30 min, 3/day are direct, others require change to train or bus in Bad Krozingen; only 7/day Sun, with none before 11:00; don't schedule yourself too tightly because cancellations can occur on milk-run trains; after 20:00 no trains to Staufen but you can take a train to Bad Krozingen station and take a shared taxi from there to Staufen for €8—call taxi 30 min before you need it, tel. 07633/5386), **Baden-Baden** (hrly, 45 min or 1.5 hrs with 1 change), **Munich** (hrly, 4.5 hrs, transfer in Mannheim), **Mainz am Rhine** (hrly, 1.5 hrs), **Basel** (hrly, 45 min), **Bern** (hrly, 2 hrs, transfer in Basel). Train info: tel. 01805-996-633.

Staufen

Staufen makes a peaceful and delightful home base for your exploration of Freiburg and the southern trunk of the Black Forest. Hemmed in by vineyards, it's small and off the beaten path, with a quiet pedestrian zone of colorful old buildings bounded by a happy creek that actually babbles. There's nothing to do here but enjoy the marketplace atmosphere, hike through the vineyards to the ruined castle overlooking the town, and savor a good dinner with local wine.

ORIENTATION

(area code: 07633)

Tourist Information: The TI, on the main square in the Rathaus, has a good (German-only) map of the wine road and can help you find a room (Mon 9:00–12:30 & 14:00–18:00, Tue–Thu until 17:30, Fri until 17:00, Sat 9:30–12:00, closed Sun, tel. 07633/80536, www.staufen.de).

Arrival in Staufen: Everything I list is within a 10-minute walk of the station (no lockers, but try Gasthaus Bahnhof—see "Sleeping," below). To get to town, exit the station with your back to the pond and angle right up Bahnhofstrasse. Turn right at the post office on Hauptstrasse for the town center, hotels, and TI.

Winery: Weingut Wiesler offers *Weinproben*—a free taste of a wine of your choice—but they'll expect you to buy a bottle if you like it (Mon–Fri 15:00–18:30, Sat 9:00–13:30, closed Sun, behind Gasthaus Bahnhof, second house on right, at base of castle hill, Krozinger Strasse 26, tel. 07633/6905, Frau Wiesler SE).

SIGHTS

Near Staufen

Wine Road (Badische Weinstrasse)—The wine road of this part of Germany staggers from Staufen through the tiny towns of Grunern, Dottingen, Sulzburg, and Britzingen, before collapsing in Badenweiler. If you're in the mood for some tasting, look for *Winzergenossenshaft* signs, which invite visitors in to taste and buy wines, and often to tour a winery.

▲**Badenweiler**—If ever a town were a park, Badenweiler is it. This idyllic, poodle-elegant, and finicky-clean spa town is known only to the wealthy Germans who soak here (**TI** open Mon–Fri 9:00–12:30 & 13:30–1:30, March–Oct also Sat 9:00–14:00, closed Sun year-round, tel. 07632/799-300, www.badenweiler.de). Its bath, Markgrafenbad, is next to the ruins of a Roman mineral bath in a park of imported and exotic trees (including a California redwood). This prize-winning piece of architecture perfectly mixes trees and peace with an elegant indoor/outdoor swimming pool (daily 9:00–22:00, tel. 07632/799-200). The locker procedure, combined with the language barrier, makes getting to the pool more memorable than you'd expect (€9.50, €8 after 16:00 and on weekends, €5.50 after 19:00 weekdays, €2 towel rental with €10 deposit). Badenweiler is a 20-minute drive south of Staufen (take the train or bus to Mullheim and bus from there).

SLEEPING

(€1 = about $1.10, country code: 49, area code: 07633)

The TI has a list of private *Zimmer*. Prices listed are for one night, but most *Zimmer* don't like one-nighters. Except for the last listing, breakfast is included.

$$$ **Gasthaus Krone,** on the main pedestrian drag, has nine rooms that gild the lily but offer a good value in this price range (Sb-€60, Db-€75, Tb-€90, parking, balconies, Hauptstrasse 30, tel. 07633/5840, fax 07633/82903, www.die-krone.de, info@die-krone.de; Kurt Lahn, who looks a bit like Dan Rather, S a little E). Its restaurant appreciates vegetables and offers wonderful splurge meals (closed Fri–Sat).

$$ **Hotel Sonne,** at the edge of the pedestrian center, offers eight newly renovated rooms with Italian flair (Sb-€45, Db-€60, continue straight past Hotel Krone, turn right at T intersection, and take second left on Mühlegasse to reach Albert-Hugard Strasse 1, tel. 07633/95300, fax 07633/953-014). Herr DeGruttola-Vittorio (an English- and German-speaking Italian) and his family serve Italian specialties along with the traditional German fare in the hotel's restaurant (closed Tue).

$$ **Hotel Hirschen,** with a storybook location in the old pedestrian center, has a cozy restaurant (closed Mon–Tue). It's family-run, with 15 plush and thoughtfully appointed rooms, balconies, and a big roof deck (Sb-€50–55, Db-€70, Tb-€95, elevator, free and easy parking, Hauptstrasse 19 on main pedestrian street, tel. 07633/5297, fax 07633/5295, info@breisgaucity.com, Dieter and Isabel SE). They have a huge luxury penthouse for four (€130).

$ **Bahnhof Hotel** is the cheapest, simplest place in town, with a dynamite castle view from the upstairs terrace, a self-service kitchen, a *kleine* washing machine for guests, and €8 dinners served on its tree-shaded patio or in its antler-filled restaurant (S-€21, D-€41, no breakfast, across from train station, tel. 07633/6190, NSE). Seven comfortable and cheery rooms right out of grandma's house share two bathrooms. At night, master of ceremonies Lotte makes it the squeeze-box of Staufen. People come from all around to party with Lotte, so it can be noisy at night. If you want to eat red meat in a wine barrel under a tree, this is the place. For stays of three nights or longer, ask her about the rooms next door (Sb-€26, Db-€41).

Black Forest

▲▲**Short and Scenic Black Forest Joyride (by car or bus)**—This pleasant loop from Freiburg takes you through the most representative chunk of the area, avoiding the touristy, overcrowded Titisee.

By Car: Leave Freiburg on Schwarzwaldstrasse (signs to Donaueschingen), which becomes scenic road #31 down the dark Höllental (Hell's Valley) toward Titisee. Turn left at Hinterzarten onto road #500, follow signs to St. Margen and then to St. Peter—one of the healthy, go-take-a-walk-in-the-clean-air places that doctors actually prescribe for people from all over Germany. There's a fine four-mile walk between St. Margen and St. Peter, with regular buses to bring you back.

By Bus: Several morning and late-afternoon buses connect Freiburg's bus station (turn right out of train station and walk 100 yards) with St. Peter and St. Margen. Get off at St. Peter, hike four miles to St. Margen, and bus back to Freiburg (for details, contact regional bus tel. 0761/207-280 or Freiburg TI, tel. 0761/388-1880).

St. Peter: The TI, just next to the Benedictine Abbey (private), can recommend a walk (Mon–Fri 9:00–12:00 & 14:00–17:00, Sat in July–Aug 10:00–12:00, closed Sun year-round and Sat Sept–June, Klosterhoff 11, tel. 07660/910-224). Sleep at the traditional old **Gasthof Hirschen** on the main square (Sb-€41, Db-€72–82, St. Peter/Hochschwarzwald, Bertoldsplatz 1, tel. 07660/204, fax 07660/1557, www.gasthof-hirschen.de), or consider **Pension Kandelblick** (D-€36–38, no CC, Seelgutweg 5, tel. 07660/349).

Extension for Drivers: From St. Peter, wind through idyllic Black Forest scenery up to Kandel (mountain). At the summit is the Berghotel Kandel. You can park here and take a short walk to the 4,000-foot peak for a great view. Then the road winds steeply through a dense forest to Waldkirch, where a fast road takes you to the Freiburg Nord autobahn entrance. With a good car and no stops, you'll get from Staufen/Freiburg to Baden-Baden via this route in three hours.

▲▲**Extended Black Forest Drive**—Of course, you could spend much more time in the land of cuckoo clocks and healthy hikes. For a more thorough visit, still connecting with Baden-Baden, try this drive: As described above, drive from Staufen or Freiburg down Höllental. After a short stop in St. Peter, wind up in Furtwangen with the impressive Deutsches Uhrenmuseum (German Clock Museum, €3, daily April–Oct 9:00–18:00, Nov–March 10:00–17:00, tel. 07723/920-117). More than a chorus of cuckoo clocks, this museum traces (in English) the development of clocks from the Dark Ages to the space age. It has an upbeat combo of mechanical musical instruments as well.

Triberg—Deep in the Black Forest, Triberg is famous for its Gutach Waterfall (which falls 500 feet in several bounces, €2.50 to see it) and, more important, the Black Forest Museum, which gives a fine look at the costumes, carvings, and traditions of the local culture (€3.50, daily 10:00–17:00, closed mid-Nov–Christmas and possibly several weeks in Jan–March, check Web site or ask at TI, tel. 07722/4434, www .schwarzwaldmuseum.de). Touristy as Triberg is, it offers an easy way for travelers without cars to enjoy the Black Forest (TI tel. 07722/953-231, closed Sun, www.triberg.de).

▲**Black Forest Open-Air Museum (Schwarzwälder Freilichter-museum)**—This offers the best look at this region's traditional folk life. Built around one grand old farmhouse, the museum is a collection of several old farms filled with exhibits on the local dress and lifestyles (€4.50, daily March–Nov 9:00–18:00, last entry at 17:00, closed in winter, English descriptions and €6 guidebook, north of Triberg, through Hornberg to Hausach/Gutach on road B33, tel. 07831/93560, www.vogtsbauernhof.org). The surrounding shops and restaurants are awfully touristy. Try your *Schwarzwald Kirschtorte* (Black Forest cherry cake) elsewhere.

Continue north through Freudenstadt, the capital of the northern Black Forest, and onto the Schwarzwald-Hochstrasse, which takes you along a ridge through 30 miles of pine forests before dumping you right on Baden-Baden's back porch.

ROTHENBURG AND THE ROMANTIC ROAD

From Munich or Füssen to Frankfurt, the Romantic Road takes you through Bavaria's medieval heartland, a route strewn with picturesque villages, farmhouses, onion-domed churches, Baroque palaces, and walled cities.

Linger in Rothenburg (ROE-ten-burg), Germany's best-preserved walled town. Countless travelers have searched for the elusive "untouristy Rothenburg." There are many contenders (such as Michelstadt, Miltenberg, Bamberg, Bad Windsheim, and Dinkelsbühl), but none holds a candle to the king of medieval German cuteness. Even with crowds, overpriced souvenirs, Japanese-speaking night watchmen, and, yes, even *Schneebälle,* Rothenburg is best. Save time and mileage and be satisfied with the winner.

Planning Your Time

The best one-day drive through the heartland of Germany is the Romantic Road. The road is clearly marked for drivers, and well described in the free brochure available at any TI. Those without wheels can take the bus tour; see the end of this chapter for details (railpass holders get a 60 percent discount, so the entire Frankfurt–Munich trip costs €29). Apart from Würzburg, with its Prince Bishop's Residenz (see Würzburg chapter), the only stop worth more than a few minutes is Rothenburg. Twenty-four hours is ideal for this town. With two nights and a day, you'll be able to see the essentials and actually relax a little.

Rothenburg

In the Middle Ages, when Frankfurt and Munich were just wide spots on the road, Rothenburg ob der Tauber was Germany's second-largest free imperial city, with a whopping population of 6,000. Today it's her

Rothenburg

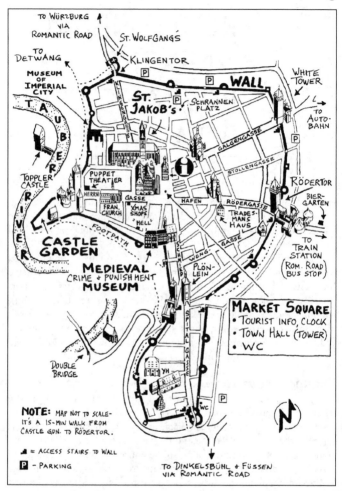

TO WÜRZBURG
VIA
ROMANTIC ROAD

ST. WOLFGANG'S

TO
DETWANG

KLINGENTOR

MUSEUM
OF
IMPERIAL
CITY

WHITE
TOWER

WALL

ST.
JAKOB'S

SCHRANNEN
PLATZ

TO
AUTO-
BAHN

T
A
U
B
E
R

GALGENGASSE

STOLLENGASSE

TOPPLER
CASTLE

PUPPET
THEATER

RÖDERTOR

R
I
V
E
R

HERRN
GASSE
FRAN.
CHURCH
XMAS
SHOPS
"HELL"

HAFEN

RÖDERGASSE

BIER-
GARTEN

TRADES-
MANS
HAUS

CASTLE
GARDEN

FOOTPATH

GASSE

WENG

TO
TRAIN
STATION
(ROM. ROAD
BUS STOP)

MEDIEVAL
CRIME + PUNISHMENT
MUSEUM

PLÖN-
LEIN

MARKET SQUARE
• TOURIST INFO, CLOCK
• TOWN HALL (TOWER)
• WC

S
P
I
T
A
L
G
A
S
S
E

YH

DOUBLE
BRIDGE

WC

NOTE: MAP NOT TO SCALE-
IT'S A 15-MIN WALK FROM
CASTLE GDN. TO RÖDERTOR.

= ACCESS STAIRS TO WALL

P = PARKING

TO DINKELSBÜHL + FÜSSEN
VIA ROMANTIC ROAD

best-preserved medieval walled town, enjoying tremendous tourist popularity without losing its charm. Get medievaled in Rothenburg.

During Rothenburg's heyday, from 1150 to 1400, it was the crossing point of two major trade routes: Tashkent–Paris and Hamburg–Venice. Today the great trade is tourism; two-thirds of the townspeople are employed to serve you. Too often, Rothenburg brings out the shopper in visitors before they've had a chance to see the historic city. True, this is a great place to do your German shopping, but appreciate the town's great history and sights first. While 2.5 million people visit each year, a mere 500,000 spend the night. Rothenburg is most enjoyable early and late, when the tour groups are gone. Rothenburg is very busy through the summer and in the Christmas Market month of December. Spring and fall are great, but it's pretty bleak from January through March—when most locals are hibernating or on vacation.

Rothenburg in a day is easy, with five essential experiences: the Medieval Crime and Punishment Museum, the Riemenschneider wood carving in St. Jakob's Church, the city walking tour, a walk along the wall, and the entertaining Night Watchman's Tour. With more time, there are several mediocre but entertaining museums, walking and biking in the nearby countryside, and lots of cafés and shops. Make a point to spend at least one night. The town is yours after dark, when the groups vacate and the town's floodlit cobbles wring some romance out of any travel partner.

ORIENTATION

(area code: 09861)

To orient yourself in Rothenburg, think of the town map as a human head. Its nose—the castle garden—sticks out to the left, and the neck is the skinny lower part, with the hostel and some of the best hotels in the Adam's apple. The town is a joy on foot. No sight or hotel is more than a 15-minute walk from the train station or each other.

Most of the buildings you'll see were built by 1400. The city was born around its long-gone castle—built in 1142, destroyed in 1356—which was located on the present-day site of the castle garden. You can see the shadow of the first town wall, which defines the oldest part of Rothenburg, in its contemporary street plan. A few gates from this wall still survive. The richest and biggest houses were in this central part. The commoners built higgledy-piggledy (read: picturesquely) farther from the center near the present walls.

Tourist Information: The TI is on Market Square (April–Oct Mon–Fri 9:00–12:00 & 13:00–18:00, Sat-Sun 10:00–15:00, Nov–March shorter hours and closed Sun, tel. 09861/40492, www.rothenburg .de). If there's a long line, just raid the rack where they keep all the free pamphlets. The map and guide comes with a virtual walking guide to the town. The "Information" monthly lists all the events and entertainment. Ask about the daily 14:00 English walking tour (April–Oct). There's free Internet access in the TI lobby (1 terminal). Visitors who arrive late can check the handy map with all hotels—highlighting which ones still have rooms available, with a free direct phone connection to them—just outside the door. The best town map is available free with this book at the Friese shop, two doors west from the TI (toward St. Jakob's Church; see "Shopping," page 142).

Arrival in Rothenburg

By Train: It's a 10-minute walk from the station to Rothenburg's Market Square (following the brown *Altstadt* signs, exit left from station, turn right on Ansbacher Strasse, and head straight into the Middle Ages). Day-trippers can leave luggage in station lockers (€2, on platform) or at the Friese shop on Market Square. Arrange train and *couchette*/sleeper reservations at the travel agency in the station (no charge for quick questions, Mon–Fri 9:00–18:00, Sat 9:00–13:00, closed Sun, tel. 09861/4611). The nearest WCs are at the snack bar next door to the station. Taxis wait at the station (€5 to any hotel).

By Car: Driving in town can be a nightmare, with many narrow, one-way streets. Park outside the walls and walk five minutes to the center. Parking lots line the town walls, ranging from free (the P5 parking lot just outside Klingentor) to €4 per day. Only those with a hotel reservation can park within the walls after hours (but not during festivals; easiest entry often via Spittaltor).

Helpful Hints

Laundry: A handy launderette is near the station off Ansbacher Strasse (€5.50/load, includes soap, English instructions, opens at 8:00, last load in Mon–Fri at 18:00, Sat at 14:00, closed Sun, Johannitergasse 8, tel. 09861/2775).

Swimming: Rothenburg has a fine modern recreation center with an indoor/outdoor pool and sauna. It's just a few minutes' walk down the Dinkelsbühl Road (*Hallenbad,* adult-€3, child-€1.50, swimsuit and towel rental-€2 each, Mon 14:00–21:00, Tue–Thu 9:00–21:00, Fri–Sun 9:00–18:00, Nordlingerstrasse 20, tel. 09861/4565).

Festivals

Rothenburgers dress up in medieval costumes and beer gardens spill out into the street to celebrate Mayor Nusch's Meistertrunk victory (Whitsun weekend, May 28–31 in 2004, see story below under "Rothenburg Town Walk—Meistertrunk Show") and 700 years of history in the Imperial City Festival (Sept 3–5 in 2004, with fireworks).

Christmas Market: Rothenburg is dead in November, January, and February, but December is its busiest month—the entire town cranks up the medieval cuteness with concerts and costumes, shops with schnapps, stalls filling squares, hot spiced wine, giddy nutcrackers, and mobs of earmuffed Germans. Christmas markets are big all over Germany, and Rothenburg's is considered one of the best. The festival takes place each year in the four weeks leading up to the last Sunday before Christmas (Nov 26–Dec 22 in 2004). Virtually all sights listed in this chapter are open longer hours during these four weeks. Try to avoid Saturdays and Sundays, when big-city day-trippers really clog the grog.

TOURS

▲▲**Night Watchman's Tour**—This tour is flat-out the most entertaining hour of medieval wonder anywhere in Europe. The Night Watchman (a.k.a. Hans Georg Baumgartner) lights his lamp and takes tourists on his one-hour rounds, telling slice-of-gritty-life tales of medieval Rothenburg (€4, April–Dec nightly at 20:00, in English, meet at Market Square, www.nightwatchman.de). This is the best evening activity in town.

Old Town Historic Walk—The TI on Market Square offers 90-minute guided walking tours in English (€4, April–Oct daily at 14:00 from Market Square). Take this for the serious history of Rothenburg and to make sense of its architecture. Alternatively, you can hire your own **private guide**—a local historian can really bring the ramparts alive. Gisela Vogl (€50/90 min, €70/2 hr, tel. 09861/4957, werner.vogl @t-online.de) and Anita Weinzierl (tel. 09868/7993) are both good. Martin Kamphans, a potter, also works as a guide (tel. 09861/7941, kamphans@t-online.de)

Horse-and-Buggy Rides—These give you a relaxing 30-minute clip-clop through the old town, starting from Market Square or Schrannen-platz (private buggy for €30, or wait for one to fill up for €5 per person).

SIGHTS

Rothenburg Town Walk

This one-hour walk weaves together Rothenburg's top sights. Start the walk on Market Square.

Market Square Spin Tour—Stand at the bottom of Market Square (10 feet below the wooden post on the corner) and—ignoring the little white arrow—spin 360 degrees clockwise, starting with the city hall tower. Now do it again slower, following these notes:

Town Hall and Tower: The city's tallest spire is the **town hall tower.** At 200 feet, it stands atop the old city hall, a white, Gothic, 13th-century building. Notice the tourists enjoying the best view in town from the black top of the tower (€1 and a rigorous but interesting climb, 214 steps, narrow and steep near the top—watch your head, April–Oct daily 9:30–12:30 & 13:00–17:00, Nov–March Sat–Sun 12:00–15:00 only, enter on Market Square through middle arch of new town hall). After a fire burned down part of the original building, a **new town hall** was built alongside what survived of the old one (fronting the square). This is in Renaissance style from 1570.

Meistertrunk Show: At the top of Market Square stands the proud **Councillors' Tavern** (clock tower from 1466). In its day, the city council drank here. Today, it's the TI and the focus of most tourists' attention when the little doors on either side of the clock flip open and the

Rothenburg Town Walk

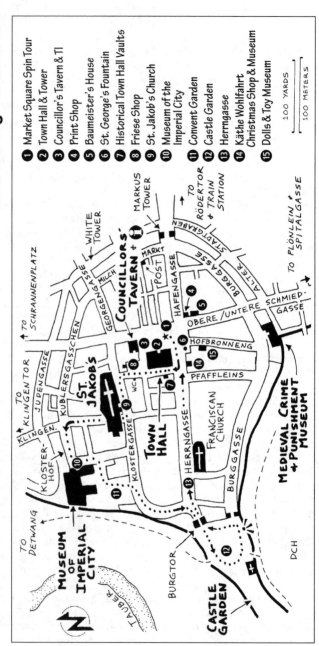

1. Market Square Spin Tour
2. Town Hall & Tower
3. Councillor's Tavern & TI
4. Print Shop
5. Baumeister's House
6. St. George's Fountain
7. Historical Town Hall Vaults
8. Friese Shop
9. St. Jakob's Church
10. Museum of the Imperial City
11. Convent Garden
12. Castle Garden
13. Herrngasse
14. Käthe Wohlfahrt Christmas Shop & Museum
15. Dolls & Toy Museum

100 YARDS
100 METERS

wooden figures (from 1910) do their thing. Be on Market Square at 11:00, 12:00, 13:00, 14:00, 15:00, 20:00, 21:00, or 22:00 for the ritual gathering of the tourists to see the less-than-breathtaking reenactment of the Meistertrunk story. In 1631, the Catholic army took the Protestant town and was about to do its rape, pillage, and plunder thing when, as the story goes, the mayor said, "Hey, if I can drink this entire three-liter tankard of wine in one gulp, will you leave us alone?" The invading commander, sensing he was dealing with an unbalanced person, said, "Sure." Mayor Nusch drank the whole thing, the town was saved, and he slept for three days.

While this is a nice story, it was dreamed up in the late 1800s for a theatrical play designed to promote a romantic image of the town. In actuality, Rothenburg was occupied and ransacked several times in the Thirty Years' War, and it never recovered—which is why it's such a well-preserved time capsule today. Hint: For the best show, don't watch the clock; watch the open-mouthed tourists gasp as the old windows flip open. At the late shows, the square flickers with camera flashes.

Bottom of Market Square: On the bottom end of the square, the cream-colored building has a fine **print shop** (upstairs—see "Shopping," page 142). Adjoining that is the **Baumeister's House,** a touristy restaurant with a fine courtyard (see "Eating," page 149), featuring a famous Renaissance facade with statues of the seven virtues and the seven vices—the former supporting the latter. The statues are copies; the originals are in the Reichsstadt Museum (listed below). The green house below that is the former house of the 15th-century Mayor Toppler (it's now the recommended Greifen Guesthouse); next to it is a famous Scottish restaurant (with arches). Keep circling to the big 17th-century **St. George's fountain.** The long metal gutters slid, routing the water into the villagers' buckets. Rothenburg's many fountains had practical functions beyond providing drinking water. The water was used for fighting fires, and some fountains were stocked with fish during times of siege. Two fine buildings behind the fountain show the old-time lofts with warehouse doors and pulleys on top for hoisting. All over town, lofts were filled with grain and corn. A year's supply was required by the city so they could survive any siege. The building behind the fountain is an art gallery (free, usually daily 11:00–17:00) showing off the work of Rothenburg's top artists. To the right is an old-time pharmacy mixing old and new in typical Rothenburg style.

The broad street running under the town hall tower is **Herrngasse.** The town originated with its castle (built in 1142 but now long gone; only the castle garden remains). Herrngasse connected the castle to Market Square. The last leg of this circular walking tour will take you from the castle garden up Herrngasse to where you now stand. For now, walk a few steps down Herrngasse to the arch under the town hall tower (between the new and old town halls). On the left wall are the town's measuring rods—a reminder that medieval Germany was made of 300 independent little countries, each with its own weights and measures. Merchants and shoppers knew that these were the local standards: the rod (4.3 yards), the *Schuh* (or shoe, roughly a foot), and the ell (from elbow to fingertip—4 inches longer than mine...try it). Notice the protruding cornerstone. These are all over town—originally to protect buildings from reckless horse carts (and vice versa). Under the arch, you'll find the...

▲**Historical Town Hall Vaults**—This museum gives a waxy but good look at Rothenburg during the Catholics-vs.-Protestants Thirty Years' War. With fine English descriptions, it offers a look at "the fateful year 1631," a replica of the famous Meistertrunk tankard, and a dungeon complete with three dank cells and some torture lore (€2, May–Oct daily 9:30–17:30, less off-season).

From the museum, walk toward St. Jakob's Church (just northwest of Market Square). You'll pass the public WC (on your left) and the recommended **Friese shop** (see "Shopping," page 142) tucked into the small square on your right.

Outside the church, you'll see a scene of Jesus praying at Gethsemane, a common feature of Gothic churches. Downhill, notice the nub of a sandstone statue—a rare original, looking pretty bad after 500 years of weather and, more recently, pollution. Original statues are now in the city museum. Better-preserved statues you see on the church are copies. If it's your wedding day, take the first entrance. Otherwise, use the second (downhill) door to enter...

▲▲**St. Jakob's Church**—Built in the 14th century, this church has been Lutheran since 1544. Take a close look at the Twelve Apostles altar in front (from 1546, left permanently in its open festival-day position). Below Christ are statues of six saints. St. James (Jakob in German, pronounced YAH-kohp) is the one with the shell. He's the saint of pilgrims, and this church was a stop on the medieval pilgrimage route to Santiago (St. James in Spanish) de Compostela in Spain. Study the painted panels—ever see Peter with spectacles? Around the back of the altarpiece (upper left) is a great painting of Rothenburg's Market Square in the 15th century—looking like it does today. Before leaving the front of the church, notice the old medallions above the carved choir stalls featuring the coats of arms of Rothenburg's leading families and portraits of city and church leaders.

Stairs in the back of the church, behind the pipe organ, lead to the artistic highlight of Rothenburg and perhaps the most wonderful wood carving in all of Germany: the glorious 500-year-old, 35-foot-high *Altar of the Holy Blood*. Tilman Riemenschneider, the Michelangelo of German woodcarvers, carved this from 1499 to 1504 to hold a precious rock-crystal capsule, set in a cross that contains a scrap of tablecloth miraculously stained in the shape of a cross by a drop of communion wine. Below, in the scene of the Last Supper, Jesus gives Judas a piece of bread, marking him as the traitor, while John lays his head on Christ's lap. Everything is portrayed exactly as described in the Bible. On the left: Jesus enters Jerusalem. On the right: Jesus prays in the Garden of Gethsemane. Notice how Judas, with his big bag of cash, could be removed from the scene—illustrated by photos on the wall nearby—as was the tradition for the four days leading up to Easter (€1.50, April–Oct Mon–Sat 9:00–17:15, Sun 10:45–17:15, Nov–March daily 10:00–12:00 & 14:00–16:00, free helpful English info sheet).

For an interesting walk to the nearby Reichsstadt Museum (listed below), leave the church and from its outside steps, walk around the corner to the right and under the chapel. Go two blocks down **Klingengasse** and stop at **Klosterhof street.** (I've marked your spot with a small circular plaque in the middle of the road.) Looking down Klingengasse, you see the Klingentor (cliff tower). This tower was Rothenburg's water cistern. From 1595 until 1910, a copper cistern high in the tower provided clean spring drinking water to the privileged. To the right of Klingentor is a good stretch of wall rampart to walk. To the left, the wall is low and simple, lacking a rampart because it guards only a cliff. Now find the shell decorating a building on the street corner next to you. That's the symbol of St. James (pilgrims commemorated their visit to Santiago de Compostela with a shell), indicating that this building is associated with the church. Walk under the shell, down Klosterhof (passing the colorful Altfränkische Weinstube; see "Eating," page 149) to the city history museum, housed in the former Dominican convent. Cloistered nuns used the lazy Susan embedded in the wall (to the right of museum door) to give food to the poor without being seen.

▲▲**Museum of the Imperial City (Reichsstadt Museum)**—You'll get a scholarly sweep through Rothenburg's history here. Highlights include *The Rothenburg Passion,* a 12-panel series of paintings from 1492 showing scenes leading up to Christ's crucifixion (in the *Konventsaal*); an exhibit of Jewish culture through the ages in Rothenburg *(Judaika);* a 14th-century convent kitchen *(Klosterküche);* romantic paintings of the town *(Gemäldegalerie);* and the fine Baumann collection of weapons and armor. Follow the *Rundgang Tour* signs (€3, €6 combo-ticket that includes Medieval Crime and Punishment Museum saves a whopping €0.20, April–Oct daily 9:30–17:30, Nov–March daily 13:00–16:00, English info sheet and descriptions, no photos, tel. 09861/939-043, www.reichsstadtmuseum.rothenburg.de).

Leaving the museum for the Castle Garden (listed below), go around to the right and into the **convent garden** (free, same hours as museum)—a peaceful place to work on your tan...or mix a poison potion. Angle left through the nun's garden (site of the now-gone Dominican church), eventually leaving via an arch at the far end. But enjoy the herb garden first. Monks and nuns, who were responsible for concocting herbal cures in the olden days, often tended herb gardens. Smell (but don't pick) the *Pfefferminze, Juniper* (gin), *Chamomilla* (disinfectant), and *Origanum*. Don't smell the plants in the poison corner (potency indicated by the number of crosses...like spiciness stars in a Chinese restaurant).

Exiting opposite where you entered, you see the back end of an original barn (behind a mansion fronting Herrngasse). Go downhill to the town wall (view through bars). This part of the wall takes advantage of the natural fortification provided by the cliff and is therefore much smaller than the ramparts. Angle left along the wall to Herrngasse, then right under the tower *(Burgtor)*. Notice the tiny "eye of the needle" door cut into the big door. If trying to get into town after curfew, you could bribe the guard to let you through this door (which was small enough to keep out any fully armed attackers).

Step through the gate and outside the wall. Look around and imagine being locked out in the year 1400. This was a wooden drawbridge (see the chain slits above). Notice the "pitch nose" mask—designed to pour boiling Nutella on anyone attacking. High above is the town coat of arms: a red castle **(roten Burg)**.

Castle Garden—The garden before you was once that red castle (destroyed in the 14th century). Today it's a picnic-friendly park with a viewpoint at the far end (considered the best place to kiss by romantic local teenagers). But the views of the lush Tauber River Valley below (a.k.a. Tauber Riviera) are just as good from either side of the tower on this near end of the park. To the right, a path leads down to the village of Detwang (you can see the church spire below)—a town even older than Rothenburg. To the left is a fine view of the fortified Rothenburg. Return to the tower, cross carefully under the pitch nose, and hike back up Herrngasse to your starting point.

Herrngasse—Many towns have a Herrngasse—where the richest patricians and merchants (the *Herren*) lived. Predictably, it's your best chance to see the town's finest old mansions. Strolling back to Market Square, you'll pass the old-time puppet theater (German only, on left), the Franciscan church (from 1285, oldest in town, on right), and the Eisenhut Hotel (Rothenburg's fanciest, worth a peek inside, on right). The shop next door at #11 retains the original old courtyard. The Käthe Wohlfahrt Christmas shop (at Herrngasse 1, see "Shopping," page 142) is your last, and perhaps greatest, temptation before reaching your starting—and ending—point: Market Square.

Museums within a Block of Market Square

▲▲**Medieval Crime and Punishment Museum**—This museum is the best of its kind, full of fascinating old legal bits and *Kriminal* pieces, instruments of punishment and torture—even a special cage complete with a metal gag for nags. As a bonus, you get exhibits on marriage traditions and witches. Follow the yellow arrows. Exhibits are tenderly described in English (€3.20, €6 combo-ticket includes €3 Imperial City Museum, April–Oct daily 9:30–18:00, Nov and Jan–Feb daily 14:00–16:00, Dec and March daily 10:00–16:00, last entry 45 min before closing, fun cards and posters, tel. 09861/5359, www.kriminalmuseum.rothenburg.de).

▲**Dolls and Toy Museum**—Two floors of historic *Kinder* cuteness is a hit with many. Pick up the free English binder for an extensive description of the exhibits (€4, family ticket-€10, daily March–Dec 9:30–18:00, Jan–Feb 11:00–17:00, just off Market Square, downhill from the fountain at Hofbronneng 13).

▲**German Christmas Museum**—Herr Wohlfahrt's passion is collecting and sharing historic Christmas decorations. This excellent museum, upstairs in the giant Käthe Wohlfahrt Christmas shop, features a unique and thoughtfully described collection of Christmas-tree stands, mini-trees sent in boxes to WWI soldiers at the front, early Advent calendars, old-time Christmas cards, 450 clever ways to crack a nut, and a look at tree decorations through the ages—including the Nazi era and when you were a kid (€4, April–Dec daily 10:00–18:00, Jan–March only Sat–Sun 10:00–18:00, hours often change off-season, Herrngasse 1).

More Sights in Rothenburg

▲▲**Walk the Wall**—Just over a mile and a half around, providing great views and a good orientation, this walk can be done by those under six feet tall and without a camera in less than an hour. The hike requires no special sense of balance. Photographers go through lots of film, especially before breakfast or at sunset, when the lighting is best and the crowds are fewest. The best fortifications are in the Spitaltor (south end). Walk from there counterclockwise to the "forehead." Climb the Rödertor en route. The names you see along the way are people who donated money to rebuild the wall after World War II and those who've recently donated €1,000 per meter for the maintenance of Rothenburg's heritage.

▲**Rödertor**—The wall tower nearest the train station is the only one you can climb. It's worth the 135 steps for the view and a fascinating rundown on the bombing of Rothenburg in the last weeks of World War II, when the east part of the city was destroyed (€1, unreliable hours, usually open daily but closed for lunch April–Oct, closed Nov–March, photos of WWII damage with English translations). If you climb this, you can skip the city hall tower.

Sightseeing Lowlights—St. Wolfgang's Church is a fortified Gothic church built into the medieval wall at Klingentor. Its dungeon-like passages and shepherd's dance exhibit are pretty lame (€1.50, April–Sept daily 11:00–13:00 & 14:00–17:00, Oct until 16:00, closed Nov–March). The cute-looking Farming Museum (Bäuerliches Museum) next door is even worse. The 700-year-old Tradesman's House (Rothenburger

Handwerkerhaus) shows the everyday life of a Rothenburger in the town's heyday (€2.20, April–Oct daily 9:00–18:00, Nov–Dec Mon–Fri 14:00–16:00, Sat–Sun 10:00–16:00, closed Jan–March, Alter Stadtgraben 26, near Markus Tower, tel. 09861/94280).

Excursions

▲A Walk in the Countryside—Just below the *Burggarten* (castle garden) in the Tauber Valley is the cute, skinny, 600-year-old castle/summer home of the medieval Mayor Toppler. The **Topplerschlösschen** ("Toppler's little castle")—the size and shape of a fortified treehouse—is in a farmer's garden and can be open whenever he's around and willing to let you in (€1.50, Fri–Sun 13:00–16:00, closed Mon–Thu and Nov, 1 mile from town center at Taubertalweg 100, tel. 09861/7358). People say the mayor had this valley-floor escape to get people to relax about leaving the fortified town...or to hide a mistress.

Walk on past the covered bridge and huge trout to the peaceful village of Detwang. Detwang is actually older than Rothenburg (from 968, the second-oldest village in Franconia). It also has a Riemenschneider altarpiece in its church. For a scenic return, loop back to Rothenburg through the valley along the river. Just past the double-arcaded bridge, follow the footpath back to town.

Franconian Bike Ride—For a fun, breezy look at the countryside around Rothenburg, rent a bike from Rad & Tat (€2.50/hr, €7.50/half-day, €10/full day, Mon–Fri 9:00–18:00, Sat 9:00–14:00, closed Sun, Bensenstrasse 17, outside of town near corner of Bensenstrasse and Erlbacherstrasse, passport number required, free Taubertal bike route maps, tel. 09861/87984, Daniel Lorenz SE). For a pleasant half-day pedal, bike along Topplerweg to Spittaltor and down into the Tauber Riviera, over the double-arcaded bridge, and along the small riverside road to Detwang, passing the cute Topplerschlösschen (described above). From Detwang, follow *Liebliches Taubertal* bike path signs as far up the Tauber River (direction Bettwar) as you like.

Franconian Open-Air Museum—A 20-minute drive from Rothenburg in the undiscovered "Rothenburgy" town of Bad Windsheim is an open-air folk museum that, compared with others in Europe, isn't much. But it tries very hard and gives you the best look around at traditional rural Franconia (€4.50, daily March–Sept 9:00–18:00, Oct–Nov 10:00–17:00, closed Dec–Feb, last entry 1 hour before closing, tel. 09841/66800, www.freilandmuseum.de).

SHOPPING

Be warned...Rothenburg is one of Germany's best shopping towns. Do it here and be done with it. Lovely prints, carvings, wineglasses, Christmas-tree ornaments, and beer steins are popular.

The Käthe Wohlfahrt Christmas trinkets phenomenon is spreading across the half-timbered reaches of Europe. In Rothenburg, tourists flock to two **Käthe Wohlfahrt Christmas Villages** (on either side of Herrngasse, just off Market Square). This Christmas wonderland is filled with enough twinkling lights to require a special electric hookup, instant Christmas mood music (best appreciated on a hot day in July), and American and Japanese tourists hungrily filling little woven shopping baskets with €5–8 goodies to hang on their trees. Let the spinning flocked tree whisk you in, but pause at the wall of Steiffs, jerking uncontrollably and mesmerizing little kids. (OK, I admit it, my Christmas tree sports a few KW ornaments.) Note: Prices are padded with tour-guide incentives (Mon–Fri 9:00–18:00, Sat 9:00–16:00, Sun 10:00–18:00, tel. 09861/4090, www.wohlfahrt.de). The new **Christmas Museum** upstairs (see "Museums within a Block of Market Square," page 140) is very good but dumps you back in the store, compelled now by the fascinating history to buy even more. Factor this likely extra expense into the museum's already steep €4 admission fee.

The **Friese shop** offers a charming contrast (just off Market Square, west of TI, on corner across from public WC). Cuckoo with friendliness, trinkets, and souvenirs, it gives shoppers with this book tremendous service: a 10 percent discount, 16 percent tax deducted if you have it mailed, and a free map (normally €1.50). Anneliese, who runs the place with her sons Frankie and Berni and grandson Rene (who played American football), charges only her cost for shipping and money exchange, and lets tired travelers leave their bags in her back room for free. For fewer crowds and better service, visit after 14:00 (Mon–Sat 8:00–17:00, Sun 9:30–17:00, tel. & fax 09861/7166).

The Ernst Geissendörfer **print shop** sells fine prints, etchings, and paintings. Show this book for 10 percent off marked prices on all cash purchases (or minimum €50 credit-card purchases) and a free shot of German brandy to sip while you browse (Mon–Sat 10:00–18:00, Sun 10:00–17:00, late Dec–April closed Sun, enter through bear shop on corner where Market Square hits Schmiedgasse, go up 1 floor, tel. 09861/2005).

For characteristic wineglasses, oenology gear, and local wine from the town's oldest wine-makers, drop by the **Weinladen am Plönlein** (daily 8:30–18:00, Plönlein 27—see "Evening Fun," below, for info on wine-tasting).

Shoppers who mail their goodies home can get handy €1.50 boxes at the **post office** in the shopping center across from the train station (Mon–Fri 9:00–17:30, Sat 9:00–12:00).

Those who prefer to eat their souvenirs shop the *Bäckereien* (bakeries). Their succulent pastries, pies, and cakes are pleasantly distracting...but skip the bad-tasting Rothenburger *Schneebälle*.

SLEEPING

In the Old Town

$$$ **Gasthof Greifen,** once the home of Mayor Toppler, is a big, traditional, 600-year-old place with large rooms and all the comforts. It's run by a fine family staff and creaks with rustic splendor (small Sb-€38, Sb-€48, Db-€60–82, Tb-€97–102, Qb-€105–122, 10 percent off for 3-night stay, self- or full-service laundry, free and easy parking, half a block downhill from Market Square at Obere Schmiedgasse 5, tel. 09861/2281, fax 09861/86374, www.gasthof-greifen.rothenburg.de, info@gasthof-greifen.rothenburg.de, Brigitte and Klingler family). The family also runs a restaurant, serving basic meals in the garden or dining room.

$$$ **Hotel Gerberhaus,** a classy new hotel in an old building, is warmly run by Inge and Kurt, who mix modern comforts into 20 bright and airy rooms while maintaining a sense of half-timbered elegance. Enjoy the pleasant garden in back (Sb-€48–56, Db-€56–79, Tb-€94–99, Qb-€104–114, prices depend on room size, 2-room apartment with kitchen-€89/2 people, €120/4 people, 5 percent off and a free *Schneeball* if you stay 2 nights and pay cash, some non-smoking rooms, some rooms with canopied 4-poster *Himmel* beds, free Internet access, laundry-€4/load, Spitalgasse 25, tel. 09861/94900, fax 09861/86555, www.gerberhaus.rothenburg.de, gerberhaus@t-online.de). The downstairs café serves good soups, salads, and light lunches.

$$$ **Hotel Kloster-Stüble,** deep in the old town near the castle garden, is my classiest listing. Jutta greets her guests while husband Rudolf does the cooking, and Erika (SE) is the fun and energetic first mate who really runs the show (Sb-€50, Db-€75–90, Tb-€110, family rooms-€110–155, luxurious apartment with kitchen and balcony-€105 for 2 or up to €200 for 6, €3 extra on weekends, family deals, Heringsbronnengasse 5, tel. 09861/6774, fax 09861/6474, www.klosterstueble.de, hotel@klosterstueble.de).

$$ **Gasthof zur Goldenen Rose** is a classic family-run place—simple, traditional, comfortable, and a great value—where scurrying Karin serves breakfast and stately Henni (SE) keeps everything in good order. The hotel has one shower per floor, but the rooms are clean, and you're surrounded by cobbles, flowers, and red-tiled roofs (S-€21, D-€36, Ds-€46, Db-€49, some triples, spacious family apartment-€107/4 people, €128/5 people, kid-friendly, streetside rooms can be noisy, closed Jan–Feb, Spitalgasse 28, tel. 09861/4638, fax 09861/86417, www.thegoldenrose.de, info@thegoldenrose.de). The Favetta family also serves good, reasonably priced meals (restaurant closed Wed). Keep your key to get in after hours (side gate in alley).

$$ **Hotel Altfränkische Weinstube am Klosterhof** is the place for well-heeled bohemians. Mario and lovely Hanne rent six cozy rooms above their dark and smoky pub in a 600-year-old building. It's an

SLEEP CODE

(€1 = about $1.10, country code: 49, area code: 09861)

Sleep Code: **S** = Single, **D** = Double/Twin, **T** = Triple, **Q** = Quad, **b** = bathroom, **s** = shower only, **no CC** = Credit Cards not accepted, **SE** = Speaks English, **NSE** = No English. Unless otherwise noted, credit cards are accepted, English is spoken, and breakfast is included.

To help you sort easily through these listings, I've divided the rooms into three categories, based on the price for a standard double room with bath:

   $$$ **Higher Priced**—Most rooms €65 or more.
    $$ **Moderately Priced**—Most rooms between €40–65.
     $ **Lower Priced**—Most rooms €40 or less.

Rothenburg is crowded with visitors, but most are day-trippers. Except for the rare Saturday night and festivals (see "Festivals," above), finding a room is easy throughout the year.

Many hotels and guest houses will pick up tired heavy-packers at the station. You may be greeted at the station by *Zimmer* skimmers who have rooms to rent. If you have reservations, resist them and honor your reservation. But if you haven't booked ahead, try talking yourself into one of these more desperate bed-and-breakfast rooms for a youth-hostel price. Be warned: These people are notorious for taking you to distant hotels and then charging you for the ride back if you decline a room.

If you're driving and unable to find your place, stop and give them a call. They will likely rescue you.

upscale Monty Python atmosphere, with TVs, modern showers, open-beam ceilings, and *Himmel* beds—canopied four-poster "heaven" beds (Sb-€45, Db-€50–60, Db suite-€70, Tb-€70, prefer cash, kid-friendly, off Klingengasse at Klosterhof 7, tel. 09861/6404, fax 09861/6410, www .romanticroad.com/altfraenkische-weinstube). Their pub is a candlelit classic, serving hot food until 22:30 and closing at 1:00. Drop by on Wednesday evening (19:30–24:00) for the English Conversation Club (see "Meet the Locals," page 152).

$$ Pension Elke, run by the spry Erich Endress and his son Klaus, rents 10 bright, airy, and comfy rooms above the family grocery store (S-€25, Sb-€35, D-€38–46, Db-€58–62, prices depend on size, extra

Rothenburg Hotels

1. Gasthof Greifen
2. Hotel Gerberhaus
3. Hotel Kloster-Stüble
4. Gasthof zur Goldenen Rose
5. Hotel Altfränkische Weinstube am Klosterhof
6. Pension Elke
7. Hotel Café Uhl
8. Gästehaus Flemming
9. Gästehaus Viktoria
10. Gästehaus Raidel
11. Gasthof Marktplatz
12. Pension Pöschel
13. Frau Liebler Rooms
14. Rossmühle Youth Hostel
15. Hotel Hornburg
16. Gasthof Rödertor
17. Pension Fuchsmühle

bed-€15, 10 percent discount with this book when you stay at least 2 nights, no CC, reception in grocery store until 19:00, otherwise go around corner onto Alter Stadtgraben to first door on left and ring bell at top of stairs, near Markus Tower at Rodergasse 6, tel. 09861/2331, fax 09861/935-355, www.pension-elke-rotherburg.de).

$$ Hotel Café Uhl offers 10 fine rooms over a bakery (Sb-€30–35, Db-€50–65, prices depend on size, third person-€18, fourth person-€13, 10 percent discount with this book and cash, non-smoking rooms, parking-€3/day, reception in café, closed Jan, Plönlein 8, tel. 09861/4895, fax 09861/92820, www.hotel-uhl.de, info@hotel-uhl.de, Paul and Robert the baker SE).

$$ Gästehaus Flemming has seven tastefully modern, fresh, and comfortable rooms and a peaceful garden behind St. Jakob's Church (Sb-€45, Db-€55, Tb-€75, no CC, Klingengasse 21, tel. 09861/92380, fax 09861/976-384, Regina SE).

$$ Gästehaus Viktoria is a cheery little place right next to the town wall. Its three rooms overflow with furniture, ribbons, and silk flowers, and lovely gardens surround the house (Db-€45–50, Tb-€60, no CC, breakfast served at nearby Hotel Altfränkische Weinstube, a block from Klingentor at Klingenschütt 4, tel. 09861/87682, Hanne SE).

$$ Gästehaus Raidel, a creaky 500-year-old house filled with beds and furniture all hand-made by Herr Raidel himself, rents 14 large rooms with cramped facilities down the hall. The forlorn ambience and staff make me want to sing the *Addams Family* theme song—but it works in a pinch (S-€20, Sb-€35, D-€38, Db-€48, Tb-€71, no CC, Wenggasse 3, tel. 09861/3115, fax 09861/935-255, www.romanticroad.com/raidel, gaestehaus-raidel@t-online.de, Herr Raidel SE).

$$ Gasthof Marktplatz, right on Market Square, rents nine tidy rooms with 1970s-era wallpaper and unenthusiastic staff (S-€21, D-€38, Ds-€43, Db-€48, T-€50, Ts-€57, Tb-€62, no CC, Grüner Markt 10, tel. & fax 09861/6722, www.gasthof-marktplatz.de, Herr Rosner SE). The maddening town hall bells ring throughout the night.

$ Pension Pöschel is friendly, with seven bearskin-cozy rooms in a concrete but pleasant building with an inviting garden out back (S-€20, D-€35, Db-€45, T-€45, Tb-€55, small kids free, no CC, Wenggasse 22, tel. 09861/3430, pension.poeschel@t-online.de, Bettina SE).

$ Frau Liebler rents two large, modern, ground-floor rooms with kitchenettes and hardwood floors (Db-€40, no CC, breakfast in room, off Market Square behind Christmas shop, Pfaffleinsgasschen 10, tel. 09861/709-215, fax 09861/709-216).

$ Hostel: Here in Bavaria, hostelling is limited to those under 27, except for families traveling with children under 18. The fine **Rossmühle Youth Hostel** has 184 beds in two buildings. The droopy-eyed building (the old town horse mill, used when the town was under siege and the river-powered mill was inaccessible) houses groups and the office. The adjacent hostel is mostly for families and individuals (dorm beds-€17, bunk-bed Db- €40, includes breakfast and sheets, dinner-€5.10, self-serve laundry-€4, Internet access, entrance on Rossmühlgasse, tel. 09861/94160, fax 09861/941-620, www.djh.de, jhrothenburg @djh-bayern.de). Reserve long in advance.

Outside the Wall

The first two places are a hundred yards outside the wall on the train-station side of town (less than a 10-min walk from the center) and are among the nicest rooms I recommend in town. The third is a rustic adventure below the town in what feels like a wilderness.

$$$ **Hotel Hornburg,** a grand 100-year-old mansion with groomed grounds and 10 spacious, tastefully decorated rooms a two-minute walk outside the wall, is a super value (Sb-€49–64, Db-€69–95, Tb-€90–110, ground-floor rooms, non-smoking rooms, family-friendly, avoid if you're allergic to dogs, parking-€2/day, bikes for guests-€10/day, exit station and go straight on Ludwig-Siebert Strasse, turn left on Mann Strasse until you're 100 yards from town wall, Hornburgweg 28, tel. 09861/8480, fax 09861/5570, www.hotel-hornburg.de, hotelhornburg @t-online.de, friendly Gabriele and Martin SE).

$$$ **Gasthof Rödertor** offers 15 decent rooms in a quiet setting one block outside the Rödertor. This guesthouse has an inviting breakfast room with a farmhouse flair, a popular beer garden, and a restaurant dedicated to the potato (see "Evening Fun and Beer Drinking," page 151). Guest rooms in an annex inside the wall are slightly cheaper (Db-€65–80, Tb-€70–105, Qb-€90–125, kids sleep free, 10 percent discount with this book and cash, Ansbacher Strasse 7, tel. 09861/2022, fax 09861/86324, www.roedertor.com, hotel@roedertor.com, Frau Teutscher and her daughter Katie SE).

$$ **Pension Fuchsmühle** is a B&B in a renovated old mill on the river below the castle end of Rothenburg. The place is a work-in-progress, with kids and a linoleum-floor feel, but if you want a rustic, countryside experience, it's great. Alex and Heidi Molitor rent six rooms and take good care of their guests (Db-€45–55, Tb-€67–75, Qb-€75–85, prices depend on length of stay, non-smoking, healthy farm-fresh breakfasts, piano, free bikes for guests, free pickup at station, across the street from Toppler's little castle at Taubertalweg 103, tel. 09861/92633, www.fuchsmuehle.de, fuchsmuehle@t-online.de). It's a steep but pleasant 15-minute hike from the Fuchsmühle to Market Square. The Molitors provide flashlights for your return after dark.

EATING

Most restaurants serve meals only 11:30–13:30 and 18:00–20:00. All places listed are within a five-minute walk of Market Square. While all survive on tourism, many still feel like local hangouts. Your choices are typical Franconian or ethnic.

Traditional Franconian Restaurants

Restaurant Glocke, a *Weinstube* (wine bar) popular with locals, is run by Rothenburg's oldest wine-makers, the Thürauf family. Their seasonal menu is complemented by their family wine, served under an atmospheric, big-beamed ceiling. The menu is in German only because the friendly staff wants to explain your options in person. Don't miss their €4 deal to sample five Franconian wines (€10–15, Mon–Sat 10:30–23:00, Sun 10:30–14:00, vegetarian options, Plönlein 1, tel. 09861/958-990).

At **Zur Goldenen Rose,** Reno cooks up traditional German fare at good prices, as Henni stokes your appetite (Tue 11:30–14:00, Thu–Mon 11:30–14:00 & 17:30–20:30, closed Wed, Spitalgasse 28; leafy garden terrace out back open in sunny weather).

Extremely picturesque and touristy, **Baumeister Haus,** tucked deep behind a streetside pastry counter and antlered dining room, fills an inviting courtyard with people who don't understand a German menu (€8–15, daily 8:00–23:00, closes earlier off-season and when slow, a few doors below Market Square, Obere Schmiedgasse 3, tel. 09861/94700).

For cellar dining under medieval murals and pointy pikes, consider **Bürgerkeller,** where Herr Terian and his family pride themselves in quality local cuisine and offer a small but inviting menu and reasonable prices (€7–14, daily 12:00–14:00 & 18:00–21:00, near bottom of Herrngasse at #24, tel. 09861/2126).

Reichs-Küchenmeister is a typical big-hotel restaurant, but on a balmy evening, its pleasant tree-shaded terrace overlooking St. Jakob's Church is hard to beat (€8–16, daily 11:00–22:00, non-smoking room, nouveau German menu, some veggie choices, Kirchplatz 8, tel. 09861/9700).

Hotel Restaurant Klosterstüble, deep in the old town near the castle garden, is a classy place for good traditional cuisine. Rudy's food is better than his English, but head waitress Erika makes sure communication goes smoothly. The shady terrace is nice on a warm summer evening (€10–15, daily 11:00–14:00 & 18:00–21:00, Heringsbronnengasse 5, tel. 09861/6774).

Bohemians enjoy the **Altfränkische Weinstube am Klosterhof.** This dark and smoky pub is classically candlelit in a 600-year-old building (€5–11, hot food served 18:00–22:30, closes at 1:00, off Klingengasse at Klosterhof 7, tel. 09861/6404). Drop by on Wednesday evening

Rothenburg Restaurants

MARKET SQUARE
- TOURIST INFO, CLOCK
- TOWN HALL (TOWER)
- WC

NOTE: MAP NOT TO SCALE—IT'S A 15-MIN WALK FROM CASTLE GDN. TO RÖDERTOR.

= ACCESS STAIRS TO WALL
P = PARKING

1 Restaurant Glocke
2 Zur Goldenen Rose
3 Baumeister Haus
4 Bürgerkeller
5 Reichs-Küchenmeister
6 Hotel Restaurant Klosterstüble
7 Altfränkische Weinstube am Klosterhof

8 Altstadt-Café Alter Keller
9 Unter den Linden
10 Lotus China
11 Pizzeria Roma
12 Gasthof Rödertor
13 Trinkstube zur Hölle ("Hell")

(19:30–24:00) for the English Conversation Club (see "Meet the Locals," page 152).

For a light meal—indoors or out—try the beautifully restored **Altstadt-Café Alter Keller,** a local favorite, central but without the crazy crowds. Its walls are festooned with old pots and jugs, and Herr Hufnagel, a baker and pastry chef, whips up giant meringue cookies and other treats (Wed–Mon 11:00–20:00, Sun until 18:00, closed Tue, Alter Keller 8, tel. 09861/2268).

In the valley along the river and worth the 20-minute hike is the **Unter den Linden** beer garden (daily in season with decent weather 10:00–22:00 and sometimes later, self-service food and good beer, call first to confirm it's open, tel. 09861/5909).

Ethnic Breaks from Pork and Potatoes

Lotus China is a peaceful world apart, serving good Chinese food (€8 plates, daily 11:30–14:30 & 17:30–23:00, 2 blocks behind TI near church, Eckele 2, tel. 09861/86886).

Pizzeria Roma is smoky because it's the locals' favorite for €6.50 pizza, pastas, and Italian wine. Service can be slow (Thu–Tue 11:30–24:00, closed Wed, also has schnitzel fare, Galgengasse 19, tel. 09861/4540).

You'll find a **Turkish** place on Schrannengasse and a **Greek** restaurant just outside the wall opposite Spitaltor.

A **supermarket** is near Rödertor, just outside the wall (Mon–Fri 8:00–20:00, Sat 8:00–16:00, closed Sun, on left as you exit wall).

Evening Fun and Beer Drinking

Beer Gardens and Discos at Rothenburg's "Bermuda Dreieck": For beer-garden fun on a balmy summer evening (for dinner or beer), Rothenburgers pick **Gasthof Rödertor,** just outside the wall through the Rödertor gate (May–Sept daily 17:00–24:00, look for wood gate). Their *Kartoffeln Stube* inside is dedicated to the potato (€6–10, daily 11:00–23:00, tel. 09861/2022). Two popular **discos** are just down the street: Black Out (Ansbacher 15, in alley next to Sparkasse bank, open Wed and Fri–Sat 22:00–3:00, closed Sun–Tue and Thu) and Club 23 (around corner from bank on Adam Hörber Strasse, open Thu–Sat from 22:00, closed Sun–Mon, tel. 09861/933-045).

Wine Drinking in the Old Center: Trinkstube zur Hölle ("Hell") is dark and foreboding, but they offer thick wine-drinking atmosphere with lots of locals and a short menu until late (a block past Criminal Museum on Burggasse, with devil hanging out front, tel. 09861/4229). Mario's **Altfränkische Weinstube** (see "Traditional Franconian Restaurants," page 149) is similarly atmospheric. Wine-lovers enjoy **Restaurant Glocke**'s *Weinstube* (recommended above); for €4, you can sample five of their Franconian wines—choose dry or half-dry

(Mon–Sat 10:30–23:00, Sun 10:30–14:00, Plönlein 1, tel. 09861/958-990). You're welcome to enjoy just the wine without eating.

Meet the Locals

For a rare chance to mix it up with locals who aren't selling anything, bring your favorite slang and tongue twisters to the **English Conversation Club** at Mario's Altfränkische Weinstube am Klosterhof (Wed 19:30–24:00, Anneliese from Friese shop and Hermann the German are regulars; see restaurant listed under "Traditional Franconian Restaurants," page 149). This group of intrepid linguists just celebrated their 1,000th meeting in 2003.

TRANSPORTATION CONNECTIONS

By bus: The Romantic Road bus tour takes you in and out of Rothenburg each afternoon (April–Oct), heading to Munich, Frankfurt, or Füssen. See the Romantic Road bus schedule on page 154 (or check www.euraide.de/ricksteves).

By train: A tiny train line connects Rothenburg to the outside world via **Steinach** (almost hrly, 15 min). If you plan to arrive in Rothenburg by train, note that the last train to Rothenburg departs nightly from Steinach at 20:30 (if you arrive in Steinach after 20:30, call one of the **taxi** services for a €22 ride to Rothenburg; ideally order the taxi at least an hour in advance: tel. 09861/2000, 09861/7227, or 09861/95100). For those leaving Rothenburg by train, the first train to Steinach departs at 6:00, the last train to Steinach at 20:00.

Steinach by train to: Rothenburg (almost hrly, 15 min, last train at 20:30), **Würzburg** (hrly, 1 hr), **Nürnberg** (2/hr, 1–1.5 hr, most change in Ansbach or Neustadt an der Aisch), **Munich** (hrly, 3 hrs, 2 changes), **Frankfurt** (hrly, 2.5 hrs, change in Würzburg). Train connections in Steinach are usually within a few minutes (to Rothenburg generally from track 5). Train info: tel. 01805/996-633.

Route Tips for Drivers

The autobahn serves Würzburg, Rothenburg, and Dinkelsbühl very efficiently, making the drive from Frankfurt to Munich with these stops very fast. But if you have the time and inclination to meander, the Romantic Road—the small and carefully signposted road tracing the medieval trade route between the Rhine and the Roman road that went over the Alps south of Munich—is worth the effort.

Arriving from the north via the Romantic Road, you'll hit Rothenburg at Klingentor. The P5 parking lot just outside the gate is free and easy for anyone sleeping in that end of town. Arriving from the autobahn, turn left at the blue gas station to get to Spitaltor. While much of the town is closed to traffic, anyone with a hotel reservation can drive in and through pedestrian zones to get to their hotel (though driving here is stressful—if you're packing light, just park outside the walls). The easiest way to enter and leave is generally via Spittalgasse (and the Spitaltor, south end).

Heading south from Rothenburg, get an early start to enjoy the quaint hills and rolling villages of what was Germany's major medieval trade route. The views of Rothenburg from the west, across the Tauber Valley, are magnificent.

After a quick stop in the center of Dinkelsbühl, cross the baby Danube River (Donau) and continue south along the Romantic Road to Füssen. Drive by Neuschwanstein Castle just to sweeten your dreams before crossing into Austria to get set up at Reutte (see Bavaria and Tirol chapter).

If detouring past Oberammergau, you can drive through Garmisch, past Germany's highest mountain (Zugspitze), into Austria via Lermoos, and on to Reutte. Or you can take the small scenic shortcut to Reutte past Ludwig's Linderhof castle and along the windsurfer-strewn Plansee.

Romantic Road (Romantische Strasse)

The Romantic Road winds you past the most beautiful towns and scenery of Germany's medieval heartland. Once Germany's medieval trade route, now it's the best way to connect the dots between Füssen, Munich, and Frankfurt (www.romantischestrasse.de).

Wander through quaint hills and rolling villages, and stop wherever the cows look friendly or a town fountain beckons. My favorite sections are from Füssen to Landsberg and Rothenburg to Weikersheim. (If you're driving with limited time, connect Rothenburg and Munich by autobahn.) Caution: The similarly promoted "Castle Road," which runs between Rothenburg and Mannheim, sounds intriguing but is nowhere near as interesting.

Throughout Bavaria, you'll see colorfully ornamented maypoles decorating town squares. Many are painted in Bavaria's colors, blue and white. The decorations that line each side of the pole symbolize the crafts or businesses of that community. Each May Day, they are festively replaced. Traditionally, rival communities try to steal each other's maypole. Locals will guard their new pole night and day as May Day approaches. Stolen poles are ransomed only with lots of beer for the clever thieves.

Getting around the Romantic Road

By Bus: The Deutsche Touring company runs buses daily between Frankfurt and Füssen in each direction (April–Oct, tel. 069/790-350,

ROMANTIC ROAD BUS SCHEDULE
(DAILY, APRIL–OCTOBER)

Two different buses run roughly parallel routes (one connecting Rothenburg and Munich, the other linking Frankfurt and
Füssen). You can switch between these buses as you wish at the
stops they have in common (for example, you have to change in
Rothenburg or Dinkelsbühl to get from Frankfurt to Munich).
The following times are based on the 2003 schedule. Check
www.euraide.de/ricksteves for any changes.

North to South

Depart Frankfurt	8:00	—
Depart Würzburg	10:00	—
Arrive Rothenburg	12:50	—
Depart Rothenburg	14:30	14:30
Arrive Dinkelsbühl	15:25	15:25
Depart Dinkelsbühl	15:40	15:45
Arrive Munich	—	19:20
Arrive Füssen	19:55	—

South to North

Depart Füssen	8:00	—
Arrive Wieskirche	8:42	—
Depart Wieskirche	8:55	—
Depart Munich	—	9:00
Arrive Dinkelsbühl	12:45	12:45
Depart Dinkelsbühl	14:00	14:00
Arrive Rothenburg	14:50	14:50
Depart Rothenburg	16:00	—
Depart Würzburg	18:25	—
Arrive Frankfurt	20:00	

www.deutsche-touring.com). A second route goes daily between
Munich and Rothenburg (you can transfer at Rothenburg to the other
route). Confirm departures and arrivals when you buy your ticket, as
special events can temporarily change bus stop locations and schedules.

Buses usually leave from train stations (in towns large enough to
have one). The ride (€70 and 11 hrs if you go all the way from Frankfurt
to Munich, pay on the bus, add €1.50 per bag) is offered at a 60 percent

The Romantic Road

discount to travelers who have a German railpass, Eurailpass, or Eurail Selectpass (if Germany is one of the selected countries). Buses stop in Rothenburg (about 2 hrs) and Dinkelsbühl (about 1 hr) and too briefly at a few other attractions. The grim drivers usually hand out maps and brochures and play a tape-recorded narration of the journey highlights in English. Bus reservations are almost never necessary. But they are free and easy, and, technically, without one you can lose your seat to someone who has one (call 069/790-350 to reserve). You can start, stop, and switch over where you like. There is no quicker or easier way to travel across Germany and get such a hearty dose of its countryside.

By Car: Follow the brown *Romantische Strasse* signs and the free tourist brochure (available all over the place) that describes the journey.

SIGHTS

Along the Romantic Road

These sights are listed from north to south.

Frankfurt—The northern terminus of the Romantic Road is in this country's Manhattan (covered in its own chapter).

Würzburg—With its fancy palace and chapel, historic Würzburg can make a good overnight stop (see next chapter).

Weikersheim—This untouristy town has a palace with fine Baroque gardens (luxurious picnic spot), a folk museum, and a picturesque town square.

▲**Herrgottskapelle**—This peaceful church is graced with Tilman Riemenschneider's greatest carved altarpiece (Easter–Oct daily 9:15–17:30, less off-season, tel. 07933/508). Across the street is the Fingerhut (thimble, literally "finger hat") museum (€2, April–Oct daily 9:00–18:00, less off-season, tel. 07933/370). The south-bound Romantic Road bus stops here for 15 minutes, long enough to see one or the other. The church and museum are a mile south of Creglingen (TI tel. 07933/631, www.creglingen.de).

▲▲▲**Rothenburg**—See above for information on Germany's best medieval town.

▲**Dinkelsbühl**—Rothenburg's little sister is cute enough to merit a short stop. A moat, towers, gates, and a beautifully preserved medieval wall surround this town. Dinkelsbühl's history museum is meager and without a word of English. The Kinderzeche children's festival turns Dinkelsbühl wonderfully on end for a week at the end of July. The helpful TI on the main street sells maps with a short walking tour and can help find rooms (Mon–Fri 9:00–18:00, Sat 10:00–13:00 & 14:00–16:00, Sun 10:00–13:00, shorter hours off-season, tel. 09851/90240, www.dinkelsbuehl.de).

Rottenbuch—This nondescript village has an impressive church in a lovely setting.

▲▲**Wieskirche**—This is Germany's most glorious Baroque-rococo church, beautifully restored and set in a sweet meadow. Heavenly! Northbound Romantic Road buses from Füssen stop here for 15 minutes. (See the Bavaria and Tirol chapter.)

Füssen—This town, the southern terminus of the Romantic Road, is three miles from the stunning Neuschwanstein Castle, worth a stop on any sightseeing agenda. (See the Bavaria and Tirol chapter for description and accommodations.)

WÜRZBURG

A historic city—though freshly rebuilt since World War II—Würzburg is worth a stop to see its impressive Prince Bishop's Residenz, the bubbly Baroque chapel (Hofkirche) next door, and the palace's sculpted gardens. Surrounded by vineyards and filled with atmospheric *Weinstuben*, this small, tourist-friendly town is easy to navigate by foot or streetcar. Today, 25,000 of its 130,000 residents are students—making the town feel young and very alive.

ORIENTATION

(area code: 0931)
Tourist Information: Würzburg's helpful TI is in the rococo Falken Haus on the Marktplatz (April–Dec Mon–Fri 10:00–18:00, Sat 10:00–14:00, May–Oct also Sun 10:00–14:00, Jan–March Mon–Fri 10:00–16:00, Sat 10:00–13:00, closed Sun, tel. 0931/372-398, www.wuerzburg.de). Their free *Visitor's Guide* pamphlet and map covers the tourist's Würzburg well. The TI also books rooms for free (in person only, not by phone) and sells detailed maps for biking through the local wine country. If you'll be continuing on the Romantic Road (see previous chapter), the TI also has the *Romantische Strasse* brochure, a list of car rental options, and bus schedules. The TI also sells the bad-value Würzburg Welcome Card, offering minimal discounts on a few sights and restaurants (€2/7 days).

    Arrival in Würzburg: Würzburg's train station is user-friendly and filled with handy services (€2 lockers in main hall, WCs between main hall and tunnel to platforms). Walk out of the train station to the small square in front. A big **city map** board provides a quick orientation (on small building to the right). Farther right is the **post office** (Mon–Fri 7:00–19:00, Sat 8:00–13:00, closed Sun) and the Romantic Road bus stop (track 13, curb closest and parallel to station building, look for very

WÜRZBURG'S BEGINNINGS

The city was born centuries before Christ at an easy-to-ford part of the Main River under an easy-to-defend hill. A Celtic fort stood where the fortress stands today. Later, three Irish missionary monks came here to Christianize the local barbarians. In A.D. 686, they were beheaded, and their relics put Würzburg on the pilgrimage map. About 500 years later, since the town was the seat of a bishop, Holy Roman Emperor Frederick Barbarossa came here to get the bishop's OK to divorce his wife. The bishop said "No problem," and the HRE thanked him by giving him secular rule of the entire region of Franconia. From then on, the bishop was also a prince, and the Prince Bishop of Würzburg answered only to the Holy Roman Emperor.

small yellow *Romantische Strasse* sign and schedule). Around the corner on the left, Fahrrad-Station rents good **bikes** (€6 from 13:00–18:30, or €10/24 hrs, no helmets, April–Oct Tue–Fri 9:30–18:30, Sat 9:30–14:30, Sun 10:00–13:00, closed Mon, shorter hours off-season, passport number required, ask for a basket, tel. 0931/57445).

From the cul-de-sac in front of the station, **trams** (#1, #3, #4, or #5) take you one stop to recommended hotels (except Hotel-Pension Spehnkuch near station) or 2 stops to the Market Square and TI. By **foot,** cross over the busy Röntgenring and head up the shop-lined Kaiserstrasse. For the **Residenz,** it's either a 15-minute walk or a short bus ride (on #14, #16, #20, #26, or #28).

Getting around Würzburg

You can easily walk to everything but the hill-top fortress. A single city bus or tram ride costs €1.50 (good for 1 hour). A 24-hour ticket covers buses and trams around town, as well as the bus to the fortress (€4.10, ticket purchased on Sat also good on Sun). Either ticket can be purchased from the driver or at a streetside machine (select ticket type—*Einzel-Fahrausweis* for single trip, or *24-Stunden-Karte* for the full day—then choose Zone K for the center of town and pay amount displayed). Transit info: tel. 0931/362-321.

Helpful Hints

Internet Access: Try the **Stadtbücherei** (library, a.k.a. *Stabü*) next to the TI (€3/hr, Mon–Fri 10:00–18:00, Thu until 19:00, Sat 10:00–14:00, closed Sun, wise to call for reservations, check in with info desk on first floor, Falken Haus, Marktplatz, tel. 0931/373-439).

Festivals: Würzburg turns 1,300 years old in 2004, and the city is planning several special events throughout the year (concerts, festivals, and marathons). Check the city Web site for details (www .wuerzburg.de) or pick up a schedule of events at the TI. Würzburg—ever clever with trade—schedules its three annual festivals (wine, Mozart, and the Kiliani-Volksfest) in rapid succession to keep things busy from June 1 through late July.

Local Guide: Maureen Aldenhoff (raised in Liverpool but for 30 years married to a Würzburger) gives good private walking tours (€78/2 hrs, €90/3 hrs, tel. 0931/52135, maureen.aldenhoff@web.de).

SIGHTS

Würzburg's Residenz

This Franconian Versailles with grand rooms, 3-D art, and a massive fresco by Tiepolo is worth ▲▲▲.

Cost, Hours, Location: €4, under 18 free, April–Oct daily 9:00–18:00, Nov–March daily 10:00–16:00, last entry 30 min before closing, no photos, tel. 0931/355-170 or 0931/355-1712. Don't confuse the Residenz (a 15-min walk southeast of the train station) with Marienberg Fortress (on the hilltop). Easy parking is available in front of the Residenz (€1/hr, pay before you leave your car).

Tours and Information: English tours, offered daily at 11:00 and 15:00, give you access to the normally closed South Wing rooms, including the Mirror Kabinett (May–Oct, 45 min, confirm at TI or call ahead, covered in entry price, but tips are welcome if the guide is good). The €3 English guidebook is dry and lengthy. Few English descriptions are provided in the Residenz; follow the self-guided tour, below, for an overview.

Residenz Grounds: The elaborate Hofkirche Chapel is next door (as you exit the palace, go left), and the entrance to the picnic-worthy garden is just beyond (for more on both, see below).

Self-Guided Tour: The following self-guided tour gives you the basics to appreciate this fine palace. Begin at the entrance.

1. Vestibule: The grand circular driveway was just right for six-horse carriages to drop off their guests. The elegant stairway comes with low steps, enabling high-class ladies to glide gracefully up, heads tilted back to enjoy Europe's largest and grandest fresco opening up above them. Ascend the stairs and look up at the...

2. Tiepolo Fresco: In 1752, the Venetian master Tiepolo was instructed to make a grand fresco illustrating the greatness of Europe, Würzburg, and the Prince Bishop. And he did—in only 13 months. Find the four continents, each symbolized by a woman on an animal and pointing to the Prince Bishop in the medallion above Europe.

Würzburg

TO VEITSHOCHHEIM

TRAIN STATION

POST
BUS STN.
BIKE RENTAL

RÖNTGENRING
HAUGERRING

FRIEDENS BRÜCKE

RIVER CRUISES

JULIUS-PROM

KOELLIKER

KAISER

BAHN HOF

STIFT HAUG

MAIN

SCHOL

BORN

EICHHORN STR.

ZELLER STR.

PATH

ALTE MAIN
MARKT
RAT-HAUS STR.
DOM

BRÜCKE

MARTINSTR.

THEATER STR.

RESIDENZ
RENNWEG

HOF-STRASSE

HOFGARTEN

MAINKAI

NEUBAU STR.

OLD UNIVERSITY

OTTO STR.

SAALGASSE

RIVER

HOSTEL

LEIST-EN STR.

FORTRESS MARIEN-BURG

LUDWIGS BRÜCKE

DCH

1/4 MILE

400 METERS

❶ Hotel Sankt Josef
❷ Hotel Schönleber
❸ Hotel Barbarossa
❹ Altstadt Hotel & Gianni's Bistro
❺ Hotel-Pension Spehnkuch
❻ Restaurant/Weinhaus zum Stachel
❼ Würzburger Ratskeller
❽ Backöfele Restaurant
❾ Restaurant Martinsklause
❿ Café Two Jours
⓫ Wirtshaus zum Lämmle
⓬ Weinstube Maulaffenbäck
⓭ Weinstube Bürgerspital
⓮ Romantic Road Bus Stop

America—desperately uncivilized—sits naked with feathers in her hair on an alligator among severed heads. She's being served hot chocolate, a favorite import and nearly a drug for Europeans back then. Africa sits on a camel in a land of trade and fantasy animals (based on secondhand reports). Asia rides her elephant in the birthplace of Christianity and the alphabet. And Europe is shown as the center of high culture—Lady Culture points her brush not at Rome, but at Würzburg. The Prince Bishop had a healthy ego. The ceiling features Apollo and a host of Greek gods, all paying homage to the PB. The fresco is undergoing a three-year refurbishment. In the meantime, about 20 percent of the fresco will be covered at all times, but drapery copies of certain sections keep the fresco interesting.

3. The White Hall: This hall—actually gray—was kept plain to punctuate the colorful rooms on either side. It's a rococo-stucco fantasy. (The word *rococo* comes from the Portuguese word for the frilly rocaille shell.) Straight ahead is the palace gift shop, but continue to your left, following signs for *Rundgang*.

4. The Imperial Hall: This hall is the ultimate example of Baroque: harmony, symmetry, illusion, and the bizarre; lots of light and mirrors facing windows; and all with a foundation of absolutism (a divine monarch, inspired by Louis XIV). Take a moment to marvel at all the 3-D tricks in the ceiling. The room features three scenes: on the ceiling, find Father Main (the local river) amusing himself with a nymph. The two walls tell more history. On one, the bishop presides over the marriage of a happy Barbarossa. Opposite that is the pay-off: Barbarossa, now the Holy Roman Emperor, gives the bishop Franconia and the secular title of prince. From this point onward, the Prince Bishop rules. Before leaving the room, survey the garden (explained below) from the balcony.

5. The North Wing: This wing is a string of lavish rooms—evolving from fancy Baroque to fancier rococo—used for the Prince Bishop's VIP guests. It's a straight shot, with short English descriptions in each room to the Green Room in the corner.

6. The Green Lacquer Room: This room is named for its silver-leaf walls, painted green. The Escher-esque inlaid floor was painstakingly restored after WWII bombings. Have fun multiplying in the mirrors before leaving. The nearby hall shows photos of the city in rubble in 1945—and craftsmen bringing the palace back to its original splendor soon after.

▲▲**Hofkirche Chapel**—This sumptuous chapel was for the exclusive use of the Prince Bishop (private altar upstairs with direct entrance to his residence) and his court (ground floor). The decor and design is textbook Baroque. Architect Balthasar Neumann was stuck with the existing walls. His challenge was to bring in light and create symmetry—essential to any Baroque work. He did it with mirrors and hidden windows. All the gold is real—if paper-thin—gold leaf. The columns are "manufactured marble," which isn't marble at all but marbled plaster. This method was popular because it was cheap and the color could be controlled. Pigment was mixed into plaster, which was rolled onto the stone or timber core of the column. This half-inch veneer was then polished. You can tell if a "marble" column is real or fake by resting your hand on it. If it warms up...it's not marble. The faded painting high above the altar shows three guys in gold robes losing their heads (monks who were martyred, see "Würzburg's Beginnings" page 158). The two side paint-

ings are by the great fresco artist Tiepolo. Since the plaster wouldn't dry
in the winter, Tiepolo spent his downtime painting with oil (free, daily
April–Oct 9:00–18:00, Nov–March 10:00–16:00, closed during 10:00
Sun Mass; facing the palace, use separate entrance at far right just before
garden entrance).

Residenz Garden—One of Germany's finest Baroque gardens is a
delightful park (enter next to the chapel). The Italian section, just inside
the gate, features statues of Greek gods, carefully trimmed 180-year-old
yew trees, and an orangerie (WCs in far right corner). The French section, directly behind the palace around to the left, is grand à la Versailles
but uses terraces to create the illusion of spaciousness (since it was originally hemmed in by the town wall).

Würzburg Old Town Walk

This brief walk gets you from the Residenz to the old bridge (Alte
Mainbrücke) through the key old-town sights.

Fountain of Franconia—In 1814, the Prince Bishop got the boot, and
Franconia was secularized. The region was given to Bavaria to be ruled
by the Wittelsbach family, so Franconia is technically a part of Bavaria
(which is like Ireland being part of Britain—never call a Franconian a
Bavarian). This statue—a gift from the townspeople to their new royal
family—turns its back to the palace and faces the town. It celebrates the
artistic and intellectual genius of Franconia with statues of three great
hometown boys (a medieval bard, the woodcarver Riemenschneider, and
the painter Grünewald). If Franconia hopped down and ran 300 yards
ahead down Hofstrasse, she'd hit the red-spired cathedral. Meet her there.

St. Kilian's Cathedral (Dom)—This is the fourth-largest Romanesque
cathedral in Germany. The building's core is Romanesque (1040–1188),
with Gothic spires and Baroque additions to the transepts. Enter
through the back (end nearest you, on the right-hand side) and leave
through the main entrance. From here, you can make a quick stop at
the brand-new Cathedral Museum (through passageway on your right-
hand side).

Cathedral Museum (Museum am Dom)—New in 2003, this museum
features a bizarre combination of old and new religious art. It pairs 11th-
to 18th-century works with modern interpretations, sprinkles it all with
a Christian theme, and wraps it in a shiny new building (€3, Tue–Sun
April–Oct 10:00–19:00, Nov–March 10:00–17:00, closed Mon, tel.
0931/3866-5600, www.museum-am-dom.de).

Upon leaving, you'll see Domstrasse leading down to the spire of
the town hall and the old bridge (where this walk will end). But we're
looping right. Go a block up Kurschner Hof. On your right, you'll pass
the entrance to the...

Neumünster Basilica—Like the *Dom*, this church has a Romanesque
body with a Baroque face. Go up the stairs to take a look inside, then

continue up the street. Notice the quiet of the pedestrian zone. Locals wouldn't have it any other way—electric trolleys, bikes, and pedestrians. **Upper Market Square (Marktplatz)**—Enter the square with the two-tone church. The fancy yellow-and-white rococo House of the Falcon once had three different facades. To fix it, the landlady gave a wandering band of stucco artists a chance to show their stuff and ended up with this (TI and library with Internet access).

Marienkapelle—The two-tone, late-Gothic church was the merchants' answer to the Prince Bishop's cathedral. Since Rome didn't bankroll the place, it's ringed with "swallow shops" (like swallows' nests cuddled up against a house)—enabling the church to run little businesses. The sandstone statues (replicas of Riemenschneider originals) are the 12 Apostles and Jesus. Walk downhill along the church to the lower marketplace, where the city's **produce market** bustles daily except Sunday (8:00–16:00). The famous Adam and Eve statues (flanking the side entrance to the church) show off Riemenschneider's mastery of the body. Continue around the church to the west portal (main entrance), where the carved Last Judgment shows kings, ladies, and bishops—some going to heaven, others making up the chain gang bound for hell, via the monster's mouth. (This was commissioned by those feisty town merchants tired of snooty blue-bloods.) Continue around to the next entry to see the Annunciation, with a cute angel Gabriel telling Mary (who is a virgin, symbolized by the lilies) the good news. Notice how God whispers through a speaking tube as baby Jesus slips down and into her ear. Head back around to the lower market (Adam-and-Eve side) and leave downhill towards the yellow building with the clock. Follow Langgasse left (past a public WC) to the fountain facing the city hall and bridge.

City Hall (Rathaus)—Würzburg's city hall is relatively humble because of the power of the Prince Bishop. A side room on the left holds the Gedenkraum 16. März (March) 1945—a memorial to the 20-minute Allied bombing that created a firestorm, destroying (and demoralizing) the town just six weeks before the end of World War II. Check out the sobering models, ponder the names (lining the ceiling) of those killed, and read the free English flier (city hall free and always open).

Old Bridge (Alte Mainbrücke)—This bridge, from 1133, is the second-oldest in Germany. The 12 statues lining the bridge are Würzburg saints and Prince Bishops. Walk to the St. Kilian statue (with the golden sword)—one of the three monks who were shown being beheaded in the Residenz Hofkirche Chapel. Stand so you can't see the white power-plant tower and enjoy the best view in town. Marienberg Fortress caps the hill (see page 164). Squint up at Kilian pointing to God...with his head on.

The hillside is blanketed with grapevines—destined to become the fine Stein Franconian wine. Johann Wolfgang von Goethe, the German

Shakespeare, ordered 900 liters of this vintage annually. A friend once asked Goethe what he thought were the three most important things in life. He said, "Wine, women, and song." When asked if he had to give one up, which it would be, without hesitating, Goethe answered "Song." Then, when asked what he would choose if he had to give up a second, Goethe paused and said, "It depends on the vintage."

Your walking tour is over. From here, consider paying a visit to fortress on the hill above you.

Marienberg Fortress (Festung Marienberg)

This 13th-century fortified retreat was the original residence of Würzburg's Prince Bishops. After being stormed by the Swedish army during the Thirty Years' War, the fortress was rebuilt in Baroque style. The fortress contains two museums: a **city history museum** (€2.50, €4 combo-ticket for both museums, April–mid-Oct Tue–Sun 9:00–18:00, closed Mon, less off-season, tel. 0931/43838) and the **Mainfränkisches Museum,** which highlights the work of Riemenschneider, Germany's top wood-carver and onetime mayor of Würzburg (€3, €4 combo-ticket for both museums, few English explanations, €3 audioguide, Tue–Sun 10:00–17:00, Nov–March until 16:00, closed Mon year-round, tel. 0931/205-940, www.mainfraenkisches-museum.de; Riemenschneider fans will also find his work throughout Würzburg's many churches). The **fortress grounds** (free) provide fine city views. The gift shop sells a good €2.60 guide explaining the fortress' history, courtyard buildings, and museums. For **restaurants** at the fortress, see "Eating," below.

Getting to Marienberg Fortress: Take **bus** #9 (€1.50 one-way, runs daily 10:00–18:00 every 40 min, departs from Residenzplatz, Barbarossaplatz, and Juliuspromenade). To **walk,** cross the Alte Mainbrücke and follow small Festung Marienberg signs to the right uphill for a heart-thumping 20 minutes (signs pointing left indicate a longer path through vineyards).

SLEEPING

Near Theaterstrasse

These hotels cluster within a block on Theaterstrasse (7-min walk from station: head up Kaiserstrasse to circular awning at Barbarossaplatz, angle left toward McDonald's for Theaterstrasse). Quieter rooms are in back, front rooms have street noise, and all are entertained by church bells.

$$$ **Hotel Schönleber** has 32 good rooms, but the two hotels listed below offer a better value (S–€40, Sb-€58–64, D-€58, Ds-€64–82, Db-€86–92, Tb-€107–112, elevator, Theaterstrasse 5, tel. 0931/304-8900, fax 0931/16012, www.hotel-schoenleber.de, reservierung@hotel-schoenleber.de).

SLEEP CODE

(€1 = about $1.10, country code: 49, area code: 0931)
Sleep Code: **S** = Single, **D** = Double/Twin, **T** = Triple, **Q** = Quad, **b** = bathroom, **s** = shower only, **no CC** = Credit Cards not accepted, **SE** = Speaks English, **NSE** = No English spoken. Unless otherwise noted, credit cards are accepted, English is spoken, and breakfast is included.

To help you sort easily through these listings, I've divided the rooms into three categories, based on the price for a standard double room with bath:

$$$ Higher Priced—Most rooms €85 or more.
$$ Moderately Priced—Most rooms between €70–85.
$ Lower Priced—Most rooms €70 or less.

Würzburg's good-value hotels provide a stress-free first or last night when flying in or out of Frankfurt. Hourly trains connect the two cities in 90 minutes (see "Transportation Connections," below). All listings include breakfast.

$$ Hotel Barbarossa, tucked peacefully away on the fourth floor, rents 17 fresh and comfortable rooms (Ss-€40, Sb-€45, Db-€70, Tb-€85, these discounted prices are promised through 2004 with this book and cash only, elevator, across from McDonald's, Theaterstrasse 2, tel. 0931/321-370, fax 0931/321-3737, marchiorello@t-online.de, Martina Marchiorello SE). Martina's husband, Gianni, runs the Altstadt Hotel just down the street.

$$ Altstadt Hotel comes with good rooms and a Venetian twist—since it's run by charming Gianni and his family above their wonderfully fragrant Italian restaurant (Ds-€50, Db-€70, like Barbarossa, these prices are good only with this book and cash, Theaterstrasse 7, tel. 0931/321-640, fax 0931/321-6464, marchiorello@t-online.de; Gianni SE).

Elsewhere in Würzburg

The first two listings are closer to the station; the third is across the river.

$$$ Sankt Josef Hotel has 33 sharp rooms and a pleasant breakfast room (Sb-€50, Db-€80–90 depending on size, non-smoking rooms, reserve ahead for parking-€8/day, left off Theaterstrasse to Semmelstrasse 28, tel. 0931/308-680, fax 0931/308-6860, hotel.st.josef@t-online.de, Herr and Frau Casagrande S some E). The hotel also has a restaurant (Thu–Tue from 17:00, closed Wed).

$ **Hotel-Pension Spehnkuch** is the best budget hotel near the station. Overlooking a busy street but quiet behind double-paned windows, it's friendly, simple, clean, and comfortable (S–€29, D–€52, T–€75, no CC, 3-min walk from station, exit station and take a right onto first street, walk 500 feet to Röntgenring 7, on first floor, tel. 0931/54752, fax 0931/54760, www.pension-spehnkuch.de, spehnkuch@web.de, Markus SE).

$ Würzburg's **hostel,** across the river, has 226 beds (€17/bed in 4- to 10-bed rooms, includes sheets and breakfast, non-members-€3 extra, no CC, must be under 27, family rooms, lunch and dinner available, 1:00 curfew, 20-min walk from station, cross Alte Mainbrücke and turn left on Saalgasse, Burkarderstrasse 44, tel. 0931/42590, jghwuerzburg @djh-bayern.de).

EATING

Zum Stachel, the town's oldest *Weinhaus,* originated as the town's tithe barn—where people deposited 10 percent of their produce as tax. In 1413, it began preparing the produce and selling wine. Today, it's a worthy splurge serving gourmet Franconian meals in an elegant stone-and-ivy courtyard and woody dining room. The ceiling depicts a medieval *Stachel* (mace) in deadly action (€20, Mon–Tue 17:00–24:00, Wed–Sat 11:00–24:00, closed Sun, reservations smart, dressy, from Marktplatz head toward river, turn right on Gressengasse to intersection with Marktgasse, Gressengasse 1, tel. 0931/52770, www.weinhaus-stachel.de).

At **Würzburger Ratskeller,** choose from three seating options: an inviting courtyard (weather permitting), a stately restaurant, or a cozy multi-room *Weinstube* below (€8–15, daily 11:30–24:00, reservations smart, next to town hall, Langasse 1, tel. 0931/13021).

Gianni's Bistro features fine pasta—handmade fresh daily by Gianni himself—and veggie options (€8–15, Mon–Sat 11:30–14:00 & 17:30–23:00, closed Sun, below recommended Altstadt Hotel, Theaterstrasse 7, tel. 0931/321-640).

Backöfele is a fun hole-in-the-wall (literally) offering a rustic menu full of local specialties. Named "the oven" for its entryway, this place is a hit with Germans (€6–16, daily 11:30–24:00, reservations smart, with your back to town hall go straight on Augustinerstrasse, take first left onto Wolfhartsgasse and first right to Ursulinergasse 2, tel. 0931/59059).

At **Martinsklause,** a 12th-century cellar near the cathedral, the bar is an old confessional, and the booths are made from cut-up church pews. You'll find local wines and specialties on the menu (Tue–Sun 18:00–24:00, closed Mon, Martinstrasse 21, tel. 0931/353-9291). Upstairs, **Martinz** (open Tue–Sun from 11:00, closed Mon) serves a long list of sweet and savory pancakes *(Pfannkuchen),* salads, steaks, and soups. In good weather, try the *Biergarten* terrace.

Café Two Jours, trendy with the student crowd, serves up inexpensive soups, salads, and sandwiches while paying homage to pop magazine culture (€4–6, daily 9:00–24:00, Juliuspromenade 40, tel. 0931/571-003).

For a beer garden under the trees, consider **Wirtshaus zum Lämmle** behind the TI (€6–10, Mon–Sat 11:00–22:00, closed Sun, plenty of fish and meaty fare, Marienplatz 5, tel. 0931/54748). Half a block away, **Weinstube Maulaffenbäck** is a tiny and characteristic place for cheap Franconian meals and good wine (€5–7, April–Nov Mon–Sat 10:00–24:00, closed Sun, Oct–March Mon–Sat 16:00–23:00, closed Sun, Maulhardgasse 9, tel. 0931/52351).

Eating at Marienberg Fortress: A self-service cafeteria/*Biergarten* next to the Mainfränkisches Museum has typical sausage-and-pretzel fare (meals €4–8), as does the *Burggaststätte* next to the city history museum (meals €6–10, same hours as museum, closed Mon, tel. 0931/47012).

Wine-Drinking to Support the Needy

Würzburg has several large wineries that produce the area's distinctive, bulbous *Bocksbeutel* bottles. These institutions, originally founded as homes for the old and poor, began making wine to pay the bills. Today, these grand Baroque complexes, which still make wine and serve the needy, have restaurants, wine shops, and extensive wine cellars (for serious buyers only). After more than 600 years, the **Bürgerspital** now cares for about a hundred local seniors, funding its work by selling its wine. Its characteristic restaurant and wine bar are right downtown. The funky little **wine store** is a time warp, filled with locals munching B.Y.O. sandwiches while sipping a glass of wine (Mon–Fri 9:00–18:00, Sat 9:00–15:00, closed Sun, corner of Theaterstrasse and Semmelstrasse, Theaterstrasse 19, tel. 0931/350-3403, www.buergerspital.de). Its **Weinstube Bürgerspital** is a classy, candle-lit restaurant with a cloistered feel (€4–8, daily 10:00–24:00, Theaterstrasse 19, tel. 0931/352-880).

TRANSPORTATION CONNECTIONS

By train to: Rothenburg (hrly, 1 hr, change in Steinach; the tiny Steinach–Rothenburg train often leaves from track 5 shortly after the Würzburg train arrives), **Frankfurt Airport** (hrly, 90 min), **Nürnberg** (2–3/hr, 1–1.25 hrs), **Munich** (2/hr, 2.5 hrs, usually with 1 or 2 changes), **Köln** (hrly, 3.5 hrs), **Berlin** (hrly, 4 hrs, 1 change). Train info: tel. 01805/996-633.

FRANKFURT

Frankfurt, the northern terminus of the Romantic Road, offers a good look at today's no-nonsense modern Germany. There's so much more to this country than castles and old cobbled squares.

You might fly into or out of Frankfurt am Main (nicknamed "Mainhattan" by locals because it's on the Main River), or at least pass through. While Frankfurt is Germany's trade and banking capital, leading the country in skyscrapers—mostly bank headquarters—one third of the city is green space. Especially in the area around the train station, you'll notice the fascinating multi-ethnic flavor of the city. A third of its 650,000 residents carry foreign passports.

Even two or three hours in Frankfurt leaves you with some powerful impressions. The city's great sights are 15 minutes from its train station, which is 15 minutes from its airport. For years, Frankfurt was a city to avoid...but today, it has a special energy that makes it worth a look.

ORIENTATION

(area code: 069)

Tourist Information: Frankfurt has several TIs. The handiest is inside the train station's main entrance, offering an abundance of brochures and a free hotel-booking service (Mon–Fri 8:00–21:00, Sat–Sun 9:00–18:00, tel. 069/2123-8800, www.frankfurt-tourismus.de). Buy the city/subway map (the basic €0.50 version is fine—skip the detailed €1 map) and consider the "Frankfurt Welcome" brochure (€0.50). The TI sells the all-day city transit pass (*Tageskarte*, €4.60), Museum Ticket (€8, valid 2 days, covers 24 museums), and Frankfurt Card (see below), and offers bus tours of the city (see below). You'll find other TIs in Römerberg (Mon–Fri 9:30–17:30, Sat–Sun 10:00–16:00), on the pedestrian shopping street Zeil, and at the airport.

Frankfurt

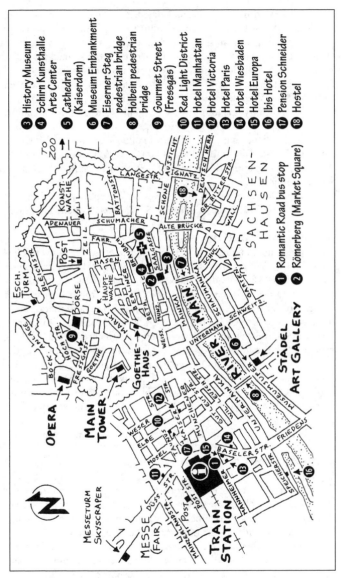

③ History Museum
④ Schirn Kunsthalle Arts Center
⑤ Cathedral (Kaiserdom)
⑥ Museum Embankment
⑦ Eiserner Steg pedestrian bridge
⑧ Holbein pedestrian bridge
⑨ Gourmet Street (Fressgas)
⑩ Red Light District
⑪ Hotel Manhattan
⑫ Hotel Victoria
⑬ Hotel Paris
⑭ Hotel Wiesbaden
⑮ Hotel Europa
⑯ Ibis Hotel
⑰ Pension Schneider
⑱ Hostel

❶ Romantic Road bus stop
❷ Römerberg (Market Square)

The **Frankfurt Card** (€7.50/1 day, €11/2 days, sold at TI) gives you a transit pass (including connections to and from the airport), 50 percent off all major museums, and 25 percent off the city bus tour (which virtually pays for the pass). If you're touring like mad for a day, this card can be worthwhile. Note that most museums are closed Monday and, depending on what the city decides, may be free and open until 20:00 on Wednesday (confirm at any TI).

The basic **city bus tour** gives a 2.5-hour orientation to Frankfurt, including Römerberg, Goethe's House, and (summer only) the Main Tower (€25, 25 percent discount with Frankfurt Card, recorded narration, April–Oct daily at 10:00 and 14:00, Nov–March daily at 14:00). The bus picks up at the Römerberg TI first, then 15 minutes later at the Hauptbahnhof TI.

Local Guide: Elisabeth Lücke loves her city and shares it very well (€45/hr, reserve in advance, tel. 06196/45787, www.elisabeth-luecke.de).

Arrival in Frankfurt

By Train: The Frankfurt train station *(Hauptbahnhof)* bustles with travelers. The TI is in the main hall just inside the front door. Lockers and baggage check (€2/day, daily 6:00–20:00) are in the main hall across from the TI. More lockers are at track 24, across from the post office (Mon–Fri 7:00–19:30, Sat 8:00–16:00, closed Sun, automatic stamp machine outside). WCs (€0.60) are under track 9/10. Inquire about train tickets in the Reisezentrum across from track 9 (daily 6:00–23:00). Pick up a snack at the fine food court across from tracks 4 and 5. Above the Reisezentrum is a peaceful lounge with a snack bar, clean WCs, telephones, and a children's play area (free entry with ticket or railpass, free coffee and juice in first-class lounge). The station is a five-minute walk from the convention center *(Messe)*, a three-minute subway ride from the center, or a 12-minute shuttle train from the airport.

By Plane: See "Frankfurt's Airport" at the end of this chapter.

Getting around Frankfurt

By Subway: Frankfurt's subway is easy to use, but a 10-minute wait for a train can be normal. From the train station, follow signs for U-Bahn (U, blue) or S-Bahn (S, green). Buy your tickets *(Fahrkarten)* from an RMV machine. Find your destination on the chart, key in the number, choose your ticket type, then pay. Choose *Einzelfahrt* for a regular single ticket (€2), *Kurzstrecke* for a short ride (€1.15, three stops or less), or *Tageskarte* for an all-day pass (€4.60 without the airport, €7.10 with). A one-way ticket to the airport costs €3.20.

By Taxi: A taxi stand is just outside the main entrance of the train station to your left. An average ride to Römerberg should cost you €6 (more in slow traffic). To get to the airport from any of my recommended hotels, count on at least €22.

SIGHTS

Römerberg

This 30-minute sightseeing walk connects the main sights around Römerberg, Frankfurt's lively Market Square. The walk begins at the...

Train Station—This is Germany's busiest train station: 350,000 travelers make their way to 25 platforms to catch 1,800 trains every day. While it was big news when it opened in the 1890s, it's a dead-end station, which, with today's high-speed trains, makes it outdated. In fact, the speedy ICE trains are threatening to bypass Frankfurt altogether unless it digs a tunnel to allow for a faster pass-through stop (a costly project is now in the discussion stage).

To get to Römerberg, it's a 20-minute walk (up Kaiserstrasse), a €6 taxi ride (without traffic) or three-minute subway ride. To take the subway, buy a ticket (see "Getting around Frankfurt," above) and follow signs to U-4 (direction Seckbacher Landstrasse) or U-5 (direction Preungesheim). Choose the track with the soonest *Nächste Abfahrt* (next departure) time and go two stops to Römerberg. Exit the station following signs for Römerberg (not Domplatz). As you surface, you'll see the tall, red tower of the cathedral behind you, where we'll end this walk. For now, walk around the building in front of you and downhill to...

▲**Römerberg**—Frankfurt's Market Square was the birthplace of the city. The town hall *(Römer)* houses the *Kaisersaal,* or Imperial Hall, where Holy Roman Emperors celebrated their coronations. Today, the *Römer* houses the city council and mayor's office. The cute row of half-timbered houses (rebuilt in 1983) opposite the *Römer* is typical of Frankfurt's quaint old center before World War II. Walk past the red-and-white church downhill toward the river to Frankfurt's...

History Museum (Historisches Museum)—Most won't want to hike through the actual museum upstairs (€4, 2 floors of artifacts, paintings, and displays without a word of English, Tue, Thu, and Sun 10:00–17:00, Wed 16:00–20:00, Fri 10:00–14:00, Sat 13:00–17:00, closed Mon, Saalgasse 19, tel. 069/2123-0702, www.historisches -museum.frankfurt.de), but the models in the ground-floor annex are fascinating (€1, follow signs to *Altstadtmodelle,* English film and explanations). Study the maps of medieval Frankfurt. The wall surrounding the city was torn down in the early 1800s to make the ring of parks and lakes you see on your modern map. The long, densely packed row of houses on the eastern end of town was Frankfurt's Jewish ghetto from 1462–1796. The five original houses that survive make up today's Jewish Museum. (Frankfurt is the birthplace of Anne Frank and the Rothschild banking family.) The big model in the middle of the room shows the town in the 1930s. Across from it, you can see the horror that befell the town in 1940, 1943, and on the "fatal night" of March 23, 1944. This last Allied bombing accomplished its goal of demoralizing the city. Find the facade of the destroyed city hall—where you just were. The film behind this model is a good 15-minute tour of Frankfurt through the ages (ask them to change the language for you—"*Auf Englisch, bitte?*"). At the model of today's Frankfurt, orient yourself, then locate the riverfront (a nice detour with a grassy park and fun Eiserner Steg pedestrian bridge, to the left as you leave this museum), and the long, skinny "pistol" (the Schirn arts exhibition center) pointing at the cathedral—where you're going next. Leaving the museum, turn right to...

Saalgasse—Literally "hall street," this lane of postmodern buildings echoes the higgledy-piggledy buildings that stood here until World War II. In the 1990s, famous architects from around the world were each given a ruined house of the same width and told to design a new building to reflect the building that stood there before the war. As you continue down the street, guess which one is an upside-down half-timbered house with the stars down below. (Hint: Animals are on the "ground floor.") Saalgasse leads to some ancient Roman ruins in front of the cathedral. The grid of stubs was the underfloor of a Roman bath (allowing the floor to be heated). The small monument in the middle of the ruins commemorates the 794 meeting of Charlemagne (king of the Franks and first Holy Roman Emperor) with the local bishop—the first official mention of a town called Frankfurt. When Charlemagne and the Franks fled from the Saxons, a white deer led them to the easiest place to cross the Main—where the Franks could ford the river—hence, Frankfurt. The skyscraper with the yellow emblem in the distance is the tallest office block in Europe (985 feet). Next to it, with the red-and-white antenna, is the Main Tower (open to the public—highly recommended and described below).

St. Bartholomew's Cathedral (Kaiserdom)—Ten Holy Roman Emperors were elected and crowned in this cathedral between 1562 and 1792. The church was destroyed in World War II, rebuilt, and reopened in 1955. Twenty-seven scenes from the life of St. Bartholomew (Bartholomäus, in German) flank the high altar and ring the choir. Everything of value was moved to safety before the bombs came. But the delightful red sandstone chapel of Sleeping Mary (to the left of high altar), carved and painted in the 15th century, was too big to move—so it was fortified with sandbags. The altarpiece and fine stained glass next to it survived the bombing (free, Sat–Thu 9:00–12:00 & 14:30–17:00, closed Fri, enter on side opposite river). In 2004, the newly restored tower should be open for tourists to climb.

From the cathedral, it's a short walk back to Römerberg or to the Zeil, Frankfurt's lively department-store-lined pedestrian boulevard. Or you can explore more of Frankfurt's sights.

Between Römerberg and the Station

▲**Main Tower**—Finished in 2000, this tower houses the Helaba Bank and offers the best public viewpoint from a Frankfurt skyscraper. A 45-second, ear-popping elevator ride—and then 50 steps—takes you to the 55th floor, 650 feet above the city (€4.50, daily 10:00–21:00, Fri–Sat until 23:00, enter at Neue Mainzer Strasse 52, near corner of Neue Schlesingerstrasse, tel. 069/913-201). Here, from Frankfurt's ultimate viewpoint, survey the city circling clockwise, starting with the biggest skyscraper (with the yellow emblem).

1. Commerce Bank building: Designed by Norman Foster (of Berlin Reichstag fame), the Commerce Bank building was finished in 1997. It's 985 feet high, with nine winter gardens spiraling up its core. Just to the left is Römerberg—the old town center. Look to the right (clockwise).

2. European Central Bank: The blue-and-gold euro symbol (€) decorates the front yard of the Euro Tower, home of the European Central Bank (a.k.a. "City of the Euro"). Its 1,000 employees administer the all-Europe currency from here. Typical of skyscrapers in the 1970s, it's slim—to allow maximum natural light into all workplaces inside. The euro symbol in the park was unveiled on January 1, 2002, the day the euro went into circulation in the 12 Eurozone countries.

The Museum Embankment lines Schaumainkai (see "Sights—Across the River," page 175) on the far side of the Main River, just beyond the Euro Tower.

3. Airport: The Rhine-Main Airport, in the distance, is the largest employment complex in Germany (62,000 workers). Frankfurt's massive train station dominates the foreground. From the station, the grand Kaiserstrasse cuts through the city to Römerberg.

4. *Messe:* The Frankfurt fair *(Messe),* marked by the skyscraper with the pointy top, is a huge convention center—the size of 40 soccer fields. It sprawls behind the skyscraper that looks like a classical column sporting a visor-like capital. (The protruding lip of the capital is heated so that icicles don't form, break off, and impale people on the street below.) Frankfurt's fair originated in 1240, when the emperor promised all participating merchants safe passage (www.messefrankfurt.com). The black twin towers of the Deutsche Bank in the foreground are typical of mid-1980s mirrored architecture.

5. West End and good living: The West End—with vast green spaces and the telecommunications tower—is Frankfurt's trendiest residential quarter. The city's "good-living spine" cuts from the West End to the right. Stretching from the classic-looking **Opera House** are broad and people-filled boulevards made to order for eating and shopping. Your skyscraper spin-tour is over. Why don't you go join them?

Opera House, Gourmet Street, and Zeil—From the Opera House to pedestrian boulevards, this is Frankfurt's good-living spine. The Opera

House was finished in 1880 to celebrate high German culture and the newly created nation. With both Mozart and Goethe flanking the entrance, all are reminded that this is a house of both music and theater. The original opera house was destroyed in World War II. Over the objections of a mayor nicknamed "Dynamite Rudy," the city rebuilt it in the original style (U-Bahn: Alte Oper). Facing the opera, turn right and walk down a restaurant-lined boulevard (Grosse Bockenheimer) nicknamed "Gourmet Street" *(Fressgass)*. (Frankfurt's Fifth Avenue, lined with top fashion shops, is the parallel Goethe Strasse.) Gourmet Street leads to Zeil, a lively, tree-lined festival-of-life pedestrian boulevard and department-store strip.

▲**Goethe House (Goethehaus)**—Johann Wolfgang von Goethe (1749–1832), a scientist, minister, poet, lawyer, politician, and playwright, was a towering figure in the early Romantic age. His birthplace, now a fine museum, is a five-minute walk northwest of Römerberg. It's furnished as it was in the mid-18th century, when the boy destined to become the German Shakespeare grew up here. Sixteen rooms on four floors tell his story: how his father dedicated his life and wealth to cultural pursuits, and how his mother told young Goethe fairy tales every night, stopping just before the ending so that the boy could exercise his own creativity. Goethe's family gave him all the money he needed to travel and learn. His collection of 2,000 books was sold off in 1795. Recently, 800 of these have been located and repurchased by the museum (you'll see them in the library). This building honors the man who inspired the Goethe Institute, dedicated to keeping the German language strong. It's no wonder, then, that there's not a word of English in the place—the €1.50 English booklet is essential (€5, covered by €8 Museum Ticket, April–Sept Mon–Fri 9:00–18:00, Sat–Sun 10:00–16:00, Oct–March closes at 16:00, Grosser Hirschgraben 23, 15-min walk from Hauptbahnhof up Kaiserstrasse, turn right on Am Salzhaus, tel. 069/138-800, www.goethehaus-frankfurt.de).

▲**Frankfurt's Red Light District**—A browse through Frankfurt's sleazy red light district offers a fascinating way to kill time between trains. From the station, Taunusstrasse leads two blocks to Elbestrasse, where you'll find a zone of 20 "eros towers"—each a five-story-tall brothel filled with prostitutes. Climbing through a few of these may be one of the more memorable experiences of your European trip (€25, daily). While hiking through the towers feels safe, the aggressive girls at the neighboring strip shows can be pretty unsettling. Ever since the Middle Ages, Frankfurt's thriving prostitution industry has gone hand-in-hand with its trade fairs. Today, it thrives with the *Messe*. Prostitutes note that business varies with the theme of the trade show—while the auto show is boom time, they complain that Frankfurt's massive book fair is a bust. Frankfurt's prostitutes are legal and taxed. Since they pay taxes, they are organizing to get the same benefits that any other taxed worker gets.

This area can be dangerous if you're careless. If you take a wrong turn, you'll find creepy streets littered with drug addicts. In 1992, Frankfurt began offering "pump rooms" to its hard-drug users. These centers provide clean needles and a safe and caring place for addicts to go to maintain their habit and get counseling. Ten years later, while locals consider the program a success, wasted people congregate in neighborhoods like this one.

Across the River

The Schaumainkai riverside promenade (across the river, over Eiserner Steg pedestrian bridge from Römerberg) is great for an evening stroll or people-watching on any sunny day. Keep your eyes peeled for nude sunbathers. On Saturdays, the museum strip street is closed off for a sprawling flea market.

Sachsenhausen District and Frankfurt's Culinary Specialties—Rather than beer-garden ambience, Frankfurt offers an apple-wine pub district. For a traditional eating-and-drinking zone with more than a hundred characteristic apple-wine pubs (and plenty of ethnic and other options), visit cobbled and cozy Sachsenhausen (wander to the east end of Schaumainkai, or, from the train station, take tram #16 to Schweizerplatz). *Apfelwein,* drunk around here since Charlemagne's time 1,200 years ago, became more popular in the 16th century, when local grapes were diseased. It enjoyed another boost two centuries later, when a climate change meant that grapes grew poorly in the area. Apple wine is about the strength of beer (5.5 percent alcohol). It's served spiced and warm in winter, cold in summer. To complement your traditional drink with a traditional meal, try Frankfurt sausage, pork chops and kraut, or green sauce (of seven herbs) on boiled eggs and beef.

Frankfurt's Museum Embankment (Museumsufer)—The Museum Embankment features nine museums lining the Main River along Schaumainkai (mostly west of Eiserner Steg pedestrian bridge). In the 1980s, Frankfurt decided that it wanted to buck its "Bankfurt" and "Krankfurt" (*krank* means sick) image. It went on a culture kick and devoted 11 percent of the city budget to the arts and culture. The result: Frankfurt has become a city of art. Today, locals and tourists alike enjoy an impressive strip of museums housed in striking buildings. These nine museums (including architecture, film, world cultures, and great European masters—the Städel Collection) and a dozen others are all well described in the TI's Museumsufer brochure (covered by €8 Museum Ticket sold at TI and participating museums, good for 2 days, most museums Tue–Sun 10:00–17:00, Wed until 20:00, closed Mon, www.kultur.frankfurt.de). Some of the museums may be free on Wednesdays.

SLEEP CODE

(€1 = about $1.10, country code: 49, area code: 069)

Sleep Code: **S** = Single, **D** = Double/Twin, **T** = Triple, **Q** = Quad, **b** = bathroom, **s** = shower only, **no CC** = Credit Cards not accepted, **SE** = Speaks English, **NSE** = No English. Unless otherwise noted, credit cards are accepted, English is spoken, and breakfast is included.

To help you sort easily through these listings, I've divided the rooms into three categories, based on the price for a standard double room with bath:

$$$ **Higher Priced**—Most rooms €90 or more.
 $$ **Moderately Priced**—Most rooms between €70–90.
  $ **Lower Priced**—Most rooms €70 or less.

Avoid driving or sleeping in Frankfurt, especially during the city's numerous trade fairs (about 7 days a month—normally not in summer), which send hotel prices skyrocketing. (Fairs will fill Frankfurt on these dates in 2004: Jan 14–18, 31; Feb 1–4, 20–24; March 5–8, 31; April 1–4, 18–22; May 15–20; June 6–10, 22–25; Aug 27–31; and Sept 14–19; visit www .messefrankfurt.com for a more complete schedule.) Pleasant Rhine or Romantic Road towns are just a quick drive or train ride away. But if you must spend the night in Frankfurt, here are some places within a block of the train station (and its fast and handy train to the airport; to sleep at the airport itself, see "Frankfurt's Airport," page 178). This isn't the safest neighborhood; don't wander into seedy-feeling streets, and be careful after dark.

For a rough idea of directions to hotels, stand with your back to the main entrance of the station: Using a 12-hour clock, Hotel Manhattan is across the street at 10:00, Pension Schneider at 12:00, Hotel Victoria at 1:00, Hotel Europa and Wiesbaden at 4:00, and Hotel Paris at 5:00. The Ibis Hotel is on a nicer street two blocks beyond Hotel Paris. The hostel is a bus ride away.

SLEEPING

$$$ Hotel Manhattan, with 60 sleek, arty rooms, is beautifully located across from the station. An unusual mix of warm and accommodating staff with all the business-class comforts, it's a good splurge on a first or last night in Europe (Sb-€87, Db-€102, show this book to get a 10 percent break during non-convention times, further discount when really slow—including weekends, kids under 12 free, elevator, free Internet access, Düsseldorfer Strasse 10, tel. 069/269-5970, fax 069/2695-97777, www.manhattan-hotel.com, manhattan-hotel@t-online.de, manager Michael Rosen SE).

$$$ Hotel Victoria, not as friendly, is midway between the station and the old town on the grand Kaiserstrasse (75 rooms, Sb-€65–85, Db-€75–95, suite-€120, Kaiserstrasse 59, on corner with Elbestrasse, tel. 069/273-060, fax 069/2730-6100, www.victoriahotel.de).

$$ Hotel Paris has 30 fine but worn rooms (Sb-€60, Db-€80, Karlsruherstrasse 8, tel. 069/273-9963, fax 069/2739-9651, www.hotel-paris.de, info@hotelparis.de).

$$ Hotel Wiesbaden has 39 faded rooms (can be smoky), unfortunate hallways, and kind management (Sb-€65, Db-€85, Db-€75 or less in summer, Tb-€90–105, Qb-€115, elevator, Baseler Strasse 52, tel. 069/232-347, fax 069/252-845).

$ Ibis Hotel Frankfurt Friedensbrücke, a bargain-price chain hotel, is the best value, with 233 identical rooms on a quiet riverside street away from the station riffraff (Sb/Db-€69, €125 during fairs, Tb-€85, breakfast-€9 per person, non-smoking rooms, elevator, parking-€8/day, exit station to right and follow Baseler Strasse 3 blocks, before river turn right on Speicherstrasse to #3, tel. 069/273-030, fax 069/237-024, www.ibishotel.com, h1445@accor-hotels.com).

$ Pension Schneider is a strange little oasis of decency and quiet three floors above the epicenter of Frankfurt's red light district, in a run-down building two blocks in front of the train station. Its 10 big, worn rooms work just fine (S-€40, D-€55, Ds-€65, Db-€70, Tb-€85, elevator, on creepy corner of Moselstrasse at Taunusstrasse 43, tel. 069/251-071, fax 069/259-228, speak only a leetle English).

$ Hotel Europa, with 46 rooms, is a decent value (Sb-€50, Db-€70, Tb-€90, prices soft on weekends and in summer, 3rd floor has non-smoking rooms but rest of hotel is smoky, elevator, garage-€8/day but free with multi-night stay, Baseler Strasse 17, tel. 069/236-013, fax 069/236-203, hoteleuropa-frankfurt@t-online.de, Luigi SE).

$ Hostel: The hostel is open to members of any age (€19 per bed in 8- and 12-bed rooms, includes sheets and breakfast, 470 beds, €4.70 for lunch or dinner, Internet access, laundry, 2:00 curfew, bus #46 goes 3/hr from station to Frankenstein Platz, Deutschherrnufer 12, tel. 069/610-0150, fax 069/6100-1599, jugendherberge€frankfurt@t-online.de).

TRANSPORTATION CONNECTIONS

Frankfurt am Main

By train to: Rothenburg (hrly, 3 hrs, changes in Würzburg and Steinach; the tiny Steinach–Rothenburg train often leaves from track 5, shortly after the Würzburg train arrives), **Würzburg** (hrly, 2 hrs), **Nürnberg** (hrly, 2 hrs), **Munich** (hrly, 4 hrs, 1 change), **Baden-Baden** (2/hr, 1.5 hrs, up to 3 changes), **Bacharach** (hrly, 1.5 hrs, change in Mainz; first train to Bacharach departs at 6:00, last train at 20:45), **Freiburg** (hrly, 2 hrs, change in Mannheim), **Bonn** (hrly, 2 hrs, 1 change), **Koblenz** (hrly, 1.5 hrs, 1 change), **Köln** (hrly, 2 hrs, change in Mainz), **Berlin** (hrly, 6 hrs), **Amsterdam** (8/day, 5 hrs, up to 3 changes), **Bern** (hrly, 4.5 hrs, changes in Mannheim and Basel), **Brussels** (hrly, 5 hrs, change in Köln), **Copenhagen** (6/day, 9 hrs, change in Hamburg), **London** (6/day, 8 hrs, 3 changes), **Milan** (hrly, 9 hrs, 2 changes), **Paris** (9/day, 6.5 hrs, up to 3 changes), **Vienna** (8/day, 8 hrs, 2 changes). Train info: tel. 01805-996-633.

Romantic Road Bus: If you're taking the bus out of Frankfurt, you can buy your ticket at the Deutsche Touring office, which is part of the train station complex but has an entrance outside (Mon–Fri 7:30–18:00, Sat 7:30–14:00, Sun 7:30–14:00, entrance at Mannheimer Strasse 4, to your right as you leave station, tel. 069/230-735 or 069/79030, www.deutsche-touring.com); or pay cash when you board the bus. While the company claims you're 90 percent safe without a reservation, you can book a seat for free by calling 069/79030. The Frankfurt–Munich bus trip costs €70. Segments of the journey cost proportionately less, but if you buy the whole journey, you don't have to complete the entire trip in one day. Travelers with railpasses (German, Eurail, or Eurail Selectpass) get a 60 percent discount. The bus departs from in front of the Deutsche Touring office promptly at 8:00 (April–Oct, confirm time at TI, Deutsche Touring office, or www.euraide.de/ricksteves).

Frankfurt's Airport *(Flughafen)*

The airport is user-friendly. There are two separate terminals (know your terminal, call the airline). All trains and subways operate out of Terminal 1 (but taxis serve both). A skyline train connects the two terminals. The airport offers showers, a baggage check desk (daily 6:00–22:00, €3.50 per bag/day), lockers (€3–5/24 hrs, depending on size), ATMs, fair banks with long hours, a grocery store (daily 6:30–21:45, Terminal 1, on level 0 between sectors A and B), a post office, a train station, a business lounge (Europe City Club—€15 for anyone with a plane ticket, on departure level), easy rental-car pickup, plenty of parking, an information booth, a pharmacy (7:00–21:30, Terminal 1), a casino, and even McBeer. McWelcome to Germany. If you're meeting someone, each terminal has a hard-to-miss "meeting point" near where those arriving pop out.

Airport Info (in English): For flight information, call 01805/372-4636 (www.frankfurt-airport.de). The airport operator (tel. 069/6900) can transfer you to any of the airlines for booking or confirmation. Or contact the airlines directly (wait for an announcement in English): Lufthansa—tel. 01803/803-803, American Airlines—tel. 01803/242-324, Delta—tel. 01803/337-880, Northwest/KLM—toll tel. 0190/510-045 (€0.62/min). Pick up the free brochure "Your Airport-Assistant" for a map and detailed information on airport services (available at the airport and at most Frankfurt hotels).

Getting to the Airport: The airport is a 12-minute train ride from downtown (€3.20, 4/hr, ride included in €7.50 Frankfurt Card but not in €4.60 all-day *Tageskarte* transit pass). Figure around €22 for a taxi from any of my recommended hotels.

Trains: The airport has its own train station (Terminal 1). Train travelers can validate railpasses or buy tickets at the airport station. **By train to: Rothenburg** (hrly, 3 hrs, with transfers in Würzburg and Steinach), **Würzburg** (2/hr, 2 hrs), **Nürnberg** (hrly, 2 hrs), **Munich** (2/hr, 4 hrs, 1 change), **Baden-Baden** (hrly, 1.5 hrs, 1 change), **Bacharach** (hrly, 1 hr, change in Mainz; first train to Bacharach departs at 6:00, last train at 21:00), and **international destinations** (such as Paris, London, Milan, Amsterdam, Vienna, and many more).

Flying Home from Frankfurt: Some of the trains from the Rhine stop at the airport on their way into Frankfurt (e.g., hrly 90-min rides direct from Bonn; hrly 90-min rides from Bacharach with a change in Mainz; earliest train from Bacharach to Frankfurt leaves about 5:40, last train at 21:30). By car, head toward Frankfurt on the autobahn and follow the little airplane signs to the airport.

Sleeping at Frankfurt Airport

You can sleep at the airport, but you'll pay a premium and miss out on seeing Frankfurt. Considering the ease of the shuttle train from Frankfurt (12 min, 4/hr), I don't advise it. But if you must, the airport **Sheraton** has 1,000 international business-class rooms (rates vary wildly depending on season and conventions, but Db usually around €200–250, about 25 percent discount with major corporate ID—try anything, AAA and senior discounts, kids up to 18 free in the room, includes big breakfast, non-smoking rooms, fitness club, Terminal 1, tel. 069/69770, fax 069/6977-2351, www.sheraton.com/frankfurt, salesfrankfurt@sheraton.com).

The **Ibis** has cheaper rooms in the same neighborhood, but it isn't as handy and the staff is rude (Db-€80–100, breakfast-€9 per person, Langer Kornweg 9a–11, Kelsterbach, tel. 06107/9870, fax 06107/987-444, www.ibishotel.com, h2203@accor-hotels.com).

Route Tips for Drivers

Frankfurt to Rothenburg: The three-hour autobahn drive from the airport to Rothenburg is something even a jet-lagged zombie can handle. It's a 75-mile straight shot to Würzburg on A-3; just follow the blue autobahn signs to Würzburg. While you can carry on to Rothenburg by autobahn, for a scenic back-road approach, leave the freeway at the Heidingsfeld–Würzburg exit. If going directly to Rothenburg, follow signs south to Stuttgart/Ulm/Road 19, then continue to Rothenburg via a scenic slice of the Romantic Road. If stopping at Würzburg, leave the freeway at the Heidingsfeld–Würzburg exit and follow *Stadtmitte*, then *Centrum* and *Residenz* signs from the same freeway exit. From Würzburg, Ulm/Road 19 signs lead to Bad Mergentheim and Rothenburg.

Frankfurt to the Rhine: Driving from Frankfurt to the Rhine or Mosel takes 90 minutes (follow blue autobahn signs from airport, major cities are signposted).

The Rhine to Frankfurt: From St. Goar or Bacharach, follow the river to Bingen, then autobahn signs to Mainz, then Frankfurt, then *Messe*, then *Hauptbahnhof* (train station); the Hauptbahnhof garage (€15/day) is under the station near all recommended hotels.

RHINE VALLEY

The Rhine Valley is storybook Germany, a fairy-tale world of legends and robber-baron castles. Cruise the most castle-studded stretch of the romantic Rhine as you listen for the song of the treacherous Loreley. For hands-on castle thrills, climb through the Rhineland's greatest castle, Rheinfels, above the town of St. Goar. Castle connoisseurs will enjoy the fine interior of Marksburg Castle. Spend your nights in a castle-crowned village, either Bacharach or St. Goar. With more time, mosey through the neighboring Mosel Valley (see next chapter).

Planning Your Time

The Rhineland does not take much time to see. The blitziest tour is an hour at Köln's cathedral (see Köln chapter) and an hour looking at the castles from your train window. But for a better look, cruise in, tour a castle or two, sleep in a genuine medieval town, and take the train out. If you have limited time, cruise less and explore Rheinfels Castle.

Ideally, spend two nights here, sleep in Bacharach, cruise the best hour of the river (from Bacharach to St. Goar), and tour the Rheinfels Castle. Those with more time can ride the riverside bike path. With two days and a car, visit the Rhine and the Mosel. With two days by train, see the Rhine and Köln.

The Rhine

Ever since Roman times, when this was the empire's northern boundary, the Rhine has been one of the world's busiest shipping rivers. You'll see a steady flow of barges with 1,000- to 2,000-ton loads. Tourist-packed buses, hot train tracks, and highways line both banks.

Many of the castles were "robber-baron" castles, put there by petty rulers (there were 300 independent little countries in medieval

Rhine Overview

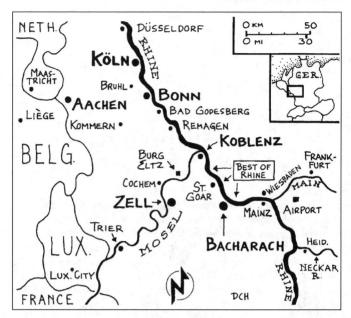

Germany) to levy tolls on passing river traffic. A robber baron would put his castle on, or even in, the river. Then, often with the help of chains and a tower on the opposite bank, he'd stop each ship and get his toll. There were 10 customs stops in the 60-mile stretch between Mainz and Koblenz alone (no wonder merchants were early proponents of the creation of larger nation-states).

Some castles were built to control and protect settlements, and others were the residences of kings. As times changed, so did the lifestyles of the rich and feudal. Many castles were abandoned for more comfortable mansions in the towns.

Most Rhine castles date from the 11th, 12th, and 13th centuries. When the pope successfully asserted his power over the German emperor in 1076, local princes ran wild over the rule of their emperor. The castles saw military action in the 1300s and 1400s, as emperors began reasserting their control over Germany's many silly kingdoms.

The castles were also involved in the Reformation wars, in which Europe's Catholic and Protestant dynasties fought it out using a fragmented Germany as their battleground. The Thirty Years' War (1618–1648) devastated Germany. The outcome: Each ruler got the freedom to decide if his people would be Catholic or Protestant, and one-third of Germany was dead. Production of Gummi bears ceased entirely.

The French—who feared a strong Germany and felt the Rhine was the logical border between them and Germany—destroyed most of the castles prophylactically (Louis XIV in the 1680s, the revolutionary army in the 1790s, and Napoleon in 1806). They were often rebuilt in neo-Gothic style in the Romantic age—the late 1800s—and today are enjoyed as restaurants, hotels, hostels, and museums.

For information on Rhine castles, visit www.burgen-am-rhein.de. For more on the Rhine, visit www.loreleytal.com (heavy on hotels but has maps, photos, and a little history).

Getting around the Rhine

While the Rhine flows north from Switzerland to Holland, the scenic stretch from Mainz to Koblenz hoards all the touristic charm. Studded with the crenellated cream of Germany's castles, it bustles with boats, trains, and highway traffic. Have fun exploring with a mix of big steamers, tiny ferries *(Fähre)*, trains, and bikes (see "More Rhine Sights," page 191).

By Boat: While many travelers do the whole trip by boat, the most scenic hour is from St. Goar to Bacharach. Sit on the top deck with your handy Rhine map-guide (or the kilometer-keyed tour in this chapter) and enjoy the parade of castles, towns, boats, and vineyards.

There are several boat companies, but most travelers sail on the bigger, more expensive, and romantic Köln-Düsseldorfer (K-D) line (free with a consecutive-day Eurailpass or with dated Eurail Flexipass, Eurail Selectpass, or German railpass—but it uses up a day of any Flexipass, otherwise about €8.40 for the first hour, then progressively cheaper per hour; the recommended Bacharach–St. Goar trip costs €8.40 one-way, €10.20 round-trip; half-price days: Tue for bicyclists, Mon and Fri for seniors over 60, tel. 06741/1634 in St. Goar, tel. 06743/1322 in Bacharach, www.k-d.com). Boats run daily in both directions from April through October, with no boats off-season. Complete, up-to-date schedules are posted in any station, Rhineland hotel, TI, bank, current Thomas Cook Timetable, or at www.euraide .de/ricksteves. Purchase tickets at the dock up to five minutes before departure. (Confirm times at your hotel the night before.) The boat is rarely full. Romantics will plan to catch the old-time *Goethe*, which sails each direction once a day (see "Rhine Cruise Schedule" in this chapter; confirm time locally).

The smaller Bingen-Rüdesheimer line is slightly cheaper than K-D (railpasses not valid, buy tickets on boat, tel. 06721/14140, www.bingen-ruedesheimer.com), with three two-hour round-trip St. Goar–Bacharach trips daily in summer (about €7.50 one-way, €9.50 round-trip; departing St. Goar at 11:00, 14:10, and 16:10, departing Bacharach at 10:10, 12:00, and 15:00).

Drivers have these options: (1) skip the boat; (2) take a round-trip cruise from St. Goar or Bacharach; (3) draw pretzels and let the loser drive, prepare the picnic, and meet the boat; (4) rent a bike, bring it on the boat for free, and bike back; or (5) take the boat one-way and return by train. When exploring by car, don't hesitate to pop onto one of the many little ferries that shuttle across the bridgeless-around-here river (see below).

By Ferry: While there are no bridges between Koblenz and Mainz, you'll see car-and-passenger ferries (usually family-run for generations) about every three miles. Ferries near St. Goar and Bacharach cross the river every 10 minutes daily in the summer from about 6:00 to 20:00, connecting Bingen–Rüdesheim, Lorch–Niederheimbach, Engelsburg–Kaub, and St. Goar–St.Goarshausen (adult-€1, car and driver-€2.80, pay on the boat).

By Train: Hourly milk-run trains down the Rhine hit every town: St. Goar–Bacharach, 12 min; Bacharach–Mainz, 60 min; Mainz–Frankfurt, 45 min. Some train schedules list St. Goar but not Bacharach as a stop, but any schedule listing St. Goar also stops at Bacharach. Tiny stations are unmanned—buy tickets at the platform machines or on the train. Prices are cheap (for example, €2.60 between St. Goar and Bacharach).

SIGHTS

The Romantic Rhine

These sights are listed from north to south, Koblenz to Bingen.

▲▲▲**Der Romantische Rhein Blitz Zug Fahrt**—One of Europe's great train thrills is zipping along the Rhine in this fast train tour. Here's a quick and easy, from-the-train-window tour (also works for car, bike, or best by boat; you can cut in anywhere) that skips the syrupy myths filling normal Rhine guides. For more information than necessary, buy the handy *Rhine Guide from Mainz to Cologne* (€4.50 book with foldout map, at most shops or TIs). Or for skimpy information and a longer, prettier map, try the *Long Rhine Tour* map (€5.20).

Sit on the left (river) side of the train or boat going south from Koblenz. While nearly all the castles listed are viewed from this side, clear a path to the right window for the times I yell, "Cross over!"

You'll notice large black-and-white kilometer markers along the riverbank. I erected these years ago to make this tour easier to follow. They tell the distance from the Rhinefalls, where the Rhine leaves Switzerland and becomes navigable. Now the river-barge pilots have accepted these as navigational aids as well. We're tackling just 36 miles (58 kilometers) of the 820-mile-long (1,320 kilometer) Rhine. Your Blitz Rhine Tour starts at Koblenz and heads upstream to Bingen. If you're going the other direction, it still works. Just hold the book upside down.

Km 590: Koblenz—This Rhine blitz starts with Romantic Rhine thrills—at Koblenz. Koblenz is not a nice city (it was really hit hard in

Best of the Rhine

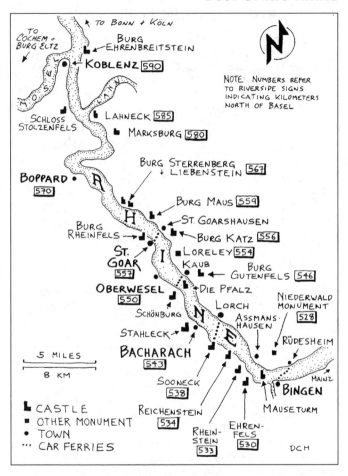

TO BONN + KÖLN

TO COCHEM + BURG ELTZ

BURG EHRENBREITSTEIN

KOBLENZ 590

M O S.

LAHN

N

NOTE: NUMBERS REFER TO RIVERSIDE SIGNS INDICATING KILOMETERS NORTH OF BASEL

SCHLOSS STOLZENFELS

LAHNECK 585

MARKSBURG 580

BURG STERRENBERG + LIEBENSTEIN 567

BOPPARD 570

R H I N E

BURG MAUS 559

ST. GOARSHAUSEN

BURG RHEINFELS

BURG KATZ 556

ST. GOAR 557

LORELEY 554

KAUB

BURG GUTENFELS 546

OBERWESEL 550

DIE PFALZ

SCHÖNBURG

LORCH

NIEDERWALD MONUMENT 528

STAHLECK

ASSMANS-HAUSEN

RÜDESHEIM

BACHARACH 543

MAINZ

SOONECK 538

BINGEN

REICHENSTEIN 534

EHREN-FELS 530

MAUSETURM

RHEIN-STEIN 533

DCH

5 MILES

8 KM

L CASTLE
■ OTHER MONUMENT
● TOWN
⋯ CAR FERRIES

World War II), but its place as the historic *Deutsche Eck* (German corner)—the tip of land where the Mosel joins the Rhine—gives it a certain historic charm. Koblenz, from the Latin for "confluence," has Roman origins. Walk through the park, noticing the reconstructed memorial to the kaiser. Across the river, the yellow Ehrenbreitstein Castle now houses a hostel. It's a 30-minute hike from the station to the Koblenz boat dock.

Km 585: Burg Lahneck—Above the modern autobahn bridge over the Lahn River, this castle *(Burg)* was built in 1240 to defend local silver mines; the castle was ruined by the French in 1688 and rebuilt in the

RHINE CRUISE SCHEDULE

Boats run May through September and on a reduced schedule for parts of April and October; no boats run November through March. These times are based on the 2003 schedule. Check www.euraide.de/ricksteves for any changes.

Koblenz	Boppard	St. Goar	Bacharach
—	9:00	10:15	11:25
*9:00	*11:00	*12:20	*13:35
11:00	13:00	14:15	15:25
14:00	16:00	17:15	18:25
13:10	11:50	10:55	10:15
14:10	12:50	11:55	11:15
—	13:50	12:55	12:15
18:10	16:50	15:55	15:15
*20:10	*18:50	*17:55	*17:15

*Riding the "Nostalgic Route," you'll take the 1913 steamer Goethe, with working paddle wheel and viewable engine room (departing Koblenz at 9:00 and Bacharach at 17:15).

1850s in neo-Gothic style. Burg Lahneck faces another Romantic rebuild, the yellow Schloss Stolzenfels (out of view above the train, a 10-min climb from tiny car park, open for touring, closed Mon).

Km 580: Marksburg—This castle (black and white with the 3 modern chimneys behind it, just after town of Spay) is the best-looking of all the Rhine castles and the only surviving medieval castle on the Rhine. Because of its commanding position, it was never attacked. It's now open as a museum with a medieval interior second only to the Mosel's Burg Eltz (see self-guided tour of Marksburg, page 191; for all the details on Burg Eltz, see next chapter). The three modern smoke-stacks vent Europe's biggest car-battery recycling plant just up the valley.

Km 570: Boppard—Once a Roman town, Boppard has some impressive remains of fourth-century walls. Notice the Roman towers and the substantial chunk of Roman wall near the train station, just above the main square.

If you visit Boppard, head to the fascinating church below the main square. Find the carved Romanesque crazies at the doorway. Inside, to the right of the entrance, you'll see Christian symbols from Roman times.

Also notice the painted arches and vaults. Originally most Romanesque churches were painted this way. Down by the river, look for the high-water *(Hochwasser)* marks on the arches from various flood years. (You'll find these flood marks throughout the Rhine and Mosel Valleys.)

Km 567: Burg Sterrenberg and Burg Liebenstein—These are the "Hostile Brothers" castles across from Bad Salzig. Take the wall between the castles (actually designed to improve the defenses of both castles), add two greedy and jealous brothers and a fair maiden, and create your own legend. Burg Liebenstein is now a fun, friendly, and affordable family-run hotel (9 rooms, Db-€90, suite-€110, giant king-and-the-family room-€180, easy parking, tel. 06773/308, www.castle-liebenstein.com, hotel-burg-liebenstein@rhinecastles.com, Nickenig family).

Km 560: While you can see nothing from here, a 19th-century lead mine functioned on both sides of the river with a shaft actually tunneling completely under it.

Km 559: Burg Maus—The Maus (mouse) got its name because the next castle was owned by the Katzenelnbogen family. (*Katz* means "cat.") In the 1300s, it was considered a state-of-the-art fortification...until Napoleon had it blown up in 1806 with state-of-the-art explosives. It was rebuilt true to its original plans around 1900. Today, the castle hosts a falconry show (€6.50, daily at 11:00 and 14:30, 20-min walk up, tel. 06771/7669, www.burg-maus.de).

Km 557: St. Goar and Rheinfels Castle—Cross to the other side of the train. The pleasant town of St. Goar was named for a sixth-century hometown monk. It originated in Celtic times (really old) as a place where sailors would stop, catch their breath, send home a postcard, and give thanks after surviving the seductive and treacherous Loreley crossing. St. Goar is worth a stop to explore its mighty Rheinfels Castle. (For information, a guided castle tour, and accommodations, see below.)

Km 556: Burg Katz—Burg Katz (Katzenelnbogen) faces St. Goar from across the river. Together, Burg Katz (built in 1371) and Rheinfels Castle had a clear view up and down the river and effectively controlled traffic. There was absolutely no duty-free shopping on the medieval Rhine. Katz got Napoleoned in 1806 and rebuilt around 1900. Today, it's under a rich and mysterious Japanese ownership. It's technically a hotel—Germany wouldn't allow its foreign purchase for private use—but it's so expensive, nobody's ever stayed there. Below the castle, notice the derelict grape terraces—worked since the eighth century, but abandoned only in the last generation. The Rhine wine is particularly good because the slate absorbs the heat of the sun and stays warm all night, resulting in sweeter grapes. Wine from the flat fields above the Rhine gorge is cheaper and good only as table wine. The wine from the steep side of the Rhine gorge—harder to grow and harvest—is tastier and more expensive.

RHINE RIVER TRADE AND BARGE-WATCHING

The Rhine is great for barge-watching. There's a constant parade of action, and each boat is different. Since ancient times, this has been a highway for trade. Today, the world's biggest port (Rotterdam) waits at the mouth of the river.

Barge workers are almost a subculture. Many own their own ships. The captain (and family) live in the stern. Workers live in the bow. The family car often decorates the bow like a shiny hood ornament. In the Rhine town of Kaub, there was a boarding school for the children of the Rhine merchant marine—but today it's closed, since most captains are Dutch, Belgian, or Swiss. The flag of the boat's home country flies in the stern (German; Swiss; Dutch—horizontal red, white, and blue; or French—vertical red, white, and blue). Logically, imports go upstream (Japanese cars, coal, and oil) and exports go downstream (German cars, chemicals, and pharmaceuticals). A clever captain manages to ship goods in each direction.

Tugs can push a floating train of up to five barges at once. Upstream it gets steeper and they can push only one at a time. Before modern shipping, horses dragged boats upstream (the faint remains of towpaths survive at points along the river). From 1873 to 1900, they laid a chain from Bonn to Bingen, and boats with cogwheels

About Km 555: A statue of the Loreley, the beautiful but deadly nymph (see next listing for legend), combs her hair at the end of a long spit—built to give barges protection from vicious icebergs that occasionally rage down the river in the winter. The actual Loreley, a cliff, is just ahead.

Km 554: The Loreley—Steep a big slate rock in centuries of legend and it becomes a tourist attraction, the ultimate Rhinestone. The Loreley (flags on top, name painted near shoreline), rising 450 feet over the narrowest and deepest point of the Rhine, has long been important. It was a holy site in pre-Roman days. The fine echoes here—thought to be ghostly voices—fertilized the legendary soil.

Because of the reefs just upstream (at kilometer 552), many ships never made it to St. Goar. Sailors (after days on the river) blamed their misfortune on a *wunderbares Fräulein* whose long blonde hair almost covered her body. Heinrich Heine's *Song of Loreley* (the Cliffs Notes version is on local postcards) tells the story of a count who sent his men to kill or capture this siren after she distracted his horny son, causing him to drown. When the soldiers cornered the nymph in her cave, she called and steam engines hoisted themselves upstream. Today, 265 million tons travel each year along the 530 miles from Basel on the Swiss border to Rotterdam on the Atlantic.

Riverside navigational aids are of vital interest to captains who don't wish to meet the Loreley. Boats pass on the right unless they clearly signal otherwise with a large blue sign. Since downstream ships can't stop or maneuver as freely, upstream boats are expected to do the tricky do-si-do work. Cameras monitor traffic all along and relay warnings of oncoming ships by posting large triangular signals before narrow and troublesome bends in the river. There may be two or three triangles per signpost, depending upon how many "sectors," or segments, of the river are covered. The lowest triangle indicates the nearest stretch of river. Each triangle tells whether there's a ship in that sector. When the bottom side of a triangle is lit, that sector is empty. When the left side is lit, an oncoming ship is in that sector.

The **Signal and Riverpilots Museum,** located at the signal triangles at the upstream edge of St. Goar, explains how barges are safer, cleaner, and more fuel-efficient than trains or trucks (Wed and Sat 14:00–17:00, outdoor exhibits always open).

her father (Father Rhine) for help. Huge waves, the likes of which you'll never see today, rose from the river and carried Loreley to safety. And she has never been seen since.

But alas, when the moon shines brightly and the tour buses are parked, a soft, playful Rhine whine can still be heard from the Loreley. As you pass, listen carefully ("Sailors...sailors...over my bounding mane").

Km 552: Killer reefs, marked by red-and-green buoys, are called the "Seven Maidens." Okay, one goofy legend: The prince of Schönburg Castle (*ober* Oberwesel) had seven spoiled daughters who always dumped men because of their shortcomings. Fed up, he invited seven of his knights up to the castle and demanded that his daughters each choose one to marry. But they complained that each man had too big a nose, was too fat, too stupid, and so on. The rude and teasing girls escaped into a riverboat. Just downstream, God turned them into the seven rocks that form this reef. While this story probably isn't entirely true, there's a lesson in it for medieval children: Don't be hard-hearted.

Km 550: Oberwesel—Cross to the other side of the train. Oberwesel was a Celtic town in 400 B.C., then a Roman military station.

It now boasts some of the best Roman-wall and medieval-tower remains on the Rhine, and the commanding Schönburg Castle. Notice how many of the train tunnels have entrances designed like medieval turrets—they were actually built in the Romantic 19th century. OK, back to the river side.

Km 546: Burg Gutenfels and Pfalz Castle: The Classic Rhine View—Burg Gutenfels (see white-painted Hotel sign) and the ship-shape Pfalz Castle (built in the river in the 1300s) worked very effectively to tax medieval river traffic. The town of Kaub grew rich as Pfalz raised its chains when boats came and lowered them only when the merchants had paid their duty. Those who didn't pay spent time touring its prison, on a raft at the bottom of its well. In 1504, a pope called for the destruction of Pfalz, but a six-week siege failed. Notice the overhanging outhouse (tiny white room—with faded medieval stains—between two wooden ones). Pfalz is tourable but bare and dull (€2 ferry from Kaub, €2.10 entry, April–Sept Tue–Sun 9:00–13:00 & 14:00–18:00, Oct–March until 17:00, last entry 60 min before closing, closed Mon and Dec, tel. 06774/570 or 0172/262-2800).

In Kaub, a green statue honors the German general Blücher. He was Napoleon's nemesis. In 1813, as Napoleon fought his way back to Paris after his disastrous Russian campaign, he stopped at Mainz—hoping to fend off the Germans and Russians pursuing him by controlling that strategic bridge. Blücher tricked Napoleon. By building the first major pontoon bridge of its kind here at the Pfalz Castle, he crossed the Rhine and outflanked the French. Two years later, Blücher and Wellington teamed up to defeat Napoleon once and for all at Waterloo.

Km 544: "The Raft Busters"—Immediately before Bacharach, at the top of the island, buoys mark a gang of rocks notorious for busting up rafts. The Black Forest is upstream. It was poor, and wood was its best export. Black Foresters would ride log booms down the Rhine to the Ruhr (where their timber fortified coal-mine shafts) or to Holland (where logs were sold to shipbuilders). If they could navigate the sweeping bend just before Bacharach and then survive these "raft busters," they'd come home reckless and romantic, the German folkloric equivalent of American cowboys after payday.

Km 543: Bacharach and Burg Stahleck—Cross to the other side of the train. Bacharach is a great stop (see details and accommodations below). Some of the Rhine's best wine is from this town, whose name means "altar to Bacchus." Local vintners brag that the medieval Pope Pius II ordered Bacharach wine by the cartload. Perched above the town, the 13th-century Burg Stahleck is now a hostel.

Km 540: Lorch—This pathetic stub of a castle is barely visible from the road. Notice the small car ferry (3/hr, 10 min), one of several along the bridgeless stretch between Mainz and Koblenz.

Km 538: Castle Sooneck—Cross back to the other side of the train. Built in the 11th century, this castle was twice destroyed by people sick and tired of robber barons.

Km 534: Burg Reichenstein, and **Km 533: Burg Rheinstein**— Stay on the other side of the train to see two of the first castles to be rebuilt in the Romantic era. Both are privately owned, tourable, and connected by a pleasant trail.

Km 530: Ehrenfels Castle—Opposite Bingerbrück and the Bingen station, you'll see the ghostly Ehrenfels Castle (clobbered by the Swedes in 1636 and by the French in 1689). Since it had no view of the river traffic to the north, the owner built the cute little *Mäuseturm* (mouse tower) on an island (the yellow tower you'll see near the train station today). Rebuilt in the 1800s in neo-Gothic style, it's now used as a Rhine navigation signal station.

Km 528: Niederwald Monument—Across from the Bingen station on a hilltop is the 120-foot-high Niederwald monument, a memorial built with 32 tons of bronze in 1877 to commemorate "the reestablishment of the German Empire." A lift takes tourists to this statue from the famous and extremely touristy wine town of Rüdesheim.

From here, the Romantic Rhine becomes the industrial Rhine, and our tour is over.

More Rhine Sights

▲▲**Marksburg Castle**—Thanks to its formidable defenses, invaders decided to give Marksburg a miss. This best-preserved castle on the Rhine can be toured only with a guide, and tours are generally in German only (4/hr in summer, 1/hr in winter). Still, it's an awesome castle, and my self-guided walking tour (below) fits the 50-minute German-language tour (€4.50, family card-€12.50, daily April–Oct 10:00–18:00, last tour departs at 17:00, Nov–March 11:00–17:00, last tour at 16:00, call ahead to see if a rare English tour is scheduled, tel. 02627/206, www.marksburg.de). Marksburg caps a hill above the Rhine town of Braubach (a short hike or shuttle train from the boat dock). Our tour starts inside the castle's first gate.

1. Inside the First Gate: While the dramatic castles lining the Rhine are generally Romantic rebuilds, Marksburg is the real McCoy— nearly all original construction. It's littered with bits of its medieval past, like the big stone ball that was swung on a rope to be used as a battering ram. Ahead, notice how the inner gate—originally tall enough for knights on horseback to gallop through—was made smaller, therefore safer from enemies on horseback. Climb the Knights' Stairway carved out of slate rock and pass under the murder hole—handy for pouring boiling pitch on invaders. (Germans still say someone with bad luck "has pitch on his head.")

2. Coats of Arms: Colorful coats of arms line the wall just inside the gate. These are from the noble families who have owned the castle since 1283. In 1283, financial troubles drove the first family to sell to the powerful and wealthy Katzenelnbogen family (who made the castle into what you see today). When Napoleon took this region in 1803, an Austrian family who sided with the French got the keys. When Prussia took the region in 1866, control passed to a friend of the Prussians who had a passion for medieval things—typical of this Romantic period. Then it was sold to the German Castles Association in 1900. Its offices are in the main palace at the top of the stairs.

3. Romanesque Palace: White outlines mark where the larger original windows were located, before they were replaced by easier-to-defend smaller ones. On the far right, a bit of the original plaster survives. Slate, which is soft and vulnerable to the elements, needs to be covered—in this case, by plaster. Because this is a protected historic building, restorers can use only the traditional plaster methods...but no one knows how to make plaster that works as well as the 800-year-old surviving bits.

4. Cannons: The oldest cannon here—from 1500—was back-loaded. This was good because many cartridges could be preloaded. But since the seal was leaky, it wasn't very powerful. The bigger, more modern cannons—from 1640—were one piece and therefore airtight, but had to be front-loaded. They could easily hit targets across the river from here. Stone balls were rough, so they let the explosive force leak out. The best cannonballs were stones covered in smooth lead—airtight and therefore more powerful and more accurate.

5. Gothic Garden: Walking along an outer wall, you'll see 160 plants from the Middle Ages—used for cooking, medicine, and witchcraft. The *Schierling* (hemlock, in the first corner) is the same poison that killed Socrates.

6. Inland Rampart: This most vulnerable part of the castle had a triangular construction to better deflect attacks. Notice the factory in the valley. In the 14th century, this was a lead, copper, and silver mine. Today's factory—Europe's largest car-battery recycling plant—uses the old mine shafts as a vent (see the 3 modern smokestacks).

7. Wine Cellar: Since Roman times, wine has been the traditional Rhineland drink. Because castle water was impure, wine—less alcoholic than today's beer—was the way knights got their fluids. The pitchers on the wall were their daily allotment. The bellows were part of the barrel's filtering system. Stairs lead to the...

8. Gothic Hall: This hall is set up as a kitchen, with an oven designed to roast an ox whole. The arms holding the pots have notches to control the heat. To this day, when Germans want someone to hurry up, they say, "give it one tooth more." Medieval windows were thin alabaster or skins. A nearby wall is peeled away to show the wattle-and-daub construction (sticks, straw, clay, mud, then plaster) of a castle's inner walls. The iron plate to the left of the next door enabled servants to stoke the heater without being seen by the noble family.

9. Bedroom: This was the only heated room in the castle. The canopy kept in heat and kept out critters. In medieval times, it was impolite for a lady to argue with her lord in public. She would wait for him in bed to give him what Germans still call "a curtain lecture." The deep window seat caught maximum light for needlework and reading. Women would sit here and chat (or "spin a yarn") while working the spinning wheel.

10. Hall of the Knights: This was the dining hall. The long table is an unattached plank. After each course, servants could replace it with another preset plank. Even today, when a meal is over and Germans are ready for the action to begin, they say, "Let's lift up the table." The "action" back then was traveling minstrels who sang and told of news gleaned from their travels.

The outhouse locked from the outside because any invader knew that the toilet—which simply hung over thin air—was a weak point in the castle's defenses.

11. Chapel: This chapel is still painted in Gothic style with the castle's namesake, St. Mark, and his lion. Even the chapel was designed with defense in mind. The small doorway kept out heavily armed attackers. The staircase spirals clockwise, favoring the sword-wielding defender (assuming he was right-handed).

12. Linen Room: Around 1800, the castle—with diminished military value—housed disabled soldiers. They'd earn a little extra money working raw flax into linen.

13. Two Thousand Years of Armor: Follow the evolution of armor since Celtic times. Because helmets covered the entire head, soldiers identified themselves as friendly by tipping their visor up with their right hand. This evolved into the military salute that is still used around the world today. Armor and the close-range weapons along the back were made obsolete by the invention of the rifle. Armor was replaced with breastplates—pointed (like the castle itself) to deflect enemy fire. This design was used as late as the start of World War I. A medieval lady's armor hangs over the door. While popular fiction has men locking their women up before heading off to battle, chastity belts were actually used by women as protection against rape when traveling.

14. The Keep: This served as an observation tower, a dungeon (with a 22-square-foot cell in the bottom), and a place of last refuge. When all was nearly lost, the defenders would bundle into the keep and burn the wooden bridge, hoping to outwait their enemies.

15. Horse Stable: The stable shows off bits of medieval crime and punishment. Cheaters were attached to stones or pillories. Shame masks punished gossipmongers. A mask with a heavy ball had its victim crawling around with his nose in the mud. The handcuffs with a neck hole were for the transport of prisoners. The pictures on the wall show various medieval capital punishments. Many times the accused was simply taken into a torture dungeon to see all these tools and, guilty or not, confessions spilled out of him. On that cheery note, your tour is over.

The Myth of the Loreley Visitors' Center—This lightweight exhibit reflects on Loreley, traces her myth, and explores the landscape, culture, and people of the Rhine Valley. Displays in English tell the history well, but the highlight for any kid-at-heart are the echo megaphones in the little theater that (with English headphones) tells the legend of the siren (€1, April–Oct daily 10:00–18:00, often closed Nov–March, tel. 06771/9100, www.loreley-touristik.de). From the exhibit, a five-minute walk (marked as 30 minutes) takes you to the impressive viewpoint overlooking the Rhine Valley from atop the famous rock. From there, it's a steep 15-minute hike down to the riverbank.

Biking the Rhine—In Bacharach, you can rent bikes at Hotel Hillen (€7/half-day, €10/full day, cheaper for guests, 30 bikes) and at Pension Malerwinkel if you're a guest (€6/day), or get a free loaner bike if you're staying at Pension Winzerhaus. In St. Goar, Hotel am Markt rents bikes to its guests.

You can bike on either side of the Rhine, but for a designated bike path, stay on the west side, where a 35-mile path runs between Koblenz and Bingen. While the stretch between Bacharach and Bingen hugs the riverside, I'd join the in-line skaters along the fine and more interesting roadside bike lane connecting Bacharach and St. Goar in six miles. In 2004, new sections of the bike path will be finished between Bacharach and Bingen, making the trip completely road-free.

Consider taking a bike on the Rhine boats (free with ticket) and then biking back, or designing a circular trip using the fun and frequent shuttle ferries. A good target might be Kaub (where a tiny boat shuttles sightseers to the better-from-a-distance castle on the island).

Hiking the Rhine—For a good two-hour hike from St. Goar to the Loreley viewpoint, catch the ferry across to St. Goarshausen (€1.50 round-trip, 6/hr until 20:00, then 2/hr, May–Oct until 23:00, Nov–April until 21:00), follow green Burg Katz (Katz Castle) signs up Burgstrasse under the train tracks to find steps on right (Loreley über Burg Katz) leading to the Katz Castle (now a private hotel for Japanese elite) and beyond. Traverse the hillside, always bearing right toward the river. You'll pass through a residential area, hike down a 50-yard path through trees, then cross a wheat field until you reach an amphitheater adjacent to the Loreley Visitors Center (shops and restaurants, see above) and rock-capping viewpoint. From here, it's a steep 15-minute hike down to the river, where a riverfront trail takes you back to St. Goarshausen and the St. Goar ferry.

Bacharach

Once prosperous from the wine and wood trade, Bacharach (BAHKH-ah-rahkh, with a guttural *kh* sound) is now just a pleasant half-timbered village of a thousand people working hard to keep its tourists happy.

Tourist Information: The TI is on the main street in the Posthof courtyard next to the church (April–Oct Mon–Fri 9:00–17:00, Sat 10:00–16:00, closed Sun, Nov–March Mon–Fri 9:00–12:00, closed Sat–Sun, Internet access-€6/hr, Oberstrasse 45, from train station turn right and walk 5 blocks down main street with castle high on your left, tel. 06743/919-303, www.bacharach.de or www.rhein-nahe-touristik.de, Herr Kuhn and his team SE). The TI stores bags for day-trippers, provides ferry schedules, and sells the handy *Rhine Guide from Mainz to Cologne* (€4.50). For accommodations, see "Sleeping," page 199.

Shopping: The **Jost** beer-stein stores carry most everything a shopper could want. One shop is across from the church in the main square, the other—which offers more deals—is a block away next to the post office at Rosenstrasse 16 (post office closed 12:30–14:00; Jost store hours: Mon–Fri 8:30–18:00, Sat 8:30–17:00, Sun 10:00–17:00, Rosenstrasse shop closed Sun, ships overseas, 10 percent discount with this book, tel. 06743/1224, www.phil-jost-germany.com). Herr and Frau Jost offer sightseeing advice, send faxes, and reserve German hotels for travelers (reasonable charge for phone and fax fees). **Woodburn House,** which engraves woody signs and knickknacks, lets travelers store bags while they look for a room and gives readers with this book a 10 percent discount (across from Altes Haus, Oberstrasse 60, Frances Geuss SE).

Local Guides: Get acquainted with Bacharach by taking a walking tour. Charming Herr Rolf Jung, retired headmaster of the Bacharach school, is a superb English-speaking guide (€30, 90 min, call to reserve, tel. 06743/1519). If Herr Jung is not available, the TI has a list of other English-speaking guides, or take the self-guided walk, described below.

INTRODUCTORY BACHARACH WALK

Start at the Köln-Düsseldorfer ferry dock (next to a fine picnic park). View the town from the parking lot—a modern landfill. The Rhine used to lap against Bacharach's town wall, just over the present-day highway. Every few years the river floods, covering the highway with several feet of water. The **castle** on the hill is a youth hostel. Two of its original 16 towers are visible from here (up to 5 if you look real hard). The huge roadside wine keg declares this town was built on the wine trade.

Reefs up the river forced boats to unload upriver and reload here. Consequently, Bacharach became the biggest wine trader on the Rhine.

Bacharach

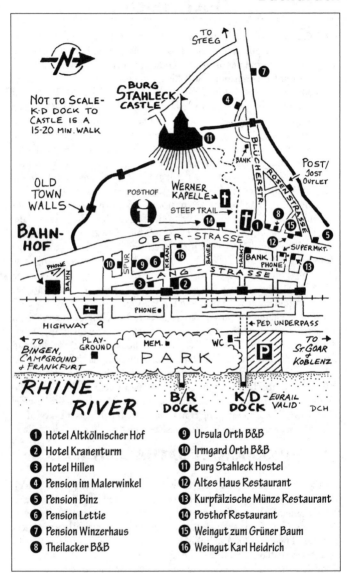

1. Hotel Altkölnischer Hof
2. Hotel Kranenturm
3. Hotel Hillen
4. Pension im Malerwinkel
5. Pension Binz
6. Pension Lettie
7. Pension Winzerhaus
8. Theilacker B&B
9. Ursula Orth B&B
10. Irmgard Orth B&B
11. Burg Stahleck Hostel
12. Altes Haus Restaurant
13. Kurpfälzische Münze Restaurant
14. Posthof Restaurant
15. Weingut zum Grüner Baum
16. Weingut Karl Heidrich

A riverfront crane hoisted huge kegs of prestigious "Bacharach" wine (which in practice was from anywhere in the region). The tour buses next to the dock and the flags of the biggest spenders along the highway remind you that today's economy is basically tourism.

At the big town map and public WC (€0.30, daily 9:00–18:00), take the underpass, ascend on the right, make a U-turn, then—if you are less than 2.3 meters tall—walk under the train tracks through the medieval gate (1 out of an original 15 14th-century gates) and to the two-tone Protestant **church,** which marks the town center.

From this intersection, Bacharach's main street (Oberstrasse) goes right to the half-timbered, red-and-white Altes Haus (from 1368, the oldest house in town) and left way down to the train station. To the left (or south) of the church, a golden horn hangs over the old **Posthof** (TI, free WC upstairs in courtyard open from 11:00). The post horn symbolizes the postal service throughout Europe. In olden days, when the postman blew this, traffic stopped and the mail sped through. This post station dates from 1724, when stagecoaches ran from Köln to Frankfurt.

Step into the courtyard—once a carriage house and inn that accommodated Bacharach's first VIP visitors. Notice the fascist eagle (from 1936, on the left as you enter) and the fine view of the church and a ruined chapel above. The Posthof is the home of the **Rhineland Museum,** which hopes to open in 2004 with a cultural landscape exhibit on the Rhine Valley. Manager Bitz's vision even includes wine-tasting (www.mittelrheintal.de).

Two hundred years ago, Bacharach's main drag was the only road along the Rhine. Napoleon widened it to fit his cannon wagons. The steps alongside the church lead to the castle. Return to the church, passing the **Italian Ice Cream** café, where friendly Mimo serves his special invention: Riesling wine–flavored gelato (quite tasty, €0.60 per scoop, opposite Posthof at Oberstrasse 48).

Inside the church (daily 9:00–18:00, English info on table near door), you'll find grotesque capitals, brightly painted in medieval style, and a mix of round Romanesque and pointed Gothic arches. Left of the altar, some medieval frescoes survive where an older Romanesque arch was cut by a pointed Gothic one.

Continue down Oberstrasse past the Altes Haus to the **old mint** *(Münze),* marked by a crude coin in its sign. Across from the mint, the wine garden of Fritz Bastian is the liveliest place in town after dark (see "Eating," page 202). Above you in the vineyards stands a ghostly black-and-gray tower—your destination.

Take the next left (Rosenstrasse) and wander 30 yards up to the **well.** Notice the sundial and the wall painting of 1632 Bacharach with its walls intact. Climb the tiny-stepped lane behind the well up into the vineyard and to the tower. The slate steps lead to a small path through the vineyard that deposits you at a viewpoint atop the stubby remains of the old town wall (if signs indicate that the path is closed, get as close to the tower base as possible).

A grand medieval town spreads before you. When Frankfurt had 15,000 residents, medieval Bacharach had 4,000. For 300 years (1300–1600), Bacharach was big, rich, and politically powerful.

From this perch you can see the chapel ruins and six surviving **city towers.** Visually trace the wall to the castle. The castle was actually the capital of Germany for a couple of years in the 1200s. When Holy Roman Emperor Frederick Barbarossa went away to fight the Crusades, he left his brother (who lived here) in charge of his vast realm. Bacharach was home of one of seven electors who voted for the Holy Roman Emperor in 1275. To protect their own power, these elector-princes did their best to choose the weakest guy on the ballot. The elector from Bacharach helped select a two-bit prince named Rudolf von Hapsburg (from a no-name castle in Switzerland). The underestimated Rudolf brutally silenced the robber barons along the Rhine and established the mightiest dynasty in European history. His family line, the Hapsburgs, ruled much of Central Europe until 1918.

Plagues, fires, and the Thirty Years' War (1618–1648) finally did Bacharach in. The town, with a population of about a thousand, has slumbered for several centuries. Today, the castle houses commoners—40,000 overnights annually by youth hostelers.

In the mid-19th century, painters such as J. M. W. Turner and writers such as Victor Hugo were charmed by the Rhineland's romantic mix of past glory, present poverty, and rich legend. They put this part of the Rhine on the old "grand tour" map as the "Romantic Rhine." Victor Hugo pondered the ruined 15th-century chapel that you see under the castle. In his 1842 travel book, *Rhein Reise (Rhine Travels),* he wrote, "No doors, no roof or windows, a magnificent skeleton puts its silhouette against the sky. Above it, the ivy-covered castle ruins provide a fitting crown. This is Bacharach, land of fairy tales, covered with legends and sagas." If you're enjoying the Romantic Rhine, thank Victor Hugo and company.

To get back into town, take the level path that leads along the wall up the valley past the next tower. Then cross the street into the parking lot. Pass Pension Malerwinkel on your right, being careful not to damage the old arch with your head. Follow the creek past a delightful little series of half-timbered homes and cheery gardens known as Painters' Corner *(Malerwinkel).* Resist looking into some pervert's peep show (on the right) and continue downhill back to the village center. Nice work.

SLEEP CODE

(€1 = about $1.10)

Sleep Code: **S** = Single, **D** = Double/Twin, **T** = Triple, **Q** = Quad, **b** = bathroom, **s** = shower only, **no CC** = Credit Cards not accepted, **SE** = Speaks English, **NSE** = No English. All hotels speak some English. Breakfast is included and credit cards are accepted unless otherwise noted.

To help you sort easily through these listings, I've divided the rooms into three categories, based on the price for a standard double room with bath:

> $$$ **Higher Priced**—Most rooms €70 or more.
> $$ **Moderately Priced**—Most rooms between €50–70.
> $ **Lower Priced**—Most rooms €50 or less.

The Rhine is an easy place for cheap sleeps. *Zimmer* and *Gasthäuser* with €20 beds abound (and *Zimmer* normally discount their prices for longer stays). Rhine-area hostels offer €14 beds to travelers of any age. Each town's TI is eager to set you up, and finding a room should be easy any time of year (except for winefest weekends in September and October). Bacharach and St. Goar, the best towns for an overnight stop, are 10 miles apart, connected by milk-run trains, riverboats, and a riverside bike path. Bacharach is a much more interesting town, but St. Goar has the famous castle (see "St. Goar," page 202). Parking in Bacharach is simple along the highway next to the tracks (3-hr daytime limit is generally not enforced) or in the boat parking lot. Parking in St. Goar is tighter; ask at your hotel.

SLEEPING

(country code: 49, area code: 06743)

See map on page 196 for locations. Ignore guest houses and restaurants posting "Recommended by Rick Steves" signs. If they're not listed in the current edition of this book, I do not recommend them.

$$$ **Hotel Altkölnischer Hof,** a grand old building near the church, rents 20 rooms with modern furnishings (and some balconies) over an Old World restaurant. Public rooms are old-time elegant (Sb-€48–70, small or dark Db-€62–65, bright new Db-€72–82, new Db with balcony-€80–105, elevator, closed Nov–March, tel. 06743/1339

or 06743/2186, fax 06743/2793, www.hotel-bacharach-rhein.de, altkoelnischer-hof@t-online.de).

$$ Hotel Kranenturm offers castle ambience without the climb—a good combination of hotel comfort with *Zimmer* coziness, a central location, and a medieval atmosphere. Run by hardworking Kurt Engel and his intense but friendly wife, Fatima, this hotel is actually part of the medieval fortification. Its former *Kran* (crane) towers are now round rooms. When the riverbank was higher, cranes on this tower loaded barrels of wine onto Rhine boats. Hotel Kranenturm is 15 feet from the train tracks, but a combination of medieval sturdiness, triple-paned windows, and included earplugs makes the riverside rooms sleepable (Sb-€40–43, Db-€55–60, bigger Db-€60–70, Tb-€75–85, lower price is for off-season or stays of at least 3 nights in high season, family deals, kid-friendly, cash preferred, Rhine views come with ripping train noise, back rooms are quieter, Internet access-€5/hour and laundry service-€12.50/load for guests only, Langstrasse 30, tel. 06743/1308, fax 06743/1021, hotel-kranenturm@t-online.de). Kurt, a good cook, serves €6–18 dinners (guests can have full dinner for €10); try his ice-cream special for dessert. Trade travel stories on the terrace with new friends over dinner, letting screaming trains punctuate your conversation. Drivers park along the highway at the Kranenturm tower. Eurailers walk down Oberstrasse, then turn right on Kranenstrasse.

$$ Hotel Hillen, a block south of the Hotel Kranenturm, has less charm and similar train noise, with spacious rooms, friendly owners, good food, and lots of rental bikes. To minimize train noise, ask for *ruhige Seite,* the quiet side (S-€28, Sb-€36, D-€42, Ds-€52, Db-€57, Tb-€75, 10 percent less for 3 nights, 15 percent discount on rooms with this book, closed Nov–March, family rooms, Langstrasse 18, tel. 06743/1287, fax 06743/1037, hotel-hillen@web.de, kind Iris speaks some English).

$$ Pension im Malerwinkel sits like a grand gingerbread house just outside the wall at the top end of town in a little neighborhood so charming it's called "Painters' Corner" *(Malerwinkel)*. The Vollmer family's 20-room place is super-quiet and comes with a sunny garden on a brook and easy parking (Sb-€35, Db-€55–58 for 1 night, €50 for 2 nights, €47 for 3 nights, no CC, some rooms have balconies but most face parking lot, bike rental-€6/day, from town center go uphill and up the valley 5 min until you pass the old town gate and look left to Blücherstrasse 41, tel. 06743/1239, fax 06743/93407, www.im-malerwinkel.de, pension@im-malerwinkel.de).

$$ Pension Binz offers four large, bright rooms and a plain apartment in a serene location (Sb-€33, Db-€51, third person-€18, apartment with 2-night minimum-€61, fine breakfast, Koblenzer Strasse 1, tel. 06743/1604, pension.binz@freenet.de, cheery Karla speaks a little English).

$ At **Pension Lettie,** effervescent and eager-to-please Lettie offers four bright rooms. Lettie speaks good English (she worked for the U.S. Army before they withdrew) and does laundry—€10.50 per load (Sb-€34, Db-€45, Tb-€61, family room for 4-€75, for 5-€95, for 6-€105, prices valid with this book, discount for 2-night stays, 6 percent more if paying with plastic, strictly non-smoking, buffet breakfast with waffles and eggs, no train noise, a few doors inland from Hotel Kranenturm, Kranenstrasse 6, tel. & fax 06743/2115, pension.lettie@t-online.de).

$ **Pension Winzerhaus,** a 10-room place run by friendly Sybille and Stefan, is 200 yards up the valley from the town gate, so the location is less charming, and the train noise is replaced by street noise. But the parking is easy, and rooms are simple, clean, and modern (Sb-€26, Db-€45, Tb-€60, Qb-€65, 10 percent off with this book, no CC, free bikes for guests, non-smoking rooms, Blücherstrasse 60, tel. 06743/1294, fax 06743/937-779, winzerhaus@compuserve.de).

$ **Herr und Frau Theilacker** run a cozy, German-feeling *Zimmer* just off the main street with four comfortable rooms, vine-covered trellises, and a breakfast room filled with their family photos. They're likely to have a room when others don't (S-€18, D-€36, no CC, in town center behind Altkölnischer Hof, take short lane between Altkölnischer Hof and Altes Haus straight ahead to Oberstrasse 57, no outside sign, tel. 06743/1248, NSE).

$ **Orth** *Zimmer:* Delightful sisters-in-law run two fine little B&Bs across the lane from each other (from station walk down Oberstrasse, turn right on Spurgasse, look for *Orth* sign). **Ursula Orth** rents five rooms and speaks a smidge of English (Sb-€20, D-€31, Db-€34, Tb-€45, no CC, rooms 4 and 5 on ground floor, Spurgasse 3, tel. 06743/1557). **Irmgard Orth** rents two fresh rooms. She speaks no English but is exuberantly cheery and serves homemade honey with breakfast (Sb-€20, Db-€34, no CC, Spurgasse 2, tel. 06743/1553).

$ **Jugendherberge Stahleck** hostel is a 12th-century castle on the hilltop—500 steps above Bacharach—with a royal Rhine view. Open to travelers of any age, this is a newly redone gem with eight beds and a private modern shower and WC in most rooms. A steep 20-minute climb on the trail from the town church, the hostel is warmly run by Evelyn and Bernhard Falke (FALL-kay), who serve hearty, €6, all-you-can-eat buffet dinners. The hostel pub serves cheap local wine until midnight (€16 dorm beds with breakfast and sheets, €3.10 extra for non-members or in a double, couples can share one of five €37 Db, no smoking in rooms, open all day but 22:00 curfew, laundry machine, beds normally available but call and leave your name, they'll hold a bed until 18:00, tel. 06743/1266, fax 06743/2684, jh-bacharach@djh-info.de). If driving, don't go in the driveway; park on the street and walk 200 yards.

EATING

You can easily find inexpensive (€10–15), atmospheric restaurants offering indoor and outdoor dining. The first three places are neighbors.

Altes Haus, the oldest building in town, serves reliably good food with Bacharach's most romantic atmosphere (€9–15, Thu–Tue 12:00–15:30 & 18:00–21:30, closed Wed and Dec–Easter, dead center by the church, tel. 06743/1209). Find the cozy little dining room with photos of the opera singer who sang about Bacharach, adding to its fame.

Kurpfälzische Münze is more expensive but a popular standby for its sunny terrace and classy candlelit interior (€7–21, daily 10:00–22:00, in the old mint, a half-block down from Altes Haus, tel. 06743/1375).

Posthof Restaurant is a historic carriage house—a stopping place for centuries of guests—newly opened as a restaurant. The menu is trendier, with free German tapas (ask), seasonal specials, and local "as organic as possible" produce. You'll sit in a half-timbered cobbled courtyard (€5–15, good salads and veggie dishes, fun kids' play area, daily 11:00 until late, Oberstrasse 45, tel. 06743/599-663).

Hotel Kranenturm is another good value with hearty meals and good main course salads (restaurant closed Nov–Feb, see hotel listing on page 200).

Wine-Tasting: Drop in on entertaining Fritz Bastian's **Weingut zum Grüner Baum** wine bar (also offers soup and cold cuts, good ambience indoors and out, just past Altes Haus, Mon–Wed and Fri from 13:00, Sat–Sun from 12:00, closed Thu and Feb–mid-March, tel. 06743/1208). As the president of the local vintner's club, Fritz is on a mission to give travelers an understanding of the subtle differences among the Rhine wines. Groups of 2–6 people pay €13.50 for a "carousel" of 15 glasses of 14 different white wines, one lonely red, and a basket of bread. Your mission: Team up with others with this book to rendezvous here after dinner. Spin the lazy Susan, share a common cup, and discuss the taste. Fritz insists, "After each wine, you must talk to each other."

For a fun, family-run wine shop and *Stube* in the town center, visit **Weingut Karl Heidrich** (on Oberstrasse, directly in front of Hotel Kranenturm), where American Susanne and German Markus proudly share their family's wine.

St. Goar

St. Goar is a classic Rhine town—its hulk of a castle overlooking a half-timbered shopping street and leafy riverside park busy with sightseeing ships and contented strollers. From the boat dock, the main drag—a

St. Goar

BURG RHEINFELS CASTLE

DCH

TRAIL TO BACHARACH

TRAIN STATION

TO BACHARACH + FRANKFURT

ULMENHOF TOWER

SCHLOSSBERG

BISMARCK

YOUTH HOSTEL

PHONE

OBER STRASSE

HEER-STRASSE

PHONE

HEER STRASSE

HIGHWAY 9

WC

HARBOR

P

PARK

BUS PARKING

TO BOPPARD + KOBLENZ

BR DOCK

FERRY

KD DOCK (EURAIL VALID)

RHINE RIVER

TO LORELEY

ST. GOARSHAUSEN

NOT TO SCALE
K·D DOCK TO CASTLE = 15 MIN. WALK

❶ Hotel am Markt
❷ Hotel Hauser
❸ Hotel Montag
❹ Hotel zur Post
❺ Frau Kurz rooms
❻ Tourist Office
❼ Post Office
❽ Supermarket

pedestrian mall without history—cuts through town before winding up to the castle. Rheinfels Castle, once the mightiest on the Rhine, is the single best Rhineland ruin to explore.

The helpful St. Goar **TI,** which books rooms and offers a free left-luggage service, is on the pedestrian street, three blocks from the K-D boat dock and train station (May–Oct Mon–Fri 8:00–12:30 & 14:00–17:00, Sat 10:00–12:00, closed Sun, Nov–April until 16:30 and closed Sat–Sun, sells *Rhine Guide from Mainz to Cologne;* from train station, go downhill around church and turn left on Heer Strasse; tel. 06741/383).

St. Goar's waterfront park is hungry for a picnic. The small Edeka **supermarket** on the main street is great for picnic fixings (Mon–Fri 8:00–18:30, Sat 8:00–13:00, closed Sun).

The friendly and helpful Montag family runs the Hotel Montag (Michael) and three **shops** (steins—Misha, Steiffs—Maria, and cuckoo clocks—Marion), all at the base of the castle hill road. The stein shop under the hotel has Rhine guides, fine steins, and copies of this year's *Rick Steves' Germany, Austria & Switzerland* guidebook. All three shops offer 10 percent off any of their souvenirs (including Hummels) for travelers with this book (€5 minimum purchase). On-the-spot VAT refunds cover about half your shipping costs (if you're not shipping, they'll give you VAT form to claim refund at airport). The hotel offers expensive coin-op **Internet** access (€8/hr).

SIGHTS

St. Goar's Rheinfels Castle

Sitting like a dead pit bull above St. Goar, this mightiest of Rhine castles rumbles with ghosts from its hard-fought past. Burg Rheinfels *was* huge—once the biggest castle on the Rhine (built in 1245). It withstood a siege of 28,000 French troops in 1692. But in 1797, the French revolutionary army destroyed it. The castle was used for ages as a quarry, and today—while still mighty—it's only a small fraction of its original size. This hollow but interesting shell offers your single best hands-on ruined-castle experience on the river.

Cost and Hours: €4, family card-€10, mid-March–Oct daily 9:00–18:00, last entry at 17:00, Nov–mid-March only Sat–Sun 11:00–17:00.

Tours and Information: Call in advance or gather 10 English-speaking tourists and beg to get an English tour—perhaps from Günther, the "last knight of Rheinfels" (tel. 06741/7753). Otherwise, follow my self-guided tour, below. The castle map is mediocre; the English booklet is better, with history and illustrations (€2). If it's damp, be careful of slippery stones. A handy WC (€0.30) is in the castle courtyard under the stairs to the restaurant entry.

Let There Be Light: If planning to explore the mine tunnels, bring a flashlight, buy a tiny one (€2.60 at entry), or do it by candlelight (museum sells candles with matches, €0.50).

Getting to the Castle: From St. Goar's boat dock or train station, take a steep 15-minute hike, a €5 taxi ride (€6 for a minibus, tel. 06741/7011), or the kitschy "tschu-tschu" tourist train (€2 one-way, €3 round-trip, 7 min to the top, 3/hr, daily 10:00–17:00, runs from square between station and dock, also stops at Hotel Montag, complete with lusty music, tel. 06741/2030).

Self-Guided Tour: Rather than wander aimlessly, visit the castle by following this tour: From the ticket gate, walk straight. Pass *Grosser Keller* on the left (where we'll end this tour), walk through an internal gate past the *zu den gedeckten Wehrgängen* sign on the right (where we'll pass later) uphill to the museum (daily 9:30–12:00 & 13:00–17:30) in the only finished room of the castle.

1. Museum and Castle Model: The seven-foot-tall carved stone immediately inside the door (marked *Keltische Säule von Pfalzfeld*)—a

St. Goar's Rheinfels Castle

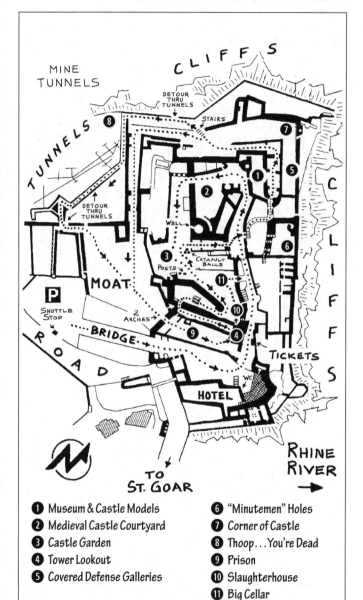

1. Museum & Castle Models
2. Medieval Castle Courtyard
3. Castle Garden
4. Tower Lookout
5. Covered Defense Galleries
6. "Minutemen" Holes
7. Corner of Castle
8. Thoop...You're Dead
9. Prison
10. Slaughterhouse
11. Big Cellar

tombstone from a nearby Celtic grave—is from 400 years before Christ. There were people here long before the Romans...and this castle. Find the old wooden library chair near the tombstone. If you smile sweetly, the man behind the desk may demonstrate—pull the back forward and it becomes stairs for getting to the highest shelves.

The sweeping castle history exhibit in the center of the room is well described in English. The massive fortification was the only Rhineland castle to withstand Louis XIV's assault during the 17th century. At the far end of the room is a model reconstruction of the castle (not the one with the toy soldiers) showing how much bigger it was before French revolutionary troops destroyed it in the 18th century. Study this. Find where you are (hint: Look for the tall tower). This was the living quarters of the original castle, which was only the smallest ring of buildings around the tiny central courtyard (13th century). The ramparts were added in the 14th century. By 1650, the fortress was largely complete. Ever since its destruction by the French in the late 18th century, it's had no military value. While no WWII bombs were wasted on this ruin, it served St. Goar as a quarry for generations. The basement of the museum shows the castle pharmacy and an exhibit of Rhine-region odds and ends, including tools and an 1830 loom. Don't miss the photos of ice-breaking on the Rhine—which, thanks to global warming, hasn't been necessary since 1963.

Exit the museum and walk 30 yards directly out, slightly uphill into the castle courtyard.

2. Medieval Castle Courtyard: Five hundred years ago, the entire castle circled this courtyard. The place was self-sufficient and ready for a siege with a bakery, pharmacy, herb garden, brewery, well (top of yard), and livestock. During peacetime, 300–600 people lived here; during a siege, there would be as many as 4,000. The walls were plastered and painted white. Bits of the original 13th-century plaster survive.

Continue through the courtyard, out *Erste Schildmauer,* turn left into the next courtyard, and walk straight to the two old, wooden, upright posts. Find the pyramid of stone catapult balls on your left.

3. Castle Garden: Catapult balls like these were too expensive not to recycle—they'd be retrieved after any battle. Across from the balls is a well—essential for any castle during the age of siegeing. Look in. The old posts are for the ceremonial baptizing of new members of the local trading league. While this guild goes back centuries, it's now a social club that fills this court with a huge wine party the third weekend of each September.

If weary, skip to #5; otherwise, climb the cobbled path up to the castle's best viewpoint—up where the German flag waves.

4. Highest Castle Tower Lookout: Enjoy a great view of the river, castle, and the forest that was once all part of this castle. Remember, the fortress once covered five times the land it does today. Notice how the other castles (across the river) don't poke above the top of the Rhine canyon. That would make them easy for invading armies to see.

Return to the catapult balls, walk down the road, go through the tunnel, veer left through the arch marked *zu den gedeckten Wehrgängen*, go down two flights of stairs, and stop at the top of the next staircase before turning left into the dark covered passageway. From here, we will begin a rectangular walk taking us completely around the perimeter of the castle. But first, take a look at the...

5. Covered Defense Galleries: Soldiers—the castle's "minutemen"—had a short commute: defensive positions on the outside, home in the holes in the wall you see below. Even though these living quarters were padded with straw, life was unpleasant. A peasant was lucky to live beyond age 45.

Now let's walk left through the dark gallery and to the corner of the castle, where you'll see a white painted arrow at eye level. Stand with your back to the arrow on the wall.

6. Corner of Castle: Look up. A three-story, half-timbered building originally rose beyond the highest stone fortification. The two stone tongues near the top just around the corner supported the toilet. (Insert your own joke here.) Turn around and face the wall. The crossbow slits below the white arrow were once steeper. The bigger hole on the riverside was for hot pitch.

Follow that white arrow along the outside to the next corner. Midway you'll pass stairs on the right leading down *zu den Minengängen* (sign on upper left). Adventurers with flashlights can detour here (see "Optional Detour—Into the Mine Tunnels," page 208). You may come out around the next corner. Otherwise, stay with me, walking level to the corner. At the corner, turn left.

7. Thoop...You're Dead. Look ahead at the smartly placed crossbow slit. While you're lying there, notice the stonework. The little round holes were for scaffolds used as they built up. They indicate this stonework is original. Notice also the fine stonework on the chutes. More boiling pitch...now you're toast, too.

Continue along the castle wall around the corner. At the railing, look up the valley and uphill where the sprawling fort stretched. Below, just outside the wall, is land where attackers would gather. The mine tunnels are under there, waiting to blow up any attackers (read below).

Continue along the perimeter, jog left, go down five steps and into an open field, and walk toward the wooden bridge. You may detour here into the passageway (on right) marked *13 Hals Graben.* The "old" wooden bridge is actually modern. Angle left through two arches (before the bridge) and through the rough entry to the *Verliess* (prison) on the left.

8. Prison: This is one of six dungeons. You walked through an entrance prisoners only dreamed of 400 years ago. They came and went through the little square hole in the ceiling. The holes in the walls supported timbers that thoughtfully gave as many as 15 residents something to sit on to keep them out of the filthy slop that gathered on the floor. Twice a day, they were given bread and water. Some prisoners actually survived longer than two years in here. While the town could torture and execute, the castle only had permission to imprison criminals in these dungeons. Consider this: According to town records, the two men who spent the most time down here—2.5 years each—died within three weeks of regaining their freedom. Perhaps after a diet of bread and water, feasting on meat and wine was simply too much.

Continue through the next arch, under the white arrow, and turn left and walk 30 yards to the *Schlachthaus*.

9. Slaughterhouse: Any proper castle was prepared to survive a six-month siege. With 4,000 people, that's a lot of provisions. The cattle that lived within the walls were slaughtered in this room. The castle's mortar was congealed here (by packing all the organic waste from the kitchen into kegs and sealing it). Notice the drainage gutters. "Running water" came through from drains built into the walls (to keep the mortar dry and therefore strong...and less smelly).

Back outside, climb the modern stairs to the left. A skinny, dark passage (yes, that's the one) leads you into the...

10. Big Cellar: This *Grosser Keller* was a big pantry. When the castle was smaller, this was the original moat—you can see the rough lower parts of the wall. The original floor was 13 feet deeper. The drawbridge rested upon the stone nubs on the left. When the castle expanded, the moat became this cellar. Halfway up the walls on the entrance side of the room, square holes mark spots where timbers made a storage loft, perhaps filled with grain. In the back, an arch leads to the wine cellar (sometimes blocked off) where finer wine was kept. Part of a soldier's pay was wine...table wine. This wine was kept in a single 180,000-liter stone barrel (that's 47,550 gallons), which generally lasted about 18 months.

The count owned the surrounding farmland. Farmers got to keep 20 percent of their production. Later, in more liberal feudal times, the nobility let them keep 40 percent. Today, the German government leaves the workers with 60 percent...and provides a few more services.

You're free. Climb out, turn right, and leave. For coffee on a great view terrace, visit the Rheinfels Castle Hotel, opposite the entrance (WC at base of steps).

Optional Detour—Into the Mine Tunnels: To protect their castle around 1600, the Rheinfellers cleverly booby-trapped the land just outside their walls by building tunnels topped with thin slate roofs and packed with explosives. By detonating the explosives when under attack, they could kill hundreds of invaders. In 1626, a handful of underground

Protestant Germans blew 300 Catholic Spaniards to—they figured—hell. You're welcome to wander through a set of never-blown-up tunnels. But be warned: It's 600 feet long, assuming you make no wrong turns; it's pitch-dark, muddy, and claustrophobic, with confusing dead-ends; and you'll never get higher than a deep crouch. It cannot be done without a light (flashlights available at entrance—see above). At stop #6 of the above tour, follow the stairs on the right leading down *zu den Minengängen* (sign on upper left).

The *Fuchsloch* sign welcomes you to the foxhole. Walk level (take no stairs) past the first steel railing (where you hope to emerge later) to the second steel railing. Climb down. The "highway" in this foxhole is three feet high. The ceiling may be painted with a white line indicating the correct path. Don't venture into the narrower side aisles. These were once filled with the gunpowder. After a small decline, take the second right. At the T-intersection, go right (uphill). After about 10 feet, go left. Take the next right and look for a light at the end of the tunnel. Head up a rocky incline under the narrowest part of the tunnel and you'll emerge at that first steel railing. The stairs on the right lead to freedom. Cross the field, walk under the bigger archway, and continue uphill toward the old wooden bridge. Angle left through two arches (before the bridge) and through the rough entry to the *Verliess* (prison) on the left. Rejoin the tour here at stop #8.

SLEEPING

(country code: 49, area code: 06741)

$$$ **Hotel Montag,** with 28 rooms, is on the castle end of town just across the street from the world's largest free-hanging cuckoo clock. Manfred and Maria Montag and their son Mike speak New Yorkish. Even though the hotel gets a lot of bus tours, it's friendly, laid-back, and comfortable (Sb-€35–45, Db-€70–80, Tb-€90–100, coin-op Internet access-€8/hr, Heer Strasse 128, tel. 06741/1629, fax 06741/2086, hotelmontag@01019freenet.de). Check out their adjacent crafts shop (heavy on beer steins).

$$$ **Rheinfels Castle Hotel** is the town splurge. Actually part of the castle but an entirely new building, this luxury 57-room place is good for those with money and a car (Db-€130–154 depending on river views and balconies, extra bed €34, elevator, free parking, indoor pool and sauna, dress-up restaurant, Schlossberg 47, tel. 06741/8020, fax 06741/802-802, www.schlosshotel-rheinfels.de, info@burgrheinfels.de).

$$ **Hotel am Markt,** well-run by Herr and Frau Velich, is rustic with all the modern comforts. It features a hint of antler with a pastel flair, 18 bright rooms, and a good restaurant where the son does the cooking. It's a good value and a stone's throw from the boat dock and train station (S-€35, Sb-€43, standard Db-€59, bigger riverview Db-€69,

Tb-€82, Qb-€88, 20 percent cheaper off-season, closed Nov–Feb, Am Markt 1, tel. 06741/1689, fax 06741/1721, www.hotelammarkt1.de, hotel.am.markt@gmx.de). Rental bikes are available to guests (€5/day).

$$ **Hotel Hauser,** facing the boat dock, is another good deal, warmly run by another Frau Velich. Its 12 rooms sit over a fine restaurant (S-€21.50, D-€45, Db-€50, great Db with Rhine-view balconies-€56, show this book and pay cash to get these prices, Db cheaper off-season, costs more with credit card, small bathrooms, restaurant, Heer Strasse 77, tel. 06741/333, fax 06741/1464, www.hotelhauser.de, hotelhauser@t-online.de).

$$ **Hotel zur Post,** with creaky parquet floors and 12 forgettable, well-worn rooms, is a reasonable value a block off the riverfront (Sb-€37, Db-€62, a block from the station at Bahnhofstrasse 3, tel. 06741/ 339, fax 06741/2708, www.hotelzurpost-online.de, zurposthotel@gmx.de, family Bergweiler).

$ **Frau Kurz** offers St. Goar's best *Zimmer* deal, with a breakfast terrace, garden, fine view, and homemade marmalade (S-€22, D-€36–38, Db-€43, showers-€2.60, more for 1-night stays, no CC, free and easy parking, confirm prices, honor your reservation or call to cancel, Ulmenhof 11, tel. & fax 06741/459, some English spoken). It's a steep five-minute hike from the train station (exit left from station, take immediate left at the yellow phone booth, pass under tracks to paved path, go up stairs and follow zigzag path to Ulmenhof, *Zimmer* is just past tower).

$ **St. Goar Hostel,** the big beige building under the castle (on road to castle, veer right just after railroad bridge) has a 22:00 curfew (but you can borrow the key) and hearty €6 dinners (S-€15, dorm beds-€12, up to 12 beds per room, includes breakfast, no CC, open all day, check-in preferred 17:00–18:00 & 19:00–20:00, Bismarckweg 17, tel. 06741/388, fax 06741/2689, jh-st-goar@djh-info.de).

EATING

Hotel am Markt serves good traditional meals (with plenty of game and fish) at fair prices (€5–16) with good atmosphere and service. For your Rhine splurge, walk, taxi, or drive up to **Rheinfels Castle Hotel** for its incredible view terrace in an elegant setting (€8–15 dinners, daily 18:30–21:15, reserve a table by the window, see hotel listing above).

TRANSPORTATION CONNECTIONS— RHINE VALLEY

Milk-run trains stop at all Rhine towns each hour starting as early as 6:00. Koblenz, Boppard, St. Goar, Bacharach, Bingen, and Mainz are each about 15 minutes apart. From Koblenz to Mainz takes 75 minutes.

To get a faster big train, go to Mainz (for points east and south) or Koblenz (for points north, west, and along Mosel). Train info: tel. 01805-996-633.

From Mainz to: Bacharach/St. Goar (hrly, 1 hr), **Cochem** (hrly, 2.5 hrs, change in Koblenz), **Köln** (3/hr, 90 min, change in Koblenz), **Baden-Baden** (hrly, 1.5 hrs), **Munich** (hrly, 4 hrs), **Frankfurt** (3/hr, 45 min), **Frankfurt Airport** (4/hr, 25 min).

From Koblenz to: Köln (4/hr, 1 hr), **Berlin** (2/hr, 5.5 hrs, up to 2 changes), **Frankfurt** (3/hr, 1.5 hrs, 1 change), **Cochem** (2/hr, 50 min), **Trier** (2/hr, 2 hrs), **Brussels** (12/day, 4 hrs, change in Köln), **Amsterdam** (12/day, 4.5 hrs, up to 5 changes).

From Frankfurt to: Bacharach (hrly, 1.5 hrs, change in Mainz; first train to Bacharach departs at 6:00, last train at 20:45), **Koblenz** (hrly, 90 min, changes in Mannheim or Wiesbaden), **Rothenburg** (hrly, 3 hrs, transfers in Würzburg and Steinach), **Würzburg** (hrly, 2 hrs), **Nürnberg** (hrly, 2 hrs), **Munich** (hrly, 4 hrs, 1 change), **Amsterdam** (8/day, 5 hrs, up to 3 changes), **Paris** (9/day, 6.5 hrs, up to 3 changes).

From Bacharach to: Frankfurt Airport (hrly, 1.5 hrs, change in Mainz, first train to Frankfurt airport departs about 5:40, last train 21:30).

MOSEL VALLEY

The misty Mosel is what some visitors hoped the Rhine would be—peaceful, sleepy, romantic villages slipped between the steep vineyards and the river; fine wine; a sprinkling of castles (Burg Eltz is tops); and lots of friendly *Zimmer*. Boat, train, and car traffic here is a trickle compared to the roaring Rhine. While the swan-speckled Mosel moseys 300 miles from France's Vosges mountains to Koblenz, where it dumps into the Rhine, the most scenic piece of the valley lies between the towns of Bernkastel-Kues and Cochem. I'd savor only this section. Cochem and Trier (see next chapter) are easy day trips from each other (1 hr by train, 55 miles by car). Cochem is the handiest home base unless you want the peace of Beilstein.

Throughout the region on summer weekends and during the fall harvest, wine festivals with oompah bands, dancing, and colorful costumes are powered by good food and wine. You'll find a wine festival in some nearby village any weekend, June through September. The tourist season lasts from April through October. Things close down tight through the winter.

Look for the booklet *The Castles of the Moselle* (€3.80, at local TIs), with information on castles from Koblenz to Trier (including Burg Eltz, Cochem, and Metternich in Beilstein). The booklet not only has historical and structural information, but also some drawings of what the now-ruined castles looked like originally.

Getting around the Mosel Valley

By Train and Bus: The train zips you to Cochem, Bullay, or Trier in a snap. Bullay has bus connections with Zell (nearly hrly, 10 min) and with Beilstein (4/day). Cochem has more frequent bus connections with Beilstein (bus #8060, hrly, less on weekends, 20 min, last bus departs Beilstein about 18:30). A one-way taxi from Cochem to Beilstein costs about €15. Pick up bus schedules at train stations or TIs.

Mosel Valley

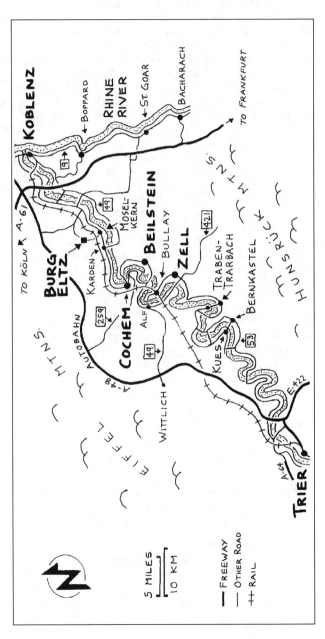

By Boat: Daily departures on the Undine-Kolb Line allow you to cruise the most scenic stretch between Cochem, Beilstein, and Zell (tel. 02673/1515, www.kolb-mosel.de): between **Cochem and Zell** (1–2/day, May–Oct, but none on Fri and Mon May–June, 3 hrs, €14 one-way, €20 round-trip), between **Cochem and Beilstein** (5/day, 1 hr, €8 one-way, €11 round-trip), and between **Zell and Beilstein** (1–2/day May–Oct, but none on Fri and Mon May–June, 2 hrs, €11 one-way, €15 round-trip). You can also take the boat from **Cochem to Karden**, near Burg Eltz (3/day, daily mid-July–mid-Aug; Wed and Sat–Sun only May–mid-July & mid-Aug–Oct, 45 min, €7 one-way, €10 round-trip). To get from Karden to Burg Eltz, choose between a long hike or a taxi ride (see "Getting to Burg Eltz," page 219).

The K-D (Köln-Düsseldorfer) line sails once a day in each direction, but only between Cochem and Koblenz (mid-June–Sept daily, May–mid-June and most of Oct Fri–Mon only, none in winter, Koblenz to Cochem 9:45–15:00, or Cochem to Koblenz 15:40–20:00, free with consecutive-day Eurailpass or a dated Eurail Flexipass, Eurail Selectpass, or German railpass, uses up a day of a Flexipass, tel. 02671/980-023, www.k-d.com). In early to mid-June, the locks close for 10 days of annual maintenance, and no boats run between Cochem, Koblenz, Beilstein, and Zell. With all the locks, Mosel cruises can be pretty slow.

By Car: The easygoing Mosel Wine Route turns anyone into a relaxed Sunday driver. Pick up a local map at a TI or service station. Koblenz and Trier are linked by two-lane roads that run along both riverbanks. While riverside roads are a delight, the river is very windy and shortcuts overland can save serious time—especially between Burg Eltz and Beilstein (see "Getting to Burg Eltz," page 219) and from the Mosel to the Rhine (note the Brodenback–Boppard shortcut). Koblenz, Cochem, and Trier have car-rental agencies.

By Bike: Biking along the Mosel is the rage among Germans. You can rent bikes in most Mosel towns (see village listings below). A fine bike path follows the river (with some bits still sharing the road with cars) from Koblenz to Zell. From Cochem, allow an hour to Beilstein and 2.5 hours for the full trip to Zell. Many pedal one way and relax with a return cruise.

By Ferry: About a dozen car-and-passenger ferries *(Fähre)* cross the Mosel between Koblenz and Trier. These are marked AF for auto and PF for pedestrian on the *Moselle Wine Road/Mosellauf* brochure.

Cochem

With a majestic castle and picturesque medieval streets, Cochem is the very touristic hub of this part of the river. For accommodations, see "Sleeping," page 216.

Tourist Information

The information-packed TI is by the bridge at the main bus stop. Most of the pamphlets (free map with town walk, town history flier) are kept behind the desk—ask. Their thorough 24-hour room listing in the window comes with a free phone connection. The TI also has information on special events, wine-tastings held by local vintners, public transportation to Burg Eltz, area hikes, and the informative €2.60 *Moselle Wine Road (Mosellauf)* brochure. The *Tips and Information from A to Z* brochure (often out of stock) lists everything from car rental agencies to saunas and babysitters (May–Oct Mon–Sat 9:00–17:00, Fri until 18:00, also Sun 10:00–12:00 in July–Oct, off-season closed weekends and at lunch, tel. 02671/60040, www.cochem.de).

Arrival in Cochem

Make a hard right out of the train station (lockers available, €1-2/day, no WC) and walk about 10 minutes to the town center and TI (just past the bus lanes on your left under the bridge).

Drivers can park near the bridge. To get to the main square *(Markt)* and colorful medieval town center, continue under the bridge (€0.30 WC), then angle right and follow Bernstrasse.

Helpful Hints

The Edeka **supermarket** is on Ravenestrasse, a five-minute walk from the TI toward the train station. For **Internet access,** try COCbit-Kommunikation (€5/hr, Mon–Fri 10:00–18:00, Sat 10:00–13:00, closed Sun, on street facing river across from boat ticket booths, Mosel-promenade 7, tel. 02671/211). The only **launderette** in town is across the bridge in a little mall near the youth hostel. Cochem's biggest **wine festival** is held the last weekend in August.

SIGHTS

Cochem Castle—This pointy castle is the work of overly imaginative 19th-century restorers (€4, mid-March–mid-Nov daily 9:00–17:00, closed mid-Nov–mid-Dec & Jan–mid-March, open last half of Dec, 20-min walk from Cochem, follow one of the frequent 40-min German-language tours while reading English explanation sheets or gather 12 English speakers and call a day ahead to schedule an English tour, tel. 02671/255, www.reichsburg-cochem.de). A bus shuttles castle-seekers between the bridge near the TI and the road below the castle (€2 one-way, 2/hr, walk last 10 min uphill to castle).

Town and River Activities—Stroll pleasant paths along the idyllic riverbank, play "life-size chess," or just grab a bench and watch Germany at play.

For great views, you could ride the *Sesselbahn* chairlift (open April–mid-Nov, €4 one-way, €5.50 round-trip, www.cochemer-sesselbahn.de) or **hike** up to the *Aussichtspunkt* (the cross—Pinnerkreuz—on the hill opposite the castle, find trailhead behind train station parking lot).

A little yellow **train** does a sightseeing loop (€2, 2/hour, 30 min).

You can rent **bikes** from the K-D boat kiosk at the dock (€4/4 hrs, €7/full day, May–Oct only) or from Kreutz behind the pumps at the Shell station at Ravenestrasse 42 (Mon–Fri 9:00–18:00, Sat 9:00–13:00, closed Sun, open year-round, €4/4 hrs, €7/full day, includes helmet, no deposit required, just your passport number, tel. 02671/91131). Consider taking a bike on the boat and riding back.

The Tanz Party mit Live Musik **cruise** is popular with German vacationers (€13.40, 20:15–22:30, nightly mid-July–Aug, Tue and Sat May–mid-July, and Tue, Thu, and Sat Sept–Oct, 2-man schmaltzy band, tel. 02671/7387). For Mosel cruises, see "Getting around the Mosel Valley," above.

SLEEPING

(country code: 49, area code: 02671)

August is very tight, with various festivals and generally inflated prices.

$$$ Rustic **Hotel Lohspeicher,** just off the main square on a street with tiny steps, is for those who want a real hotel—high prices—in the thick of things. Its nine high-ceilinged rooms have modern comforts (Sb-€39, Db-€78, about 10 percent higher mid-July–mid-Nov, elevator, breakfast in a fine stone-and-timber room, restaurant, parking-€4.50/day, closed Feb, Obergasse 1, tel. 02671/3976, fax 02671/1772, www.lohspeicher.de, service@lohspeicher.de, Ingo SE).

$$$ **Hotel am Hafen,** across the river, offers views of Cochem (some rooms have balconies; Db-€80–120, €10 extra for 1-night stays, air-con, Uferstrasse 3, tel. 02671/97720, fax 02671/977-227, www.hotel-am-hafen.de, hotel-am-hafen@t-online.de).

$ **Weingut Rademacher** rents six beautiful ground-floor rooms. Wedged between vineyards and train tracks, with a pleasant garden and a big common kitchen, it's a great value. Charming hostess Andrea and her husband Hermann (both SE) give tours of their wine cellar when time permits (earlier is better); guests enter for free. If there's no tour, visitors are welcome to taste the wine (Sb-€26.50, Db on train side-€43, Db on vineyard side-€49, less for 3 nights, family deals, non-smoking, free parking, go right from station on Ravenestrasse, turn right on Pinnerstrasse, walk under tracks and curve right to Pinnerstrasse 10, tel. 02671/4164, fax 02671/91341).

$ **Haus Andreas** has 10 clean, modern rooms at fair prices (Sb-

SLEEP CODE

(€1 = about $1.10)

Sleep Code: **S** = Single, **D** = Double/Twin, **T** = Triple, **Q** = Quad, **b** = bathroom, **s** = shower only, **no CC** = Credit Cards not accepted, **SE** = Speaks English, **NSE** = No English. Unless otherwise noted, credit cards are accepted, English is spoken, and breakfast is included.

To help you sort easily through these listings, I've divided the rooms into three categories based on the price for a standard double room with bath:

$$$ **Higher Priced**—Most rooms €70 or more.
$$ **Moderately Priced**—Most rooms between €50–70.
$ **Lower Priced**—Most rooms €50 or less.

€23, Db-€36–40, Tb-€54, no CC, Schlossstrasse 9, reception is often across the street in shop at #16, tel. 02671/1370 or 02671/5155, fax 02671/1370, Frau Pellny S a little E). From the main square, take Herrenstrasse; after a block, angle right up the steep hill on Schlossstrasse.

$ Cochem's **hostel,** just opened in 2003, is a huge family-friendly complex with 142 beds, picnic tables, grill pit, playground, game room, bar, restaurant, and a sundeck over the Mosel (dorm bed–€17, Db-€44, more for non-members, includes sheets and breakfast, half- and full-board options available at extra cost, Klottenstrasse 9, tel. 02671/8633, fax 02671/8568, jh-cochem@djh-info.de).

EATING

Zum Stüffje is a traditional half-timbered *Weinstube* with simple food and veggie options (Wed–Mon 11:30–14:00 & 17:30–21:00, closed Tue, Oberbachstrasse 14, tel. 02671/7260).

Gaststätte Noss, with fine food served inside or out, is open later than most other restaurants (closed Thu, Moselpromenade 4, tel. 02671/7067).

Locals go to "Arthur's place," officially named **Alte Gutschänke,** for a glass of wine in a cozy cellar seated at long wooden get-to-know-your-neighbor tables (extensive wine list and basic food, Mon–Fri from 18:00, Sat–Sun from 14:00, open Easter–Oct, closed winter, just up the hill at Schlossstrasse 6, tel. 02671/8950, Arthur SE).

TRANSPORTATION CONNECTIONS

By train to: Koblenz (hrly, 60 min), **Bullay** (near Zell, hrly, 10 min), and **Trier** (hrly, 60 min). Train info: tel. 01805-996-633, Cochem train info: tel. 02671/240. Bus info: tel. 02671/8976.

Burg Eltz

My favorite castle in all of Europe lurks in a mysterious forest. It's been left intact for 700 years and is furnished throughout as it was 500 years ago. Thanks to smart diplomacy and clever marriages, Burg Eltz was never destroyed. (It survived one 5-year siege.) It's been in the Eltz family for 820 years.

Eltz means stream. The first *Burg* on the *Eltz* (castle on the stream) appeared in the 12th century to protect a trade route. By 1472, the castle looked like it does today, with the homes of three big land-lord families gathered around a tiny courtyard within one formidable fortification. Today, the excellent 45-minute tour winds you through two of those homes, while the third remains the fortified quarters of the Eltz family. The elderly countess of Eltz—whose family goes back 33 generations here (you'll see a photo of her family)—enjoys flowers. Each week for 40 years, she's had grand arrangements adorn the public castle rooms.

It was a comfortable castle for its day: 80 rooms made cozy by 40 fireplaces and wall-hanging tapestries. Its 20 toilets were automatically flushed by a rain drain. The delightful chapel is on a lower floor. Even though "no one should live above God," this chapel's placement was acceptable because it fills a bay window—which floods the delicate Gothic space with light. The three families met—working out common problems as if sharing a condo—in the large "conference room." A carved jester and a rose look down on the big table, reminding those who gathered that they were free to discuss anything ("fool's freedom"— jesters could say anything to the king), but nothing discussed could leave the room (the "rose of silence"). In the bedroom, have fun with the suggestive decor: the jousting relief carved into the canopy, and the fertile and phallic figures hiding in the lusty green wall paintings.

Near the exit, the €2.50 treasury fills the four higgledy-piggledy floors of a cellar with the precious, eccentric, and historic mementos of this family that once helped elect the Holy Roman Emperor and, later, owned a sizable chunk of Croatia (Hapsburg favors).

Cost, Hours, Information: €6 castle entry, plus €2.50 for treasury, April–Oct daily from 9:30 with the last tour departing at 17:30, closed Nov–March, tel. 02672/950-500, www.burg-eltz.de.

Tours: The only way to see the castle is with a 45-minute tour

Burg Eltz Area

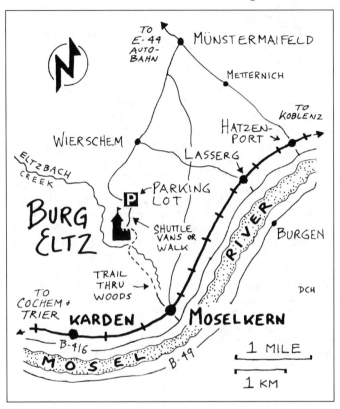

(included in entry price). German tours go constantly (with helpful English fact sheets, €0.50). Guides speak English and thoughtfully collect English speakers into their own tours—well worth waiting for (never more than 20 minutes). It doesn't hurt to call ahead to see if an English tour is scheduled—or organize your own by corralling 20 English speakers in the inner courtyard, then push the red button on the white porch and politely beg for an English guide.

Getting to Burg Eltz: By **train,** Get off at the Moselkern station midway between Cochem and Koblenz (hrly trains, no lockers at station, but if you ask kindly, clerk will store luggage in office—ring at the window if necessary). Leaving the station, exit right and follow Burg Eltz signs for about 20 minutes up, down, and inland along a residential street (signs are sparse, but have faith and stay on the main road). Then take the marked trail (slippery when wet, slightly steep near end). It's a pleasant 60-minute hike between the station and castle through a pine forest where sparrows carry crossbows, and maidens, disguised as falling leaves, whisper "watch out."

Alternatively, you can **taxi** from Cochem (30 min, €40 one-way for up to 4 people, Cochem taxi tel. 02671/8080) and then enjoy the hike downhill back to the train station in Moselkern. A cheaper taxi option is to train to either Moselkern or Karden, then call a cab from there (15 min, €18 from Moselkern, €23 from Karden, taxi tel. 02672/1407).

A more romantic option is to take a **boat** from Cochem to Karden, then choose between a hike up to the castle (ask boat crew for hiking directions, allow 90 min) or a taxi (see above).

The easiest option is by **car**: From Koblenz, leave the river at Hatzenport following the white Burg Eltz signs through the towns of Münstermaifeld and Wierschem. From Cochem, following the Münstermaifeld signs from Moselkern saves about 10 minutes. (Note that the Eltz signs at Moselkern lead to a trailhead for the hour-long hike to the castle. To drive directly to the castle, ignore the Eltz signs until you reach Münstermaifeld.) The castle parking lot (€1.50/day, daily 9:00–18:00) is 1.25 miles past Wierschem. From the lot, hike 10 minutes downhill to the castle or wait (maximum 10 min) for the red castle shuttle bus (€1.50 one-way). There are three Burg Eltz parking lots; only this lot (1.25 miles south of Wierschem) is close enough for an easy walk. Another option is to park at the Moselkern station (free) and follow the park-and-walk signs (see above).

If driving between Burg Eltz and Beilstein or Zell, you'll save 30 minutes with this **shortcut**: from Eltz, cross the river at Karden, go through town, and bear right at the swimming pool (direction Bruttig-Fankel). This overland route deposits you in Bruttig, a scenic riverside three-mile drive from Beilstein (21 miles from Zell).

Beilstein

Upstream from Cochem is the quaintest of all Mosel towns. Beilstein (BILE-shtine) is Cinderella-land—extremely peaceful except for its territorial swans. Its 180 residents run 30 or so hotels and eateries. Herr Nahlen rents bikes for pleasant riverside rides (ring bell at Bachstrasse 47, €6/day, tel. 02673/1840). Parking is free in any space along the riverside road you can find. For accommodations, see "Sleeping," page 222.

Beilstein has no real tourist office, but several cafés advertise that they have town info. Buses go about hourly from Beilstein to Cochem (see "Getting around the Mosel Valley," page 212).

INTRODUCTORY BEILSTEIN WALK

Explore the narrow lanes, ancient wine cellar, resident swans, and ruined castle by following this short walk.

1. Beilstein's Riverfront: Stand where the village hits the river. In 1963, the big road and the Mosel locks were built, making the river so peaceful today. Before then, access to Beilstein was limited to a tiny one-way lane and the small ferry. The cables that tether the ferry once allowed the motorless craft to go back and forth powered only by the current and an angled rudder. Today, it shuttles people (€1), bikes, and cars constantly from 9:00 to 18:00. The campground across the river is typical of German campgrounds—80 percent of its customers set up their trailers and tents at Easter and use them as summer homes until October, when the regular floods chase them away for the winter. If you stood where you are now through the winter, you'd have cold water up to your crotch five times. Look inland. The Earl of Beilstein—who ruled from his castle above town—built the Altes Zollhaus in 1634 to levy tolls from river traffic. Today, the castle is a ruin, the once-mighty monastery (see the big church high on the left) is down to one monk, and the town's economy is based only on wine and tourists.

Beilstein's tranquility is thanks to Germany's WWI loss. This war cost Germany the region of Alsace (now part of France). Before World War I, the Koblenz–Trier train line—which connects Alsace to Germany—was the busiest in Germany. It tunnels through the grape-laden hill across the river in what was the longest train tunnel in Germany. The construction of a supplemental line destined to follow the riverbank (like the lines that crank up the volume on the Rhine) was stopped in 1914 and, since Alsace went to France in 1918, the plans were scuttled.

Follow Bachstrasse into town. You'll notice blue plaques on the left marking the high-water *(Hochwasser)* points of historic floods.

At the first corner, Furst-Metternich Strasse leads left to the monastery (climb stairs marked the *Klostertreppe*). While its population is down to one Carmelite, Rome maintains an oversized-for-this-little-town church that runs a view restaurant.

Bachstrasse—literally "creek street"—continues straight through Beilstein, covering up the brook that once flowed through town providing a handy disposal service 24/7. Today, Bachstrasse is lined by wine cellars. The only way for a small local vintner to make any decent money these days is to sell his wine directly to customers in inviting little places like these. Your first right leads to the...

2. Market Square: For centuries, neighboring farmers sold their goods on Marktplatz. The *Zehnthaus* (tithe house) was the village IRS, where locals would pay one-tenth *(Zehnte)* of their produce to their landlord (either the Church or the earl). Pop into the Zehnthauskeller.

Packed with peasants' offerings 400 years ago, it's now packed with vaulted medieval ambience. It's fun at night for candlelit wine-tasting, soup and cold cuts, and schmaltzy music (live Fri and Sat). The Bürgerhaus (above the fountain) had nothing to do with medieval fast food. First the village church, then the *Bürger*'s (like a mayor) residence, today it's *the* place for a town party or wedding. Haus Lipmann (on the riverside, now a recommended hotel and restaurant—see "Sleeping," below) dates from 1727. It was built by the earl's family as a residence after the French destroyed his castle. Haus Lipmann's main dining hall was once the knights' hall. The stepped lane leads uphill (past the Zehnthaus, follow signs for Burgruine Metternich) to...

3. Beilstein's Castle: Beilstein once rivaled Cochem as the most powerful town on this part of the Mosel. Its castle (Burg Metternich) is a sorry ruin today, but those who hike up are rewarded with a postcard Mosel view and a chance to hike even higher to the top of its lone surviving tower (€2, daily 9:00–18:00, July-Aug until 19:00, closes earlier off-season, view café/restaurant).

For more exercise and an even better view, continue up behind the castle and follow the road that leads uphill. A hundred yards above the castle (take the left fork), you'll find the ultimate "castle–river bend–carpets of vineyards" photo stop. The derelict roadside vineyard is a sign of recent times—the younger generation is abandoning the family plots, opting out of all that hard winemaking work. A surprising sight—the most evocative Jewish cemetery this side of Prague *(Judenfriedhof)*—is 200 yards farther up the road.

During the 700 years leading up to 1942, Beilstein hosted a Jewish community. As in the rest of Europe, wealthy Jews could buy citizenship and enjoy all the protections afforded to residents. These *Schutzjuden,* or "protected Jews," were shielded from the often crude and brutal "justice" of the Middle Ages. In 1840, 25 percent of Beilstein's 300 inhabitants were Jewish. But no payment could shield this community from Hitler—so there are no Jews in today's Beilstein. (A small Jewish community in Koblenz maintains this lovely cemetery.)

From here, you can return to the castle gate, ring the bell *(Klingel)* and show your ticket to get back in and retrace your steps, or continue on the road, which curves and leads downhill (a gravel path at the next bend on the left leads back into town).

SLEEPING

(country code: 49, area code: 02673)

Between Cochem and Zell, cozier Beilstein is very small and quiet (no train; hourly buses to nearby Cochem, fewer buses on weekends, 15 min; taxi to Cochem-€15). Many hotels shut down from mid-November through March.

$$$ Hotel Haus Lipmann is your chance to live in a medieval mansion with hot showers and TVs. A prizewinner for atmosphere, it's been in the Lipmann family for 200 years. The creaky wooden staircase and the elegant dining hall, with long wooden tables surrounded by antlers, chandeliers, and feudal weapons, will get you in the mood for your castle sightseeing, but the riverside terrace may mace your momentum (Sb-€75, Db-€85, no CC, 5 rooms, closed Nov–April, Marktplatz 3, tel. 02673/1573, fax 02673/1521, www.hotel-haus-lipmann.com, hotel.haus.lipmann@t-online.de). The entire Lipmann family—Marion and Jonas, their hardworking son David, and his wife Anja (all SE)—hustles for its guests.

Marion's brother Joachim Lipmann (SE) runs two hotels of his own: The half-timbered, riverfront **$$$ Altes Zollhaus Gästezimmer** packs all the comforts into eight tight, bright, and modern rooms (Sb-€45, Db-€60, deluxe Db-€80, no CC, closed Nov–March, tel. 02673/1850, fax 02673/1287, www.hotel-lipmann.de, lipmann@t-online.de). **$$$ Hotel Am Klosterberg** is a big modern place at the extremely quiet top of town (up the main street 200 yards inland) with 16 comfortable rooms (Db-€60–80, Auf dem Teich 8, same contact info as Altes Zollhaus).

$$ Hotel Gute Quelle offers half-timbers, a good restaurant, and 13 comfortable rooms, plus seven in an annex across the street (Sb-€35, D-€52, Db-€60, less for longer stays, closed Dec–March, Marktplatz 34, tel. 02673/1437, fax 02673/1399, www.hotel-gute-quelle.de, helpful Susan speaks Irish).

$ The comfortable **Gasthaus Winzerschenke an der Klostertreppe** is a great value, right in the tiny heart of town (5 rooms, Sb-€26, Db-€44, bigger Db-€54, no CC, discount for 2-night stays, closed Nov–Easter, go up main street and take second left onto Furst-Metternich-Strasse, reception in restaurant, tel. 02673/1354, fax 02673/962-371, www.winzerschenke-beilstein.de, Frau Sausen NSE, her son Christian SE).

EATING

You'll have no problem finding a characteristic dining room or a relaxing riverview terrace. **Restaurant Haus Lipmann** serves good fresh food with daily specials on a glorious leafy riverside terrace (daily 10:00–23:00). The **Zehnthauskeller** on the Marktplatz is *the* place for wine-tasting with soup, cold plates, and lively *Schlager* (kitschy German folk-pop) while old locals on holiday sit under a dark medieval vault (Tue–Sun 11:00–23:00, closed Mon, off-season until 18:00).

Zell

Peaceful, with a fine riverside promenade, a pedestrian bridge over the water, and plenty of *Zimmer,* Zell makes a good overnight stop. Zell has a long pedestrian zone filled with colorful shops, restaurants, and *Weinstuben* (wine bars). A fun oompah folk band plays on weekend evenings on the main square, making evenings here a delight.

The **TI** is on the pedestrian street, four blocks downriver from the pedestrian bridge (Mon–Fri 8:00–12:30 & 13:30–17:00, Sat 10:00–13:00, closed Sun, off-season also closed Sat, tel. 06542/4031, www.zell-mosel .de). The little **Wein und Heimatmuseum** features Mosel history (same building as TI, Wed and Sat 15:00–17:00). For a village **view,** walk up to the medieval wall's gatehouse and through the cemetery to the old munitions tower. Frau Klaus rents **bikes** (€10/day, 1.25 miles out of town, downstream at Hauptstrasse 5, tel. 06542/2589, NSE). Berliner Kaffe-Kännchen offers **Internet access** (2 terminals, €6.80/hr, Mon–Tue and Thu–Fri 8:00–18:30, Sat until 18:00, Sun 14:00–18:00, closed Wed, across pedestrian bridge opposite bus stop at Baldninen Strasse 107, tel. 06542/5450).

Locals know Zell for its Schwarze Katze (Black Cat) wine. Peter Weis (SE) runs the F. J. Weis winery and gives an entertaining and free tour of his 40,000-bottle-per-year **wine cellar.** The clever 20-minute tour starts at 17:00 (call ahead to reserve, open daily April–Nov 10:30–19:00, closed Dec–March but call and they might fit you in for a tasting, tel. 06542/41398); buy a bottle or two to keep this fine tour going. A blue flag marks his *Weinkeller* south of town, 200 yards past the bridge toward Bernkastel, riverside at Notenau 30.

SLEEPING

(country code: 49, area code: 06542)

Zell's hotels are a disappointment, but its private homes are a fine value. The owners speak almost no English and discount their rates if you stay more than one night. They don't take reservations long in advance for one-night stays; just call a day ahead.

Trains go hourly from Cochem or Trier to Bullay, where the bus takes you to little Zell (€1.50, 2/hr, 10 min; bus stop is across street from Bullay train station, check yellow MB schedule for times, last bus at about 19:00). The central Zell stop is called Lindenplatz.

$$$ Hotel zum Grünen Kranz is the place if you're looking for room service, a sauna, a pool, and an elevator (32 rooms, Sb-€45–60, Db-€86–120, non-smoking rooms, Balduinstrasse 13, tel. 06542/98610, fax 06542/986-180, www.zum-gruenen-kranz.de). In the annex across the street, they rent 10 immense apartments (prices on request).

$$ Hotel Ratskeller, just off the main square on a pedestrian street, rents 14 sharp rooms with tile flooring and fair rates (Sb-€42, Db-€72, cheaper Nov–mid-April, above a pizzeria, Balduinstrasse 36, tel. 06542/98620, fax 06542/986-244, ratskeller-zellmosel@web.de, Gardi SE).

$$ Weinhaus Mayer, a stressed-out old pension, is perfectly central with Mosel-view rooms (12 rooms, Db-€70–72, Balduinstrasse 15, tel. 06542/4530, fax 06542/61160, NSE). They have 16 newly renovated rooms with top comforts, many with riverview balconies, at their *Neues Gästehaus* (Db-€82, no CC, tel. 06542/61169, fax same as above).

$$ Peter Weis Apartments, of the F. J. Weis winery (recommended above), rents two luxurious apartments (Db-€55, less for 2 or more nights, extra person-€7, he'll get breakfast for you-€6, or you can walk to bakery and buy it yourself, 200 yards beyond bridge on Bernkastel road, riverside at Notenau 30, tel. 06542/41398, fax 06542/961-178, f.j.weis@t-online.de).

$ Gasthaus Gertrud Thiesen is classy, with a TV-living-breakfast room and a river view. The Thiesen house has four big, bright rooms and is on the town's first corner overlooking the Mosel from a great terrace (D-€41, no CC, closed Nov–Feb, Balduinstrasse 1, tel. 06542/4453).

$ Weinhaus zum Fröhlichen Weinberg offers four cheap, basic rooms (D-€36, no CC, family *Zimmer*, Mittelstrasse 6, tel. & fax 06542/4308) above a *Weinstube* restaurant (can be noisy, especially weekends; jolly Jürgen SE).

$ Homey **Gästehaus am Römerbad,** near the church, rents six cheap and sleepable rooms (Sb-€21, Db-€41, no CC, Am Römerbad 5, tel. 06542/41602, Elizabeth Münster SE).

$ Gästezimmer Rosa Mesenich is a little place facing the river (Db-€40, no CC, Brandenburg 48, tel. 06542/4297, NSE).

$ Nearby, the vine-strewn doorway of **Gastehaus Eberhard** leads to gregarious owners, cushy rooms, and potential wine-tastings (Db-€38, no CC, Brandenburg 42, tel. 06542/41216, NSE).

TRIER

Germany's oldest city lies at the head of the scenic Mosel Valley, near the Luxembourg border. An ancient Roman capital, Trier brags that it was inhabited by Celts for 1,300 years before Rome even existed. Today Trier is thriving and feels very young. A short stop here offers you a look at Germany's oldest Christian church, one of its most enjoyable market squares, and its best Roman ruins.

Founded by Augustus in 16 B.C., Trier served as the Roman town Augusta Treverorum for 400 years. When Emperor Diocletian (who ruled A.D. 285–305) divided his overextended Roman Empire into four sectors, he made Trier the capital of the west: roughly modern-day Germany, France, Spain, and England. For most of the fourth century, this city of 80,000, with a four-mile wall, four great gates, and 47 round towers, was the favored residence of Roman emperors. Emperor Constantine used the town as the capital of his fading Western Roman Empire. Many of the Roman buildings were constructed under Constantine before he left for Constantinople. In 480, Trier fell to the Franks. Today, Trier's Roman sights include the huge city gate (Porta Nigra), basilica, baths, and amphitheater.

ORIENTATION

(area code: 0651)

Tourist Information: Trier's small but helpful TI is just through the Porta Nigra. You can pay €2 for an easily readable map, but cheapskates and those with good eyes can squint at the free small-print map, which suffices for navigating Trier's key sights. They also sell a useful little guide to the city called *Trier: A Guide to Monuments* (€3.40) as well as the *Holiday Region Trier* brochure (€1, lists opening hours of Trier's sights, info on city tours, Mosel boat excursions, events, leisure activities, and more). Consider also the booklet *Walking Tours through Trier* (€3), which has little information on sights but a great map and proposed walking routes (Roman, medieval, Jewish, rainy day). The TI also books rooms for free (April–Oct Mon–Sat 9:00–18:00, Sun 10:00–15:00, March & Nov–Dec Mon–Sat 9:00–18:00, Sun 10:00–13:00, Jan–Feb Mon–Sat 10:00–17:00, closed Sun, tel. 0651/978-080, www.trier.de).

Discount Cards: The **Trier Card** allows free use of city buses and discounts on city tours, museums, and Roman sights (€9, family-€15, valid for 3 days, sold at TI). Since the town is small and walkable, this is only a good deal if you'll be here for two or three days and plan to visit lots of sights. If you're visiting at least three Roman sights (including baths, Porta Nigra, and amphitheater, but not the archaeological museum), buy the **Roman sights combo-ticket** instead (€6.20, family ticket-€14.80, available at participating sights).

Walking Tours: The TI offers a two-hour walking tour in English on Saturday at 13:30 (€6, May–Oct only), private 2-hour tours (€65), and a few audioguides (€6, get there early or call ahead to reserve, tel. 0651/978-080).

Arrival in Trier

By Train: From the train station (lockers-€1–2/day, WC-€0.50), walk 15 boring minutes and four blocks up Theodor-Heuss-Allee to the big black Roman gate and turn left under the gate to find the TI. From here the main pedestrian mall (Simeonstrasse) leads into the town's charm: the Market Square and cathedral (a 5-min walk) and basilica (5 more min).

By Car: Drivers get off at Trier Verteilerkreis and follow signs to *Zentrum*. There is parking near the gate and TI.

Helpful Hints

Internet Access: Try **Altaxx** (daily 16:00–23:00, from Porta Nigra take underground passage beneath busy street, Paulinstrasse 80, tel. 0651/991-9303, www.altaxx.com).

Laundry: A well-maintained, self-service launderette is near the Marx Museum (€8 for the works, daily 8:00–22:00, Brückenstrasse 19).

Bus Tours of Trier

The old town is walkable. But if you're tired and want an overview, consider hopping on the hokey little red-and-yellow tourist train, the **Römer-Express,** for its 35-minute loop of Trier's major old town sights (€6, April–Oct 2/hr daily 10:00–18:00, March & Nov hourly daily 11:00–17:00, Dec–Feb on request 11:00–16:00, recorded narration in English, departs from TI, buy tickets from driver or at TI, tel. 0651/9935-9525).

For a live guide and a big, air-conditioned bus, take the one-hour **bus tour** offered by the TI (€6, May–Oct daily at 13:00 in English).

For a hop-on, hop-off option, try the city bus **Trier Tour** to see the Roman sights (except the cathedral) and the Petrisberg hillside view-point (€5.60, April–Oct daily 10:00–18:00, 2/hr, pick up route map at TI, includes free travel on all city buses for the day).

SIGHTS

These sights are listed in the order you'll reach them from the Porta Nigra.

▲**Porta Nigra**—Roman Trier was built as a capital. Its architecture mirrored the grandeur of the empire. Of the four-mile wall's four huge gates, only this north gate survives. This most impressive Roman fortification in Germany was built without mortar—only iron pegs hold the sandstone blocks together. While the other three gates were destroyed by medieval metal and stone scavengers, this "black gate" (originally red sandstone, but darkened by time) survived because it became a church. Saint Simeon—a pious Greek recluse—lived inside the gate for seven years. After his death in 1035, the Saint Simeon monastery was established, and the gate was made into a two-story church—lay church on the bottom, monastery church on top. Napoleon had everything non-Roman about the structure destroyed in 1803, but the 12th-century Romanesque apse—the round part at the east end—survived. You can climb around the gate, but there's little to see aside from a fine town view. Just inside the entrance, look for pictures of how the gate looked during various eras, including its church phase (€2.10, April–Sept daily 9:00–18:00, Oct–March daily 9:00–17:00).

Trier's main pedestrian drag, which leads away from the gate, is named for Saint Simeon. The arcaded courtyard and buildings of the monastery of Saint Simeon remain (now home to the city museum and TI).

City Museum (Städtisches Museum Simeonstift)—This museum traces Trier's long, interesting history. Just inside the entrance (on the right) are some free city models, good for orientation. The huge model is Trier in 1800, complete with city walls and towers (find Porta Nigra, #1, on the window side). A smaller model in the same room shows the cathedral in 1944, after Allied bombings. The rest of the museum (€2.60 entry) houses the original A.D. 958 market cross and figures from St. Peter's Fountain (you'll see copies soon on market square—see next page), as well as other sculptures, porcelain, furniture, and paintings (Easter–Oct daily 9:00–17:00; Nov–Easter Tue–Fri 9:00–17:00, Sat–Sun 9:00–13:00, closed Mon, tel. 0651/718-2449, www.museum-trier.de)

As you walk to the market square, you'll see—about halfway down on your left at Simeonstrasse 19, the...

House of the Three Magi (Dreikönigshaus)—Now a restaurant, this colorful Venetian-style building was constructed in the 13th century as a

Trier

- **1** Hotel zum Christophel
- **2** Hotel Römischer Kaiser
- **3** Hotel Frankenturm
- **4** Hotel Pieper
- **5** Hotel Monopol
- **6** Hotel Kolpinghaus Warsberger Hof
- **7** Restaurant Krim
- **8** Restaurant zum Domstein
- **9** Launderette

keep. Look for the floating door a story above the present-day entrance. A wooden staircase to this door was once the only way in or out. If the town was in danger, the staircase could be burned or torn down, in order to fend off enemies and protect inhabitants. (Look for another medieval keep with a floating door—the Frankenturm—just off market square near the recommended hotel of the same name.)

▲▲**Market Square (Hauptmarkt)**—Trier's Hauptmarkt square is a people-filled swirl of fruit stands, flowers, painted facades, and fountains (with a handy public WC). This is one of Germany's most in-love-with-life marketplaces.

For an orientation to the sights, go to the square's centerpiece, a market cross, and stand on the side of the cross (east) closest to the big stone cathedral a block away. This cathedral was the seat of the archbishop. In medieval times, the cathedral was its own walled city, and the archbishop of Trier was one of the seven German electors who chose the Holy Roman Emperor. This gave the archbishop tremendous political, as well as spiritual, power (for more on the cathedral, see below).

The pink-and-white building (now an H&M department store) on the corner of the lane leading to the cathedral was a **palace** for the archbishop. Notice the seal above the door: a crown flanked by a crosier, representing the bishop's ecclesiastical power, and a sword, demonstrating his political might. This did not sit well with the townspeople of Trier. The square you're standing in was the symbolic battlefield of a centuries-long conflict between Trier's citizens and the bishop.

The stone **market cross** (a replica of the 958 original, now in the City Museum—see above) next to you celebrates the trading rights given to the archbishop by King Otto the Great. This was a slap in the face to Trier townspeople, since trading rights were usually reserved for free cities—which they wanted to become.

Look across the square from the lane to the cathedral, to the 15th-century **town hall** (with a knight on each second-story corner). The people of Trier wanted a town hall, but the bishop wouldn't allow it—so they built this "assembly hall" instead. The knight on the left, facing the Market Square, has his mask up, watching over his people. The other knight, facing the cathedral and the bishop, has his mask down and his hand on his sword, ready for battle.

Tensions mounted 30 years later. Look to the left, at the tall white steeple with yellow trim. This is the Gothic tower of the **Church of St. Gangolf,** the medieval townspeople's church and fire watchman's post. (From medieval times until the present day, a bell has rung nightly at 22:00, reminding local drunks to go home. When the automatic bell-ringer broke last winter, concerned locals flooded the mayor with calls.) In 1507, Trier's mayor built this new Gothic tower to make the people's church higher than the cathedral. A Latin Bible verse adorns the top in gold letters: "Stay awake and pray." In retaliation, the bishop raised one tower of his cathedral (all he could afford). He topped it with a threatening message of his own, continuing the town hall's verse: "For you never know the hour when the Lord will come."

Look farther to the left, to the Renaissance **St. Peter's Fountain** (1595). This fountain symbolizes thoughtful city government, with allegorical statues of justice (sword and scale), fortitude (broken column), temperance (wine and water), and prudence (snake and mirror—missing for generations). The ladies represent idealized cardinal virtues—but notice the rude monkeys hiding on the column behind them, showing the way things are really done.

Find the recommended **Zum Domstein** restaurant near the fountain. In Trier, you can't even put a rec room in your basement without tripping over Roman ruins. The owner of this restaurant discovered a Roman column in her cellar. Upstairs, she still sells traditional German food. Downstairs, you'll find the column, a mini-museum of Roman crockery, and expensive cuisine (€22–30) based on ancient Roman recipes (daily 12:00–14:00 & 18:00–21:00, or just sneak in for a peek, Am Hauptmarkt 5).

The rest of the square is a textbook of architectural styles. Notice the half-timbered houses at the north end of the square (toward Porta Nigra), marking Trier's 14th-century Jewish ghetto. Nearby, look for the Art Deco hotel that now houses a McDonald's (whose famous arches are dubbed by locals "the golden horn"). You'll also see the overpriced and uninspired **Spielzeug (Toy) Museum** (€4, daily 11:00–17:00, tel. 0651/75850, www.spielzeugmuseum-trier.de). When you're finished on the square, head down the lane to the cathedral.

▲▲**Cathedral (Dom)**—This is the oldest church in Germany. St. Helena, the mother of Emperor Constantine (who legalized Christianity in the Roman Empire in A.D. 312) and an important figure in early Christian history, let part of her palace be used as the first church on this spot. In 326, to celebrate the 20th anniversary of his reign, Constantine began the construction of St. Peter's in Rome and this huge cathedral in Trier—also called St. Peter's. The Dom information center is on the courtyard across from the cathedral; ask if any excavations from the very first part of Constantine's cathedral are open for public viewing.

Begin your visit in the large front courtyard of the cathedral. As you face the cathedral, look in the corner behind you and to your left (near the pink palace); you'll see a large patch of light-colored bricks in an L shape in the ground. The original Roman cathedral was more than four times its present size; these light-colored bricks mark one corner of this massive "double cathedral." (The opposite corner was at the back of the smaller Liebfrau church, waaay across the courtyard.) The plaque by the corner shows the floor plan of the original Roman cathedral.

Enter the cathedral (free, April–Oct daily 6:30–18:00, Nov–March daily 6:30–17:30, €0.10 English info flyer, www.trierer-dom.de). You'll see many altars lining the nave, dedicated not to saints, but to bishops. These ornate funeral altars were a fashionable way for the powerful archbishop-electors to memorialize themselves. Even the elaborate black-and-white altar at the back of the church (where you entered) is not a religious shrine, but a memorial for a single rich bishop.

The "pilgrim's walk" (the stairway at the right front of the church) leads to the chapel holding the cathedral's most important relic, the Holy Robe of Christ, found by St. Helena on a pilgrimage to Jerusalem (rarely on view, but you can see its reliquary, look for photos of the actual robe after the first flight of stairs). The second flight of stairs leads to the **treasury** (Dom Schatzkammer), displaying huge bishops' rings, the sandal of St. Andrew (in a box topped with a golden foot), and a holy nail supposedly from the Crucifixion (€1.50, April–Oct Mon–Sat 10:00–16:45, Sun 14:00–16:45; Nov–March Mon–Sat 11:00–15:45, Sun 14:00–15:45). From the treasury, you can fight the crowds the last few stairs up to the chapel (same hours as treasury). Back down the stairs, the door on your left leads to the peaceful Domkreuzgang cloister between the *Dom* and the Liebfrau church. As you leave the cathedral the way you came in, notice the controversial modern (1972) paintings at the back of the church, representing the Alpha (Paradise/Creation, to the left) and the Omega (the Last Judgment, to the right).

If you want to visit the Diocesan Museum (described below), go right as you exit the cathedral's main door and turn down the first street on your right (Windstrasse). As you walk with the cathedral on your right, you'll be able to see the different eras of its construction. The big red cube that makes up the back half of the present-day cathedral is all that remains of the enormous original fourth-century Roman construction (at one time twice as tall as what you see here). Arched bricks in the facade show the original position of Roman windows and doors. Around this Roman nucleus, chunks were grafted on over a millennium and a half of architectural styles: the front half of the cathedral facing the big courtyard, added in the 11th century; the choir on the back, from the 12th century; and the transept and round Baroque shrine on the far back, from the 18th century.

If you look at the original Roman construction squarely, you'll see that it's not perfectly vertical. Locks were built along the Mosel River in the 1960s, depleting groundwater—which was the only thing preserving the church's original wooden foundation. The foundation disintegrated, and the walls began to sag. Architects competed to find a way to prevent the cathedral from collapsing, and the winner—a huge steel bracket above the main nave, holding the walls up with cables—seems to be working.

Just past the cathedral on Windstrasse to the left is the...

▲**Diocesan Museum (Museum am Dom)**—This cathedral museum offers exhibits on the history of the cathedral. Inside and to the right, find the small model of the original Roman church, and the bigger model showing some of the present-day excavations of its various pieces. Don't miss the pieced-together remains of fine ceiling frescoes (dating from A.D. 310–320) from a Roman palace. The palace was destroyed around A.D. 325, and the Dom was built over it. The 50,000 pieces of the frescoes were discovered while cleaning up from WWII bombs. The vivid reds, greens, and blues of the restored works depict frolicking cupids, bejeweled women, and a philosopher clutching his scroll (all described in German). A good €3.60 English book clearly explains the palace ceiling's elaborate structure and the fresco restoration process. Elsewhere in the museum, the stone capitals, gold chalices, vestments, and icons are meaningless to most, unless you can read German (€2, April–Oct Mon–Sat 9:00–17:00, Sun 13:00–17:00, Nov–March closed Mon, Windstrasse 6, tel. 0651/710-5255, www.museum.bistum-trier.de).

Liebfrau Church—Claimed to be the oldest Gothic church in

Germany, it's connected to the *Dom*'s right side, on the southeast corner of the original Roman church site. Dating from 1235, it was built when Gothic was in vogue, so French architects were brought in—and paid with money borrowed from the bishop of Köln when funds ran dry. It's now filled with colorful, modern stained glass (daily April–Oct 7:30–18:00, Nov–March until 17:30).

▲▲**Basilica/Imperial Throne Room (Konstantin Basilika)**—Two blocks south of the *Dom*, this 200-foot-by-100-foot building is the largest intact Roman structure outside of Rome. It's best known a basilica, but it actually started as a throne room. Go inside and look up: Each of the squares in the ceiling above you is 10 feet by 10 feet—as big as your hotel room. Picture this throne room in ancient times, decorated with golden mosaics, rich marble, colorful stucco, and busts of Constantine and his family filling the seven niches. The emperor sat in majesty under a canopy on his altar-like throne. The windows in the apse around him were smaller than the ones along the side walls, making his throne seem even bigger.

The last emperor moved out in A.D. 395, and petty kings set up camp in the building throughout the Middle Ages. By the 12th century, the bishops had taken it over and converted it to a five-story palace. The building became a Lutheran church in 1856, and remains the only Lutheran church in Trier. It was badly damaged by WWII bombs, and later partially restored. A good €1.30 English booklet brings the near-empty shell to life (free, April–Oct Mon–Sat 10:00–18:00, Sun 12:00–18:00, Nov–March Tue–Sat 11:00–12:00 & 15:00–16:00, Sun 12:00–13:00, closed Mon, tel. 0651/72468).

A rococo wing, the Elector's Palace, was added to the basilica in the 18th century to house the archbishop-elector; today it houses local government offices (closed to the public). This faces a fragrant garden, which leads to three sights: an interesting archaeological museum, the remains of a Roman bath, and a 25,000-seat amphitheater (all described below).

▲**Archaeological Museum (Rheinisches Landesmuseum)**—This is not only a museum, but also an active excavation and research center. Upstairs, in the back and to the right, is a huge model of Roman Trier (try to pick out the buildings you're visiting today: cathedral, basilica, baths). Downstairs, explore the huge funerary monuments. Once these were all painted like the replica in the courtyard; today, they tell archaeologists volumes about daily life in Roman times. Find the woman visiting a beauty salon (hint: She's on the tallest monument). The mosaics room is a highlight. On the wall, find the mosaic of four horses surrounding the superstar charioteer Polydus (mosaic floors were the *Sports Illustrated* covers of the Roman world), discovered intact at the Imperial Baths (€5.50, Tue–Fri 9:30–17:00, Sat–Sun 10:30–17:00, closed Mon, few English descriptions but good audioguide free with entry, tel. 0651/97740, www.landesmuseum-trier.de).

To reach the Imperial Baths and amphitheater, exit the Landesmuseum to the left and follow the stone wall for 200 yards to the busy street. To reach the Imperial Bath ruins, go right through the opening in the wall (see below). For the unexceptional **amphitheater** (April–Sept daily 9:00–18:00, Oct–March until 17:00, tel. 0651/97740), take the marked pedestrian underpass, then follow Hermesstrasse another half-mile as it curves up the hill (ignore signs pointing you to the right).

Imperial Baths (Kaiserthermen)—Built by Constantine, this is the biggest of Trier's three Roman baths and the most intricate bath of the Roman world. Trier's cold northern climate, the size of the complex, and the enormity of Constantine's ego meant that these Imperial Baths required a two-story subterranean complex of pipes, furnaces, and slave galleys to keep the water at a perfect 47 degrees Celsius (120 degrees Fahrenheit). Explore the underground tunnels (nearly a mile's worth), noticing the chest-high holes in the walls that used to hold the floor (slaves above, pipes below). It's an impressive complex—too bad the baths never quite worked right and were left unfinished after Constantine left (€2.10, included in Roman combo-ticket, April–Sept daily 9:00–18:00, Oct–March daily 9:00–17:00).

Another, less interesting Roman bath is a 10-minute walk away: a modern glass box covers bath excavations at the **Viehmarkt Museum.** Locals grouse that the ruins sat in the rain for years before their tax money was used to build this expensive new house. The red bricks in the marketplace outside show the intersection of the original Roman roads, laid out as a grid (€2.10, included in Roman combo-ticket, Tue–Sun 9:00–17:00, closed Mon, last entry 30 min before closing, €1.50 English brochure, 10-min walk from Market Square down Brotstrasse, right on Fahrstrasse to Viehmarktplatz, tel. 0651/994-1057).

Karl Marx's House—Communists can lick their wounds at Karl Marx's house. Early manuscripts, letters, and photographs of the influential economist/philosopher fill several rooms of his birth house. Oblivious to their slide out of a shrinking middle class, people still sneer (€2, Mon 13:00–18:00, Tue–Sun 10:00–18:00, Nov–March closes 13:00–14:00 and at 17:00, 15-min film in English at 20 min after each hour, a reasonable amount of English description, or buy €0.30 brochure or €5 book, tel. 0651/970-680, www.fes.de/marx). From the Market S quare, it's a 10-minute walk down Fleischstrasse—which becomes Brückenstrasse—to the house at Brückenstrasse 10.

SLEEPING

Near Porta Nigra

$$$ The classy **Hotel zum Christophel** offers top comfort in its 11 sharp rooms above a fine restaurant with a kind owner (Sb-€55–60, Db-€85–90, elevator, Am Porta Nigra Platz, Simeonstrasse 1, tel. 0651/979-

SLEEP CODE

(€1 = about $1.10, country code: 49, area code: 0651)
Sleep Code: **S** = Single, **D** = Double/Twin, **T** = Triple, **Q** = Quad, **b** = bathroom, **s** = shower only, **no CC** = Credit Cards not accepted, **SE** = Speaks English. Unless otherwise noted, credit cards are accepted, English is spoken, and breakfast is included.

To help you sort easily through these listings, I've divided the rooms into three categories, based on the price for a standard double room with bath:

$$$ Higher Priced—Most rooms €85 or more.
  $$ Moderately Priced—Most rooms between €50–85.
    $ Lower Priced—Most rooms €50 or less.

4200, fax 0651/74732, www.zumchristophel.de, info@zumchristophel.de).

$$$ Hotel Römischer Kaiser next door is a lesser value, charging more for a polished lobby and comparable rooms (43 rooms, Sb-€67–77, Db-€98–108, includes parking, elevator, Am Porta Nigra Platz, tel. 0651/97700, fax 0651/977-099, www.hotels-trier.de).

Near Market Square

$$ Hotel Frankenturm, decked out in modern style with track lighting and cheery color schemes, is above a lively saloon next to a medieval keep of the same name. The six rooms with a private bath are on the first floor up; the other six rooms are two floors up with a shared bath (S-€40, Sb-€60, D-€50, Db-€80, T-€60, Tb-€90, no elevator, Dietrichstrasse 3, tel. 0651/978-240, fax 0651/978-2449, frankenturm @t-online.de).

$ Kolpinghaus Warsberger Hof is the best value for cheap sleeps in town. This Catholic Church–run place is clean, with 150 beds—some in single and double rooms—and it serves inexpensive meals in its pleasant restaurant, which is open to the public (€15/bed in 3- to 6-bed dorm rooms, sheets-€2.50, S-€22, D-€42, T-€60, Q-€76, showers down the hall, breakfast not included, a block to the right at the end of market square, Dietrichstrasse 42, tel. 0651/975-250, fax 0651/975-2540, www.warsberger-hof.de, info@warsberger-hof.de).

Near the Station

$$ Hotel Pieper is less central and run by the friendly Becker family (he cooks and she keeps the books). They rent 21 comfortable rooms furnished with dark wood over a pleasant neighborhood restaurant (Sb-€44, Db-€70, Tb-€88, 12-min walk from station, 2 blocks off main drag, Thebäerstrasse 39, tel. 0651/23008, fax 0651/12839, www.hotel-pieper-trier.de, info@hotel-pieper-trier.de). From the station, follow Theodor-Heuss-Allee (toward Roman gate) to the second big intersection, angle right onto Göbenstrasse, and continue as the road curves and becomes Thebäerstrasse.

$$ **Hotel Monopol,** at the train station, has 35 older but clean rooms. It's dark but handy (S-€31–36, Sb-€39–47, D-€52–67, Db-€62–77, Tb-€93, Qb-€112, elevator, Bahnhofsplatz 7, tel. 0651/714-090, fax 0651/714-0910, www.hotel-monopol-trier.de).

EATING

Good eateries abound on the side streets leading away from the pedestrian drag of Simeonstrasse and the Market Square. On Dietrichstrasse, try the restaurants in the recommended hotels **Warsberger Hof** (daily 11:00–24:00, outdoor courtyard seating) or **Frankenturm** (Mon–Sat 11:30–1:00, Sun 18:00–1:00). Young locals enjoy trendy Mediterranean cuisine at **Krim,** also just off the Market Square (daily 9:00–24:00, Glockenstrasse 7, tel. 0651/73943). The popular **Zum Domstein** serves pricey Roman fare in a cellar and cheaper German fare upstairs (daily 12:00–14:00 & 18:00–21:00, Am Hauptmarkt 5, tel. 0651/74490; see "Sights," page 228).

TRANSPORTATION CONNECTIONS

By train to: Cochem (hrly, 45 min), **Köln** (7/day, 3 hrs), **Koblenz** (hrly, 75 min), **Bullay** (with buses to Zell, hrly, 40 min), **St. Goar/Bacharach** (hrly, 2.5 hrs), **Baden-Baden** (hrly, long 4 hrs, with 1–2 changes). Train info: tel. 01805/996-633.

KÖLN AND THE UNROMANTIC RHINE

(Cologne)

Romance isn't everything. Köln is an urban Jacuzzi that keeps the Rhine churning. It's home to Germany's greatest Gothic cathedral and its best collection of Roman artifacts, a world-class art museum, and a healthy dose of German urban playfulness.

Peaceful Bonn, which offers good people-watching and fun pedestrian streets, used to be the capital of West Germany. The small town of Remagen had a bridge that helped defeat Hitler in World War II, and unassuming Aachen (near the Belgian border) was once the capital of Europe.

Köln

Germany's fourth-largest city, Köln has a compact, lively center. The Rhine was the northern boundary of the Roman Empire and, 1,700 years ago, Constantine—the first Christian emperor—made Colonia the seat of a bishopric. Five hundred years later, under Charlemagne, Köln became the seat of an archbishopric. With 40,000 people within its walls, it was the largest German city and an important cultural and religious center throughout the Middle Ages. Today, the city is most famous for its toilet water. Eau de Cologne was first made here by an Italian chemist in 1709.

Even though WWII bombs destroyed 95 percent of Köln (population down from 800,000 to 40,000), it has become, after a remarkable recovery, a bustling commercial and cultural center as well as a fun, colorful, and pleasant-smelling city.

ORIENTATION

(area code: 0221)

Köln's old-town core, bombed out then rebuilt quaint, is traffic-free and includes a park and bike path along the river. From the cathedral/TI/train station, Hohe Strasse leads into the shopping action.

The Roman arch in front of the cathedral reminds us that even in Roman times, this was an important trading street and a main road through Köln. In medieval times, when Köln was a major player in the heavyweight Hanseatic Trading League, two major trading routes crossed here. This high street thrived. Following its complete destruction in World War II, it emerged once again as an active trading street—the first pedestrian shopping mall in Germany.

For a quick old-town ramble, stroll down Hohe Strasse and take a left at the city hall *(Rathaus)* to the river (where K-D Rhine cruises start). Enjoy the quaint old town and the waterfront park. The Hohenzollernbrücke, crossing the Rhine at the cathedral, is the busiest railway bridge in the world (30 trains/hr all day long).

Tourist Information

Köln's energetic TI, opposite the church entrance, has free city maps, a program of private guided tours (including, architecture, medieval Köln, Romanesque churches; call TI to reserve), and several brochures (Mon–Sat 9:00–21:00, Sun 10:00–18:00, July–Aug Mon–Sat until 22:00, Unter Fettenhennen 19, tel. 0221/2213-0400, www.koelntourismus.de). Köln's **WelcomeCard** (€9/24 hrs, €14/48 hrs) provides use of the city's transit system, a 50 percent discount on major museums (Römisch-Germanisches, Ludwig, and Wallraf-Richartz), and smaller discounts on other museums (like the Chocolate Museum). Note that many of Köln's museums are closed on Monday. For information on the museums, visit www.museenkoeln.de.

Two-hour German/English **city bus tours** leave daily from the TI (€14, discount with WelcomeCard, April–Oct daily at 10:00, 12:30, and 15:00, and a shorter version at 17:30 on Sat–Sun, Nov–March daily at 11:00 and 14:00). To get tickets to concerts, the opera, and the theater, stop by **KölnMusik Ticket** next to the Roman Museum (Mon–Fri 9:00–18:30, Sat 9:00–16:00, closed Sun, tel. 0221/2040-8160, can book ahead at www.koelnticket.de).

Arrival in Köln

Köln couldn't be easier to visit—its three important sights cluster within two blocks of its TI and train station. This super pedestrian zone is a constant carnival of people.

Köln's bustling **train station** has everything you need: a drugstore, food court, juice bar, shopping mall with grocery store, pricey WC (€1), travel center *(Reisezentrum,* Mon–Fri 5:30–23:00, Sat–Sun until 22:30),

Köln

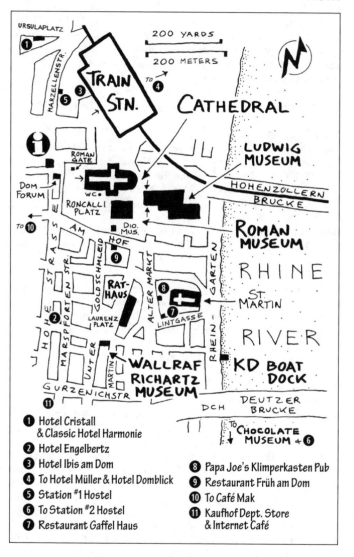

200 YARDS

200 METERS

URSULAPLATZ

❶

MARZELLENSTR.

TRAIN STN.

❸

❺

TO ❹

CATHEDRAL

i

ROMAN GATE

LUDWIG MUSEUM

DOM FORUM

WC.

RONCALLI PLATZ

HOHENZOLLERN BRÜCKE

TO ❿

AM HOF

STRASSE

DIO. MUS.

❾

ROMAN MUSEUM

RHINE

PFORTEN STR.

GOLDSCHMIED

RAT-HAUS

ALTER MARKT

RHEIN-GARTEN

❽

❷

LAURENZ PLATZ

❼

LINTGASSE

ST. MARTIN

HOHE

MARS

UNTER

MARTIN

WALLRAF RICHARTZ MUSEUM

RHEIN-

RIVER

KD BOAT DOCK

GÜRZENICHSTR.

❶❶

DCH

DEUTZER BRÜCKE

TO CHOCOLATE MUSEUM + ❻

- ❶ Hotel Cristall
  & Classic Hotel Harmonie
- ❷ Hotel Engelbertz
- ❸ Hotel Ibis am Dom
- ❹ To Hotel Müller & Hotel Domblick
- ❺ Station #1 Hostel
- ❻ To Station #2 Hostel
- ❼ Restaurant Gaffel Haus
- ❽ Papa Joe's Klimperkasten Pub
- ❾ Restaurant Früh am Dom
- ❿ To Café Mak
- ❶❶ Kaufhof Dept. Store
  & Internet Café

and lockers (€2/24 hrs, put money in and wait 30 seconds for door to open; next to *Reisezentrum*).

For questions about bus travel, visit the Deutsche Touring office one block behind the station (Mon–Fri 9:00–18:00, Sun 9:00–13:00, closed Sat, can answer questions about Romantic Road bus, Johanis-strasse 43-45, tel. 0221/759-8660).

Exiting the front of the station (the end near track 1), you'll find yourself smack-dab in the shadow of the Dom. If your jaw drops, pick it up. Up the steps and to the right is the main entrance to the Dom (TI across street). For hotels Müller and Domblick, leave the station from the back (the end near track 11).

If you **drive** to Köln, follow signs to *Zentrum,* then continue to the huge Parkhaus am Dom pay lot under the cathedral (€1.50/hr, €13/day).

Helpful Hints

Internet Access: Consider the **Internet/Call Center** a block from the station at Marzellenstrasse 3–5 (€3/hour, daily 9:30–24:00, tel. 0221/139-96200), or **Surf Inn,** on the third floor of the Kaufhof department store (€4/hr, Mon–Fri 9:30–20:00, Sat 9:00–16:00, closed Sun, Hohe Strasse 41–53 at intersection with Schildergasse, tel. 0221/925-3301).

Bike Rental: You can rent bikes from the riverside Kölner Fahrradverleih, a 10-minute walk from the station (marked on free TI map; €2/hour, €10/day, ask for recommended route, Sedanstrasse 27, tel. 0221/723-627). They also offer German-English guided **bike tours** of the city (€15, 3 hrs, daily April–Oct at 13:30, rain poncho provided just in case, max 10 people, reservations recommended, mobile 0171/629-8796). Consider biking the path along the Rhine River up past the convention center *(Messe)* and to the Rheinpark for a picnic.

SIGHTS

Köln's Cathedral

▲▲▲**Cathedral (Dom)**—The Gothic Dom, Germany's most exciting church, looms immediately up from the train station (daily 6:00–19:30, no tourist visits during church services daily 6:30–10:00 & 18:30, Sun also at 12:00 & 17:00, get schedule at Dom Forum office or www.koelner-dom.de). The one-hour English-only **tours** are reliably excellent (€4, Mon–Sat at 10:30 and 14:30, Sun at 14:30, meet inside front door of Dom, tel. 0221/9258-4730). Your tour ticket also gives you free entry to the English-language 20-minute video in the Dom Forum directly following the tour (see "Dom Forum," page 244). If you don't take the tour, follow this seven-stop walk (note that stops 3–7 are closed during confession Mon–Fri 7:00–9:00, Sat 14:00–18:00):

1. Roman gate and cathedral exterior: The square in front of the cathedral has been a busy civic meeting place since ancient times. A Roman temple stood where the cathedral stands today. The north gate of the Roman city, from A.D. 50, marks the start of Köln's 2,000-year-old main street.

Köln Cathedral

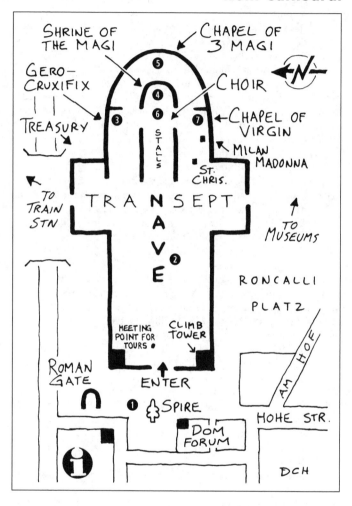

Look for the life-size replica tip of a spire. The real thing is 515 feet above you. The cathedral facade, finished according to the original 13th-century plan, is "neo-Gothic" from the 19th century.

Postcards show the church after the 1945 bombing. The red brick building—off to your right as you face the church—is the Diocesan Museum. The Roman museum is between that and the cathedral, and the modern-art museum is behind that.

Step inside the church. Grab a pew in the center of the nave.

2. Nave: If you feel small, you're supposed to. The 140-foot-tall ceiling reminds us of our place in the vast scheme of things. Lots of stained glass—enough to cover three football fields—fills the church with light, representing God.

The church was begun in 1248. The choir—the lofty area from the center altar to the far end ahead of you—was finished in 1322. Later, with the discovery of America and routes to the Indies by sea, trade shifted away from inland ports like Köln. Funds dried up and eventually the building stopped. For 300 years, the finished end of the church was walled off and functioned as a church, while the unfinished torso (where you now sit) waited. For centuries, the symbol of Köln's skyline was a huge crane that sat atop the unfinished west spire.

With the rise of German patriotism in the early 1800s, Köln became a symbol of German unity. And the Prussians—the movers and shakers behind German unity—mistakenly considered Gothic a German style. They initiated a national tax that funded the speedy completion of this gloriously Gothic German church. Seven hundred workers (compared to 100 in the 14th century) finished the church in just 38 years (1842–1880). The great train station was built in the shadow of the cathedral's towering spire.

The glass windows in the front of the church are medieval. The glass surrounding you in the nave is not as old, but it's precious nevertheless. The glass on the left is Renaissance. That on the right—a gift from Ludwig I, father of Mad King Ludwig of touristic fame—is 19th-century Bavarian.

While 95 percent of Köln was destroyed by WWII bombs, the structure of the cathedral survived fairly well. In anticipation of the bombing, the glass and art treasures were taken to shelters and saved. The new "swallow's nest" organ above you was installed to celebrate the cathedral's 750th birthday in 1998. Relics (mostly skulls) fill cupboards on each side of the nave. The guys in the red robes are cathedral cops, called Schweizers (after the Swiss guard at the Vatican); if a service is getting ready to start, they might hustle you out (unless you'd like to stay for the service).

3. Gero-Crucifix: As you step through the gate into the oldest part of the church, look for the mosaic of the ninth-century church on the floor. It shows a saint holding the Carolingian Cathedral, which stood on this spot for several centuries before this one was built.

Ahead of you on the left, the Chapel of the Cross features the oldest surviving monumental crucifix from north of the Alps. Carved in 976 with a sensitivity 300 years ahead of its time, it shows Jesus not suffering and not triumphant—but with eyes closed...dead. He paid the price for our sins. It's quite a two-fer: great art and powerful theology in one. The cathedral has three big pilgrim stops: this crucifix, the Shrine of the Magi, and the *Madonna of Milan* (both coming up).

Continue to the front end of the church, stopping to look at the big golden reliquary in the glass case behind the high altar.

4. Shrine of the Magi: Relics were a big deal in the Middle Ages. Köln's acquisition of the bones of the Three Kings in the 12th century put it on the pilgrimage map and brought in enough money to justify the construction of this magnificent place. By some stretch of medieval Christian logic, these relics also justified the secular power of the local king. This reliquary, made in about 1200, is the biggest and most splendid I've seen. It's seven feet of gilded silver, jewels, and enamel. Old Testament prophets line the bottom, and 12 New Testament apostles— with a wingless angel in the center—line the top.

Inside sit the bones of the Magi...three skulls with golden crowns. So what's the big deal about these three kings of Christmas-carol fame? They were the first to recognize Jesus as the savior and the first to come as pilgrims to worship him. They inspired medieval pilgrims and countless pilgrims since. For a thousand years, a theme of this cathedral has been that life is a pilgrimage...a search for God.

5. Chapel of the Three Magi: The center chapel, at the far end, is the oldest. It also has the church's oldest window (center, from 1265). It has the typical design: a strip of Old Testament scenes on the left with a theologically and visually parallel strip of New Testament scenes on the right (such as, on bottom panels: to the left, the birth of Eve; to the right, the birth of Mary with her mother Anne on the bed).

Later, glass (which you saw lining the nave) was painted and glazed. This medieval window is actually colored glass, which is assembled like a mosaic. It was very expensive. The size was limited to what pilgrim donations could support. Notice the plain, budget design higher up.

6. Choir: Peek into the center zone between the high altar and the carved wooden central stalls. (You can usually only get inside if you take the tour.) This is surrounded by 13th- and 14th-century art: carved oak stalls, frescoed walls, statues painted as they would have been, and original stained glass high above. Study the fanciful oak carvings. The woman cutting the man's hair is a Samson-and-Delilah warning to the sexist men of the early Church.

7. Chapel of the Virgin: The nearby chapel faces one of the most precious paintings of the important Gothic "School of Köln."

The Patron Saints of Köln was painted in 1442 by Stefan Lochner. Notice the photographic realism and believable depth. There are literally dozens of identifiable herbs in the grassy foreground. During the 19th century, the city fought to have it in the museum. The Church went to court to keep it. The judge ruled that it could stay in the cathedral only as long as a Mass was said before it every day. For more than a hundred years, that happened at 18:30. Now, 21st-century comfort has trumped 19th-century law; in winter, services take place in the warmer Sacraments

Chapel instead. (For more on the School of Köln art style, see "Wallraf-Richartz Museum," page 245).

Overlooking the same chapel, the *Madonna of Milan* sculpture (1290), associated with miracles, was a focus of pilgrims for centuries.

As you head for the exit, find the statue of St. Christopher (with Jesus on his shoulder and the pilgrim's staff). Since 1470, pilgrims and travelers have looked up at him and taken solace in the hope that their patron saint is looking out for them. Go in peace.

Church Spire Climb—For 509 steps and €2, you can enjoy a fine city view from the cathedral's south tower (May–Sept daily 9:00–18:00, March–April & Oct until 17:00, Nov–Feb until 16:00, €5 combo-ticket also includes treasury). From the *Glockenstube* (only 400 steps up), you can see the Dom's nine huge bells, including Dicke Peter (24-ton Fat Peter), claimed to be the largest free-swinging church bell in the world.

Treasury—The newly built treasury sits outside the cathedral's left transept (when you exit through the front door, turn right and continue right around the building to the gold pillar that reads *Schatzkammer*). The six dim, hushed rooms are housed in the cathedral's 13th-century stone cellar vaults (€4, €5 combo-ticket also includes spire, daily 10:00–18:00, lockers at entry with €1 coin deposit, tel. 0221/1794-0300). Spotlights shine on black cases filled with gilded chalices and crosses, medieval reliquaries (bits of chain, bone, cross, and cloth in gold-crusted glass capsules), and plenty of fancy bishop garb: intricately embroidered miters and vestments, rings with fat gemstones, and six-foot gold crosiers. Displays come with brief English descriptions, but the fine little €4 book sold inside the cathedral shop provides extra information.

Dom Forum—This helpful visitor center, across from the entrance of the cathedral, is a good place to take a break (Mon–Fri 10:00–18:30, Sat 10:00–17:00, Sun 13:00–17:00, plenty of info, welcoming lounge with €0.50 coffee, free WC downstairs, tel. 0221/9258-4720). They offer an English-language "multi-vision" video on the history of the church daily at 11:30 and 15:30 (starts slow but gets a little better, 20 min, €1.50 or included with church tour, www.domforum.de).

Diocesan Museum—This museum contains some of the cathedral's finest art (free, Fri–Wed 10:00–18:00, closed Thu, brick building to right of Roman Museum, Koncalliplatz 2, tel. 0221/257-7672, www.kolumba.de).

More Sights

▲▲**Römisch-Germanisches Museum**—Germany's best Roman museum offers minimal English among its elegant and fascinating display of Roman artifacts: fine glassware, jewelry, and mosaics (€3.60, 50 percent discount with WelcomeCard, Tue–Sun 10:00–17:00, closed Mon, Roncalliplatz 4, tel. 0221/2212-4590). The permanent collection is downstairs and upstairs; temporary exhibits are on the ground floor.

Budget travelers can view the museum's prize piece, a fine mosaic floor, free from the front window. Once the dining-room floor of a rich merchant, this is actually its original position (the museum was built around it). It shows scenes from the life of Dionysus...wine and good times, Roman-style. The tall monument over the Dionysus mosaic is the mausoleum of a first-century Roman army officer. Upstairs, you'll see a reassembled, arched original gate to the Roman city with the Roman initials for the town, CCAA, still legible, and incredible glassware that Roman Köln was famous for producing. The gift shop's €0.50 brochure provides too little information, and the €12 book too much (detailed descriptions for this museum and about Roman artifacts displayed in other German cities).

▲▲**Ludwig Museum**—Next door and more enjoyable, this museum—in a slick and modern building—offers a stimulating trip through the art of the last century and American Pop and post-WWII art. Artists include German and Russian expressionists, the Blue Rider school, and Picasso. The floor plan is a mess. Just enjoy the art. The Agfa History of Photography exhibit is three rooms with no English; look for the pigeon with the tiny vintage camera strapped to its chest (€5.10, often more due to special exhibitions, 50 percent discount with WelcomeCard, Tue 10:00–20:00, Wed–Fri 10:00–18:00, Sat–Sun 11:00–18:00, closed Mon, last entry 30 min before closing, exhibits are fairly well described in English, classy but pricey cafeteria with reasonable salad bar at entry level, Bischofsgartenstrasse 1, tel. 0221/2212-6165).

▲▲**Wallraf-Richartz Museum**—Housed in a cinderblock of a building near the city hall, this minimalist museum features a world-class collection of old masters, from medieval to northern Baroque and Impressionist. You'll see the best collection anywhere of Gothic School of Köln paintings (1300–1550), offering an intimate peek into those times. Included is German, Dutch, Flemish, and French art by masters such as Dürer, Rubens, Rembrandt, Hals, Steen, van Gogh, Renoir, Monet, Munch, and Cézanne (€5.10, 50 percent discount with WelcomeCard, Tue 10:00–20:00, Wed–Fri 10:00–18:00, Sat–Sun 11:00–18:00, closed Mon, English descriptions, Martin Strasse 39, tel. 0221/2212-1119).

Assorted Museums and Tours—The TI has information on lots more museums. Consider the following:

Chocoholics love the **Imhoff-Stollwerck Chocolate Museum** (cleverly billed as the "Mmmuseum"). The museum takes you on a well-described-in-English tour from the origin of the cocoa bean to the finished product. You can see displays on the culture of chocolate and watch treats trundle down the conveyor belt in the functioning chocolate factory, the museum's highlight. The top floor's exhibit of chocolate advertising is fun. Sample sweets from the chocolate fountain, or take some home from the fragrant, choc-full gift shop (€5.50, €5 with

WelcomeCard, Tue–Fri 10:00–18:00, Sat–Sun 11:00–19:00, closed Mon, last entry 1 hr before closing, Rheinauhafen 1a, an easy walk south on riverfront between Deutzer and Severins bridges, or take the handy Schoko-Express tourist train from the TI, 2/hr, €2 each way; tel. 0221/931-8880, www.schokoladenmuseum.de).

The **Käthe Kollwitz Museum** offers the largest collection of this woman's powerful expressionist art, welling from her experiences living in Berlin during the tumultuous first half of the last century (€3,

SLEEP CODE

(€1 = about $1.10, country code: 49, area code: 0221)
Sleep Code: **S** = Single, **D** = Double/Twin, **T** = Triple, **Q** = Quad, **b** = bathroom, **s** = shower only, **no CC** = Credit Cards not accepted, **SE** = Speaks English, **NSE** = No English. Unless otherwise noted, credit cards are accepted, English is spoken, and breakfast is included.

To help you sort easily through these listings, I've divided the rooms into three categories, based on the price for a standard double room with bath:

$$$ **Higher Priced**—Most rooms €100 or more.
$$ **Moderately Priced**—Most rooms between €75–100.
$ **Lower Priced**—Most rooms €75 or less.

Köln is *the* convention town in Germany. Consequently, the town is either jam-packed with hotels in the €180 range, or empty and hungry. Unless otherwise noted, prices listed are the non-convention weekday rates. You'll find that prices are much higher during conventions, but soft on weekends (always ask) and for slow-time drop-ins. In 2004, conventions are scheduled for these dates: January 19–25; February 1–4, 9–13, and 25–29; March 14–17 and 26–28; April 2–4 and 16–25; May 16–19; June 10–13; July 9–11 (coincides with Köln's Lichter festival on July 10, with fireworks and lots of boats on the river); August 16–18; September 5–7, 16–19, and 22–23; October 19–23 and 28–31; and November 1–7, 16–21, and 26–28. For an update, visit www .koelnmesse.de. Unlisted smaller conventions can lead to small price increases. Big conventions in nearby Düsseldorf can also fill up rooms and raise rates in Köln. Outside of convention times, the TI can always get you a discounted room in a business-class hotel (for a €3 fee).

Tue–Fri 10:00–18:00, Sat–Sun 11:00–18:00, closed Mon, Neumarkt 18–24, tel. 0221/227-2363, www.kollwitz.de). To find the museum, enter Neumarkt Passage and walk to the glass-domed center courtyard. Take the glass elevator to the fifth floor.

SLEEPING

Sleeping in Class on Ursulaplatz

Two good business-class splurge hotels stand side-by-side a five-minute walk northwest of the station (exit straight, then turn right on Marzellenstrasse, up to Ursulaplatz). These can be pricey but are an excellent value on non-convention weekends.

$$$ Classic Hotel Harmonie is all class, striking a perfect balance between modern and classic. Its 72 rooms include some luxurious "superior" rooms (with hardwoods and swanky bathrooms, including a foot-warming floor) that become affordable on weekends. So *this* is how the other half lives (Sb-€75–95, Db-€115, €20 less on non-convention weekends if you ask, superior room-€20 extra, some rooms have train noise so request quiet room, non-smoking rooms, air-con, elevator, Ursulaplatz 13–19, tel. 0221/16570, fax 0221/165-7200, www.classic-hotel-harmonie.de, harmonie@classic-hotels.com).

$$$ Hotel Cristall is a modern "designer hotel" with 84 cleverly appointed rooms (enjoy the big easel paintings and play human chess on the carpet). The deeply hued breakfast room and lounge are so hip that German rock stars have photo shoots here (Sb-€82, Db-€108 but drops to €95 on weekends, request quiet room to escape street and train noise, air-con, non-smoking rooms, elevator, Ursulaplatz 9–11, tel. 0221/16300, fax 0221/163-0333, www.hotelcristall.de, hotelcristall@t-online.de).

Near the Pedestrian Zone

These moderately priced places, centrally located along the pedestrian zone, are more convenient than charming.

$$ Hotel Engelbertz is a fine, family-run, 40-room place an eight-minute walk from the station and cathedral at the end of the pedestrian mall (specials for readers with this book who request a discount during non-convention times: Sb-€50 and Db-€65 if you call to book on same day or day before, Sb-€62 and Db-€82 if you reserve in advance; regular rate Sb-€68 and Db-€96, convention rate Db-€186, elevator, just off Hohe Strasse at Obenmarspforten 1-3, tel. 0221/257-8994, fax 0221/257-8924, www.hotel-engelbertz.de, info@hotel-engelbertz.de).

$$ Hotel Ibis am Dom, a huge budget chain with a 71-room modern hotel right at the train station, offers all the comforts in a tidy affordable package (Sb-€77, Db-€89; convention rate: Sb-€109, Db-€121; breakfast-€9 extra per person, air-con, non-smoking rooms, elevator, Hauptbahnhof, entry across from station's *Reise-zentrum*, tel. 0221/912-8580, fax 0221/9128-58199, www.ibis-hotel .de, h0739@accor-hotels.com).

Sleeping Cheap behind the Station

Affordable, family-run hotels line Domstrasse and Brandenburger Strasse behind (northeast of) the train station in a quieter neighborhood. To reach these hotels, exit the station away from the cathedral (the end near track 11).

$ **Hotel Müller,** run by a family of the same name, has 15 rooms with 3-star quality at 2-star prices (because it doesn't have an elevator), an outdoorsy basement breakfast room/bar, and a courtyard terrace (Sb-€45, Db-€65, prices can double during big conventions, Internet access, Brandenburger Strasse 20, exit behind station to Breslauer Platz, walk up Johannisstrasse two blocks, left on Brandenburger Strasse, tel. 0221/912-8350, fax 0221/9128-3517, www.hotel-mueller-koeln.de, hotel-mueller-koeln@t-online.de).

$ **Hotel Domblick** offers 23 basic but well-maintained rooms behind a creepy eye-plus-Dom logo—are we looking at the cathedral, or is it looking at us? (Sb-€60, Db-€75, elevator, exit behind station to Breslauer Platz, walk left two blocks, turn right on Domstrasse, and walk 2 blocks up to #28, tel. 0221/123-742, fax 0221/125-736, www.hotel -dom-blick.de).

Hostels

$ **Station Hostels** have two locations in the city with some cheap doubles (www.hostel-cologne.de). Sheets are included; breakfast is extra.

Station 1, with 60 beds, is a two-minute walk from the train station (dorm bed-€15–18, S-€27, D-€40, key deposit-€10, no curfew, free Internet access, laundry, kitchen, bike rental-€7/day, tel. 0221/912-5301, fax 0221/912-5303, exit station on Dom side, walk straight 1 block, turn right on Marzellenstrasse to #44-48).

Station 2, near the river, offers 50 beds a 15-minute walk south of the train station (dorm bed-€16-19, S-€27, D-€42, curfew: Mon–Fri 1:00, Sat–Sun 3:00, public bar downstairs, tel. 0221/230-247, fax 0221/801-6970, Rheingasse 34–36).

EATING

Kölsch is both the dialect spoken here and the city's distinct type of beer (pale, hoppy, and highly fermented). You'll find plenty of places to enjoy both in the streets around Alter Markt (2 blocks off river).

These three eateries are open daily for lunch and dinner: **Gaffel Haus** serves good local food (near Lintgasse at Alter Markt 20–22, tel. 0221/257-7692). **Papa Joe's Klimperkasten,** in a dark pub packed with memorabilia and nightly live jazz, wins the atmosphere award (Alter Markt 50–52, tel. 0221/258-2132). Closer to the cathedral and station, touristy **Früh am Dom** offers three floors of drinking and dining options (Am Hof 12–14, tel. 0221/261-3211).

For non-*Bräuhaus* dining, sophisticated locals enjoy light fare at **Café Mak** (Tue–Sun 11:00–17:00, Wed until 20:00, closed Mon, just across Hohe Strasse from Dom in Museum of Applied Arts at An der Rechtschule 1, inside front door and down the stairs, smoky inside, courtyard seating outside, tel. 0221/278-0783).

TRANSPORTATION CONNECTIONS

By train to: Cochem (2/hr, 1.75 hrs), **Bacharach** or **St. Goar** (hrly, 1.5 hrs, 1 change), **Frankfurt Airport** (every 2 hrs direct, or 3/hr, 2 hrs, change in Mainz), **Koblenz** (4/hr, 1 hr), **Bonn** (6/hr, 20 min), **Trier** (3/hr, 3 hrs, change in Koblenz), **Aachen** (3/hr, 1 hr), **Paris** (7/day, 4 hrs), **Amsterdam** (every 2 hrs, 3.5 hrs, up to 4 changes). Train info: tel. 01805-996-633.

Unromantic Rhine

▲**Bonn**—Bonn was chosen for its sleepy, cultured, and peaceful nature as a good place to plant Germany's first post-Hitler government. After Germany became one again, Berlin took over its position as capital.

Today, Bonn is sleek, modern, and, by big-city standards, remarkably pleasant and easygoing. The pedestrian-only old town stretching out from the station will make you wonder why the United States can't trade in its malls for real, people-friendly cities. The market square and Münsterplatz—filled with street musicians—are a joy. People-watching doesn't get much better, though the actual sights are disappointing. There's a sparse exhibit at **Beethoven's House** (€4, April–Oct Mon–Sat 10:00–18:00, Sun 11:00–16:00, Nov–March Mon–Sat 10:00–17:00, Sun 11:00–16:00, last entry 30 min before closing, free English brochure, tel. 0228/981-7525).

The **TI** is a five-minute walk in front of the station (Mon–Fri 9:00–18:30, Sat 9:00–16:00, Sun 10:00–14:00, room-finding service–€2, go straight on Windechstrasse, next to Karstadt department store, tel. 0228/775-000).

▲**Remagen**—Midway between Koblenz and Köln are the scant remains of the Bridge at Remagen, of WWII (and movie) fame. But the memorial and the bridge stubs are enough to stir the emotions of Americans who remember when it was the only bridge that remained, allowing the Allies to cross the Rhine and race to Berlin in 1945. A small museum tells the bridge's fascinating story in English. It was built during World

War I to help supply the German forces on the Western Front—ironic that this was the bridge Eisenhower said was worth its weight in gold for its service against Germany. Hitler executed four generals for their failure to blow it up. Ten days after the Americans arrived, the bridge did collapse, killing 28 Americans (€3.50, March–mid-Nov daily 10:00–17:00, May–Oct until 18:00, on the Rhine's west bank, south side of Remagen town, follow Brücke von Remagen signs, Remagen TI tel. 02642/20187, www.remagen.de).

▲Aachen (Charlemagne's Capital)—This city was the capital of Europe in A.D. 800, when Charles the Great (Charlemagne) called it Aix-la-Chapelle. The remains of his rule include an impressive Byzantine/Ravenna–inspired church with his sarcophagus and throne. See the headliner newspaper museum and great fountains, including a clever arrange-'em-yourself version.

Sightseeing Lowlights

Heidelberg—This famous old university town attracts hordes of Americans. Any surviving charm is stained almost beyond recognition by commercialism. It doesn't make it into Germany's top 20 days.

Mainz, Wiesbaden, and Rüdesheim—These towns are all too big or too famous. They're not worth your time. Mainz's Gutenberg Museum is also a disappointment.

NÜRNBERG

Nürnberg (sometimes spelled Nuremberg in English), Bavaria's second city, is packed with interesting sights. The red sandstone Gothic buildings in its charming old town make the city feel far smaller than its population of 500,000. Nürnberg is known for its glorious medieval architecture, its important Germanic history museum, its famous Christmas market (Germany's biggest), its tragic Nazi past, and its tiny little Bratwurst.

ORIENTATION

(area code: 0911)

Nürnberg's old town (containing virtually all important non-Nazi sites) is surrounded by fragments of its old wall and moat, and just beyond that, a ring road. Just outside the southern ring is the train station, and just inside that ring, the Frauentor. From this medieval city gate, sights cluster along a straight line (Königstrasse) downhill to the small Pegnitz River, then back uphill through the market square (Hauptmarkt) to the castle (Kaiserburg). The Nazi Documentation Center—at the former Nazi Rally Grounds—is southeast of the center (easily accessible by tram or S-Bahn; see "Nazi Sites," page 260).

Tourist Information: Nürnberg's handy and helpful **TI** is in the modern building just inside the Frauentor (Mon–Sat 9:00–19:00, closed Sun, across ring road from station at Bahnhofplatz, tel. 0911/233-6131, www.nuernberg.de). Pick up the free city map (with updated sight hours and prices on the back) and get information about bus and walking tours. The TI also books rooms (no fee) and sells transit passes and the Nürnberg Card (see below). The TI's second branch, at the Hauptmarkt, may close in 2004.

Nürnberg Card: The Nürnberg Card covers all of your local transportation and admission to all of Nürnberg's museums, plus a few other

Nürnberg Center

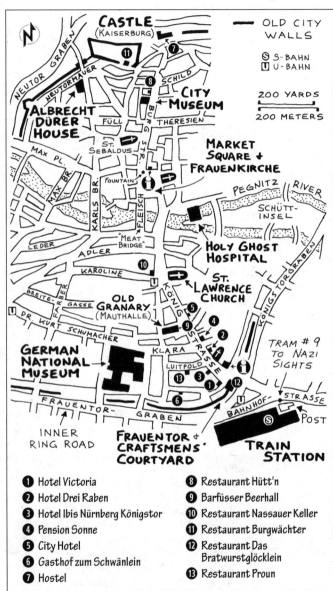

— OLD CITY WALLS

Ⓢ S-BAHN
Ⓤ U-BAHN

200 YARDS
200 METERS

❶ Hotel Victoria
❷ Hotel Drei Raben
❸ Hotel Ibis Nürnberg Königstor
❹ Pension Sonne
❺ City Hotel
❻ Gasthof zum Schwänlein
❼ Hostel

❽ Restaurant Hütt'n
❾ Barfüsser Beerhall
❿ Restaurant Nassauer Keller
⓫ Restaurant Burgwächter
⓬ Restaurant Das Bratwurstglöcklein
⓭ Restaurant Proun

discounts (€18/2 days). The catch: It's only available to those who spend at least one night in Nürnberg. If you're staying one night and two full days, and plan to visit lots of museums, this is a good value. But for a quick one-day visit or day trip, it won't pay for itself.

Internet Access: Try **TelePost,** just inside the Frauentor (€3/hr, Königstrasse 65).

Planning Your Time

Nürnberg is a handy stop between other German destinations, and an easy add-on to an itinerary that includes Munich, Würzburg, and Rothenburg. For the quickest visit to Nürnberg, toss your bag in a locker at the station and head out to the Nazi Documentation Center. With more time, stroll from the station up to the castle (following the route described below). On the way back to the station (or your hotel), stop off at the German National Museum.

Tours of Nürnberg

Walking tours of Nürnberg's old town in English leave from the Hauptmarkt every day May through October at 13:00 (€7.50 plus castle admission, 2.5 hrs, book in advance at TI or just show up and pay guide).

Bus tours (which include some walking) leave daily at 9:30 May through October from the old granary at Hallplatz, two blocks up from the Frauentor TI (€11, 2.5 hrs, in German and English, tel. 0911/202-2910).

For a lower-key tour, hop on the **tourist train** that makes the rounds in the old town (€4, 30 min, leaves Hauptmarkt about hourly 10:30–16:00).

Doris Ritter is a very good **local guide** (€80/2 hrs, €100/3 hrs, tel. 0911/518-1719, doris.ritter@nuernberg-tours.de).

Arrival in Nürnberg

Nürnberg's stately old Hauptbahnhof—with a shiny new interior—is conveniently located at the southern edge of the center, just outside the old city walls. The station has WCs, lockers, ATMs, and lots of shops. You can get train information and buy tickets at the *Reisezentrum* in the main hall (center of building). To reach Frauentor—the medieval city's southern gate, and the perfect starting point for a stroll through town—take the escalators down into the underpass, then follow signs for *Altstadt* (old town). When you emerge, the TI is on your right and the Frauentor tower is on your left.

To go directly to the Nazi Documentation Center from the station, leave through the exit by the McDonald's and catch tram #9 (see "Nazi Sites," page 260).

Getting around Nürnberg

Most of Nürnberg's sights are in the strollable old town, but the Nazi sites are beyond easy walking distance. Nürnberg's public transportation network, run by VGN, has trams, buses, U-Bahns (subways), and S-Bahns (faster suburban train network). All work on the same tickets, which you can buy at the TI, vending machines, or on board. A single ticket (good for 90 min of travel in one direction, including transfers) costs €1.40. A day ticket (*TagesTicket Solo,* good for one calendar day) is €3.60. A day ticket also earns you minor discounts at state museums—ask. Public transit info: tel. 0911/270-7599, www.vgn.de.

SIGHTS

Nürnberg's Old Town

Nürnberg's best sights are conveniently clustered along a straight-line thoroughfare connecting the Hauptbahnhof with the market square *(Hauptmarkt)* and the castle (Kaiserburg). For a good orientation, take the following self-guided stroll. Plan on an hour, not including stops. Begin at the Frauentor (right where you emerge from the Hauptbahnhof underpass).

Frauentor—This tower guards one of the four medieval entrances to Nürnberg's old town. In the Middle Ages, Nürnberg did not have abundant natural resources or a navigable waterway—instead, its people made their living through trade and crafts, such as making scientific instruments, weapons, and armor. The German emperors took note of this industrious little town, and gave it economic privileges (in 1219, the city earned the right to answer only to the Holy Roman Emperor himself). This started a boom for Nürnberg that eventually led to the construction of these walls. Of the three miles of wall that once surrounded the city, most is still intact. Many Central European cities of this size tore down their walls to make way for expansion in the 1800s, and Nürnberg almost did the same. Now they're glad they didn't—it's better for tourism. Between the walls just next to the gate, you'll see the entrance to the...

Craftsmen's Courtyard (Handwerkerhof)—This hokey collection of half-timbered houses was built in the 1970s to give tourists a medieval vibe as they entered the old town from the station. It's packed with replicas of medieval shops, where artisans actually make—and, of course, sell—leather, pottery, and brass goods. (There's also a good place to sample the tiny local Bratwurst—see "Eating," below.) In the Middle Ages, this area between the walls was not a medieval mall but *Passkontrolle*—where all visitors had to register before they could enter the town.

When you're finished poking around the courtyard, head into town (with the train station at your back) on...

Königstrasse—Though it had always been one of the four primary entrances to Nürnberg, this street became the city's main drag only after the train station was built around the turn of the century. It's lined with key sights, several recommended hotels and restaurants, and some wonderful Gothic architecture.

Nürnberg hit its peak in the 14th century, when the Golden Bull law (1356) regularized the election of the Holy Roman Emperor. From then throughout the Middle Ages, German emperors were elected in Frankfurt, crowned in Aachen—and had their first Imperial Diet (a gathering of German nobles and VIPs) right here in Nürnberg.

Nürnberg's low point came during World War II. By the end of the war, 90 percent of the old town was destroyed—the only German city that had it worse was Dresden. If a building was only damaged, it was repaired in the original Gothic style—check out the building with the Peschke shop on the right. But some buildings were completely destroyed. Instead of rebuilding these exactly as they were, or replacing them with brand-new-style buildings, Nürnbergers compromised, creating a style that was at once modern and traditional. Look at the Burger King building on the left (#72). The design is modern, but it incorporates Gothic elements and uses the same distinctive red sandstone as older buildings.

Just after the Burger King on the left, you'll see a small **church** (Klarakirche). In the Middle Ages, Nürnberg had nine monasteries like this one. When the Reformation hit, Nürnberg turned Lutheran, and most of the monasteries were torn down. When they fell, so did Nürnberg's importance; while the city was now Lutheran, its emperors were still Catholic. The ever-important Imperial Diet—once Nürnberg's claim to fame—moved to Regensburg.

If you want to visit the German National Museum now, turn left on the next street (Klaragasse) and walk two blocks (see below). Otherwise, continue along Königstrasse and double back to the museum later.

Across the street from Klarakirche, look for Mary on the second-story corner. You'll see statues like this all over Nürnberg. In the Middle Ages, when most people were illiterate, these landmarks were more useful than addresses for finding the right building. Even after more people began to read, the tradition stuck.

After another block, the street becomes pedestrians-only. Königstrasse used to have more cars and trams than any other street in town. But in the 1970s, the U-Bahn came, and this part of the street became traffic-free. About where the pedestrian street begins, on the left you'll see the...

Old Granary (Mauthalle)—Medieval Nürnberg had 10 of these huge granaries—to ensure that they'd have enough food in case of famine or siege. The grain was stored up above in the attic (behind all of those little dormer windows). Today the cellar is home to a lively beer hall,

Barfüsser (see "Eating," page 265).

Continue another two blocks to...

▲▲St. Lawrence Church (Lorenzerkirche)—Though this is a massive house of worship, it's not a cathedral—because Nürnberg never had a bishop (a fact they were very proud of...a bishop would just order them around, and they prized their independence). Though you've been walking on Königstrasse (King's Street), the street name is misleading. When most kings came to town, they preferred instead to come through the west gate—so they could approach this masterful facade head-on.

The church exterior was completed around 1360. The darker-colored blocks are older; as they've deteriorated, some have been replaced with the stronger, lighter-colored blocks. The entire church was badly damaged in World War II, but was rebuilt quickly (completed in 1952) thanks to an American donor.

Look closely at the main doorway. You'll see Adam and Eve to the right and left of the doors, respectively. In the first row above the left door, you'll see two scenes: Jesus' birth on top, and the visit from the Magi on the bottom. Over the right door, you'll see the Slaughter of the Innocents (with a baby skewered by a Roman sword—classic medieval subtlety), and below that, the presentation of Jesus in the temple and the flight to Egypt. Above those scenes are, from lowest to highest, Jesus' Passion; people coming out of their graves for the Final Judgment (notice the jaws of Hell on the right); and above it all, Saint Peter with his key.

It's worth a few minutes to step inside (enter around right side; €1 suggested donation, Mon–Sat 9:00–17:00, Sun 12:00–16:00). The interior wasn't completely furnished until more than a century after the church was built—just in time for the Reformation (so the new Catholic decor suddenly adorned a Lutheran church). Most of the decorations inside were donated by wealthy Nürnbergers trying to cut down on their time in purgatory. There are two important pieces. First, suspended over the altar, is a woodcarving by one of medieval Germany's best woodcarvers (and Nürnberg native), Viet Stoss. Second, notice the frilly tabernacle to the left of the altar. The man holding the tabernacle on his shoulders is a statue of the artist who created it, Adam Kraft. In the Middle Ages, it was unthinkable for a simple artist to draw attention to himself—he was a faceless artisan, no more important than a blacksmith or a stonemason. But in the 1490s, when this was created, the Renaissance was in the air, and artists like Kraft began putting themselves into their works. Kraft's contemporary, the painter Albrecht Dürer, actually signed his works—an incredible act in Germany at that time (see "Albrecht Dürer House," page 259).

As you leave the church, notice the castle-like building on the corner across from the facade. This is the only remaining **tower house** in Nürnberg. It was built in 1200—when there was no city wall, and the locals had to fend for themselves. It's basically a one-family castle. (In the basement, you'll find an appropriately medieval restaurant—complete with suits of armor—called the Nassauer Keller; see "Eating," page 265.)

Continue downhill to the river. When you get to the bridge, look to the right. You can't miss the...

▲**Holy Ghost Hospital (Heilig-Geist-Spital)**—This river-spanning building was donated to Nürnberg in 1339 by the city's richest resident, eager to do his part to help the poor...and hopefully skip purgatory altogether. (You can see a statue of him hanging out on the second-story corner of the Spital Apotheke, the first building after the bridge.) He funded this very scenic hospital to care for ill, disabled, and elderly Nürnbergers. Beneath the middle window under the turret, find the dove—symbol of the Holy Ghost, the hospital's namesake.

If you look in the distance to the right—beyond the hospital and the next two bridges—you'll see a half-timbered fragment of the town wall. The big white building to the right of that is Germany's biggest multiplex, with 20 screens (most of them underground).

Now cross to the other side of the bridge, and look at the next bridge over (the Meat Bridge). Look familiar? It's based on Venice's Rialto Bridge. This is the narrowest point of the river, and flooding was a big concern. Since this bridge doesn't have any piers, there's less chance of a collapse. When this was built in 1596, it was considered an engineering feat—the most high-tech bridge in Central Europe.

Now continue across the bridge, jogging left at the fork, past the monument—depicting characters from a 15th-century satire called *The Ship of Fools (Das Narrenschiff)*—and enter the...

▲**Market Square (Hauptmarkt)**—When Nürnberg boomed in the 13th century, it consisted of two distinct walled towns separated by the river. Very quickly, it was obvious that the two should merge so the middle wall came down, and this market square, built by the Holy Roman Emperor Charles IV, became the center of the newly united city. Though Charles is more often associated with Prague (he's the namesake for the Charles Bridge and Charles University), he also loved Nürnberg—visiting here 60 times during his reign.

The church on the square **(Frauenkirche)** is located on the site of a former synagogue (inside, there's a Star of David on the floor). When Nürnberg's towns were separate, Jewish residents were encouraged to live in this swampy area close to the river and outside the walls. When the towns merged and this land became valuable, Charles IV allowed his subjects to force out the Jews—and 600 were killed in the process...a somber reminder that Hitler was not the first person in Nürnberg to persecute Jews.

Year-round, the market square is lively with fruit, flower, and souvenir stands. For a few weeks before Christmas, it hosts Germany's largest **Christmas market** (*Christkindlmarkt*, over 2 million visitors each year). Walk across the square to the pointy gold fountain.

Medieval tanneries, slaughterhouses, and the hospital you just saw dumped their byproducts into the river. This **Beautiful Fountain** (Schöner Brunnen) brought clean drinking water into the square.

Of course, it's packed with allegorical meaning. The eight figures on the bottom, outermost ring represent the arts (such as philosophy, music, and astronomy). On the pillars just above them are the four church fathers and the four evangelists, showing that religion is higher than the arts. On the column itself, the lowest figures are the seven electors of the Holy Roman Emperor and nine heroes—three Catholic (like King Arthur and Charlemagne); three Jewish (like King David); and three heathen (like Julius Caesar). At the very top are eight prophets, hovering above—and granting legitimacy to—worldly power. On the side of the fountain facing the river, you'll probably see tourists fussing over a gold ring. If you believe in such silly tour-guide tales, spinning this ring three times brings good luck...okay, go ahead and spin it.

Leave the square straight uphill from the fountain, heading for the castle. Along the way, you'll pass Saint Sebaldus (Sebaldkirche), Nürnberg's second great Gothic church. (When Nürnberg was two towns, each one had its own church.) Beyond that on the left, you'll see the...

City Museum (Stadtmuseum Fembohaus)—This museum, packed with information about the city, is worth a visit primarily for the three interesting models of historic Nürnberg on the fourth floor (€1 for models only, €4 for whole museum, Tue–Sun 10:00–17:00, Thu 10:00–20:00, closed Mon, Burgstrasse 15, tel. 0911/231-2595).

Now huff your way the rest of the way up to the...

▲**Imperial Castle (Kaiserburg)**—Holy Roman Emperors stayed here when they paid a visit to Nürnberg. This huge complex is actually two different castles. The castle on the right, which used to house the Holy Roman Emperor's right-hand man, is now a youth hostel (see "Sleeping," below). On the left is the castle for the emperor himself. Under the tall tower is a courtyard with a superb view over the city. The castle interior and museum are standard fare; the most interesting bits here are the so-called Deep Well (which, at 165 feet, is...well, deep) and the Romanesque double-decker chapel (higher nobility in the upper chapel, lower nobility down below—plus a special balcony for the emperor). Unfortunately, you can see these sights only with a German tour, unless you go with the TI's English tour of the entire old town, which includes the castle (see "Tours of Nürnberg," page 253). Otherwise, wander the half-timbered courtyard, enjoy the town view, and head on to the next sight (castle grounds free; entry to buildings only with German tours: €4.50 for 1-hr tour of museum, palace, and chapel, €5 also includes tour of well and climbing the tower on your own; €2 to climb tower and join German tour only for the well; April–Sept daily 9:00–18:00, Oct–March daily 10:00–16:00, tel.

0911/225-726).

After you leave the castle, consider a stroll to one of Nürnberg's oldest neighborhoods. Leave the castle to the right, then take the lower fork. In a couple of blocks, you'll reach Tiergärtnertorplatz. Near the top of the square, you'll see a huge rabbit. This is a 3-D depiction of one of the best-known paintings by medieval Nürnberg artist Albrecht Dürer, *The Hare* (the original painting, badly deteriorating, is hiding in a Vienna vault). Just behind the monument, the small gate marked N was one of the original gates of the city. (The bigger gate on the left is newer.) The half-timbered building at the bottom of the square is the...

Albrecht Dürer House (Albrecht-Dürer-Haus)—Nürnberg's most famous son lived here for the last 20 years of his life. Albrecht Dürer (1471–1528) was a contemporary of Michelangelo who studied in Venice and brought the Renaissance to stodgy medieval Germany. He did things that were unthinkable to other Northern European artists of his time—such as signing his works, or painting things like hares simply for study (not on commission).

Nothing in the museum is original (all of the paintings are replicas—the only Dürer originals in Nürnberg are in the German National Museum, listed below). But it does a fine job of capturing the way that Dürer actually lived, including a replica of the workshop where he printed his woodcuts. On Saturdays at 14:00, you can take an English tour of the house with an actress playing Dürer's wife, Agnes (€4, includes audioguide, Agnes tour-€2.50 extra, €1.50 English brochure also available, Tue–Sun 10:00–17:00, Thu until 20:00, closed Mon, Albrecht-Dürer-Strasse 39, tel. 0911/231-2568).

You've walked from the southern gate of Nürnberg to the northern gate, and your tour is over. On your way back to the Frauentor—if you haven't already been—consider a detour to the...

▲German National Museum (Germanisches Nationalmuseum)—This massive museum is dedicated to the cultural history of the German-speaking world. While the museum has some great pieces, the collection sprawls and English information is sparse (descriptions posted on only the most important works; official guidebook in German, but a €1.50 English audioguide is planned for 2004).

For a quick walk-through, focus on the best bits. Room 103 is devoted to the world's oldest existing globe. Since it dates from 1491, the Americas are conspicuously missing. Straight ahead in the next room (#114) are some paintings by Nürnberg's own Albrecht Dürer—ranging from the small, intimate portrait of his teacher, Michael Wolgemut, to the larger-than-life paintings of Holy Roman Emperors Charlemagne and Sigismund. In the Middle Ages, when Nürnberg was important, the HRE crown and other imperial accessories (Charlemagne's wearing them) were brought here to display. Dürer painted these to go with the imperial treasures. Today, the crown is on view in Vienna's Hofburg

Treasury...flanked by copies of these same two Dürer paintings.

There's plenty else to see here, from suits of armor and pocket watches to musical instruments and 20th-century chairs that look like the one back in your hotel room—plus halls and halls of mediocre Germanic art from every era. While the museum has few truly world-class pieces, it's fun to wander.

Hitler refused to visit here. This museum documents the full range of Germanic experience, but Hitler had a much narrower vision of what it meant to be German—and didn't approve of everything under this roof (€4, €5 during some special exhibitions, free Wed 18:00–21:00, free English tours every other Sun at 14:00, Tue–Sun 10:00–18:00, Wed 10:00–21:00, 2 blocks west of Königstrasse at Kartäusergasse 1, entrance on far side of building, tel. 0911/133-1284, www.gnm.de).

Nazi Sites

Today, Nürnberg is coming to terms with its Nazi past, with an excellent museum—the Nazi Documentation Center—at the heart of the chilling remains of Hitler's enormous Rally Grounds (now Luitpoldhain park).

▲▲▲**Nazi Documentation Center (Dokumentationszentrum)**— Visitors to Europe's Nazi and Holocaust sights inevitably ask the same haunting question: How could this happen? This superb museum does its best to provide an answer. It meticulously traces the evolution of the National Socialist (Nazi) movement, focusing on how it both energized and terrified the German people (the exhibit's official title is "Fascination and Terror"). A good audioguide takes you through the exhibit. Special attention is paid to Nürnberg's role in the Nazi movement, including the construction and use of the Rally Grounds, where Hitler's most massive demonstrations took place. This is not a World War II or a Holocaust museum; those events are almost an afterthought. Instead, the Center frankly analyzes the Nazi phenomenon, to understand how it happened—and to prevent it from happening again.

Cost, Hours, Information: €5, includes audioguide, €2 English guidebook is a must, €6 combo-ticket includes Nürnberg Trials Courtroom (see below), Mon–Fri 9:00–18:00, Sat–Sun 10:00–18:00, Bayernstrasse 110, tel. 0911/231-5666, www.museen.nuernberg.de.

Getting to the Nazi Documentation Center and Rally Grounds: The museum is located in one small wing of Hitler's enormous, unfinished Congress Hall—the largest surviving example of Nazi architecture. The side of the building has been pierced with a shaft of modern architecture—the museum entrance—symbolically crippling Hitler's ideals.

The Nazi Documentation Center and Rally Grounds are at Luitpoldhain park, southeast of the old town. From the Hauptbahnhof, you have two easy options: tram or S-Bahn. Tram #9 leaves from in front of the McDonald's at the train station every 10 minutes (direction

NAZIS IN NÜRNBERG

It's no coincidence that Nürnberg appealed to Hitler. The city is centrally located in Germany, making it a convenient meeting point for Nazi supporters. Hitler also had a friend here, Julius Streicher (a.k.a. the Franconian Führer), who fanned the flames of Nazism and anti-Semitism (particularly though his inflammatory newspaper *Der Stürmer*—The Storm Trooper). But of greater importance, Nürnberg was steeped in German history. As one of the most important cities of medieval Europe, Nürnberg appealed to Hitler as a way to legitimize his Third Reich by invoking Germany's glorious past. Hitler loved the idea of staging his rallies within sight of the imposing Kaiserburg castle, a symbol of the First Reich, the Holy Roman Empire.

When Hitler took power in 1933, he made Nürnberg the site of his *Reichsparteitage*—**Nazi Party Rallies.** Increasingly elaborate celebrations of Nazi culture, ideology, and power took place here annually for the next six years. The chilling images from Leni Riefenstahl's documentary *Triumph of the Will* were filmed at the 1934 rallies. At the 1935 rallies, the Nazis devised the first laws, called the **Nürnberg Laws,** that legally defined Jews as second-class citizens.

Hitler and his favorite architect, Albert Speer, designed staggeringly massive buildings (such as a stadium seating 400,000 spectators) to host the proceedings. The **Rally Grounds** were the ultimate example of Hitler's preferred architecture style: stark, huge, and neoclassical. Only a few of the plans were completed before World War II broke out in 1939, forcing the construction budget to be reassigned to the war effort. Today it's possible to walk around the still-unfinished remains of Hitler's megalomaniacal super-structures (see "Rally Grounds" on the next page).

As the war drew to a close, the world puzzled over what to do with the Nazi officers who had overseen some of the most gruesome atrocities in the history of humankind. It was finally decided that they should be tried as war criminals by an international tribunal (spearheaded by the U.S. and based on the Anglo-American code of law). These trials took place right here in the Nürnberg Trials Courtroom (see page 263). The **Nürnberg Trials**—the first ever such war-crimes tribunal—brought about a new concept of international law, which continues today in The Hague, Netherlands.

Doku-Zentrum, trip takes about 15 min); the last stop is at the doorstep of the Documentation Center. S-Bahn #2 is slightly faster (10 min, stop Dutzendteich), but less frequent (every 20 min), and it drops you off farther away from the museum. From the Hauptmarkt, you can hop on the made-for-tourists bus #36. All three options cost the same (€1.40 one-way, covered by €3.60 transit day pass).

▲**Rally Grounds (Reichsparteitagsgelände)**—Albert Speer, Hitler's favorite architect, designed this immense complex of buildings (over 4 square miles) for the Nazi rallies. You'll get the best sense of the rally grounds simply from the exhibits inside the Documentation Center. Not much of Hitler's ambitious plans were completed. To visit the surviving fragments, you'll have to make quite a hike (plan on an hour round-trip from the Documentation Center)—and there's precious little to see. But it does give you a sense of the mind-boggling scale of what Hitler and Speer planned.

Begin at the Nazi Documentation Center, in the **Congress Hall** (Kongresshalle). This huge building—big enough for an audience of 50,000—was originally intended to be topped with a roof and skylight. As you leave the Documentation Center, turn right and walk along the side of the building. When you get to the end, turn right again and continue walking with the Congress Hall on your right. Continue past the end of the building, and then turn left (under the *Kommen Sie gut nach Hause* sign) onto the Great Road.

As you walk along the **Great Road** (Grosse Strasse), with a lake on either side, consider the gigantic scale of this complex. At 200 feet wide, the Great Road was big enough to be used as a runway by the Allies after the war. The road is pointed toward Nürnberg's imperial palace, Kaiserburg—Hitler's symbolic connection to the First Reich.

Near the end of the lake, ahead and to the right, was to be the site of the **German Stadium** (Deutsches Stadion)—the biggest in the world (with 400,000 seats). They got as far as digging a foundation before funding was redirected to the war effort. Today, the site of the stadium is a park surrounding the big Silbersee—which was the stadium's foundation.

If you'd like to detour to the German Stadium site, you can—but it's time-consuming, without much to see. Instead, walk down the first lakeside path on your left as you reach the end of the Great Road. Continue along the lake for a good 15 minutes until you dead-end into the parking lot. To your right is the huge Zeppelin Field.

Zeppelin Field (Zeppelinwiese) was the site of the Nazis' biggest rallies, including those famously filmed by Leni Riefenstahl. You can actually climb up on the grandstand and stand on the platform in front of the Zeppelin Tribune, where Hitler stood to survey the masses (up to 100,000 people at a time). The Tribune is based on the design of the ancient Greek Pergamon altar (now in Berlin's Pergamon Museum); it was originally topped by an enormous swastika, which was detonated by

Nazi Sites in Nürnberg

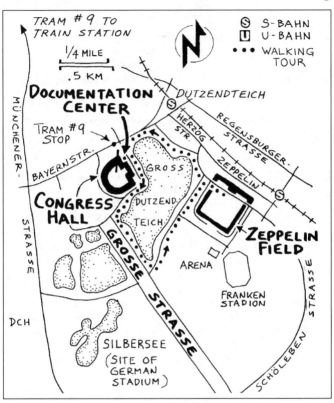

TRAM #9 TO TRAIN STATION

¼ MILE
.5 KM

DOCUMENTATION CENTER

MÜNCHENER-

TRAM #9 STOP

BAYERNSTR.

CONGRESS HALL

GROSSE STRASSE

STRASSE

DCH

SILBERSEE (SITE OF GERMAN STADIUM)

S S-BAHN
U U-BAHN
••• WALKING TOUR

DUTZENDTEICH

HERZOG STR.

REGENSBURGER STRASSE

GROSS

DUTZEND-TEICH

ZEPPELIN

ZEPPELIN FIELD

ARENA

FRANKEN STADION

SCHÖLEBEN STRASSE

STRASSE

the Allies soon after the end of the war.

From here, hike along the lake (with the lake on your left) back towards the Congress Hall. When you dead-end at the busy road, the S-Bahn station is to the right, and the tram stop is in front of the museum to your left.

Nürnberg Trials Courtroom (Nürnberger Prozesse)—In 1945, in courtroom *(Saal)* #600 of Nürnberg's Palace of Justice (Justizgebäude), 21 Nazi war criminals stood trial before an international tribunal of judges appointed by the four victorious countries. After nearly two years of trials and deliberations, 11 Nazis were sentenced to death and the rest to life imprisonment. One of the death sentences was for Hitler's right-hand man, Hermann Göring. He wanted to be shot by firing squad—a proper military execution—but his request was denied. Instead, two hour before his scheduled hanging, Göring committed suicide with poison he had smuggled into his cell, infuriating many who thought that

SLEEP CODE

(€1 = about $1.10, country code: 49, area code: 0911)
Sleep Code: **S** = Single, **D** = Double/Twin, **T** = Triple, **Q** =
Quad, **b** = bathroom, **s** = shower only, **no CC** = Credit Cards
not accepted. Unless otherwise noted, credit cards are accepted,
English is spoken, and breakfast is included.

To help you sort easily through these listings, I've divided
the rooms into three categories, based on the price for a standard double room with bath:

$$$ **Higher Priced**—Most rooms €90 or more.
$$ **Moderately Priced**—Most rooms between €60–90.
$ **Lower Priced**—Most rooms €60 or less.

Several Nürnberg hotels cluster around the Frauentor, on or
close to Königstrasse. This handy neighborhood is convenient
to the station and city sightseeing, just inside the old town walls.
The mini–red light district on nearby Luitpoldstrasse—a sprinkling of strip clubs and sex shops—is harmless. At most
Nürnberg hotels, you can expect higher prices during major
conventions in the spring and fall (expect around 25 percent
increase for most conventions, but as much as 75 percent for
the huge toy fair—Feb 5–10 in 2004). Prices also go up in
December, especially weekends, when the Christmas market is
going on. From June through August, convention season is
over, the tourists hit town, and prices are low.

this death was too easy for him.

While this historic courtroom is still in active use, you can tour it
on weekends (€2, €6 combo-ticket includes Nazi Documentation
Center, tours Sat–Sun at the top of each hr 13:00–16:00, west of center
at Fürther Strasse 10, enter on Bärenschanzstrasse, take U-1 to
Bärenschanze, tel. 0911/231-5666).

SLEEPING

$$$ **Hotel Victoria** offers friendly staff and 66 fresh, new-feeling rooms
just inside the Frauentor. The standard rooms are a better value than
the slightly bigger business rooms (standard rooms: S-€49, Sb-€74, Db-
€99; business rooms: Sb-€84, Db-€109, discounts on slow summer
weekends, rates 20–30 percent higher during conventions, non-smoking

floor, elevator, parking lot-€5.50/day, Königstrasse 80, tel. 0911/24050, fax 0911/227-432, www.hotelvictoria.de, mail@hotelvictoria.de).

$$$ Hotel Drei Raben is an artsy and fun splurge, with a super-stylish lobby, 25 comfortable rooms, and lots of elegant touches. The standard rooms are plenty nice, but the "myth rooms" come with Franconian fairy tales painted on the wall. All guests get a free book of local folk tales (standard rooms: Sb-€80, Db-€120; myth rooms: Sb/Db-€150; junior suites: Sb/Db-€185; ask for special summer discounts—especially on weekends, when you can get myth rooms for standard prices or lower; prices go up for toy fair but not for other conventions, non-smoking rooms, elevator, Königstrasse 63, tel. 0911/274-380, fax 0911/232-611, www.hotel-drei-raben.de, hotel-drei-raben@t-online.de).

$$ Ibis Nürnberg Königstor offers 53 good-value, cookie-cutter rooms in a great location (Sb/Db-€63 Mon–Thu, €57 Fri–Sun, €92 during conventions, breakfast-€9 extra per person, elevator, Königstrasse 74, tel. 0911/232-000, fax 0911/209-684, www.ibis-hotel.de, h1069 @accor-hotels.com).

$ Pension Sonne offers some of the best cheap beds in town, with a refreshing professionalism and 13 well-maintained rooms (S-€30, D-€50, T for a family-€74, no CC, Königstrasse 45, tel. 0911/227-166, Ittner family speaks just enough English).

$ City Hotel, with 20 old, worn rooms, has great prices for the location and amenities (Sb-€40, Db-€50; convention rates: Sb-€67, Db-€87; elevator, Königstrasse 25–27, tel. 0911/232-645, fax 0911/203-999, Widtmann family).

$ Gasthof zum Schwänlein has 16 good, cheap rooms above a restaurant serving Czech and Franconian cuisine. This cozy place is on a quiet street, but the squeaky floors, loud plumbing, and thin walls can make for a noisy night. Bring earplugs (S-€28, Ss-€34, Sb-€36, D-€42, Ds-€48–49, Db-€54, Tb-€67, no CC, Hintere Sterngasse 11, tel. 0911/225-162, fax 0911/241-9008, Hlatky family).

$ Nürnberg's **youth hostel** is romantically situated inside the Kaiserburg at the top of the old town. It's scenic, but can be crowded with school groups in summer. As with all Bavarian hostels, travelers over 26 are not allowed (bed in 2- to 6-bed dorm-€19, S-€35, D-€42, less for longer stays, more for non-members, includes breakfast and sheets, curfew-1:00, tel. 0911/230-9360, fax 0911/2309-3611, jhnuernberg @djh-bayern.de).

EATING

Nürnberg is famous for its pinkie-sized Bratwurst (called, like local residents, *Nürnberger*). Nürnbergers—the people—insist that size doesn't matter; they maintain that *in der Kürze liegt die Würze*—in the shortness, therein lies the tastiness. (Sounds like they're overcompensating for something...). It's quickest to eat them three at a time, side-by-side, in a hamburger-like bun (sold at little stands on the street). Nürnberg is packed with atmospheric old places to try this or other regional specialties. For convenience, I've listed restaurants that are on (or just off of) Königstrasse, the main drag connecting the station to the castle.

A couple of blocks below the castle is **Hütt'n,** where happy locals dine on big plates of regional fare (Mon–Fri 16:00–24:00, Sat 11:00–24:30, Sun 10:00–22:30, Burgstrasse 19, tel. 0911/201-9881).

In the basement of the old grain storehouse *(Mauthalle)* is the massive **Barfüsser** brewery and beer cellar—packed with jovial Germans dining on meat-on-the-bone (from pork knuckle to duck) and swilling beer by the mini–wooden barrel. This is good, smoky, German fun (daily 11:00–24:00, Hallplatz 2, tel. 0911/204-242).

Across from the St. Lawrence Church, the small door to the **Nassauer Keller** leads down steep steps into a 13th-century vaulted cellar—filled with suits of armor, happy eaters, and traditional food (Mon–Sat 12:00–15:00 & 18:00–24:00, closed Sun, Karolinienstrasse 2–4, tel. 0911/225-967).

Burgwächter serves up German cuisine either indoors in its cozy restauant or outdoors on big old picnic tables on the covered patio. It's just under the castle and gets a mix of tourists and local clientele (daily 11:00–24:00, Am Ölberg 10, tel. 0911/222-126).

Tourists come to **Das Bratwurstglöcklein** for its location—in the middle of the Craftsmen's Courtyard, just inside the Frauentor. But locals enjoy the food, too. It's a convenient place to sample Nürnberg's famous Bratwurst (Mon–Sat 10:00–21:30, closed Sun, Rathausplatz 1, tel. 0911/227-625).

For a break from German fare, visit the trendy **Proun,** with international cuisine in a mod, subdued setting (Tue–Sat 10:00–1:00, Sun 10:00–19:00, across from super-modern Design Museum at Luitpoldstrasse 3, tel. 0911/237-3181).

TRANSPORTATION CONNECTIONS

By train to: Rothenburg (at least hrly, 1.25–2 hrs, change in Steinach), **Würzburg** (2–3/hr, 1–1.25 hrs), **Munich** (hrly, 1.75 hrs), **Frankfurt** (hrly, 2 hrs). Train info: tel. 0911/219-1053 or 01805/996-633.

DRESDEN

Dresden, the capital of Saxony, surprises visitors with fine Baroque architecture and impressive museums. It's historical, intriguing, and fun. While the city is packed with tourists, 85 percent of them are German. Until Americans rediscover Dresden's Baroque glory, you'll feel like you're in on a secret.

At the peak of its power in the 18th century, the capital of Saxony ruled most of present-day Poland and Eastern Germany from the bank of the Elbe River. Dresden native Augustus the Strong was both prince elector of Saxony and king of Poland. He imported artists from all over Europe, peppering his city with stunning Baroque buildings. Dresden's architecture and dedication to the arts—along with the gently rolling hills surrounding the city—earned it the nickname "Florence on the Elbe."

Sadly, Dresden is today best known for its destruction in World War II. American and British pilots firebombed the city on the night of February 13, 1945. More than 50,000 people were killed and 85 percent of the historical center was destroyed. (American Kurt Vonnegut, who was a POW in Dresden during the firebombing, later memorialized the event in his novel *Slaughterhouse-Five*.) Dresden is still rebuilding.

When Germany was divvied up at the end of World War II, Dresden wound up in the Soviet sector. Forty years of Communist rule left its outskirts—and even some of its center—a nightmare of blocky, utilitarian Stalinist architecture. But older Dresdeners feel some nostalgia for the Red old days, when "everyone had a job." Today, Saxony's unemployment rate is 19 percent. Even so, Dresden is a young and vibrant city, crawling with happy-go-lucky students who barely remember Communism.

ORIENTATION

(area code: 0351)

Dresden's city center lies at a curve in the Elbe River. The Old Town (Altstadt) is south of the Elbe, and the New Town (Neustadt) is to the north. Dresden is big, with half a million residents, but virtually all of its sights are within easy strolling distance along the south bank of the Elbe in the Old Town. The main train station (Hauptbahnhof) is a 5-minute tram ride or a 15-minute walk south of the historical center, partly along the heavily Communist-influenced Prager Strasse. The New Town, to the north of the river, is more residential. It boasts virtually no sights, but can be fun to explore and has some recommended hotels and restaurants.

Planning Your Time

Dresden, conveniently located halfway between Prague and Berlin, is well worth a stop. If you're short on time, Dresden's top sights can be seen in a midday break on your Berlin–Prague train ride (it's about 2.5 hours from both). Catch the early train, throw your bag in a locker in the station (€2), do the self-guided tour (below), and visit some museums before taking an evening train out. If you have more time, Dresden merits an overnight stay.

Tourist Information

Dresden has two TIs: in the heart of the Altstadt in the neoclassical Schinkelwache building at **Theaterplatz** (next to the Zwinger, Mon–Fri 10:00–18:00, Sat–Sun 10:00–16:00) and in a freestanding kiosk at the train-station end of **Prager Strasse** (Mon–Fri 9:30–18:00, Sat 9:30–16:00, closed Sun, general TI tel. 0351/491-920, www.dresden-tourist .de). Both tourist offices book rooms (€3 per person), sell concert and theater tickets, and operate travel agencies. Get the handy, free one-page map of Dresden with a listing of key sights, hours, and prices on the back. Also ask for the free *Kultur Quartier Dresden* brochure, with English information on the city's cultural sights.

The **Dresden City Card** sold at the TIs gives you admission to all of Dresden's top museums, discounts on some lesser museums, and unlimited use of the city's transit system (€18/48 hrs; €29 for 72-hr "Regional" version, including outlying areas). If you are only here for the day, skip it—instead, buy a one-day museum pass, called a *Tageskarte* (€10, covers all state museums, including all listed below; available at participating museums).

Many of Dresden's museums (including all Zwinger museums, the Royal Palace, and Watchman's Tower) are closed on Monday. The Albertinum (including the New Masters Gallery and Green Vault) is closed on Thursday. The Web site for all Dresden museums is www .skd-dresden.de.

Central Dresden

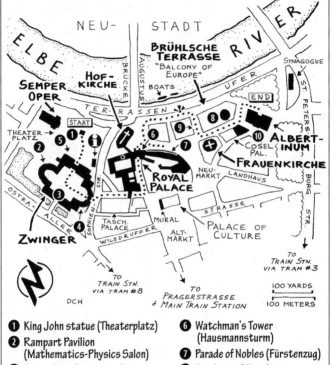

1. King John statue (Theaterplatz)
2. Rampart Pavilion (Mathematics-Physics Salon)
3. Crown Gate (Kronentor)
4. Glockenspielpavillon (Porcelain Collection)
5. Semper Gallery (Old Masters Gallery and Royal Armory)
6. Watchman's Tower (Hausmannsturm)
7. Parade of Nobles (Fürstenzug)
8. Academy of Fine Arts ("lemon juicer" dome)
9. Münzgasse
10. Frauenkirche Visitors' Center

Local Guide: Dr. Günther Kirsch, a good guide, authored one of the souvenir picture books you'll see around town (€28/hr, reserve several weeks ahead if possible, tel. 0351/459-1601).

Arrival in Dresden

Dresden has two major train stations. If you're coming for the day and want easiest access to the sights, use the Hauptbahnhof, just south of the Old Town. Exit the station following signs for taxis and trams, cross the tracks to the opposite side, and take tram #8 (departing to your left), which zips you to the historical center (Theaterplatz stop). If you'd rather walk to the Old Town (15 min), you'll get a dose of the Communist era as you stroll the Soviet-style Prager Strasse (turn left out of station, go under railway overpass, and take pedestrian walkway over construction zone).

The Neustadt station serves the New Town north of the river, near some recommended hotels. From the Neustadt station, tram #11 runs to Am Zwingerteich, a park in the center right next to the sights. Trains run between the Hauptbahnhof and Neustadt station every 10 minutes (€3, 10-min ride; also connected by slower tram #3).

Getting around Dresden

The city is well connected by slick new trams and buses. Buy tickets at the machines in the backs of trams. One ride costs €1.50 (or €0.90 for a *Kurzstrecke*—short stretch—of fewer than 4 stops). A 24-hour ticket *(Tageskarte)* costs €4. Free use of the public transit is included with the City Card (see above).

DO-IT-YOURSELF DRESDEN BAROQUE BLITZ TOUR

Dresden's main sights are conveniently clustered along a delightfully strollable promenade next to the Elbe. Though Dresden has a long and colorful history, focus on the three eras that have shaped it the most: Dresden's golden age in the mid-18th century under Augustus the Strong; the city's WWII destruction by firebombs; and the Communist regime that took over at the war's end and continued until 1989.

The following walk laces together all of Dresden's top sights. It should take you about an hour, not counting museum stops (which could be substantial). Unless otherwise noted, Dresden's museums are light on English information (no audioguides) but heavy on sightseeing value.

Theaterplatz—Begin at Theaterplatz (convenient drop-off point for tram #8 from Hauptbahnhof). Face the equestrian statue (King John, an unimportant mid-19th-century ruler) in the middle of the square. In front of you, behind the statue, is the Saxon State Opera House—nicknamed the **Semper Oper** after its architect, Gottfried Semper (can be toured with a German-speaking guide, €5, 1 hr, enter on right side, tel. 0351/491-1496). Three opera houses have stood in this spot: the first was destroyed by a fire in 1869, the second by firebombs in 1945. The Semper Oper continues to be a world-class venue, and tickets for the Saxon State Orchestra (the world's oldest) are hard to come by (on sale a year in advance; box office in Schinkelwache TI across the square, Mon–Fri 10:00–18:00, Sat 10:00–13:00, closed Sun, tel. 0351/491-1705, fax 0351/491-1700, www.semperoper.de).

Let's get oriented. Behind you is the Hofkirche, with its distinctive openwork steeple, and behind that is the sprawling Royal Palace

Dresden

TO BERLIN

NEUSTADT STATION

TO PFUND'S DAIRY

BAUTZ-NER STR.

❸

ANTON

THERES.

KÖNIG.

HAIN

ALBERTPLATZ

N E U S T A D T

❹

❾

❽

ALBERT STR.

WIGARDSTR.

MARIEN-BRÜCKE

PALAIS PLATZ

GR. MEISS.

HAUPTSTR.

KÖPCKE STR.

CAROLA BRÜCKE

R I V E R

E L B E

HOF-KIRCHE

AUGUSTUS BRÜCKE

PATH

BOATS

BRÜHLSCHE TERRASSE

SYNA-GOGUE

SEMPER OPER

THEATER PLATZ

❻

ALBERT-INUM

TO YENIDZE & SLAUGHTER HOUSE-FIVE

OSTRA-

ROYAL PALACE

NEU-MARKT

FRAUEN-KIRCHE

ZWINGER

WILSD. STR.

ALT-MARKT

❼

RATHAUS

¼ MILE

400 METERS

A L T S T A D T

ST. PETERSBURGER STR.

❶ = KEY TRAM STOP

ALLEE

WAISENHAUSER

REITBAHN STR.

PRAGERSTRASSE

ST. PETERSBURGER STR.

MAIN STATION

❶ Hotel Rest. Kipping
❷ Hotels Bastei, Königstein & Lilienstein
❸ Hotel Bayerischer Hof Dresden
❹ Hotel Martha Hospiz
❺ AHA (Apart Hotel Akzent)
❻ Münzgasse (Hilton Hotel, Rest. Kleppereck & Dampf Schiff Bierhaus)
❼ Restaurant Altmarkt Keller
❽ Wenzel Prager Bierstuben
❾ Ausonia Restaurant

❷

❶ LIND.

TO PRAGUE VIA E-55

(both described below). When facing the Opera House, on your left is the neoclassical Schinkelwache (Guardhouse, houses the TI). The big building behind it and to its right is the Semper Gallery, the east wing of the Zwinger (your next stop). All the buildings you see here—Dresden's Baroque treasures—are replicas. The originals were destroyed by American and British bombs in a single night. For almost 60 years, Dresden has been rebuilding—and there's lots more work to do.

Walk through the passageway into the Zwinger courtyard (to your left as you face the Semper Oper), noticing the Crown Gate on the opposite site lowering majestically into view. Stop in the middle of the courtyard, where we'll survey all four wings.

The Zwinger—This palatial building is a Baroque masterpiece, the pride and joy of the Wettin dynasty. The Wettins ruled Saxony for nearly 900 years—right up until the end of the First World War. At its peak, Saxony had not a king, but an elector. The prince elector of Saxony—one of a handful of nobles who elected the Holy Roman Emperor—was one of Germany's most powerful people. The 18th century was Saxony's golden age. Friedrich Augustus I, prince elector of Saxony, wheeled and dealed—and converted from his Saxon Protestantism to a more Polish-friendly Catholicism—to become King Augustus II of Poland. Legends paint Augustus as a macho, womanizing, powerful, ambitious, properly Baroque man—a real Saxon superstar. A hundred years after his death, historians—or was it the Saxon tourist office?—dubbed him "the Strong." Today tour guides love to impart silly legends about Augustus, who supposedly fathered 365 children and could break a horseshoe in half with his bare hands.

Like most Wettins, Augustus the Strong was unlucky at war, but a clever diplomat and a lover of the arts. We can thank Augustus and the rest of the Wettins—and the nobles who paid them taxes—for Dresden's rich architectural and artistic heritage. Anticipating WWII bombs, Dresdeners preserved their town's art treasures by storing them in underground mines and cellars in the countryside.

The courtyard where the Zwinger now stands was the site of a fortress in the Middle Ages. By Augustus' time, it was used for celebrations of Saxon royalty. Face the west wing (with the Crown Gate on your left). You're looking at the **Rampart Pavilion (Wallpavillon),** the first wing of the palace—an orangery built for Augustus' fruit trees. Stairs lead to a fine Zwinger view from the terrace above. This wing of the Zwinger houses the fun **Mathematics-Physics Salon** (see "Sights—Dresden's Zwinger," page 276). Turn to the left, facing the **Crown Gate (Kronentor);** its golden crown is topped by four eagles, symbolizing Polish royalty (remember, Augustus was also king of Poland). Turn again to the left to see the **Glockenspielpavillon.** The **glockenspiel** near the top of the gate has 40 bells. Because they are made of Meissen porcelain, they can play half-tones (sharps and flats), giving them a bigger repertoire than metal-bell glockenspiels (bells chime every 15 min and play melodies at 11:15, 14:15, and 17:15). Above the glockenspiel stands Hercules, with the Earth on his back—a fitting symbol for Augustus the Strong. This wing of the Zwinger also houses Augustus the Strong's **Porcelain Collection** (see "Sights—Dresden's Zwinger," page 276). Turn once more to the left (with the Crown Gate behind you) to see the **Semper Gallery.** This Zwinger wing was added to the original courtyard a hundred years later by Gottfried Semper (of opera house fame). It houses Dresden's best museum, the **Old Masters Gallery,** as well as the **Royal Armory**.

Take time to enjoy some of the Zwinger's excellent museums. When you're finished, exit the Zwinger through the Glockenspiel-pavillon (east gate). Halfway through the corridor, notice the timelines telling the history of the Zwinger in German: to the right, its construction, and to the left, its destruction and reconstruction. Notice the Soviet spin: On May 8, 1945, the Soviet army liberated Dresden from "fascist tyranny" *(faschistischen Tyrannei),* and from 1945 to 1964, the Zwinger was rebuilt with the "power of the workers and peasants" *(Arbeiter- und Bauern-Macht).*

As you exit the corridor, jog to the left, cross the street and the tram tracks, and walk down the perpendicular Taschenberg Strasse with the yellow Taschenberg Palace on your right. Go under the passageway between the Royal Palace and the yellow palace. Ahead of you and to the right, the blocky modern building is the...

Palace of Culture (Kulturpalast)—This theater, built by the Communist government in 1969, is still used for concerts today. The faded green tarp near the top covers a mural depicting Communist themes: workers; strong women; care for the elderly; teachers and students; and, of course, the red star and the seal of the former East Germany. The tarp went up soon after the Communists went out—supposedly because the mural was in disrepair—and it's been up ever since. This is an interesting commentary on the way Dresdeners have adapted to a post-Communist world.

Now turn left (with the Palace of Culture behind you). Walk toward the tallest tower ahead on the left (the climbable **Watchman's Tower,** described below). On your left is the east wing of the sprawling...

Royal Palace (Residenzschloss)—The palace is still being repaired from the WWII firebombing; the farther you walk, the more destruction you'll see. Its reconstruction will take many years. When finished, the Royal Palace will house civic offices and the city's massive art collection—only one-third of which is currently in museums.

Just before you reach the tunnel, look for the bombed-out gap in the wall to your left. This was the palace's **Great Courtyard.** Across the courtyard you see the black-and-white decoration on the inside of the western wing. These images, called sgraffito, are scratched into plaster over charcoal. Continue through the tunnel. Halfway through the tunnel on your right-hand side is a door to the Palace Museum and access to the Watchman's Tower for a great view (see "More Sights in Dresden," page 277). When you're finished climbing the tower, exit the tunnel. You have just come through the Georgenbau gate into the **Palace Square.** Ahead of you and to the left is the...

Hofkirche (Cathedral)—Why does Dresden, a stronghold of local-boy Martin Luther's Protestant Reformation, boast such a beautiful Catholic cathedral? When Augustus the Strong died, his son wanted to continue as king of Poland, like his father. The pope wouldn't allow it unless Augustus Junior agreed to build a Catholic church in Dresden. Today, the Hofkirche is the largest church in Saxony—although just 5 percent of Saxons are Catholic. The passageway connecting the church with the palace allowed the royal family to avoid walking in the street with commoners. The cathedral's roof is ringed by sculptures of 78 religious and allegorical figures by Lorenzo Mattelli. Go inside and find the Memorial Chapel (behind you and to the right as you face the main altar), dedicated to those who died in the firebombing and to all victims of violence. The evocative *pietà* altarpiece (1973) is made of Meissen porcelain. The basement houses the royal crypt, including the heart of the still-virile Augustus the Strong—which, according to legend, beats when a pretty woman comes near (free, enter through side door facing palace, Mon–Thu and Sat 8:00–19:00, Fri 13:00–19:00, Sun 7:00 –19:00, access to crypt only with free German tour, schedule posted by door, tel. 0351/484-4712, www.kathedrale-dresden.de). The 3,000-pipe organ is played for the public on Wednesdays and Saturdays at 11:30 (April–Dec only).

As you leave the Hofkirche, look back at the palace. To the left, next to the palace's main entrance, you'll see a long, yellow mural called the...

Parade of Nobles (Fürstenzug)—This mural shows the 35 members of Saxon royalty, in chronological order, dating back to the Middle Ages. It was created out of the Saxons' need to commemorate their heritage, particularly after Saxony became a part of Germany in 1870. Painted on 24,000 tiles of Dresden china, the mural is longer than a football field (335 feet) and longer than the Watchman's Tower is tall. At the end of the parade, notice the non-royals: students, painters, and teachers. Behind them, you'll see commoners: a miner, a farmer, and a carpenter. The smug-looking fellow at the very end is the creator of the mural, Wilhelm Walther. Walk about 20 yards along the mural and find Augustus the Strong, atop a white stallion rearing up (labeled with his Polish name, Augustus II): dynamic, powerful, perfectly Baroque. Although the entire parade passes through plants and flowers, only the lady-killer Augustus' horse tramples a rose.

When you're finished looking at the mural, return to the Palace

Square facing the river. Climb the big staircase on your right and walk along the...

Brühlsche Terrasse—This "Balcony of Europe" was once Dresden's defensive rampart—look ahead along the side of the terrace facing the river to see openings for cannons and other weapons. By Baroque times, fortresses were no longer necessary, and this became one of Europe's most charming promenades. Stroll, and enjoy the leafy canopy of linden trees. Past the first fountain and the café, belly up to the railing facing the Elbe River.

Elbe River Overview—Dresden has the world's largest and oldest fleet of historic **paddleboat steamers:** nine riverboats from the 19th century (some of which still have plaques bragging, "10-year warranty"). The hills in the distance are home to Saxon vineyards, producing Germany's northernmost wine. Because only a small amount of the land is suitable for vineyards, Saxon wine is expensive and enjoyed mostly by locals. Below you to the left is the bridge called **Augustusbrücke,** connecting Dresden's Old Town with the New Town. Look under the bridge. The water during the massive flood in August of 2002 filled about two-thirds of the arches.

Look across the bridge to the **New Town.** While 85 percent of Dresden's Old Town was decimated by Allied firebombs, much of the New Town survived. The 18th-century apartment buildings here were restored—giving the area a Baroque look instead of the blocky Soviet style predominant on the Old Town side of the river. At the far end of the Augustusbrücke, look for the golden equestrian statue, a symbol of Dresden—Augustus the Strong, the **Goldene Reiter** (golden rider), facing east to his kingdom of Poland. Behind that, the **Three Kings Church** (Dreikönigskirche) marks a neighborhood with some recommended restaurants (see "Eating," below). To the right of Augustusbrücke are some governmental buildings, and upriver to the far right, lots of Soviet-style apartments. The interesting mosque-shaped building in the distance to the far left (marked Yenidze) was originally a tobacco factory designed to advertise Turkish cigarettes, and is now an office building with restaurants and nightclubs.

Continue walking along the Brühlsche Terrasse. Pass the pastel Baroque building on the right—once a gallery, now owned by Hilton and home to restaurants. Ahead on the right, you'll see the glass domes of the **Academy of Fine Arts.** (Locals call the big dome on the right "the lemon juicer.") Just before you get to this building, go down the stairs on your right and head toward the huge scaffolding. You'll walk along **Münzgasse,** which has lots of trendy restaurants with outdoor seating (see "Eating," below). This street re-creates the lively café scene of prewar Dresden. When the Frauenkirche (ahead of you) is rebuilt, the streets around it will teem with restaurants and cafés like these. At the end of Münzgasse, you'll see the massive reconstruction project of the...

Frauenkirche (Church of Our Lady)—Augustus the Strong grew jealous of the mighty Catholic domes of Venice and London, and demanded that a proper Lutheran church be built in Dresden. Completed in 1743, this was Germany's biggest Protestant church (310 feet high). Its unique central stone cupola design gave it the nickname "handbell church"—like St. Peter's in Rome. (Pictures of the church can be found around the reconstruction site and on postcard racks around Dresden.) Then, on the night of February 13, 1945, the firebombs came. When the smoke cleared the next morning, the Frauenkirche was still standing. It burned for two days before finally collapsing. After the war, the Frauenkirche was kept in rubble as a peace monument and the site of many memorial vigils.

In 1992, the reconstruction of the church began. The restorers are using as many of the church's original stones as possible, fitting the church together like a giant jigsaw puzzle. One third of the finished church will be original stones, and new pieces are custom-made to fill in the gaps. The project is due to be completed in 2005, a year before the city's 800th anniversary. The reconstruction will cost more than €100 million—90 percent of which has come from donors around the world.

The site is well described by signs (most in English). Look closely at the church facade: You can see where the original, dark stones meet the new, brighter pieces. Around the church to the right is the small square of Neumarkt; here you'll see rows of scaffolding where chunks of the church—old and new—are sorted and cataloged. For more information, visit the nearby **Frauenkirche Visitors Center,** which features models and photographs of how the Frauenkirche once looked—and how it will look again in 2005 (Mon–Fri 10:00–18:00, Sat–Sun until 17:00, grayish-green building beyond yellow palace at Georg-Treu-Platz 3, follow signs for Treffpunkt Frauenkirche, tel. 0351/486-7757 or 0351/656-0660).

When you're finished exploring the Frauenkirche or munching along Münzgasse, you could end your Dresden walk with a visit to the nearby **Albertinum,** which houses the rest of Dresden's top museums (19th- and 20th-century art and breathtaking treasury items, see "More Sights—Dresden," below; to reach Albertinum, go up stairs at end of courtyard across from Frauenkirche Visitors' Center, then turn right).

SIGHTS

Dresden's Zwinger
All museums in the Zwinger have the same hours: Tue–Sun 10:00–18:00, closed Mon (tel. 0351/491-4678 or 0351/491-4622).

▲▲▲**Old Masters Gallery (Gemäldegalerie Alte Meister)**— Dresden's best museum features works by Raphael, Titian, Rembrandt,

Rubens, Vermeer, and more. Find the cityscapes of Dresden, painted during its golden age by Canaletto. These paintings of mid-18th-century Dresden feature the Hofkirche (still under construction) and the newly completed Frauenkirche. (Upstairs, you'll find paintings of Venice by his more famous uncle, also called "Canaletto.") Other highlights include Vermeer's pensive *Girl at a Window Reading a Letter,* the extensive Rubens collection, and Rembrandt's jaunty self-portrait—with Saskia on his lap and a glass of ale held aloft. But you'll kick yourself if you miss Raphael's masterful *Sistine Madonna.* The portrait features Madonna and Child, Saints Sixtus and Barbara, and wispy angel faces in the clouds. But more recently, the stars of this painting are the pair of whimsical angels in the foreground. These lovable tykes—of T-shirt and poster fame—connect the heavenly world of the painting with you and me (€6, includes Royal Armory entry, included in day ticket, no English explanations so consider the good €10.20 English guidebook, Tue–Sun 10:00–18:00, in Zwinger's Semper Gallery, tel. 0351/491-4678 or 0351/491-4622).

Royal Armory (Rüstkammer)—Packed with swords and suits of armor, the armory is especially fun for its tiny children's armor and the jousting exhibit in the back (€3 alone, or free with entry to Old Masters Gallery, included in day ticket, Tue–Sun 10:00–18:00, in Zwinger across passage from Old Masters Gallery).

Mathematics-Physics Salon (Mathematisch-Physikalischer Salon)—This fun collection features globes, lenses, and clocks from the 16th to 19th centuries (€3, included in day ticket, Tue–Sun 10:00–18:00, in Zwinger).

Porcelain Collection (Porzellansammlung)—Augustus the Strong was obsessed with fancy china; he liked to say he had "porcelain sickness." Here you can enjoy some of his symptoms (€5, included in day ticket, Tue–Sun 10:00–18:00, in Zwinger).

More Sights in Dresden

▲▲**Albertinum**—This historic building houses several of Dresden's best collections. **The Sculpture Collection** (Skulpturensammlung) is on the ground floor, but the best parts are upstairs: The **Green Vault** (Grünes Gewölbe), a treasure-trove of Saxon royalty, features extravagant ivory, silver, and gold knickknacks. Examine the incredibly elaborate diorama of the Delhi Court birthday celebration of a mogul (a thinly veiled stand-in for Augustus the Strong). The adjacent **Coin Cabinet** (Münzkabinett) is also interesting. The **New Masters Gallery** (Gemäldegalerie Neue Meister) features works by 19th- and 20th-century greats such as Renoir, Rodin, van Gogh, Degas, and Klimt. My favorites include Otto Dix's moving triptych *War* (painted between the two World Wars), Gustav Klimt's *Buchenwald,* and Rodin's *Thinker* at the top of the main stairwell (€6, included in day ticket, Fri–Wed 10:00–18:00, closed Thu, at far end of Brühlsche Terrasse, tel. 0351/491-4714 or 0351/491-4622).

▲**Dresden Royal Palace Exhibition and Watchman's Tower (Dresdner Schlossausstellung und Hausmannsturm)**—While the museum—detailing the history and reconstruction of the palace—is skippable, the Watchman's Tower is well worth the 160 steps for a panoramic view of Dresden. On the way up, you'll see exhibits (in German but with interesting photos and blueprints) about the tower's construction and reconstruction (€2.50 for tower and museum, included in day ticket, Tue–Sun 10:00–18:00, closed Mon, tower closed but museum open Nov–March, entrance inside Royal Palace's Georgenbau gate next to Parade of Nobles mural, tel. 0351/491-4678 or 0351/491-4622).

Prager Strasse—This pedestrian mall—connecting the train station and the historic center—was built by the Communists after the war. This street reflects Soviet ideals: big, blocky, functional buildings without extraneous ornamentation. As you stroll down Prager Strasse, imagine these buildings without any of the color or advertising. (Stores "advertised" with simple signs reading Milk, Bread, or simply Products.) In October 1989, special trains carrying Eastern Europeans came through Dresden, heading from the West German embassy in Prague to sanctuary in Western Europe. This street was jammed with people hoping to get on those trains. (The Wall fell a few weeks later.) Today, the street is filled with corporate logos, shoppers with lots of choices, and scruffy, loitering teenagers.

SLEEPING

In the Old Town (Altstadt)

$$$ Hilton Dresden has 340 luxurious rooms in heart of the Altstadt, one block from the river, some with views of the Frauenkirche. Complete with porters, fitness club, pool, and several restaurants, it's everything you would expect from a four-star chain hotel (Sb-€155–190, Db-€170–205, breakfast-€18, An der Frauenkirche 5, tel. 0351/864-2777, fax. 0351/864-2889, www.dresden.hilton.com, rm_dresden @hilton.com).

$$ Hotel Kipping is tidy, located right by the Hauptbahnhof, and professionally run by the friendly and proper Kipping brothers (Ranier and Peter). The building was one of few in this area to survive the fire-bombing—in fact, several people took shelter here during the attack (Sb-€70–95, Db-€85–115, suite for 1-€115–130, for 2-€130–145, child's bed-€20, prices guaranteed through 2004 with this book, elevator, free parking, Winckelmannstrasse 6, tram #8 whisks you to the center, tel. 0351/478-500, fax 0351/478-5099, www.hotel-kipping.de, reception@hotel-kipping.de).

$ Hotels Bastei, Königstein, and Lilienstein are cookie-cutter members of the Ibis chain, goose-stepping single-file up Prager Strasse (listed in order from the station to the center). Each is practically identical,

SLEEP CODE

(€1 = about $1.10, country code: 49, area code: 0351)

Sleep Code: **S** = Single, **D** = Double/Twin, **T** = Triple, **Q** = Quad, **b** = bathroom, **s** = shower only, **no CC** = Credit Cards not accepted, **SE** = Speaks English, **NSE** = No English. Unless otherwise noted, credit cards are accepted, English is spoken, and breakfast is included.

To help you sort easily through these listings, I've divided the rooms into three categories, based on the price for a standard double room with bath:

   $$$ **Higher Priced**—Most rooms €120 or more.
   $$ **Moderately Priced**—Most rooms between €80–120.
   $ **Lower Priced**—Most rooms €80 or less.

Dresden is packed with big, conference-style hotels; characteristic, family-run places are harder to come by. Most buildings in the old center were destroyed by the firebombing and replaced by big, blocky buildings—the Communists weren't fans of quaint. The TI has a room-booking service (€3 per person).

with 360 rooms (newly renovated Bastei is a couple euros more in high season). Though utterly lacking in charm, they are an excellent value at a convenient location between the Hauptbahnhof and the Old Town (Sb-€56–66, Db-€68–84, apartment-€95, breakfast-€9 extra per person, air-con, elevator, Internet access-€6/hr, parking-€6.50/day, can't miss them on Prager Strasse; Bastei reservation tel. 0351/4856-6661, fax 0351/4856-5555, hotel-bastei@ibis-dresden.de; Königstein reservation tel. 0351/4856-6662, fax 0351/4856-6666, hotel-koenigstein@ibis-dresden.de; Lilienstein reservation tel. 0351/4856-6663, fax 0351/4856-7777, hotel-lilienstein@ibis-dresden.de; Web site for all three: www.ibis-hotel.de). Skip their overpriced, below-average hotel restaurants. Instead, eat in the Old Town—or, closer, at Hotel Kipping (see "Eating," page 280).

In the New Town (Neustadt)

These hotels are in tidy residential neighborhoods north of the Elbe, best reached via the Neustadt train station. All three hotels are connected to the center by tram #11.

$$$ Hotel Bayerischer Hof Dresden, across from the Neustadt train station, offers 50 rooms and classy, grand public spaces (Sb-€90–100, Db-€120–135, junior suite-€130–145, suite-€140–170, elevator, non-smoking rooms, free parking, Antonstrasse 33–35, yellow building across from station, tel. 0351/829-370, fax 0351/801-4860, www .bayerischer-hof-dresden.de, info@bayerischer-hof-dresden.de).

$$ **Hotel Martha Hospiz,** near the recommended restaurants on Königstrasse, is a bright, cheery, 50-room place. The two old buildings that make up the hotel have been smartly renovated and connected in back with a glassed-in winter garden and an outdoor breakfast terrace on a charming garden. It's a 10-minute walk to the historical center and a five-minute walk to the Neustadt station (S-€54, Sb-€72–84, Db-€102–118, extra bed-€26, elevator, leaving Neustadt station, turn right on Hainstrasse, left on Theresenstrasse, and then right on Nieritzstrasse to #11, tel. 0351/81760, fax 0351/817-6222, www.vch.de/marthahospiz .dresden, marthahospiz.dresden@t-online.de).

$ **AHA (Apart Hotel Akzent),** run by friendly and accommodating Albrecht (SE), has a homey and welcoming ambience. This place rents 29 simple but neat apartments with kitchens; all except the top floor have balconies. It's a bit farther from the center—10 minutes by foot east of Albertplatz, a 20-minute walk or a quick ride on tram #11 from the center—but its friendliness, coziness, and good value make it a winner (Sb-€60–65, Db-€70–90, twin Db-€90–100, elevator, Bautzner Strasse 53, tel. 0351/800-850, fax 0351/8008-5114, www.ahahotel.de, info@ahahotel.de).

EATING

Dresden's ancient beer halls were destroyed in the firebombing and were not replaced by the Communists. As Dresden comes back to life after 40 years of Communist repression, every restaurant seems bright, shiny, and modern.

In the Old Town

Closest to the city's key sights, you'll find several tasty, affordable restaurants with outdoor seating along **Münzgasse,** the street that connects the Brühlsche Terrasse and the Frauenkirche. **Restaurant Kleppereck** serves hearty German food and some Saxon specialties (entrées €10–15, Mon–Fri 11:00–24:00, Sat–Sun 11:00-22:00, Münzgasse 10, tel. 0351/496-5123). Across the street, **Dampf Schiff Bierhaus** serves similar fare with equal helpings of trendy, traditional, and nautical (daily 11:00–24:00, tel. 0351/864-2826).

Altmarkt Keller, a few blocks farther from the river on Altmarkt, is a festive beer cellar that serves Saxon and Bohemian food and has several Czech beers on tap. The lively crowd, cheesy music, and jolly murals add to the fun. The giant mural inside the entryway—representing the friendship between Dresden and Prague—reads, "The sunshine of life is drinking and being happy" (entrées €8–10, daily 11:00–24:00, Altmarkt 4 by the McDonald's, tel. 0351/481-8130).

Restaurant Kipping, in the recommended hotel of the same name, serves international cuisine and Saxon specialties. Their sauerbraten is *wunderbar* (entrées €9–12, Mon–Sat 18:00–22:30, closed Sun, Winckelmannstrasse 6, tel. 0351/478-500).

In the New Town

If you want to venture farther for dinner, consider the New Town, across the Augustusbrücke. Although the main drag of the New Town is glum (lots of Communist architecture), just a block away is the charming Baroque Königstrasse, where you'll find these restaurants.

Wenzel Prager Bierstuben is a woodsy bar that spills out into an airy, glassed-in gallery (entrées €8–10, daily 11:00–24:00, Königstrasse 1, tel. 0315/804-2010).

Ausonia, an Italian restaurant run by Luigi Murolo and his family, will give you a break from mustard and kraut (€7–9 pizza or pasta, daily 11:30–23:30, Königstrasse 9, tel. 0351/803-3123).

Erlebnisgastronomie (Experience Gastronomy)

All the rage among Dresdeners (and German tourists in Dresden) is *Erlebnisgastronomie.* Elaborately decorated theme restaurants have sprouted next to the biggest-name sights all over town, with over-the-top theme-park decor and historically costumed waitstaff. These can offer a fun change of pace and aren't the bad value you might suspect. Consider **Pulver Turm** (soldiers in the Powder Tower, An Der Frauenkirche 12a, tel. 0351/262-600), **Sophienkeller** (royal wait staff in the Taschenberg Palace, even has a rotating carousel table with suspended swing-chairs you sit in while you eat, daily 11:00–24:00, Taschenberg 3, tel. 0351/497-260, www.sophienkeller-dresden.de), or **Silber Stolln** (silver mine in the New Town at Hauptstrasse 1a, tel. 0351/808-220).

TRANSPORTATION CONNECTIONS

By train to: Berlin (every 2 hrs, 2.25 hrs), **Prague** (7/day, 3 hrs), **Munich** (every 2 hrs, 7 hrs, transfer in Leipzig, Nürnberg, or Fulda), **Frankfurt** (every 2 hrs, 4.5 hrs). Train info: tel. 01805-996-633.

BERLIN

No tour of Germany is complete without a look at its historic and reunited capital, a construction zone called Berlin. Stand over ripped-up tracks and under a canopy of cranes and watch the rebirth of a European capital. Enjoy the thrill of walking over what was the Wall and through Brandenburg Gate.

Berlin has had a tumultuous recent history. After the city was devastated in World War II, it was divided by the Allied powers: The American, British, and French sectors became West Berlin, and the Russian sector, East Berlin. The division was set in stone when the East built the Berlin Wall in 1961. The Berlin Wall lasted 28 years. In 1990, less than a year after the Wall fell, the two Germanys officially became one. When the dust settled, Berliners from both sides of the once-divided city faced the monumental challenge of reunification.

The last decade has taken Berlin through a frenzy of rebuilding. And while there's still plenty of work to be done, a new Berlin is emerging. Berliners joke they don't need to go anywhere because the city's always changing. Spin a postcard rack to see what's new. A five-year-old guidebook on Berlin covers a different city.

Reunification has had its negative side, and locals are fond of saying "the Wall survives in the minds of some people." Some "Ossies" (impolite slang for Easterners) miss their security. Some "Wessies" miss their easy ride (military deferrals, subsidized rent, and tax breaks). For free spirits, walled-in West Berlin was a citadel of freedom within the East.

The city government has been eager to charge forward with little nostalgia for anything that was Eastern. Big corporations and the national government have moved in, and the dreary swath of land that was the Wall has been transformed. City planners are boldly taking Berlin's reunification and the return of the national government as a good opportunity to make Berlin a great capital once again.

ORIENTATION

(area code: 030)
Berlin is huge, with nearly four million people. But the tourist's Berlin can be broken into four digestible chunks:

1. The area around Bahnhof Zoo and the grand Kurfürstendamm Boulevard, nicknamed "Ku'damm" (transportation, tours, information, hotel, shopping hub).

2. Former downtown East Berlin (Brandenburg Gate, Unter den Linden boulevard, Museum Island (Pergamon), the area around Oranienburger Strasse, and Alexanderplatz).

3. The new city center: Kulturforum museums, Potsdamer Platz, the Jewish Museum, and Wall-related sights.

4. Charlottenburg Palace and museums, on the outskirts of the city.

Planning Your Time

Because of the city's location, try to enter and/or leave by either night train or plane. On a three-week trip through Germany, Austria, and Switzerland, I'd give Berlin two days and spend them this way:

Day 1: 10:00-Take a guided walking tour (offered by Original Berlin Walks, see "Tours," page 287). After lunch, take my Do-It-Yourself Orientation Tour (described on page 288), stopping midway

Berlin Sightseeing Modules

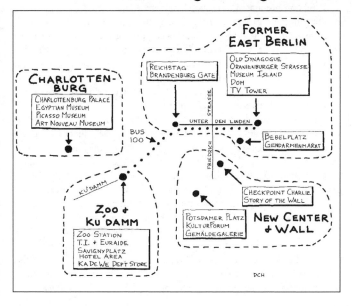

to scale the new dome of the Reichstag building, then finishing with a walk through eastern Berlin. End your day at the Pergamon Museum.

Day 2: Spend the morning lost in the painted art of the Gemälde-galerie. After lunch, hike or taxi via Potsdamer Platz to the Topography of Terror exhibit and along the surviving Zimmerstrasse stretch of Wall to the Museum of the Wall at Checkpoint Charlie. With extra time, consider visiting the Jewish Museum.

If you are maximizing your sightseeing, you could squeeze a hop-off, hop-on bus tour into Day 1 and start Day 2 with a visit to the Egyptian and Picasso museums at Charlottenburg. Remember that the Museum of the Wall is open late and most museums are closed on Monday.

Tourist Information

Berlin's TIs are run by a for-profit agency working for the city's big hotels, which colors the information they provide. The main TI is five minutes from the Bahnhof Zoo, in the Europa Center (with Mercedes symbol on top, enter outside to left at Budapester Strasse 45, April–Oct Mon–Sat 8:30–20:30, Sun 10:00–18:30, Nov–March Mon–Sat 10:00–19:00, Sun 10:00–18:00; call toll tel. 0190/016-316 €1/min; tel. from U.S.: 011-49-700/8623-7546, www.berlin-tourism.de). Smaller TIs are in the Brandenburg Gate (daily April–Oct 9:30–19:00, Nov–March 10:00–18:00) and at the bottom of the TV Tower at Alexanderplatz (April–Oct daily 9:00–20:00, Nov–March daily 10:00–18:00).

The TIs sell a good city map (€0.50—get it), the *Berlin Programm* (a €1.60 comprehensive German-language monthly that lists upcoming events and museum hours, www.berlin-programm.de), the Museumspass (a.k.a. *Schaulust*, €10, 3-day pass to several museums, including many of the biggies, see "Helpful Hints," page 286), and the German-English bimonthly *Berlin Calendar* magazine (€1.20, with timely features on Berlin and a partial calendar of events). The TIs also offer a €3 room-finding service (but only to hotels that give them kickbacks—many don't). Most hotels have free city maps.

EurAide's information office, in the Bahnhof Zoo, provides a great service. They have answers to all your questions about Berlin or train travel around Europe. It's staffed by Americans (so communication is simple), and they have a knack for predicting your needs, then publishing free fliers to serve them (Mon–Fri 8:30–12:00 & 13:00–16:30, Sat 8:30–12:00, closed Sun, closed Sat–Sun Oct–March, closed Jan, located in the train station *Reisezentrum*, great opportunity to get future *couchette* reservations nailed down ahead of time, Prague Excursion passes available—see "Transportation Connections" on page 327, www.euraide.de). EurAide also sells all public transit tickets, including the one-day bus/metro pass (€6.10), the Welcome Card (see "Getting around Berlin" page 285), and city maps—making a trip to the TI probably unnecessary. To get the most out of EurAide, organize your questions and needs before your visit.

Arrival in Berlin

By Train at Bahnhof Zoo: Berlin's central station is called Bahnhof Zoologischer Garten (because it's near Berlin's famous zoo), or "Zoo" for short (rhymes with "toe"). Coming from Western Europe, you'll probably land at Zoo. It's small, well organized, and handy (lockers and baggage check available in back of station).

Upon arrival by train, orient yourself like this: Inside the station, follow signs to Hardenbergplatz. Step into this busy square filled with city buses, taxis, the transit office, and derelicts. The Original Berlin Walks start from the curb immediately outside the station at the top of the taxi stand (see "Tours," page 287). Between you and the McDonald's across the street is the stop for bus #100 (departing to the right for the Do-It-Yourself Orientation Tour). Turn right and tiptoe through the riffraff to the eight-lane highway, Hardenbergstrasse. Walk to the median strip and stand with your back to the tracks. Ahead you'll see the black, bombed-out hulk of the Kaiser Wilhelm Memorial Church and the Europa Center (Mercedes symbol spinning on roof), which houses the main TI. Just ahead on the left, amid the traffic, is the BVG transport information kiosk (buy a €6.10 day pass covering the subway and buses, and pick up a free subway map). If you're facing the church, my recommended hotels are behind you to your right.

If you arrive at Berlin's other train stations (trains from most of Eastern Europe arrive at Ostbahnhof), no problem: Ride another train (fastest option) or the S-Bahn or U-Bahn (runs every few min) to Bahnhof Zoo and pretend you arrived here.

By Plane: See "Transportation Connections," page 327.

Getting around Berlin

Berlin's sights spread far and wide. Right from the start, commit yourself to the fine public transit system.

By Subway and Bus: The U-Bahn (*Untergrund-Bahn,* Berlin's subway), S-Bahn (*Schnell-Bahn,* or fast train, mostly above ground and with fewer stops), *Strassenbahn* (streetcars), and all buses are consolidated into one "BVG" system that uses the same tickets. Here are your options:

• Basic ticket *(Einzel Fahrschein)* for two hours of travel on buses or subways (€2.10; *Erwachsener* means adult—anyone 14 or older).

• A day pass *(Tageskarte)* covering zones A and B—the city proper—€6.10, good until 3:00 the morning after. To get out to Potsdam, you need a ticket covering zone C (€6.30). (For longer stays, a 7-day *Tageskarte* is also available—€22, or €28 including zone C; or buy two WelcomeCards, see below.)

• A cheap short-ride ticket *(Kurzstrecke Erwachsener)* for a single short ride of six bus stops or three subway stations, with one transfer (€1.20).

• The Berlin/Potsdam **WelcomeCard** gives you three days of transportation in zones A, B, and C, and those same three days of minor discounts on lots of minor and a few major museums (including Checkpoint Charlie), sightseeing tours (including the recommended Berlin Walks), and music and theater events (€19, valid for an adult and up to 3 kids younger than 14). The WelcomeCard is a good deal for a three-day trip (since three one-day transit cards alone cost only €0.70 less than the WelcomeCard) and worth considering for a two-day trip.

Buy your tickets or cards from machines at U- or S-Bahn stations or at the BVG pavilion in front of Bahnhof Zoo (English instructions). To use the machine, first select the type of ticket you want, then load in the coins or paper. Punch your ticket in a red or yellow clock machine to validate it (or risk a €40 fine). The double-decker buses are a joy (can buy ticket on bus), and the subway is a snap. The S-Bahn (but not U-Bahn) is free with a validated Eurailpass (but it uses a Flexipass day).

Sections of the U- or S-Bahn sometimes close temporarily for repairs. In this situation, a bus route replaces the train (*Ersatzverkehr*, or "replacement transportation").

By Taxi: Taxis are easy to flag down, and taxi stands are common. A typical ride within town costs €5–8, and a cross-town trip (for example, Zoo to Alexanderplatz) will cost you around €14. A local law designed to help people get safely and affordably home from their subway station late at night is handy for tourists any time of day: A short ride of no more than two kilometers (1.25 miles) is a flat €3. (Ask for "*Kurzstrecke, drei euro, bitte.*") To get this cheap price, you must hail a cabbie on the street rather than go to a taxi stand (from a stand, it's a minimum €5 charge). Cabbies aren't crazy about the law, so insist on the price and be sure to keep the ride short.

By Bike: Be careful: In Berlin, motorists don't brake for bikers (and bikers don't brake for pedestrians). Fortunately, some roads and sidewalks have special red-painted bike lanes. Just don't ride on the regular sidewalk—it's *nicht erlaubt* (not allowed—that's *verboten* to you and me).

In western Berlin, you can rent good bikes at the **Bahnhof Zoo** left-luggage counter (in back of station, next to lockers; they come with lock, airpump, and mounted basket, €10/day, €23/3 days, €35/7 days, daily 6:15–21:00, passport required, €50 cash deposit); in the east, go to **Fahrradstation** at Hackesche Höfe (€15/day, Mon–Fri 8:00–20:00, Sat–Sun 10:00–16:00, Rosenthaler Strasse 40, tel. 030/2045-4500).

Helpful Hints

Monday Activities: Most museums are closed on Monday. Save Monday for Berlin Wall sights, the Reichstag building, the Do-It-Yourself Orientation Tour (see below), walking/bus tours, the Jewish Museum, churches, the zoo, or shopping along Kurfürstendamm (Ku'damm) Boulevard or at the Kaufhaus des Westens

(KaDeWe) department store. (When Monday is a holiday—as it is several times a year—museums are open then and closed Tuesday.)

Museums: All **state museums,** including the Pergamon Museum and Gemäldegalerie (plus others as noted in "Sights," page 302), are free on the first Sunday of each month. There are two different types of discount passes for Berlin's state museums (www.smpk.de, different from the mostly private museums and sights covered by the WelcomeCard—"Getting around Berlin," above). The state museums are covered by a **one-day ticket** (*Tageskarte*, €6, not valid for special exhibitions, purchase at participating museums, not sold at TI). Entry at most of these museums costs €6, so admission to one essentially includes all of the others on the same day. For longer stays, consider the three-day "*Schaulust*" **Museumspass,** which covers most of the state museums as well as several others (including the Jewish Museum). Only €4 more than the day ticket, it's valid for three times as long and is an excellent value if you'll be doing more than two days of museum-hopping (€10, not valid for special exhibitions, purchase at TI or at participating museums). Note that if a museum is closed on one of the days of your Museumspass, you have access to that museum on the fourth day to make up for lost time.

Addresses: Many Berlin streets are numbered with odd and even numbers on the same side of the street, often with no connection to the other side (for example, Ku'damm #212 can be across the street from #14). To save steps, check the white street signs on curb corners; many list the street numbers covered on that side of the block.

Travel Agency: Last Minute Flugbörse can help you find a flight in a hurry (next to TI in Europa Center, tel. 030/2655-1050, www .lastminuteflugboerse.de).

Internet Access: You'll find cheap, fast Internet access at easyInternetcafé (daily 24 hrs, Ku'damm 224, 10-min walk from Bahnhof Zoo and near recommended hotels, buy ticket at self-service machines, instructions in English).

Laundry: Schnell und Sauber Waschcenter is a handy launderette near my recommended hotels (daily 6:00–23:00, €5–9 wash and dry, Leibnizstrasse 72, four blocks west of Savignyplatz, near intersection with Kantstrasse).

TOURS

▲▲▲**City Walking Tours**—The Original Berlin Walks offers a variety of worthwhile tours led by enthusiastic guides who are native English speakers. The company, run by Englishman Nick Gay, offers a three-hour **Discover Berlin** introductory walk daily year-round at 10:00 and also at 14:30 from April through October for €12 (€9 if you're under 26 or with WelcomeCard). Just show up at the taxi rank in front of Bahnhof Zoo (or 20 min later in eastern Berlin, at the Kilkenny Irish Pub entrance inside Hackescher Markt S-Bahn station). Their high-quality, high-energy guides also offer other tours: **Infamous Third Reich Sites** (€10, €7.50 with WelcomeCard, at 10:00 May–Sept Wed, Fri, and Sat–Sun; March–April and Oct Sat–Sun only), **Jewish Life in Berlin** (€10, €7.50 with WelcomeCard, Mon at 10:00 May–Sept), and **Potsdam** (€15, €11.20 with WelcomeCard, see "Sights—Near Berlin," page 316). Many of the Third Reich and Jewish history sights are difficult to pin down without these excellent walks. Also consider their six-hour trip to the **Sachsenhausen** Concentration Camp, intended "to challenge preconceptions," according to Nick (€15, €11.20 with WelcomeCard, at 10:15 May–Sept Tue, Thu, and Sat–Sun; March–April and Oct Tue and Sat; requires transit day ticket with zone C—or buy from guide, call office for tour specifics). Confirm tour schedules at EurAide or by phone with Nick or his wife and partner, Serena (private tours also available, tel. 030/301-9194, www.berlinwalks.com, berlinwalks@snafu.de).

For a more exhaustive (or, for some, exhausting) walking tour of Berlin, consider **Brewer's Berlin Tours,** run by Terry, a former British embassy worker in East Berlin, and his well-trained staff. These daily tours—especially the in-depth Total version—are legendary for their length, and best for those with a long attention span and a serious interest in Berlin (€10 for either tour, all-day Total Berlin starts at 10:00 and can last 5–8 hrs, 4-hr Classic Berlin starts at 12:00, both meet at taxi stand in front of Friedrichstrasse S-Bahn station, look for red sign, also does Potsdam tours twice weekly, mobile 0179/739-5389, www .brewersberlin.com).

▲**City Bus Tours**—For bus tours, you have two choices:

1. Full-blown, three-hour bus tours. Contact Severin & Kühn (€22, daily 10:00 and 14:00, live guides in 2 languages, from Ku'damm 216, tel. 030/880-4190) or take BVG buses from Ku'damm 18 (€20, 2.5 hrs, leave every 30–60 min daily 10:00–17:00, tel. 030/885-9880).

2. Hop-on, hop-off circle tours. Several companies make a circuit of the city (City-Circle Sightseeing is good, offered by Severin & Kühn). The TI has all the brochures. The tour offers unlimited hop-on, hop-off privileges for its 14-stop route with a good English narration (€18, 10:00–18:00, last bus leaves from Ku-damm at 16:00, 2–4/hr, 2-hr loop, taped commentary). Just hop on where you like and pay the driver. On a sunny day when some double-decker buses go topless, these are a photographer's delight, cruising slowly by just about every top sight in town.

Do-It-Yourself Orientation Tour

Here's an easy ▲▲▲ introduction to Berlin. Half the tour is by bus, the other half is on foot. Berlin's bus #100 (direction Mollstrasse and Prenzlauer Allee) is a sightseer's dream, stopping at Bahnhof Zoo,

Europa Center/Hotel Palace, Siegessäule, Reichstag, Brandenburg Gate, Unter den Linden, Pergamon Museum, and ending at Alexanderplatz. If you have the €18 and two hours for a hop-on, hop-off bus tour (described above), take that instead. But this short €2.10 bus ride is a fine city introduction. Buses leave from Hardenbergplatz in front of the Bahnhof Zoo (and nearly next door to the Europa Center TI, in front of Hotel Palace). Buses come every 10 minutes, and single tickets are good for two hours—so take advantage of hop-on-and-off privileges. Climb aboard, stamp your ticket (giving it a time), and grab a seat on top. You could ride the bus all the way, but I'd get out at the Reichstag and walk to Alexanderplatz.

Part 1: By Bus #100 from Bahnhof Zoo to the Reichstag

(This is about a 10-min ride. Note: The upcoming stop will light up on the reader board inside the bus.)

☛ On your left and then straight ahead, before descending into the tunnel, you'll see the bombed-out hulk of the **Kaiser Wilhelm Memorial Church,** with its postwar sister church (described below) and the **Europa Center.** This is the west-end shopping district, a bustling people zone with big department stores nearby. When the Wall came down, East Berliners flocked to this area's department stores (especially KaDeWe, described below). Soon after, the biggest, swankiest new stores were built in the East. Now the West is trying to win those shoppers back by building even bigger and better shopping centers around Europaplatz. Across from the Zoo station, the under-construction Zoofenster tower will be taller than all the buildings you see here.

Emerging from the tunnel, on your immediate right you'll see the Berlin tourist information office.

☛ At the stop in front of Hotel Palace: on the left, the elephant gates mark the entrance to the **Berlin Zoo** and its aquarium (described below).

☛ Driving down Kurfürstenstrasse, you'll pass several Asian restaurants—a reminder that, for most, the best food in Berlin is not German. Turning left, with the huge Tiergarten in the distance ahead, you'll cross a canal and see the famous **Bauhaus Archive** (an off-white, blocky building) on the right. The Bauhaus movement ushered in a new age of modern architecture that emphasized function over beauty, giving rise to the blocky steel-and-glass skyscrapers in big cities around the world. On the left is Berlin's new embassy row. The big turquoise wall marks the communal home of all five Nordic embassies.

☛ The bus enters a 400-acre park called the **Tiergarten,** packed with cycle paths, joggers, and nude sunbathers. The Victory Column (Siegessäule, with the gilded angel, described below) towers above this vast city park that was once a royal hunting grounds, now nicknamed the "green lungs of Berlin."

BERLIN AT A GLANCE

▲▲▲**Reichstag** Germany's historic Parliament building, topped with a striking dome you can ascend. **Hours:** Daily 8:00–24:00, last entry 22:00.

▲▲▲**Museum of the Wall at Checkpoint Charlie** Moving museum near the former site of the famous border checkpoint between the American and Soviet sectors, with stories of brave escapes during the Cold War and the gleeful days when the wall fell. **Hours:** Daily 9:00–22:00.

▲▲▲**Gemäldegalerie** Germany's top collection of 13th- through 18th-century European paintings, featuring Dürer, Van Eyck, Rubens, Titian, Raphael, Caravaggio, and more. **Hours:** Tue–Sun 10:00–18:00, Thu until 22:00, closed Mon.

▲▲**Brandenburg Gate** One of Berlin's most famous landmarks, a multi-arched gateway, at the former border of East and West. **Hours:** Always open.

▲▲**Unter den Linden** Leafy boulevard through the heart of former East Berlin, lined with some of the city's top sights. **Hours:** Always open.

▲▲**Pergamon Museum** The only essential museum on Museum Island (just off Unter den Linden), featuring the fantastic second-century B.C. Greek Pergamon Altar. **Hours:** Tue–Sun 10:00–18:00, Thu until 22:00, closed Mon.

▲▲**Berlin Wall** Mostly gone, but parts of the wall are still visible, including the East Side Gallery and a chunk near the Topography of Terror (former SS and Gestapo headquarters). **Hours:** Always open.

▲▲**Jewish Museum Berlin** User-friendly museum celebrating Jewish culture, in a highly conceptual building. **Hours:** Daily 10:00–20:00, Mon until 22:00.

▲▲**Gendarmenmarkt** Inviting square bounded by twin churches, a chocolate shop, and the concert hall. **Hours:** Always open.

▲▲**New Synagogue** Largest prewar synagogue in Berlin, destroyed by Nazis, with a facade that has since been rebuilt. **Hours:** Sun–Thu 10:00–18:00, Fri 10:00–14:00, closed Sat, May–Aug Sun–Mon until 20:00 and Fri until 17:00.

▲▲Egyptian Museum Proud home of the exquisite 3,000-year-old bust of Queen Nefertiti. **Hours:** Tue–Sun 10:00–18:00, closed Mon.

▲Kaiser Wilhelm Memorial Church Evocative destroyed church in the heart of the former West Berlin, with a modern annex. **Hours:** Church open Mon–Sat 10:00–16:00, closed Sun, annex open daily 9:00–19:00.

▲Kurfürstendamm West Berlin's main boulevard (nicknamed Ku'damm), packed with tourists and upscale shops. **Hours:** Always open.

▲Käthe Kollwitz Museum Features the black-and-white art of the local artist who conveyed the suffering of Berlin's stormiest century. **Hours:** Wed–Mon 11:00–18:00, closed Tue.

▲Kaufhaus des Westens (KaDeWe) The "department store of the West"—the biggest on the Continent—is where East Berliners flocked when the wall came down. **Hours:** Mon–Fri 9:30–20:00, Sat 9:00–16:00, closed Sun.

▲Potsdamer Platz The Times Square of old Berlin, long a postwar wasteland, now rebuilt with huge glass skyscrapers (can ascend 300-foot-tall Kollhoff tower), an underground train station, and—covered with a huge canopy—the Sony Center mall with eateries. **Hours:** Always open.

▲Music Instruments Museum Impressive collection of historic instruments. **Hours:** Tue–Fri 9:00–17:00, Sat–Sun 10:00–17:00, closed Mon.

▲Charlottenburg Palace Skippable Baroque Hohenzollern palace on the edge of town, across street from Egyptian Museum. **Hours:** Tue–Sun 10:00–17:00, closed Mon.

▲Berggruen Collection Notable works by Picasso, Matisse, van Gogh, Cézanne, and Paul Klee. **Hours:** Tue–Fri 10:00–18:00, Sat–Sun 11:00–18:00, closed Mon.

▲Bröhan Museum Collection of Art Nouveau and art deco furnishings. **Hours:** Tue–Sun 10:00–18:00, closed Mon.

Tiergarten Berlin's "Central Park," stretching two miles from Bahnhof Zoo to Brandenburg Gate, with the Siegessäule (Victory Column) in the
(continued on page 292)

center. **Hours:** Park always open, column climbable April–Sept Mon–Thu 9:30–18:30, Fri–Sun 9:30–19:00, Oct–March daily 9:30–17:30, closes in the rain.

Bebelplatz Square on Unter den Linden bounded by great buildings and an interesting book-burning memorial. **Hours:** Always open.

Neue Wache Touching memorial to the victims of fascism. **Hours:** Always open.

Berlin Cathedral Towering church over popular Lustgarten park on Museum Island. **Hours:** Mon–Sat 9:00–20:00, Sun 11:30–18:00, summer Thu until 22:00.

Fernsehturm A 1,200-foot-tall TV tower with observation deck, in eastern Berlin. **Hours:** March–Oct daily 9:00–1:00, Nov–Feb daily 10:00–24:00.

☛ On the left, a block after leaving the Siegessäule: The 18th-century, late-rococo **Bellevue Palace** is the German White House. Formerly a Nazi VIP guest house, it's now the residence of the federal president (whose power is mostly ceremonial). If the flag's out, he's in.

☛ Driving along the Spree River: This park area was a residential district before World War II. Now, on the left-hand side, it's filled with the buildings of the **new national government.** The huge brick "brown snake" complex was built to house government workers—but it didn't sell—so now its apartments are available to anyone. A Henry Moore sculpture entitled *Butterfly* floats in front of the slope-roofed House of World Cultures (Berliners have nicknamed this building "the pregnant oyster"). The modern tower (next on left) is a carillon with 68 bells (1987).

☛ While you could continue on bus #100, it's better on foot from here. Leap out at the Platz der Republik. Through the trees on the left you'll see Germany's new and sprawling chancellery. Started during the more imperial rule of Helmut Kohl, it's now considered overly grand. The big park is the Platz der Republik, where the Siegessäule stood until Hitler moved it. The gardens were recently dug up to build underground train tracks to serve Berlin's new main train station (the Lehrter Bahnhof, across the field). Watch your step—excavators found a 250-pound undetonated American bomb.

☛ Just down the street stands the **Reichstag.** As you approach the old building with the new dome, look for the row of slate slabs imbedded in the ground (looks like a fancy slate bicycle rack). This is a memorial to

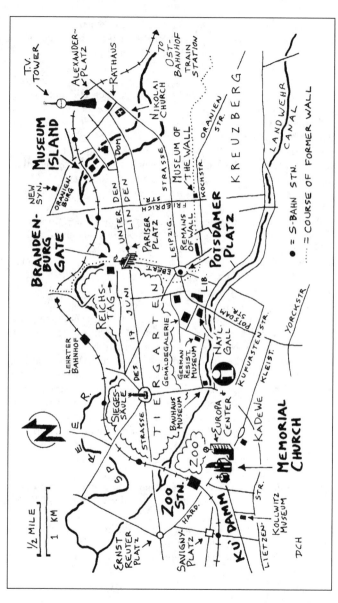

the 96 politicians who were murdered and persecuted because their politics didn't agree with Chancellor Hitler's. Each slab is marked with a name and the party that politician belonged to—mostly KPD (Communists) and SPD (Socialists).

Throughout Berlin, you'll see posters advertising a play called *Ich bin's nicht, Adolf Hitler es gewesen* (It wasn't me, Adolf Hitler did it). The photo is of a model by Hitler's architect Albert Speer of what Berlin was to look like when the Nazis controlled the planet. Hitler planned to rename his capital city "Germania Metropolis." The enormous dome is the Great Hall of the People. Below it and to the right is the tiny Reichstag. Imagine this huge 950-foot-high dome dwarfing everything in Berlin (in the field to your left as you face the Reichstag).

Now visit the Reichstag (open late, no lines in evening) and continue the walk below.

▲▲▲Reichstag Building—The Parliament building—the heart of German democracy—has a short but complicated and emotional history. When it was inaugurated in the 1890s, the last emperor, Kaiser Wilhelm, disdainfully called it the "house for chatting." It was from here that the German Republic was proclaimed in 1918. In 1933, this symbol of democracy nearly burned down. While the Nazis blamed a Communist plot, some believe that Hitler himself planned the fire, using it as a handy excuse to frame the Communists and grab power. As World War II drew to a close, Stalin ordered his troops to take the Reichstag from the Nazis by May 1 (the workers' holiday). More than 1,500 Nazis made their last stand here—extending World War II by two days. On April 30, 1945, it fell to the Allies. It was hardly used from 1933 to 1999. For its 101st birthday, in 1995, the Bulgarian-American artist Christo wrapped it in silvery-gold cloth. It was then wrapped again in scaffolding, rebuilt by British architect Lord Norman Foster, and turned into the new parliamentary home of the Bundestag (Germany's lower house). To many Germans, the proud resurrection of the Reichstag—which no longer has a hint of Hitler—symbolizes the end of a terrible chapter in German history.

The **glass cupola** rises 155 feet above the ground, and a double staircase winds 755 feet to the top for a grand view. Inside the dome, a cone of 360 mirrors reflects natural light into the legislative chamber below. Lit from inside at night, this gives Berlin a memorable nightlight. The environmentally friendly cone also helps with air circulation, drawing hot air out of the legislative chamber and pulling in cool air from below.

Hours: Free, daily 8:00–24:00, last entry 22:00, most crowded 10:00–16:00 (wait in line to go up—good street musicians, metal detectors, no big luggage allowed, some hour-long English tours when parliament is not sitting, tel. 030/2273-2152, www.bundestag.de).

Line-Beating Tip: Those with table reservations at the Dachgarten rooftop restaurant don't wait in the long lines. Go straight to the front and tell them you have a reservation. Reserve in advance by phone or e-mail (Dachgarten, €15–26 entrées with a view, daily 9:00–16:30 & 18:30–24:00, tel. 030/2262-9933, kaeferreservierung.berlin@feinkost-kaefer.de).

Self-Guided Tour: As you approach the building, look above the door, surrounded by stone patches from WWII bomb damage, to see the motto and promise: *Dem Deutschen Volke* (to the German people). The open and airy lobby towers 100 feet high with 65-foot-tall colors of the German flag. Glass doors show the **central legislative chamber.** The message: There will be no secrets in government. Look inside. The seats are "Reichstag blue," a lilac-blue color designed by the architect to brighten the otherwise gray interior. The German eagle (a.k.a. the "fat hen") spreads his wings behind the podium. Notice the doors marked "Yes," "No," and "Abstain"...the Bundestag's traditional "sheep jump" way of counting votes (for critical and close votes, all 669 members leave and vote by walking through the door of their choice).

Ride the elevator to the base of the glass **dome.** Take time to study the photos and read the circle of captions—an excellent exhibit telling the Reichstag story. Then study the surrounding architecture: a broken collage of old on new, like Germany's history. Notice the dome's giant and unobtrusive sunscreen that moves as necessary with the sun. Peer down through the skylight to look over the shoulders of the elected representatives at work. For Germans, the best view is down—keeping a close eye on their government.

Start at the ramp nearest the elevator and wind up to the top of the **double ramp.** Take a 360-degree survey of the city as you hike: First, the big park is the **Tiergarten,** the "green lungs" of Berlin. Beyond that is the **Teufelsberg,** or Devil's Hill (built of rubble from the bombed city in the late 1940s and famous during the Cold War as a powerful ear of the West—notice the telecommunications tower on top). Given the violent and tragic history of Berlin, a city blown apart by bombs and covered over by bulldozers, locals say, "You have to be suspicious when you see the nice green park." Find the **Seigessäule,** the Victory Column (moved by Hitler in the 1930s from in front of the Reichstag to its present position in the Tiergarten). Next, scenes of the new Berlin spiral into your view—**Potsdamer Platz,** marked by the conical glass tower that houses Sony's European headquarters. The yellow building to the right is the Berlin Philharmonic Concert Hall. Continue circling left, and find the green chariot atop the **Brandenburg Gate.** A monument to the Gypsy Holocaust will be built between the Reichstag and Brandenburg Gate. (Gypsies, as disdained by the Nazis as the Jews, lost the same percentage of their population to Hitler.) Another Holocaust memorial will be built just south of Brandenburg Gate. Next, you'll see **former East Berlin** and the city's next huge construction zone, with a forest of 300-foot-tall skyscrapers in the works. Notice the TV tower (with the Pope's Revenge—explained below), the Berlin Cathedral's massive dome, the red tower of the city hall, the golden dome of the New Synagogue, and the Reichstag's **roof garden restaurant** (see above). Follow the train tracks in the distance to the left toward a huge construction zone marking the future central Berlin train station, Lehrter Bahnhof. Just in front of it, alone in a field, is the Swiss Embassy. This used to be surrounded by buildings, but now it's the only one left. Complete your spin tour with the blocky **Chancellery,** nicknamed by locals "the washing machine." It may look like a pharaoh's tomb, but it's the office and home of Germany's most powerful person, the chancellor and his team.

Let's continue our walk and cross what was the Berlin Wall. Leaving the Reichstag, turn left around the building. You'll see the Brandenburg Gate ahead on your right.

Part 2: Walking Tour from Brandenburg Gate up Unter den Linden to Alexanderplatz

Allow a comfortable hour for this walk through eastern Berlin, including time for dawdling (but not including museum stops).

▲▲**Brandenburg Gate**—The historic Brandenburg Gate (1791, the last survivor of 14 gates in Berlin's old city wall—this one led to the city of Brandenburg), crowned by a majestic four-horse chariot with the Goddess of Peace at the reins, was the symbol of Prussian Berlin...and later the symbol of a divided Berlin. Napoleon took the statue to the Louvre in Paris in 1806. When the Prussians got it back, she was renamed the Goddess of Victory. The gate sat unused, part of a sad circle dance called the Wall, for more than 25 years. Now postcards all over town show the ecstatic day—November 9, 1989—when the world enjoyed the sight of happy Berliners jamming the gate like flowers on a parade float. Pause a minute and think about struggles for freedom—past and present. (There's actually a "quiet room" built into the gate for this purpose, daily 11:00–18:00.) Around the gate, look at the information boards with pictures of how much this area changed throughout the 20th century. The latest chapter: The shiny white gate was completely restored in 2002 (financed mostly by Deutsche Telekom). The TI within the gate is open daily April–Oct 9:30–19:00, Nov–March 10:00–18:00.

▲**Pariser Platz**—From in front of Brandenburg Gate, face Pariser Platz (toward the east). Unter den Linden leads to the TV tower in the distance (the end of this walk). The space used to be filled with important government buildings—all bombed to smithereens. Today, Pariser Platz is unrecognizable as the deserted no-man's-land it became under the Communist regime. Sparkling new banks, embassies (the French Embassy rebuilt where it was before World War II), and a swanky hotel have filled in the void.

Unter den Linden

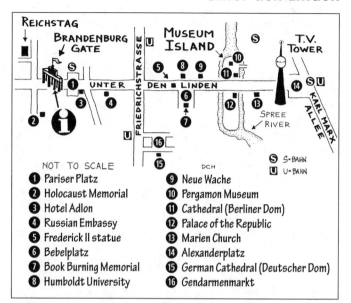

REICHSTAG

BRANDENBURG GATE

MUSEUM ISLAND

T.V. TOWER

FRIEDRICHSTRASSE

UNTER   DEN ■ LINDEN

SPREE RIVER

KARL MARX ALLEE

NOT TO SCALE

DCH

S S·BAHN
U U·BAHN

❶ Pariser Platz
❷ Holocaust Memorial
❸ Hotel Adlon
❹ Russian Embassy
❺ Frederick II statue
❻ Bebelplatz
❼ Book Burning Memorial
❽ Humboldt University

❾ Neue Wache
❿ Pergamon Museum
⓫ Cathedral (Berliner Dom)
⓬ Palace of the Republic
⓭ Marien Church
⓮ Alexanderplatz
⓯ German Cathedral (Deutscher Dom)
⓰ Gendarmenmarkt

Crossing through the gate, look to your right to a construction site—formerly the "death strip." The **U.S. Embassy** once stood here, and a new one will stand in the same spot (due to be completed in 2006). This new embassy has been controversial; for safety's sake, Uncle Sam wanted it away from other buildings, but the Germans preferred it in its original location. A compromise was reached, building the embassy by the gate—but rerouting several major roads to reduce the security risk. The new **Holocaust memorial,** consisting of more than 2,500 gravestone-like pillars, will be completed in 2004 and will stand behind the new embassy.

The **DZ Bank building** (next to the old-new site of the U.S. Embassy) is by Frank Gehry, the unconventional American architect famous for Bilbao's golden Guggenheim, Prague's Dancing House, and Seattle's EMP. Gehry fans might be surprised at the DZ Bank building's low profile. Structures on Pariser Platz are expected to be bland so as not to draw attention away from the Brandenburg Gate. (The glassy facade of the Academy of Arts, next to Gehry's building, is controversial for that very reason.) For your fix of the good old Gehry, step into the lobby and check out its undulating interior.

Brandenburg Gate, the center of old Berlin, sits on a major boulevard, running east–west through Berlin. The western segment, called Strasse des 17. Juni, stretches for four miles from the Siegessäule (past the flea market—see page 305) to the Olympic Stadium. For our walk, we'll follow this city axis in the opposite direction, east, up what is known as Unter den Linden—into the core of old imperial Berlin and past what was once the palace of the Hohenzollern family who ruled Prussia and then Germany. The palace—the reason for just about all you'll see—is a phantom sight, long gone (though some Berliners hope to rebuild it).

▲▲Unter den Linden—This is the heart of former East Berlin. In Berlin's good old days, Unter den Linden was one of Europe's grand boulevards. In the 15th century, this carriageway led from the palace to the hunting grounds (today's big Tiergarten). In the 17th century, Hohenzollern princes and princesses moved in and built their palaces here so they could be near the Prussian emperor.

Named centuries ago for its thousand linden trees, this was the most elegant street of Prussian Berlin before Hitler's time and the main drag of East Berlin after his reign. Hitler replaced the venerable trees—many 250 years old—with Nazi flags. Popular discontent actually drove him to replant linden trees. Today, Unter den Linden is no longer a depressing Cold War cul-de-sac, and its pre-Hitler strolling café ambience is returning.

As you walk toward the giant TV tower, the big building you see jutting out into the street on your right is the **Hotel Adlon.** It hosted such notables as Charlie Chaplin, Albert Einstein, and Greta Garbo. (This was where Garbo said, "I want to be alone," during the filming of *Grand Hotel.*) Destroyed in World War II, the grand Adlon was rebuilt in 1996. See how far you can get inside.

The Unter den Linden S-Bahn station ahead of you is one of Berlin's former **ghost subway stations.** During the Cold War, most underground train tunnels were simply blocked at the border. But a few Western lines looped through the East. To make a little hard Western cash, the Eastern government rented the use of these tracks to the West, but the stations (which happened to be in East Berlin) were strictly off-limits. For 28 years, the stations were unused, as Western trains slowly passed through, seeing only eerie DDR (East German) guards and lots of cobwebs. Literally within days of the fall of the Wall, these stations were reopened, and today they are a time-warp (with dreary old green tiles and original signage). Go down into the station, walk along the track, and exit on the other side, following signs to *Russische Botschaft*...the Russian Embassy.

The **Russian Embassy** was the first big postwar building project in East Berlin. It's built in the powerful, simplified, neoclassical style Stalin liked. While not as important now as it was a few years ago, it's immense as ever. It flies the Russian white, red, and blue. Find the hammer-and-sickle motif decorating the window frames. Continuing past the Aeroflot Airline offices, look across the street to the right to see the back of the **Komische Oper** (comic opera; program and view of ornate interior posted in window). While the exterior is ugly, the fine old theater interior, amazingly missed by WWII bombs, survives. The shop ahead on your right is an amusing mix of antiques, local guide-books, knickknacks, and East Berlin nostalgia souvenirs.

The West lost no time in consuming the East; consequently, some are feeling a wave of nostalgia—*Ost*-algia—for the old days of East Berlin. In recent local elections, nearly half of East Berlin's voters—and 6 percent of West Berliners—voted for the old Communist Party. One symbol of that era has been given a reprieve. As you continue to Friedrichstrasse, look at the DDR–style pedestrian lights, and you'll realize that someone had a sense of humor back then. The perky red and green men—*Ampelmännchen*—were under threat of replacement by the far less jaunty Western signs. Fortunately, the DDR signals will be kept after all.

At **Friedrichstrasse,** look right. Before the war, the Unter den Linden/Friedrichstrasse intersection was the heart of Berlin. In the 1920s, Berlin was famous for its anything-goes love of life. This was the cabaret drag, a springboard to stardom for young and vampy entertain-ers like Marlene Dietrich. (Born in 1901, Dietrich starred in the first German "talkie" and then headed straight to Hollywood.) Today, this boulevard, lined with super department stores (such as Galeries Lafayette, with its cool marble and glass waste-of-space interior, Mon–Fri 9:30–20:00, Sat 9:00–16:00, closed Sun; belly up to its amaz-ing ground floor viewpoint) and big-time hotels (such as the Hilton and Four Seasons), has slowly begun to replace Ku'damm as the grand com-merce and café boulevard of Berlin—though the West is retaliating with some new stores of its own. Across from Galeries Lafayette is American Express (handy for any train ticket needs, Mon–Fri 9:00–19:00, Sat 10:00–13:00, closed Sun, travel agency tel. 030/201-7400, to replace traveler's checks, call 0800/185-3100).

If you continued down Friedrichstrasse, you'd wind up at the Checkpoint Charlie Museum in about 10 minutes (see "Sights—Eastern Berlin," page 308). But for now, continue along Unter den Linden. You'll notice big, colorful water pipes around here, and throughout Berlin. As long as the city remains a big construction zone, it will be laced with these drainage pipes—key to any building project. Berlin's high water table means any new basement comes with lots of pumping out.

Continue down Unter den Linden a few more blocks, past the large equestrian statue of **Frederick II** ("the Great"), and turn right into the square (Bebelplatz). Stand on the glass window in the center. (Construction of an underground parking lot might prevent you from reaching the glass plate.)

Frederick the Great—who ruled from 1740 to 1786—established Prussia as a military power. This square was the center of the "new Rome" Frederick envisioned. Much of Frederick's palace actually survived

World War II but was torn down by the Communists since it symbolized the imperialist past. Now some Berliners want to rebuild the palace, from scratch, exactly as it once was. Other Berliners insist that what's done is done.

Bebelplatz is bounded by great buildings. The German State Opera was bombed in 1941, rebuilt to bolster morale and to celebrate its centennial in 1943, and bombed again in 1945. The former state library is where Lenin studied much of his exile away (climb to the second floor of the library to see a stained glass window depicting his life's work with almost biblical reverence; there's a good café with light food, Tim's Canadian Deli, downstairs). The round Catholic St. Hedwig's Church—nicknamed the "upside-down teacup"—was built to placate the subjects of Catholic lands Frederick added to his empire. (Step inside to see the cheesy DDR government renovation.)

Humboldt University, across Unter den Linden, was one of Europe's greatest. Marx and Lenin (not the brothers or the sisters) studied here as did Grimm (both brothers) and more than two dozen Nobel Prize winners. Einstein—who was Jewish—taught here until taking a spot at Princeton in 1932 (smart guy).

Look down through the glass you're standing on: The room of empty bookshelves is a memorial to the notorious Nazi **book burning.** It was on this square in 1933 that staff and students from the university threw 20,000 newly forbidden books (like Einstein's) into a huge bonfire on the orders of the Nazi propaganda minister Joseph Goebbels.

Continue down Unter den Linden. The next square on your right holds the Opernpalais' restaurants (see "Eating," page 325). On the university side of Unter den Linden, the Greek temple–like building is the **Neue Wache** (the emperor's New Guardhouse, from 1816). When the Wall fell, this memorial to the victims of fascism was transformed into a new national memorial. Look inside where a replica of the Käthe Kollwitz statue, *Mother with Her Dead Son,* is surrounded by thought-provoking silence. This marks the tombs of Germany's unknown soldier and the unknown concentration camp victim. The inscription in front reads, "To the victims of war and tyranny." Read the entire statement in English (on wall, right of entrance).

After the Neue Wache, the next building you'll see is the **German History Museum** (Deutsches Historisches Museum im Zeughaus, Thu–Tue 10:00–18:00, Thu until 20:00, closed Wed, tel. 030/203-040, www.dhm.de), but I find its new I. M. Pei–designed annex with a spiraling glass staircase more interesting (to find it, go down the street—Hinter dem Giesshaus—to the left of the museum).

Just before the bridge, wander left along the canal through a tiny but colorful arts-and-crafts market (weekends only, a larger flea market is just outside the Pergamon Museum; see page 308). Canal tour boats leave from here.

Go back out to the main road and cross the bridge to **Museum Island,** home of Germany's first museums and today famous for its Pergamon Museum (see "Sights—Eastern Berlin," page 308). Eventually, all of the museums on this island will be connected by underground tunnels and consolidate the art collections of East and West Berlin—creating a massive complex intended to rival the Louvre. Today, the museum complex starts with an imposing red neoclassical facade on the left (a musty museum of antiquities; Pergamon is behind it). For 300 years, the square (Lustgarten) has flip-flopped between military parade ground and people-friendly park—depending upon the political tenor of the time. In 1999, it was made into a park again (read history posted in corner opposite church).

The towering church is the 100-year-old **Berlin Cathedral** (Berliner Dom, €4, €5 includes access to dome gallery, Mon–Sat 9:00–20:00, Sun 11:30–18:00, on summer Thu church—but not dome gallery—open until 22:00, www.berliner-dom.de; May–Sept organ concerts offered most Wed,–Fri at 15:00, free with regular admission, for other concerts visit ticket office on Lustgarten side, Mon–Fri 10:00–17:30, closed Sat–Sun, tel. 030/2026-9136). Inside, the great reformers (Luther, Calvin, and company) stand around the brilliantly restored dome like stern saints guarding their theology. Frederick I rests in an ornate tomb (right transept, near entrance to dome). The 270-step climb to the outdoor dome gallery is tough, but offers pleasant, breezy views of the city at the finish line (last entry 30 min before closing, dome closes in bad weather and at 17:00 in winter). The crypt downstairs is not worth a look.

Across the street is the decrepit **Palace of the Republic** (with the copper-tinted windows). A symbol of the Communist days, it was East Berlin's parliament building and futuristic entertainment complex. Although it officially has a date with the wrecking ball, many Easterners want it saved, and its future is still uncertain.

Before crossing the next bridge (and leaving Museum Island), look right. The pointy twin spires of the 13th-century Nikolai Church mark the center of medieval Berlin. This Nikolai-Viertel (district) was restored by the DDR and was trendy in the last years of socialism. Today, it's dull and, with limited time, not worth a visit. As you cross the bridge, look left in the distance to see the gilded **New Synagogue,** rebuilt after WWII bombing (described below). Across the river to the left of the bridge is the construction site of a new shopping center with a huge aquarium in the center. The elevator will go right through the middle of an undersea world.

Walk toward **Marien Church** (from 1270, interesting but very faded old *Dance of Death* mural inside door) at the base of the TV tower. The big, red-brick building past the trees on the right is the **city hall,** built after the revolution of 1848 and arguably the first democratic building in the city. In the park are grandfatherly statues of Marx and Engels (nicknamed by locals "the old pensioners"). Surrounding them are stainless steel monoliths depicting the struggles of the workers of the world.

The 1,200-foot-tall **Fernsehturm (TV Tower)** offers a fine view from halfway up (€6.50, March–Oct daily 9:00–1:00, Nov–Feb daily 10:00–24:00, tel. 030/242-3333). The tower offers a handy city orientation and an interesting view of the flat, red-roofed sprawl of Berlin—including a peek inside the city's many courtyards *(Höfe)*. Consider a kitschy trip to the observation deck for the view and lunch in its revolving restaurant (reservations smart for dinner, same phone number). Built (with Swedish know-how) in 1969, the tower was meant to show the power of the atheistic state at a time when DDR leaders were having the crosses removed from church domes and spires. But when the sun shined on their tower, the greatest spire in East Berlin, a huge cross, reflected on the mirrored ball. Cynics called it "The Pope's Revenge." East Berliners dubbed the tower "The Big Asparagus." They joked that if it fell over, they'd have an elevator to the West.

Farther east, pass under the train tracks into **Alexanderplatz.** This area—especially the Kaufhof—was the commercial pride and joy of East Berlin. Today, it's still a landmark, with a major U- and S-Bahn station.

For a ride through workaday eastern Berlin, with its Lego-hell apartments (dreary even with their new face-lifts), hop back on bus #100 from here. It loops five minutes to the end of the line and then, after a couple minutes' break, heads on back. (This bus retraces your route, finishing at Bahnhof Zoo.) Consider extending this foray into eastern Berlin to Karl Marx Allee (see "Sights—Eastern Berlin," page 308).

SIGHTS

Western Berlin

Western travelers still think of Berlin's "West End" as the heart of the city. While it's no longer that, the West End still has the best infrastructure to support your visit and works well as a home base. Here are a few sights within an easy walk of your hotel and the Zoo station.

▲**Kurfürstendamm**—West Berlin's main drag, Kurfürstendamm boulevard (nicknamed "Ku'damm"), starts at Kaiser Wilhelm Memorial Church and does a commercial cancan for two miles. In the 1850s, when Berlin became a wealthy and important capital, her new rich chose Kurfürstendamm as their street. Bismarck made it Berlin's Champs-Elysées. In the 1920s, it became a chic and fashionable drag of cafés and boutiques. During the Third Reich, as home to an international community of diplomats and journalists, it enjoyed more freedom than the rest of Berlin. Throughout the Cold War, economic subsidies from the West made sure that capitalism thrived on Ku'damm. And today, while much of the old charm has been hamburgerized, Ku'damm is still a fine

Western Berlin

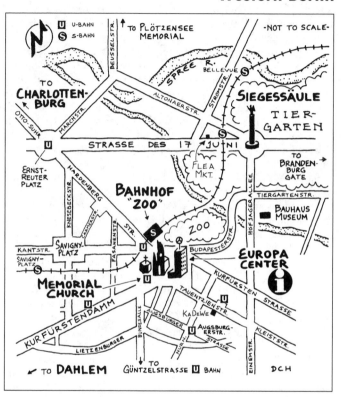

place to feel the pulse of the city and enjoy the elegant shops (around Fasanenstrasse), department stores, and people-watching.

▲**Kaiser Wilhelm Memorial Church (Gedächtniskirche)**—The church was originally a memorial to the first emperor of Germany, who died in 1888. Its bombed-out ruins have been left standing as a memorial to the destruction of Berlin in World War II. Under a fine mosaic ceiling, a small exhibit features interesting photos about the bombing and before-and-after models of the church (free, Mon–Sat 10:00–16:00, closed Sun, www.gedaechtniskirche.com).

After the war, some Berliners wanted to tear the church down and build it anew. Instead, it was decided to keep the ruin as a memorial, and stage a competition to design a modern add-on section. The winning selection—the short, modern building (1961) next to the church—offers a world of 11,000 little blue windows (free, daily 9:00–19:00). The blue glass was given to the church by the French as a reconciliation gift. For more information on both churches, pick up the English booklet (€2.60). The lively square between the churches and the Europa Center (a shiny high-rise shopping center built as a showcase of Western capitalism during the Cold War) usually attracts street musicians.

▲**Käthe Kollwitz Museum**—This local artist (1867–1945), who experienced much of Berlin's stormiest century, conveys some powerful and mostly sad feelings about motherhood, war, and suffering through the black-and-white faces of her art (€5, €1 pamphlet has English explanations of a few major works, Wed–Mon 11:00–18:00, closed Tue, a block off Ku'damm at Fasanenstrasse 24, tel. 030/882-5210, www.kaethe-kollwitz.de).

▲**Kaufhaus des Westens (KaDeWe)**—The "department store of the West," with a staff of 2,100 to help you sort through its vast selection of 380,000 items, claims to be the biggest department store on the Continent. You can get everything from a haircut and train ticket (basement) to souvenirs (third floor). The theater and concert box office on the sixth floor charges an 18 percent booking fee, but they know all your options (cash only). The sixth floor is also a world of gourmet taste treats. The biggest selection of deli and exotic food in Germany offers plenty of classy opportunities to sit down and eat. Ride the glass elevator to the seventh floor's glass-domed Winter Garden self-service cafeteria—fun but pricey (Mon–Fri 9:30–20:00, Sat 9:00–16:00, closed Sun, tel. 030/21210, U-Bahn Wittenbergplatz). The Wittenbergplatz U-Bahn station (in front of KaDeWe) is a unique opportunity to see an old-time station. Enjoy its interior.

Berlin Zoo—More than 1,400 different kinds of animals call Berlin's famous zoo home—or so the zookeepers like to think. Germans enjoy seeing the pandas at play (straight in from the entrance). I enjoy seeing the Germans at play (€9 for zoo or world-class aquarium, €14 for both, children half price, daily 9:00–18:30, Nov–Feb until 17:00, aquarium closes at 18:00, feeding times—*Fütterungszeiten*—posted on map just inside entrance, enter near Europa Center in front of Hotel Palace or opposite Bahnhof Zoo on Hardenbergplatz, Budapester Strasse 32, tel. 030/254-010).

Erotic Art Museum—This offers three floors of graphic (mostly 18th-century) Oriental art, a tiny theater showing erotic silent movies from the early 1900s, and a special exhibit on the queen of German pornography, the late Beate Uhse. This amazing woman, a former test pilot for the Third Reich and groundbreaking purveyor of condoms and sex ed in the 1950s, was the female Hugh Hefner of Germany and CEO of a huge chain of porn shops. If you're traveling far and are sightseeing selectively, the sex museums in Amsterdam or Copenhagen are much better. This one, though well described in English, is little more than prints and posters (€5, daily 9:00–24:00, last entry 23:00, hard-to-beat gift shop, at corner of Kantstrasse and Joachimstalerstrasse, a block from

Bahnhof Zoo, tel. 030/886-0666). If you just want to see sex, you'll see much more for half the price in a private video booth next door.

Central Berlin

Hitler and the Third Reich—While many come to Berlin to see Hitler sights, these are essentially invisible. The German Resistance Museum (described below) is in German only and difficult for the tourist to appreciate. The Topography of Terror (SS and Gestapo headquarters) is a fascinating exhibit but—again—only in German, and all that remains of the building is its foundation. (Both museums have helpful audioguides in English.) Hitler's bunker is completely gone (near Potsdamer Platz). Your best bet for "Hitler sites" is to take the Infamous Third Reich Sites walking tour offered by Berlin Walks (see "Tours," page 287). EurAide has a good flier listing and explaining sites related to the Third Reich.

Tiergarten/Siegessäule—Berlin's "Central Park" stretches two miles from Bahnhof Zoo to Brandenburg Gate. Its centerpiece, the Siegessäule (Victory Column), was built to commemorate the Prussian defeat of France in 1870. The pointy-helmeted Germans rubbed it in, decorating the tower with French cannons and paying for it all with francs received as war reparations. The three lower rings commemorate Bismarck's victories. I imagine the statues of Moltke and other German military greats—which lurk in the trees nearby—goose-stepping around the floodlit angel at night. Originally standing at the Reichstag, the immense tower was actually moved to this position by Hitler in 1938 to complement his anticipated victory parades. At the first level, notice how WWII bullets chipped the fine marble columns. Climbing its 285 steps earns you a breathtaking Berlin-wide view and a close-up look at the gilded angel made famous in the U2 video (€2.20, April–Sept Mon–Thu 9:30–18:30, Fri–Sun 9:30–19:00, Oct–March daily 9:30–17:30, closes in the rain, WCs for paying guests only, no elevator, bus #100, 030/8639-8560). From the tower, the grand Strasse des 17. Juni (named for a workers' uprising against the DDR government in the 1950s) leads east to the Brandenburg Gate.

Flea Market—A colorful flea market with great antiques, more than 200 stalls, collector-savvy merchants, and fun German fast-food stands thrives weekends beyond Siegessäule on Strasse des 17. Juni (S-Bahn Tiergarten).

German Resistance Memorial (Gedenkstätte Deutscher Widerstand)—
This memorial and museum tells the story of the German resistance to Hitler. The Benderblock was a military headquarters where an ill-fated attempt to assassinate Hitler was plotted (the actual attempt occurred in Rastenburg, eastern Prussia). Stauffenberg and his co-conspirators were shot here in the courtyard. While explanations are in German only, the spirit that haunts the place is multi-lingual (free, Mon–Fri

9:00–18:00, Thu until 20:00, Sat–Sun 10:00–18:00, free and good English audioguide with passport, €3 printed English translation, no crowds, near Kulturforum just south of Tiergarten at Stauffenbergstrasse 13, enter in courtyard, door on left, main exhibit is on third floor, bus #129, tel. 030/2699-5000).

▲**Potsdamer Platz**—The Times Square of Berlin, and possibly the busiest square in Europe before World War II, Potsdamer Platz was cut in two by the Wall and left a deserted no-man's-land for 40 years. This immense commercial/residential/entertainment center (with the European corporate headquarters of Sony and others), sitting on a futuristic transportation hub, was a vision begun in 1991 when it was announced that Berlin would resume its position as capital of Germany. Sony, Daimler-Chrysler, and other huge corporations have turned it once again into a center of Berlin. While most of the complex just feels big (the arcade is like any huge, modern, American mall), the entrance to the complex and Sony Center Platz are worth a visit.

For an overview of the new construction, and a scenic route to Sony Center Platz, go to the east end of Potsdamer Strasse, facing the skyscrapers (the opposite end from Kulturforum), at main intersection of Potsdamer Strasse/Leipziger Strasse and Ebert Strasse/Stressemanstrasse, U-Bahn: Potsdamer Platz). Find the green hexagonal clock tower with the traffic lights on top. This is a replica of the first automatic **traffic light** in Europe, which once stood at the six-street intersection of Potsdamer Platz. On either side of Potsdamer Strasse, you'll see huge cubical entrances to the brand-new underground Potsdamer Platz train station (due to open in 2005). Near these entrances, notice the **glass cylinders** sticking out of the ground. The mirrors on the tops of the tubes move with the sun to collect the light and send it underground. Now go in one of the train station entrances and follow signs to "Sony Center." (While you're down there, look for the other ends of the big glass tubes.)

You'll come up the escalator into **Sony Center** under a grand canopy. At night, multicolored floodlights play on the underside of this tent. Office workers and tourists eat here by the fountain, enjoying the parade of people. The modern Bavarian Lindenbrau beer hall—the Sony boss wanted a *Bräuhall*—serves good traditional food (big salads, 3-foot-long taster boards of 8 different beers, daily 11:00–24:00, tel. 030/2575-1280). The adjacent Josty Bar is built around a surviving bit of a venerable hotel that was a meeting place for Berlin's rich and famous before the bombs (daily 9:00–1:00, tel. 030/2575-9702). You can browse the futuristic Sony Style Store, visit the Filmhaus (a museum with an exhibit on Marlene Dietrich), and do some surfing at Web Free TV (on the street).

Across Potsdamer Strasse, you can ride what's billed as "the fastest elevator in Europe" to skyscraping rooftop **views.** You'll travel at nearly 30 feet per second to the top of the 300-foot-tall Kollhoff tower (€3.50,

Tue–Sun 11:00–20:00, closed Mon, in red brick building at Potsdamer Platz 1, tel. 030/2529-4372, www.panoramapunkt.de).

Kulturforum, in Central Berlin

Just west of Potsdamer Platz, with several top museums and Berlin's concert hall, is the city's cultural heart (admission to all sights covered by €6 day card or 3-day *Schaulust* Museumspass, free on first Sun of month). Of its sprawling museums, only the Gemäldegalerie is a must. The tourist info telephone number for all Kulturforum museums is 030/266-2951. To reach the Kulturforum, take the S- or U-Bahn to Potsdamer Platz, then walk along Potsdamer Platz and Potsdamer Strasse. From the Zoo station, you can also take bus #200 to Philharmonie. Across Potsdamer Strasse from the Kulturforum is the huge National Library (free English periodicals).

▲▲▲**Gemäldegalerie**—Germany's top collection of 13th- through 18th-century European paintings (more than 1,400 canvases) is beautifully displayed in a building that is a work of art in itself. Follow the excellent free audioguide. The North Wing starts with German paintings of the 13th to 16th centuries, including eight by Dürer. Then come the Dutch and Flemish—Jan Van Eyck, Brueghel, Rubens, Van Dyck, Hals, and Vermeer. The wing finishes with German, English, and French 18th-century art, such as Gainsborough and Watteau. An octagonal hall at the end features a fine stash of Rembrandts. The South Wing is saved for the Italians—Giotto, Botticelli, Titian, Raphael, and Caravaggio (€6, Tue–Sun 10:00–18:00, Thu until 22:00, closed Mon, clever little loaner stools, great salad bar in cafeteria upstairs, Matthäikirchplatz 4).

New National Gallery (Neue Nationalgalerie)—This features 20th-century art, with ever-changing special exhibits (€6, Tue–Fri 10:00–18:00, Thu until 22:00, Sat–Sun 11:00–18:00, closed Mon, café downstairs).

Museum of Arts and Crafts (Kunstgewerbemuseum)—Wander through a thousand years of applied arts—porcelain, fine *Jugendstil* (art nouveau) furniture, Art Deco, and reliquaries. There are no crowds and no English descriptions (€3, Tue–Fri 10:00–18:00, Sat–Sun 11:00–18:00, closed Mon).

▲**Musical Instruments Museum**—This impressive hall is filled with 600 exhibits from the 16th century to modern times. Wander among old keyboard instruments and funny-looking tubas. There's no English, aside from a €0.10 info sheet, but it's fascinating if you're into pianos (€3, Tue–Fri 9:00–17:00, Sat–Sun 10:00–17:00, closed Mon, the low-profile white building east of the big, yellow Philharmonic Concert Hall, tel. 030/254-810).

Poke into the lobby of Berlin's Philharmonic Concert Hall and see if there are tickets available during your stay (ticket office open Mon–Fri 15:00–18:00, Sat–Sun 11:00–14:00, must purchase tickets in person, box office tel. 030/2548-8132).

Eastern Berlin

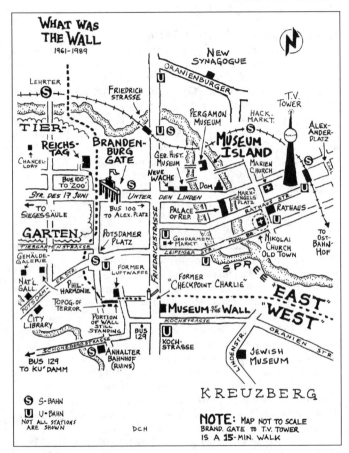

WHAT WAS
THE WALL
1961-1989

NEW SYNAGOGUE

ORANIENBURGER

LEHRTER

FRIEDRICH STRASSE

PERGAMON MUSEUM

HACK. MARKT.

T.V. TOWER

TIER-

REICHS-TAG

CHANCEL-LORY

BRANDEN-BURG GATE

GER. HIST. MUSEUM

MUSEUM ISLAND

ALEX-ANDER-PLATZ

BUS 100 TO ZOO

NEUE WACHE

MARIEN CHURCH

STR. DES 17 JUNI

UNTER DEN LINDEN

DOM

TO .. SIEGESSÄULE

BUS 100 TO ALEX. PLATZ

PALACE OF REP.

MARX-ENGELS-PLATZ

RATHAUS

RATHAUS STR.

GARTEN

POTSDAMER PLATZ

GENDARMEN-MARKT

NIKOLAI CHURCH OLD TOWN

TO OST-BAHN-HOF

TIERGARTENSTRASSE

GEMÄLDE-GALERIE

LEIPZIGER STR.

MÜHL. BR.

SPREE

NAT'L. GALL.

PHIL-HARMONIE

FORMER LUFTWAFFE

FORMER "CHECKPOINT CHARLIE"

"EAST"

POTSDAM.

TOPOG. OF TERROR

PORTION OF WALL STILL STANDING

MUSEUM OF THE WALL

"WEST"

CITY LIBRARY

KOCHSTRASSE

ORANIEN STR.

SCHÖNEBERGSTRASSE

BUS 129

BUS 129 TO KU'DAMM

ANHALTER BAHNHOF (RUINS)

KOCH-STRASSE

LINDENSTR.

JEWISH MUSEUM

KREUZBERG

S   S-BAHN
U   U-BAHN
NOT ALL STATIONS ARE SHOWN

DCH

NOTE: MAP NOT TO SCALE
BRAND. GATE TO T.V. TOWER
IS A 15-MIN. WALK

Eastern Berlin

▲▲**Pergamon Museum**—Of the museums on Museumsinsel (Museum Island), just off Unter den Linden, only the Pergamon is essential. Its highlight is the fantastic Pergamon Altar. From a second-century B.C. Greek temple, it shows the Greeks under Zeus and Athena beating the giants in a dramatic pig pile of mythological mayhem. Check out the action spilling onto the stairs. The Babylonian Ishtar Gate (glazed blue tiles from sixth century B.C.) and many ancient Greek and Mesopotamian treasures are also impressive (€6, covered by Museumspass, Tue–Sun 10:00–18:00, Thu until 22:00, closed Mon, free on first Sun of month, courtyard café, behind Museum Island's red stone museum of antiquities, Am Kupfergraben, tel. for all sights on Museum Island: 030/2090-5577 or 030/209-050). The excellent audioguide (free with admission) covers the museum's highlights. Don't mind the scaffolding. Renovation projects (due to last until 2008) may cause small sections of the museum to close temporarily in 2004, but the museum will remain open.

Old National Gallery—Also on Museum Island, this gallery shows 19th-century German Romantic art: man against nature, Greek ruins dwarfed in enchanted forests, medieval churches, and powerful mountains (€6, covered by Museumspass, Tue–Sun 10:00–18:00, Thu until 22:00, closed Mon, free on first Sun of month, tel. 030/2090-5801).

▲▲**The Berlin Wall**—The 100-mile "Anti-Fascist Protective Rampart," as it was called by the East German government, was erected almost overnight in 1961 to stop the outward flow of people (3 million leaked out between 1949 and 1961). The 13-foot-high Wall *(Mauer)* had a 16-foot tank ditch, a no-man's-land that was 30 to 160 feet wide, and 300 sentry towers. During its 28 years, there were 1,693 cases when border guards fired, 3,221 arrests, and 5,043 documented successful escapes (565 of these were East German guards). The carnival atmosphere of those first years after the Wall fell is gone, but hawkers still sell "authentic" pieces of the Wall, DDR (East German) flags, and military paraphernalia to gawking tourists. Pick up the free brochure *Berlin: The Wall*, available at EurAide or the TI, which traces the history of the Wall and helps you find the remaining chunks and other Wall-related sights in Berlin. You can also rent a *Here We Go* audioguide about the Wall, which starts at Checkpoint Charlie, guides you along Zimmerstrasse to Potsdamer Platz, and then brings you back via Leipziger Strasse and Mauerstrasse (€5, 80 min).

▲▲▲**Museum of the Wall at Checkpoint Charlie (Mauermuseum Haus am Checkpoint Charlie)**—While the famous border checkpoint between the American and Soviet sectors is long gone, its memory is preserved by one of Europe's most interesting museums: The House at Checkpoint Charlie. During the Cold War, it stood defiantly—spitting distance from the border guards—showing off all the clever escapes over, under, and through the Wall.

Today, while the drama is over and hunks of the Wall stand like victory scalps at its door, the museum still tells a gripping history of the Wall, recounts the many ingenious escape attempts (early years with a cruder wall saw more escapes), and includes plenty of video and film coverage of those heady days when people-power tore down the Wall (€7.50, assemble 10 tourists and get in for €4.50 each, €3 audioguide, discount with WelcomeCard but not covered by Museumspass, cash only, daily 9:00–22:00, U-6 to Kochstrasse or—better from Zoo—line 2 to Stadtmitte, Friedrichstrasse 43–45, tel. 030/253-7250, www.mauermuseum.de). If you're pressed for time, this is a good after-dinner sight.

Americans—the Cold War victors—have the biggest appetite for Wall-related sights. Where the gate once stood, notice the thought-provoking post with larger-than-life posters of a young American soldier facing east and a young Russian soldier facing west. Around you are reconstructions of the old checkpoint. It's not named for a person, but for Number Three—as in Alpha (at the East–West German border, a hundred miles west of here), Bravo (as you enter Berlin proper), and Charlie (the most famous because it was the only place where foreigners could pass). A few yards away (on Zimmerstrasse), a glass panel describes the former checkpoint. From there, a double row of cobbles in Zimmerstrasse marks where the Wall once stood (these innocuous cobbles run throughout the city, tracing the former Wall's path). Follow it one very long block to Wilhelmstrasse and a surviving stretch of Wall.

When it fell, the Wall was literally carried away by the euphoria. What did manage to survive has been nearly devoured by a decade of persistent "Wall peckers." The park behind the Zimmerstrasse/Wilhelmstrasse bit of Wall marks the site of the command center of Hitler's Gestapo and SS (explained by English plaques throughout). It's been left undeveloped as a memorial to the tyranny once headquartered here. In the park is...

The Topography of Terror—Because of the horrible things planned here, rubble of the Gestapo and SS buildings will always be left as rubble. The SS, Hitler's personal bodyguards, grew to become a state-within-a-state, with its talons in every corner of German society. Along an excavated foundation of the building, an exhibit tells the story of National Socialism and its victims in Berlin (free, info booth open May–Sept daily 10:00–20:00, Oct–April daily 10:00–18:00 or until dark, free English audioguide with your passport as a deposit, tel. 030/2548-6703).

Across the street (facing the Wall) is the German Finance Ministry (Bundesministerium der Finanzen). Formerly the headquarters of the Nazi air force, this is the only major Hitler-era government building that survived the war's bombs. The Communists used it to house their—no joke—Ministry of Ministries. Walk up Wilhelmstrasse (to the north) to see an entry gate (on your left) that looks much like it did when Germany occupied nearly all of Europe. On the north side of the building (farther up Wilhelmstrasse, at corner with Leipziger Strasse) is a wonderful example of Communist art. The mural (from the 1950s) is classic Social Realism, showing the entire society—industrial laborers, farmworkers, women, and children—all happily singing the same patriotic song. This was the Communist ideal. For the reality, look at the ground in the courtyard in front of the mural to see an enlarged photograph from a 1953 uprising here against the Communists—quite a contrast.

▲▲**Jewish Museum Berlin**—This new museum is one of Europe's best Jewish sights. The highly conceptual building is a sight in itself, and the museum inside—an overview of the rich culture and history of Europe's Jewish community—is excellent. The Holocaust is appropriately remembered, but it doesn't overwhelm this celebration of Jewish life.

Designed by the American architect Daniel Libeskind, the zinc-walled building's zigzag shape is pierced by voids symbolic of the irreplaceable cultural loss caused by the Holocaust. Enter the museum through the 18th-century Baroque building next door, then go through an underground tunnel to reach the main exhibit. While underground, you can follow the Axis of Exile to a disorienting slanted garden with 49 pillars, or to the Axis of Holocaust, an eerily empty tower shut off from the outside world.

When you emerge from underground, climb the stairs to the engaging, thought-provoking, and accessible museum. There are many interactive exhibits (spell your name in Hebrew) and pieces of artwork (the *Fallen Leaves* sculpture in the building's largest void is especially powerful), and it's all very kid-friendly (peel the giant garlic and climb through a pomegranate tree). English explanations interpret both the exhibits and the design of the very symbolic building. The museum is in a nondescript residential neighborhood a 10-minute walk from the Checkpoint Charlie museum, but it's well worth the trip (€5, covered by Museumspass, discount with WelcomeCard, daily 10:00–20:00, Mon until 22:00, closed on Jewish holidays, tight security includes bag check and metal detectors, U-Bahn line 1, 6, or 15 to Hallesches Tor, take exit marked Jüdisches Museum, exit straight ahead, then turn right on Franz-Klühs-Strasse, museum is 5 min ahead on your left at Lindenstrasse 9, tel. 030/2599-3300, www.jmberlin.de). The museum has a good café/restaurant (lunch 12:00–16:00, daily special-€9, snacks at other times, tel. 030/2593-9760).

East Side Gallery—The biggest remaining stretch of the Wall is now "the world's longest outdoor art gallery." It stretches for nearly a mile and is covered with murals painted by artists from around the world. The murals are routinely whitewashed, so new ones can be painted. This length of the Wall makes a poignant walk. For a quick look, just go to Ostbahnhof station and look around (exit towards river and turn left on Mühlenstrasse; the freshest and most colorful art is at this end). The gallery only survives until a land ownership dispute can be solved, when it will likely be developed like the rest of the city. (Given the recent history, imagine the complexity of finding rightful owners of all this suddenly very-valuable land.) If you walk the entire length, you'll find a small Wall souvenir shop at the end (they'll stamp your passport with the former East German stamp) and a bridge crossing the river to a subway station at Schlesisches Tor (in Kreuzberg).

Kreuzberg—This district—once abutting the dreary Wall and inhabited mostly by poor Turkish guest laborers and their families—is still run-down, with graffiti-riddled buildings and plenty of student and Turkish street life. It offers a gritty look at melting-pot Berlin in a city where original Berliners are as rare as old buildings. Berlin is the fourth-largest Turkish city in the world, and Kreuzberg is its "downtown." But to call it a "little Istanbul" insults the big one. You'll see *döner kebab* stands, shops decorated with spray paint, and mothers wearing scarves. For a dose of Kreuzberg without getting your fingers dirty, joyride on bus #129 (catch it near Jewish Museum). For a colorful stroll, take U-Bahn to Kottbusser Tor and wander—ideally on Tuesday and Friday between 12:00 and 18:00, when the Turkish Market sprawls along the bank of the Maybachufer Canal.

▲▲**Gendarmenmarkt**—This delightful and historic square is bounded by twin churches, a tasty chocolate shop, and the concert hall (designed by Schinkel, the man who put the neoclassical stamp on Berlin and Dresden) for the Berlin symphony. In summer, it hosts a few outdoor cafés, *Biergartens,* and sometimes concerts. The name of the square—part French and part German—reminds us that in the 17th century, a fifth of all Berliners were French émigrés, Protestant Huguenots fleeing Catholic France. Back then, tolerant Berlin was a magnet for the persecuted. The émigrés vitalized the city with new ideas and know-how.

The Deutscher Dom (German Cathedral, described below) has a history exhibit worthwhile for history buffs. The Franzosischer Dom (French Cathedral) offers a humble museum on the Huguenots (€1.50, Tue–Sun 12:00–17:00, closed Mon) and a chance to climb 254 steps to the top for a grand city view (€1.50, daily 9:00–19:00).

Fassbender & Rausch, on the corner near the Deutscher Dom, is Europe's biggest **chocolate store.** After 150 years of chocolate-making, this family-owned business proudly displays its sweet delights—250 different kinds—on a 55-foot-long buffet. Truffles are sold for about €0.50 each. The shop's evangelical Herr Ostwald (a.k.a. Benny) would love you to try his best-seller: tiramisu (Mon–Fri 10:00–20:00, Sat 10:00–16:00, closed Sun, corner of Mohrenstrasse at Charlottenstrasse 60, tel. 030/2045-8440).

German Cathedral—The Deutscher Dom houses the thought-provoking "Milestones, Setbacks, Sidetracks" (Wege, Irrwege, Umwege) exhibit, which traces the history of the German parliamentary system. The exhibit is well done and more interesting than it sounds. There are no English descriptions, but you can follow a fine and free 90-minute-long audioguide (passport required for deposit; to start, follow the blue arrows downstairs) or buy the detailed €10 guidebook (free, June–Aug Tue–Sun 10:00–19:00, Tue until 22:00, closed Mon, Sept–May Tue–Sun 10:00–18:00, Tue until 22:00, closed Mon, on Gendarmenmarkt just off Friedrichstrasse, tel. 030/2273-0431).

▲▲**New Synagogue**—A shiny gilded dome marks the New Synagogue, now a museum and cultural center on Oranienburger Strasse. Only the dome and facade have been restored, and a window overlooks a vacant field marking what used to be the synagogue. The largest and finest synagogue in Berlin before World War II, it was desecrated by Nazis on Crystal Night in 1938, bombed in 1943, and partially rebuilt in 1990. Inside, past tight security, there's a small but moving exhibit on the Berlin Jewish community through the centuries with some good English descriptions (ground floor and first floor). On its facade, the *Vergesst es nie* message—added by East Berlin Jews in 1966—means "Never forget." East Berlin had only a few hundred Jews, but now that the city is united, the Jewish community numbers about 12,000 (€3, Sun–Thu 10:00–18:00, Fri 10:00–14:00, closed Sat, May–Aug Sun–Mon until 20:00 and Fri until 17:00, last entry 30 min before closing, U-Bahn Oranienburger Tor, Oranienburger Strasse 28/30, tel. 030/8802-8300, www.cjudaicum.de).

Oren, a popular near-kosher café, is next to the synagogue (see "Eating—Eastern Berlin," page 326). If you're heading for the Pergamon Museum next, take a shortcut by turning left after leaving the synagogue, then right on Monbijoustrasse. Cross the canal and turn left to the museum.

A block from the synagogue, walk 50 yards down Grosse Hamburger Strasse to a little park. This street was known for 200 years as the "street of tolerance" because the Jewish community donated land to Protestants so that they could build a church. Hitler turned it into the "street of death" *(Todes Strasse)*, bulldozing 12,000 graves of the city's oldest Jewish cemetery and turning a Jewish old-folks home into a deportation center. Note the two memorials—one erected by the former East Berlin government and one built later by the city's unified government. Somewhere nearby, a plainclothes police officer keeps watch over this park.

▲**Oranienburger Strasse**—Berlin is developing so fast, it's impossible to predict what will be "in" next year. The area around Oranienburger Strasse is definitely trendy (but is being challenged by hip Friedrichshain, farther east).

While the area immediately around the synagogue is dull, 100 yards away things get colorful. The streets behind Grosse Hamburger Strasse flicker with atmospheric cafés, *Kneipen* (pubs), and art galleries.

At night, techno-prostitutes line Oranienburger Strasse. Prostitution is legal here, but there's a big debate about taxation. Since they don't get unemployment insurance, why should they pay taxes?

A block in front of the Hackescher Markt S-Bahn station is **Hackesche Höfe**—with eight courtyards bunny-hopping through a wonderfully restored 1907 *Jugendstil* building. It's full of trendy restaurants, theaters, and cinema (playing movies in their original languages).

This is a fine example of how to make huge city blocks livable—
Berlin's apartments are organized around courtyard after courtyard off
the main roads.

Karl Marx Allee—The buildings along Karl Marx Allee in East Berlin
(just beyond Alexanderplatz) were completely leveled by the Soviets in
1945. When Stalin decided this main drag should be a showcase street,
he had it rebuilt with lavish Soviet aid and named it Stalin Allee. Today,
this street, done in the bold "Stalin Gothic" style so common in Moscow
back in the 1950s, has been restored (and named after Karl Marx), providing a rare look at Berlin's Communist days. Cruise down Karl Marx
Allee by taxi or ride the U-Bahn to Strausberger Platz and walk to
Schillingstrasse. There are some fine Social Realist reliefs on the buildings, and the lampposts incorporate the wings of a phoenix (rising from
the ashes) in their design.

Natural History Museum (Museum für Naturkunde)—This place is
worth a visit just to see the largest dinosaur skeleton ever assembled.
While you're there, meet "Bobby" the stuffed ape (€3.50, Tue–Fri
9:30–17:00, Sat–Sun 10:00–18:00, closed Mon, last entry 30 min before
closing, U-Bahn line 6 to Zinnowitzer Strasse, Invalidenstrasse 43, tel.
030/2093-8591).

Around Charlottenburg Palace

The Charlottenburg district—with a cluster of fine museums across the
street from a grand palace—makes a good side-trip from downtown.
Ride U-2 to Sophie-Charlotte Platz and walk 10 minutes up the tree-
lined boulevard Schlossstrasse (following signs to *Schloss*), or—much
faster—catch bus #145 (direction Spandau) direct from Bahnhof Zoo.

For a Charlottenburg lunch, the **Luisen Bräu** is a comfortable
brewpub restaurant with a copper and woody atmosphere, good local
"microbeers" (*dunkles* are dark, *helles* light), and traditional German grub
(€5–8 meals, daily 9:00–24:00, fun for groups, across from palace at
Luisenplatz 1, tel. 030/341-9388).

▲**Charlottenburg Palace (Schloss)**—If you've seen the great palaces of
Europe, this Baroque Hohenzollern palace comes in at about number
10 (behind Potsdam, too). It's even more disappointing since the main
rooms can be toured only with a German guide (€8 includes 50-min
tour, €2 to see just upper floors without tour, €7 to see palace grounds
excluding tour areas, last tour 1 hr before closing, cash only, Tue–Sun
10:00–17:00, closed Mon, tel. 030/320-911).

The **Knöbelsdorff Wing** features a few royal apartments. Go
upstairs and take a substantial hike through restored-since-the-war,
gold-crusted white rooms (€5 depending on special exhibitions, free
English audioguide, Tue–Fri 10:00–18:00, Sat–Sun 11:00–18:00, closed
Mon, last entry 30 min before closing, when facing the palace walk
toward the right wing, tel. 030/3209-1202).

Charlottenburg Palace Area

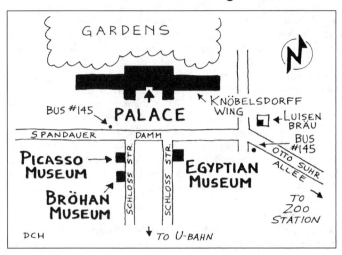

▲▲Egyptian Museum—Across the street from the palace, the Egyptian Museum offers one of the great thrills in art appreciation—gazing into the still-young and beautiful face of 3,000-year-old Queen Nefertiti, the wife of King Akhenaton (€6, covered by Museumspass, Tue–Sun 10:00–18:00, closed Mon, free on first Sun of month, free English audioguide, Schlossstrasse 70, tel. 030/343-5730).

This bust of Queen Nefertiti, from 1340 B.C., is perhaps the most famous piece of Egyptian art in Europe. Discovered in 1912, it shows the Marilyn Monroe of the early 20th century, with all the right beauty marks: long neck, symmetrical face, and just the right makeup (she's called "Berlin's most beautiful woman"). The bust never left its studio, but served as a master model for all other portraits of the queen. (That's probably why the left eye was never inlaid.) Buried for over 3,000 years, she was found by a German team who, by agreement with the Egyptian government, got to take home any workshop models they found. Although this bust is not representative of Egyptian art, it has become a symbol for Egyptian art by popular acclaim. Don't overlook the rest of the impressive museum, wonderfully lit and displayed, but with little English aside from the audioguide.

The Egyptian section of the 19th-century Royal Prussian Museum was originally in the Neues Museum on Museum Island. After World War II, the collection was divided between East and West. Plans are in the works to reunite the collection in its original Museum Island building, the Bodesmuseum, which is currently under renovation (due to be completed in 2010).

▲**Berggruen Collection: Picasso and His Time**—This tidy little museum is a pleasant surprise. Climb three floors through a fun and substantial collection of Picasso. Along the way, you'll see plenty of notable work by Matisse, van Gogh, and Cézanne. Enjoy a great chance to meet Paul Klee (€6, covered by Museumspass, Tue–Fri 10:00–18:00, Sat–Sun 11:00–18:00, closed Mon, free the first Sun of month, Schlossstrasse 1, tel. 030/3269-580).

▲**Bröhan Museum**—Wander through a dozen beautifully furnished art nouveau *(Jugendstil)* and art deco living rooms, a curvy organic world of lamps, glass, silver, and posters. English descriptions are posted on the wall of each room on the main floor. While you're there, look for the fine collection of Impressionist paintings by Karl Hagemeister (€4–6 depending on special exhibits, covered by Museumspass excluding special exhibits, Tue–Sun 10:00–18:00, closed Mon, Schlossstrasse 1A, tel. 030/3269-0600, www.broehan-museum.de).

Near Berlin

▲**Sanssouci Palace, New Palace, and Park, Potsdam**—With a lush park strewn with the extravagant whimsies of Frederick the Great, the sleepy town of Potsdam has long been Berlin's holiday retreat. Frederick's super-rococo Sanssouci Palace is one of Germany's most dazzling. His equally extravagant New Palace (Neues Palais), built to disprove rumors that Prussia was running out of money after the costly Seven Years' War, is on the other side of the park (it's a 30-min walk between palaces).

Your best bet for seeing Sanssouci Palace is to take the Potsdam TI's walking tour (see below). Otherwise, to make sense of all the ticket and tour options for the two palaces, stop by the palaces' TI (TI is across the street from windmill near Sanssouci entrance, helpful English-speaking staff, tel. 0331/969-4202).

Sanssouci Palace: Even though *sans souci* means "without a care," it can be a challenge for an English speaker to have an enjoyable visit. The palaces of Vienna, Munich, and even Würzburg offer equal sightseeing thrills with far fewer headaches. While the grounds are impressive, the interior of Sanssouci Palace can be visited only by a one-hour tour in German (with a borrowed English text), and these tours get booked up quickly. The only English option is the Potsdam TI's tour (see next page).

If you take a German tour of Sanssouci, you must be at the palace in person to get your ticket and the appointment time for your tour. In the summer, if you arrive by 9:00, you'll get right in. If you arrive after 10:00, plan on a wait. If you arrive after 12:00, you may not get in at all (€8, April–Oct Tue–Sun 9:00–17:00, closed Mon, Nov–March Tue–Sun 9:00–16:00, closed Mon, tel. 0331/969-4190).

New Palace: Use the English texts to tour Frederick's New Palace

Greater Berlin

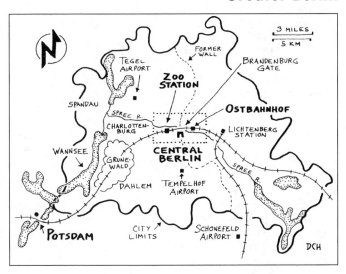

(€5, plus €1 for optional live tour in German, May–Oct Sat–Thu 9:00–17:00, closed Fri, Nov–April Sat–Thu 9:00–16:00, closed Fri). If you also want to see the king's apartments, you must take a required 45-minute tour in German (€5, offered May–Oct daily at 11:00 and 14:00). Off-season (Nov–April), the king's apartments are closed, and you can visit the rest of the New Palace only on a German tour (€5); it can take up to an hour for enough people to gather.

Walking Tours: The Potsdam TI's handy walking tour includes Sanssouci Palace, offering the only way to get into the palace with an English-speaking guide (€25 covers walking tour, palace, and park, 11:00 daily except Mon, 3.5 hrs, departs from Film Museum across from TI, reserve by phone, in summer reserve at least 2 days in advance, tel. 0331/275-5850, Potsdam TI hours: April–Oct Mon–Fri 9:00–19:00, Sat–Sun 10:00–16:00, less off-season, 5-min walk from Potsdam S-Bahn station, walk straight out of station and take first right onto An der Orangerie, Friedrich-Ebert Strasse 5, tel. 0331/275-5850).

A "Discover Potsdam" walking tour (which doesn't include Sanssouci Palace) is offered by "The Original Berlin Walks" and led by a native English-speaking guide. The tour leaves from Berlin at 9:40 on Saturdays May through October (€15, or €11.20 if under age 26 or with WelcomeCard, meet at taxi stand at Zoo Station, public transportation not included but can buy ticket from guide, no booking necessary, tel. 030/301-9194). The guide takes you to Cecilienhof Palace (site of postwar Potsdam conference attended by Churchill, Stalin, and Truman), through pleasant green landscapes to the historic heart of Potsdam for lunch, and to Sanssouci Park.

What to Avoid: Potsdam's much-promoted Wannsee boat rides are torturously dull.

Getting to Potsdam: Potsdam is easy to reach from Berlin (17 min on direct Regional Express/RE trains from Bahnhof Zoo every 30 min, or 30 min direct on S-Bahn #7 from Bahnhof Zoo to Potsdam station; both covered by transit pass with zones A, B, and C). If you're taking the Potsdam TI's tour, walk to the TI from the Potsdam S-Bahn stop (see "Walking Tours," above, for directions). If not taking the TI tour, catch bus #695 from the Potsdam station to the palaces (3/hr, 20 min). Use the same bus #695 to shuttle between the sights in the park. For a more scenic approach, take tram #96 or #X98 from the Potsdam station to Luisenplatz, then walk 15 minutes through the park and enjoy a classic view of Sanssouci Palace.

Other Day Trips—EurAide has researched and printed a *Get Me Outta Here* flier describing good day trips to small towns and another flier on the nearby Sachsenhausen concentration camp (which many think is as interesting as Dachau; a Sachsenhausen day trip is also offered by The Original Berlin Walks, see "City Walking Tours," page 287).

NIGHTLIFE

For the young and determined sophisticate, *Zitty* and *Tip* are the top guides to alternative culture (in German, sold at kiosks). Also pick up the free schedules *Flyer* and *030* in bars and clubs. *Berlin Programm* lists a nonstop parade of concerts, plays, exhibits, and cultural events (in German, www.berlin-programm.de); the *Ex-Berliner* has less information but is entirely in English (both sold at kiosks and TIs).

Oranienburger Strasse's trendy scene (see "Sights—Eastern Berlin," page 308) is already being eclipsed by the action at Friedrichshain and Kollwitzplatz farther east. Tourists stroll the Ku'damm after dark.

Visit KaDeWe's ticket office for your music and theater options (sixth floor, 18 percent fee but access to all tickets). Ask about "competitive improvisation" and variety shows.

For jazz (blues and boogie, too) near recommended Savignyplatz hotels, consider **A Trane Jazz Club** (daily, 21:00–2:00, Bleibtreustrasse 1, tel. 030/313-2550) and **Quasimodo Live** (Kantstrasse 12a, under Delphi Cinema, tel. 030/312-8086). For quality blues and New Orleans–style jazz, stop by **Ewige Lampe** (from 21:00, Niebuhrstrasse 11a).

Bar Jeder Vernunft offers modern-day cabaret a short walk from the recommended hotels. This variety show under a classic old tent perched atop a modern parking lot is a hit with German speakers, but can still be worthwhile for non–German speakers (as some of the music shows are in a sort of "Dinglish"). Even some Americans perform here periodically. Tickets are generally around €15, and shows change regularly (shows start at 20:30, closed Sun, seating can be a bit cramped, Schaperstrasse 24, tel. 030/883-1582).

To spend an evening enjoying Europe's largest revue theater, consider **Revue Berlin** at the Friedrichstadt Palast. The show basically depicts the history of Berlin, and is choreographed in a funny and musical way that's popular with the Lawrence Welk–type German crowd. It's even entertaining for your entire English-speaking family (€13–51, Tue–Sat 20:00, also Sat–Sun at 16:00, U-Bahn Oranienburger Tor, tel. 030/284-8830, www.friedrichstadtpalast.de).

SLEEPING

Near Savignyplatz and Bahnhof Zoo

These hotels and pensions are a 5- to 15-minute walk from Bahnhof Zoo (or take S-Bahn to Savignyplatz). Hotels on Kantstrasse have street noise. Ask for a quieter room in back. The area has an artsy charm going back to the cabaret days in the 1920s, when it was the center of Berlin's gay scene. Of the accommodations listed in this area, Pension Peters offers the best value for budget travelers.

$$$ **Pension Savoy** rents 16 comfortable and colorfully decorated rooms with all the amenities. You'll love the cheery old pastel breakfast room and the friendly staff (who speak just enough English). Most rooms overlook a quiet courtyard (Ss-€62, Sb-€73, Db-€102–109, extra person-€34–46, elevator, Meinekestrasse 4, tel. 030/881-3700, fax 030/882-3746, www.hotel-pension-savoy.de).

$$$ **Hotel Astoria** is a friendly, three-star, business-class hotel with 32 comfortably furnished rooms and affordable summer and weekend rates (high season Db-€117–128; prices drop to Sb-€86–97, Db-€94–118 during low season of July–Aug, Nov–Feb, or any 2 weekend nights or if slow; breakfast-€10 extra, rooms with showers are cheaper than rooms with baths, non-smoking floors, elevator, free Internet access, parking-€13/day, around corner from Bahnhof Zoo at Fasanenstrasse 2, tel. 030/312-4067, fax 030/312-5027, www.hotelastoria.de, info@hotelastoria.de).

$$$ **Hecker's Hotel** is an ultramodern, four-star business hotel with 69 rooms and all the sterile Euro-comforts (Sb-€125, Db-€150, breakfast-€15, weekends breakfast included, all rooms-€200 during conferences, non-smoking rooms, elevator, parking-€9/day, between Savignyplatz and Ku'damm at Grolmanstrasse 35, tel. 030/88900, fax 030/889-0260, www.heckers-hotel.com).

$$$ **Hotel Atlanta** has 30 newly renovated rooms in an older building with big leather couches, half a block south of Ku'damm. It's next to Gucci, on an elegant shopping street (Ss-€40–70, Sb-€60–99, Db-€80–120, Tb-€100-140, Qb-€120–160, non-smoking rooms,

SLEEP CODE

(€1 = about $1.10, country code: 49, area code: 030)

Sleep Code: **S** = Single, **D** = Double/Twin, **T** = Triple, **Q** = Quad, **b** = bathroom, **s** = shower only, **no CC** = Credit Cards not accepted, **SE** = Speaks English, **NSE** = No English. Unless otherwise noted, credit cards are accepted, English is spoken, and breakfast is included.

To help you sort easily through these listings, I've divided the rooms into three categories, based on the price for a standard double room with bath:

$$$ **Higher Priced**—Most rooms €100 or more.
 $$ **Moderately Priced**—Most rooms between €80–100.
  $ **Lower Priced**—Most rooms €80 or less.

I have concentrated my hotel recommendations around Savignyplatz. While Bahnhof Zoo and Ku'damm are no longer the center of Berlin, the trains, TI, and walking tours are all still handy to Zoo. And the streets around the tree-lined Savignyplatz (a 10-min walk behind the station) have a neighborhood charm. While towering new hotels are being built in the new center, simple, small, and friendly good-value places abound only here. My listings are generally located a couple of flights up in big, run-down buildings. Inside, they are clean, quiet, and spacious enough so that their well-worn character is actually charming. Rooms in back are on quiet courtyards.

The city is packed and hotel prices go up on holidays, including Green Week in mid-January, Easter weekend, the first weekend in May, Ascension weekend in May, the Love Parade (a huge techno-Woodstock, second weekend in July), Germany's national holiday (Oct 2–4), Christmas, and New Year's.

During slow times, the best values are actually business-class rooms on the push list booked through the TI. But as the world learns what a great place Berlin is to visit, a rising tide of tourists will cause these deals to fade away.

Fasanenstrasse 74, tel. 030/881-8049, fax 030/881-9872, www.hotelatlanta.de, hatlanta68266759@aol.com).

$$$ Hotel Askanischerhof is the oldest *Zimmer* in Berlin, posh as can be with 16 sprawling antique-furnished rooms. Photos on the walls brag of famous movie-star guests. Frau Glinicke offers Old World

Berlin's Savignyplatz Neighborhood

S — S-BAHN
U — U-BAHN

① Pension Savoy
② Hotel Astoria
③ Hecker's Hotel
④ Hotel Askanischerhof
⑤ Hotel Atlanta
⑥ Hotel-Pension Funk
⑦ Hotel Bogota
⑧ Hotel Carmer 16
⑨ Hotel Imperator
⑩ Pension Peters
⑪ Pension Alexis
⑫ Hotel Crystal Garni
⑬ Jugendgastehaus am Zoo Hostel
⑭ To Hotels Austriana, Insel Rügen, Bella & Curtis; To Weyers Café Rest.
⑮ Dicke Wirtin Pub
⑯ Restaurant Die Zwölf Apostel
⑰ Ristorante San Marino
⑱ Restaurant Zillemarkt
⑲ Restaurant Tomasa
⑳ A Trane Jazz Club
㉑ Käthe Kollwitz Museum
㉒ To Launderette

service and classic Berlin atmosphere (Sb-€95–110, Db-€117–145, extra bed-€25, free parking, non-smoking rooms, elevator, Ku'damm 53, tel. 030/881-8033, fax 030/881-7206, www.askanischer-hof.de, info @askanischer-hof.de).

$$$ **Hotel Carmer 16,** with 30 bright, airy rooms, feels like a big, professional hotel with all the comfy extras but with a cold reception staff (Sb-€76–93, Db-€93–122, extra person-€35, some rooms have balconies, elevator and a few stairs, beauty parlor and mini-spa upstairs, Carmerstrasse 16, tel. 030/3110-0500, fax 030/3110-0510, carmer16 @t-online.de).

$$ **Hotel-Pension Funk,** the former home of a 1920s silent-movie star, is delightfully quirky. Kind manager Herr Michael Pfundt offers 14 elegant old rooms with rich art nouveau furnishings (S-€34–57, Ss-€41–72, Sb-€52–82, D-€52–82, Ds-€72–93, Db-€82–113, extra

person-€23, prices guaranteed through 2004 with this book, cash preferred, Fasanenstrasse 69, a long block south of Ku'damm, tel. 030/882-7193, fax 030/883-3329, www.hotel-pensionfunk.de, berlin@hotel-pensionfunk.de).

$$ **Hotel Bogota** has 125 unique rooms and several large lounges in a sprawling, drab old maze of a building that once housed the Nazi Chamber of Culture. (After the war, German theater stars were "denazified" here before they could go back to work.) Pieces of the owner's modern art collection lurk around every corner. Take a peek at the bizarre collage in the atrium, with mannequins suspended from the ceiling (S-€44, Ss-€55–57, Sb-€66–72, D-€66–69, Ds-€74–77, Db-€94–98, extra bed-€20, children under 12 free, prices guaranteed through 2004 with this book, non-smoking rooms, elevator, bus #109 from Bahnhof Zoo to Schlüterstrasse 45, tel. 030/881-5001, fax 030/883-5887, www.hotelbogota.de, hotel.bogota@t-online.de).

$$ **Hotel-Pension Imperator** fills a sprawling floor of a grand building with 11 big, quiet, and Old World–elegant rooms and a clientele that includes the occasional actor or musician (S-€42, Ss-€58, Sb-€65, D-€78, Ds-€88–93, Db-€98, Ts-€118, no CC, elevator, Meinekestrasse 5, tel. 030/881-4181, fax 030/885-1919).

$ **Pension Peters,** run by a German-Swedish couple, is sunny and central with a cheery breakfast room. Decorated sleek Scandinavian, with every room renovated, it's a winner (S-€36, Ss-€46, Sb-€58, D-€51, Ds-€67, Db-€66–77, extra bed-€8, kids under 12 free, family room, 3 percent extra if you pay with plastic, prices guaranteed through 2004 with this book, Internet access, 10 yards off Savignyplatz at Kantstrasse 146, tel. 030/3150-3944, fax 030/312-3519, www.pension-peters-berlin.de, penspeters@aol.com, Annika and Christoph SE). The same family also runs a larger hotel just outside of Berlin (see Hotel Pankow under "More Berlin Hotels," below) and rents apartments (ideal for small groups and longer stays).

$ **Pension Alexis** is a classic old-European four-room pension in a stately 19th-century apartment run by Frau and Herr Schwarzer. The shower and toilet facilities are older and cramped, but this, more than any other Berlin listing, has you feeling at home with a faraway aunt (S-€42, D-€65, T-€97, Q-€128, no CC, big rooms, handheld showers, Carmerstrasse 15, tel. 030/312-5144, enough English spoken).

$ **Hotel Crystal Garni** is professional and offers small, well-worn, comfortable rooms and a *vollkorn* breakfast room (S-€36, Sb-€41, D-€47, Ds-€57, Db-€66–77, elevator, a block past Savignyplatz at Kantstrasse 144, tel. 030/312-9047, fax 030/312-6465, run by John and Dorothy Schwarzrock and Herr Vasco Flascher).

$ **Jugendgastehaus am Zoo** is a bare-bones, cash-only youth hostel that takes no reservations and hardly has a reception desk. It's far less comfortable and only marginally cheaper than simple hotels (85 beds, dorm beds-€18, S-€25, D-€44, includes sheets, no breakfast, no CC, Hardenbergstrasse 9a, tel. 030/312-9410, fax 030/312-5430).

South of Ku'damm

Several small hotels are nearby in a charming, café-studded neighborhood 300 yards south of Ku'damm, near the intersection of Sächsische Strasse and Pariser Strasse (bus #109 from Bahnhof Zoo, direction: Airport Tegel). They are less convenient from the station than most of the Savignyplatz listings above.

$$ **Hotel Austriana,** with 25 modern and bright rooms, is warmly and energetically run by Thomas (S-€33–43, Ss-€41–48, Sb-€49–67, Ds-€62–69, Db-€78–89, Ts-€78–96, Qs-€96–104, prices higher for holidays and conferences, half the rooms have balconies, elevator, Pariser Strasse 39, tel. 030/885-7000, fax 030/8857-0088, www.austriana.de, austriana@t-online.de).

$$ **Insel Rügen Hotel,** in the same building as the Austriana, has 31 rooms and ornate, Eastern decor (S-€28, Ss-€39, D-€51, Ds-€61–66, Db-€77–82, elevator, Pariser Strasse 39, tel. 030/884-3940, fax 030/8843-9437, www.insel-ruegen-hotel.de, ir-hotel@t-online.de).

$$ **Hotel-Pension Bella,** a clean, simple, masculine-feeling place with high ceilings, rents nine big, comfortable rooms but is a lesser value (S-€30–45, Ss/Sb-€45–65, D-€50–65, Ds-€70–85, Db-€80–90, extra person-€10, apartment also available, elevator, bus #249 from Zoo, Ludwigkirchstrasse 10a, tel. 030/881-6704, fax 030/8867-9074, www.pension-bella.de, pension.bella@t-online.de).

$ **Hotel-Pension-Curtis,** in the same building as the Austriana and Insel Rügen (recommended above), has 10 hip, piney, basic rooms (S-€32–37, Ss-40–45, Ds-€60–70, Ts-€75–83, Qs-€90–100, no CC, elevator, Pariser Strasse 39, tel. 030/883-4931, fax 030/885-0438).

More Berlin Hotels

Away from the Center

$ **Hotel Pankow** is a new, fresh, colorful 43-room place run by friendly Annika and Christoph (from the Pension Peters, above). It's a 30-minute commute north of downtown but a good value (S-€29, Sb-€44, D-€39, Db-€59, T-€49, Tb-€69, Q-€55, Qb-€75, family rooms, children under 16 free in room with parents, elevator, Internet access, free parking in lot or €3/day in garage, tram station in front of hotel takes you to the center in 30 min, Pasewalker Strasse 14-15, tel. 030/486-2600, fax 030/4862-6060, www.hotel-pankow-berlin.de, hotelpankow@aol.com).

Near Augsburgerstrasse U-Bahn Stop

$$ Consider **Hotel-Pension Nürnberger Eck** (S-€45, Sb-€60, D-€70, Db-€92, Nürnberger Strasse 24a, tel. 030/235-1780, fax 030/2351-

7899) or **Hotel Arco** (Sb-€64–75, Db-€82–92, Geisbergerstrasse 30, tel. 030/235-1480, fax 030/2147-5178, www.arco-hotel.de).

Near Güntzelstrasse U-Bahn Stop

$ Choose between **Pension Güntzel** (Ds-€59, Db-€69–79, single rooms €16 less, Güntzelstrasse 62, tel. 030/857-9020, fax 030/853-1108, www.pension-guentzel.de), **Pension Finck** (S-€39, Ss-€42, D-€45, Ds-€59, €3 extra for 1-night stays, no CC, Güntzelstrasse 54, tel. 030/861-2940, fax 030/873-8223), or **Hotel Pension München** (S-€40, Sb-€55, Db-€75, also Güntzelstrasse 62, tel. 030/857-9120, fax 030/8579-1222, www.hotel-pension-muenchen-in-berlin.de).

In Eastern Berlin

$$$ **Hotel Unter den Linden** is ideal for those nostalgic for the days of Soviet rule, although nowadays at least, the management tries to be efficient and helpful. Formerly one of the best hotels in the DDR, this huge, blocky place, right on Unter den Linden in the heart of what was East Berlin, is reasonably comfortable and reasonably priced. Built in 1966, with prison-like corridors, it has 331 modern, plain, and comfy rooms (Sb-€67–87, Db-€109–123, non-smoking rooms, at intersection of Friedrichstrasse, Unter den Linden 14, tel. 030/238-110, fax 030/2381-1100, www.hotel-unter-den-linden.de, reservation @hotel-unter-den-linden.de).

Hostels in South and Eastern Berlin

Berlin is known among budget travelers for its fun, hip hostels. Here are four good bets (all prices listed per person): **Studentenhotel Meininger 10** (€23 per person, includes sheets and breakfast, no CC, no curfew, elevator, free parking, near city hall on JFK Platz, Meiningerstrasse 10, U-Bahn: Rathaus Schoneberg, tel. 030/7871-7414, fax 030/7871-7412, www.meininger-hostels.de), **Mitte's Backpacker Hostel** (€15 dorm beds, S-€30, D-€23–28, T-€20, Q-€18, sheets-€2.50, no breakfast, could be cleaner, no curfew, Internet access-€6/hr, laundry, bike rental-€15/day, English newspapers, U-Bahn: Zinnowitzerstrasse, Chauseestrasse 102, tel. 030/2839-0965, fax 030/2839-0935, www.backpacker.de, info@backpacker.de), **Circus** (dorm bed-€13–15, S-€28–32, D-€21–24, T-€18–20, Q-€16–18, 2-person apartment with kitchen-€65–75, 4-person apartment-€115-130, breakfast-€4, sheets-€2, no CC, no curfew, Internet access, 2 locations, U-Bahn: Rosa-Luxemburg Platz, Rosa-Luxemburg Strasse 39, or U-Bahn: Rosenthaler Platz, Weinbergsweg 1a, both tel. 030/2839-1433, fax 030/2839-1484, www.circus-berlin.de, info@circus-berlin.de), or **Clubhouse** (dorm bed-€14, bed in 5- to 7-bed room-€17, S-€32, D-€23, T-€20, breakfast-€3, sheets-€2, no CC, Internet access, on second floor, nightclub below, in hip Oranienburger Strasse area, S- or U-Bahn:

Friedrichstrasse, Kalkscheunenstrasse 4-5, tel. 030/2809-7979, fax 030/2809-7977, www.clubhouse-berlin.de, info@clubhouse-berlin.de).

EATING

Don't be too determined to eat "Berlin-style." The city is known only for its mildly spicy sausage. Still, there is a world of restaurants in this ever-changing city to choose from. Your best approach may be to choose a neighborhood, rather than a particular restaurant.

For quick and easy meals, colorful pubs—called *Kneipen*—offer light meals and the fizzy local beer, Berliner Weiss. Ask for it *mit Schuss* for a shot of fruity syrup in your suds. If the kraut is getting *Wurst,* try one of the many Turkish, Italian, or Balkan restaurants. Eat cheap at *Imbiss* snack stands, bakeries (sandwiches), and falafel/kebab places. Bahnhof Zoo has several bright and modern fruit-and-sandwich bars and a grocery (daily 6:00–24:00).

Western Berlin
Near Savignyplatz
Several good places are on or within 100 yards of Savignyplatz. Take a walk and survey these: **Dicke Wirtin** is a smoky old pub with traditional old-Berlin *Kneipe* atmosphere, famously cheap *Gulaschsuppe,* and salads (daily 12:00–4:00, just off Savignyplatz at Carmerstrasse 9, tel. 030/312-4952). **Die Zwölf Apostel** restaurant is trendy for leafy candlelit ambience and Italian food. A dressy local crowd packs the place for €10 pizzas and €15 to €30 meals. Late-night partygoers appreciate Apostel's great breakfast (daily, 24 hrs, no CC, outside seating in summer until 10:00, immediately across from Savigny S-Bahn entrance, Bleibtreustrasse 49, tel. 030/312-1433). **Ristorante San Marino,** on the square, is another good Italian place, serving cheaper pasta and pizza (daily 11:00–1:00, Savignyplatz 12, tel. 030/313-6086). **Zillemarkt Restaurant,** which feels like an old-time Berlin beer garden, serves traditional Berlin specialties in the garden or in the rustic candlelit interior (€10 meals, daily 10:00–24:00, near the S-Bahn tracks at Bleibtreustrasse 48a, tel. 030/881-7040).

Tomasa is most popular for its weekend breakfast (reservations smart) but also has a nice dinner atmosphere with a completely German crowd (€15 dinner plates, daily 10:00–24:00, a block off Savignyplatz at Knesebackstrasse 22, tel. 030/312-8310).

Weyers Café Restaurant, serving quality international and German cuisine, is a great value and worth a short walk. It's sharp, with white tablecloths, but not stuffy. On a sunny day, its patio is packed with locals (€10 dinner plates, daily 8:00–2:00, seating indoors or outside on the leafy square, Pariser Strasse 16, reservations smart after 20:00, tel. 030/881-9378).

Ullrich Supermarkt is the neighborhood grocery store (Mon–Fri 9:00–20:00, Sat 9:00–16:00, closed Sun, Kantstrasse 7, under the tracks near Bahnhof Zoo). There's plenty of fast food near Bahnhof Zoo and on Ku'damm.

Near Bahnhof Zoo

Self-Service Cafeterias: The top floor of the famous department store, **KaDeWe,** holds the Winter Garden Buffet view cafeteria, and its sixth-floor deli/food department is a picnicker's nirvana. Its arterials are clogged with more than 1,000 kinds of sausage and 1,500 types of cheese (Mon–Fri 9:30–20:00, Sat 9:00–16:00, closed Sun, U-Bahn: Wittenbergplatz). **Wertheim** department store, a half-block from the Memorial Church, has cheap food counters in the basement and a city view from its fine self-service cafeteria, Le Buffet, located up six banks of escalators (Mon–Fri 9:30–20:00, Sat 9:00–16:00, closed Sun, U-Bahn: Ku'damm). **Marche,** a chain that's popped up in big cities all over Germany, is another inexpensive, self-service cafeteria within a half block of the Kaiser Wilhelm church (Mon–Thu 8:00–22:00, Fri–Sat 8:00–24:00, Sun 10:00–22:00, plenty of salads, fruit, made-to-order omelettes, Ku'damm 14, tel. 030/882-7578).

At Bahnhof Zoo: Terrassen am Zoo is a good restaurant right in the station, offering peaceful decency amidst a whirlwind of travel activity (daily 6:00–22:00, upstairs, next to track 1, tel. 030/315-9140).

Eating in Eastern Berlin
Along Unter den Linden

The Opernpalais, preening with fancy prewar elegance, hosts a number of pricey restaurants. Its **Operncafé** has the best desserts and the longest dessert bar in Europe (daily 8:00–24:00, across from university and war memorial at Unter den Linden 5, tel. 030/202-683); sit down and enjoy perhaps the classiest coffee stop in Berlin. The beer and tea garden in front has a cheap food counter (from 10:00, depending on weather). More students and fewer tourists eat in the student facilities at Humboldt University across the street (go through courtyard, enter building through main door, follow signs to cafeteria on right or cheaper, government-subsidized *Mensa* on left, both closed weekends).

Oren Restaurant and Café is a trendy, stylish, near-kosher/vegetarian place next to the New Synagogue. The food is pricey but good, and the ambience is happening (daily 12:00–1:00, Sun open at 10:00, Sat until 3:00, north of Museum Island about 5 blocks away at Oranienburger Strasse 28, tel. 030/282-8228).

Near Pergamon Museum

Try the **Kupfer Keller,** a small basement restaurant, for a short list of traditional German grub, including *Berliner Kartoffelsuppe*—Berlin potato soup (Tue–Sun 11:00–18:00, closed Mon, at corner of Bauhof Strasse and Am Kupfergraben, across from Pergamon).

Deponie3 is a trendy Berlin *Kneipe* usually filled with students from the nearby Humboldt University. Garden seating in the back is nice if you don't mind the noise of the S-Bahn passing directly above you. The interior is a cozy, wooden wonderland of a bar, serving basic sandwiches, salads, and daily specials (sometimes with live music, open Mon–Fri from 9:00, Sat–Sun from 10:00, Georgenstrasse 5, 1 block from Pergamon under S-Bahn tracks, tel. 030/2016-5740).

Near Checkpoint Charlie

Lekkerbek, a busy little bakery and cafeteria, sells inexpensive and tasty salads, soups, pastas, and sandwiches (Mon–Fri 6:00–18:00, Sat 7:00–13:00, closed Sun, a block from Checkpoint Charlie museum at Kochstrasse subway stop, Friedrichstrasse 211, tel. 030/251-7208). For a classier sit-down meal, try **Café Adler,** across the street from the museum (Mon–Sat 10:00–24:00, Sun 10:00–19:00, Friedrichstrasse 20b, tel. 030/251-8965).

TRANSPORTATION CONNECTIONS

Berlin has three train stations (with more on the way). Bahnhof Zoo was the West Berlin train station and still serves Western Europe: Frankfurt, Munich, Hamburg, Paris, and Amsterdam. The Ostbahnhof (former East Berlin's main station) still faces east, serving Prague, Warsaw, Vienna, and Dresden. The Lichtenberg Bahnhof (eastern Berlin's top U- and S-Bahn hub) also handles a few eastbound trains. Expect exceptions. All stations are conveniently connected by subway and even faster by train. Train info: tel. 01805-996-633.

By train to: Frankfurt (14/day, 5 hrs), **Munich** (14/day, 7 hrs, 10 hrs overnight), **Köln** (hrly, 6.5 hrs), **Amsterdam** (4/day, 7 hrs), **Budapest** (2/day, 13 hrs; 1 goes via Czech Republic and Slovakia, so Eurail is not valid), **Copenhagen** (4/day, 8 hrs, change in Hamburg), **London** (4/day, 15 hrs), **Paris** (6/day, 13 hrs, change in Köln, 1 direct night train), **Zürich** (12/day, 10 hrs, 1 direct night train), **Prague** (4/day, 5 hrs, no overnight trains), **Warsaw** (4/day, 8 hrs, 1 night train from Lichtenberg Stn; reservations required on all Warsaw-bound trains), **Kraków** (2/day, 10 hrs), **Vienna** (2/day, 12 hrs via Czech Republic; for second-class ticket, Eurailers pay an extra €23 if under age 26 or €31 if age 26 or above; otherwise, take the Berlin–Vienna via Passau train—nightly at 20:00).

Eurailpasses don't cover the Czech Republic. The **Prague Excursion pass** picks up where Eurail leaves off, getting you from any border into Prague and then back out to Eurail country again within seven days (first class-€50, second class-€40, youth second class-€35, buy from EurAide at Berlin's Bahnhof Zoo or Munich's Hauptbahnhof and get reservations—€3—at the same time).

There are **night trains** from Berlin to Amsterdam, Munich, Köln, Brussels, Paris, Vienna, Budapest, Kraków, Warsaw, Stuttgart, Basel, and Zürich, but there are no night trains from Berlin to anywhere in Italy or Spain. A *Liegeplatz,* or berth (€15–21), is a great deal; inquire at EurAide at Bahnhof Zoo for details. Beds cost the same whether you have a first- or second-class ticket or railpass. Trains are often full, so get your bed reserved a few days in advance from any travel agency or major train station in Europe. Note: Since the Paris–Berlin night train goes through Belgium, railpass holders cannot use a Eurail Selectpass to cover this ride unless they've selected Belgium.

Berlin's Three Airports

Allow €20 for a taxi ride to or from any of Berlin's airports. **Tegel Airport** handles most flights from the United States and Western Europe (4 miles from center, catch the faster bus #X9 to Bahnhof Zoo, or bus #109 to Ku'damm and Bahnhof Zoo for €2; bus TXL goes to Alexanderplatz in East Berlin). Flights from the east and on Buzz Airlines usually arrive at **Schönefeld Airport** (12.5 miles from center, short walk to S-Bahn, catch S-9 to Zoo Station). **Templehof Airport**'s future is uncertain (in Berlin, bus #119 to Ku'damm or U-Bahn 6 or 7). The central telephone number for all three airports is 01805-000-186. For British Air, call 01805-266-522, Delta at 01803-337-880, SAS at 01803-234-023, or Lufthansa at 01803-803-803.

AUSTRIA
(Österreich, the Kingdom of the East)

- 32,000 square miles (the size of South Carolina, or two Switzerlands)
- 8 million people (240 per square mile and holding, 78 percent Catholic)
- 1 euro (€) = about $1.10

During the grand old Hapsburg days, Austria was Europe's most powerful empire. Its royalty built a giant kingdom of more than 60 million people by making love, not war (having lots of children and marrying them into the other royal houses of Europe).

Today, this small, landlocked country does more to cling to its elegant past than any other nation in Europe. The waltz is still the rage. Austrians are very sociable; it's important to greet people in the breakfast room and those you pass on the streets or meet in shops. The Austrian's version of "Hi" is a cheerful "*Grüss Gott*" ("May God greet you"). You'll get the correct pronunciation after the first volley—listen and copy.

While they speak German and talked about unity with Germany long before Hitler ever said "*Anschluss*," the Austrians cherish their distinct cultural and historical traditions. They are not Germans. Austria is mellow and relaxed compared to Deutschland. *Gemütlichkeit* is the local word for this special Austrian cozy-and-easy approach to life. It's good living—whether engulfed in mountain beauty or bathed in lavish high culture. The people stroll as if every day were Sunday, topping things off with a cheerful visit to a coffee or pastry shop.

It must be nice to be past your prime—no longer troubled by being powerful, able to kick back and celebrate life in the clean, untroubled

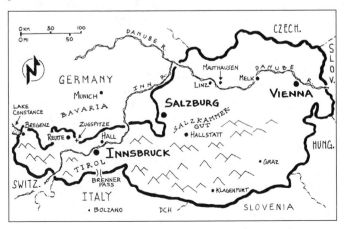

mountain air. While the Austrians make less money than their neighbors, they enjoy a short workweek and a long life span.

Prices in Austria are lower than in Germany and much lower than in Switzerland. Shops are open from 8:00 to 17:00 or 18:00.

Austrians eat on about the same schedule we do. Treats include Wiener schnitzel (breaded veal cutlet), *Knödel* (dumplings), *Apfelstrudel,* and fancy desserts like the Sacher torte, Vienna's famous chocolate cake. Bread on the table sometimes costs extra (if you eat it). Service is included in restaurant bills, but it's polite to leave a little extra (about 5 percent).

In Austria, all cars must have a ***Vignette*** motorway toll sticker stuck to the inside of their windshield. These are sold at all border crossings (24 hours a day), big gas stations near borders, and car rental agencies. Stickers cost €8 for 10 days (€22 for 2 months). Not having one earns you a stiff fine.

In the following section, I'll cover Austria's top cities *except* for Reutte, in Tirol. For this book, Reutte has been annexed by Germany. You'll find it in the Bavaria and Tirol chapter.

Austrian History

Austria's history marches in step with Germany's, but there are some differences that give Austria its distinct culture.

c. A.D. 1: The Romans occupy and defend the "crossroads of Europe," where the west–east Danube River crosses the north–south Brenner Pass through the Alps.

c. 800: Charlemagne designates Austria as one boundary of his European empire—the "eastern state," or *Osterreich.*

1273: An Austrian noble from the Hapsburg family (Rudolf I) is elected Holy Roman Emperor, ruling Austria, Germany, and north Italy. From 1438 until 1806, every Emperor but one is a Hapsburg. The Hapsburgs arrange strategic marriages for their children with other prominent royalty around Europe, gaining power through international connections.

1493: Maximilian I is crowned emperor. His marriage to Mary of Burgundy weds two kingdoms together, and their grandson, Charles V, will inherit a vast empire.

1519: Charles V (r. 1519–1556) is the most powerful man in Europe, ruling Austria, Germany, the Low Countries, parts of Italy, and Spain (with her New World possessions). Charles is responsible for trying to solve the problems of all those lands, including battling Turks in Vienna and Lutherans in Germany. While many lands north of the Danube would turn Protestant, Austria remains Catholic.

1522: Charles gives Austria (and the Turkish problem) to his little brother, Ferdinand, who four years later marries into the Bohemian and Hungarian crowns, as well.

1529: Muslim Turks besiege Vienna, beginning almost two centuries of battles between Austria and the Turks. In the course of the wars, Austria gains possession of Hungary.

1556: Charles V retires from the throne to enter a monastery, leaving his kingdom to his son (King Philip II of Spain), and to his brother, Ferdinand I of Austria, the crown of Holy Roman Emperor. From now on, Austria's rulers would concentrate on ruling their "Austro-Hungarian" empire, which includes Austria, Hungary, the Czech Republic, Slovakia, Slovenia, Bosnia, north Italy (Venice), and later, parts of Poland.

1648: The Thirty Years' War ends, leaving the "Holy Roman Empire" an empire only in name: a figurehead emperor of a scattered group of German-speaking people mainly in Austria and Germany.

1683: 200,000 Muslims from Ottoman Turkey surround the city of Vienna. The Turks are driven off, leaving behind bags of coffee that help fuel a beverage craze around Europe. Vienna's first coffeehouse opens (soon followed by a Starbucks across the street).

1672–1714: Three wars with Louis XIV of France (including War of the Spanish Succession) drain Austria.

1740: Maria Theresa (r. 1740–1780) has 16 children and still finds time to fight two wars in 25 years, defending her right to rule. Adored by her subjects for her down-to-earth personality, she brings Austria international prestige by marrying her daughters to Europe's royalty.

1781: Maria Theresa's son Joseph II, who frees the serfs and takes piano lessons from Mozart, rules as an "enlightened despot." Vienna becomes the world capital of symphonic music, home to Haydn (1732–1809), Mozart (1756–1791), and Beethoven (1770–1827).

1792: When his aunt, Marie-Antoinette, is imprisoned and (later) beheaded by Revolutionaries in Paris, Austria's Emperor Franz II seeks revenge, beginning two decades of wars between revolutionary France and monarchist Austria.

1805: Napoleon defeats Austria at Austerlitz, his greatest triumph over the forces of monarchy. Napoleon forces Holy Roman Emperor Franz II to hand over the imperial crown (1806), ending a thousand years of Empire, and he even marries Franz II's daughter, Marie-Louise.

1814–1815: An Austrian, Chancellor Metternich, heads the Congress of Vienna, reinstalling kings and nobles in lands now free of Napoleon.

1848: Emperor Franz Josef (Emperor of Austria, not of the Holy Roman Empire) rules for the next 68 years, maintaining white-gloved tradition while overseeing great change—Austria's decline as an empire and entrance into the modern industrial world.

1849: 100,000 Viennese attend the funeral of violinist Johann Strauss, poularizer of the dance craze called the waltz. His son, Johann

Strauss, Jr. (1825–1899), takes the baton of the Strauss Orchestra and waltzes to the next level, writing "The Blue Danube."

1866: Prussia provokes war and defeats Austria, effectively freezing Austria out of any involvement in a modern German nation.

1914: Austria fires the opening shots of World War I to avenge the assassination of their heir to the throne.

1919: After its defeat in World War I, the Austro-Hungarian empire is divided into separate democratic nations, with Austria assigned the borders it has today.

1932: Mirroring events in Germany, a totalitarian government (of Engelbert Dollfuss) replaces a weak democracy floundering in economic depression.

1938: Nazi Germany—using the threat of force and riding a surge of Germanic nationalism—annexes Austria in the *Anschluss,* and leads it into World War II.

1945: Like Germany, a defeated Austria is divided by the victors into occupied zones, but Austria's do not remain permanent.

1955: Modern Austria is born with the blessing of the international community.

1995: Austria joins the European Union.

2000: The European Union places sanctions on Austria (lifted a few months later) when the far-right Freedom Party—campaigning under the slogan "*Überfremdung:* Too many foreigners"—gains seats in Austria's parliament.

2002: The Freedom Party does badly in elections.

VIENNA

(Wien)

Vienna is a head without a body. For 640 years the capital of the once-grand Hapsburg empire, she started and lost World War I, and with it her far-flung holdings. Today, you'll find an elegant capital of 1.6 million people (20 percent of Austria's population) ruling a small, relatively insignificant country. Culturally, historically, and from a sightseeing point of view, this city is the sum of its illustrious past. The city of Freud, Brahms, Maria Theresa's many children, a gaggle of Strausses, and a dynasty of Holy Roman Emperors ranks right up there with Paris, London, and Rome.

Vienna has always been the easternmost city of the West. In Roman times, it was Vindobona, on the Danube facing the Germanic barbarians. In medieval times, Vienna was Europe's bastion against the Ottoman Turks (a horde of 200,000 was repelled in 1683). Though the ancient walls held out the Turks, World War II bombs destroyed nearly a quarter of the city's buildings. In modern times, Vienna took a big bite out of the USSR's Warsaw Pact buffer zone.

The truly Viennese person is not Austrian, but a second-generation Hapsburg cocktail, with grandparents from the distant corners of the old empire—Poland, Serbia, Hungary, Romania, the Czech Republic, Slovakia, and Italy. Vienna is the melting-pot capital of a now-collapsed empire that, in its heyday, consisted of 60 million people—only 8 million of whom were Austrian.

In 1900, Vienna's 2.2 million inhabitants made it the world's fifth-largest city (after New York, London, Paris, and Berlin). But the average Viennese mother today has 1.3 children, and the population is down to 1.6 million. (Dogs are the preferred "child.")

Some ad agency has convinced Vienna to make Elisabeth, wife of Emperor Franz Josef, with her narcissism and difficulties with royal life, the darling of the local tourist scene. You'll see "Sissy" all over town. But stay focused on the Hapsburgs who mattered.

Vienna Overview

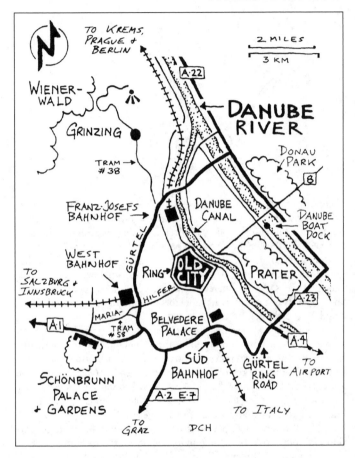

Of the Hapsburgs who ruled Austria from 1273 to 1918, Maria Theresa (ruled 1740–1780) and Franz Josef (ruled 1848–1916) are the most famous. People are quick to remember Maria Theresa as the mother of 16 children (10 survived). This was actually no big deal back then (one of her daughters had 18 kids, and a son fathered 16). Maria Theresa's reign followed the Austrian defeat of the Turks, when Europe recognized Austria as a great power. She was a strong and effective queen. (Her rival, the Prussian emperor, said, "When at last the Hapsburgs get a great man, it's a woman.")

Maria Theresa was a great social reformer. During her reign, she avoided wars and expanded her empire by skillfully marrying her children into the right families. After daughter Marie Antoinette's marriage into the French Bourbon family (to Louis XVI), for instance, a country that had been an enemy became an ally. (Unfortunately for Marie, she arrived in time for the Revolution, and she lost her head.)

A great reformer and in tune with her era, Maria Theresa employed Robin Hood policies to help Austria glide through the age of revolution without turmoil. She taxed the Church and the nobility, provided six years of obligatory education to all children, and granted free health care to all in her realm. She also welcomed the boy genius Mozart into her court.

As far back as the 12th century, Vienna was a mecca for musicians—both sacred and secular (troubadours). The Hapsburg emperors of the 17th and 18th centuries were not only generous supporters of music but fine musicians and composers themselves. (Maria Theresa played a mean double bass.) Composers like Haydn, Mozart, Beethoven, Schubert, Brahms, and Mahler gravitated to this music-friendly environment. They taught each other, jammed together, and spent a lot of time in Hapsburg palaces. Beethoven was a famous figure, walking—lost in musical thought—through Vienna's woods.

After the defeat of Napoleon and the Congress of Vienna in 1815 (which shaped 19th-century Europe), Vienna enjoyed its violin-filled belle époque, which shaped our romantic image of the city—fine wine, chocolates, cafés, and waltzes. "Waltz King" Johann Strauss and his brothers kept Vienna's 300 ballrooms spinning.

This musical tradition continues into modern times, leaving some prestigious Viennese institutions for today's tourists to enjoy: the Opera, the Boys' Choir, and the great Baroque halls and churches, all busy with classical and waltz concerts.

ORIENTATION

(area code: 01)
Vienna—Wien in German (veen)—sits between the Vienna Woods (Wienerwald) and the Danube (Donau). To the southeast is industrial sprawl. The Alps, which arc across Europe from Marseille, end at Vienna's wooded hills. These provide a popular playground for walking and new-wine–drinking. This greenery's momentum carries on into the city. More than half of Vienna is parkland, filled with ponds, gardens, trees, and statue-maker memories of Austria's glory days.

Think of the city map as a target. The bull's-eye is the cathedral, the first circle is the Ring, and the second is the Gürtel. The old town—snuggling around towering St. Stephan's Cathedral south of the Danube—is bound tightly by the Ringstrasse. The Ring, marking what was the city wall, circles the first district (or *Bezirk*). The Gürtel, a broader ring road, contains the rest of downtown (*Bezirkes* 2–9).

Addresses start with the *Bezirk,* followed by street and building number. Any address higher than the ninth *Bezirk* is beyond the Gürtel, far from the center. The middle two digits of Vienna's postal codes show the *Bezirk.* The address "7, Lindengasse 4" is in the seventh district, #4 on Linden Street. Its postal code would be 1070. Nearly all your sightseeing will be done in the core first district or along the Ringstrasse. As a tourist, concern yourself only with this compact old center. When you do, sprawling Vienna suddenly becomes manageable.

Planning Your Time

For a big city, Vienna is pleasant and laid-back. Packed with sights, it's worth two days and two nights on the speediest trip. It seems like Vienna was designed to help people just meander through a day. To be grand-tour efficient, you could sleep in and sleep out on the train (Berlin, Venice, Rome, the Swiss Alps, Paris, and the Rhine are each handy night trains away). But then you'd miss the Danube and Melk. I'd come in from Salzburg via Hallstatt, Melk, and the Danube and spend two days this way:

Day 1: 9:00-Circle the Ring by tram, following the self-guided tour (see "Do-It-Yourself Tram Orientation Tour," page 340), 10:00-Drop by TI for any planning and ticket needs, then see the sights in Vienna's old center (described below): Monument against War and Fascism, Kaisergruft crypt, Kärntner Strasse, St. Stephan's Cathedral, and Graben, 12:00-Finger sandwiches for lunch at Buffet Trzesniewski, 13:00-Tour the Hofburg and treasury, 16:00-Time to hit one more museum or shop, or browse and people-watch, 19:30-Choose classical music (concert or opera), House of Music museum, or *Heurige* wine garden.

Day 2: 9:00-Schönbrunn Palace (drivers: This is conveniently on the way out of town toward Salzburg; horse-lovers: You'll need to rearrange—or rush the palace—to see the Lipizzaner stallions' morning practice), 12:00-Lunch at Rosenberger Markt, 13:00-Tour the Opera, 14:00-Kunsthistorisches Museum, 16:00-Your choice of the many sights left to see in Vienna, Evening-See Day 1 evening options.

Tourist Information

Vienna has one real tourist office, a block behind the Opera House at Albertinaplatz (daily 9:00–19:00, tel. 01/24555, www.info.wien.at). Confirm your sightseeing plans and pick up the free and essential city map with a list of museums and hours (also available at most hotels), the monthly program of concerts (called *Wien-Programm*), and the youth guide *(Ten Good Reasons for Vienna)*. The TI also books rooms (for a €2.90 fee). While hotel and ticket booking agencies answer questions and give out maps and brochures at the train stations and airport, I'd rely on the TI if possible.

Consider the TI's handy €3.60 *Vienna from A to Z* booklet. Every important building sports a numbered flag banner that keys into this guidebook. A to Z numbers are keyed into the TI's city map. When lost, find one of the "famous-building flags" and match its number to your map. If you're at a famous building, check the map to see what other key numbers are nearby, then check the A to Z book description to see if you want to go in. This system is especially helpful for those just wandering aimlessly among Vienna's historic charms.

The much-promoted €17 Vienna Card might save the busy sightseer a few euros. It gives you a 72-hour transit pass (worth €12) and discounts of 10–50 percent at the city's museums.

Arrival in Vienna

By Train at the West Station (Westbahnhof): Train travelers arriving from Munich, Salzburg, and Melk land at the Westbahnhof. The *Reisebüro am Bahnhof* books hotels (for a €4 fee), has maps, answers questions, and has a train info desk (daily 7:30–21:00). To get to the city center (and most likely, your hotel), catch the U-3 metro (buy your ticket or transit pass—described below—from a *Tabak* shop in the station or from a machine—good on all city transit). U-3 signs lead down to the metro tracks. If your hotel is along Mariahilfer Strasse, your stop is on this line (direction Simmering; see "Sleeping," page 370). If you're sleeping in the center or just sightseeing, ride five stops to Stephansplatz, escalate in the exit direction Stephansplatz, and you'll hit the cathedral. The TI is a five-minute stroll down the busy Kärntner Strasse pedestrian street.

The Westbahnhof has a grocery store (daily 5:30–23:00), ATMs, Internet access, change offices, and storage facilities. Airport buses and taxis wait in front of the station.

By Train at the South Station (Südbahnhof): Those arriving from Italy and Prague land here. The Südbahnhof has all the services, left luggage, and a TI (daily 9:00–19:00). To reach Vienna's center, follow the S *(Schnellbahn)* signs to the right and down the stairs, and take any train in the direction Floridsdorf; transfer in two stops (at Landsstrasse/Wien Mitte) to the U-3 line, direction Ottakring, which goes directly to Stephansplatz and Mariahilfer Strasse hotels. Also, tram D goes to the Ring, and bus #13A goes to Mariahilfer Strasse.

By Train at Franz Josefs Station: If you're coming from Krems (in the Danube Valley), you'll arrive at Vienna's Franz Josefs station. From here, take tram D into town. Better yet, get off at Spittelau (the stop before Josefs) and use its handy U-Bahn station.

By Plane: Vienna's airport (12 miles from town, tel. 01/7007-22233 for info and to connect with various airlines, www.viennaairport.com) is connected by S-Bahn to the very central Wien-Mitte station (€3, 2/hr, 24 min). Beginning in 2004, an even speedier new train connects the airport to Wien-Mitte (€8, 16 min). With these new, faster options now available, the express airport bus (€6, 3/hr, 20 min) will likely be phased out. Taxis into town cost about €35 (including €10 airport surcharge). Hotels arrange for fixed-rate car service to the airport (€30, 30-min ride).

Getting around Vienna

By Bus, Tram, and Metro: Take full advantage of Vienna's simple, cheap, and super-efficient transit system. Buses, trams, and the metro all use the same tickets. Buy your tickets from *Tabak* shops, station machines, or *Vorverkauf* offices in the station. You have lots of choices:

• single tickets (€1.50, €2 if bought on tram, good for 1 journey with necessary transfers)

• 24-hour pass (€5)

• 72-hour pass (€12)

• 7-day pass (€12.50, pass always starts on Mon)

• *Acht Tage Karte:* eight all-day trips for €24 (can be shared, for example, 4 people for 2 days each). With a per-person cost of €3/day (compared to €5/day for a 24-hour pass) this can be a real saver for groups. Kids under 15 travel free on Sundays and holidays.

Take a moment to study the eye-friendly city-center map on metro station walls to internalize how the metro and tram system can help you (metro routes are designated by the end-of-the-line stop). I use the tram mostly to zip along the Ring (tram #1 or #2) and take the metro to outlying sights or hotels. The free tourist map has essentially all the lines marked, making the too-big €1.50 transit map unnecessary. Numbered lines (such as #38) are trams, numbers followed by an *A* (such as #38A) are buses. Lines that begin with *U* (e.g., U-3) are subways, or *U-Bahnen.* And blue lines are the speedier S-Bahns *(Schnellbahnen).*

Stamp a time on your ticket as you enter the system or tram (stamp it only the first time for a multiple-use pass). Cheaters pay a stiff €44 fine if caught—and then they make you buy a ticket. Rookies miss stops because they fail to open the door. Push buttons, pull latches—do whatever it takes. Study the excellent wall-mounted street map before you exit the metro. Choosing the right exit—signposted from the moment you step off the train—saves lots of walking (for information call 01/790-9105).

By Taxi: Vienna's comfortable, civilized, and easy-to-flag-down taxis start at €2. You'll pay about €8 to go from the Opera to the West Train Station (Westbahnhof). Consider the luxury of having your own car and driver. Johann (John) Lichtl is a kind, honest, English-speaking cabbie who can take up to four passengers in his car (€25/1 hr, €20/hr for 2 or more hours, mobile 0676/670-6750).

By Bike: Handy as you'll find the city's transit system, you may want to rent a bike (list of rental places at the TI). If the tram's not your style, you can circle the Ring on a convenient bike path.

By Buggy: Rich romantics get around by traditional horse and buggy. You'll see the horse buggies, called *Fiakers*, clip-clopping tourists on tours lasting 20 minutes (€40—old town), 40 minutes (€65—old town and the Ring), or one hour (€95—all of the above, but more thorough). You can share the ride and cost with up to five people. Because it's a kind of guided tour, before settling on a carriage, talk to a few drivers and pick one who's fun and speaks English.

Helpful Hints

Banking: ATMs are everywhere. Banks are open weekdays roughly from 8:00 to 15:00 and until 17:30 on Thursday. After-hours, you can change money at train stations, the airport, post offices, or the American Express office (Mon–Fri 9:00–17:30, Sat 9:00–12:00, closed Sun, Kärntner Strasse 21-23, tel. 01/5154-0456).

Post Offices: Choose from the main post office (Postgasse in center, open 24 hrs daily, handy metered phones), West Train Station (daily 6:00–23:00), South Train Station (daily 7:00-22:00), or near the Opera (Mon–Fri 7:00–19:00, closed Sat–Sun, Krugerstrasse 13).

English Bookstores: Consider the **British Bookshop** (Mon–Fri 9:30–18:30, Sat 9:30–17:00, closed Sun, at corner of Weihburggasse and Seilerstätte, tel. 01/512-1945; same hours at branch at Mariahilferstrasse 4, tel. 01/522-6730) or **Shakespeare & Co.** (Mon–Sat 9:00–19:00, closed Sun, north of Höher Markt square, Sterngasse 2, tel. 01/535-5053).

Internet Access: The TI has a list of Internet cafés. BigNet is the dominant outfit (about €3/hr, cheaper if you buy snack or drink, www.bignet.at), with lots of stations at Kärntner Strasse 61 (daily 10:00–24:00), Mariahilfer Strasse 27 (daily 8:00–2:00), and Hoher Markt 8–9 (daily 10:00–24:00). Surfland Internet Café is near the Opera (€1.40 to start, then €0.08/min, daily 10:00–23:00, Krugerstrasse 10, tel. 01/512-7701).

TOURS

Walks—The *Walks in Vienna* brochure at the TI describes Vienna's guided walks. The basic 90-minute Vienna First Glance introductory walk is given daily throughout the summer (€11, 14:00 from TI, in English and German, tel. 01/894-5363, www.wienguide.at).

Local Guides—The tourist board Web site (www.info.wien.at) has a long list of local guides with specialties and contact information. Lisa Zeiler is a good English-speaking guide (2-hr walks for €120—if she's booked, she can set you up with another guide, tel. 01/402-3688, lisa.zeiler@gmx.at).

Bus Tours—The Yellow Cab Sightseeing company offers a one-hour, €12, quickie double-decker bus tour with a tape-recorded narration, departing at the top of each hour (10:00–17:00) from in front of the

Opera (corner of Operngasse). Vienna Sightseeing offers hop-on, hop-off tours covering the 13 predictable sightseeing stops. Given Vienna's excellent public transportation and this outfit's meager one-bus-per-hour frequency, I'd take this not to hop on and off, but only to get the narrated orientation drive through town (recorded narration in 8 languages, €20 for 24-hr ticket, or €12 if you stay on for the 60-minute circular ride). Their basic Vienna city sights tour includes a visit to the Schönbrunn Palace and a bus tour around town (€33, 3/day April–Nov, 2/day Dec–March, 3.5 hrs; to book this or get info on other tours, call 01/7124-6830).

Do-It-Yourself Tram Orientation Tour

In the 1860s, Emperor Franz Josef had the city's ingrown medieval wall torn down and replaced with a grand boulevard 190 feet wide. The road, arcing nearly three miles around the city's core, predates all the buildings that line it—so what you'll see is neoclassical, neo-Gothic, and neo-Renaissance. One of Europe's great streets, it's lined with many of the city's top sights. Trams #1 and #2 and a great bike path circle the whole route—and so should you.

This self-service tram tour, rated ▲▲, gives you a fun orientation and a ridiculously quick glimpse of the major sights as you glide by (€1.50, 30-min circular tour). Tram #1 goes clockwise; tram #2, counterclockwise. Most sights are on the outside, so use tram #2 (sit on the right, ideally in the front seat of the front car; or—for maximum view and minimum air—sit in the bubble-front seat of the second car). Start immediately across the street from the Opera House.

You can jump on and off as you go (trams come every 5 min). Read ahead and pay attention—these sights can fly by. Let's go:

☞ Immediately on the left: The city's main pedestrian drag, Kärntner Strasse, leads to the zigzag roof of **St. Stephan's Cathedral.** This tram tour makes a 360-degree circle around the cathedral, staying about this same distance from it.

☞ At first bend (before first stop): Look right toward the tall fountain and the guy on a horse. Schwartzenberg Platz shows off its **equestrian statue** of Prince Charles Schwartzenberg, who fought Napoleon. Behind that is the Russian monument (behind the fountain), which was built in 1945 as a forced thanks to the Soviets for liberating Austria from the Nazis. Formerly a sore point, now it's just ignored.

☞ Going down Schubertring, you reach the huge **Stadtpark** (city park) on the right, which honors many great Viennese musicians and composers with statues. At the beginning of the park, the gold-and-cream concert hall behind the trees is the **Kursalon,** opened in 1867 by the Strauss brothers, who directed many waltzes here. The touristy Strauss concerts are held here (see "Summer Music Scene," page 364).

Vienna

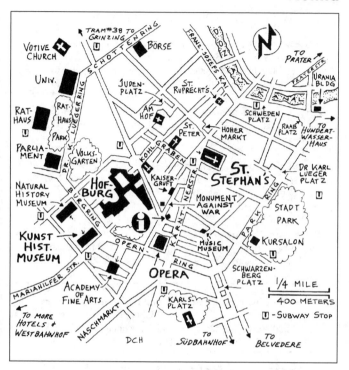

Immediately after next stop, look right: In the same park, the gilded statue of Waltz King **Johann Strauss** holds a violin as he did when he conducted his orchestra, whipping his fans into a two-stepping frenzy.

At next stop at end of park: On the left, a green statue of Dr. Karl Lueger honors the popular man who was mayor of Vienna until 1910.

At next bend: On the right, the quaint white building with military helmets decorating the windows was the Austrian ministry of war—back when that was a big operation. Field Marshal Radetzky, a military big shot in the 19th century under Franz Josef, still sits on his high horse. He's pointing toward the post office, the only art nouveau building facing the Ring. Locals call the architecture along the Ring "**historicism**" because it's all neo-this and neo-that—generally fitting the purpose of the particular building (for example, farther along the Ring, we'll see a neo-Gothic city hall—recalling when medieval burghers ran the city government in Gothic days, a neoclassical parliament building—celebrating ancient Greek notions of democracy, and a neo-Renaissance opera house—venerating the high culture filling it).

VIENNA AT A GLANCE

▲▲▲**Opera** Dazzling, world-famous opera house. **Hours:** Visit by 35-min tour only, daily in English, July–Aug at 11:00, 13:00, 14:00, 15:00, and often at 10:00 and 16:00; Sept–June fewer tours, afternoon only, confirm tour times by calling.

▲▲▲**Hofburg Treasury** The Hapsburgs' collection of jewels, crowns, and other valuables—the best on the Continent. **Hours:** Wed–Mon 10:00–18:00, closed Tue.

▲▲▲**Schönbrunn Palace** Spectacular summer residence of the Hapsburgs, similar in grandeur to Versailles. **Hours:** April–Oct daily 8:30–17:00, July–Aug until 18:00, Nov–March daily 8:30–16:30, reservations recommended.

▲▲▲**Kunsthistorisches Museum** World-class exhibit of the Hapsburgs' art collection, including Raphael, Titian, Caravaggio, Bosch, and Brueghel. **Hours:** Tue–Sun 10:00–18:00, Thu until 21:00, closed Mon.

▲▲**St. Stephan's Cathedral** Beautiful, enormous Gothic cathedral in the center of Vienna. **Hours:** Church doors open Mon–Sat 6:00–22:00, Sun 7:00–22:00, officially only open for tourists Mon–Sat 8:30–11:30 & 13:00-16:30, Sun 13:00-16:30.

▲▲**Stephansplatz, Graben, and Kohlmarkt** Atmospheric pedestrian squares and streets around the cathedral. **Hours:** Always open.

▲▲**Hofburg Imperial Apartments** Lavish main residence of the Hapsburgs. **Hours:** Daily 9:00–17:00.

▲▲**Hofburg New Palace Museums** Uncrowded collection of armor, musical instruments, and ancient Greek statues, in the elegant halls of a Hapsburg palace. **Hours:** Wed–Mon 10:00–18:00, closed Tue.

▲▲**Kaisergruft** Crypt for the Hapsburg royalty. **Hours:** Daily 9:30–16:00.

▲▲**KunstHausWien** Modern art museum dedicated to zany local artist/environmentalist Hundertwasser. **Hours:** Daily 10:00–19:00.

▲▲**Haus der Musik** Modern musuem with interactive exhibits on Vienna's favorite pastime. **Hours:** Daily 10:00–22:00.

▲**Monument against War and Fascism** Powerful four-part statue remembering victims of the Nazis. **Hours:** Always open.

▲**Albertina Museum** Newly opened Hapsburg residence with ho-hum apartments and world-class permanent and temporary exhibits. **Hours:** Daily 10:00–18:00, Wed until 21:00.

▲**Kärntner Strasse** Vienna's lively main pedestrian drag, connecting the Opera with the cathedral. **Hours:** Always open.

▲**Lipizzaner** Museum Displays dedicated to the regal Lipizzaner Stallions; horse-lovers should check out their practice sessions. **Hours:** Museum open daily 9:00–18:00, stallions practice across the street roughly Feb–June and Sept–Oct, Tue–Sat 10:00–12:00 when the horses are in town, call to confirm.

▲**Augustinian Church** Hapsburg marriage church, now hosting an 11:00 Sunday Mass with wonderful music. **Hours:** Open daily.

▲**Imperial Furniture Collection** Eclectic collection of Hapsburg furniture. **Hours:** Tue–Sun 10:00–18:00, closed Mon.

▲**Academy of Fine Arts** Small but exciting collection with works by Bosch, Botticelli, Rubens, Guardi, and Van Dyck. **Hours:** Tue–Sun 10:00–16:00, closed Mon.

▲**Belvedere Palace** Elegant palace of Prince Eugene of Savoy, with a collection of 19th- and 20th-century Austrian art (including Klimt). **Hours:** Tue–Sun 10:00–18:00, closed Mon.

▲**Dorotheum** Vienna's highbrow auction house. **Hours:** Mon–Fri 10:00–18:00, Sat 9:00–17:00, closed Sun.

☛ At next corner: The white-domed building over your right shoulder as you turn is the Urania, Franz Josef's 1910 **observatory.** Lean forward and look behind it for a peek at the huge red cars of the giant 100-year-old Ferris wheel in Vienna's Prater Park (fun for families, described in "Top People-Watching and Strolling Sights," page 364).

☛ Now you're rolling along the **Danube Canal.** This "Baby Danube" is one of the many small arms of the river that once made up the Danube at this location. The rest have been gathered together in a mightier modern-day Danube, farther away. This neighborhood was thoroughly bombed in World War II. The buildings across the canal are typical of postwar architecture (1960s). This was the site of the original Roman town, Vindobona. In three long blocks, on the left (opposite the BP station, be ready—it passes fast), you'll see the ivy-covered walls and round Romanesque arches of St. Ruprechts, the oldest church in Vienna (built in the 11th century on a bit of Roman ruins). Remember, medieval Vienna was defined by that long-gone wall which you're tracing on this tour. Relax for a few stops until the corner.

☛ Leaving the canal, turning left up Schottenring, at first stop: On the left, the orange-and-white, neo-Renaissance temple of money, the **Börse,** is Vienna's stock exchange.

☛ Next stop, at corner: The huge, frilly, neo-Gothic church on the right is a "votive church," built as a thanks to God when an 1853 assassination attempt on Emperor Franz Josef failed. Ahead on the right (in front of tram stop) is the Vienna University building (established in 1365, it has no real campus as the buildings are scattered around town). It faces (on the left, behind a gilded angel) a chunk of the old city wall.

☛ At next stop on right: The neo-Gothic city hall, flying the flag of Europe, towers over **Rathaus Platz,** a festive site in summer with a huge screen showing outdoor movies, operas, and concerts. Immediately across the street (on left) is the **Hofburg Theater,** Austria's national theater.

☛ At next stop on right: The neo-Greek temple of democracy houses the **Austrian Parliament.** The lady with the golden helmet is Athena, goddess of wisdom. Across the street (on left) is the royal park called the "Volksgarten."

☛ After the next stop on the right is the **Natural History Museum,** the first of Vienna's huge twin museums. It faces the **Kunsthistorisches Museum,** containing the city's greatest collection of paintings. The **MuseumsQuartier** behind them completes the ensemble with a collection of mostly modern-art museums. A hefty statue of Empress Maria Theresa sits between the museums, facing the grand gate to the **Hofburg,** the emperor's palace (on left). Of the five arches, only the center one was used by the emperor. (Your tour is essentially finished. If you want to jump out here, you're at many of Vienna's top sights.)

☛ Fifty yards after the next stop, on the left through a gate in the black iron fence, is the statue of Mozart. It's one of many charms in the

Burggarten, which until 1880 was the private garden of the emperor. Vienna had more than its share of intellectual and creative geniuses. A hundred yards farther (on left, just out of the park), the German philosopher Goethe sits in a big, thought-provoking chair playing trivia with Schiller (across the street on your right). Behind the statue of Schiller is the Academy of Fine Arts.

☛ Hey, there's the **Opera** again. Jump off the tram and see the rest of the city.

SIGHTS

Vienna's Old Center

▲▲▲**Opera (Staatsoper)**—The Opera, facing the Ring and near the TI, is a central point for any visitor. While the critical reception of the building 130 years ago led the architect to commit suicide, and though it's been rebuilt since the WWII bombings, it's still a dazzling place (€4.50, by guided 35-min tour only, daily in English, July–Aug at 11:00, 13:00, 14:00, 15:00, and often at 10:00 and 16:00; Sept–June fewer tours, afternoon only). Tours are often canceled for rehearsals and shows, so check the posted schedule or call 01/514-442-613.

The Vienna State Opera—with musicians provided by the Vienna Philharmonic Orchestra in the pit—is one of the world's top opera houses. There are 300 performances a year, except in July and August, when the singers rest their voices. Since there are different operas nearly nightly, you'll see big trucks out back and constant action backstage—all the sets need to be switched each day. Even though the expensive seats normally sell out long in advance, the opera is perpetually in the red and subsidized by the state.

Tickets for seats: For ticket information, call 01/513-1513 (phone answered daily 10:00–21:00, www.culturall.com or www.wiener-staatsoper.at). If seats aren't sold out, last-minute tickets (for pricey seats—up to €100) are sold for €30 from 9:00 to 14:00 only the day before the show.

Standing room: Unless Pavarotti is in town, it's easy to get one of 567 *Stehplätze* (standing-room spots, €2 at the top or €3.50 downstairs). While the front doors open 60 minutes early, a side door (on the Operngasse side, the door under the portico nearest the fountain) is open 80 minutes before curtain time, giving those in the know an early grab at standing-room tickets. Just walk in straight, then head right until you see the ticket booth marked *Stehplätze* (tel. 01/5144-42419). If fewer than 567 people are in line, there's no need to line up early. You can even buy standing-room tickets after the show has started—in case you want only a little taste of opera (see "Rick's crude tip," page 346). Dress is casual (but do your best) at the standing-room bar. Locals save their spot along the rail by tying a scarf to it.

Rick's crude tip: For me, three hours is a lot of opera. But just to see and hear the Opera House in action for half an hour is a treat. You can buy a standing-room spot and just drop in for part of the show. Ushers don't mind letting tourists with standing-room tickets in for a short look. Ending time is posted in the lobby—you could stop by for just the finale. If you go at the start or finish, you'll see Vienna dressed up. With all the time you save, consider stopping by...

Sacher Café, home of every chocoholic's fantasy, the Sacher torte, faces the rear of the Opera. While locals complain that the cakes have gone downhill, a coffee and slice of cake here is €8 well invested. For maximum elegance, sit inside (daily 8:00–23:30, Philharmoniker Strasse 4, tel. 01/51456). The adjacent Café Mozart is better for a meal.

The U-Bahn station in front of the Opera is actually a huge underground shopping mall with fast food, newsstands, lots of pickpockets, and even an Opera Toilet Vienna experience (€0.50, *mit Musik*).

▲**Monument against War and Fascism**—A powerful four-part statue stands behind the Opera House on Albertinaplatz. The split white monument, *The Gates of Violence,* remembers victims of the 1938–1945 Nazi rule of Austria. A montage of wartime images—clubs and gas masks, a dying woman birthing a future soldier, slave laborers—sits on a pedestal of granite cut from the infamous quarry at Mauthausen, a nearby concentration camp. The hunched-over figure on the ground behind is a Jew forced to wash anti-Nazi graffiti off a street with a toothbrush. The statue with its head buried in the stone reminds Austrians of the consequences of not keeping their government on track. Behind that, the 1945 declaration of Austria's second republic is cut into the stone. This monument stands on the spot where several hundred people were buried alive while hiding in the cellar of a building demolished in a WWII bombing attack.

Austria was pulled into World War II by Germany, which annexed the country in 1938, saying Austrians were wannabe Germans, anyway. But Austrians are not Germans—never were, never will be. They're quick to tell you that while Austria was founded in 976, Germany wasn't born until 1870. For seven years during World War II (1938–1945), there was no Austria. In 1955, after 10 years of joint occupation by the victorious Allies, Austria regained total independence.

Across the square from the TI, you'll see what looks like a big terrace overlooking the street. This was actually part of Vienna's original defensive rampart. Next to it is the...

▲**Albertina Museum**—For years, this building—the oldest of the Hapsburgs' Vienna residences—was closed for reconstruction. Now it has re-opened its doors so that commoners like you and me can wander its regal halls and enjoy some world-class artwork.

The Albertina consists of various components. First, you can stroll through the Hapsburg state rooms (French classicism—lots of white marble—but pretty ho-hum stuff compared to the apartments in the

Hofburg up the street). Second, the Albertina routinely borrows world-famous artwork for special exhibitions; in 2004, you'll see Paul Klee (Feb–April), Rembrandt (April–June), and Piet Mondrian (mid-Oct 2004 through Feb 2005). Finally, the Albertina also has its own spectacular collection of works by Michelangelo, Rubens, Rembrandt, and Raphael, plus a huge sampling of precise drawings by Albrecht Dürer. They're still experimenting with how to exhibit these masterpieces—so ask if your favorite artist is on display (state rooms only-€4, more for other exhibitions, audioguide also available for both permanent and temporary exhibits, daily 10:00–18:00, Wed until 21:00, overlooking Albertinaplatz across from TI and Opera House, tel. 01/534-830).

▲▲**Kaisergruft (Remains of the Hapsburgs)**—The crypt for the Hapsburg royalty, a block down the street from the Monument against War and Fascism, is covered in detail under "More Hofburg Sights," page 356.

▲**Kärntner Strasse**—This grand, mall-like street (traffic-free since 1974) is the people-watching delight of this in-love-with-life city. It points south in the direction of the southern Austrian state of Kärnten (for which it's named). Starting from the Opera, you'll find lots of action—shops, street music, the city casino (at #41), American Express (#21–23), and then, finally, the cathedral.

▲▲**St. Stephan's Cathedral**—Stephansdom is the Gothic needle around which Vienna spins. It has survived Vienna's many wars and symbolizes the city's freedom (church doors open Mon–Sat 6:00–22:00, Sun 7:00–22:00, officially only open for tourists Mon–Sat 8:30–11:30 & 13:00–16:30, Sun 13:00–16:30, otherwise closed for services; during services, you can enter back of church and get to north tower elevator, but unless you're attending Mass, you cannot enter main nave; entertaining English tours daily April–Oct at 15:45, €4, information board inside entry has tour schedules).

This is the third church to stand on this spot. (In fact, an older Romanesque chapel—the Virgilkapelle—is on display in the adjacent metro station.) The last bit of the 13th-century Romanesque church, the portal, round windows of the towers, and fascinating carvings in the tympanum, can be seen on the west end (above the entrance). The church survived the bombs of World War II, but, in the last days of the war, fires from the street fighting between Russian and Nazi troops leapt to the rooftop; the original timbered Gothic rooftop burned, and the cathedral's huge bell crashed to the ground. With a financial outpouring of civic pride, the roof of this symbol of Austria was rebuilt in its original splendor by 1952. The ceramic tiles are purely decorative (locals who contributed to the postwar reconstruction each "own" one for their donation).

Inside, find the Gothic sandstone **pulpit** in the middle of the nave (on left). A spiral stairway winds up to the lectern, surrounded and supported by the four Latin Church fathers: Saints Ambrose, Jerome,

Gregory, and Augustine. The railing leading up swarms with symbolism: lizards (animals of light), battle toads (animals of darkness), and the "Dog of the Lord" standing at the top to be sure none of those toads pollutes the sermon. Below the toads, wheels with three parts (the Trinity) roll up, while wheels with four parts (standing for the four seasons, symbolizing mortal life) roll down. This work, by Anton Pilgram, has all the elements of flamboyant Gothic in miniature. But this was around 1500, and the Renaissance was going strong in Italy. While Gothic persisted in the North, the Renaissance spirit had already arrived. Pilgram included what's thought to be a rare self-portrait bust in his work (the guy with sculptor's tools, looking out a window under the stairs). Gothic art was done for the glory of God. Artists were anonymous. In the more humanist Renaissance, man was allowed to shine— and artists became famous.

You can ascend both towers, the north (via crowded elevator inside on the left) and the south (outside right transept, by spiral staircase). The north shows you a big **bell** (the 21-ton Pummerin, cast from the cannon captured from the Turks in 1683, supposedly the second biggest bell in the world that rings by swinging) but a mediocre view (€4, daily 8:30–17:30, July–Aug until 18:00, Nov–March until 17:00). The 450-foot-high **south tower,** called St. Stephan's Tower, offers a great view— 343 tightly wound steps up the spiral staircase (€3, daily 9:00–17:30, this hike burns about 1 Sacher torte of calories). From the top, use your *Vienna from A to Z* to locate the famous sights.

The forlorn **Cathedral Museum** (Dom Museum, outside left transept past horses) gives a close-up look at piles of religious paintings, statues, and a treasury (€5, Tue–Sat 10:00–17:00, closed Sun–Mon, Stephansplatz 6, tel. 01/515-523-560).

▲▲**Stephansplatz, Graben, and Kohlmarkt**—The atmosphere of the church square, Stephansplatz, is colorful and lively. At nearby Graben Street (which was once a *Graben,* or ditch—originally the moat for the Roman military camp), top-notch street entertainers dance around an exotic **plague monument** (at Bräuner Strasse). In medieval times, people did not understand the causes of plagues and figured they were a punishment from God. It was common for survivors to thank God with a monument like this one from the 1600s. Find Emperor Leopold, who ruled during the plague and made this statue in gratitude. (Hint: The typical inbreeding of royal families left him with a gaping underbite.) Below Leopold, Faith (with the help of a disgusting little cupid) tosses old naked women—symbolizing the plague—into the abyss.

Just before the plague monument is Dorotheergasse, leading to the Dorotheum auction house (see "More Sights in Vienna," page 359). Just beyond the monument, you'll pass a fine set of public WCs before dead-ending at the recommended restaurant Julius Meinl am Graben (see "Eating," page 376). Turning left on **Kohlmarkt,** you enter Vienna's most elegant shopping street (except for "American Catalog Shopping," at #5, second floor) with the emperor's palace at the end. Strolling Kohlmarkt, daydream about the edible window displays at **Demel** (#14). These delectable displays change about weekly, reflecting current happenings in Vienna. Drool through the interior (coffee and cake-€7.50). Shops like this boast "K. u. K."—good enough for the *König und Kaiser* (king and emperor—same guy). Just beyond Demel and across the street, at #1152, you can pop into a charming little Baroque carriage courtyard, with the surviving original carriage garages.

Kohlmarkt ends at Michaelerplatz, with a scant bit of Roman Vienna exposed at its center. On the left are the fancy Laden Plankl shop, with traditional formal wear, and the stables of the Spanish Riding School. Study the grand entry facade to the Hofburg Palace—it's neo-Baroque from around 1900. The four heroic giants are Hercules wrestling with his great challenges (much like the Hapsburgs, I'm sure). Opposite the facade, notice the modern Loos House, which was built at about the same time. It was nicknamed the "house without eyebrows" for the simplicity of its windows. This anti–art nouveau statement was actually shocking at the time. To quell some of the outrage, the architect added flower boxes. Enter the Hofburg Palace by walking through the gate, under the dome, and into the first square (In der Burg).

Vienna's Hofburg Palace

▲▲**Hofburg**—The complex, confusing, and imposing Imperial Palace, with 640 years of architecture, demands your attention. This first Hapsburg residence grew with the family empire from the 13th century until 1913, when the last "new wing" opened. The winter residence of the Hapsburg rulers until 1918, it's still the home of the Spanish Riding School, the Vienna Boys' Choir, the Austrian president's office, 5,000 government workers, and several important museums.

Rather than lose yourself in its myriad halls and courtyards, focus on three sections: the Imperial Apartments, Treasury, and Neue Burg (New Palace).

Hofburg orientation from In der Burg Square: The statue is of Emperor Franz II, grandson of Maria Theresa, grandfather of Franz Josef, and father-in-law of Napoleon. Behind him is a tower with three kinds of clocks (the yellow disk shows the stage of the moon tonight). On the right, a door leads to the Imperial Apartments. Franz faces the oldest part of the palace. The colorful gate, which used to have a drawbridge, leads to the 13th-century Swiss Court (named for the Swiss mercenary guards once stationed here), the Schatzkammer (treasury), and the Hofburgkapelle (palace chapel, where the Boys' Choir sings the Mass). For the Heroes' Square and the New Palace, continue opposite the way you entered In der Burg, passing through the left-most tunnel (with a tiny but handy sandwich bar—Hofburg Stüberl, Mon–Fri 7:00–18:00,

Vienna's Hofburg Palace

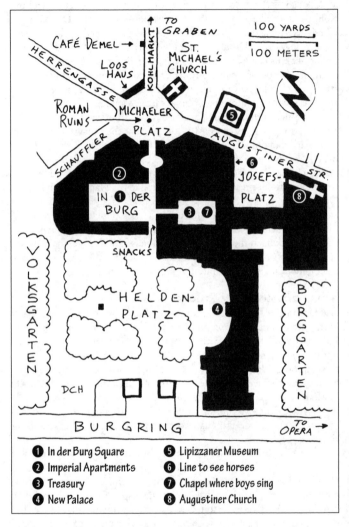

❶ In der Burg Square	❺ Lipizzaner Museum
❷ Imperial Apartments	❻ Line to see horses
❸ Treasury	❼ Chapel where boys sing
❹ New Palace	❽ Augustiner Church

Sat 9:00–15:00, Sun 10:00–15:00—your best bet if you need a bite or drink before touring the Imperial Apartments).

▲▲**Imperial Apartments (Kaiserappartements)**—These lavish, Versailles-type, "wish-I-were-God" royal rooms are the downtown version of the grander Schönbrunn Palace. If you're rushed and have time for only one palace, do this (€7.50, daily 9:00–17:00, last entry 16:30, from courtyard through St. Michael's Gate, just off Michaelerplatz, tel. 01/533-7570). Palace visits are a one-way romp through 20 rooms. You'll find some helpful English information within, and, with that and the following description, you won't need the €6.90 Hofburg guidebook. The €3.20 audioguide is only worthwhile for a Hapsburg history buff. Tickets include the royal silver and porcelain collection *(Silberkammer)* near the turnstile. If touring the silver and porcelain, do it first to save walking.

Get your ticket, study the big model of the palace complex, and (just after the turnstile) notice the family tree tracing the Hapsburgs from 1273 to their messy WWI demise. The first two rooms give an overview (in English) of Empress Elisabeth's fancy world—her luxury homes and fairy-tale existence. Throughout the tour, banners describe royal life.

Amble through the first several furnished rooms to the...

Waiting room for the audience room: A map and mannequins from the many corners of the Hapsburg realm illustrate the multi-ethnicity of the empire. Every citizen had the right to meet privately with the emperor. Three huge paintings entertained guests while they waited. They were propaganda, showing crowds of commoners enthusiastic about their Hapsburg royalty. On the right: An 1809 scene of the emperor returning to Vienna, celebrating news that Napoleon had begun his retreat. Left: The return of the emperor from the 1814 Peace of Paris, the treaty that ended the Napoleonic wars. (The 1815 Congress of Vienna that followed was the greatest assembly of diplomats in European history. Its goal: to establish peace through a "balance of power" among nations. While rulers ignored nationalism in favor of continued dynastic rule, this worked for about 100 years, until a colossal war—World War I—wiped out Europe's royal families.) Center: Less important, the emperor makes his first public appearance to adoring crowds after recovering from a life-threatening illness (1826). The chandelier—considered the best in the palace—is Baroque, made of Bohemian crystal.

Audience room: Suddenly, you were face-to-face with the emp. The portrait on the easel shows Franz Josef in 1915, when he was over 80 years old. Famously energetic, he lived a spartan life dedicated to duty. He'd stand at the high table here to meet with commoners, who came to show gratitude or make a request. (Standing kept things moving.) On the table, you can read a partial list of 56 appointments he had on January 3, 1910 (family name and topic of meeting).

Conference room: The emperor presided here over the equivalent of cabinet meetings. Remember, after 1867, he ruled the Austro-Hungarian Empire, so Hungarians sat at these meetings. The paintings on the wall show the military defeat of a popular Hungarian uprising...subtle.

EMPEROR FRANZ JOSEF

Franz Josef I—who ruled for 68 years (1848–1916)—was the embodiment of the Hapsburg Empire as it finished its six-century-long ride. Born in 1830, Franz Josef had a stern upbringing that instilled in him a powerful sense of duty and—like so many men of power—a love of things military. His uncle, Ferdinand I, was a dimwit, and, as the revolutions of 1848 were rattling royal families throughout Europe, the Hapsburgs replaced him, putting 18-year old Franz Josef on the throne. FJ was very conservative. But worse, he figured he was a talented military tactician, leading Austria into disastrous battles against Italy (which was fighting for its unification and independence) in the 1860s. His army endured severe, avoidable casualties. It was clear: FJ was a disaster as a general. Wearing his uniform to the end, he never saw what a dinosaur his monarchy was becoming, and never thought it strange that the majority of his subjects didn't even speak German. He had no interest in democracy and pointedly never set foot in Austria's parliament building. But, like his contemporary Queen Victoria, he was the embodiment of his empire—old-fashioned but sacrosanct. His passion for low-grade paperwork earned him the nickname "Joe bureaucrat." Mired in these petty details, he missed the big picture. He helped start a world war that ultimately ended the age of monarchs. The year 1918 marked the end of Europe's big royal families: Hohenzollerns (Prussia), Romanovs (Russia), and Hapsburgs (Austria).

Emperor Franz Josef's study: The desk was originally between the windows. Franz Josef could look up from his work and see his lovely, long-haired empress Elisabeth's reflection in the mirror. Notice the trompe l'oeil paintings above each door, giving the believable illusion of marble relief.

The walls between the rooms are wide enough to hide servants' corridors (the door to his valet's room is in the back left corner). The emperor lived with a personal staff of 14: three valets, four lackeys, two doormen, two manservants, and three chambermaids.

Emperor's bedroom: This features his famous spartan iron bed and portable washstand (necessary until 1880, when the palace got running water). A small painted porcelain portrait of the newlywed royal couple sits on the dresser. Franz Josef lived here after his estrangement from Sissy. An etching shows the empress—an avid hunter—riding sidesaddle

SISSY

Empress Elisabeth, Emperor Franz Josef's mysterious, narcissistic, and beautiful wife, is in vogue. She was mostly silent, worked out frantically to maintain her Barbie Doll figure, and spent hours each day tending to her ankle-length hair. Sissy's main goals in life seem to have been preserving her reputation as a beautiful empress and maintaining her fairy-tale hair. In spite of severe dieting and fanatic exercise, age took its toll. After turning 30, she allowed no more portraits to be painted and was generally seen in public with a delicate fan covering her face (and bad teeth). Complex and influential, she was adored by Franz Josef, whom she respected. Her personal mission and political cause was promoting Hungary's bid for nationalism. Her personal tragedy was the death of her son Rudolf, the crown prince, by suicide. Disliking Vienna and the confines of the court, she traveled more and more frequently. Over the years, the restless Sissy and her hardworking husband became estranged. In 1898, while visiting Geneva, Switzerland, she was murdered by an Italian anarchist. Sissy has been compared to Princess Diana because of her beauty, bittersweet life, and tragic death.

while jumping a hedge. The big ornate stove in the corner was fed from behind. Through the 19th century, this was a standard form of heating.

Great salon: See the paintings of the emperor and empress in grand gala ballroom outfits from 1865.

Small salon: This is dedicated to the memory of the assassinated Emperor Maximilian of Mexico (bearded portrait, Franz Josef's brother, killed in 1867). This was also a smoking room—necessary in the early 19th century, when smoking was newly fashionable (but only for men—never in the presence of women).

Empress' bedroom and drawing room: This was Sissy's, refurbished neo-rococo in 1854. She lived here—the bed was rolled in and out daily—until her death in 1898.

Sissy's dressing/exercise room: Servants worked two hours a day on Sissy 's famous hair here. She'd exercise on the wooden structure. While she had a tough time with people, she did fine with animals. Her favorite circus horses, Flick and Flock, prance on the wall.

Sissy's bathroom: Detour into the behind-the-scenes palace. In the narrow passageway, you'll walk by Sissy's hand-painted porcelain WC (on the right). In the main bathroom, you'll see her huge copper tub (with the original wall coverings behind it). Sissy was the first

Hapsburg to have running water in her bathroom. From here, you can wander (over the first linoleum ever used in Vienna—from around 1880) through the servants' quarters, with tropical scenes painted by Bergl in 1766. As you leave these rooms and re-enter the imperial world, look back to the room on the left.

Empress' great salon: The room is painted with Mediterranean escapes, the 19th-century equivalent of travel posters. The statue is of Elisa, Napoleon's oldest sister (by the neoclassical master, Canova). In the next room, at the end of the hall, admire the empress' hard-earned thin waist (20 inches at age 16, 21 inches at age 50...after giving birth to 4 children). Turn the corner and pass through the anterooms of Alexander's apartments.

Red salon: The Gobelin wall hangings were a 1776 gift from Marie Antoinette and Louis XVI in Paris to their Viennese counterparts.

Dining room: It's dinnertime, and Franz Josef has called his extended family together. The settings are modest...just silver. Gold was saved for formal state dinners. Next to each name card was a menu with the chef responsible for each dish. (Talk about pressure.) While the Hofburg had tableware for 4,000, feeding 3,000 was a typical day. The cellar was stocked with 60,000 bottles of wine. The kitchen was huge—50 birds could be roasted on the hand-driven spits at once.

After a few more rooms and the shop, you're back on the street. Two quick lefts take you back to the palace square (In der Burg), where you can pass through the black, red, and gold gate and to the treasury.

▲▲▲**Treasury (Weltliche und Geistliche Schatzkammer)**—This Secular and Religious Treasure Room contains the best jewels on the Continent. Slip through the vault doors and reflect on the glitter of 21 rooms filled with scepters, swords, crowns, orbs, weighty robes, double-headed eagles, gowns, gem-studded bangles, and an eight-foot-tall, 500-year-old unicorn horn (or maybe the tusk of a narwhal)—which was considered incredibly powerful in the old days, giving its owner the grace of God. These were owned by the Holy Roman Emperor—a divine monarch. The well-produced, included audioguide provides a wealth of information (€7.50, Wed–Mon 10:00–18:00, closed Tue, follow Schatzkammer signs to the Schweizerhof, tel. 01/52524).

Room 2: The personal crown of Rudolf II has survived since 1602—it was considered too well-crafted to cannibalize for other crowns. This crown is a big deal because it's the adopted crown of the Austrian Empire, established in 1806 after Napoleon dissolved the Holy Roman Empire (so named because it tried to be the grand continuation of the Roman Empire). Pressured by Napoleon, the Austrian Francis II—who had been Holy Roman Emperor—became Francis I, Emperor of Austria. Francis I/II (the stern guy on the wall) ruled from 1792 to 1835. Look at the crown. Its design symbolically merges the typical medieval king's crown and a bishop's miter.

Rooms 3 and 4: These contain some of the coronation vestments and regalia needed for the new Austrian emperor.

Room 5: Ponder the Throne Cradle. Napoleon's son was born in 1811 and made king of Rome. The little eagle at the foot is symbolically not yet able to fly, but glory-bound. Glory is symbolized by the star, with dad's big *N* raised high.

Room 11: The collection's highlight is the 10th-century crown of the Holy Roman Emperor. The imperial crown swirls with symbolism "proving" that the emperor was both holy and Roman. The jeweled arch over the top is reminiscent of the parade helmet of ancient Roman emperors whose successors the HRE claimed to be. The cross on top says the HRE ruled as Christ's representative on earth. King Solomon's portrait (on the crown, right of cross) is Old Testament proof that kings can be wise and good. King David (next panel) is similar proof that they can be just. The crown's eight sides represent the celestial city of Jerusalem's eight gates. The jewels on the front panel symbolize the Twelve Apostles.

The nearby 11th-century Imperial Cross preceded the emperor in ceremonies. Encrusted with jewels, it carried a substantial chunk of *the* cross and *the* holy lance (supposedly used to pierce the side of Jesus while on the cross; both items displayed in the same glass case). Look behind the cross to see how it was actually a box that could be clipped open and shut. You can see bits of the "true cross" anywhere, but this is a prime piece—with the actual nail hole.

The other case has jewels from the reign of Karl der Grosse (Charlemagne), the greatest ruler of medieval Europe. Notice Charlemagne modeling the crown (which was made a hundred years after he died) in the tall painting adjacent.

Room 12: The painting shows the coronation of Josef II in 1764. He's wearing the same crown and royal garb you've just seen.

Room 16: Most tourists walk right by perhaps the most exquisite workmanship in the entire treasury, the royal vestments (15th century). Look closely—they are painted with gold and silver threads.

▲Heroes' Square and the New Palace (Heldenplatz and the Neue Burg)—This last grand addition to the palace, from just before World War I, was built for Franz Ferdinand but never used. (It was tradition for rulers not to move into their predecessor's quarters.) Its grand facade arches around Heldenplatz, or Heroes' Square. Notice statues of the two great Austrian heroes on horseback: Prince Eugene of Savoy (who beat the Turks that had earlier threatened Vienna) and Archduke Charles (first to beat Napoleon in a battle, breaking Nappy's image of invincibility and heralding the end of the Napoleonic age). The frilly spires of Vienna's neo-Gothic city hall break the horizon, and a line of horse-drawn carriages await their customers.

▲▲New Palace Museums: Armor, Music, and Ancient Greek Statues—The Neue Burg—technically part of the Kunsthistorisches

Museum across the way—houses three fine museums (same ticket): an armory (with a killer collection of medieval weapons), historical musical instruments, and classical statuary from ancient Ephesus. The included audioguide brings the exhibits to life and lets you actually hear the fascinating old instruments in the collection being played. An added bonus is the chance to wander all alone among those royal Hapsburg halls, stairways, and painted ceilings (€7.50, Wed–Mon 10:00–18:00, closed Tue, almost no tourists, tel. 01/5252-4484).

More Hofburg Sights

These sights are near—and associated with—the palace.

▲**Lipizzaner Museum**—A must for horse-lovers, this tidy museum in the Renaissance Stallburg Palace shows (and tells in English) the 400-year history of the famous riding school. Lipizzaner fans have a warm spot in their hearts for General Patton, who, at the end of World War II—knowing that the Soviets were about to take control of Vienna—ordered a raid on the stable to save the horses and ensure the survival of their fine old bloodlines. Videos show the horses in action on TVs throughout the museum. The "dancing" originated as battle moves: *pirouette* (quick turns) and *courbette* (on hind legs to make a living shield for the knight). The 45-minute movie in the basement theater also has great horse footage (showings alternate between German and English).

A highlight for many is the opportunity to view the stable from a museum window and actually see the famous white horses just sitting there looking common. Don't bother waving...it's a one-way mirror (€5, daily 9:00–18:00, Reitschulgasse 2 between Josefsplatz and Michaelerplatz, tel. 01/533-8658).

Seeing the Lipizzaner Stallions: Seats for performances by Vienna's prestigious Spanish Riding School book up months in advance, but standing room is often available the same day (tickets-€35–105, standing room-€24–28, March–June and Sept–Oct Sun at 11:00, sometimes also Fri at 18:00). Lucky for the masses, training sessions (with music) in a chandeliered Baroque hall are open to the public (€11.50 at the door, roughly Feb–June and Sept–Oct, Tue–Sat 10:00–12:00 when the horses are in town, tel. 01/533-9031, www.srs.at). Tourists line up early at Josefsplatz, gate 2. Save money and avoid the wait by buying the €14.50 combo-ticket that covers both the museum and the training session (and lets you avoid that ticket line). Or, better yet, simply show up late. Tourists line up for hours to get in at 10:00, but almost no one stays for the full two hours—except for the horses. As people leave, new tickets are printed continuously, so you can just waltz in with no wait at all. If you arrive at 10:45, you'll see one group of horses finish and two more perform before they quit at noon.

▲**Augustinian Church**—The Augustinerkirche (on Josefsplatz) is the Gothic and neo-Gothic church where the Hapsburgs latched, then buried, their hearts (weddings took place here and the royal hearts are in the vault). Don't miss the exquisite, tomb-like Canova memorial (neo-classical, 1805) to Maria Theresa's favorite daughter, Maria Christina, with its incredibly sad white-marble procession. The church's 11:00 Sunday Mass is a hit with music-lovers—both a Mass and a concert, often with an orchestra accompanying the choir. To pay, contribute to the offering plate and buy a CD afterwards. (Programs are available at the table by the entry all week.)

▲▲**Kaisergruft, the Remains of the Hapsburgs**—Visiting the imperial remains is not as easy as you might imagine. These original organ donors left their bodies—about 150 in all—in the unassuming Kaisergruft (Capuchin Crypt), their hearts in the Augustinian Church (church open daily, but to see the goods you'll have to talk to a priest; Augustinerstrasse 3), and their entrails in the crypt below St. Stephan's Cathedral. Don't tripe.

Upon entering the Kaisergruft (€4, daily 9:30–16:00, last entry 15:40, behind Opera on Neuer Markt), buy the €0.50 map with a Hapsburg family tree and a chart locating each coffin.

The double coffin of Maria Theresa and her husband is worth a close look for its artwork. Maria Theresa outlived her husband by 15 years—which she spent in mourning. Old and fat, she installed a special lift enabling her to get down into the crypt to be with her dead husband (even though he had been far from faithful). The couple recline—Etruscan style—atop their fancy lead coffin. At each corner are the crowns of the Hapsburgs—the Holy Roman Empire, Hungary, Bohemia, and Jerusalem. Notice the contrast between the rococo splendor of Maria Theresa's tomb and the simple box holding her more modest son, Josef II (at his parents' feet). An enlightened monarch, Josef mothballed the too-extravagant Schönbrunn, secularized the monasteries, established religious tolerance within his realm, and freed the serfs. Josef was a model of practicality (he even invented a reusable coffin)—and very unpopular with other royals.

Franz Josef (1830–1916) is nearby in an appropriately austere military tomb. Flanking Franz Josef are the tombs of his son, Rudolf II, and Empress Elizabeth. Rudolf committed suicide in 1898 and—since the Church wouldn't allow such a burial for someone who took his own life—it took considerable legal hair-splitting to win Rudolf this spot (after examining his brain, it was determined that he was physically retarded and therefore incapable of knowingly killing himself). *Kaiserin* Elisabeth (1837–1898), a.k.a. Sissy, always gets the "Most Flowers" award.

In front of those three is the most recent Hapsburg tomb. Empress Zita was buried in 1989. Her burial procession was probably the last such Old Regime event in European history. The monarchy died hard in Austria.

Rather than chasing down all these body parts, remember that the magnificence of this city is the real remains of the Hapsburgs. Pan up. Watch the clouds glide by the ornate gables of Vienna.

▲**Imperial Furniture Collection (Kaiserliches Hofmobiliendepot)**— Bizarre, sensuous, eccentric, or precious, this is your peek at the Hapsburgs' furniture—from grandma's wheelchair to the emperor's spittoon—all thoughtfully described in English. The Hapsburgs had many palaces, but only the Hofburg was permanently furnished. The rest were furnished on the fly—set up and taken down by a gang of royal roadies called the "Depot of Court Movables" (Hofmobiliendepot). When the monarchy was dissolved in 1918, the state of Austria took possession of the Hofmobiliendepot's inventory—165,000 items. Now this royal storehouse is open to the public in a fine, new, sprawling museum. Don't go here for the Biedermeier or *Jugendstil* furnishings. The older Baroque and rococo pieces are the most impressive and tied most intimately to the royals. Combine a visit to this museum with a stroll down the lively shopping boulevard, Mariahilfer Strasse (€7, Tue–Sun 10:00–18:00, closed Mon, Mariahilfer Strasse 88, tel. 01/5243-3570).

Schönbrunn Palace

▲▲▲**Schönbrunn Palace**—Among Europe's palaces, only Schloss Schönbrunn rivals Versailles. Located four miles from the center, it was the Hapsburgs' summer residence. It's big (1,441 rooms), but don't worry—only 40 rooms are shown to the public. (The families of 260 civil servants actually rent simple apartments in the rest of the palace.)

While the exterior is Baroque, the interior was finished under Maria Theresa in let-them-eat-cake rococo. The chandeliers are either of hand-carved wood with gold-leaf gilding or of Bohemian crystal. Thick walls hid the servants as they ran around stoking the ceramic stoves from the back, and so on. Most of the public rooms are decorated in neo-Baroque, as they were under Franz Josef (ruled 1848–1916). When WWII bombs rained on the city and the palace grounds, the palace itself took only one direct hit. Thankfully, that bomb, which crashed through three floors—including the sumptuous central ballroom—was a dud.

Reservations and Hours: Schönbrunn suffers from crowds. To avoid the long delays in July and August (mornings are worst), make a reservation by telephone (tel. 01/8111-3239, answered daily 8:00–17:00). You'll get an appointment time and a ticket number. Check in at least 30 minutes early. Upon arrival, go to the group desk, give your number, pick up your ticket, and jump in ahead of the masses. If you show up in peak season without calling first, you deserve the frustration. Wait in line, buy your ticket, and wait until the listed time to enter (which could be tomorrow). Kill time in the gardens or coach museum (palace open April–Oct daily 8:30–17:00, July–Aug until 18:00, Nov–March daily

8:30–16:30). Crowds are worst from 9:30 to 11:30, especially on week-ends and in July and August; it's least crowded from 12:00 to 14:00 and after 16:00.

Cost and Tours: The admission price is the price of the tour you select. Choose between two recorded audioguide tours: the Imperial Tour (22 rooms, €8, 35 min, Grand Palace rooms plus apartments of Franz Josef and Elisabeth) or the Grand Tour (40 rooms, €10.50, 50 min, adds apartments of Maria Theresa). The Schönbrunn Pass Classic includes the Grand Tour, Gloriette viewing terrace, maze, court bakery, and privy garden (€18, available April–Oct only; more info: www .schoenbrunn.at). I'd go for the Grand Tour.

Getting to Palace: Take tram #58 from Westbahnhof directly to the palace, or ride U-4 to Schönbrunn and walk 400 yards. The main entrance is in the left side of the palace as you face it.

Coach Museum Wagenburg—The Schönbrunn coach museum is a 19th-century traffic jam of 50 impressive royal carriages and sleighs. Highlights include silly sedan chairs, the death-black hearse carriage (used for Franz Josef in 1916, and most recently for Empress Zita in 1989), and an extravagantly gilded imperial carriage pulled by eight Cinderella horses. This was rarely used other than for the coronation of Holy Roman Emperors, when it was disassembled and taken to Frankfurt for the big event (€4.50, April–Oct daily 9:00–18:00, Nov–March daily 10:00–16:00, last entry 30 min before closing time, closed Mon in winter, 200 yards from palace, walk through right arch as you face palace, tel. 01/877-3244).

Palace Gardens—After strolling through all the Hapsburgs tucked neatly into their crypts, a stroll through the emperor's garden with count-less commoners is a celebration of the natural evolution of civilization from autocracy into real democracy. As a civilization, we're doing well.

The sculpted **gardens** (with a palm house, €3.50, May–Sept daily 9:30–18:00, Oct–April daily 9:30–17:00) lead past Europe's oldest **zoo** *(Tiergarten,* built by Maria Theresa's husband for the entertainment and education of the court in 1752; €12, May–Sept daily 9:00–18:30, less off-season, tel. 01/877-9294) up to the **Gloriette,** a purely decorative mon-ument celebrating an obscure Austrian military victory and offering a fine city view (viewing terrace-€2.30, included in €18 Schönbrunn Pass Classic, April–Sept daily 9:00–18:00, July–Aug until 19:00, Oct until 17:00, closed Nov–March). The park itself is free (daily sunrise to dusk, entrance on either side of the palace). A touristy choo-choo train makes the rounds all day, connecting Schönbrunn's many attractions.

More Sights in Vienna

▲▲▲**Kunsthistorisches Museum**—This exciting museum, across the Ring from the Hofburg Palace, showcases the grandeur and opulence of the Hapsburgs' collected artwork. There are European masterpieces galore, all well hung on one glorious floor, plus a fine display of Egyptian, classical, and applied arts.

Starting with the Italian wing of the museum, you get an immediate sense of the richness of this collection—you've walked right into the High Renaissance. Here, you'll see Raphael's graceful *Madonna of the Meadow* and Correggio's voluptuous *Jupiter and Io.* Meander through the Venetian Renaissance rooms to spend time with Titian, and land (with a thud) in the heart of Realism. (Caravaggio's still-shocking *David with the Head of Goliath* shows the artist was distinctly ahead of his time.)

The Baroque rooms offer pudgy winged babies galore—quite a contrast to the simple, direct, and down-to-earth Northern paintings by Dutch and Flemish artists only steps away. Enjoy Hieronymus Bosch's bizarrely crowded work and linger at the paintings by Peter Brueghel, the undisputed master of the slice-of-life village scene. Giuseppe Arcimboldo's *Summer* and *Water* (with faces made of produce and fish, respectively) are always crowd-pleasers. Try the helpful, included audio-guide for the full picture (€9, Tue–Sun 10:00–18:00, Thu until 21:00, closed Mon, tel. 01/525-240).

Sadly, one of the jewels in the museum's crown is now missing. Cellini's *Salt Cellar,* a divine golden salt bowl valued at €50 million, was stolen (to the anguish of the Vienna art world) in 2003 by expert thieves.

▲**Natural History Museum**—In the twin building facing the art museum, you'll find moon rocks, dinosaur stuff, and the fist-sized *Venus of Willendorf*—at 30,000 years old, the world's oldest sex symbol, found in the Danube Valley (€6.50, Wed–Mon 9:00–18:30, Wed until 21:00, closed Tue, tel. 01/521-770).

MuseumsQuartier—This sprawling collection of blocky, modernist museums is housed within the Baroque facade of the former imperial stables. The centerpiece is the **Leopold Museum,** which features modern Austrian art, including the best collection of works by Egon Schiele (1890–1918) and a few works by Kokoschka and Klimt (€9, Wed–Mon 10:00–19:00, Fri 10:00–21:00, closed Tue, behind Kunsthistorisches Museum, U-2 or U-3: Volkstheater/Museumsplatz, Museumsplatz 1–5, tel. 01/525-700).

The new **Museum of Modern Art** (Museum Moderner Kunst Stiftung Ludwig, a.k.a. Mumok), also in the MuseumsQuartier, is Austria's leading modern-art gallery. Its huge, state-of-the-art building displays revolving exhibits showing off art of the last generation—including Klee, Picasso, and Pop (€8, Tue–Sun 10:00–18:00, Thu until 21:00, closed Mon, tel. 01/525-001-440, www.mumok.at). Rounding out the sprawling MuseumsQuartier are an architecture museum, Transeuropa, Electronic Avenue, children's museum, and the Kunsthalle Wien—an exhibition center for contemporary art. Various combo-tickets are available for those interested in more than just the Leopold Museum (visit www.mqw.at). Walk into the center from the Hofburg side, where the main entrance (with visitor center and info room) leads to a big courtyard with cafés, fountains, and huge lounging sponges surrounded by the quarter's various museums.

▲**Academy of Fine Arts**—This small but exciting collection includes works by Bosch, Botticelli, and Rubens; a Venice series by Guardi; and a self-portrait by 15-year-old Van Dyck (€5, Tue–Sun 10:00–16:00, closed Mon, 3 blocks from Opera at Schillerplatz 3, tel. 01/5881-6225). As you wander the halls of this academy, ponder how history might have been different if Hitler—who applied to study architecture here but was rejected—had been accepted as a student.

▲▲**KunstHausWien: Hundertwasser Museum**—This "make yourself at home" museum is a hit with lovers of modern art. It mixes the work and philosophy of local painter/environmentalist Hundertwasser. Stand in front of the colorful checkerboard building and consider Hundertwasser's style. He was against "window racism." Neighboring houses allow only one kind of window. But $100H_2O$'s windows are each different—and he encouraged residents to personalize them. He recognized tree tenants as well as human tenants. His buildings are spritzed with a forest and topped with dirt and grassy little parks—close to nature, good for the soul. Floors and sidewalks are irregular—to "stimulate the brain" (although current residents complain it just causes wobbly furniture and sprained ankles). Thus $100H_2O$ waged a one-man fight—during the 1950s and 1960s, when concrete and glass ruled—to save the human soul from the city. (Hundertwasser claimed that "straight lines are godless.") Inside the museum, start with his interesting biography (which ends in 2000). His fun-loving paintings are half *Jugendstil* ("youth style") and half just kids' stuff. Notice the photographs from his 1950s days as part of Vienna's bohemian scene. Throughout the museum, notice the fun philosophical quotes from an artist who believed, "If man is creative, he comes nearer to his creator" (€8 for Hundertwasser Museum, €14 combo-ticket includes special exhibitions, half price on Mon, daily 10:00–19:00, extremely fragrant and colorful garden café, U-3: Landstrasse, Weissgerberstrasse 13, tel. 01/712-0491).

The KunstHausWien provides by far the best look at Hundertwasser. For an actual lived-in apartment complex by the green master, walk five minutes to the one-with-nature **Hundertwasserhaus** (free, at Löwengasse and Kegelgasse). This complex of 50 apartments, subsidized by the government to provide affordable housing, was built in the 1980s as a breath of architectural fresh air in a city of boring, blocky apartment complexes. While not open to visitors, it's worth visiting for its fun-loving and colorful patchwork exterior and the Hundertwasser festival of shops across the street. Don't miss the view from Kegelgasse to see the "tree tenants" and the internal winter garden residents enjoy.

▲**Belvedere Palace**—This is the elegant palace of Prince Eugene of Savoy—the still-much-appreciated conqueror of the Turks. Eugene, a

Frenchman considered too short and too ugly to be in the service of Louis XIV, offered his services to the Hapsburgs. While he was short and ugly indeed, he became the greatest military genius of his age. Today, his palace houses the Austrian gallery of 19th- and 20th-century art. Skip the lower palace and focus on the garden and the upper palace *(Oberes Belvedere)* for a winning view of the city, a fine collection of *Jugendstil* art, and Vienna's best look at the dreamy work of Gustav Klimt (€7.50, Tue–Sun 10:00–18:00, closed Mon, entrance at Prinz Eugen Strasse 27, tel. 01/7955-7134). Your ticket includes the Austrian Baroque and Gothic art in the Lower Palace.

▲▲**Haus der Musik**—Vienna's House of Music has a small first-floor exhibit on the Vienna Philharmonic, and upstairs you'll enjoy fine audiovisual exhibits on each of the famous hometown boys (Haydn, Mozart, Beethoven, Strauss, and Mahler). But the museum is unique for its effective use of interactive touch-screen computers and head-phones to actually explore the physics of sound. You can twist, dissect, and bend sounds to make your own musical language, merging your voice with a duck's quack or a city's traffic roar. Wander through the "sonosphere" and marvel at the amazing acoustics—I could actually hear what I thought only a piano tuner could hear. Pick up a virtual baton to conduct the Vienna Philharmonic Orchestra (each time you screw up, the orchestra stops and ridicules you). A computer will help you compose your own waltz by throwing dice. Really seeing the place takes time. It's open late and makes a good evening activity (€10, daily 10:00–22:00, 2 blocks from Opera at Seilerstatte 30, tel. 01/51648, www.hdm.at).

▲**Vienna's Auction House, the Dorotheum**—For an aristocrat's flea market, drop by Austria's answer to Sotheby's, the Dorotheum. Its five floors of antique furniture and fancy knickknacks have been put up either for immediate sale or auction, often by people who inherited old things they don't have room for (Mon–Fri 10:00–18:00, Sat 9:00–17:00, closed Sun, classy little café on second floor, between Graben and Hofburg at Dorotheergasse 17, tel. 01/515-600). Fliers show schedules for actual auctions, which you are welcome to attend.

Judenplatz Memorial and Museum—Judenplatz marks the location of Vienna's 15th-century Jewish community, one of Europe's largest at the time. The square, once filled with a long-gone synagogue, is now dom-inated by a blocky memorial to the 65,000 Austrian Jews killed by the Nazis. The memorial—a library turned inside out—symbolizes Jews as "people of the book" and causes one to ponder the huge loss of culture, knowledge, and humanity that took place during 1938 to 1945.

The Judenplatz Museum, while sparse, has displays on medieval Jewish life and a well-done video re-creating community scenes from five centuries ago. Wander the scant remains of the medieval synagogue below street level—discovered during the construction of the Holocaust

JUGENDSTIL

Vienna gave birth to its own curvaceous brand of art nouveau around the early 1900s: *Jugendstil* ("youth style"). The TI has a brochure laying out Vienna's 20th-century architecture. The best of Vienna's scattered *Jugendstil* sights: the Belvedere Palace collection, the clock on Hoher Markt (which does a musical act at noon), and the gilded, cabbage-domed building at the Ring end of the Naschmarkt (U-1, U-2, or U-4: Karlsplatz, and follow signs to Secession). This gallery (housing a huge Beethoven frieze by Klimt) proclaims the movement's slogan: "To each century its art, and to art its liberty." Klimt, Wagner, and friends (who called themselves the Vienna Secession) first exhibited their "liberty-style" art here in 1897.

memorial. This was the scene of a medieval massacre. Since Christians weren't allowed to lend money, Jews were Europe's moneylenders. As so often happened in Europe, when Christian locals fell too deeply into debt, they found a convenient excuse to wipe out the local ghetto—and their debts at the same time. In 1421, 200 of Vienna's Jews were burned at the stake. Others who refused a forced conversion committed mass suicide in the synagogue (€3, €7 combo-ticket includes a synagogue and Jewish Museum of the City of Vienna, Sun–Thu 10:00–18:00, Fri 10:00–14:00, closed Sat, Judenplatz 8, tel. 01/535-0431).

Honorable Mention—There's much, much more. The city map lists everything. If you're into butterflies, Esperanto, undertakers, tobacco, clowns, firefighting, Freud, or the homes of dead composers, you'll find them all in Vienna. Several good museums that try very hard but are submerged in the greatness of Vienna include: **Jewish Museum of the City of Vienna** (€5, or €7 combo-ticket includes synagogue and Judenplatz Museum—listed above, Sun–Fri 10:00–18:00, Thu until 20:00, closed Sat, Dorotheergasse 11, tel. 01/535-0431, www.jmw.at), **Historical Museum of the City of Vienna** (Tue–Sun 9:00–18:00, closed Mon, Karlsplatz), **Folkloric Museum of Austria** (Tue–Sun 10:00–17:00, closed Mon, Laudongasse 15, tel. 01/406-8905), and **Museum of Military History**, one of Europe's best if you like swords and shields (Heeresgeschichtliches Museum, Sat–Thu 9:00–17:00, closed Fri, Arsenal district, Objekt 18, tel. 01/795-610). The vast **Austrian Museum of Applied Arts** (Österreichisches Museum für Angewandte Kunst, or MAK) is Vienna's answer to London's Victoria & Albert collection. The museum shows off the fancies of local aristocratic society, including a fine *Jugendstil* collection (€8, free Sat, open Tue–Sun

10:00–18:00, Tue until 24:00, closed Mon, Stubenring 5, tel. 01/711-360, www.mak.at).

For a walk in the **Vienna Woods,** catch the U-4 metro to Heiligenstadt, then bus #38A to Kahlenberg, for great views and a café overlooking the city. From there, it's a peaceful 45-minute downhill hike to the *Heurigen* of Nussdorf or Grinzing to enjoy some wine (see "Vienna's Wine Gardens," page 366).

Top People-Watching and Strolling Sights

▲**City Park**—Vienna's Stadtpark is a waltzing world of gardens, memorials to local musicians, ponds, peacocks, music in bandstands, and locals escaping the city. Notice the *Jugendstil* entrance at the Stadtpark metro station. The Kursalon, where Strauss was the violin-toting master of waltzing ceremonies, hosts daily touristy concerts in 3/4 time.

▲**Prater**—Vienna's sprawling amusement park tempts many visitors with its huge 220-foot-tall, famous, and lazy Ferris wheel *(Riesenrad),* roller coaster, bumper cars, lilliputian railroad, and endless eateries. Especially if you're traveling with kids, this is a fun, goofy place to share the evening with thousands of Viennese (daily 9:00–24:00 in summer, but quiet after 22:00, U-1: Praterstern). For a local-style family dinner, eat at Schweizerhaus (good food, great beer) or Wieselburger Bierinsel.

Sunbathing—Like most Europeans, the Austrians worship the sun. Their lavish swimming centers are as much for tanning as swimming. To find the scene, follow the locals to their "Danube Sea" and a 20-mile, skinny, man-made beach along Danube Island. It's traffic-free concrete and grass, packed with in-line skaters and bikers, with rocky river access and a fun park (easy U-Bahn access on U-1 to Donauinsel).

▲**Naschmarkt**—Vienna's ye olde produce market bustles daily near the Opera along Wienzeile Street. It's likeably seedy and surrounded by sausage stands, Turkish *döner kebab* stalls, cafés, and theaters. Each Saturday, it's infested by a huge flea market where, in olden days, locals would come to hire a monkey to pick little critters out of their hair (Mon–Fri 7:00–18:00, Sat 6:00–18:00, closed Sun, closes earlier in winter, U-4: Kettenbruckengasse). For a picnic park, walk a block down Schleifmuhlgasse.

SUMMER MUSIC SCENE

Vienna is Europe's music capital. It's music *con brio* from October through June, reaching a symphonic climax during the Vienna Festival each May and June. Sadly, in July and August, the Boys' Choir, the Opera, and many more music companies are—like you—on vacation. But Vienna hums year-round with live classical music. In the summer, you have these basic choices:

Touristy Mozart and Strauss Concerts—If the music comes to you, it's touristy—designed for flash-in-the-pan Mozart fans. Powdered-wig orchestra performances are given almost nightly in grand traditional settings (€25–50). Pesky wigged-and-powdered Mozarts peddle tickets in the streets with slick sales pitches about the magic of the venue and the quality of the musicians. Second-rate orchestras, clad in historic costumes, perform the greatest hits of Mozart and Strauss. While there's not a local person in the audience, the tourists generally enjoy the evening. To sort through all your options, check with the ticket office in the TI (same price as on the street but with all venues to choose from).

Strauss Concerts in the Kursalon—For years, Strauss concerts have been held in the Kursalon, where the Waltz King himself directed wildly popular concerts 100 years ago (€32–49, 4 concerts nightly April–Oct, 1 concert nightly other months, tel. 01/512-5790). Shows are a touristy mix of ballet, waltzes, and a 15-piece orchestra in wigs and old outfits. For the cheap option, enjoy a summer afternoon coffee concert (free if you buy a drink weekends and maybe also weekdays July–Aug 15:00–17:00).

Serious Concerts—These events, including the Opera, are listed in the monthly *Wien-Programm* (available at TI). Tickets run from €36 to €75 (plus a stiff 22 percent booking fee when booked in advance or through a box office like the one at the TI). If you call a concert hall directly, they can advise you on the availability of (cheaper) tickets at the door. Vienna takes care of its starving artists (and tourists) by offering cheap standing-room tickets to top-notch music and opera (1 hour before show time).

Vienna's **Summer of Music Festival** assures that even from June through September, you'll find lots of great concerts, choirs, and symphonies (special *Klang Bogen* brochure at TI; get tickets at Wien Ticket pavilion off Kärntner Strasse next to Opera House or go directly to location of particular event; Summer of Music tel. 01/42717).

Musicals—The Wien Ticket pavilion sells tickets to contemporary American and British musicals (€10–95 with €2.50 standing room) and offers these tickets at half price from 14:00 until 17:00 the day of the show. Or you can reserve (full-price) tickets for the musicals by calling up to one day ahead (call combined office of the 3 big theaters at tel. 01/58885).

Vienna Boys' Choir—The boys sing (heard but not seen, from a high balcony) at Mass in the Imperial Chapel *(Hofburgkapelle)* of the Hofburg (entrance at Schweizerhof, from Josefs Platz go through tunnel) 9:15–10:30 on Sundays, except in July and August. While seats must be reserved two months in advance (€5–29, reserve by fax, e-mail, or mail: fax 011-431-533-992-775 from the U.S., hmk@aon.at, or write Hofmusikkapelle, Hofburg-Schweizerhof, 1010 Wien; tel. for information only—cannot book tickets—01/533-9927), standing room inside is free and open to the first 60 who line up. Rather than line up early, you can simply swing by and stand in the narthex just outside, where you can hear the boys and see the Mass on a TV monitor. Boys' Choir concerts (on stage at the Musikverein) are also given Fridays at 16:00 in May, June, September, and October (€35–48, standing room goes on sale at 15:30 for €15, Karlsplatz 6, U-1, U-2, or U-4: Karlsplatz, tel. 01/5880-4141). They're nice kids, but, for my taste, not worth all the commotion. Remember, many churches have great music during Sunday Mass. Just 200 yards from the Boys' Choir chapel, Augustinian Church has a glorious 11:00 service each Sunday.

VIENNA'S CAFÉS

In Vienna, the living room is down the street at the neighborhood coffeehouse. This tradition is just another example of Viennese expertise in good living. Each of Vienna's many long-established (and sometimes even legendary) coffeehouses has its individual character (and characters). They offer newspapers, pastries, sofas, elegance, smoky ambience, and "take all the time you want" charm for the price of a cup of coffee. Order it *melange* (with a little milk) or *schwarzer* (black). Rather than buy the *Herald Tribune* ahead of time, buy a cup of coffee and read it for free, Vienna-style.

These are my favorites: **Café Hawelka,** with a dark, "brooding Trotsky" atmosphere, paintings by struggling artists who couldn't pay for coffee, a saloon-wood flavor, chalkboard menu, smoked velvet couches, an international selection of newspapers, and a phone that rings for regulars (Wed–Mon 8:00–2:00, Sun from 16:00, closed Tue, just off Graben, Dorotheergasse 6); **Café Central,** with *Jugendstil* decor and great *Apfelstrudel* (high prices and stiff staff, Mon–Sat 8:00–22:00, Sun 10:00-18:00, Herrengasse 14, tel. 01/533-376-326); the **Café Sperl,** dating from 1880 with furnishings identical to the day it opened, from the coat tree to the chairs (Mon–Sat 7:00–23:00, Sun 11:00–20:00 except closed Sun July–Aug, just off Naschmarkt near Mariahilfer Strasse, Gumpendorfer 11, tel. 01/586-4158); and the basic, untouristy **Café Ritter** (daily 7:30–23:30, Mariahilfer Strasse 73, U-3: Neubaugasse, near several recommended hotels, tel. 01/587-8237).

VIENNA'S WINE GARDENS

The *Heurige* is a uniquely Viennese institution celebrating the *Heurige,* or new wine. When the Hapsburgs let Vienna's vintners sell their own wine tax-free, several hundred families opened *Heurigen* (wine-garden restaurants clustered around the edge of town), and a tradition was born. Today, they do their best to maintain the old-village atmosphere, serving the homemade new wine (the last vintage, until November 11, when a new vintage year begins) with light meals and strolling musicians.

Most *Heurigen* are decorated with enormous antique presses from their vineyards. Wine gardens might be closed on any given day; always call ahead to confirm, if you have your heart set on a particular place. (For a near-*Heurige* experience right downtown, drop by Gigerl Stadtheuriger; see "Eating," page 376.)

At any *Heurige,* fill your plate at a self-serve cold-cut buffet (€6–9 for dinner). Dishes to look out for: *Stelze* (grilled knuckle of pork), *Fleischlaberln* (fried ground meat patties), *Schinkenfleckerln* (pasta with cheese and ham), *Schmalz* (a spread made with pig fat), *Blunzen* (black pudding...sausage made from blood), *Presskopf* (jellied brains and innards), *Liptauer* (spicy cheese spread), *Kornspitz* (whole-meal bread roll), and *Kummelbraten* (crispy roast pork with caraway). Waitresses will then take your wine order (€2.20 per quarter liter, about 8 oz). Many locals claim it takes several years of practice to distinguish between *Heurige* and vinegar.

There are more than 1,700 acres of vineyards within Vienna's city limits, and countless *Heurige* taverns. For a *Heurige* evening, rather than go to a particular place, take a tram to the wine-garden district of your choice and wander around, choosing the place with the best ambience.

Getting to the *Heurigen:* You have three options: trams and buses, a 15-minute taxi ride, or a goofy tourist train.

Trams make a trip to the Vienna Woods quick and affordable. The fastest way is to ride U-4 to its last stop, Heiligenstadt, where trams and buses in front of the station fan out to the various neighborhoods. Ride tram D to its end point for Nussdorf. Ride bus #38A for Grinzing and on to the Kahlenberg viewpoint—#38A's end station (note that tram #38—different from bus #38A—starts at the Ring and finishes at Grinzing). To get to Neustift am Walde, ride U-6 to Nussdorfer Strasse and catch bus #35A. Connect Grinzing and Nussdorf with bus #38A and tram D (transfer at Grinzingerstrasse).

The **Heuriger Express** train is tacky but handy and relaxing, chugging you on a hop-on, hop-off circle from Nussdorf through Grinzing and around the Vienna Woods (€7.30, 50 min, daily April–Oct 12:00–19:00, departs from end station of tram D in Nussdorf at the top of every hr, tel. 01/479-2808).

Here are four good *Heurige* neighborhoods:

Grinzing: Of the many *Heurige* suburbs, Grinzing is the most famous, lively...and touristy. Many people precede their visit to Grinzing by riding bus #38A to its end (up to Kahlenberg for a grand Vienna view) and then ride 20 minutes back into the *Heurige* action. From the Grinzing tram stop, follow Himmelgasse uphill toward the onion-top dome. You'll pass plenty of wine gardens—and tour buses—on your way up. Just past the dome, you'll find the heart of the *Heurige.*

Pfarrplatz: Between Grinzing and Nussdorf, this area features several decent spots, including the famous and touristy **Beethovenhaus**

(Mon–Sat 16:00–24:00, Sun 11:00–24:00, bus #38A stop: Fernsprechamt/Heiligenstadt, walk 5 min uphill on Dübling Nestelbachgasse to Pfarrplatz 2, tel. 01/370-3361). Beethoven lived—and composed his Sixth Symphony—here in 1817. He hoped the local spa would cure his worsening deafness. **Weingut and Heuriger Werner Welser,** a block uphill from Beethoven's place, is lots of fun, with music nightly from 19:00 (daily 15:30–24:00, Probusgasse 12, tel. 01/318-9797).

Nussdorf: A less-touristy district—characteristic and popular with locals—Nussdorf has plenty of *Heurige* ambience. Right at the end station of tram D, you'll find three long and skinny places side by side: **Heuriger Kierlinger** (daily 15:30–24:00, Kahlenbergerstrasse 20, tel. 01/370-2264), **Steinschaden** (daily 15:00–24:00, Kahlenbergerstrasse 18, tel. 01/370-1375), and **Schübel-Auer Heuriger** (Tue–Sat 16:00–24:00, closed Sun–Mon, Kahlenbergerstrasse 22, tel. 01/370-2222). Walk through any of these and you pop out on Kahlenbergerstrasse, where a walk uphill takes you to some more eating and drinking fun: **Bamkraxler** (the tree jumper), the only beer garden amid all these vineyards. It's a fun-loving, youthful place with fine keg beer and a regular menu, rather than the *Heurige* cafeteria line (€6–10 meals, veggie options, Tue–Sat 16:00–24:00, Sun 11:00–24:00, closed Mon, Kahlenbergerstrasse 17, tel. 01/318-8800).

Neustift am Walde: This neighborhood has lots of *Heurigen,* plenty of charm, and the fewest tourists of all (U-6: Nussdorferstrasse, then bus #35A stop: Neustift am Walde). A line of big, venerable places invite you through welcoming arches that lead up terraced backyards filled with rough tables until you hit the actual vineyards. Pop into **Weingut Wolff** (Wed–Sun 16:00–24:00, closed Mon–Tue, Rathstrasse 50, tel. 01/440-3727) and **Fuhrgassl Huber Weingut** (daily 14:00–24:00, live music Tue–Sat 19:00–24:00, Neustift am Walde 68, tel. 01/440-1405) and take your choice. If you want to really be rural—surrounded by vineyards—hike 10 minutes from there to **Weinhof Zimmermann** (Mon–Fri 15:00–23:00, Sat–Sun 12:00–23:00, Mitterwurzergasse 20, tel. 01/440-1207). Find Mitterwurzergasse—the lane behind the two places listed above—and hike to the right. Look for the sign taking you uphill into a farm. There you'll see 50 rough picnic tables between the farmhouse and the vines.

NIGHTLIFE

If old music and new wine aren't your thing, Vienna has plenty of alternatives. For an up-to-date rundown on fun after dark, get the TI's free *Ten Good Reasons for Vienna* booklet. An area known as the "Bermuda Dreieck" (Triangle), north of the cathedral between Rotenturmstrasse and Judengasse, is the hot local nightspot, with lots of classy pubs, or *Beisl* (such as Krah Krah, Salzamt, Slammer, and Bermuda Bräu), and

Hotels and Restaurants in Central Vienna

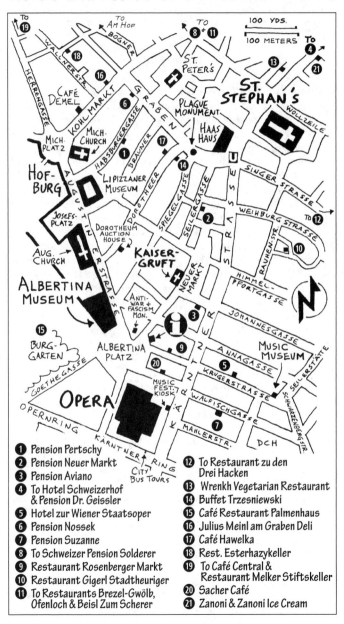

1. Pension Pertschy
2. Pension Neuer Markt
3. Pension Aviano
4. To Hotel Schweizerhof & Pension Dr. Geissler
5. Hotel zur Wiener Staatsoper
6. Pension Nossek
7. Pension Suzanne
8. To Schweizer Pension Solderer
9. Restaurant Rosenberger Markt
10. Restaurant Gigerl Stadtheuriger
11. To Restaurants Brezel-Gwölb, Ofenloch & Beisl Zum Scherer
12. To Restaurant zu den Drei Hacken
13. Wrenkh Vegetarian Restaurant
14. Buffet Trzesniewski
15. Café Restaurant Palmenhaus
16. Julius Meinl am Graben Deli
17. Café Hawelka
18. Rest. Esterhazykeller
19. To Café Central & Restaurant Melker Stiftskeller
20. Sacher Café
21. Zanoni & Zanoni Ice Cream

music spots. On balmy summer evenings, the liveliest scene is at Danube Island (especially during the Summer Stage festival). If you just want a good movie, the English Cinema Haydn plays three different English-language movies nightly (Mariahilfer Strasse 57, tel. 01/587-2262).

SLEEPING

Within the Ring, in the Old City Center

You'll pay extra to sleep in the atmospheric old center, but if you can afford it, staying here gives you the best classy Vienna experience.

$$$ **Pension Pertschy** circles an old courtyard and is bigger and more hotelesque than the others listed here. Its 50 rooms are huge, but well-worn and a bit musty. Those on the courtyard are quietest (Sb-€77, Db-€112–162 depending on size, cheaper off-season, extra bed-€30, non-smoking rooms, elevator, U-1 or U-3: Stephensplatz, Hapsburgergasse 5, tel. 01/534-490, fax 01/534-4949, www.pertschy.com, pertschy @pertschy.com).

$$$ **Pension Neuer Markt** is a four-star place that feels family-run, with 37 quiet, comfy, old-feeling rooms in a perfectly central locale (Ss-€81, Sb-€95, Ds-€88, Db-€112, prices can vary with season and room size, extra bed-€20, elevator, Seilergasse 9, tel. 01/512-2316, fax 01/513-9105, www.hotelpension.at/neuermarkt, neuermarkt@hotelpension.at).

$$$ **Pension Aviano** is another peaceful four-star place, with 17 comfortable rooms on the fourth floor above lots of old center action (Sb-€82, Db-€122–142 depending on size, 15 percent cheaper Nov–March, extra bed-€30, elevator, non-smoking rooms, between Neuer Markt and Kärntner Strasse at Marco d'Avianogasse 1, tel. 01/512-8330, fax 01/5128-3306, aviano@pertschy.com).

$$$ **Hotel Schweizerhof** is a classy 55-room place with big rooms, three-star comforts, and a more formal ambience. It's centrally located midway between St. Stephan's Cathedral and the Danube canal, with all its rooms at least four floors above any street noise (Sb-€84–88, Db-€109–131, Tb-€131–146, low prices are for July–Aug and slow times, with cash and this book get your best price and then claim a 10 percent discount, elevator, Bauernmarkt 22, U-1 or U-3: Stephansplatz, tel. 01/533-1931, fax 01/533-0214, www.schweizerhof.at, office@schweizerhof.at).

$$$ **Hotel zur Wiener Staatsoper** (the Schweizerhof's sister hotel) is quiet and rich. Its 22 tight rooms come with high ceilings, chandeliers, and fancy carpets on parquet floors—ideal for people whose hotel tastes are a cut above mine. The singles are tiny, with beds too short for anyone over six feet tall (Sb-€76–88, Db-€109–131, Tb-€131–146, extra bed-€22, prices depend on season, July–Aug and Dec–March are cheaper, elevator, U-1, U-2, or U-4: Karlsplatz, a block from Opera at Krugerstrasse 11, tel. 01/513-1274, fax 01/513-127-415, www .zurwienerstaatsoper.at, office@zurwienerstaatsoper.at).

SLEEP CODE

(€1 = about $1.10, country code: 43, area code: 01)

Sleep Code: **S** = Single, **D** = Double/Twin, **T** = Triple, **Q** = Quad, **b** = bathroom, **s** = shower only, **no CC** = Credit Cards not accepted. English is spoken at each place. Unless otherwise noted, credit cards are accepted and breakfast is included.

To help you sort easily through these listings, I've divided the rooms into three categories, based on the price for a standard double room with bath:

$$$ **Higher Priced**—Most rooms €110 or more.
$$ **Moderately Priced**—Most rooms between €75–110.
$ **Lower Priced**—Most rooms €75 or less.

Book accommodations by phone a few days in advance. Most places will hold a room without a deposit if you promise to arrive before 17:00. My recommendations stretch mainly from the center, and along the likeable Mariahilfer Strasse, to the Westbahnhof (West Station). Even places with elevators often have a few stairs to climb, too.

$$ At **Pension Nossek,** an elevator takes you above any street noise into Frau Bernad's and Frau Gundolf's world, where the children seem to be placed among the lace and flowers by an interior designer. Right on the wonderful Graben, this is a particularly good value (26 rooms, S-€46–54, Ss-€58, Sb-€66–88, Db-€105, €25 extra for sprawling suites, extra bed-€35, no CC, elevator, U-1 or U-3: Stephansplatz, Graben 17, tel. 01/5337-0410, fax 01/535-3646, www.pension-nossek.at, reservation@pension-nossek.at).

$$ **Pension Suzanne,** as Baroque and doily as you'll find in this price range, is wonderfully located a few yards from the Opera. It's small, but run with the class of a bigger hotel; the 26 rooms are packed with properly Viennese antique furnishings. Streetside rooms come with some noise (Sb-€72, Db-€90–111 depending on size, extra bed-€30, spacious apartment for up to 6 also available, discounts in winter, elevator, a block from Opera, U-1, U-2, or U-4: Karlsplatz, follow signs for the Opera exit, Walfischgasse 4, tel. 01/513-2507, fax 01/513-2500, www.pension-suzanne.at, info@pension-suzanne.at).

$$ **Schweizer Pension Solderer,** family-owned for three generations, is run by Anita. She runs an extremely tight ship (lots of rules), but offers 11 homey rooms, parquet floors, and lots of tourist info

(S-€35–42, Ss-€51–55, Sb-€58–62, D-€55–62, Ds-€65–75, Db-€80–85, Tb-€95–105, Qb-€120–125, prices depend on season and room size, no CC, non-smoking, elevator, laundry-€11/load, U-2 and U-4: Schottenring, Heinrichsgasse 2, tel. 01/533-8156, fax 01/535-6469, www.schweizerpension.com, schweizer.pension@chello.at).

$$ Pension Dr. Geissler has 23 comfortable rooms on the eighth floor of a modern building about 10 blocks northeast of St. Stephan's, near the canal (S-€43, Ss-€63, Sb-€72, D-€60, Ds-€72, Db-€90, 20 percent less in winter, elevator, U-1 and U-4: Schwedenplatz, Postgasse 14, tel. 01/533-2803, fax 01/533-2635, www.hotelpension.at/dr-geissler, dr.geissler@hotelpension.at).

Hotels and Pensions along Mariahilfer Strasse

Lively Mariahilfer Strasse connects the West Station and the city center. The U-3 metro line, starting at the Westbahnhof, goes down Mariahilfer Strasse to the cathedral. This very Viennese street is a tourist-friendly and vibrant area filled with local shops and cafés. Most hotels are within a few steps of a metro stop, just one or two stops from the West Train Station (direction from the station: Simmering).

$$$ NH Hoteles, a Spanish chain, runs two stern, passionless business hotels a few blocks apart on Mariahilfer Strasse. Both rent ideal-for-families suites, each with a living room, two TVs, bathroom, desk, and kitchenette (rack rate: Db suite-€170, going rate usually closer to €105, plus €13 per person for optional breakfast, cheaper Sat–Sun, apartments for 2–3 adults, kids under 12 free, non-smoking rooms, elevator). The 78-room **NH Atterseehaus** is at Mariahilfer Strasse 78 (U-3: Zieglergasse, tel. 01/5245-6000, fax 01/524-560-015, nhattersee-haus@nh-hotels.com), and the **NH Wien** has 106 rooms at Mariahilfer Strasse 32 (U-3: Neubaugasse, tel. 01/521-720, fax 01/521-7215, nhwien@nh-hotels.com). The Web site for both is www.nh-hotels.com.

$$ Pension Corvinus is bright, modern, and warmly run by a Hungarian family: Miklos, Judit, and Zoltan. Its eight comfortable rooms are spacious with small yacht-type bathrooms (Sb-€58, Db-€91, Tb-€105, extra bed-€26, non-smoking rooms, portable air-con-€10, elevator, free Internet access, parking garage-€11/day, on the third floor at Mariahilfer Strasse 57–59, tel. 01/587-7239, fax 01/587-723-920, www.corvinus.at, hotel@corvinus.at). If heading for the Corvinus, don't be pirated by the people in the Haydn Hotel (below).

$$ Pension Mariahilf is a four-star place offering a clean, aristocratic air in an affordable and cozy pension package. Its 12 rooms are spacious but outmoded, with an art deco flair. You'll find the latest American magazines and even free Mozart balls at the reception desk (Sb-€59–66, Db-€95–102, Tb-€124, lower prices are for longer stays, elevator, U-3: Neubaugasse, Mariahilfer Strasse 49, tel. 01/586-1781, fax 01/586-178-122, penma@atnet.at, warmly run by Frau and Herr Ender).

Vienna: Hotels and Restaurants Outside the Ring

U = SUBWAY

¼ MILE

400 METERS

N

RAT-HAUS

OLD CITY

KUNST HIST. MUSEUM

SPITTEL-BERG QUARTER

WEST-BAHNHOF

EUROPA-PLATZ

HILFER

IMPERIAL FURN. COLL.

NASCH-MARKT

TRAM 58

TO SCHÖNBRUNN

DCH

1 Hotel NH Atterseehaus

2 Hotel NH Wien

3 Hotel Ibis Wien

4 Hotel Fürstenhof

5 Pension Corvinus & Haydn Hotel

6 Pension Mariahilf

7 Hotel Admiral

8 Pension Hargita

9 Pension Lindenhof

10 K&T Boardinghouse

11 Budai Ildiko Rooms & Maria Pribojszki Rooms

12 To Hilde Wolf Rooms

13 To Pension Fünfhaus, Wombats City Hostel & Hostel Ruthensteiner

14 Westend City Hostel

15 Hostels Myrthengasse & Believe It or Not

16 Spittelberg Quarter Restaurants

17 Restaurant Beim Novak

18 Café Sperl

19 Café Ritter

20 Internet Café

$$ Haydn Hotel, in the same building the Pension Corvinus (listed above), is a big, fancy, dark place with 40 spacious rooms that have seen better days (Sb-€58–70, Db-€72–100, suites and family apartments, extra bed-€30, portable air-con-€12, elevator, free Internet access, Mariahilfer Strasse 57–59, tel. 01/587-4414, fax 01/586-1950, www.haydn-hotel.at, info@haydn-hotel.at).

$$ Hotel Admiral is a huge, quiet, family-run hotel with 80 large, comfortable rooms. Alexandra works hard to keep her guests happy, though others on the staff are less friendly (Sb-€66, Db-€91, extra bed-€23, prices promised through 2004 with this book, cheaper in winter, breakfast-€5 per person, free parking, U-2 or U-3: Volkstheater, a block off Mariahilfer Strasse at Karl Schweighofer Gasse 7, tel. 01/521-410, fax 01/521-4116, www.admiral.co.at, hoteladmiralwien@aon.at).

$ Pension Hargita rents 24 generally small, bright, and tidy rooms (mostly twins) with Hungarian decor. This spick-and-span, well-run, well-located place is an excellent value (S-€31, Ss-€35, Sb-€50, D-€45, Ds-€52, Db-€60, Ts-€63, Tb-€71, Qb-€87, breakfast-€3 per person, credit card adds 3 percent to cost and not for 1-night stays, U-3: Zieglergasse, corner of Mariahilfer Strasse and Andreasgasse, Andreasgasse 1, tel. 01/526-1928, fax 01/526-0492, www.hargita.at, pension @hargita.at, classy Amalia SE).

$ Pension Lindenhof rents 19 worn but clean rooms and is filled with plants (S-€29, Sb-€36, D-€49, Db-€65, no CC, elevator, U-3: Neubaugasse, Lindengasse 4, tel. 01/523-0498, fax 01/523-7362, pensionlindenhof@yahoo.com, Gebrael family, Zara and Keram SE).

$ K&T Boardinghouse rents four big, comfortable rooms facing the bustling Mariahilfer Strasse above a sex shop (S-€40, D-€50, Db-€60, Tb-€80, Qb-€100, 2-night minimum, no breakfast, no CC, non-smoking, free Internet access, 3 flights up, no elevator, Mariahilfer Strasse 72, tel. 01/523-2989, fax 01/522-0345, www.kaled.at, kaled @chello.at, Tina SE).

Two women rent rooms out of their dark and homey apartments in the same building at Lindengasse 39 (classic old elevator). Each has high ceilings and Old World furnishings, with two cavernous rooms sleeping two to four and a skinny twin room, all sharing one bathroom. These places are great if you're on a tight budget and wish you had a grandmother to visit in Vienna: **$ Budai Ildiko** lives on the mezzanine level and speaks English (S-€29, D-€44, T-€64, Q-€82, no breakfast but free coffee, no CC, laundry, apt. #5, tel. 01/523-1058, tel. & fax 01/526-2595, budai@hotmail.com). **$ Maria Pribojszki** lives on the first floor (D-€48, D for 2 nights-€44, T-€69, Q-€88, breakfast-€4 per person, no CC, no clothes-washing in room, smoky place, apt. #7, tel. 01/523-9006, b&b@aon.at).

$ Hilde Wolf, with the help of her grandson, Patrick, shares her homey apartment with travelers. Her four huge but stuffy rooms are like old libraries (S-€33, D-€48, T-€70, Q-€90, breakfast-€4, no CC, U-2: Karlsplatz, 3 blocks below Naschmarkt at Schleifmühlgasse 7, tel. 01/ 586-5103, fax 01/689-3505, www.schoolpool.at/bb, santa.claus@aon.at).

Near the Westbahnhof Train Station

$$ Hotel Ibis Wien, a modern high-rise hotel with American charm, is ideal for anyone tired of quaint old Europe. Its 340 cookie-cutter rooms are bright, comfortable, and modern and have all the conveniences (Sb-€64, Db-€79, Tb-€94, prices €5 more per room May–June, Aug, and Sept–Oct, breakfast-€9 per person extra, non-smoking rooms, elevator, parking garage-€10/day, exit Westbahnhof to the right and walk 400 yards, Mariahilfer Gürtel 22-24, tel. 01/59998, fax 01/597-9090, h0796@accor-hotels.com).

$$ Hotel Fürstenhof, right across from the station, charges top euro for its 58 spacious but borderline-musty rooms. This venerable hotel has an Old World maroon-velvet feel (S-€44, Sb-€67–92, D-€62, Db-€108, Tb-€114, Qb-€120, elevator, Internet access-€6/hr, Europaplatz 4, tel. 01/523-3267, fax 01/523-326-726, www.hotel-fuerstenhof.com, reception@hotel-fuerstenhof.com).

$ Pension Fünfhaus is big, clean, stark, and quiet—almost institutional. Although the neighborhood is run-down and comes with a few ladies loitering late at night, this 47-room place is a good value (S-€30, Sb-€38, D-€44, Db-€51, T-€66, Tb-€72, apartments for 4 people-€90, prices promised through 2004 with this book, no CC, closed mid-Nov–Feb, Sperrgasse 12, tel. 01/892-3545 or 01/892-0286, fax 01/892-0460, Frau Susi Tersch). Half the rooms are in the fine main building and half are in the annex, which has good rooms but is near the train tracks and a bit scary on the street at night. From the station, ride tram #52 or #58 two stops down Mariahilfer Strasse to Kranzgasse stop, then backtrack two blocks to Sperrgasse.

Cheap Dorms and Hostels near Mariahilfer Strasse

$ Believe It or Not is a tiny, basic place with two coed rooms for up to 10 travelers and the cheapest beds in town. Hardworking and friendly Gosha warns that this place is appropriate only for the young at heart. It's locked up from 10:00 to 12:30, has kitchen facilities, and has no curfew (bed-€13.50, €10 Nov–Easter, no CC, Myrthengasse 10, ring apt. #14, tel. 01/526-4658, www.believe-it-or-not-vienna.at, believe_it_or_not_vienna@hotmail.com, SE).

$ Jugendherberge Myrthengasse is a well-run youth hostel (260 beds-€16–18 each in 3- to 6-bed rooms, includes sheets and breakfast, non-members pay €3.50 extra, some private rooms for couples and families, Myrthengasse 7, tel. 01/523-6316, fax 01/523-5849, hostel@chello.at).

$ Westend City Hostel, just a block from the West Station and

Mariahilfer Strasse, is new, with 180 beds in 4- to 12-bed dorms (€16–18 per bed including sheets, breakfast, and a locker, no CC, laundry, Internet access-€4.40/hr, Fügergasse 3, tel. 01/597-6729, fax 01/597-672-927, www.westendhostel.at, westendcityhostel@aon.at, SE).

$ Other hostels with €14 beds near Mariahilfer Strasse are **Wombats City Hostel** (Grangasse 6, tel. 01/897-2336, wombats@chello.at) and **Hostel Ruthensteiner** (also has doubles for €20 per person, Robert-Hamerling-Gasse 24, tel. 01/893-4202, info@hostelruthensteiner.com).

EATING

The Viennese appreciate the fine points of life, and right up there with waltzing is eating. The city has many atmospheric restaurants. As you ponder the Slavic and Eastern European specialties on menus, remember that Vienna's diverse empire may be gone, but its flavor lingers.

While cuisines are routinely named for countries, Vienna claims to be the only *city* with a cuisine of its own: Vienna soups come with fillings (semolina dumpling, liver dumpling, or pancake slices). *Gulasch* is a beef ragout of Hungarian origin (spiced with onion and paprika). Of course, Viennese schnitzel (Wiener schnitzel) is a breaded and fried veal cutlet. Another meat specialty is boiled beef *(Tafelspitz)*. While you're sure to have *Apfelstrudel,* try the sweet cheese strudel, too (*Topfenstrudel,* wafer-thin strudel pastry filled with sweet cheese and raisins).

On nearly every corner, you can find a colorful *Beisl* (Viennese tavern) filled with poetry teachers and their students, couples loving without touching, housewives on their way home from cello lessons, and waiters who enjoy serving hearty food and good drink at an affordable price. Ask at your hotel for a good *Beisl.*

Wherever you're eating, some vocabulary will help. Try the *grüner Veltliner* (dry white wine), *Traubenmost* (a heavenly grape juice—alcohol-free but on the verge of wine), *Most* (the same thing but lightly alcoholic), and *Sturm* (stronger than *Most,* autumn only). The local red wine (called *Portugieser*) is pretty good. Since the Austrian wine is often sweet, remember the word *trocken* (dry). You can order your wine by the *Viertel* (quarter liter, 8 oz) or *Achtel* (eighth liter, 4 oz). Beer comes in a *Krügel* (half liter, 17 oz) or *Seidel* (0.3 liter, 10 oz).

Near St. Stephan's Cathedral

All of these places are within a five-minute walk of the cathedral.

Gigerl Stadtheuriger offers a near-*Heurige* experience (à la Grinzing, see "Vienna's Wine Gardens," page 366), often with accordion or live music—without leaving the city center. Just point to what looks good. Food is sold by the weight; 200 grams is about a quarter of a pound (cheese and cold meats cost about €2.50–5 per 100 grams, salads are about €2 per 100 grams; price sheet is posted on the wall to right of buffet line, 10 *dag* equals 100 grams). They also have menu entrées, along with spinach strudel, quiche, *Apfelstrudel,* and, of course, casks of new and local wines. Meals run €7–11 (daily 15:00–24:00, indoor/outdoor seating, behind cathedral, a block off Kärntner Strasse, a few cobbles off Rauhensteingasse on Blumenstock, tel. 01/513-4431).

Am Hof square (U-3: Herrengasse) is surrounded by a maze of atmospheric medieval lanes; the following places are all within a block of the square. **Restaurant Ofenloch** serves good, old-fashioned Viennese cuisine with friendly service, both indoors and out. This 300-year-old eatery, with great traditional ambience, is central, but not overrun with tourists (main dishes €15–22, Tue–Sat 11:30–24:00, Mon 18:00–24:00, closed Sun, Kurrentgasse 8, tel. 01/533-8844). **Brezel-Gwölb,** a wonderfully atmospheric wine cellar with outdoor dining on a quiet square, serves delicious light meals, fine *Krautsuppe,* and old-fashioned local dishes. It's ideal for a romantic late-night glass of wine (daily 11:30–1:00, leave Am Hof on Drahtgasse, then take first left to Ledererhof 9, tel. 01/533-8811). Around the corner, **Beisl "Zum Scherer"** is just as untouristy, with indoor or outdoor seating, a soothing woody atmosphere, intriguing decor, and local specialties (Mon–Sat 11:00–24:00, closed Sun, Judenplatz 7, tel. 01/533-5164). Just below Am Hof, the ancient and popular **Esterhazykeller** has traditional fare deep underground or outside on a delightful square (Mon–Fri 11:00–23:00, Sat–Sun 16:00–23:00, self-service buffet in lowest cellar or from menu, Haarhof 1, tel. 01/533-2614).

These wine cellars are fun and touristy but typical, in the old center, with reasonable prices and plenty of smoke: **Melker Stiftskeller,** less touristy, is a *Stadtheurige* in a deep and rustic cellar with hearty, inexpensive meals and new wine (Tue–Sat 17:00–24:00, closed Sun–Mon, between Am Hof and Schottentor metro stop at Schottengasse 3, tel. 01/533-5530). **Zu den Drei Hacken** is famous for its local specialties (Mon–Sat 11:00–23:00, closed Sun, indoor/outdoor seating, Singerstrasse 28, tel. 01/512-5895).

Wrenkh Vegetarian Restaurant and Bar is popular for its high vegetarian cuisine. Chef Wrenkh offers daily lunch menus (€8–10) and dinner plates (€8–13) in a bright, mod bar or in a dark, smoke-free, fancier restaurant (daily 11:30–24:00, Bauernmarkt 10, tel. 01/533-1526).

Buffet Trzesniewski is an institution—justly famous for its elegant and cheap finger sandwiches and small beers (€0.70 each). Three different sandwiches and a *kleines Bier (Pfiff)* make a fun, light lunch. Point to whichever delights look tasty and pay for them and a drink. Take your drink tokens to the lady on the right. Sit on the bench and scoot over to a tiny table when a spot opens up (Mon–Fri 8:30–19:30, Sat 9:00–17:00, closed Sun, 50 yards off Graben, nearly across from brooding Café Hawelka, Dorotheergasse 2, tel. 01/512-3291). This is a good opportunity to try the fancy grape juices—*Most* or *Traubenmost* (see page 376).

Julius Meinl am Graben has been famous since 1862 as a top-end delicatessen with all the gourmet fancies (including a highly rated restaurant upstairs, shop open Mon–Fri 8:00–19:30, Sat 8:30–17:00, closed Sun, restaurant Mon–Sat until 24:00, closed Sun, Am Graben 19, tel. 01/532-3334).

Akakiko Sushi: If you're just schnitzeled out, this small chain of Japanese restaurants with an easy sushi menu may suit you. The bento box meals are tasty. Three locations are very convenient (all open daily 10:00–24:00): Singerstrasse 4 (a block off Kärntner Strasse near the cathedral), Heidenschuss 3 (near other recommended eateries just off Am Hof), and Mariahilfer Strasse 42–48 (fifth floor of Kaufhaus Gerngross, near many recommended hotels).

Ice Cream! For a gelato treat or fancy dessert with a mob of happy Viennese, stop by the thriving **Zanoni & Zanoni** (daily 7:00–24:00, 2 blocks up Rotenturmstrasse from cathedral at Lugeck 7, tel. 01/512-7979).

Near the Opera

Café Restaurant Palmenhaus, overlooking the palace garden *(Burggarten),* tucked away in a green and peaceful corner two blocks behind the Opera in the Hofburg's backyard, is a world apart. If you want to eat modern Austrian cuisine with palm trees rather than tourists, this is it. And at the edge of a huge park, it's great for families (€11 lunches, €15 dinners, daily 10:00–2:00, serious vegetarian dishes, fish, and an extensive wine list, indoors in greenhouse or outdoors, at Burggarten, tel. 01/533-1033). While nobody goes to the Palmenhaus for good prices, the **Palmenhaus BBQ**—a cool parkside outdoor pub just below that uses the same kitchen—is a wonderful value with more casual service (summer Wed–Sat from 20:00, closed Sun–Tue, open in good weather only, informal with €8 BBQ and meals posted on chalkboard).

Rosenberger Markt Restaurant is my favorite for a fast, light, and central lunch. Just a block toward the cathedral from the Opera, this place—while not cheap—is brilliant. Friendly and efficient, with special theme rooms for dining, it offers a fresh, smoke-free, and healthy cornucopia of food and drink (daily 10:30–23:00, lots of fruits, veggies, fresh-squeezed juices, addictive banana milk, ride the glass elevator downstairs, Maysedergasse 2, tel. 01/512-3458). You can stack a small salad or veggie plate into a tower of gobble for €2.50.

Spittelberg Quarter

A charming cobbled grid of traffic-free lanes and Biedermeier apartments has become a favorite place for Viennese wanting a little dining charm between the MuseumsQuartier and Mariahilfer Strasse (handy to many recommended hotels; take Stiftgasse from Mariahilfer Strasse, or wander over here after you close down the Kunsthistorisches or Leopold Museum). Tables tumble down sidewalks and into breezy courtyards filled with appreciative locals enjoying dinner or a relaxing drink. Stroll Spittelberggasse, Schrankgasse, and Gutenberggasse and pick your favorite place. Check out the courtyard inside Spittelberggasse 3, and don't miss the vine-strewn wine garden inside Schrankgasse 1. I ate well and cheaply at **Plutzer Bräu** (daily 11:00–2:00, good daily specials and beer from the keg, Schrankgasse 4, tel. 01/526-1215). For traditional Viennese cuisine with tablecloths, consider the classier **Witwe Bolte** (Mon–Fri 11:30–15:00 & 17:30–23:30, Sat–Sun 11:30–23:20, Gutenberggasse 13, tel. 01/523-1450).

Near Mariahilfer Strasse

Mariahilfer Strasse is filled with reasonable cafés serving all types of cuisine. **Restaurant Beim Novak** serves good local cuisine away from the modern rush (Mon–Fri 11:30–15:00 & 18:00–22:00, open Sat for dinner Sept–March, closed Sun, a block down Andreasgasse from Mariahilfer Strasse at Richtergasse 12, tel. 01/523-3244).

Naschmarkt is Vienna's best Old World market, with plenty of fresh produce, cheap local-style eateries, cafés, and *döner kebab* and sausage stands (Mon–Fri 7:00–18:00, Sat 6:00–18:00, closed Sun, closes earlier in winter, U-4: Kettenbrückengasse).

TRANSPORTATION CONNECTIONS

Vienna has two main train stations: the Westbahnhof (West Train Station), serving Munich, Salzburg, Melk, and Budapest; and the Südbahnhof (South Train Station), serving Italy, Budapest, Prague, Poland, Slovenia, and Croatia. A third station, Franz Josefs, serves Krems and the Danube Valley (but Melk is served by the Westbahnhof). Metro line U-3 connects the Westbahnhof with the center, tram D takes you from the Südbahnhof and the Franz Josefs station to downtown, and tram #18 connects West and South stations. Train info: tel. 051717 (wait through long German recording for operator).

By train to: Melk (hrly, 75 min, sometimes change in St. Pölten), **Krems** (hrly, 1 hr), **Salzburg** (hrly, 3 hrs), **Innsbruck** (every 2 hrs, 5.5 hrs), **Budapest** (6/day, 3 hrs), **Prague** (4/day, 4.5 hrs), **Český Krumlov** (5/day, 6–7 hrs, up to 3 changes), **Munich** (hrly, 5.25 hrs, change in Salzburg, a few direct trains), **Berlin** (2/day, 10 hrs, longer on night train), **Zürich** (3/day, 9 hrs), **Ljubljana** (7/day, 6–7 hrs, convenient early-morning direct train, others change in Villach or Maribor), **Zagreb** (8/day, 6.5–10.5 hrs, 3 direct, others with up to 3 changes including Villach and Ljubljana), **Kraków** (4/day, 6.5–9 hrs, 2 direct including a night train), **Warsaw** (4/day, 7.5–10 hrs, 2 direct including a night train), **Rome** (1/day, 13.5 hrs), **Venice** (3/day, 7.5 hrs, longer on night train), **Frankfurt** (4/day, 7.5 hrs), **Amsterdam** (1/day, 14.5 hrs).

To Eastern Europe: Vienna is the springboard for a quick trip to

Prague and Budapest—three hours by train from Budapest (€37 one-way, €47 round-trip if you stay 4 days or less, free with Eurail) and four hours from Prague (€41 one-way, €82 round-trip, €53 round-trip with Eurail). Americans don't need a visa to enter the Czech Republic, but Canadians do; neither nationality needs a visa for Hungary. Purchase tickets at most travel agencies. Eurail passholders bound for Prague must pay to ride the rails in the Czech Republic; for details, see "Transportation Connections" in the Berlin chapter.

Route Tips for Drivers

Driving in and out of Vienna: Navigating in Vienna isn't bad. Study the map. As you approach from Krems, you'll cross the North Bridge and land on the *Gürtel,* or outer ring. You can continue along the Danube canal to the inner ring, called the *Ringstrasse* (clockwise traffic only). Circle around either thoroughfare until you reach the "spoke" street you need.

Vienna West to Hall in Tirol (280 miles): To leave Vienna, follow the signs past the Westbahnhof to Schloss Schönbrunn (Schönbrunn Palace), which is directly on the way to the West A-1 autobahn to Linz. Leave the palace by 15:00, beating rush hour, and follow autobahn signs to West A-1, passing Linz and Salzburg, nipping through Germany, and turning right onto Route 93 in the direction of Kufstein, Innsbruck, and Austria at the Dreieck Inntal (autobahn intersection). Crossing back into Austria, you'll follow the scenic Inn River valley until you stop five miles east of Innsbruck at Hall in Tirol. There's an autobahn tourist information station just before Hall (in season daily 10:00–22:00, works for the town's hotels but still helpful).

DANUBE VALLEY

From the Black Forest in Germany to the Black Sea in Ukraine, the Danube flows 1,770 miles through a dozen countries. Western Europe's longest river (the Rhine is only half as long), it's also the only major river flowing west to east, making it invaluable for commercial transportation.

The Danube is at its romantic best just west of Vienna. Mix a cruise with a bike ride through the Danube's Wachau Valley, lined with ruined castles, beautiful abbeys, small towns, and vineyard upon vineyard. After touring the glorious abbey of Melk, douse your warm, fairy-tale glow with a bucket of Hitler at the Mauthausen concentration camp.

ORIENTATION

Planning Your Time

For a day trip from Vienna, catch the early train to Melk, tour the abbey, eat lunch, and take an afternoon trip along the river from Melk to Krems. Note that the boat goes much faster downstream (east, from Melk to Krems) than vice versa. From Krems, catch the train back to Vienna. Try a boat/bike combination or consider the DDSG boat company's convenient Kombi-ticket. This special package includes the train trip from Vienna to Melk, entry to the Melk Abbey, a boat cruise to Krems, and the return train trip to Vienna for a total of €38 (DDSG office in Vienna: Friedrichstrasse 7, tel. 01/58880, www.ddsg-blue-danube.at). While this region is a logical day trip from Vienna, with good train connections to both Krems and Melk, spending a night in Melk is a convenient detour from the main Munich/Salzburg/Vienna train line (from Salzburg to Vienna, transfer in Amstetten or Linz).

Mauthausen, farther away, should be seen en route to or from Vienna. On a three-week trip, I'd see only one concentration camp. Mauthausen is more powerful than the more convenient Dachau and worthwhile if you have a car.

Danube Valley

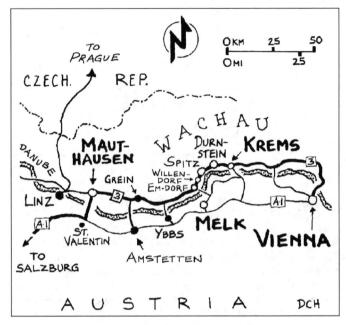

Cruising the Danube's Wachau Valley

By car, bike, or boat, the 24-mile stretch of the Danube between Krems and Melk is as pretty as they come. You'll cruise the Danube's wine road, passing wine gardens all along the river. Those hanging out a wreath of straw or greenery are inviting you in to taste. In local slang, someone who's feeling his wine is "blue." (Blue Danube?) Note that in German, Danube is Donau, as you'll see by the signs.

By Boat: Two different companies run boats run between Melk and Krems: **DDSG** (3/day in each direction May–Sept, 1/day April and Oct, tel. 01/58880, www.ddsg-blue-danube.at) and **Brandner** (2/day in each direction May–Sept, 1/day weekdays and 2/day weekends second half of April and Oct, tel. 07433/529-021, www.brandner .at). Both charge the same: €17 one-way, €22 round-trip ticket allowing stopovers, bikes ride free. In peak season (May–Sept), boats depart daily from Melk at 8:25, 11:00, 13:50 (two different boats), and 16:15 (90-min ride downstream). Boats depart from Krems at 10:10, 10:15, 13:00, 15:40, and 15:45 (because of the 6-knot flow of the Danube, the same ride upstream takes twice as long—3 hrs). The 16:15 departure from Melk and the 15:45 departure from Krems require an easy transfer in Spitz; the rest are direct. Confirm these times by calling the boat companies (see above), the Melk TI (tel. 02752/5230-7410), or the Krems TI (tel. 02732/82676). For a longer cruise, some boats start or end in Vienna.

By Bike: See the Melk–Krems Bike Ride described in "Sights—The Danube Valley," page 386. Ask any local TI or your hotel for the latest on bike rental options; some hotels rent or loan bikes.

By Bus: The bus between Melk and Krems is a good budget or rainy-day alternative to the boat (€7, 60 min; Melk to Krems: Mon–Fri 4/day, Sat 2/day, none Sun; Krems to Melk: Mon–Fri 5/day, Sat 3/day, none Sun; catch bus at train station, buy ticket on bus; for best views, sit on the driver's side from Melk to Krems or the non-driver's side from Krems to Melk).

By Train: Hourly trains connect Vienna with Krems and with Melk. Trains to Melk depart from Vienna's Westbahnhof. Trains for Krems depart from Vienna's Franz Josefs Bahnhof. If you're starting or ending your visit to the Danube Valley with Krems, consider departing from or arriving at Vienna's Spittelau (the train's first stop after the Franz Josefs Bahnhof) instead of the Bahnhof itself, because Spittelau has a U-Bahn station and Franz Josefs Bahnhof does not.

While tiny, one-car, milk-run trains chug along from village to village up the river, they don't stop at Melk (which affects bicyclists, see Bike Ride in "Sights—The Danube Valley," 386).

Melk

Sleepy and elegant under its huge abbey that seems to police the Danube, the town of Melk offers a pleasant stop.

Tourist Information: The TI, run by helpful Manfred Baumgartner, is a block off the main square (look for green signs) and has info on nearby castles, the latest on bike rental, specifics on bike rides along the river, a free town map with a self-guided walking tour, and a list of Melk hotels and *Zimmer* (July–Aug Mon–Sat 9:00–19:00, Sun 10:00–12:00 & 17:00–19:00, May–June and Sept Mon–Fri 9:00–12:00 & 14:00–18:00, Sat-Sun 10:00–12:00 & 16:00–18:00, off-season closed Sat afternoon and Sun, good picnic garden with WC behind TI, Babenbergerstrasse 1, tel. 02752/5230-7410). For accommodations, see "Sleeping," page 387.

Arrival in Melk: Walk straight out of the station (lockers-€2) for several blocks; at the curve, keep straight and go down the stairs, following the cobbled alley that dumps you into the center of the village. The abbey access is up on your right, and the TI is a block off the end of the square to your right. If you arrive by boat, turn right as you leave the boat dock and follow the canalside bike path towards the big yellow abbey (the village is beneath its far side). In about five minutes, you'll come to a flashing light (at intersection with bridge); turn left and you're steps from downtown.

To reach the boat dock from Melk, leave the town toward the river, with the abbey on your right. Turn right when you get to the busy road and follow the canal (at the fork, it's quicker to jog left onto the bike path than to follow the main road). Follow signs for "*Linienschifffahrt-Scheduled Trips-Wachau.*"

SIGHTS

Melk

▲▲**Melk Abbey (Benediktinerstift)**—Melk's newly restored abbey, beaming proudly over the Danube Valley, is one of Europe's great sights. Established as a fortified Benedictine abbey in the 11th century, it was destroyed by fire. What you see today is 18th-century Baroque. Architect Jakob Prandtauer made the building one with nature. The abbey church, with its 200-foot-tall dome and symmetrical towers, dominates the complex—emphasizing its sacred purpose.

Freshly painted and gilded throughout, it's a Baroque dream, a lily alone. The grand restoration project—financed in part by the sale of the abbey's Gutenberg Bible to Harvard—was completed by 1996 to celebrate the 1,000th anniversary of the first reference to a country named Österreich (Austria).

Cost, Hours, and Information: €6.90, May–Sept daily 9:00–18:00, April and Oct daily 9:00–17:00, last entry one hour before closing; Nov–March the abbey is open only for tours in German with a little English at 11:00 and 14:00; tel. 02752/555-232, www.stiftmelk.at.

Tours: English tours of the abbey are offered daily (May–Sept at 14:50, €8.50 includes tour and admission, private guide-€36), but it's easiest just to wander through on your own, with the help of the following self-guided tour:

1. East Facade: As you come through the first passageway and approach the grand entry, imagine the abbot on the balcony greeting you as he used to greet important guests. Flanking him are statues of Peter and Paul (leaders of the apostles and patron saints of the abbey church) and the monastery's coat of arms (crossed keys). High above are the Latin words "Glory only in the cross" and a huge copy of the Melk Cross (one of the abbey's greatest treasures—the original is hiding in the treasury and viewable only with special permission).

2. Prelate's Courtyard: Pass into the main courtyard. This is more than a museum. For 900 years, monks of St. Benedict have lived and worked here. Their task: bringing and maintaining Christianity and culture to the region. (Many of the monks live outside the abbey in the community.) They run a high school with about 800 students, a small boarding school, and a busy retreat center.

There have been low points. During the Reformation (1500s), only eight monks held down the theological fort. Napoleon made his headquarters here in 1805 and 1809. And in 1938, when Hitler annexed Austria, the monastery was squeezed into one end of the complex and nearly dissolved. But today, the institution survives—that's the point of the four modern frescoes gracing the courtyard, funded by agriculture (historically, monasteries are big landowners) and your visit. In the far left-hand corner, climb the stairs to...

3. Imperial Corridor and Abbey Museum: This 640-foot-long corridor, lined with paintings of Austrian royalty, is the spine of the Abbey Museum. Duck into the first room of the museum (on the left, near beginning of hall). Art treasures and a recently updated exhibit (with creepy sound and light effects) fill several rooms. Continue through the museum—running parallel to the corridor—and go through the room at the end with the big rotating model of the abbey.

4. Marble Hall: While the door frames are real marble, most of this large dining room/ballroom is stucco. The treasure here is the ceiling fresco (by Tirolean Paul Troger, 1731). Notice three themes: 1) The Hapsburgs liked to be portrayed as Hercules; 2) Athena, the goddess of wisdom, is included, because the Hapsburgs were smart as well as strong; and 3) The Hapsburgs were into art and culture. This is symbolized by angels figuratively reining in the forces of evil, darkness, and brutality so—through this wise moderation—goodness, beauty, art, and science can rule.

5. Balcony: Here, we enjoy dramatic views of the Danube Valley, the town of Melk, and the facade of the monastery church. The huge statue above everything shows the risen Christ, cross in hand and victorious over death—the central message of the entire place.

6. Library: The inlaid bookshelves, matching bindings, and another fine Troger fresco combine harmoniously to provide for the Marble Hall's thematic counterpart. This room celebrates not wise politics, but faith. The ceiling shows a woman surrounded by the four cardinal virtues (wisdom, justice, fortitude, and recycling)—natural traits that lead to a supernatural faith. The statues flanking the doors represent the four traditional university faculties (law, medicine, philosophy, and theology). The globes show a 17th-century view of the earth and heavens. Many of the monastery's 100,000 volumes fill the shelves (some of the oldest and most precious are in the glass display case).

7. Church: The finale is the church, with its architecture, ceiling frescoes, stucco marble, grand pipe organ, and sumptuous chapels combining in full Baroque style to make the theological point: A just battle leads to victory. The ceiling shows St. Benedict's triumphant entry into Heaven (on a fancy carpet). In the front, above the huge papal crown, saints Peter and Paul shake hands before departing for their final battles and ultimate victory. And, high above, the painting in the dome shows that victory: the Holy Trinity, surrounded by saints of particular importance to Melk, happily in Heaven.

Other Abbey Sights—Near the entrance (and exit) to the abbey, you'll find the Abbey Park (included in abbey ticket, or €3 for just the park, May–Oct daily 9:00–18:00, closed Nov–April)—home to a picturesque Baroque pavilion housing some fine Bergl frescoes and a café. Nearby, in the former orangery, is the abbey's expensive restaurant.

The Danube Valley

▲▲**Melk-to-Krems Danube Valley Bike Ride**—The three-hour pedal from Melk to Krems takes you through the Wachau Valley—steeped in tradition, blanketed with vineyards, and ornamented with cute villages. Bikers rule here, and you'll find all the amenities that make this valley so popular with Austrians on two wheels. Two hotels in Melk—Hotel zur Post and Hotel-Pension Wachau—rent bikes. For the latest on bike rental possibilities, check with the TI.

Bike routes are clearly marked with green Donau-Radwanderweg signs. The local TIs give out a free *Donau Radweg* brochure with a helpful if basic route map. As you study it, note the north bank has the best and most popular trail; it's paved all the way, winds through picturesque villages, and runs near, though not on, the river. But consider the south bank, which has less car traffic; although the bike trail merges with the actual road about half the time, it comes with better river views. (Note: The bike-in-a-red-border signs mean "no biking.")

Pedal downstream toward Krems to enjoy a gradual slope in your favor. While catching the boat back makes for a much longer day (it's slow upstream), cute one-car milk-run trains rattle up the valley stopping at most towns along the way (about hourly, 60 min from Krems to Emmersdorf opposite Melk, bike rack at rear of train—carry bike up the stairs to reach rack). If you prefer, you can go half-and-half by cruising to Spitz—a good midway point—and then hopping on a bike (or vice versa). Spitz has a boat station and train station (the bike path between Spitz and Krems is more interesting than between Melk and Spitz). Little ferries shuttle bikers and vacation-goers regularly across the river at three points.

A good day plan from Melk: Depart Melk at 8:00, bike the valley, lunch in Krems or picnic on train, and catch the 13:00 train from Krems back to Emmersdorf (across the river, 3 miles from Melk). If you run out of steam or time, you can catch a train at most towns en route.

Krems—This is a gem of a town. From the boat dock, walk a few blocks north and east to the TI and pick up a town map. Then stroll the traffic-free, shopper's-wonderland old town. If nothing else, it's a pleasant 20-minute walk from the dock to the train station (Krems–Vienna trains hrly, 60 min). The local **TI** can find you a bed in a private home (D-€40, Db-€50) if you decide to side-trip into Vienna from this small-town alternative (TI open Easter–Oct Mon–Fri 8:30–18:30, Sat 10:00–12:00 & 13:00–18:00, Sun 10:00–12:00 & 13:00–16:00; Nov–Easter Mon–Fri 8:30–17:00, closed Sat–Sun; Undstrasse 6, tel. 02732/82676).

$ Melanie Stasny's Gästezimmer is a super place to stay (€23/person in Db, Tb, or Qb, friendly with a proud vineyard and wine cellar, 300 yards from dock at Steiner Landstrasse 22, tel. 02732/82843, fax 02732/83141); when they're booked, they send travelers to their son's place down the street.

Dürnstein—This touristic flypaper lures hordes of visitors with its traffic-free quaintness and its one claim to fame (and fortune): Richard the Lion-Hearted was imprisoned here in 1193. You can probably sleep in his bedroom. The ruined castle above can be reached by a good hike with great river views.

Willendorf—This is known among art buffs as the town where the oldest piece of European art was found. There's a tiny museum in the village center (free, limited hrs). A block farther uphill (follow the signs to Venus, just under tracks follow stairs to right) you can see the monument where the well-endowed, 30,000-year-old fertility symbol, the Venus of Willendorf, was discovered. (The fist-sized original is now in Vienna's Natural History Museum.)

SLEEPING

$$$ Hotel zur Post is Melk's most modern-feeling hotel—professional and well-run by the Ebner family, with 28 comfy and tidy rooms over a good restaurant (Sb-€54, Db-€80–88 depending on size, Tb-€115, 8 percent discount with cash and this book, closed Jan–mid-Feb, elevator, Linzer Strasse 1, tel. 02752/52345, fax 02752/234-550, ebner.post @netway.at). Hotel zur Post has free bikes for guests and rents them to others (€7/half-day, €10/full day).

$$$ Hotel Stadt Melk, a block below the main square, has pink halls and drab, outmoded rooms. The moderately priced choices (below) offer better rooms for lower prices, but this will do in a pinch (Sb-€50–60, Db-€80, Hauptplatz 1, tel. 02752/52475, fax 02752/524-7519, www.tiscover.at/hotel-stadt-melk, hotel.stadtmelk@netway.at).

$$ Gasthof Goldener Stern's 11 rooms have recently been redone, with barn-flavored elegance and flowers on every pillow. The pricier canopy-bed rooms are very romantic. This lively place buzzes with locals eating in the atmospheric old restaurant—and with Regina and Kurt Schmidt's five children. It's on the small alley that veers off the main square above the twin turrets (D-€42–50, Db-€58–70, Db suite-€100, prices depend on room size, rooms for up to 5 also available, no CC, Sterngasse 17, tel. 02752/52214, fax 02752/522-144, goldenerstern .melk@aon.at).

$$ Café Fürst rents 10 clean, recently renovated rooms over its creaky restaurant. Run by the Madar family, it's right on the traffic-free main square, with a fountain outside the door and the abbey hovering overhead (Sb-€40, small Db-€58–60, big Db-€74, Tb-€75, no CC, Rathausplatz 3-5, tel. 02752/52343, fax 02752/523-434, cafe.madar @utanet.at).

$$ Hotel-Pension Wachau is a big, clean, modern place with a residential elegance in a rural-smelling modern suburb. It's a dull 20-minute walk from the center, but near the autobahn exit—so it's best for drivers. Half of the 24 rooms are non-smoking (Sb-€42–47, small Db-€65, big Db-€70, extra bed-€20, cheaper Nov–April, bike rental-€10/day for guests and non-guests, just off Wiener Strasse at Wachberg 157, tel. 02752/52531, fax 02752/525-3113, hotel.wachau@netway.at, Hipfinger family).

$ Pension Weisses Lamm has the cheapest beds in the center and absentee management. Within its Old World hallways are 20 modern rooms with bathrooms and TVs for *Zimmer* prices (Sb-€20, Db-€40, Tb-€60, no CC, Linzer Strasse 7, tel. 02752/54085, mobile 0676-323-3119).

SLEEP CODE

(€1 = about $1.10, country code: 43, area code: 02752)

Sleep Code: **S** = Single, **D** = Double/Twin, **T** = Triple, **Q** = Quad, **b** = bathroom, **s** = shower only, **no CC** = Credit Cards not accepted. Breakfast is included, credit cards are accepted unless otherwise noted, and everyone speaks at least some English.

To help you sort easily through these listings, I've divided the rooms into three categories, based on the price for a standard double room with bath:

$$$ **Higher Priced**—Most rooms €75 or more.
$$ **Moderately Priced**—Most rooms between €40–75.
$ **Lower Priced**—Most rooms €40 or less.

Melk makes a fine overnight stop. Except during August, you shouldn't have any trouble finding a good room at a reasonable rate. The TI has a long list of people renting rooms for about €20 per person. Most of these are a few miles from the center. If you stay in Melk, you are entitled to a free regional coupon book (*Gäste-card*, 10 percent discount on boats to Krems, free entry to town swimming pool, etc.)—ask.

Melk Hotels

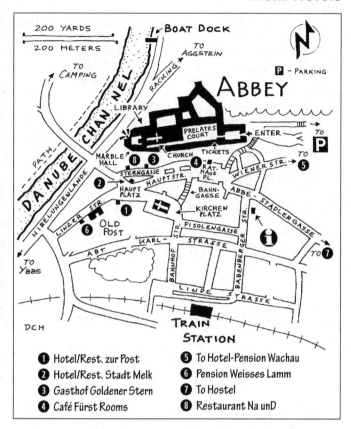

- **1** Hotel/Rest. zur Post
- **2** Hotel/Rest. Stadt Melk
- **3** Gasthof Goldener Stern
- **4** Café Fürst Rooms
- **5** To Hotel-Pension Wachau
- **6** Pension Weisses Lamm
- **7** To Hostel
- **8** Restaurant Na unD

$ Hostel: The modern, institutional **youth hostel** is a 10-minute walk from the station; turn right at the post office (25 quad rooms, beds–€15, nonmembers–€3 extra, includes sheets and breakfast, closed 12:00–16:00, closed Nov-March, Abt-Karl-Strasse 42, tel. 02752/52681, fax 02752/54257, www.jungehotels.at/melk, melk@jungehotels.at).

EATING

The recommended hotels **Gasthof Goldener Stern** and **Café Fürst** also have restaurants with fine, inexpensive local cuisine (both open daily).

Hotel Restaurant zur Post, classier and pricier, is worth the few extra euros (good local dishes, courtyard and fine streetside seating with an abbey view, daily 11:30–12:30, closed Jan–mid-Feb, Linzer Strasse 1, tel. 02752/52345). Downstairs is a fun and atmospheric wine cellar, with both local and international wines.

Melk's most elegant meals are served at **Hotel Restaurant Stadt Melk** (delicate nouvelle cuisine–type menus–€46 for standard or €56 for 8-course blowout, €20 entrées, terrace seating, reservations smart, daily 18:30–22:00, Hauptplatz 1, tel. 02752/52475). In season, look for *Marillen Knodel,* the local apricot dumpling—a dessert the Viennese come to Melk for in July and August (out of season, they're likely frozen and will take 20 minutes to cook, so order early).

Locals swear by the food at **Na unD,** with good Austrian and African dishes—run by the Ghanese-Austrian Addo family (closed Mon, Sterngasse 13, tel. 02752/51678).

TRANSPORTATION CONNECTIONS

Melk is on the autobahn and just off the Salzburg–Vienna train line.

By train to: Vienna's Westbahnhof (hrly, 1–2 hrs, some with transfer in St. Pölteu), **Salzburg** (hrly, 2 hrs, transfer in Amstetten or Linz), **Mauthausen** (nearly hrly, 75 min, transfer at St. Valentin).

Mauthausen Concentration Camp

More powerful and less tourist-oriented than Dachau, this slave-labor and death camp functioned from 1938 to 1945 for the exploitation and extermination of Hitler's opponents. More than half of its 206,000 quarry-working prisoners died here, mostly from starvation or exhaustion. Mauthausen has a strangely serene setting next to the Danube above an overgrown quarry (€2, April–Aug daily 8:00–18:00, Sept 8:00–17:00, Oct–mid-Dec and Feb–March 8:00–16:00, last entry 1 hour before closing time, closed mid-Dec–Jan, for directions to camp, see "Transportation Connections," page 391, tel. 07238/2269, TI tel. 07238/3860). You can borrow a free, tape-recorded 24-minute tour. The excellent €3 English guidebook covers the site very well (bookshop just inside entrance, closed 12:30–13:00). Allow two hours to tour the camp completely.

The camp barracks house a worthwhile museum at the far end of the camp on the right (no English). A graphic 45-minute movie is shown at the top of each hour. There are several film rooms. Find one marked English. If it's running, you can just slip in.

The most emotionally moving rooms and the gas chamber are downstairs. The spirits of the victims of these horrors can still be felt. Back outside the camp, each victim's country has erected a gripping memorial. Many yellowed photos have fresh flowers. Find the barbed-wire memorial overlooking the quarry and the "stairway of death" *(Todesstiege)* and walk at least halfway down (very uneven path). Return to the parking lot via the upper wall for a good perspective over the camp.

By visiting a concentration camp and putting ourselves through this emotional wringer, we heed and respect the fervent wish of the victims of this fascism—that we "never forget." Many people forget by choosing not to know.

SLEEPING AND EATING

Near Mauthausen

Sleeping in Enns, near Mauthausen: Just off the autobahn, less than four miles southwest of Mauthausen and 62 miles west of Vienna, Enns calls itself Austria's oldest town. **Hotel zum Goldenen Schiff,** facing Enns' delightful main square, is a decent value, with 20 comfy rooms and a quaint location (Sb-€42, Db-€62, no CC, family rooms, free parking, Hauptplatz 23, tel. 07223/86086, fax 07223/860-8615, www.tiscover.at /hotel.brunner, e-mail: wolfgang.brunner@liwest.at).

Eating: Moststub 'n Frellerhof, a farmhouse 50 yards below the Mauthausen parking lot, offers a refreshing, peaceful break after your visit. They serve *Most* (grape juice ready to become wine), homemade schnapps, and light farm-fresh meals (May–Sept daily from 13:00, playground, tel. 07238/2789).

TRANSPORTATION CONNECTIONS

Most trains stop at St. Valentin, midway between Salzburg and Vienna, where sporadic trains make the 15-minute ride to the Mauthausen station (get map from station attendant, camp is #9 on map, luggage check-€2.25).

Getting to Mauthausen Camp from Mauthausen Station: To cover the three miles between the camp and station, you can **hike** (1 hr, follow signs to *Ehemaliges KZ-Gedenkstätte Lager*) or **taxi** (minibus taxis available, about €10 one-way, ask taxi to pick you up in 2 hrs, share the cost with other tourists, tel. 07238/2439). Train info: tel. 07238/2207.

Vienna to Mauthausen by train: You can reach Mauthausen direct from Vienna's Franz Josefs Bahnhof or faster from the Westbahnhof with a transfer in St. Valentin.

St. Valentin by train to: Salzburg (hrly, 2 hrs), **Vienna** (hrly, 2 hrs).

Route Tips for Drivers

Hallstatt to Vienna, via Mauthausen, Melk, and Wachau Valley (210 miles): Leave Hallstatt early. Follow the scenic Route 145 through Gmunden to the autobahn and head east. After Linz, take exit #155, Enns, and follow the signs for Mauthausen (5 miles from freeway). Go through Mauthausen town and follow the signs to *Ehemaliges KZ-Gedenkstätte Lager*. From Mauthausen, it's a speedy 60 minutes to Melk via the autobahn, but the curvy and scenic Route 3 along the river is worth the nausea. At Melk, signs to Stift Melk lead to the *Benediktinerstift* (Benedictine Abbey). Other Melk signs lead into the town.

The most scenic stretch of the Danube is the Wachau Valley between Melk and Krems. From Melk (get a Vienna map at the TI), cross the river again (signs to *Donaubrucke*) and stay on Route 3. After Krems it hits the autobahn (A-22), and you'll barrel right into Vienna's traffic. (See "Route Tips for Drivers" in the Vienna chapter for details.)

SALZBURG

Salzburg is forever smiling to the tunes of Mozart and *The Sound of Music*. Thanks to its charmingly preserved old town, splendid gardens, Baroque churches, and Europe's largest intact medieval fortress, Salzburg feels made for tourism. It's a museum city with class. Vagabonds wish they had nicer clothes.

But even without Mozart and the von Trapps, Salzburg is steeped in history. In about A.D. 700, Bavaria gave Salzburg to Bishop Rupert for his promise to Christianize the area. Salzburg remained an independent state until Napoleon came (around 1800). Thanks in part to its formidable fortress, Salzburg managed to avoid the ravages of war for 1,200 years...until World War II. Half the city was destroyed by WWII bombs, but the historic old town survived.

Eight million tourists crawl its cobbles each year. That's a lot of Mozart balls—and all that popularity has led to a glut of businesses hoping to catch the tourist dollar. Still, Salzburg is a must.

ORIENTATION

(area code: 0662)

Salzburg, a city of 150,000 (Austria's fourth largest), is divided into old and new. The old town, sitting between the Salzach River and the 1,600-foot-high hill called Mönchsberg, holds nearly all the charm and most of the tourists.

Tourist Information: Salzburg's TIs are helpful. There are three branches: at the **train station** (April–Sept daily 9:00–18:30, July–Aug until 19:30, Oct–March until 17:45, tel. 0662/8898-7340), on **Mozartplatz** in the old center (daily 9:00–18:00, July–Aug until 19:00, sometimes closed Sun in winter, tel. 0662/8898-7330), and at the **Salzburg Süd park-and-ride** (July–Aug daily 9:00–19:00, Easter–June and Sept–Oct Mon–Sat 10:00–18:00, closed Sun, closed Nov–Easter, tel.

0662/8898-7360; central office: tel. 0662/889-870, www.salzburg.info). At any TI, you can pick up a free city center map (the €0.70 map, with more information on sights, probably isn't necessary), a brochure of sights with current hours and prices, and a bimonthly schedule of events. Book a concert upon arrival. The TIs also book rooms (€2.20 fee for up to 2 people, or €4.40 for 3 people or more).

Salzburg Card: The TI sells the Salzburg Card, which covers all your public transportation (including elevator and funicular) and admission to all the city sights (including Hellbrunn Palace). The card is pricey (€20/24 hrs, €28/48 hrs, €1 less Oct–May), but if you'd like to pop into all the sights without concern for the cost, this can save money and enhance your experience.

Planning Your Time

While Vienna measures much higher on the Richter scale of sightseeing thrills, Salzburg is simply a touristy, stroller's delight. If you're going into the nearby Salzkammergut lake country (see next chapter), skip the *Sound of Music* tour—if not, allow half a day for it. The *S.O.M.* tour kills a nest of sightseeing birds with one ticket (city overview, *S.O.M.* sights, and a fine drive through the lakes). You'll probably need two nights for Salzburg—nights are important for swilling beer in atmospheric local gardens and attending concerts in Baroque halls and chapels. Seriously consider one of Salzburg's many evening musical events (about €30–40). While the sights are mediocre, the town is an enjoyable Baroque museum of cobbled streets and elegant buildings. And to get away from it all, bike down the river or hike across the Mönchsberg.

Arrival in Salzburg

By Train: The little Salzburg station is user-friendly. The TI is at track 2A. Downstairs at street level, you'll find a place to store your luggage, buy tickets, and get train information. Bike rental is nearby (see below). The bus station is across the street (where buses #1, #5, #6, #51, and #55 go to the old center; get off at the first stop after you cross the river for most sights and city center hotels, or just before the bridge for Linzergasse hotels). Figure €6.50 for a taxi to the center. To walk downtown (15 min), leave the station ticket hall to the left and walk straight down Rainerstrasse, which leads under the tracks past Mirabellplatz, turning into Dreifaltigkeitsgasse. From here, you can turn left onto Linzergasse for many of the recommended hotels or cross the Staatsbrücke (bridge) for the old town (and more hotels). For a more dramatic approach, leave the station the same way but follow the tracks to the river, turn left, and walk the riverside path toward the fortress.

By Car: Follow *Zentrum* signs to the center and park short-term on the street or longer under Mirabellplatz. Ask at your hotel for suggestions.

Getting around Salzburg

By Bus: Single-ride tickets are sold on the bus for €1.70. At machines and *Tabak* shops, you can buy a €3.20 day pass (*Tageskarte,* good for 24 hrs) and cheaper single tickets (€1.40 each, but you must buy 5 at a time). To signal the driver you want to get off, press the buzzer on the pole. Bus info: tel. 0662/4480-6262.

By Bike: Salzburg is a biker's delight. Top Bike rents bikes from two outlets (at the river side of the train station and on the old town side of the Staatsbrücke, €3.70/hr, €13/24 hrs, tel. 06272/4656, mobile 0676-476-7259, www.topbike.at, Sabina SE). Velo-Active rents bikes on Residenzplatz under the *Glockenspiel* in the old town (€4.50/hr, €15/24 hrs, mountain bikes-€6/hr, €18/24 hrs, daily 9:00–18:00 but hours unreliable—often you'll have to call, shorter hours off-season and in bad weather, passport number for security deposit, tel. 0662/435-595, mobile 0676/435-5950). Thanks to a promotional deal they have with the train station, both companies offer 20 percent off with a valid train ticket or Eurailpass—ask for it.

By Funicular and Elevator: The old town is connected to Mönchsberg (and great views) via funicular and elevator. The **funicular** (FestungsBahn) whisks you up to the imposing Hohensalzburg fortress (€8.50 round-trip includes admission to fortress grounds, €5.50 one-way; funicular runs May–Aug daily 9:00–22:00, Sept until 21:30, Oct–Dec and mid-March–April until 17:00, closed for maintenance Jan–mid-March, www.festungsbahn.at). You can't take the funicular up without paying for entrance to the fortress grounds—unless you have a concert ticket and it's within an hour before the performance (see "Music Scene," page 408).

The **elevator** (MönchsbergAufzug) on the east side of the old town propels you to the recommended Naturfreundehaus (see "Sleeping—In or Above the Old Town," page 413), the Modern Art Museum, and lots of wooded paths (€1.60 one-way, €2.60 round-trip, summer daily 9:00–21:00, off-season until 18:00, www.moenchsbergaufzug.at).

By Taxi: Salzburg is a fine taxi town. Meters start around €3 (from train station to your hotel, allow about €6.50). As always, small groups can taxi for about the same price as riding the bus.

By Boat: Salzburg's first attempt at a Salzach River Cruise sank to the bottom—literally—when someone moored the boat with too short a rope during the August 2002 floods. Now the boat is back up and running (€10 for basic 40-min roundtrip cruise, April–Sept 8/day, more June–Aug, €13 to Hellbrunn with return on bus, April–Sept 3/day, more June–Aug, boat leaves from old-town side of river just west—downstream—of Staatsbrücke, tel. 0662/8257-6912, www.salzburgschifffahrt.at).

By Buggy: The horse buggies *(Fiaker)* that congregate at the Residenz Platz charge €35 for a 25-minute trot around the old town (www.fiaker-salzburg.at).

Helpful Hints

Internet Access: BigNet, a block off Mozartplatz at Judengasse 5, has 33 terminals (about €6/hr, daily 9:00–22:00, tel. 0662/841-470). The Internet Café is on Mozartplatz next to the TI (€9/hr, daily 9:00–24:00, off-season until 22:00, 11 terminals, Mozartplatz 5, tel. 0662/844-822).

Laundry: The launderette near recommended Linzergasse hotels at the corner of Paris-Lodron Strasse and Wolf-Dietrich Strasse is handy (€10 self-service, €15 same-day full-service, Mon–Fri 7:30–18:00, Sat 8:00–12:00, closed Sun, tel. 0662/876-381).

Guide Association: Salzburg's many guides can give you a good three-hour walk through town for €125 (tel. 0662/840-406). Barbel Schalber, who enjoys leaving the touristy places, offers my readers a two-hour walk packed with information and spicy opinions for €75 per family or group (tel. 0662/632-225, baxguide@utanet.at).

American Express: AmEx has travel agency services, but doesn't sell train tickets—and it charges no commission to cash AmEx checks (Mon–Fri 9:00–17:30, Sat 9:00–12:00, closed Sun, Mozartplatz 5, tel. 0662/8080).

SELF-GUIDED OLD TOWN WALKING TOUR

The tourist office offers two-language, one-hour guided walks of the old town. They are informative and worthwhile if you don't mind listening to a half hour of German (€8, daily at 12:15, not on Sun in winter, start at TI on Mozartplatz, tel. 0662/8898-7330—just show up and pay the guide). But you can easily do it on your own.

Here's a basic old-town orientation walk, worth ▲▲▲.

Mozartplatz—This square features a statue of Mozart erected in 1842. Mozart spent much of his first 20 years (1756–1777) in Salzburg, the greatest Baroque city north of the Alps. But the city's much older. The Mozart statue actually sits on bits of Roman Salzburg. And the pink church of St. Michael overlooking the square is from A.D. 800. The first Salzburgers settled right around here. Surrounding you are Café Glockenspiel, the Internet Café, the American Express office, and the tourist information office with a concert box office. Just around the downhill corner is a pedestrian bridge leading over the Salzach River to the quiet, most medieval street in town, Steingasse (see "Across the River," page 402). Walk toward the cathedral and into the big square with the huge fountain.

Residenz Platz—Salzburg's energetic Prince-Archbishop Wolf Dietrich (who ruled from 1587–1612) was raised in Rome, counted the Medicis as his buddies, and had grandiose Italian ambitions for Salzburg. After a convenient fire destroyed the cathedral, he set about building "the Rome of the North." This square, with his new cathedral and palace, was the centerpiece of his Baroque dream city. A series of interconnecting squares—like you'll see nowhere else—lead from here through the old town.

For centuries, Salzburg's leaders were both important church officials and princes of the Holy Roman Empire, hence the title "Prince-Archbishop"—mixing sacred and secular authority. Wolf Dietrich misplayed his power and spent his last five years imprisoned in the Salzburg castle.

The fountain is as Italian as can be, with a Triton matching Bernini's famous Triton Fountain in Rome. Lying on a busy trade route to the south, Salzburg was well aware of the exciting things going on in Italy. Things Italian were respected (as in colonial America, when a bumpkin would "stick a feather in his cap and call it macaroni"). Local artists even Italianized their names in order to raise their rates.

Residenz—Dietrich's skippable palace is connected to the cathedral by a skyway. A series of ornately decorated rooms and an art gallery are open to visitors with time to kill (€7.30 includes both palace and gallery with audioguide, €5 each for palace or picture gallery, daily 10:00–17:00, gallery closed Mon except July–Aug, entire complex closed one month around Easter, tel. 0662/8042-2690).

Opposite the old Residenz is the new Residenz, which has long been a government administration building. Today it houses the central post office and the Heimatwerk, a fine shop showing off all the best local handicrafts (Mon–Fri 9:00–18:00, Sat 9:00–13:00, closed Sun). Atop the new Residenz is the famous...

Glockenspiel—This bell tower has a carillon of 35 17th-century bells (cast in Antwerp) that chimes throughout the day and plays tunes (appropriate to the month) at 7:00, 11:00, and 18:00. There was a time when Salzburg could afford to take tourists to the top of the tower to actually see the big barrel with adjustable tabs turn (like a giant music box mechanism)...pulling the right bells in the right rhythm. Notice the ornamental top: an upside-down heart in flames surrounding the solar system (symbolizing that God loves all of creation).

Look back, past Mozart's statue, to the 4,220-foot-high Gaisberg—the forested hill with the television tower. A road leads to the top for a commanding view. Its summit is a favorite destination for local nature-lovers (by city bus or bike). Walk under the Prince-Archbishop's skyway and step into Domplatz, the cathedral square.

Salzburg Cathedral—Built in the 17th century, this was one of the first Baroque buildings north of the Alps. It was built during the Thirty Years' War to emphasize Salzburg's commitment to the Roman Catholic cause and the power of the Church here. Salzburg's archbishop was technically the top papal official north of the Alps (donation requested, May–Oct Mon–Sat 9:00–18:30, Sun 13:00–18:30, Nov–April Mon–Sat 10:00–17:00, Sun 13:00–17:00). The dates on the iron gates refer to milestones in the church's history: In 774, the previous church (long since destroyed) was founded by St. Virgil, to be replaced in 1628 by the church you see today. In 1959, the reconstruction was completed after a WWII bomb blew through the dome.

Wander inside. Built in just 14 years (1614–1628), the church boasts harmonious architecture. When the pope visited in 1998, 5,000 people filled the cathedral (dimensions: 330 feet long and 230 feet tall). The baptismal font (dark bronze, left of the entry) is from the previous cathedral (c. 1320). Mozart was baptized here (Amadeus means "beloved by God"). Gape up. The interior—with its five independent organs—is marvelous. Concert and Mass schedules are posted at the entrance; the Sunday Masses at 10:00 and 11:30 are famous for their music. Mozart, who worked here as the organist for two years, would advise you that the acoustics are best in pews immediately under the dome.

Under the skyway, a stairway leads down to the *Domgrabungen*—an **excavation site** under the church with a few second-century Christian Roman mosaics and the foundation stones of the previous Romanesque and Gothic churches (€2, May–Sept Wed–Sun 9:00–17:00, closed Mon–Tue, closed Oct–April, 0662/845-295). The **Cathedral Museum** (Dom Museum) has a rich collection of church art (entry at portico, €4.50, mid-May–Oct Mon–Sat 10:00–17:00, Sun 13:00–18:00, closed Nov–mid-May, tel. 0662/844-189).

From Cathedral Square to St. Peter's: The cathedral square is surrounded by "ecclesiastical palaces." The statue of Mary (1771) is looking away from the church, but, if you stand in the rear of the square immediately under the middle arch, you'll see how she's positioned to be crowned by the two angels on the church facade.

From the cathedral, walk toward the fortress into the next square (passing the free underground public WCs and the giant chessboard) to the pond. This was a horse bath, the 18th-century equivalent of a car wash. Notice the puzzle above it—the artist wove the date of the structure into a phrase. It says, "Leopold the Ruler Built Me," using the letters LLDVICMXVXI, which total 1732—the year it was built. A small road (back by the chessboard) leads uphill to the fortress (and fortress lift). The stage is set up for the many visiting choirs who are unable to line up a gig. They are welcome to sing here anytime at all. Leave the square through a gate on the right that reads St. Peter. It leads to a waterfall and St. Peter's Cemetery.

The **waterfall** is part of a canal system that has brought water into Salzburg from Berchtesgaden, 16 miles away, since 1150. The stream, divided from here into smaller canals, was channeled through town to power factories (more than 100 water-mill–powered firms as late as the 19th century), provide fire protection, and flush out the streets (Sat morning was flood-the-streets day). Drop into the traditional **bakery** at the waterfall. It's hard to beat their rocklike *Roggenbrot* (sold Thu–Tue

7:00–17:30, Sat until 12:00, closed Wed). Then step into the cemetery *(Katakomben)*.

St. Peter's Cemetery—This collection of lovingly tended mini-gardens abuts the Mönchberg's rock wall (April–Sept daily 6:30–19:00, Oct–March daily 6:30–18:00). Iron crosses were much cheaper than stone tombstones. The graves are cared for by relatives. (In Austria, grave sites are rented, not owned. Rent bills are sent out every 10 years. If no one cares enough to make the payment, you're gone.) Look up the cliff. Medieval hermit monks lived in the hillside—but "catacombs" they're not. For €1, you can climb lots of steps to see a few old caves, a chapel, and some fine views (May–Sept Tue–Sun 10:30–17:00, closed Mon, Oct–April Wed–Thu 10:30–15:30, Fri–Sun 10:30–16:00, closed Mon–Tue). While the cemetery the von Trapp family hid out in was actually in Hollywood, it was inspired by this one. Walk through the cemetery (silence is requested) and out the opposite end. Drop into St. Peter's Church, a Romanesque basilica done up beautifully Baroque. Continue through the arch opposite the church entry and through a modern courtyard (past dorms for student monks).

Toscanini Hof faces the 1925 Festival Hall. Its three halls seat 5,000. This is where the nervous Captain von Trapp waited before walking onstage to sing "Edelweiss" just before he escaped with Maria and his family to Switzerland. On the left is the city's 1,500-space, inside-the-mountain parking lot; ahead behind the *Felsenkeller* sign is a tunnel (generally closed) leading to the actual concert hall; and to the right is the backstage of a smaller hall where carpenters are often building stage sets (open on hot days). Walk downhill through Max Reinhardt Platz, to the right of the church and past the public WC to...

Universitätsplatz—This square comes with a busy open-air produce market—Salzburg's liveliest (mornings Mon–Sat, best on Sat). Locals are happy to pay more here for the reliably fresh and top-quality produce (half of Austria's produce is now grown organically). The market really bustles on Saturday mornings, when the farmers are in town. Public marketplaces have fountains for washing fruit and vegetables. The fountain here (notice the little ones for smaller dogs and bigger dogs)—a part of the medieval water system—plummets down a hole and to the river. The sundial is accurate (except for the daylight savings hour), showing both the time (obvious) and the date (less obvious). Continue to the end of the square (opposite cathedral), passing several characteristic and nicely arcaded medieval tunnel passages (on right) connecting the square to Getreidegasse. At the big road (across from the giant horse troughs), take two right turns and you're at the start of...

Getreidegasse—This street was old Salzburg's busy, colorful main drag. *(Schmuck* means jewelry.) Famous for its old wrought-iron signs, the street still looks much as it did in Mozart's day. On the right at #39, Sporer is known for its homemade spirits (Mon–Fri 9:00–12:30 &

14:30–19:00, Sat 8:30–17:00, closed Sun, tel. 0662/845-431). At #40, Eisgrotte serves good ice cream. Across from Eisgrotte, a tunnel leads to Bosna Grill, the local choice for the very best sausage in town (see "Eating Cheap in the Old Town," page 418). Farther along you'll see the Nordsee Restaurant, which was a more controversial addition to this street than the McDonald's—notice the medieval golden arches street sign. Wolfgang was born on this street. Find his very gold house at #9 (follow the crowds).

Mozart's Birthplace (Geburtshaus)—Mozart was born here in 1756. It was in this building—the most popular Mozart sight in town—that he composed most of his boy-genius works. Filled with scores of scores, portraits, his first violin (picked up at age 5), the clavichord (a predecessor to the piano with simple teeter-totter keys that played very softly) on which he composed *The Magic Flute* and the *Requiem,* a relaxing video concert hall, and exhibits about the life of Wolfgang on the road and Salzburg in Mozart's day, including a furnished middle-class apartment (all well-described in English), it's almost a pilgrimage (€5.50, or €9 for combo-ticket to Mozart's *Wohnhaus*—see "Sights—Across the River," page 402, July–Aug daily 9:00–19:00, Sept–June daily 9:00–18:00, last entry 30 min before closing, Getreidegasse 9, tel. 0662/844-313). Note that Mozart's *Wohnhaus* provides a more informative visit than this more-visited site.

SIGHTS

Above the Old Town

▲**Hohensalzburg Fortress**—Built on a rock 400 feet above the Salzach River, this fortress was never really used. That's the idea. It was a good investment—so foreboding, nobody attacked the town for a thousand years. One of Europe's mightiest, it dominates Salzburg's skyline and offers incredible views. You can hike up or ride the *Festungsbahn* (funicular, €8.50 round-trip includes fortress courtyard entry, €5.50 one-way, pleasant to walk down). The fortress visit has two parts—a relatively dull courtyard with some fine views (€3.60 or included in €8.50 funicular fare) and the palatial interior (worth the €3.60 extra admission). Tourists are allowed inside only with an escort, so you'll go one room at a time, listening to the entire 50-minute audioguide narration (included).

The decorations are from around 1500—fantastic animals and plants inspired by tales of New World discoveries. While the interior furnishings are mostly gone—to the museums of Vienna, Paris, London, and Munich—the rooms survived as well as they did because no one wanted to live there after 1500, so it was never modernized. Your tour includes the obligatory room dedicated to the art of "intensive questioning"—filled with tools of that gruesome trade—and a sneak preview of the room used for the nightly fortress concerts. The last rooms show

Salzburg

MIRABELL PALACE

TO CENTRAL STATION

MIRA-BELL PLATZ

INSTITUTE ST. SEBASTIAN

ST. SEB. CEM.

MIRA-BELL GDNS.

SCHWARZ

MOZARTEUM

PUPPET THEATER

MAKART PLATZ

MOZART WOHN-HAUS

KAPUZINER-BERG

MÜLLNER HAUPTSTR.

SALZ

FRANZ-JOSEF KAI

STEG

STAATS

DREI GASSE

LINZERGASSE

CAPUCHIN MONASTERY

TO AUGUS-TINER BRÄU-STÜBL

ELEV.

MOZART GEBURTS-HAUS

GETREIDEGASSE

ACH

RIVER

RUDOLFS

IMBERSTRASSE

TO HALLEIN

MODERN ART MUSEUM

NATUR-FREUNDE-HAUS

U.-PLATZ

JUDENGASSE

GOLDG.

HOFSTALLGASSE

RESIDENZ

RES. PLATZ

DOM PLATZ

BOB'S TOURS

MOZART PLATZ

NEW RES. & POST

FESTIVAL CONCERT HALLS

KAP. PL.

CATHEDRAL

YH

NEUTOR TUNNEL

TRAIL

TO MOOSSTRASSE ZIMMERS

CEM.

SCHANZL

ST. PETER'S

MÖNCHS BERG

FUNICULAR

DCH

HOHEN-SALZBURG FORTRESS

•••• WALKING TOUR ROUTE STARTING AT MOZART PLATZ & ENDING AT MOZART GEBURTSHAUS

200 YARDS

200 METERS

music, daily life in the castle, and an exhibit dedicated to the Salzburg regiment in World War I and World War II. The highlight is the commanding city view from the top of a tower (fortress open daily year-round; mid-March–mid-June: grounds 9:00–18:00, interior 9:30–17:30; mid-June–mid-Sept: grounds 9:00–19:00, interior 9:30–18:00; mid-Sept–mid-March: grounds 9:00–17:00, interior 9:30–17:00; last entry 30 min before closing, tel. 0662/8424-3011). Warning: The one-room marionette exhibit in the fortress courtyard is a bad value—you'll see more for free in its lobby than by paying to go inside.

▲**The Hills Are Alive Walk**—For a great little hike, exit the fortress by taking the trail across Salzburg's little mountain, Mönchsberg. The trail leads through the woods high above the city (stick to the high lanes, or you'll end up back in town), taking you to the Naturfreundehaus (café, light meals, cheap beds, elevator nearby for a quick descent to Neumayr Platz in the old town) and eventually to the church that marks the rollicking Augustiner Bräustübl (described in "Eating—Away from the Center," page 419).

In 1669, a huge Mönchsberg landslide killed more than 200 townspeople. Since then the cliffs have been carefully checked each spring and fall. Even today, you might see crews on the cliff, monitoring its stability.

Museum of Modern Art on Mönchsberg (Museum der Moderne auf dem Mönchsberg)—New for the summer of 2004 is a modern-art museum on top of Mönchsberg, housing Salzburg's Rupertinum Gallery, plus special exhibitions. While the collection is so-so, the restaurant has some of the best views in town (www.museumdermoderne.at).

Across the River

Salzach River—Cross the river (ideally on one of two pedestrian bridges). It's called "salt river" not because it's salty, but because of its original precious trade—the salt mines of Hallein are just nine miles upstream. Salt could be transported from here all the way to the Danube and on to Russia. The riverbanks and roads were built in 1860. Before that, the Salzach was much wider and slower-moving. Houses opposite the old town fronted the river with docks and garages for boats.

▲**Steingasse**—This street, a block in from the river, was the only street in the Middle Ages going south to Hallein. Today, it's wonderfully tranquil and free of Salzburg's touristy crush. Wander down Steingasse (from Mozartplatz, cross the river via the Mozartsteg pedestrian bridge, cross the busy Imbergstrasse, jog left and go a block farther inland to a quiet cobbled lane, and turn left).

Stroll down this peaceful chunk of old Salzburg—once the only road on this side of the river. Just after the Maison de Plaisir at #24 (for centuries, a town brothel—open from 14:00), you'll find a magnificent view of the fortress across the river. Notice the red dome marking the oldest nunnery in the German-speaking world (established in 712) under the fortress and to the left. The real Maria from *The Sound of Music* taught in this nunnery's school. In 1927, she and Herr von Trapp were married in the church you see here (not the church filmed in the movie). He was 47. She was 22. Hmmmm.

At #19, find the carvings on the old door—notices from beggars to the begging community (more numerous after the economic dislocation caused by the wars over religion following the Reformation) indicating whether the residents would give or not. The four ringers indicate four families lived at this address.

At #9, a plaque shows where Joseph Mohr, who wrote the words to "Silent Night," was born, poor and illegitimate, in 1792. Stairs lead from near here up to the monastery.

Across the street, on the corner you just passed, the wall is gouged out. This was left even after the building was restored so locals could remember the American GI who tried to get a tank down this road during a visit to #24.

By night, Steingasse is home to many trendy pubs (see "Steingasse Pub Crawl," page 420).

▲**St. Sebastian Cemetery**—Wander through this quiet place—so Baroque and so Italian (free, April–Oct daily 9:00–19:00, Nov–March daily 9:00–16:00, entry usually at Linzergasse 43). While Mozart is buried in Vienna, his father and most of his family are buried here (from the Linzergasse entrance, take 17 paces and look left). When Prince-Archbishop Wolf Dietrich had the cemetery moved from around the cathedral and put here, across the river, people didn't like it. To help popularize it, he had his mausoleum built as its centerpiece. Continuing straight past the Mozart tomb, step into his dome. Read the legalistic epitaph (posted in English) and look at the tomb through the grate in the floor. To get to the cemetery (Friedhof St. Sebastian), take Linzergasse, the best shopping street in Salzburg.

▲▲**Mozart's** *Wohnhaus*—This reconstruction of Mozart's second home (his family moved here when he was 17) is the most informative Mozart sight in town. The English-language audioguide (free with admission, keep it carefully pointed at the ceiling transmitters and don't move while listening) provides a fascinating insight into Mozart's life and music, with the usual scores, old pianos, and an interesting 30-minute-long film that runs continuously, all in English (€5.50, or €9 for combo-ticket to birthplace, guidebook-€4.50, daily 9:00–18:00, July–Aug until 19:00, last tickets sold 30 min before closing, allow 1 hr for visit, across river from old town, Makartplatz 8, tel. 0662/8742-2740).

▲**Mirabell Gardens and Palace** *(Schloss)*—The bubbly gardens, laid out in 1730, are always open and free. You may recognize the statues and the arbor featured in the *S.O.M.* A brass band plays free park concerts (May–Aug Sun 10:30 and Wed 20:30). To properly enjoy the lavish Mirabell Palace—once the prince bishop's summer palace and now the seat of the mayor—get a ticket to a *Schlosskonzert* (my favorite venue for a classical concert). Baroque music flying around a Baroque hall is a happy bird in the right cage. Tickets (€26–31, student-€14) are rarely sold out (tel. 0662/848-586). The nearby **Café Bazar** is a great place for a break (see "Eating," below).

More Salzburg Sights

▲▲**Riverside Bike Ride**—The Salzach River has smooth, flat, and scenic bike paths along each side. On a sunny day, I can think of no

SOUND OF MUSIC DEBUNKED

Rather than visit the real-life sights from the life of Maria von Trapp and family, most tourists want to see the places where Hollywood chose to film this fanciful story. Local guides are happy not to burst any *S.O.M.* pilgrim's bubble, but keep these points in mind:

• "Edelweiss" is not a cherished Austrian folk tune or national anthem. Like all the "Austrian" music in the *S.O.M.*, it was composed for Broadway by Rodgers and Hammerstein. It was, however, the last composition that the famed team wrote together, as Hammerstein died in 1960—nine months after the musical opened.

• The *S.O.M.* implies that Maria was devoutly religious throughout her life, but Maria's foster parents raised her as a socialist and atheist. Maria discovered her religious calling while studying to be a teacher. After completing school, she joined the convent as a novitiate.

• Maria's position was not as governess to all the children, as portrayed in the musical, but specifically as governess and teacher for the Captain's second-oldest daughter, Maria, who was bedridden with rheumatic fever.

• The Captain didn't run a tight domestic ship. In fact, his seven children were as unruly as most. But he did use a whistle to call them—each kid was trained to respond to a certain pitch.

• Though the von Trapp family did have seven children, the show changed all their names and even their genders. Rupert, the eldest child, responded to the often-asked tourist question, "Which one are you?" with a simple, "I'm Leisl!"

• The family never escaped by hiking to Switzerland (which is a 5-hour drive away). Rather, they pretended to go on one of their

more shout-worthy escape from the city. The nearly four-mile path to Hellbrunn Palace is easy, with a worthy destination. For a nine-mile ride, head out to Hallein (where you can tour a salt mine, see "Sights—Near Salzburg," below, the north or "new town" side of river is most scenic). Even a quickie ride across town is a great Salzburg experience. In the evening, the riverbanks are a floodlit-spires world.

▲ *Sound of Music* **Tour**—I took this tour skeptically (as part of my research chores). While quality varies per quide and readers give this tour mixed reviews, I liked it. It includes a quick but good general city tour, hits the *S.O.M.* spots (including the stately home, gazebo, and frequent mountain hikes. With only the possessions in their back-packs, they "hiked" all the way to the train station (it was at the edge of their estate) and took a train to Italy. Hitler immediately closed the Austrian borders when he learned of this. The movie scene showing them climbing into Switzerland was actually filmed near Berchtesgaden, Germany...home to Hitler's Eagle's Nest, and certainly not a smart place to flee.

- The actual von Trapp family house exists...but it's not the one in the film. The mansion in the movie is actually two different build-ings, one used for the front, the other for the back. The interiors were all filmed on Hollywood sets.

- For the film, Boris Levin designed a reproduction of Nonnberg Abbey courtyard so faithful to the original (down to its cobble-stones and stained-glass windows) that many still believe the clois-ter scenes were really shot at the abbey. And no matter what you hear in Salzburg, the graveyard scene (in which the von Trapps hide from the Nazis) was also filmed on the Fox lot.

- In 1956, a German film producer offered Maria $10,000 for the rights to her book. She asked for royalties, too, and a share of the profits. The agent explained that German law forbids film compa-nies from paying royalties to foreigners (Maria had by then become a U.S. citizen). She agreed to the contract and unknowingly signed away all film rights to her story. Only a few weeks later, he offered to pay immediately if she would accept $9,000 in cash. Because it was more money than the family had seen in all of their years of singing, she accepted the deal. Later, she discovered the agent had swindled them—no such law existed.

wedding church), and shows you a lovely stretch of the Salzkammergut. This is worthwhile for *S.O.M.* fans and those who won't otherwise be going into the Salzkammergut. Warning: Many think rolling through the Austrian countryside with 30 Americans singing "Do, a Deer" is pretty schmaltzy. Local Austrians don't understand all the commotion. Of the many companies doing the tour, consider Bob's Special Tours (usually uses a more intimate mini-bus) and the Panorama tours (more typical, professional big bus). Each one provides essentially the same tour (in English with a live and lively guide, 4 hrs, free hotel pick-up) for the same price. The *S.O.M.* tour for each company costs €35, but you'll get a €5 discount from either if you book direct and mention Rick Steves. Getting a spot is simple—just call and make a reservation. Note: Your hotel will be eager to call to reserve for you—to get their commission—but if you let them do it, you will not get the discount I've negotiated. Each company also offers an extensive array of other day trips from Salzburg (Berchtesgaden Eagle's Nest, salt mines, and Salzkammergut lakes and mountains are the most popular, with similar discounts—€5 off with this book—and big bus vs. mini-bus differences as above)—all explained in their brochures, which litter hotel lobbies all over town.

Mini-bus option: Ninety percent of **Bob's Special Tours** use a mini-bus and therefore have better access for old-town sights, promote a more casual feel, and spend less time waiting and picking up (buses leave from Bob's office along the river just east of Mozartplatz at Rudolfskai 38, daily at 9:00 and 14:00 year-round, tel. 0662/849-511, mobile 0664-541-7492, www.bobstours.com). Nearly all of Bob's tours (confirm beforehand) stop for the luge ride when the weather is dry (mountain bobsled–€4 extra). Some travelers looking for Bob's tours at Mozartplatz have been hijacked by other companies...have Bob's pick you up at your hotel or meet the bus at their office (see above).

Big-bus option: Salzburg Panorama Tours depart Mirabellplatz daily at 9:30 and 14:00 year-round (tel. 0662/874-029 or 0662/883-211, www.panoramatours.com). Many travelers appreciate their more professional feel, roomier buses, and slightly higher vantage point. While they try to stop for a luge ride, there's generally not enough time (as shopping and coffee are a priority).

▲**Hellbrunn Castle**—The attractions here are a garden full of clever trick fountains and the sadistic joy the tour guide gets from soaking tourists. (Hint: When you see a wet place, cover your camera.) The Baroque garden, one of the oldest in Europe, now features *S.O.M.*'s "I Am 16, Going on 17" gazebo (€7.50, includes 35-min tour, daily 9:00–17:30, July–Aug until 18:00 and €7 fountain tours until 22:00, April and Oct until 16:30, closed Nov–March, tel. 0662/820-372, www.hellbrunn.at). The archbishop's mediocre 17th-century palace, in the courtyard, is open by tour only (audioguide included in admission). Hellbrunn is about three miles south of Salzburg (bus #55 from station or downtown, 2/hr, 20 min). It's most fun on a sunny day or with kids, but, for many, it's a lot of trouble for a few water tricks.

Near Salzburg

▲**Bad Dürrnberg Salzbergwerke**—This salt mine tour above the town of Hallein (9 miles from Salzburg) is a fun experience. Wearing white overalls and sliding down the sleek wooden chutes, you'll cross underground from Austria into Germany while learning about the old-time salt mining process (€15.50, April–Oct daily from 9:00 with last tour at 17:00,

Greater Salzburg

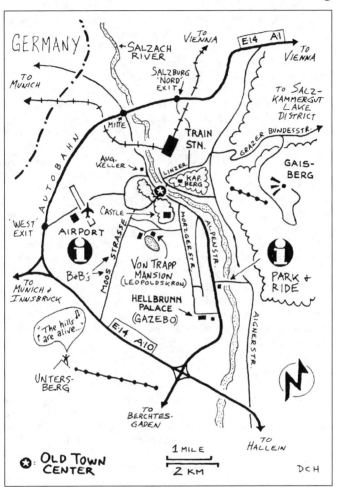

GERMANY

SALZACH RIVER

TO VIENNA

E14 A1

TO VIENNA

TO MUNICH

SALZBURG 'NORD' EXIT

TO SALZ-KAMMERGUT LAKE DISTRICT

MITTE

GRAZER BUNDESSTR.

TRAIN STN.

GAIS-BERG

AUG. KELLER

LINZER

KAP. BERG

AUTOBAHN

CASTLE

MOZARTER STR.

ALPENSTR.

'WEST' EXIT

AIRPORT

MOOS STRASSE

B+B's

VON TRAPP MANSION (LEOPOLDSKRON)

PARK + RIDE

TO MUNICH + INNSBRUCK

HELLBRUNN PALACE (GAZEBO)

AIGNERSTR.

"The hills are alive..."

E14 A10

UNTERS-BERG

TO BERCHTES-GADEN

N

TO HALLEIN

⊗: OLD TOWN CENTER

1 MILE

2 KM

DCH

Nov–March daily from 11:00 with last tour at 15:00, English-speaking guides, easy bus and train connections from Salzburg, tel. 06245/852-8515, www.salzwelten.at). A convenient "Salz Erlebnis Ticket" from Salzburg's train station covers admission, train, and shuttle bus tickets, all in one money-saving round-trip ticket (around €18, buy ticket at train station).

▲**Berchtesgaden**—This alpine ski town in the region of the same name just across the German border (12 miles from Salzburg) flaunts its attractions very successfully. During peak season, you may find yourself in a traffic jam of desperate tourists trying to turn their money into fun.

The TI is next to the train station (TI: German tel. 08652/967-150, from Austria tel. 00-49-8652/967-150). From the station, buses go to the salt mines (a 20-min walk otherwise) and the idyllic Königsee (popular €11, 1-hr scenic cruises, 2/hr, with the pilot demonstrating the lake's echo with a trumpet, stopovers anywhere, German tel. 08652/963-618, from Austria tel. 00-49-8652/963-618).

At the Berchtesgaden **salt mines,** you put on traditional miners' outfits, get on funny little trains, and zip deep into the mountain. For one hour, you'll cruise subterranean lakes; slide speedily down two long, slick, wooden banisters; and learn how they mined salt so long ago. Call for crowd-avoidance advice. When the weather gets bad, this place is mobbed. You can buy a ticket early and browse through the town until your appointed tour time (€12.50, May–mid-Oct daily 9:00–17:00, mid-Oct–April Mon–Sat 12:30–15:30, closed Sun, German tel. 08652/60020, from Austria tel. 00-49-8652/60020).

Hitler's famous **Eagle's Nest**—designed as a retreat for diplomatic meetings—towers high above Obersalzberg near Berchtesgaden. The road and building were constructed in an impressive 13 months—just in time to be given to Hitler for his 50th birthday. The view will blow your cake out. The site is open to visitors (mid-May–Oct), but little remains of the alpine retreat Hitler visited only 10 times. The round-trip bus ride up the private road and the lift to the top (a 2,000-foot altitude gain) cost €16 from the station, €13 from the parking lot. For more substance, visit the new **Nazi Documentation Center,** including a visit to the bunkers that burrow into the mountainside (€2.50, €2 for English audioguide, April–Oct daily 9:00–17:00, Nov–March Tue–Sun 10:00–15:00, closed Mon, last entry 1 hr before closing, next to parking lot, German tel. 08652/947-960, from Austria tel. 00-49-8652/947-960, www.obersalzberg.de).

Getting from Salzburg to Berchtesgaden, the bus is more scenic and direct than the train (2/hr, 30 min, bus station across street from Salzburg's train station). Some travelers visit Berchtesgaden en route from Munich (hrly trains from Munich, 2.5 hrs, with 1 change).

MUSIC SCENE

▲▲**Salzburg Festival**—Each summer, from late July to the end of August, Salzburg hosts its famous Salzburger Festspiele, founded in 1920 to employ Vienna's musicians in the summer. This fun and festive time is crowded, but there are plenty of beds (except for a few August weekends). Tickets are normally available the day of the concert unless it's a really big show (the ticket office on Mozartplatz, in the TI, prints a daily list of concerts and charges a 30 percent fee to book them). For specifics on this year's festival schedule and tickets, visit www.salzburgfestival.at, or contact the Austrian National Tourist

Office in the United States (Box 1142, New York, NY 10108-1142, 212/944-6880, fax 212/730-4568, www.austria-tourism.com, info@oewnyc .com)—but I've never planned in advance and have enjoyed great concerts with every visit.

▲▲**Musical Events outside of Festival Time**—Salzburg is busy throughout the year, with 2,000 classical performances in its palaces and churches annually. Pick up the events calendar at the TI (free, bimonthly). Whenever you visit, you'll have a number of concerts (generally small chamber groups) to choose from. There are nearly nightly concerts at the fortress (for beginners—Mozart's greatest hits) and at the Mirabell Palace (with more sophisticated programs). Both feature small chamber groups, have open seating, and charge roughly €30–36 for tickets (concerts at 19:30, 20:00, or 20:30, doors open 30 min early). The *Schlosskonzerte* at the Mirabell Palace offer a fine Baroque setting for your music (tel. 0662/848-586). The fortress concerts, called *Festungskonzerte,* are held in the "prince's chamber" (tel. 0662/825-858 to reserve, you can pick up tickets at the door). This medieval-feeling room atop the fortress has windows overlooking the city, and the concert gives you a chance to enjoy the grand city view and a stroll through the castle courtyard. (The €8.50 round-trip funicular is discounted to €3.20 within an hour of the show if you have a concert ticket.)

The **"5:00 Concert"** next to St. Peter's is cheaper, since it features young artists (€10, July–Sept daily except Wed, 45 min, tel. 0662/8445-7619, www.sbg.ac.at/mus/5.htm). While the series is formally named after the brother of Joseph Haydn, it offers music from various masters.

Salzburg's impressive **Marionette Theater** performs operas with remarkable marionettes and recorded music (€22–35, nearly nightly June–Sept except Sun, also some in May, tel. 0662/872-406, www .marionetten.at).

For those who'd like some classical music but would rather not sit through a concert, Stiftskeller St. Peter offers a **Mozart Dinner Concert,** with a traditional candlelit meal and Mozart's greatest hits performed by a string quartet and singers in historic costumes gavotting among the tables. In this elegant Baroque setting, you'll enjoy three courses of food mixed with three 20-minute courses of top-quality music (€45, almost nightly at 20:00, see "Eating," page 416, call to reserve at 0662/828-6950).

The **S.O.M. dinner show** at the Sternbräu Inn (see "Eating," page 416) is Broadway in a dirndl with tired food. But it's a good show, and *S.O.M.* fans are mesmerized by the evening. A piano player and a hard-working quartet of singers perform an entertaining mix of *Sound of Music* hits and traditional folk songs (€43 includes a schnitzel and crisp apple strudel dinner at 19:30, €29 for 20:30 show only, those booking direct get a 10 percent discount with this book, reserve ahead, fun for families, daily mid-May–mid-Oct, Griesgasse 23, tel. 0662/826-617, www.soundofmusicshow.com).

SLEEP CODE

(€1 = about $1.10, country code: 43, area code: 0662)

Sleep Code: **S** = Single, **D** = Double/Twin, **T** = Triple, **Q** = Quad, **b** = bathroom, **s** = shower only, **no CC** = Credit Cards not accepted, **SE** = Speaks English, **NSE** = No English. Unless otherwise noted, credit cards are accepted, English is spoken, and breakfast is included.

To help you sort easily through these listings, I've divided the rooms into three categories, based on the price for a standard double room with bath:

$$$ **Higher Priced**—Most rooms €90 or more.
 $$ **Moderately Priced**—Most rooms between €60–90.
  $ **Lower Priced**—Most rooms €60 or less.

Finding a room in Salzburg, even during the music festival, is usually easy. Rates rise significantly (20–30 percent) during the music festival (mid-July through Aug) and sometimes also around Easter and Christmas; these higher prices do not appear in the price ranges included in hotel listings below.

SLEEPING

Linzergasse and Rupertgasse

These listings are between the train station and the old town in a pleasant neighborhood (with easy parking), a 15-minute walk from the train station (for directions, see "Arrival in Salzburg," above) and a 10- to 15-minute walk to the old town. If you're coming from the old town, simply cross the main bridge (Staatsbrücke) to the mostly traffic-free Linzergasse.

$$$ Altstadthotel Wolf Dietrich, around the corner from Linzergasse on Wolf-Dietrich Strasse, is well located and a reasonable big-hotel option, if that's what you want. Their main hotel, at Wolf-Dietrich Strasse 7, has 27 rooms and an elevator (Sb-€54–109, Db-€100–154, family deals, €40 more during festival time, complex pricing but readers of this book get a 10 percent discount on prevailing price, garage-€12/day, pool, sauna). Their annex—the **Hotel Residenz** across the street, at #4—has 14 very similar rooms, cheaper prices, and no elevator (Db-€99–149; contact for both hotels: tel. 0662/871-275, fax 0662/882-320, www.salzburg-hotel.at, office@salzburg-hotel.at).

$$$ Hotel Trumer Stube, a few blocks from the river just off

Salzburg Center Hotels

1. Hotels Wolf Dietrich & Residenz
2. Hotel Trumer Stube
3. Hotel Goldene Krone
4. To Hotel Bergland
   & Hotel-Pension Jedermann
5. Institute St. Sebastian
6. Pension zum Jungen Fuchs
7. Blaue Gans Arthotel
8. Hotel Weisse Taube
9. Gasthaus zur Goldenen Ente
10. Hotel am Dom
11. Hotel Weisses Kreuz
12. Launderette

Linzergasse, has 20 clean, cozy rooms and a friendly, can-do owner (Sb-€56–70, Db-€89–103, Tb-€89–125, Qb-€132–140, prices depend on room size, some taller guests consider ceilings low in top-floor rooms, no CC except to hold reservation, non-smoking, elevator, small breakfast in small breakfast room, Internet access-€4/hr, Bergstrasse 6, tel. 0662/874-776, fax 0662/874-326, www.trumer-stube.at, info@trumer-stube.at, pleasant Silvia SE).

$$ Hotel Goldene Krone, about five blocks from the river, is big, quiet, and creaky-traditional but modern, with comforts rare in this price range (25 rooms, Sb-€55, Db-€80, Tb-€115, claim your 10 percent discount with this book, closed in March, elevator, relaxing backyard garden, Linzergasse 48, tel. 0662/872-300, fax 0662/8723-0066, office@hotel-goldenekrone.com, Claudia and Günther SE). Guests can watch *The Sound of Music* and other Salzburg videos in the lounge when they like. Every night at 18:00, Günther offers a free orientation talk on Salzburg. He also guides a just-for-fun, low-key, four-hour walking and biking tour of untouristy Salzburg (€5, May–Sept in good weather only, Tue, Thu, and Sat at 14:00, must reserve ahead).

$$ Pensions on Rupertgasse: These two hotels are about five blocks farther from the river up Paris-Lodron Strasse to Rupertgasse, a breeze for drivers but with more street noise than the places on Linzergasse. They're both modern and well-run—excellent values if you don't mind being a bit away from the old town. **Bergland Hotel** is charming and classy, with comfortable neo-rustic rooms (Sb-€55, Db-€85, Tb-€95, Qb-€115, elevator, Internet access-€0.15/min, English library, bike rental, Rupertgasse 15, tel. 0662/872-318, fax 0662/872-3188, www.berglandhotel.at, kuhn@berglandhotel.at, Kuhn family). The similar, boutique-like **Hotel-Pension Jedermann,** a few doors down, is also tastefully done and comfortable, with artsy decor and a backyard garden (Sb-€55, Db-€75–85, Tb-€105, Qb-€135, Internet access-€0.15/min, Rupertgasse 25, tel. 0662/873-241, fax 0662/873-2419, www.hotel-jedermann.com, office@hotel-jedermann.com).

$ Institute St. Sebastian—a somewhat sterile but very clean, historic building—houses female students from various Salzburg colleges, and rents some rooms, October through June. From July through September, they rent all 50 rooms to travelers. The building has spacious public areas, a roof garden, and some of the best rooms and dorm beds in town for the money. The immaculate doubles come with modern baths and head-to-toe twin beds (Sb-€33, Db-€54, Tb-€69, Qb-€84, elevator, includes small breakfast, self-service laundry-€3/load, reception open July–Sept 7:30–12:00 & 13:00–22:00, Oct–June 8:00–12:00 & 16:00–21:00, Linzergasse 41, enter through arch at #37, tel. 0662/871-386, fax 0662/8713-8685, www.st-sebastian-salzburg.at, office@st-sebastian-salzburg.at). Students like the €17 bunks in 4- to 10-bed dorms (€2 less if you have sheets, no lockout time, free lockers, free showers). You'll find self-service kitchens on each floor (fridge space is free; request a key).

$ Pension zum Jungen Fuchs terrifies claustrophobes and titillates troglodytes. It's plain and sometimes smelly, but sleepable and wonderfully located in a funky, dumpy old building (16 rooms, S-€27, D-€38, Db-€65, T-€50, no breakfast, no CC, just up from Hotel Krone at Linzergasse 54, tel. 0662/875-496).

In or above the Old Town

$$$ The ultramodern **Blaue Gans Arthotel** gives you a break from charming old Salzburg—with artsy public spaces and 40 sleek, Scandinavian-style rooms beautifully located right on Getreidegasse. The standard rooms are supposedly smaller than the €20-more-expensive superior rooms—but there's really not much difference (Sb-€99, standard Db-€109, superior Db-€129, deluxe Db-€159, junior suite-€169, non-smoking rooms, elevator, Getreidegasse 41–43, tel. 0662/842-4910, fax 0662/842-4919, www.blauegans.at, office@blauegans.at).

$$$ Hotel Weisse Taube is a big, quiet, old-feeling 30-room place with more comfort than character, well-located about a block off Mozartplatz (Sb-€59–67, Db-€93–122, prices depend on room size, elevator, tel. 0662/842-404, fax 0662/841-783, Kaigasse 9, www.weissetaube.at, hotel@weissetaube.at).

$$ Gasthaus zur Goldenen Ente is in a 600-year-old building with medieval stone arches and narrow stairs. Located above a good restaurant, it's as central as you can be on a pedestrian street in old Salzburg. The 17 rooms are modern yet worn, and the service is uneven—from friendly to brusque to nonexistent (Sb-€53, Db-€79 with this book, extra person-€29, in July–Aug and Dec: Sb-€61, Db-€98 with this book, elevator, parking-€6/day, Goldgasse 10, tel. 0662/845-622, fax 0662/845-6229, www.ente.at, hotel@ente.at, Robert and family Steinwender SE).

$$ Hotel am Dom is just up Goldgasse from the Goldenen Ente—and equally well-located. The 14 rooms are old, basic, but well-maintained (Sb-€76–79, Db-€79–117, extra bed-€33, prices slightly lower Nov–mid-June, non-smoking rooms, Goldgasse 17, tel. 0662/|872-765, fax 0662/8727-6555, www.amdom.at, bach@salzburg.co.at, family Bachleitner).

$$ Hotel Restaurant Weisses Kreuz is a Tolkienesque little family-run place on a cobbled backstreet under the fortress. It's away from the crowds and offers a fine restaurant, four rooms, and a peaceful roof garden (Sb-€55–73, Db-€66–90, Tb-€120, prices depend on room size, garage, Bierjodlgasse 6, tel. 0662/845-641, fax 0662/845-6419, weisses.kreuz@eunet.at).

$ Naturfreundehaus, also called "Gasthaus Stadtalm," is a local version of a mountaineer's hut and a great budget alternative. In a forest guarded by singing birds, it's snuggled in the remains of a 15th-century castle wall atop the little mountain overlooking Salzburg, with magnificent town and mountain views (€13.50/person in 2-, 4-, and 6-bed dorms, includes breakfast and shower, no CC, €6 bike rental, open mid-April–Oct, 2 min from top of €2.60 round-trip Mönchsberg elevator, Mönchsberg 19-C, tel. & fax 0662/841-729, www.stadtalm.com, Peter SE).

Away from the Center

$$$ **Hotel am Nussdorferhof** is a creatively run, 29-room place, located about halfway between the old town and the *Zimmer* on Moosstrasse (listed below). Run enthusiastically by Herbert and Ilse, the hotel has all the amenities including a sauna, whirlpool, and Internet access. It's a 15-minute walk or short bus ride from the old town (Sb-€68, Db-€98, big Db-€115, 1–2 kids sleep free, claim a 10 percent discount with this book when you reserve, some waterbeds, some theme rooms, elevator, 1 free 24-hr bus pass per person per stay, attached Italian restaurant, shuttle to/from train station or airport for a fee—just call, Moosstrasse 36, bus stop Nussdorferstrasse, tel. 0662/824-838, fax 0662/824-8389, www.nussdorferhof.at, info@nussdorferhof.at).

$ **Pension Bloberger Hof** is comfortable and friendly, with a rural location and 20 modern, good-value rooms. It's just beyond the *Zimmer* on Moosstrasse (listed below), and reached by the same bus #60 from the center (Sb-€32–46, Db-€51–55, big new Db with balcony-€79–85, extra bed-€15, family apartment, non-smoking rooms, free loaner bikes, will pick up at station, Hammerauerstrasse 4, bus stop: Hammerauerstrasse, tel. 0662/830-227, fax 0662/827-061, www.blobergerhof.at, office@blobergerhof.at).

Zimmer (Private Rooms)

These are generally roomy and comfortable and come with a good breakfast, easy parking, and tourist information. Off-season, competition softens prices. They are a bus ride from town, but, with a day pass and the frequent service, this shouldn't keep you away. In fact, most will happily pick you up at the train station if you simply telephone them and ask. Most will also do laundry for a small fee for those staying at least two nights. Unsavory *Zimmer* skimmers lurk at the station. Ignore them. I've listed prices for two nights or more. If staying only one night, expect a 10 percent surcharge.

Beyond the Train Station

$ **Brigitte Lenglachner** fills her big, traditional home with a warm welcome (S-€24, D-€37, Db-€44, T-€50, Tb-€64, Qb-€88, apartment with kitchen for up to 5, Scheibenweg 8, tel. & fax 0662/438-044, bedandbreakfast4u@yahoo.de). It's a 10-minute walk northeast of the station (cross pedestrian Pioneer Bridge, turn right, walk along the river to the third street—Scheibenweg—turn left, and it's halfway down on the right).

$ **Trude Poppenberger's** three pleasant rooms share a long, mountain-view balcony (S-€24, D-€37, T-€55; Wachtelgasse 9, tel. & fax 0662/430-094, www.trudeshome.com, mail@trudeshome.com). Call for a pick-up or walk 30 minutes northwest of the station (cross pedestrian Pioneer Bridge, turn right, walk along river 300 yards, cross canal, left on Linke Glanzeile for 3 min, right onto Wachtelgasse).

On Moosstrasse

The busy street called Moosstrasse, southwest of Mönchsberg, is lined with *Zimmer*. Those farther out are farmhouses. Handy bus #60 connects Moosstrasse to the center frequently (Mon–Fri 4/hr until 17:00, then 2/hr, Sat 4/hr until 12:00, then 2/hr)—but service drops to a frustrating once per hour on Sundays. To get to these from the train station, take bus #1, #5, #6, #51, or #55 to Makartplatz, where you'll change to #60. If you are coming from the old town, catch bus #60 from Hanuschplatz, just downstream of the Staatsbrücke near the *Tabak* kiosk. Buy a €1.70 *Einzelkarte-Kernzone* ticket (for 1 trip) or a €3.20 *Tageskarte* (for the entire day) from the streetside machine and punch it when you board the bus. If you're driving from the center, go through the tunnel, straight on Neutorstrasse, and take the fourth left onto Moosstrasse.

$ **Frau Ballwein** offers cozy, charming, fresh rooms in two buildings—one of them a 160-year-old farmhouse that feels new (S-€23, D-€40, Db-€48–50, Tb-€65–70, family deals, farm-fresh breakfasts, no CC, non-smoking, Moosstrasse 69-A, bus stop: Gsengerweg, tel. & fax 0662/824-029, www.privatvermieter.com/haus-ballwein, haus.ballwein @gmx.net).

$ **Helga Bankhammer** rents four old-feeling but pleasant rooms in a farmhouse, with a real dairy farm out back (D-€40, Db-€45, no surcharge for one-nighters, family deals, non-smoking, laundry-about €5/load, Moosstrasse 77, bus stop: Marienbad, tel. & fax 0662/830-067, www .privatzimmer.at/helga.bankhammer, helga.bankhammer@telering.at).

$ **Haus Reichl,** with three good rooms ranging from fresh to musty, feels the most remote (Db-€48, Tb-€66, Qb with balcony and view-€80, non-smoking, between Ballwein and Bankhammer B&Bs, 200 yards down Reiterweg to #52, bus stop: Gsengerweg, tel. & fax 0662/826-248, www.privatzimmer.at/haus-reichl, haus.reichl@telering.at).

Near the Train Station

$$ **Pension Adlerhof,** a plain and decent old place, is two blocks in front of the train station (left off Kaiserschutzenstrasse), but a 15-minute walk from the sightseeing action. It has a quirky staff and 35 well-maintained rooms (Sb-€55–60, D-€52–64, Db-€78–88, Tb-€90–102,

Qb-€112–120, 10 percent cheaper off-season and during slow times, no CC, Internet access-€7/hr, elevator, Elisabethstrasse 25, tel. 0662/875-236, fax 0662/873-6636, www.pension-adlerhof.com, adlerhof@pension -adlerhof.at, Kurt and Inge Pregartbauer).

$ International Youth Hotel, a.k.a. the "Yo-Ho," is the most lively, handy, and American of Salzburg's hostels (€15 in 6- to 8-bed dorms, €18 in dorms with b, D-€20/person, Db-€23/person, Q-€17/person, Qb-€20/person, prices lower for 2- or 3-night stays, sheets included, breakfast cheap, 6 blocks from station toward Linzergasse and 6 blocks from river at Paracelsusstrasse 9, tel. 0662/879-649, fax 0662/878-810, www.yoho.at, office@yoho.at). This easygoing place speaks English first; has cheap meals, 160 beds, lockers, Internet access, laundry, tour discounts, and no curfew; plays *The Sound of Music* free daily at 13:30; runs a lively bar; and welcomes anyone of any age. The noisy atmosphere and lack of a curfew can make it hard to sleep.

EATING

Salzburg boasts many inexpensive, fun, and atmospheric places to eat. I'm a sucker for big cellars with their smoky, Old World atmosphere, heavy medieval arches, time-darkened paintings, antlers, hearty meals, and plump patrons. These places, all centrally located in the old town, are famous with visitors but are also enjoyed by the locals.

Gasthaus zum Wilder Mann is the place if the weather's bad and you're in the mood for *Hofbräu* atmosphere and a hearty, cheap meal at a shared table in one small, well-antlered room (€6–8 daily specials, Mon–Sat 11:00–21:00, closed Sun, smoky, 2 min from Mozart's birthplace, enter from Getreidegasse 22 or Griesgasse 17, tel. 0662/841-787). For a quick lunch, get the *Bauernschmaus,* a mountain of dumplings, kraut, and peasant's meats (€8).

Stiftskeller St. Peter has been in business for more than 1,000 years—it was mentioned in the biography of Charlemagne. It's classy (with strolling musicians) and central as can be, serving uninspired traditional Austrian cuisine (meals €15–25, daily 11:00–24:00, indoor/outdoor seating, next to St. Peter's church at foot of Mönchsberg, restaurant tel. 0662/841-268). They host the Mozart Dinner Concert described in "Music Scene," above (€45, nearly nightly at 20:00, call 0662/828-6950 to reserve).

Gasthaus zur Goldenen Ente (see "Sleeping," page 410) serves great food in an elegant, subdued hotel dining room or on a quiet pedestrian lane. The chef, Robert, specializes in roast duck *(Ente)* and Tirolean traditions. But he'll happily replace your kraut and dumplings with a wonderful selection of steamed green and orange vegetables for no extra charge. Their *Salzburger Nockerl,* the mountainous sweet soufflé served

Salzburg Center Restaurants

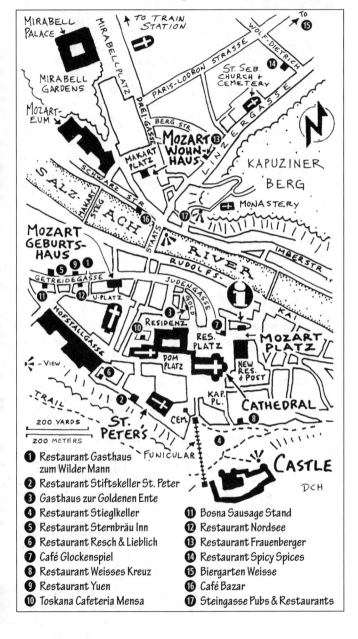

1. Restaurant Gasthaus zum Wilder Mann
2. Restaurant Stiftskeller St. Peter
3. Gasthaus zur Goldenen Ente
4. Restaurant Stieglkeller
5. Restaurant Sternbräu Inn
6. Restaurant Resch & Lieblich
7. Café Glockenspiel
8. Restaurant Weisses Kreuz
9. Restaurant Yuen
10. Toskana Cafeteria Mensa
11. Bosna Sausage Stand
12. Restaurant Nordsee
13. Restaurant Frauenberger
14. Restaurant Spicy Spices
15. Biergarten Weisse
16. Café Bazar
17. Steingasse Pubs & Restaurants

all over town, is big enough for four—try it (Tue–Sat 11:30–21:00, closed Sun–Mon, Goldgasse 10, tel. 0662/845-622).

Stieglkeller is a huge, atmospheric institution that has several rustic rooms and outdoor garden seating with a great rooftop view of the old town (May–Sept daily 10:00–23:00, closed Oct–April, 50 yards uphill from the lift to the fortress, Festungsgasse 10, tel. 0662/842-681).

Sternbräu Inn is a sprawling complex of popular eateries (traditional, Italian, self-serve, and vegetarian) in a cheery garden setting—explore both courtyards before choosing a seat (most restaurants open daily 9:00–24:00). One fancy, air-conditioned room hosts the *Sound of Music* dinner show (see "Music Scene," page 408).

Resch & Lieblich, wedged between the cliffside and the back of the big concert hall, is a rough and characteristic place popular with locals for salads, goulash, and light meals (daily 10:00–23:00, closed Sun off-season, indoor/outdoor seating in rustic little cellar or under umbrellas on square, Toscaninihof, tel. 0662/843-675).

Café Glockenspiel, on Mozartplatz 2, is the place to see and be seen. It's overpriced, but—like St. Mark's Square in Venice—it's worth it if you want to linger and enjoy the spot (daily 9:00–23:00, closes earlier off-season, tel. 0662/841-403).

Restaurant Weisses Kreuz, nestled behind the cathedral and under the fortress, serves good Balkan cuisine in a pleasant dining room (daily 11:30–14:45 & 17:00–22:45, closed Tue Oct–mid-June, Bierjodlgasse 6, tel. 0662/845-641).

For a break from the *Wurst,* consider **Restaurant Yuen,** with darn good Chinese food and friendly service (daily 11:30–23:00, in courtyard at Getreidegasse 24, tel. 0662/843-770).

Eating Cheap in the Old Town

Toskana Cafeteria Mensa is the students' lunch place, fast and cheap—with fine indoor seating and a great courtyard for sitting outside with students and teachers instead of tourists. They serve a daily soup and main course special for €3.50 (Mon–Thu 8:30–17:00, Fri 8:30–15:00, hot meals served 11:00–13:30 only, closed Sat–Sun, behind the Residenz, in the courtyard opposite Sigmund-Haffnergasse 16).

Sausage stands serve the local fast food. The best places (like the Altstadt-Imbiss on the side of the Collegiate Church just off Universitätsplatz) use the same boiling water all day, which fills the weenies with more flavor. Key words: *Weisswurst*—boiled white sausage, *Bosna*—with onions and curry, *Käsekrainer*—with melted cheese inside, *Debreziner*—spicy Hungarian, *Frankfurter*—our weenie, *frische*—fresh ("eat before the noon bells"), and *Senf*—mustard (ask for sweet—*süss* or sharp—*scharf*). Only a tourist puts the sausage in a bun like a hot dog. Munch alternately between the meat and the bread (that's why you have 2 hands), and you'll look like a local. Generally, the darker the weenie, the spicier it is. The best spicy sausage is at the 54-year-old **Bosna Stand,** run by the chatty Frau Ebner (€2.40, to go only, Mon–Fri 11:00–19:00, May–Dec also Sat 11:00–17:00, July–Dec also Sun 16:00–20:00, hiding down the tunnel marked #33 across from Getriedegasse 40).

Picnickers will appreciate the bustling morning **produce market** (daily except Sun) on Universitätsplatz, behind Mozart's house (see "Self-Guided Old Town Walking Tour," page 396).

Nordsee, a popular chain, serves good, fast, and inexpensive seafood next to Mozart's House on Getriedegasse.

Away from the Center

These two places are on the old-town side of the river, about a 15-minute walk along the river (river on your right) from the Staatsbrücke bridge.

Augustiner Bräustübl, a monk-run brewery, is rustic and crude. It's closed for lunch, but on busy nights, it's like a Munich beer hall with no music but the volume turned up. When it's cool, you'll enjoy a historic setting with beer-sloshed and smoke-stained halls. On balmy evenings, it's a Monet painting with beer breath under chestnut trees in the garden. Local students mix with tourists eating hearty slabs of schnitzel with their fingers or cold meals from the self-serve picnic counter, while children frolic on the playground kegs. Waiters only bring drinks. For food, go up the stairs, survey the hallway of deli counters, and assemble your meal (or, as long as you buy a drink, you can bring in your own picnic, open daily 15:00–23:00, Augustinergasse 4, tel. 0662/431-246; head up Müllner Hauptstrasse northwest along the river and ask for "Müllnerbräu," its local nickname). Don't be fooled by second-rate gardens serving the same beer nearby. Augustiner Bräustübl is a huge, 1,000-seat place within the Augustiner brewery. For your beer: Pick up a half-liter or full-liter mug (*shank* means self-serve price, *bedienung* is the price with waiter service), pay the lady, wash your mug, give Mr. Keg your receipt and empty mug, and you will be made happy.

For dessert—after a visit to the strudel kiosk—enjoy the incomparable floodlit view of old Salzburg from the nearby Müllnersteg pedestrian bridge and a riverside stroll home.

Krimplestätter employs 450 years of experience serving authentic old-Salzburger food in its authentic old-Austrian interior or its cheery garden (Tue–Sun 11:00–24:00, closed Mon all year and Sun Sept–April, Müllner Hauptstrasse 31, tel. 0662/432-274). For fine food with a wild finale, eat here and drink at the nearby Augustiner Bräustübl.

On or near Linzergasse

These cheaper places are near the recommended hotels on Linzergasse.

Frauenberger is friendly, picnic-ready, and inexpensive, with indoor or outdoor seating (Mon 8:00–14:00, Tue–Fri 8:00–18:00, Sat 8:00–12:30, closed Sun, *Wurst* grill open longer hours and on Sun, across from Linzergasse 16).

Spicy Spices is a trippy vegetarian-Indian restaurant serving tasty curry and rice take-out, samosas, organic salads, vegan soups, and fresh juices (€5 lunch specials, Mon–Sat 10:00–22:00, Sun 12:00–21:00, Wolf-Dietrich Strasse 1, tel. 0662/870-712).

The very local **Biergarten Weisse** is closer to the hotels on Rupertgasse and away from the tourists (Mon–Sat 10:30–2:00, Sun 16:00–24:00, on Rupertgasse east of Bayerhamerstrasse, tel. 0662/872-246).

The copper-topped **Café Bazar,** overlooking the river between the Mirabell Gardens and the Staatsbrücke, is a great place for a classy drink with an old-town and castle view (Mon–Sat 7:30–24:00, closed Sun, Schwarzstrasse 3, tel. 0662/874-278).

Steingasse Pub Crawl

For a fun post-concert activity, crawl through medieval Steingasse's trendy pubs, open until the wee hours. This is a young and very hip scene: dark bars filled with well-dressed twentysomethings lazily smoking cigarettes and talking philosophy, with avant-garde Euro-pop throbbing on the soundtrack. Most of the pubs are in cellar-like caves...extremely atmospheric. (For more on Steingasse, see "Across the River," page 402.)

At the Linzergasse end of Steingasse are a couple of places that serve food and are lively earlier in the evening. **Pepe Gonzales,** with Mexican decor, serves tapas (nightly 18:30–3:00, Steingasse 3, 0662/873-662). Next door, **Shrimps** is the least claustrophobic of these places, with international cuisine (nightly 17:00–1:00, Steingasse 5).

A block farther down Steingasse, the scene doesn't get rolling until later. The tiny **Fridrich,** with lots of mirrors and a silver ceiling fan, specializes in wine (nightly from 17:00, Steingasse 15, tel. 0662/876-218). Next door, **Soulen Sprung** wins the "Best Atmosphere" award (nightly 21:00–4:00, Steingasse 13, tel. 0662/875-918). First you have to ring the bell to get inside the locked door (don't be shy). Then you reach the hellish interior—lots of stone and red decor, with mountains of melted wax beneath age-old candlesticks.

After you close down these four places, consider the next street down—Giselakai, along the river—also lined with trendy pubs.

TRANSPORTATION CONNECTIONS

By train, Salzburg is the first stop over the German–Austrian border. This means that if Salzburg is your only stop in Austria, and you're using a Eurail Selectpass that does not include Austria, you don't have to pay extra or add Austria to your pass to get here.

By train to: **Innsbruck** (direct every 2 hrs, 2 hrs), **Vienna** (2/hr, 3.5 hrs), **Hallstatt** (hrly, 50 min to Attnang Puchheim, 20-min wait, then 90 min to Hallstatt), **Reutte** (every 2 hrs, 4 hrs, transfer to a bus in Innsbruck), **Munich** (2/hr, 1.5–2 hrs). Train info: tel. 051717 (wait through long German recording for operator).

By car: To leave town driving west, go under the Mönchsberg tunnel and follow blue A1 signs to Munich. It's 90 minutes from Salzburg to Innsbruck.

Route Tips for Drivers

Into Salzburg from Munich: After crossing the border, stay on the autobahn, taking the Süd Salzburg exit in the direction of Anif. First, you'll pass Schloss Hellbrunn (and zoo), then the TI and a great park-and-ride service. Get sightseeing information and a €3.20 one-day *Tageskarte* bus pass from the TI (July–Aug daily 9:00–19:00, Easter–June and Sept–Oct Mon–Sat 10:00–18:00, closed Sun, closed Nov–Easter, tel. 0662/8898-7360), park your car (free), and catch the shuttle bus (€1.70, included in day ticket, every 5 min, bus #49, #51, or #95) into town. Mozart never drove in the old town, and neither should you. If you don't believe in park-and-rides, the easiest, cheapest, most central parking lot is the 1,500-car Altstadt lot in the tunnel under the Mönchsberg (€14/day; note your slot number and which of the twin lots you're in, tel. 0662/846-434). Your hotel may provide discounted parking passes.

From Salzburg to Hallstatt (50 miles): Get on the Munich–Wien autobahn (blue signs), head for Vienna, exit at Thalgau, and follow signs to Hof, Fuschl, and St. Gilgen. The Salzburg-to-Hallstatt road passes two luge rides (see Hallstatt chapter), St. Gilgen (pleasant but touristy), and Bad Ischl (the center of the Salzkammergut with a spa, the emperor's villa if you need a Hapsburg history fix, and a good TI—tel. 06132/277-570).

Hallstatt is basically traffic-free. To park, try parking lot #1 in the tunnel above the town (free with guest card). Otherwise, try the lakeside lots (a pleasant 10- to 20-min walk from the town center) after the tunnel on the far side of town. If you're traveling off-season and staying downtown, you can drive in and park by the boat dock. (For more on parking in Hallstatt, see the next chapter.)

HALLSTATT AND THE SALZKAMMERGUT: AUSTRIA'S LAKE DISTRICT

Commune with nature in Austria's Lake District. "The hills are alive," and you're surrounded by the loveliness that has turned on everyone from Emperor Franz Josef to Julie Andrews. This is *Sound of Music* country. Idyllic and majestic, but not rugged, it's a gentle land of lakes, forested mountains, and storybook villages, rich in hiking opportunities and inexpensive lodging. Settle down in the postcard-pretty, lake-cuddling town of Hallstatt.

ORIENTATION

(area code: 06134)

Lovable Hallstatt is a tiny town bullied onto a ledge between a selfish mountain and a swan-ruled lake, with a waterfall ripping furiously through its middle. It can be toured on foot in about 15 minutes. The town is one of Europe's oldest, going back centuries before Christ. The symbol of Hallstatt, which you'll see all over town, is two adjacent spirals—a design based on jewelry found in Bronze Age Celtic graves high in the nearby mountains.

The charms of Hallstatt are the village and its lakeside setting. Go there to relax, nibble, wander, and paddle. While tourist crowds can trample much of Hallstatt's charm in August, the place is almost dead in the off-season. The lake is famous for its good fishing and pure water.

Tourist Information: The friendly and helpful TI, on the main drag, can explain hikes and excursions, arrange private tours of Hallstatt (€65), and find you a room (April–Oct Mon–Fri 9:00–12:00 & 14:00–17:00, in July–Aug also Sat–Sun 10:00–14:00, Nov–March Mon–Fri 9:00–13:00, closed Sat–Sun, a block from Marktplatz toward lakefront parking, above post office, Seestrasse 169, tel. 06134/8208, www.hallstatt.net or www.inneres-salzkammergut.at). On Saturdays in July and August, the TI offers a €5 tour of the town in English (check with TI for details).

Hallstatt

① Gasthof Zauner
② Pension Hallberg
③ Gasthof Simony
④ Hotel/Restaurant Bräugasthof
⑤ To Gasthof Grüner Anger & Launderette
⑥ Helga Lenz Rooms
⑦ Haus Trausner Rooms
⑧ Herta Höll Rooms
⑨ Gasthaus zur Mühle Hostel
⑩ Pension Seethaler
⑪ Pension Sarstein
⑫ Rest. Grüner Baum
⑬ Strand Café

Planning Your Time

While there are plenty of lakes and charming villages, Hallstatt is really the only one that matters. One night and a few hours to browse are all you'll need to fall in love. To relax or take a hike in the surroundings, give it two nights and a day. It's a relaxing break between Salzburg and Vienna. My best Austrian week: the two big cities (Salzburg and Vienna), a bike ride along the Danube, and a stay in Hallstatt.

Arrival in Hallstatt

By Train: Hallstatt's train station is a wide spot on the tracks across the lake. *Stefanie* (a boat) meets you at the station and glides scenically across the lake into town (€1.90, meets each train until about 18:30—don't arrive after that). The last departing boat-train connection leaves Hallstatt around 18:15, and the first boat goes in the morning at 6:50 (9:20 on Sun). Walk left from the boat dock for the TI and most hotels. Since there's no train station in town, the TI can help you find schedule information, or check www.oebb.at.

By Car: The main road skirts Hallstatt via a long tunnel above the town. Parking is tight mid-June through mid-October. Hallstatt has several numbered parking areas outside the town center. Parking lot #1 is in the tunnel above the town (swing through to check for a spot, free with guest card). Otherwise, several numbered lots are just after the tunnel. If you have a hotel reservation, the guard will let you drive into town to drop your bags (ask if your hotel has any in-town parking). It's a lovely 10- to 20-minute lakeside walk to the center of town from the lots. Without a guest card, you'll pay €4.20 per day for parking. Off-season parking in town is easy and free.

Helpful Hints

Bike Rental: Hotel Grüner Baum, facing the market square, rents bikes (€6/half-day, €11/full day).

Parks and Swimming: Green and peaceful lakeside parks line the south end of Lake Hallstatt. If you walk 10 minutes south of town to Hallstatt-Lahn, you'll find a grassy public park, playground, and swimming area *(Badestrand)* with a fun man-made play island *(Bade-Insel)*.

Views: For a great view over Hallstatt, hike above Helga Lenz's *Zimmer* as far as you like (see "Sleeping," page 430), or climb any path leading up the hill. The 40-minute steep hike down from the salt-mine tour gives the best views (see "Sights," page 426).

Internet: Try Hallstatt Umbrella Bar (€4/hr, summers only, weather permitting—since it's literally under a big umbrella, halfway between Lahn boat dock and Museum Square at Seestrasse 145).

Laundry: A small full-service launderette is at the campground up from the *Bade-Insel,* just off the main road (about €8/load, mid-April–mid-Oct daily 7:00–12:00 & 15:00–22:00, closed off-season, tel. 06134/83224). In the center, Hotel Grüner Baum does laundry for non-guests (€11/load, facing Market Square).

HALLSTATT HISTORIC TOWN WALK

This short walk starts at the dock.

Boat Landing—There was a Hallstatt before there was a Rome. In fact, because of the importance of salt mining here, an entire epoch—the Hallstatt era, from 800 to 400 B.C.—is named for this important spot. Through the centuries, salt was traded and people came and went by boat. You'll still see the traditional *Fuhr* boats, designed to carry heavy loads in shallow water.

Towering above the town is the Catholic church. Its faded St. Christopher—patron saint of travelers with his cane and baby Jesus on his shoulder—watched over those sailing in and out. Until 1875, the only way into town was by boat. Then came the train and the road. The good ship *Stefanie* shuttles travelers back and forth from here to the Hallstatt train station immediately across the lake. The *Bootverleih* sign advertises boat rentals (see "Lake Trip," below).

Notice the one-lane road out of town (with the waiting time, width, and height posted). Until 1966, when a bigger tunnel was built above Hallstatt, all the traffic crept single file right through the town.

Look down the shore at the huge homes. Several families lived in each of these houses back when Hallstatt's population was about double its present 1,000; today, many of them rent rooms to visitors.

Parking is tight here in the tourist season. Locals and hotels have cards getting them into the prime town-center lot. From October through May, the barricade is lifted and anyone can park here. Hallstatt is snowbound for about three months each winter, but the lake hasn't frozen over since 1981.

See any swans? They've patrolled the lake like they own it since the 1860s, when Emperor Franz Josef and Empress Sissy—the Princess Di of her day—made this region their annual holiday retreat. Sissy loved swans, so locals made sure she'd see them here. During this period, the Romantics discovered Hallstatt, many top painters worked here, and the town got its first hotel.

Tiny Hallstatt has two big churches—Protestant (step into its cemetery, which is actually a grassy lakeside playground) and Catholic up above (described below, with its fascinating bone chapel). After the Reformation, most of Hallstatt was Protestant. Then, under Hapsburg rule, it was mostly Catholic. Today, 60 percent of the town is Catholic. Walk over the town's stream, past the Protestant church, one block to the...

Market Square—In 1750, a fire leveled this part of town. The buildings you see now are all late-18th-century and built of stone rather than burnable wood. Take a close look at the two-dimensional, up-against-the-wall pear tree (it likes the sun-warmed wall). The statue features the Holy Trinity. Continue a block past Gasthof Simony to the pair of phone booths and step into the...

Museum Square—Because 20th-century Hallstatt was of no industrial importance, it was untouched by World War II. But once upon a time, its salt was worth defending. High above, peeking out of the trees, is Rudolf's Tower (Rudolfsturm). Originally a 13th-century watchtower protecting the salt mines, and later the mansion of a salt-mine boss, it's now a restaurant with a great view. A zigzag trail connects the town with Rudolfsturm and the salt mines just beyond. The big white houses by the waterfall were water-powered mills that once ground Hallstatt's grain. If you hike up a few blocks, you'll see the river raging through town. Around you are the town's TI, post office, a museum, city hall, and the Dachstein Sport shop (with a prehistoric basement, described below). The statue on the square is of the mine manager who excavated prehistoric graves around 1850. Much of the *Schmuck* (jewelry) sold locally is inspired by the jewelry found in the area's Bronze Age tombs.

For thousands of years, people have been leaching salt out of this mountain. A brine spring sprung here, attracting Bronze Age people around 1500 B.C. Later, they dug tunnels to mine the rock, which was 70 percent salt, dissolved it into a brine, and distilled out salt—precious for preserving meat (and making french fries so tasty). For a look at early salt-mining implements, visit the museum.

SIGHTS

▲▲**Hallstatt's Catholic Church and Bone Chapel**—The Catholic church overlooks the town from above. From near the boat dock, hike up the covered wooden stairway and follow signs to *Kath. Kirche*. The lovely church has 500-year-old altars and frescoes dedicated to St. Barbara (patron of miners) and St. Catherine (patron of foresters—lots of wood was needed to fortify the many miles of tunnels and boil the brine to distill out the salt). The last priest modernized parts of the church, but since Hallstatt is a UNESCO World Heritage Site, now they're changing it all back to its original state.

Behind the church, in the well-tended graveyard, is the 12th-century Chapel of St. Michael (even older than the church). Its bone chapel—or charnel house *(Beinhaus)*—contains more than 600 painted skulls. Each skull has been lovingly named, dated, and decorated (skulls with dark, thick garlands are oldest—18th century, those with flowers more recent—19th century). Space was so limited in this cemetery that bones had only 12 peaceful, buried years here before making way for the freshly dead. Many of the dug-up bones and skulls ended up in this chapel. They stopped this practice in the 1960s, about the same time the Catholic Church began permitting cremation (€1, mid-May–Sept daily 10:00–18:00, Easter–mid-May daily 11:00–16:00 and Oct daily 10:00–17:00 weather permitting, closed Nov–Easter).

▲**World Heritage Hallstatt Museum**—This newly redone museum tells the story of Hallstatt—with a special focus on the Hallstatt period (800–400 B.C.), when this little village was the crucial salt-mining hub of a culture that spread from France to the Balkans. Back then, Celtic tribes dug for precious salt, and Hallstatt was, as its name means, the "place of salt."

First you'll watch a video that takes you back in time 7,000 years. Then you'll walk through exhibits tracing the town's evolution to the present day. This fun museum—though pricey—is well organized into meaningful, bite-sized chunks. There are displays on everything from the region's flora and fauna to local artists and the surge in Hallstatt tourism during the Romantic age—and lots and lots of salt-mining artifacts. Everything's in German, but the €2 English guide explains most of it (€6, July–Aug daily 10:00–19:00, May–June and Sept–Oct daily 9:00–18:00, Nov–April Tue–Sun 10:00–16:00, closed Mon, Seestrasse

56, adjacent to TI, tel. 06134/828-015). The Dachstein Sport shop across from the TI dug into a prehistoric site, and now its basement is another small museum (free).

▲**Lake Trip**—For a quick boat trip, you can ride *Stefanie* across the lake and back for €3.80. It stops at the tiny Hallstatt train station for 30 minutes, giving you time to walk to a hanging bridge and enjoy the peaceful, deep part of the lake. Longer lake tours are also available (€6.50/50 min, €8/75 min, www.hallstatt.net/schiffahrt, sporadic schedules—especially off-season—so check chalkboards by boat docks for today's times). Those into relaxation can rent a sleepy electric motorboat to enjoy town views from the water (two rental places: Riedler, next to ferry dock or across from Bräugasthof, tel. 06134/8320, or Hemetsberger, near Gasthof Simony or past bridge before Bad Insel, tel. 06134/8228; both daily in-season and in good weather until 19:00; boats have 2 speeds: slow and stop; €9/hr, spend an extra €3/hr for faster 500-watt boats).

▲▲**Salt Mine Tour**—If you have yet to pay a visit to a salt mine, Hallstatt's—which claims to be the oldest in the world—is a good one. You'll ride a steep funicular high above the town (funicular-€7.90 round-trip, €4.70 one-way, May–Sept daily 9:00–18:00, Oct until 16:30, closed Nov–April), take a 10-minute hike, check your bag and put on old miners' clothes, hike 650 feet higher in your funny outfit to meet your guide, load onto the train, and ride into the mountain through a tunnel actually made by prehistoric miners. Inside, you'll watch a great video (English headsets), slide down two banisters, and follow your guide. While the tour is mostly in German, the guide is required to speak English if you ask—so ask (salt mine tour-€14.50, €19.90 combo-ticket includes entrance and round-trip funicular, can buy mine tickets at cable car station, May–Sept daily 9:30–16:30, Oct daily 9:30–15:00, the 16:00 funicular departure catches the last tour at 16:30, no children under age 4, rarely a long wait but arrive after 15:00 and you'll find no lines and a smaller group, tel. 06132/200-2400). The well-publicized ancient Celtic graveyard excavation sites nearby are really dead (precious little to see). If you skip the funicular, the scenic 40-minute hike back into town is (with strong knees) a joy.

At the base of the funicular, notice train tracks leading to the Erbstollen tunnel entrance. This lowest of the salt tunnels goes many miles into the mountain, where a shaft connects it to the tunnels you just explored. Today, the salty brine from these tunnels flows 25 miles through the world's oldest pipeline to the huge modern salt works (next to the highway) at Ebensee. You'll pass a stack of the original 120-year-old wooden pipes between the lift and the mine.

▲**Local Hikes**—Mountain-lovers, hikers, and spelunkers keep busy for days, using Hallstatt as their home base (ask the TI for ideas). Local hikes are well described in the TI's *Dachstein Hiking Guide* (€5.80, in English). A good, short, and easy walk is the two-hour round-trip up the Echerntal Valley to the Waldbachstrub waterfall and back. With a car, consider hiking around nearby Altaussee (flat, 3-hour hike) or along Grundlsee to Tolpitzsee. Regular buses connect Hallstatt with Gosausee for a pleasant hour-long walk around that lake. The TI can recommend a great two-day hike with an overnight in a nearby mountain hut.

Near Hallstatt

▲▲**Dachstein Mountain Cable Car and Caves**—For a refreshing activity, ride a scenic cable car up a mountain to visit huge, chilly caves.

Dachstein Cable Car: From Obertraun, three miles beyond Hallstatt on the main road (or right across the lake as the crow flies), a mighty gondola goes in three stages high up the Dachstein Plateau—crowned by Dachstein, the highest mountain in the Salzkammergut (over 9,000 feet). The first segment stops at Schönbergalm (4,500 feet, runs May–Oct), which has a mountain restaurant and two huge caves (described below). The second segment goes to the summit of Krippenstein (6,600 feet, runs mid-May–Oct). The third segment descends to Gjaidalm (5,800 feet, runs mid-June–Oct), where several hikes begin. For a quick high-country experience, Krippenstein is better than Gjaidalm. From Krippenstein, you'll survey a scrubby, limestone, karst landscape (which absorbs rainfall through its many cracks and ultimately carves all those caves) with 360-degree views of the surrounding mountains (round-trip cable-car ride to the caves-€13, to Krippenstein-€18.50, to Gjaidalm-€20, cheaper family rates available, last cable car back down usually around 17:00, tel. 06134/8400, www.dachstein.at).

Giant Ice Caves (*Riesen-Eishöhle*, 4,500 feet): These were discovered in 1910. Today, guides lead tours in German and English on an hour-long, half-mile-long hike through an eerie, icy, subterranean world, passing limestone canyons the size of subway stations. The limestone caverns, carved by rushing water, are named for scenes from Wagner operas—the favorite of the mountaineers who first came here. If you're nervous, note that the iron oxide covering the ceiling takes 5,000 years to form. Things are very stable.

At the lift station, report to the ticket window to get your cave appointment. While the temperature is just above freezing and the 600 steps help keep you warm, bring a sweater. Allow 90 minutes, including the 10-minute hike from the station (€8, or €12.30 combo-ticket with Mammoth Caves, open May–Oct, hour-long tours 9:00–16:00, stay in front and assert yourself for English information, tel. 06134/8400).

Drop by the little free museum near the lift station—in a local-style wood cabin designed to support 200 tons of snow—to see the huge-cave-system model, exhibits about its exploration, and info about life in the caves.

Salzkammergut

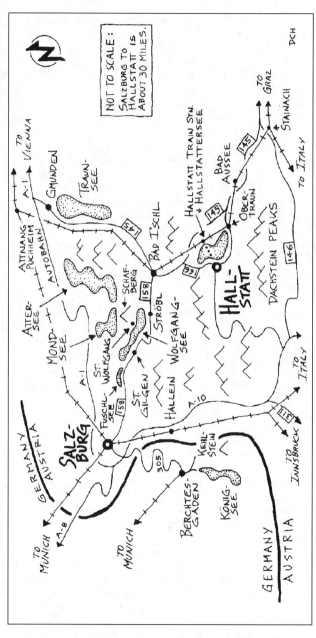

Mammoth Caves *(Mammuthöhle):* While huge and well-promoted, these are much less interesting than the ice caves and—for most—not worth the time. Of the 30-mile limestone labyrinth excavated so far, you'll walk a half-mile with a German-speaking guide (€8, or €12.30 combo-ticket with ice caves, open mid-May–Oct, hour-long tours 10:00–15:00, call a few days before to check on the schedule for an English guide, entrance a 10-min hike from lift station).

Getting to Obertraun: The cable car to Dachstein leaves from Obertraun, right across the lake from Hallstatt. From Hallstatt, the handiest option is bus (5/day June–Oct, 4/day off-season). Romantics can take the boat (€3.60, 5/day, less off-season, 15 min)—but it's a longer hike to the lift station. The adventurous or impatient can consider hitching a ride—virtually all cars leaving Hallstatt to the south will pass through Obertraun in a few minutes.

Luge Rides on the Hallstatt–Salzburg Road—If you're driving between Salzburg and Hallstatt, you'll pass two luge rides. Each is a ski lift that drags you backwards up the hill as you sit on your go-cart. At the top, you ride the cart down the winding metal course. Operating the sled is simple. Push to go, pull to stop, take your hands off your stick and you get hurt.

Each course is just off the road with easy parking. The ride up and down takes about 15 minutes. Look for *Riesen-Rutschbahn* or *Sommer-rodelbahn* signs. The one near Fuschlsee (closest to Salzburg) is half as long and cheaper (€3.50/ride, 1,970 feet, tel. 06235/7297). The one near Wolfgangsee is a double course, more scenic with grand lake views (€5.50/ride, €36/10 rides, 4,265 feet, each track is the same speed, tel. 06137/7085). Courses are open Easter through October from 10:00 to 18:00 (July–Aug 9:30–19:00)—but will close in bad weather. These are fun, but the concrete courses near Reutte are better (see Bavaria and Tirol chapter).

SLEEPING

$$$ Gasthof Zauner is a business machine offering 12 pricey, modern, pine-flavored rooms on the main square (Sb-€46–53, Db-€84–98, prices depend on season and view, closed mid-Nov–mid-Dec, Marktplatz 51, tel. 06134/8246, fax 06134/82468, www.zauner.hallstatt.net, zauner @hallstatt.at).

$$$ Pension Hallberg-Tauchergasthof (Diver's Inn), across from the TI, has six big rooms and a funky mini-museum of WWII artifacts found in the lake (Sb-€40–75, Db-€60–110, rooms for up to 5 also available, price depends on size, cash preferred, tel. 06134/8709, fax 06134/82865, www.pension-hallberg.at.tf, hallberg@aon.at, Gerda the "Salt Witch" and Eckbert Winkelmann).

$$ Gasthof Simony, my 500-year-old favorite, is on the square,

SLEEP CODE

(€1 = about $1.10, country code: 43, area code: 06134)
Sleep Code: **S** = Single, **D** = Double/Twin, **T** = Triple, **Q** =
Quad, **b** = bathroom, **s** = shower only, **no CC** = Credit Cards
not accepted, **SE** = Speaks English, **NSE** = No English. Unless
otherwise noted, credit cards are accepted, English is spoken,
and breakfast is included.

To help you sort easily through these listings, I've divided
the rooms into three categories, based on the price for a standard double room with bath:

$$$ **Higher Priced**—Most rooms €80 or more.
  $$ **Moderately Priced**—Most rooms between €50–80.
   $ **Lower Priced**—Most rooms €50 or less.

Hallstatt's TI can almost always find you a room (either in town
or at B&Bs and small hotels outside of town—which are more
likely to have rooms available and come with easy parking).
Mid-July and August can be tight. Early August is worst.
Hallstatt is not the place to splurge—some of the best rooms
are in *Zimmers,* just as nice and modern as the bigger hotels, at
half the cost. A bed in a private home costs about €20 with
breakfast. It's hard to get a one-night advance reservation. But if
you drop in and they have a spot, one-nighters are welcome.
Prices include breakfast, lots of stairs, and a silent night.
"Zimmer mit Aussicht?" means "Room with view?"—worth
asking for. Only a few of my listings accept plastic, which goes
for most businesses here.

with a lake view, balconies, creaky wood floors, slippery rag rugs, antique
furniture, a lakefront garden for swimming, and a huge breakfast.
Reserve in advance. For safety, reconfirm your room and price a day or
two before you arrive and call again if arriving late (S-€35, D-€45, Ds-
€55, Db-€75, third person-€30 extra, cash preferred, Markt 105, tel. &
fax 06134/8231, Susanna Scheutz SE).

$$ Bräugasthof Hallstatt is another creaky, friendly old place—a
former brewery—with eight cozy, mostly lakeview rooms run by
Susanna's sister and her family (Sb-€42, Db-€76, Tb-€110, Db/Tb
cheaper for 3-night stays, just past TI on the main drag at Seestrasse 120,
tel. 06134/8221, fax 06134/82214, braugasthof-fam.lobisser@aon.at,
Lobisser family).

$$ Gasthof Pension Grüner Anger is a practical, modern 11-room place away from the medieval town center—the only place in town that doesn't squeak and creak. It's big and quiet, a few blocks from the base of the salt mine lift, and a 10-minute walk from Market Square (Sb-€30, Db-€63, €3 more per room July–Aug, more for 1-night stays July–Aug, third person-€15, non-smoking, free parking, Lahn 10, tel. 06134/8397, fax 06134/83974, www.hallstatt.net/gruener.anger, anger @aon.at, Sulzbacher family).

$ Helga Lenz is a five-minute climb above the Pension Seethaler (look for the green *Zimmer* sign). This big, sprawling, woodsy house has a nifty garden perch, wins the Best View award, and is ideal for those who sleep well in tree houses (S-€17—only available April–June & Oct, D-€30, Db-€36, T-€44, Tb-€51, 1-night stays-€2 per person extra, family room, no CC, closed Nov–March, Hallberg 17, tel. & fax 06134/8508, www.demregio.at/lenz, haus-lenz@aon.at).

$ Two *Zimmers* are a few minutes' stroll south of the center, just past the bus stop/parking lot and over the bridge: **Haus Trausner** has four clean, bright, new-feeling rooms (Ds-€35, Db-€38, Ts-€52.50, less for more than 1 night, no CC, Lahnstrasse 27, tel. 06134/8710, trausner1@utanet.at, Maria Trausner SE) while **Herta Höll** rents out three rooms in a riverside house crawling with kids (Db-€40, apartment-€60, no CC, Malerweg 45, tel. 06134/8531, fax 06134/825-533, frank .hoell@aon.at).

$ Gasthaus zur Mühle Jugendherberge, below the waterfall, with the cheapest good beds in town, is popular for its great pizzas and cheap grub (21 rooms, bed in 3- to 20-bed coed dorms-€11, D-€24, sheets-€3 extra, family quads, breakfast-€3, big lockers with a €20 deposit, closed Nov, reception closed Tue Sept–mid-May—so arrange in advance if arriving on Tue, below tunnel car park, Kirchenweg 36, tel. & fax 06134/8318, toeroe.f@magnet.at, run by Ferdinand Törö).

$ Pension Seethaler is a dark, homey old lodge with 45 beds and a breakfast room mossy with antlers, perched above the lake. The confusing floor plan is like an M. C. Escher house with more fire hazards, and the staff won't win any awards for congeniality—*Zimmer* are friendlier and cheaper—but this place is a reasonable last resort (€18/person in S, D, T, or Q, €26/person in Db, Tb, or Qb, no CC, coin-op showers downstairs-€1/8 min, Dr. Morton Weg 22, find the stairs to the left of Seestrasse 116, at top of stairs turn left, tel. 06134/8421, pension .seethaler@kronline.at).

$ Ancient-feeling Pension Sarstein has 25 beds in basic, dusty rooms with flower-bedecked, lakeview balconies, in a charming building run by friendly Frau Fischer. You can swim from her lakeside garden (S-€18, D-€32, Ds-€44, Db-€50 with this book, Ds and Db have balconies, 1-night stays-€1.50 per person extra, no CC, leave the boat dock to the right and walk 200 meters to Gosaumühlstrasse 83, tel. 06134/8217, NSE).

EATING

You can enjoy good food inexpensively, with delightful lakeside settings. While everyone cooks the typical Austrian fare, your best bet here is trout. *Reinanke* trout is from Lake Hallstatt. Restaurants in Hallstatt tend to have unreliable hours and close early on slow nights, so don't wait too long to get dinner.

Feed the swans while your trout is being cooked at **Restaurant Bräugasthof** (fun menu and tasty food, May–Oct daily 10:00–21:00, closed Nov–April, tel. 06134/20012, see "Sleeping," page 430). Other lakefront options include **Restaurant Simony** (see "Sleeping," page 430) and **Hotel Grüner Baum** (May–Oct Tue–Sun 11:30–22:00, closed Mon and Nov–April, at bottom of Market Square, tel. 06134/8263).

While it lacks a lakeside setting, **Gasthof Zauner's** classy restaurant is well respected for its grilled meat and fish; the interior of its dining room is covered in real ivy that grows in through the windows (daily 11:30–14:30 & 17:30–22:00, closed Mon Feb–April, reservations smart, see "Sleeping," page 430).

For the best pizza in town with a fun-loving local crowd, chow down cheap and hearty at **Gasthaus zur Mühle** (daily 11:00–14:00 & 17:00–21:00, closed Tue and no lunch mid-Oct–mid-May, see "Sleeping," page 430).

Locals like the smoky **Strand Café,** a 10-minute lakeside hike away, near the town beach (April–Oct Tue–Sun 10:00–21:00, closed Mon and Nov–March, great garden setting on the lake, Seelande 102, tel. 06134/8234).

For your late-night drink, savor the market square from the trendy little pub called **Ruth Zimmermann** (June–Oct daily 9:00–2:00, Nov–May daily 12:00–2:00, tel. 06134/8306).

TRANSPORTATION CONNECTIONS

For tips for drivers coming here from Salzburg, see the end of the Salzburg chapter.

By train to: Salzburg (hrly, 90 min to Attnang Puchheim, short wait, 50 min to Salzburg), **Vienna** (hrly, 90 min to Attnang Puchheim, short wait, 2.5 hrs to Vienna). Day-trippers to Hallstatt can check bags at the Attnang Puchheim station. (Note: Connections there and back can be very fast—about 5 min; have coins ready for the lockers at track 1.) Train info: tel. 051717 (wait through long German recording for operator).

INNSBRUCK AND HALL

Austria's Tirol region—in the country's panhandle, south of Bavaria—is a winter sports mecca known for its mountainous panoramas. In the region's capital, Innsbruck, the Golden Roof glitters—but you'll strike it rich in neighboring Hall, which has twice the charm and none of the tourist crowds.

Innsbruck

Innsbruck is world-famous as a resort for skiers and a haven for hikers...but when compared to Salzburg and Vienna, it's stale strudel. Still, a quick look is easy and interesting. Innsbruck was the Hapsburgs' capital of the Tirol, and its medieval center—now a glitzy, tourist-filled pedestrian zone—still gives you the feel of a provincial medieval capital. The much-ogled Golden Roof *(Goldenes Dach)* is the centerpiece.

ORIENTATION

(area code: 0512)
Tourist Information: Innsbruck has two TIs: **downtown** (daily 9:00–18:00, Burggraben 3, 3 blocks in front of Golden Roof, tel. 0512/5356, www.innsbruck-information.at) and at the **train station** (summer daily 9:00–21:00, winter daily 9:00–20:00, tel. 0512/583-766). At either one, you can pick up a free city map (the €1 map, with more information on sights, isn't necessary) or book a room (€3 fee).

    Innsbruck Card: The €21, 24-hour Innsbruck Card pays for itself only if you take the Mountain Lift (also covers Igls Lift, as well as the Sightseer mini-bus, buses, trams, museums, zoo, and palace).

    Tours of Innsbruck: The TI offers two different **walking tours** of Innsbruck May through October: a basic one-hour city walk (€8, daily at

Innsbruck and Hall

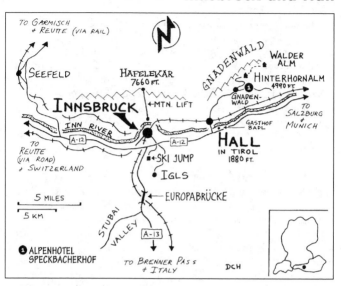

14:00) and another that adds the Hofkirche and takes 90 minutes (€12, daily at 10:00). Both tours are in English and German and start at the downtown TI (no walking tours Nov–April). There are also **bus-plus-walking tours** for €13 (summer only, daily at 12:00, 2 hrs, in English and German).

Arrival in Innsbruck

From the main train station (Hauptbahnhof), it's a 10-minute walk to the old-town center. Leave by veering right to Brixnerstrasse. Follow it past the fountain at Boznerplatz and straight until it dead-ends into Maria-Theresa Strasse. Turn right and go 300 yards into the old town (you'll pass the TI on Burggraben on your right), where you'll see the Golden Roof and Hotel Weisses Kreuz.

Helpful Hints

Laundry and Internet: Bubble Point is a handy self-service launderette with Internet terminals (€6/load, Mon–Fri 8:00-22:00, Sat–Sun 8:00–20:00, between train station and Golden Roof at Brixner-strasse 1, www.bubblepoint.com).

Getting around Innsbruck

A single ticket for Innsbruck's buses or trams costs €1.60; a day ticket is €3.30. Buy tickets from the machine at the tram stop or at a *Tabak;*

single tickets can also be purchased from the driver. Transit info: tel. 0512/530-7500, www.ivb.at.

A new made-for-tourists mini-bus called the **Sightseer** follows two popular routes around town, connecting the key sights (€2.50 for any one-way trip, €4 round-trip to a particular sight and back, headphone commentary in English, May–Oct 2/hr 9:00–17:30, Nov–April hrly 10:00–17:00). If visiting several outlying sights, you can buy a day ticket (*Tagesticket*, €8, includes funicular) and use the Sightseer as a hop-on, hop-off bus. It's pricey—more than twice the cost of a day pass on public transit—but convenient (for information and tickets, visit the TI).

SIGHTS

Innsbruck's Old Town

▲▲**The Golden Roof** (*Goldenes Dach)* **and Herzog-Friedrichstrasse**— The three-block pedestrian street (Herzog-Friedrichstrasse) in front of the Golden Roof is Innsbruck's tourism ground zero.

Stand in front of the Roof to get oriented. Emperor Maximilian I loved Innsbruck, and built a palace here—including the balcony topped with 2,657 gilded copper tiles. The **Golden Roof** (1494) offered Maximilian an impressive spot from which to view his medieval spectacles.

Most buildings along this street are Gothic (notice the entry arches), but across the street from the Golden Roof (to the left as you face the Roof) is the frilly Baroque-style **Helblinghaus** facade. Above you is the bulbous **city tower** (*Stadtturm),* which you can climb for a great view (€2.50, June–Sept daily 10:00–20:00, Oct–May 10:00–17:00, tel. 0512/561-500). This was the old town watchtower (the prison was on the second floor). Like many Austrian buildings (including the nearby Hofkirche), this originally had a pointy Gothic spire—but was replaced with this onion-shaped one when Baroque was in vogue. If you walk down the shop-lined Hofgasse (facing the Golden Roof, go right), you'll reach the Hofburg palace, Hofkirche, and Folklife Museum (see below).

A block in front of the Golden Roof—next to the McDonald's—is the historic **Hotel Weisses Kreuz.** It's built on Roman foundations, but has only been hosting guests for the last 500 years. The white cross (*weisses Kreuz)* is the symbol of the Order of Malta—knights who opened up guesthouses for Holy Land–bound pilgrims during the Crusades. In 1769, a 13-year-old Amadeus Mozart and his father stayed here on their way to Italy. A generation later, this hotel was one of the centers of resistance against Napoleon, and later still, against the Nazis (giving shelter to Jewish refugees). When the American soldiers moved in from Italy, they made the hotel their headquarters. Today, it's still a functioning hotel (see "Sleeping," below), and recently hosted Otto von Hapsburg, the Man Who Would Be Emperor, if his great-great-uncle hadn't started—and lost—World War I. Though Otto could have

EMPEROR MAXIMILIAN I

The big name in Innsbruck is Emperor Maximilian I (1459–1519), who made this city a regional capital, and built the Golden Roof. This Hapsburg emperor was a dynamic, larger-than-life Renaissance man—soldier, sculptor, and statesman (though not very good at any of these). At the same time, he clung to the last romantic fantasies of the Middle Ages; for example, he was the last Hapsburg who personally led his troops into battle.

Most people associate the Hapsburg Empire with Vienna—which was the capital of the empire's far-flung Eastern European holdings during its peak in the 17th and 18th centuries. But during Maximilian's time, two centuries earlier, the focus was on Italy—he took the "Roman" part of Holy Roman Emperor very seriously. This made Innsbruck very important, since it was the capital of Tirol (which then included much of today's northern Italy, and was on the Italian frontier). This visionary emperor hoped that once all of Italy was his, Innsbruck would become the permanent capital of his empire. In reality, he was unlucky at war and ran up huge debts...but his strategic marriage to Mary of Burgundy set the stage for the large-scale expansion of the empire. Though he wanted to be a war hero, as with most Hapsburgs, his biggest victory came with a trip to the altar.

stayed in the fanciest place in town, he chose this historic, comfortable inn instead.

▲▲**Hofkirche**—Emperor Maximilian liked Innsbruck so much, he wanted to be buried here—surrounded by 28 larger-than-life cast-bronze statues of his ancestors, relatives, in-laws...and his favorite heroes of the dying Middle Ages (such as King Arthur). The good €1 English book tells you who everyone is. Don't miss King Arthur (as you face the altar, he's the fifth from the front on the right, next to the heavy metal dude) and Mary of Burgundy, Maximilian's first—and favorite—wife (third from the front on the left). Some of these sculptures—including König Artur—were designed by German Renaissance painter Albrecht Dürer. That's Maximilian himself, kneeling on top of the huge sarcophagus. Sadly, the real Max isn't inside. By the time he died, Maximilian had become notorious for running up debts, and his men weren't allowed to bring his body here.

Just inside the door to the church, you'll find the tomb of the popular Tirolean soldier Andreas Hofer, who fought against Napoleon (church entry-€3, also included in €5 entry to Folklife Museum, Sept–June Mon–Sat 9:00–17:00, Sun 9:00–12:00, July–Aug Mon–Sat 9:00–17:30, Sun 9:00–12:00, Universitätsstrasse 2).

▲▲Tirolean Folklife Museum (Tiroler Volkskunst Museum)—This museum, next door to the Hofkirche, offers the best look anywhere at traditional Tirolean lifestyles. Fascinating exhibits range from wedding dresses and gaily painted cribs and nativity scenes, to maternity clothes and babies' trousers. The upper floors show Tirolean homes through the ages (€5, includes entry to Hofkirche, Sept–June Mon–Sat 9:00–17:00, Sun 9:00–12:00, July–Aug Mon–Sat 9:00–17:30, Sun 9:00–12:00, hard to appreciate without the €2 English guidebook, Universitätsstrasse 2, tel. 0512/584-302).

Hofburg—This 18th-century Baroque palace, built by Maria Theresa, is only worth a visit if you aren't going to the much bigger and better palaces in Vienna, Munich, or near Füssen (€6, daily 9:00–17:00, last entry 16:30, tel. 0512/587-186, www.tirol.com/hofburg-ibk).

Maria-Theresa Strasse—The fine Baroque Maria-Theresa Strasse stretches south from the medieval center. **St. Anne's Column** (Annasäule) marks the middle of the old marketplace. This was erected in the 18th century by townspeople thankful that their army had defeated an invading Bavarian army and saved the town (it's the same idea as the plague columns you see throughout Europe).

At the far end of the street, the **Triumphal Arch** is a gate Maria Theresa built to commemorate a happy and a sad occasion. The happy: Her son Leopold II, archduke of Tuscany, met and married a Spanish princess here in Innsbruck—and Maria Theresa and her husband Franz came for the ceremony. But Franz partied a little too hard, and died the day after the wedding. (Maria Theresa wore black for the rest of her life.) The south-facing side of the arch—what you see as you approach the center—shows the interlocked rings of the happy couple. But the flipside, visible as you leave town, features mournful statuary.

▲Slap Dancing—For your Tirolean folk fun, Innsbruck hotels offer an entertaining evening of slap dancing and yodeling nearly nightly at 20:30 from April through October (€20 includes a drink with 2-hour show, tickets at TI). Every summer Thursday, the town puts on a free outdoor folk show under the Golden Roof (July–Sept, weather permitting).

Into the Mountains
▲Ski Jump *(Bergisel)*—A new, modern ski jump has been built in the same location as the original ski jump (demolished in 2000) that was used for the 1964 and 1976 Olympics. It's an inviting side trip with a superb view, overlooking the city just off the Brenner Pass road on the south side of town (drivers follow signs to *Bergisel*, walkers take tram #1 from the center). For the best view, hike to the Olympic rings under the dishes that held the Olympic flame, where Dorothy Hamill and a host

of others who brought home the gold are honored. Near the car park is a memorial to Andreas Hofer, the hero of the Tirolean battles against Napoleon. The lazy can zip up to the top in a funicular, then an elevator, for a great view and a panorama cafe (€6 for 2-min funicular, or 325 steps for free, daily 9:00–17:00, www.bergisel.info).

Mountain Lifts and Hiking—A popular mountain-sports center and home of the 1964 and 1976 Winter Olympics, Innsbruck is surrounded by 150 mountain lifts, 1,250 miles of trails, and 250 hikers' huts. One lift goes right out of downtown. The first stage, a funicular, goes to the Alpine Zoo (called Hungerburgbahn, €4.20). From there, cable cars lead up into the mountains (Nordkettenbahn Seegrube-Hafelekar, €18.10). If it's sunny, consider riding the lift right out of the city to the mountaintops above (€23 total). Ask your hotel or hostel for an Innsbruck Club card, which offers overnight guests various discounts, bike tours, and free guided hikes in summer. Hikers meet in front of Congress Innsbruck daily at 8:45; each day, it's a different hike in the surrounding mountains and valleys (bring only lunch and water; boots, rucksack, and transport are provided; confirm with TI).

Alpenzoo—This zoo is one of Innsbruck's most popular attractions (understandable when the competition is the Golden Roof). You can ride the funicular up to the zoo (free if you buy your zoo ticket before boarding) and get a look at all the animals that hide out in the Alps: wildcats, owls, elk, vultures, and more (€5.80, €7.30 combo-ticket at TI includes round-trip transit, May–Sept daily 9:00–18:00, Oct–April daily 9:00–17:00, Weiherburggasse 37, tel. 0512/292-323, www.alpenzoo.at).

Near Innsbruck

▲▲**Alpine Side-Trip by Car to Hinterhornalm**—In Gnadenwald, a village sandwiched between Hall and its Alps, pay a €4.50 toll, pick up a brochure, then corkscrew your way up the mountain. Marveling at the crazy amount of energy put into such a remote road project, you'll finally end up at the rustic Hinterhornalm Berg restaurant (often closed, mobile 0664/211-2745). Hinterhornalm is a hang-gliding springboard. On good days, it's a butterfly nest. From there, it's a level 20-minute walk to Walderalm, a cluster of three dairy farms with 70 cows that share their meadow with the clouds. The cows—cameras dangling from their thick necks—ramble along ridge-top lanes surrounded by cut-glass peaks. The ladies of the farms serve soup, sandwiches, and drinks (very fresh milk in the afternoon) on rough plank tables. Below you spreads the Inn River Valley and, in the distance, tourist-filled Innsbruck.

Sleeping in Gnadenwald: **$$$ Alpenhotel Speckbacherhof** is a grand rustic hotel set between a peaceful forest and a meadow with all the comforts—mini-golf, laundry, the works (D-€44, Db-€66–90, 2 apartments as Db-€110–115 plus €12 per additional person, half board €13 extra per person, includes breakfast, closed Nov–mid-Dec, Sankt

Martin 2, tel. 05223/52511, fax 05223/525-1155). Drive 10 minutes uphill from Hall to the village of Gnadenwald. It's across the street from the Hinterhornalm toll road.

SLEEPING

$$$ Hotel Weisses Kreuz, near the Golden Roof, has been housing visitors for 500 years (see "Sights," page 436). While it still feels like an old inn, its 40 rooms are newly renovated and comfortable (S-€34–39, Sb-€57–61, D-€64–67, small Db-€84–91, the big Db at €95–109 is a better value, includes breakfast, non-smoking rooms, elevator, Internet access, 50 yards in front of Golden Roof, as central as can be in the old town at Herzog-Friedrichstrasse 31, tel. 0512/594-790, fax 0512/594-7990, www.weisseskreuz.at, hotel@weisseskreuz.at).

$$ Pension Stoi rents 17 pleasant, basic rooms 200 yards from the train station (S-€32, Sb-€37, D-€52, Db-€58, T-€58, Tb-€65, Q-€65, Qb-€80, no breakfast, no CC, free parking in alleyway behind pension; on foot, jog left as you leave the station to Salurnerstrasse, take first left on Adamgasse, then watch for signs in the courtyard on the right, Salurnerstrasse 7, tel. 0512/585-434, fax 05238/87282, www.stoi.cjb.net, info@stoi.cjb.net, Stoi family).

EATING

You'll find plenty of expensive places in the pedestrian zone around the Golden Roof; locals favor **Weinhaus Happ** (daily 11:00–23:00, on left

---

SLEEP CODE

(€1 = about $1.10, country code: 43, area code: 0512)

Sleep Code: **S** = Single, **D** = Double/Twin, **T** = Triple, **Q** = Quad, **b** = bathroom, **s** = shower only, **no CC** = Credit Cards not accepted, **SE** = Speaks English, **NSE** = No English. Unless otherwise noted, credit cards are accepted, English is spoken, and breakfast is included.

To help you sort easily through these listings, I've divided the rooms into three categories, based on the price for a standard double room with bath:

$$$ **Higher Priced**—Most rooms €70 or more.
$$ **Moderately Priced**—Most rooms between €40–70.
$ **Lower Priced**—Most rooms €40 or less.

as you face Roof at Herzog-Friedrichstrasse 14, tel. 0512/582-980) and **Ottoburg** (Tue–Sun 10:00–14:00 & 18:00–24:00, closed Mon, jog left down street in front of Roof to Herzog-Friedrichstrasse 1, tel. 0512/584-338).

To get a bit off the tourist track, consider the **Weisses Rössl** (Mon–Sat 7:00–15:00 & 17:00–24:00, closed Sun; facing Roof, go one block left to Kiebachgasse 8, tel. 0512/583-057). Or stroll across the Innbrücke (bridge over the river Inn) and go left a half-block along the waterfront street to the smoky but very local **Weisses Lamm** (Wed–Mon 8:00–24:00, closed Tue, hiding upstairs at Mariahilfstrasse 12, tel. 0512/283-156).

TRANSPORTATION CONNECTIONS

To: Hall (4 buses/hr, 25 min; hrly trains, 15 min), **Salzburg** (trains every 2 hrs, 2 hrs), **Vienna** (trains every 2 hrs, 5.5 hrs), **Reutte** (trains every 2 hrs, 2.5 hrs with transfer in Garmisch and sometimes also in Mittenwald; or by bus: 4/day, 2.5 hrs), **Bregenz** (every 2 hrs, some with transfer in Feldkirch, 2.5 hrs), **Zürich** (3/day, 4 hrs), **Munich** (every 2 hrs, 2 hrs), **Paris** (2 trains/day, transfer in Munich or Salzburg, 11 hrs), **Milan** (2/day, 5.5 hrs), **Venice** (1/day, 5 hrs). Night trains run to Vienna, Milan, Venice, and Rome. Train info: tel. 051717 (wait through long German recording for operator).

Hall

Hall was a rich salt-mining center when Innsbruck was just a humble bridge *(Brücke)* town on the Inn River. Hall actually has a larger old town than does its sprawling neighbor, Innsbruck. Hall hosts a colorful morning scene before the daily tour buses arrive, closes down tight for its daily siesta, and sleeps on Sunday. There's a brisk farmers' market on Saturday mornings. (For drivers, Hall is a convenient overnight stop on the long drive from Vienna to Switzerland.)

ORIENTATION

Tourist Information

Hall's helpful TI offers lots of town information and brochures on a wide range of topics. If it's not too busy, they can also help you find a room (June–Sept Mon–Fri 8:30–18:00, Sat 9:00–12:00, closed Sun, Oct–May Mon–Fri 8:30–12:30 & 14:00–18:00, Sat 9:00–12:00, closed Sun, just off main square at Wallpachgasse 5, tel. 05223/56269, town info: www.tiscover.com/hall, region info: www.regionhall.at).

Arrival in Hall

By Bus: Coming from Innsbruck, get off at the Unterer Stadtplatz stop, just below downtown Hall. (If you stay on the bus, it makes a long loop beyond and then back into Hall, dropping you at the *Kurhaus* at the top of town.) From the Unterer Stadtplatz bus stop, you're a five-minute uphill walk from the town square and TI. To reach the recommended Gasthof Badl, go through the door next to the bus stop (marked #17 and Burg Hasegg), cut through a couple of courtyards until you're under the castle tower, exit across the courtyard from the tower, and turn right towards the river. Go straight, then veer left to use the railroad underpass. From there, cross the old wooden bridge to the hotel.

By Train: Hall's train station is a 10-minute walk from the town center (exit straight ahead up Bahnhofstrasse, turn right at the busy road, and you'll soon reach the fountain that marks the bottom of town). To reach Gasthof Badl, leave the station to the right, follow the tracks straight ahead, veer right to access the railroad underpass, then head straight across the old wooden bridge.

By Car: Drivers approaching on the Autobahn take the Hall-Mitte exit. You'll cross a big bridge, then you'll see a convenient parking lot (5-min walk to old center, 60 min free with cardboard clock under windshield—but you may have to pay in 2004).

SIGHTS

Main Square (Oberer Sadtplatz)—Hall's quaint main square at the top of town is worth a visit (TI just up the street). In the adjacent square (Pfarrplatz) is the Town Hall *(Rathaus)* and St. Nicholas Parish Church (Pfarrkirche St. Nikolaus). This much-appended Gothic church is decorated Baroque, with fine altars, a twisted apse, and a north wall lined with bony relics.

Hall Mint in Hasegg Castle (Münze Hall in Burg Hasegg)— Beginning in the 15th century, Hall began minting coins—most notably the *Taler* (which eventually became "dollar" in English). The former town mint, housed in Hasegg Castle, is between the river and the center at the south end of town. The Hall Mint Museum was renovated and expanded in 2003 to show off the town's proud minting heritage. The centerpiece is a huge, fully-functioning replica of a 16th-century minting press—powered by water and made entirely of wood (€6, includes audioguide, April–Oct daily 10:00–17:00, Nov–March Mon–Thu 10:00–12:00 & 14:00–17:00, Fri 10:00–12:00 only, closed Sat–Sun, €5 castle tours also available—call for details, tel. 05223/585-5165, www.muenze-hall.at). The bus from Innsbruck drops you off right by the castle (stop: Unterer Stadtplatz, go through door marked #17 and "Burg Hasegg"); from Gasthof Badl, it's the first big building you'll see after crossing the old pedestrian bridge.

Salt Museum (Bergbaumuseum)—Back when salt was money, Hall was loaded. Try catching a tour at this museum, where the town has reconstructed one of its original salt mines, complete with pits, shafts, drills, tools, and a slippery but tiny wooden slide (€3, May–Sept, by guided 45-min tour only, usually Mon–Sat 11:30 and 15:30, Sun 15:30, amount of English depends on guide and makeup of group, call TI to confirm schedule and check on English-speaking guides, tel. 05223/56269). The museum is a block south of the main square at Eugenstrasse.

Walking Tours—The TI organizes one-hour town walks (€6, includes admissions, €8 also includes salt museum tour, above; May–Sept, usually Mon–Sat 10:00 and 14:00, Sun 14:00, same English situation as "Salt Museum," above). The TI can also put you in touch with an English-speaking private guide (around €80/1 hr).

Swimming—If you want to make a splash, check out Hall's magnificent *Freischwimmbad,* a huge outdoor pool complex with four diving boards, a giant lap pool, a big slide, and a kiddies' pool, all surrounded by a lush garden, sauna, mini-golf, and lounging locals (€3, mid-May–Aug daily 9:00–19:00, closed Sept–mid-May, at campground northwest of Hall, follow *Schwimmbad* signs from downtown to Scheidensteinstrasse 24, tel. 05223/454-6475, www.camping-hall.at).

Biking—You can rent bikes at the campground (about €7/day, see directions for "Swimming," above). The riverside bike path (7 miles from Hall to Volders) is a treat.

SLEEPING AND EATING

(€1 = about $1.10, country code: 43, area code: 05223)

Lovable towns that specialize in lowering the pulse of local vacationers line the Inn Valley. Hall, while the best town, has the shortest list of accommodations. Up the hill on either side of the river are towns strewn with fine farmhouse hotels and pensions. Most *Zimmer* charge about €20 per person but don't accept one-night stays.

$$ **Gasthof Badl** is a big, comfortable, friendly place run by sunny Frau Steiner and her daughter, Sonja. I like its convenience, peace, big breakfast, easy telephone reservations, and warm welcome (25 rooms, Sb-€36, Db-€58, Tb-€85, Qb-€107, elevator, rental bikes for guests for fine riverside path, Innbrücke 4, tel. 05223/56784, fax 05223/567-843, www.hotel-badl-tirol.com, badl@tirol.com). Hall's kitchens close early, but Gasthof Badl's restaurant serves excellent dinners until 21:30 (€7–11, closed Tue). They stock the essential TI brochures and maps of Hall and Innsbruck in English. It's easy for drivers to find: From the east, it's immediately off the Hall-Mitte freeway exit; you'll see the orange-lit Bed sign. From Innsbruck, take the Hall-Mitte exit and, rather than turning left over the big bridge into town, go straight. On foot, see "Arrival in Hall," page 442.

$ *Zimmer:* For a cheaper room in a private home, **Frieda Tollinger** rents out three rooms and accepts one-nighters (€16/person with breakfast, no CC, across the river from Badl and downstream about a half-mile, follow Untere Lend, which becomes Schopperweg, to #8, tel. 05223/41366, NSE).

TRANSPORTATION CONNECTIONS

Innsbruck is the nearest major train station. Hall and Innsbruck are connected by train and bus. Trains do the trip faster but leave only hourly; bus #4 takes a bit longer (25 min, €2.30 each way) but leaves four times per hour and drops you closer to town (see "Arrival in Hall," page 442). Buses go to and from the Innsbruck train station, a 10-minute walk from the old-town center. Drivers staying in freeway-handy Hall can side-trip into Innsbruck on the bus.

Route Tips for Drivers
From Hall into Innsbruck and on to Switzerland: For old Innsbruck, take the autobahn from Hall to the Innsbruck Ost exit and follow the signs to *Zentrum,* then *Kongresshaus,* and park as close as you can to the old center on the river *(Hofgarden).*

Just south of Innsbruck is the new ski jump (from the autobahn take the Innsbruck Süd exit and follow signs to *Bergisel*). Park at the end of the road near the Andreas Hofer Memorial, and climb to the empty, grassy stands for a picnic.

Leaving Innsbruck for Switzerland head west on the autobahn (direction: Bregenz). (If you're coming directly from Innsbruck's ski jump, go down into town along huge cemetery—thoughtfully placed just beyond the jump landing—and follow blue A12, Garmisch, Arlberg signs). The eight-mile-long Arlberg tunnel saves you 30 minutes on your way to Switzerland, but costs you lots of scenery and €8.50 (Swiss francs and credit cards accepted). For a joyride and to save a few bucks, skip the tunnel, exit at St. Anton, and go via Stuben.

After the speedy Arlberg tunnel, you're 30 minutes from Switzerland. Bludenz, with its characteristic medieval quarter, makes a good rest stop. Pass Feldkirch (and another long tunnel) and exit the autobahn at Rankweil/Feldkirch Nord, following signs for Altstätten and Meiningen (CH). Crossing the baby Rhine River, leave Austria.

To side-trip to Liechtenstein, follow FL signs at Feldkirch (see "Side-Trip through Liechtenstein" in the Appenzell chapter).

Leaving Hall or Innsbruck for Reutte, go west (as above, direction Switzerland) and leave the freeway at Telfs, where signs direct you to Reutte (a 90-min drive).

Side-Trip over Brenner Pass into Italy: A short swing into Italy is fast and easy from Innsbruck or Hall (45-min drive, easy border crossing). To get to Italy, take the great Europa Bridge over Brenner Pass. It costs about €8, but in 30 minutes, you'll be at the border. (Note: Traffic can be heavy on summer weekends.)

In Italy, drive to the colorful market town of Vipiteno/Sterzing. **Reifenstein Castle** is a unique and wonderfully preserved medieval castle, just south of town on the west side of the valley, down a small road next to the autobahn. The lady who lives at the castle gives tours in German, Italian, and a little English (open Easter–Oct only, entry by tour only, €3.50, tours Sat–Thu at 9:30, 10:30, 14:00, and 15:00, closed Fri and Nov–Easter, picnic spot at drawbridge, tel. from Austria 00-39-047/-765-879, in Italy: tel. 0472/765-879).

SWITZERLAND

(Schweiz, Suisse, Svizzera)

- 16,000 square miles (half the size of Ireland, or 13 Rhode Islands)
- About 6 million people (375 people per square mile, declining slightly)
- 1 Swiss franc (SF) = about 70 cents, and 1.40 SF = about $1

Switzerland is one of Europe's richest, best-organized, and most expensive countries. Like Boy Scouts, the Swiss count cleanliness, neatness, punctuality, tolerance, independence, thrift, and hard work as virtues, and they love pocketknives. Their high income, a great social security system, and the spectacular Alps give the Swiss plenty to be thankful for.

Switzerland is Europe's most mountainous country. Forty percent of the country consists of uninhabitable rocks, lakes, and rugged Alps. Its geography has given it distinct cultural regions. Two-thirds of the people speak German, 20 percent French, 10 percent Italian, and a small group in the southeast speak Romansh, a descendant of ancient Latin. The singsongy Swiss German spoken dialect is quite different from the written High German. Most Swiss are multi-lingual, and English is widely spoken.

Historically, Switzerland is one of Europe's oldest democracies (yet women didn't get the vote until 1971). Born when three states (cantons)

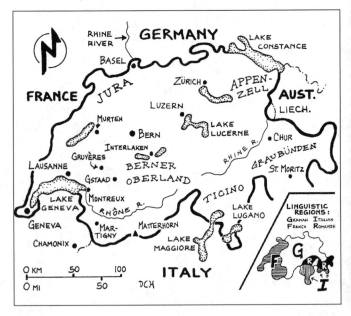

united in 1291, the Confoederatio Helvetica, as it was called in Roman times (the "CH" decal on cars doesn't stand for chocolate), grew to the 23 cantons of today. The government is decentralized, and cantonal loyalty is very strong.

Fiercely independent, Switzerland loves its neutrality and stayed out of both world wars. But it's far from lax defensively. Every fit man serves in the army and stays in the reserve. Each house has a gun and a bomb shelter. Switzerland bristles with 600,000 rifles in homes and 12,000 heavy guns in place. Swiss vacuum-packed emergency army bread, which lasts two years, is also said to function as a weapon. Airstrips hide inside mountains behind Bat Cave doors. With the push of a button, all road, rail, and bridge entries to the country can be destroyed, changing Switzerland into a formidable mountain fortress. Notice the innocent-looking but explosive patches checkerboarding the roads at key points, such as tunnel entrances and mountain summits (and hope no one invades until you get past). Sentiments are changing, and Switzerland has come close to voting away its entire military.

In 2002, Switzerland legalized marijuana use. When polls showed that over 30 percent of the country had used marijuana, the Parliament decided to decriminalize the drug rather than criminalize a third of its population. The new law is still hazy—the Swiss can possess and use pot, but can't sell large amounts of it. The drug is trendy in the Swiss military. A generation ago, new recruits had a reputation as heavy drinkers. Today, two-thirds use marijuana.

The Swiss currency is the franc, but the Swiss in touristy areas accept euros (smaller bills, no big bills or coins) and give Swiss francs in change.

Prices are high. More and more locals call sitting on the pavement around a bottle of wine "going out." Hotels with double rooms under $80 are rare. Even dormitory beds cost $15. If your budget is tight, be sure to chase down hostels (many have family rooms) and keep your eyes peeled for *Matratzenlagers* (literally, "mattress dorms"). Hiking is free, though major alpine lifts run $20–40.

The Swiss eat when we do and enjoy a straightforward, no-nonsense cuisine. Specialties include delicious fondue, rich chocolates, a melted cheese dish called raclette, fresh dairy products (try muesli yogurt), 100 varieties of cheese, and Fendant, a good, crisp, local white wine. The Co-op and Migros grocery stores are the hungry hiker's best budget bet; groceries charge about 50 percent more than U.S. prices.

While Switzerland's booming big cities are cosmopolitan, traditional culture survives in the alpine villages. Spend most of your time getting high in the Alps. On Sunday, you're most likely to enjoy traditional music, clothing, and culture. August 1 is the festive Swiss national holiday.

Transportation

Drivers: You can get anywhere quickly on Switzerland's fine road system (the world's most expensive per mile to build). Drivers pay a one-time, 40 SF fee for a permit to use Swiss autobahns—check to see if your rental car already has one; if not, buy it at the border, gas station, or car rental agency. Anyone caught driving on a Swiss autobahn without this tax sticker is likely to be cop-stopped and fined.

Flights: If you arrive in the country by plane, you'll likely land in Zürich (for information on the airport, see Zürich chapter), which has easy train connections to onward destinations.

Trains: Switzerland's public transportation is slick. The country is crisscrossed with scenic train routes, making the journey as fun as the destination.

The most famous route is the **Glacier Express,** connecting two mountain resorts (Zermatt and St. Moritz) with stunning snowy scenery. Note that Switzerland has some privately owned train lines. For instance, a large segment of the Glacier Express journey is private (see map). Private lines are usually covered by Swiss passes, but not covered by Eurail and Eurail Select passes (though these passes can get you discounts on certain trips). If your railpass doesn't cover an entire journey, pay for the "uncovered" portion at the station before you board the train. (Everyone needs to pay for any required seat reservations and meal supplements.)

Other great train trips include the **Bernina Express** (which takes you from Swiss glaciers to Italian palm trees in one day) and the lake-strewn **Golden Pass** (from graceful Luzern to jazzy Montreux via Interlaken). The **William Tell Express** connects German-speaking Luzern with Italian-speaking Lugano, starting with a three-hour cruise (from Luzern to Flüelen) and finishing with a train ride (runs only in one direction, starting in Luzern; operates May–Oct only). Reserve ahead for these special rides locally at train stations, or before you go by calling Rail Europe at 800/438-7245.

For a little country, Switzerland has a confusing array of railpasses. If you're visiting Switzerland for a few days, don't bother with them. For a visit of a week or more, they can save you money. If your Swiss travels are focused in a certain region (such as the Berner Oberland), consider a regional pass. Note that Swiss passes are valid on postal buses that reach mountain-high hamlets inaccessible by rail. For details, see www.ricksteves.com/rail.

If you're town- or mountain-hopping through Switzerland by train, you can send your baggage ahead (so you don't have to haul it around with you). Just drop it off at the station and pay up (10 SF with ticket or railpass, 40 SF without, maximum 55 pounds). Your bag will show up within 24 hours of your arrival (usually faster), and will be held free for five days (after that, you're charged 3 SF/day).

A Swiss Timeline

Switzerland forged unity from diversity. Despite four languages, diverse geography, ill-defined borders, and many religious sects—and despite being surrounded by Europe's four big powers (France, Germany, Austria, and Italy)—the Swiss cantons banded together to form an independent federal system that still works today.

500,000,000 B.C.: The ocean floor is rocked by earthquakes that fold the earth upward, creating the Alps.

53 B.C.: Julius Caesar defeats the Helvetia, a Celtic tribe. (Swiss cars today display the "CH" sticker of the traditional name, Confoederatio Helvetica.) The Romans' language, Latin, would eventually develop into the French, Italian, and Romansh languages.

c. A.D. 300: Germanic tribes invade and settle.

c. 600: An Irish missionary named Columbanus arrives and (re-)converts the Swiss to Christianity.

800: Swiss lands are part of Charlemagne's empire, later called the Holy Roman Empire, under German kings.

1256–1273: During an interregnum, in which no emperor rules, the Swiss develop a measure of independence. When Austrian Hapsburgs are brought into reign, the Swiss resent foreign control.

1291: On August 1, Swiss citizens swear the oath, "We will be a one and only nation of brothers..." and rise up against Hapsburg rule. The three cantons of Uri, Schwyz, and Unterwalden unite, proclaiming independence and democratic institutions.

In a legend of the time, the Swiss William Tell refuses to bow to the Hapsburg hat, a symbol of their power. As punishment, he's forced to shoot an apple off his own son's head. He does so, then leads a rebellion.

In fact, the Swiss often outbattled the more powerful Hapsburgs (Battle of Morgarten, 1315), but they had to fight for two full centuries to drive the Hapsburgs out, earning a reputation as Europe's fiercest warriors. Swiss mercenaries (like the Swiss Guards that protect the Vatican today) became a major export product.

1332: Luzern joins the Swiss Federation, soon followed by more cantons.

1499: A treaty makes Switzerland independent in fact, if not in name.

1500s: During the Reformation, Switzerland is bitterly divided but offers a haven for free-thinkers. Ulrich Zwingli establishes Protestantism in Zürich, John Calvin (a Frenchman) brings followers to Geneva, and Erasmus (from Holland) teaches at Basel.

1648: The Treaty of Westphalia officially makes Switzerland independent.

1798: French revolutionary forces occupy Switzerland and try to establish a strong central government. It doesn't stick, so Napoleon restores canton power (1803).

1815: The Congress of Vienna proclaims Switzerland with today's borders.

Scenic Swiss Rail Routes

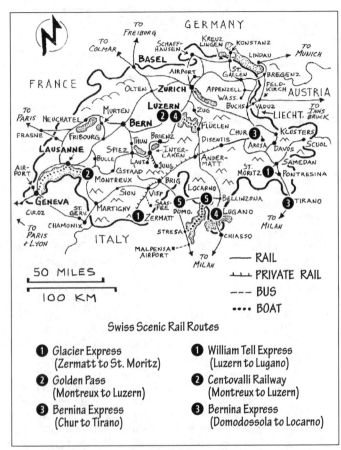

Swiss Scenic Rail Routes

- ① Glacier Express (Zermatt to St. Moritz)
- ② Golden Pass (Montreux to Luzern)
- ③ Bernina Express (Chur to Tirano)
- ① William Tell Express (Luzern to Lugano)
- ② Centovalli Railway (Montreux to Luzern)
- ③ Bernina Express (Domodossola to Locarno)

1848: Amid a Europe-wide wave of liberal reforms, Switzerland's tradition of democracy is established in a constitution. The new Confederation features a modern, bicameral parliament modeled after America's.

1864: The International Red Cross is founded by a Genevan, adopting the Swiss flag with colors reversed as its symbol.

1872–1882: The Gotthard railway is built over the Alps.

1914–1918: In World War I, Switzerland declares neutrality, and Geneva serves as the postwar seat of the League of Nations (a forerunner to the United Nations).

1939–1945: When World War II breaks out, 850,000 Swiss men grab their rifles and mobilize to protect the borders while they declare neutrality. Critics charge that, though neutral, Switzerland's open trade policies helped supply Nazi Germany.

c. 1945: After the war, their policy of neutrality leads the Swiss to refuse membership in the UN, NATO, and the EU.

1989: The final canton grants women the right to vote.

2002: Switzerland joins the United Nations but decides to hold off on EU membership.

2003: Land-locked Switzerland wins the world's most prestigious sailboat race, the America's Cup.

2004: Today, Switzerland's 26 cantons are autonomous, part of a loose federalist democracy. Four political parties rule in an ever-changing array of coalitions, as they have since World War II. The economy thrives on tourism, banking, skilled labor (especially engineering), chemicals, watches, textiles, water power...and chocolate.

ZÜRICH

There's a good chance that you'll pass through Zürich on your travels through Switzerland. It's the nation's rail and airplane hub (see "Zürich Airport" at end of chapter). Though Zürich is known mostly for its banks, there's more to Switzerland's biggest city (360,000). While Bern provides a more charming urban experience, Zürich is worth a quick visit.

ORIENTATION

Tourist Information: There's a TI at the back of the train station (April Mon–Sat 8:30–19:00, Sun 9:00–18:30, May–Oct Mon–Sat 8:00–20:30, Sun 8:30–18:30, less off-season, tel. 012-154-000, www .zuerich.com).

Getting around Zürich: A ticket for the trams and buses costs 2.10 SF (a 1-day pass is 7.20 SF). For a whirlwind visit, consider the **ZürichCARD**, which covers transportation by train, tram, bus, and boat; admission to 43 museums; and welcome drinks in many restaurants (15 SF/24 hrs, 30 SF/72 hrs, sold at TI).

Helpful Hints

Bikes: A city program called "*Züri rollt*" allows you to borrow a bike for free from May through October (leave passport and 20 SF deposit, daily 7:30–21:30, various locations, including train station track 18, Opera, and the Globus office on Bahnhofstrasse—look for *Züri rollt* signs). For more information, ask the TI, or contact Workfare (tel. 013-053-010 or 079-431-4838).

Laundry: Try Speed Wash (Mon–Sat 7:00–22:00, Sun 10:30–22:00, Weinbergstrasse 37, tel. 012-429-914).

INTRODUCTORY ZÜRICH WALK

Start at the train station. Notice the huge modern statue above you, the "Guardian Angel," protecting all travelers.

Take the southern exit and walk down Bahnhofstrasse. On your right, you'll see the only **park** on this pedestrians- and trams-only boulevard. It's dedicated to Zürich's most important teacher, Pestalozzi (1746–1827), who wanted good education to be available for everyone (not only for sons of rich families). Parks like this one are rare in central Zürich because of sky-high property values (around here, it's 20,000 SF per square foot).

Turn left to Werdmühleplatz, continue towards the Limmat River, and make a short stop at the **Police Department.** This building used to be the biggest convent in Zürich, and later became an orphanage (financed by the same Pestalozzi) before being converted into the police station. Don't be shy—enter the police headquarters to have a peek at an amazing wall painting by Swiss artist Augusto Giacometti. His famous "Hall of the Flowers" *(Blüemlihalle),* awash in bright colors, reflects the relief and joy the artist felt when World War I ended.

Continue along the river toward the lake. The small riverside street called **Schipfe** used to be the harbor of Zürich, when the city's trade depended on the river traffic. The name "Schipfe" comes from the Swiss-German word *schüpfe,* which means "push." Here boats were pushed into the water.

Continue along the Limmat River, and you'll walk under **arcaded facades.** These buildings housed medieval baths for the rich. Poor people only used the bath for special occasions, like before they got married. No one bathed in the dirty river, which got the runoff from the slaughterhouse in the gray building across the river.

Now walk up the hill on Pfalzgasse to enjoy a great view from another park: **Lindenhof.** Here stood the oldest building of Zürich, a customs house from Roman times. The Romans stayed here from 14 B.C. until the 4th century A.D., when Germanic tribes took over. The Carolingians built another fortress on top of this hill, but when Zürich became a free city in the 13th century, the townspeople destroyed it and established a law forbidding any new construction. The citizens realized that whoever resided on this hill would rule over the city—and they didn't want any more rulers.

From here, you have a great view over the far side of the Limmat River. The **university** is the largest institution in Switzerland, with 22,000 students. Next to it is Zürich's renowned technical college—the ETH (Eidgenössische Technische Hochschule, or Federal Institute of Technology), with 11,000 students. The ETH has graduated 25 Nobel Prize winners, including Albert Einstein and Wilhelm Röntgen (who discovered X-rays).

Zürich

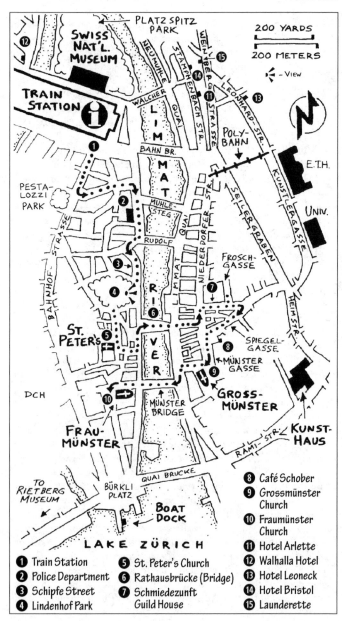

200 YARDS

200 METERS

← – VIEW

1. Train Station
2. Police Department
3. Schipfe Street
4. Lindenhof Park
5. St. Peter's Church
6. Rathausbrücke (Bridge)
7. Schmiedezunft Guild House
8. Café Schober
9. Grossmünster Church
10. Fraumünster Church
11. Hotel Arlette
12. Walhalla Hotel
13. Hotel Leoneck
14. Hotel Bristol
15. Launderette

Take the stairs next to the chess players down to Strehlgasse, and follow Glockengasse and Robert-Walser-Gasse to St. Peterhofstatt, a square with Zürich's oldest church: **St. Peter's.** The eighth-century church has Europe's largest clock face (28 feet in diameter). The town watchman used to live above the clock. His duty was to look through the windows every 15 minutes. If he spotted a fire, he had to ring the alarm and hang a flag out of the window facing the fire. This system seems to have worked—Zürich never suffered a major fire. In the 18th century this church had such a well-loved priest, Johan Kaspar Lavater (1784–1804), that people reserved their seats for Sunday Mass. The priest, a friend of Goethe, had long discussions over glasses of wine with the "German Shakespeare" in the nearby Reblaube Gaststube, which still has a "Goethestube."

Walk down the narrow Thermengasse. Under your feet are excavations of a **Roman bath,** discovered by accident 15 years ago. Before crossing the Rathausbrücke, turn right and walk one block to the best patisserie shop in the city: Teuscher, famous for their Champagne truffles (Mon–Sat 8:00–18:30, Sun 16:00–18:00, Storchengasse 9).

Continue to the **Rathausbrücke.** This is the oldest bridge in the city and was used as a market from Roman times. Cross the bridge and continue up toward the old and cozy **Niederdorf** neighborhood (you'll cross Niederdorf Strasse, lined with eateries). Head up Rindermarkt, passing Zürich's oldest guild house, the **Schmiedezunft.** The coat of arms shows the instruments of the blacksmith, but also the golden snake of doctors and dentists. In the Middle Ages, these guilds were lumped together because the blacksmith made the instruments the doctors used. Besides, the medical professions were considered dirty—dentists were not even allowed to practice within the city walls, due to the screams and the blood. Across the street, you'll find the house where the Swiss author Gottfried Keller (1821–1848) spent his happy youth—and had the many wild drinking adventures that are fodder for local legends even today.

Go up the hill and look to your left. This used to be the **Jewish quarter** until 1348. House #4 on Froschgasse was originally the synagogue and Jewish school. As in other towns throughout Europe, the Jews were held responsible for the last big plague epidemic. They were accused of poisoning the wells, and were attacked by angry locals. Not many survived.

Continue uphill. Just before entering Spiegelgasse, step into the **Stadtarchiv.** The archive displays a model of Zürich from 1800. Now head right, along the Spiegelgasse, and notice the house where **Lenin** lived for one year (1916–1917). When Lenin left for St. Petersburg, citizens wondered why he was heading to that troubled area, not suspecting he had caused many of the problems.

Turn left on Münstergasse, but not without stopping at Zürich's popular **Café Schober.** It serves the best (and most expensive) hot chocolate in the city.

The big church on your right is the **Grossmünster**. Legend says that it was founded by Charlemagne in the eighth century. It was also a monastery and school for second-born sons of noble families. Today it houses the faculty of theology of the University of Zürich. You can climb the left tower (about 200 steps) for a great view over the city (closes at 17:00). The windows are by Swiss artist Giacometti.

Cross the river to the **Fraumünster**. This church also has stained-glass windows by Giacometti, but another famous artist worked here, too. Don't miss the windows in the apse by French modern artist Marc Chagall (from 1970). Walk back to the church nave and look on your left for another Chagall window, created in 1980 (free entry, May–Sept daily 9:00–18:00, Oct–Nov and March–April daily 10:00–17:00, Dec–Feb daily 10:00–16:00).

Your tour is over. From here, consider continuing to the lake for a boat ride (see below)—or back to the station to catch your train.

SIGHTS

Limmatschiff Boat Ride—You can take a cruise on Zürich's lake (Zürichsee) and the Limmat River. From the end of the above walking tour, head for Bürkliplatz (on the lakeshore) to catch the boat (5.40 SF, included in 7.20 SF transit day pass, free with Eurail/Eurail Selectpass and Swiss railpass but uses a flexi-day, 2/hr, daily 11:00–19:00, later mid-June–Sept). After a fun 90-minute ride on the lake, the boat takes you up the Limmat River and back to Swiss National Museum (behind train station).

Swiss National Museum (Schweizerisches Landesmuseum)—This important and massive museum, in a neo-Gothic castle next to the train station, presents a wide range of artifacts from Swiss history. You'll find everything from ancient stone wheels to mountains of ecclesiastical art to halls of costumes from various eras (free, Tue–Sun 10:30–17:00, closed Mon, Museumstrasse 2, tel. 012-186-511).

Kunsthaus Zürich—This great collection of mostly modern art includes Swiss artists (Alberto Giacometti, Johann Heinrich Füssli, Ferdinand Hodler) as well as international greats such as Munch, Picasso, Kokoschka, Beckmann, Corinth, Monet, and Chagall. The younger generation is also represented, with works by Rothko, Merz Twombly, Beuys, Bacon, and Baselitz (10 SF, special exhibits 12–17 SF, Tue–Thu 10:00–21:00, Fri–Sun 10:00–17:00, Heimplatz 1, tram #3, #5, #8, or #9 or bus #31 to Kunsthaus stop, tel. 012-538-484, www.kunsthaus.ch).

Museum Rietberg—In historic villas set in a beautiful park, this museum houses art from Asia, Africa, America, and the South Pacific (14 SF, Tue–Sun 10:00–17:00, Wed 10:00–20:00, closed Mon, tram #7 to Museum Rietberg stop, Villa Wesendonck, Gablerstrasse 15, tel. 012-063-131, www.rietberg.ch).

E.G. Bührle Collection—This collection is a must for lovers of the French Impressionists, their forerunners, and their followers. Here you'll find exceptional paintings by Manet, Degas, Cézanne, Monet, Renoir, Gauguin, van Gogh, Picasso, and Braque. You'll also see a smattering of Dutch Baroque and 18th-century Venetian works, plus religious sculptures from medieval times to the Renaissance (9 SF, Tue, Fri, and Sun 14:00–17:00, Wed 17:00–20:00, closed Mon, Thu, and Sat, tram #2 or #4 to Wildbachstrasse stop, or bus #77 to Altenhofstrasse stop, Zollikerstrasse 172, tel. 014-220-086, www.buehrle.ch).

Platzspitz Park—What used to be a riverside hangout for drug addicts has been cleaned up and is now a safe, family-friendly place, ideal for picnics (free, daily 6:00–21:00, behind train station and Swiss National Museum, clean WC). From here you can take a boat down to the lake (included in 7.20 SF transit pass; see above).

SLEEPING

$$$ Hotel Arlette is a comfortable, small hotel with 30 rooms, well-located an eight-minute walk from the station (Sb-135–185 SF, Db-175–250 SF, Stampfenbachstrasse 26, tel. 012-520-032, fax 012-520-923, hotel.arlette@bluewin.ch, family Schlotter). From the station, take the north exit and cross the Limmat River over the Walchebrücke bridge. Walk through the passageway and turn right.

SLEEP CODE

(1.40 SF = about $1, country code: 41)

Sleep Code: **S** = Single, **D** = Double/Twin, **T** = Triple, **Q** = Quad, **b** = bathroom, **s** = shower only, **no CC** = Credit Cards not accepted, **SE** = Speaks English, **NSE** = No English. Unless otherwise noted, credit cards are accepted, English is spoken, and breakfast is included.

To help you sort easily through these listings, I've divided the rooms into two categories, based on the price for a standard double room with bath:

$$$ **Higher Priced**—Most rooms 200 SF or more.
$$ **Moderately Priced**—Most rooms less than 200 SF.

My listings are near the train station, ideal for those passing through or leaving on an early-morning train or plane (train to airport: 5.40 SF, 10 min, leaves every 10 min).

$$$ **Walhalla Hotel,** just behind the train station, has 48 modern, spacious rooms (Sb-100–150 SF, Db-160–220 SF, breakfast-15 SF, Limmatstrasse 5, tel. 014-465-400, fax 014-465-454).

$$ **Hotel Leoneck,** a 10-minute uphill walk from the station, offers 70 modern yet kitschy bovine-themed rooms at a good price. The hotel—and the good attached Crazy Cow restaurant (daily 6:30–24:00)—somehow manage to make Swiss cows seem cool; enjoy the moo-velous mural in your bedroom (Sb-100–140 SF, Db-150–185 SF, Tb-185–240 SF, Qb-240–290 SF, non-smoking rooms, elevator, Internet access, Leonhardstrasse 1, tel. 012-542-222, fax 012-542-200, www.leoneck.ch, info@leoneck.ch, Herr Gold and his friendly staff SE). From the station, take the Bahnhofstrasse exit and find tram #10 (direction Bahnhof Oerlikon, 2 stops to Haldenegg, look for Crazy Cow restaurant).

$$ **Hotel Bristol,** run by Martin Hämmerli and his friendly staff, offers 54 modern and cozy rooms an eight-minute walk from the station (Sb-110–150 SF, Db-150–190 SF, Tb-190–220 SF, Qb-200–240 SF, 5 percent discount with this book, includes breakfast, Internet access-5 SF/30 min, laundry-15 SF/load, Stampfenbachstrasse 34, tel. 012-584-444, fax 012-584-400, www.hotelbristol.ch, info@hotelbristol .ch). Follow the same directions as for Hotel Arlette (above), but turn left after the passageway onto Stampfenbachstrasse and look for the blue building on the right.

TRANSPORTATION CONNECTIONS

By train to: Interlaken (hrly, 2.25 hrs), **Bern** (2/hr, 1.25 hrs), **Murten** (2/hr, 2–2.5 hrs, transfer in Bern or Fribourg, Switzerland), **Lausanne** (2/hr, 2.5 hrs), **Appenzell** (2/hr, 1.75 hrs with transfer in Gossau or 2.25 hrs with transfer in St. Gallen), **Munich** (every 2 hrs, some direct in 4.5 hrs, some 5.25 hrs with transfer in Stuttgart), **Frankfurt** (at least hrly, 4–4.5 hrs, some direct but most with transfer in Basel or Stuttgart).

Zürich Airport

Smooth, compact, and user-friendly, the Zürich Airport is a major transportation hub and an eye-opening introduction to Swiss efficiency. Swiss airlines use the A concourse, and most others use the B concourse; both funnel to the same immigration line. To find a Suisse Bank exchange office (daily 6:00–22:00), upscale chocolate and watch stores, and Internet access, bypass the immigration line and go to the back wall behind the big staircase. Eateries and ATMs are plentiful before and after immigration. The train station underneath the airport (with a mini-mall, post office, and tidy grocery) can whisk you about anywhere you'd want to go in Europe, including downtown Zürich (5.40 SF, 10 min, leaves every 10 min—much cheaper than the 50 SF taxi ride). Your train ticket into Zürich can be used during the following two hours for all public transportation. For flight information, call the automated toll number: 0900300-313 (press 2 for English).

If you have to catch an early-morning flight, don't spend a fortune to stay near the airport (Hilton, Db starting at 250 SF, tel. 018-285-050). Sleep near the train station downtown (see above), then zip to the airport in the morning on the frequent and fast train.

Trains: The airport has its own station. **By train to: Interlaken** (hrly, 2.5 hrs), **Bern** (2/hr, 1.5 hrs), **Murten** (hrly, 2.75 hrs, change in Fribourg, Switzerland), **Lausanne** (2/hr, 2.75 hrs), **Munich** (4/day, 4.25 hrs), **Appenzell** (2/hr, 1.5 hrs with transfer in Gossau or 2 hrs with transfer in St. Gallen).

GIMMELWALD AND THE BERNER OBERLAND

Frolic and hike high above the stress and clouds of the real world. Take a vacation from your busy vacation. Recharge your touristic batteries up here in the Alps, where distant avalanches, cowbells, the fluff of a down comforter, and the crunchy footsteps of happy hikers are the dominant sounds. If the weather's good (and your budget's healthy), ride a gondola from the traffic-free village of Gimmelwald to a hearty breakfast at Schilthorn's 10,000-foot revolving Piz Gloria restaurant. Linger among alpine whitecaps before riding, hiking, or parasailing down 5,000 feet to Mürren and home to Gimmelwald.

Your gateway to the rugged Berner Oberland is the grand old resort town of Interlaken. Near Interlaken is Switzerland's open-air folk museum, Ballenberg, where you can climb through traditional houses from every corner of this diverse country.

Ah, but the weather's fine and the Alps beckon. Head deep into the heart of the Alps and ride the gondola to the stop just this side of heaven—Gimmelwald.

Planning Your Time

Rather than tackle a checklist of famous Swiss mountains and resorts, choose one region to savor: the Berner Oberland. Interlaken is the administrative headquarters and a fine transportation hub. Use it for business (banking, post office, laundry, shopping) and as a springboard for alpine thrills. With decent weather, explore the two areas (south of Interlaken) that tower above either side of the Lauterbrunnen Valley: Kleine Scheidegg/Jungfrau and Mürren/Schilthorn. Ideally, make the village of Gimmelwald your home base for three nights and spend a day on each side of the valley. On a speedy train trip, you can overnight into and out of Interlaken. For the fastest look, consider a night in Gimmelwald, breakfast at the Schilthorn, an afternoon doing the Männlichen–Wengen hike, and an evening or night train out.

What? A nature-lover not spending the night high in the Alps? Alpus interruptus.

Getting around the Berner Oberland

For more than 100 years, this has been the target of nature-worshiping pilgrims. And Swiss engineers and visionaries have made the most exciting alpine perches accessible by lift or train. Part of the fun (and most of the expense) here is riding the many lifts.

Generally, scenic trains and lifts are not covered on train passes, but a Eurailpass or Eurail Selectpass give you a 25 percent **discount** on even the highest lifts (without the loss of a flexi-day). Ask about discounts for early-morning and late-afternoon trips, youths, seniors, families, groups, and those staying awhile. The Junior Card for families pays for itself in the first hour of trains and lifts: Children under 16 travel free with parents (20 SF/1 child, 40 SF/2 or more children; available at Swiss train stations). Get a list of discounts and the free fare and time schedule at any Swiss train station.

Study the "Alpine Lifts in the Berner Oberland" chart in this chapter. Lifts generally go at least twice hourly, from about 7:00 until about 20:00 (sneak preview: www.jungfrau.ch). **Drivers** can park at the gondola station in Stechelberg (2 SF/2 hrs, 6 SF/day) for the lift to Gimmelwald, Mürren, and the Schilthorn, or at the train station in Lauterbrunnen (2 SF/2 hrs, 9 SF/day) for trains to Wengen and Kleine Scheidegg.

Interlaken

When the 19th-century Romantics redefined mountains as something more than cold and troublesome obstacles, Interlaken became the original alpine resort. Ever since, tourists have flocked to the Alps because they're there. Interlaken's glory days are long gone, its elegant old hotels eclipsed by the new, more jet-setty alpine resorts. Today its shops are filled with chocolate bars, Swiss army knives, and sunburned backpackers.

ORIENTATION

Efficient Interlaken is a good administrative and shopping center. Take care of business, give the town a quick look, and view the live TV coverage of the Jungfrau and Schilthorn weather in the window of the Schilthornbahn office on the main street (at Höheweg 2, Mon–Fri 8:00–12:00 & 13:30–18:00, Sat 8:00–12:00, closed Sun, tel. 033-826-0007, www.schilthorn.ch, also on TV in most hotel lobbies). Then head for the hills. Stay in Interlaken only if you suffer from alptitude sickness (see "Sleeping in Interlaken," at the end of this chapter).

Tourist Information: The TI has good information for the region, advice on alpine lift discounts, and a room-finding service (July–Sept Mon–Fri 8:00–18:30, Sat 8:00–17:00, Sun 10:00–12:00 & 16:00–18:00; Oct–June Mon–Fri 8:00–12:00 & 13:30–18:00, Sat 9:00–12:00, closed Sun, tel. 033-826-5300, www.interlakentourism .ch; attached to Hotel Metropole on the main street between West and East stations, a 10-min walk from either). While the Interlaken/Jungfrau region map costs 2 SF, good mini-versions are included in the many free transportation and hiking brochures. Pick up a Bern map if that's your next destination.

Arrival in Interlaken: Interlaken has two train stations: East (Ost) and West. Most major trains stop at the Interlaken-West station. This station's helpful and friendly train information desk answers tourists' questions (travel center for in-depth rail questions: Mon–Fri 8:00–18:00, Sat–Sun 8:00–12:00 & 14:00–18:00, Nov–March closed Mon–Fri 12:00–14:00; ticket windows: daily 6:00–20:45; tel. 033-826-4750). There's a fair exchange booth next to the ticket windows. Ask at the station about discount passes, special fares, railpass discounts, and schedules for the scenic mountain trains.

It's a pleasant 20-minute walk between the West and East stations, or an easy, frequent train connection (2/hr, 2.60 SF). From the Interlaken-East station, private trains take you deep into the mountainous Jungfrau region (see "Transportation Connections" at the end of this chapter).

Helpful Hints

Telephone: Phone booths cluster outside the post office near the West station. For efficiency, buy a phone card from a newsstand. (Gimmelwald's sole public phone—at the gondola station—takes only cards, not coins.)

Laundry: Friendly Helen Schmocker's *Wäscherei* has a change machine, soap, English instructions, and a pleasant riverside location (open daily 7:00–22:00 for self-service; for full service: Mon–Fri 8:00–12:00 & 13:30–18:00, Sat 8:00–12:00 & 13:30–16:00, closed Sun, drop off in the morning and pick up that afternoon, tel. 033-822-1566; exit left from West station and follow the main street to the post office, turn left and take Marktgasse over 2 bridges to Beatenbergstrasse 5).

Warning: On Sundays and holidays, small-town Switzerland is quiet. Hotels are open, and lifts and trains run, but many restaurants and most stores are closed. If this concerns you, call the Interlaken TI to see if a holiday falls during your visit.

Stores: A brand-new **Migros supermarket** is across the street from Interlaken West train station (Mon–Thu 8:00–18:30, Fri 8:00–21:00, Sat 7:30–16:00, closed Sun). The **Co-op Pronto** mini-

Interlaken

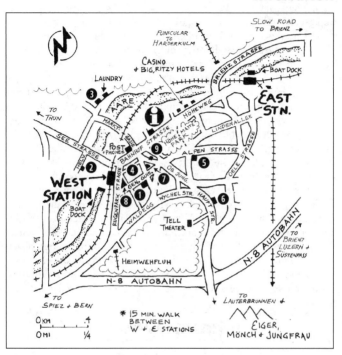

SLOW ROAD TO BRIENZ →

FUNICULAR To HARDERKULM

CASINO & BIG, RITZY HOTELS

BRIENZ STRASSE

← BOAT DOCK

LAUNDRY

❸

AARE

TO THUN

HOHEWEG

MARKT GASSE

SEE STRASSE

HOHEMATTE PARK

LINDENALLEE

EAST STN.

ℹ️

POST + PHONES

BAHNHOF STRASSE

ALPEN STRASSE

OELE STRASSE

❷

❾

❺

❹

GEN. GUIS.

❼

OB. JUNG.

WEST STATION

BOAT DOCK

RUGENPARK STRASSE

❽

❶

WALDEGG

WYCHEL STR.

HAUPT STR.

❻

N-8 AUTOBAHN

TO BRIENZ LUZERN & SÜSTENPASS

TELL THEATER

HEIMWEHFLUH

N-8 AUTOBAHN

TO SPIEZ & BERN

0 KM — .4
0 MI — ¼

* 15 MIN. WALK BETWEEN W + E STATIONS

TO LAUTERBRUNNEN &

EIGER, MÖNCH & JUNGFRAU

market has longer hours (daily 6:00–22:00, across from TI). There's lots of buzz surrounding Interlaken's **Hanf Center,** a small shop selling a wide selection of products made from hemp, including clothes, paper, noodles, and beer (Mon 13:30–18:30, Tue–Fri 10:00–12:00 & 13:30–18:30, Sat 10:00–16:00, closed Sun, Jungfraustrasse 47, near end of Höhematte Park closest to West station, tel. 033-823-1552).

SIGHTS

Boat Trips—*Interlaken* means "between the lakes"—Thun and Brienz, to be exact. You can explore these lakes on a lazy boat trip (8/day mid-June–mid-Sept, fewer off-season, free with Eurail/Eurail Selectpass but uses a flexi-day, schedules at TI or at BLS Travel Center in West station, tel. 033-826-4750 or 033-334-5211). The boats on **Lake Thun** (4 hrs, 40 SF round-trip) stop at the **St. Beatus Höhlen caves** (16 SF, April–mid-Oct daily 10:30–17:00, closed mid-Oct–March, 30-min boat ride from Interlaken, tel. 033-841-1643, www.beatushoehlen.ch) and two visit-worthy towns: Spiez (1 hr from Interlaken) and Thun (1.75 hrs). The boats on **Lake Brienz** (3 hrs, 32 SF round-trip) stop at the super-cute and quiet village of Iseltwald (45 min away) and at Brienz (1.25 hrs away, near Ballenberg Open-Air Folk Museum).

Adventure Trips—For the adventurer with money and little concern for personal safety, several companies offer high-adrenaline trips such as rafting, canyoning (rappelling down watery gorges), bungee jumping, and paragliding. Most adventure trips cost 90–180 SF. Interlaken companies include: Alpin Raft (tel. 033-823-4100, www.alpinraft.ch), Alpin Center (at Wilderswil station and across from Balmer's youth hostel, tel. 033-823-5523, www.alpincenter.ch), Swiss Adventures (tel. 033-773-7373, www.swissadventures.ch), and Outdoor Interlaken (tel. 033-826-7719, www.outdoor-interlaken.ch). For an overview of your options, visit www.interlakenadventure.com.

Recent fatal accidents have understandably hurt the adventure-sport business in the Berner Oberland. In May 2000, an American died bungee jumping from the Stechelberg–Mürren gondola (the operator used a 180-meter rope for a 100-meter jump). Also in 2000, a landslide killed several hikers. In July 1999, 21 tourists died canyoning on the Saxetenbach River, 10 miles from Interlaken; they were battered and drowned by a flash flood filled with debris. Enjoying nature up close comes with risks. Adventure sports increase those risks dramatically. Use good judgment.

Gimmelwald

Saved from developers by its "avalanche zone" classification, Gimmelwald was (before tourism) one of the poorest places in Switzerland. Its traditional economy was stuck in the hay, and its farmers, unable to make it in their disadvantaged trade, survived only by Swiss government subsidies (and working the ski lifts in the winter). For some travelers, there's little to see in the village. Others enjoy a fascinating day sitting on a bench and learning why they say, "If Heaven isn't what it's cracked up to be, send me back to Gimmelwald." Gimmelwald is my home base in the Berner Oberland (see "Sleeping in Gimmelwald," page 477).

Take a walk through the town. This place is for real. Most of the 130 residents have the same last name: von Allmen. They are tough and proud. Raising hay in this rugged terrain is labor-intensive. One family harvests enough to feed only 15 or 20 cows. But they'd have it no other way, and, unlike the absentee-landlord town of Mürren, Gimmelwald is locally owned. (When word got out that urban planners wished to develop Gimmelwald into a town of 1,000, locals pulled some strings to secure the town's bogus avalanche-zone building code.)

The huge, sheer cliff face that dominates your mountain views from Gimmelwald (and Mürren) is the Schwarzmönch (Black Monk).

Gimmelwald

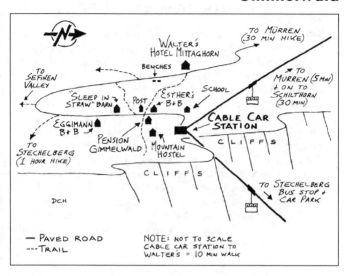

The three peaks above (or behind) it are, left to right, the Eiger, Mönch, and Jungfrau.

Do not confuse obscure Gimmelwald with touristy and commercialized Grindelwald, just over the Kleine Scheidegg ridge.

A WALK THROUGH GIMMELWALD

Gimmelwald, though tiny with one zigzag street, gives a fine look at a traditional mountain Swiss community. Here's a quick walking tour:

Gondola Station: When the lift came in the 1960s, this village's back end became Gimmelwald's front door. This was, and still is, a farm village. Stepping off the gondola, you see a sweet little hut. Set on stilts to keep out mice, the hut was used for storing cheese (the rocks on the rooftop keep the shingles on through wild winter winds). Notice the yellow alpine "street sign" showing where you are, the altitude (4,470 feet), and how many hours *(Std.)* and minutes it takes to walk to nearby points. Behind the cheese hut stands the village schoolhouse. In Catholic Swiss towns, the biggest building is the church. In Protestant towns, it's the school. Gimmelwald's biggest building is the school (2 teachers, 17 students, and a room that doubles as a chapel when the Protestant pastor makes his monthly visit). Don't let Gimmelwald's low-tech look fool you: In this school, each kid has his or her own Web site. In the opposite direction, just beyond the little playground, is Gimmelwald's Mountain Hostel.

SWISS COW CULTURE

Traditional Swiss cow farmers could make more money for much easier work in another profession. In a good year, farmers produce enough cheese to break even—they support their families on government subsidies. (The government supports traditional farming as much for the tourism as for the cheese.) But these farmers have made a lifestyle choice to keep tradition alive and to live high in the mountains. Rather than lose their children to the cities (a big issue for Rhine vintner families), Swiss farmers have the opposite problem: Kids argue over who gets to take over the family herd.

The cows' grazing ground can range in elevation by as much as 5,000 feet throughout the year. In the summer (usually mid-June), the farmer straps elaborate ceremonial bells on his herd and takes them up to a hut at high elevations. The cows hate these big bells, which can cost upwards of 2,000 SF apiece—a proud investment for a humble farmer. When the cows arrive at their summer home, the bells are hung under the eaves.

These high-elevation summer stables are called "alps." Try to find some on a Berner Oberland tourist map (e.g., Wengernalp, Grütschalp, Schiltalp). The cows stay at the alps for about 100 days. The farmers hire a team of cheese makers to work at each alp—mostly hippies, students, and city slickers eager to spend three

Walk up the lane 50 yards, past the shower in the phone booth, to Gimmelwald's...

Times Square: From this tiny intersection, we'll follow the town's main street (away from gondola station, where most yellow arrows are pointing). Most of the buildings used to house two families and are divided vertically right down the middle. The writing on the post office building is a folksy blessing: "Summer brings green, winter brings snow. The sun greets the day, the stars greet the night. This house will keep you warm. May God give us his blessings." The date indicates when it was built or rebuilt (1911).

Main Street: Walk up the road. Notice the announcement board: one side for tourist news, the other for local news. Cross the street and peek into the big new barn, dated 1995. This is part of the Sleep in Straw association, which rents out barn spots to travelers when the cows are in the high country. To the left of the door is a cow scratcher. Swiss cows have legal rights (for example, in the winter, they must be taken out for exercise at least 3 times a week). This big barn is built in a modern style. Traditionally, barns were summer months in the mountains. Each morning, the hired hands get up at 5:00 to milk the cows, take them to pasture, and make the cheese—milking the cows again when they come home in the evening.

Every alp also has a resident herd of pigs. Cheese-making leftovers (*Molke,* or whey) can damage the ecosystem if thrown out—but pigs love the stuff. Cheese makers claim that bathing in whey improves the complexion...but maybe that's just the altitude talking.

Meanwhile, the farmers—glad to be free of their bovine responsibilities—turn their attention to making hay. The average farmer has a few huts at various altitudes, each surrounded by small hay fields. The farmer follows the seasons up into the mountains, making hay and storing it above the huts. In the fall, the cows come down from the alps and spend the winter moving from hut to hut, eating the hay the farmer spent the summer preparing for them.

Throughout the year, you'll see farmers moving their herds to various elevations. If snow is in the way, farmers sometimes use tourist gondolas to move their cows. Every two months or so, Gimmelwald farmers bring together cows that aren't doing so well and herd them into the gondola to meet the butcher in the valley below.

small (like those on the hillside high above) and closer to the hay. But with trucks and paved roads, hay can be moved easier and farther, and farms need more cows to be viable. Still, even a well-run big farm hopes just to break even. The industry survives only with government subsidies (see "Swiss Cow Culture," above). Go just beyond the next barn and look to your right.

Water Fountain/Trough: This is the site of the town's historic water supply. Local kids love to bathe in this when the cows aren't drinking from it. From here, detour left down a lane about 50 yards (along a wooden fence and past pea-patch gardens) to the next trough and the oldest building in town, Husmättli, from 1658. Study the log-cabin construction. Many are built without nails.

Back on the paved road, continue uphill. Gimmelwald has a strict building code. For instance, shutters can only be natural, green, or white. Notice the cute cheese hut on the right (with stones on the shingles and alpine cheese for sale). It's full of strong cheese—up to three years old. On the left (at B&B sign) is the home of Olle and Maria, the village schoolteachers. Gimmelwald heats with wood and, since the wood needs to age a couple of years to burn well, it's stacked everywhere. Fifty yards farther along is the...

Alpenrose: At the old schoolhouse, notice the big ceremonial cowbells hanging under the uphill eave. These swing from the necks of cows during the alpine procession from the town to the high Alps (mid-June) and back down (around Sept 20). At the end of town, notice the dramatic Sefinen Valley. The road switches back at the...

Gimmelwald Fire Station: Check out the notices up above on the fire station building. Every Swiss male does a year in the military, then a few days a year in the reserves until about age 40. The 2004 Swiss Army calendar tells the reserves when and where to go. The *Schiessübungen* poster details the shooting exercises required this year. In keeping with the William Tell heritage, each Swiss man does shooting practice annually for the military (or spends 3 days in jail).

High Road: Follow the high road to Hotel Mittaghorn. The resort of Mürren hovers in the distance. And high on the left, notice the hay field with terraces. These are from WWII days, when Switzerland, wanting self-sufficiency, required all farmers to grow potatoes. From Hotel Mittaghorn, you can return to Gimmelwald's Times Square via the stepped path.

Gimmelwald after Dark—Evening fun in Gimmelwald is found at the hostel (offering a pool table, Internet access, lots of young Alp-aholics, and a good chance to share information on the surrounding mountains) or at Pension Gimmelwald's terrace restaurant next door. Walter's bar (in Hotel Mittaghorn) is a local farmers' hangout. When they've made their hay, they come here to play. Although they look like what some people would call hicks, they speak some English and can be fun to get to know. Sit outside (benches just below the rails, 100 yards down the lane from Walter's) and watch the sun tuck the mountaintops into bed as the moon rises over the Jungfrau. If this isn't your idea of nightlife, stay in Interlaken.

BERNER OBERLAND SIGHTS AND ACTIVITIES

Alpine Excursions

There are days of possible hikes from Gimmelwald. Many are a fun combination of trails, mountain trains, and gondola rides. Don't mind the fences (although wires can be solar-powered electric); a hiker has the right of way in Switzerland. However, as late as June, snow can curtail your hiking plans (the Männlichen lift doesn't even open until the first week in June). Before setting out on any hike, get advice from a knowledgeable local to confirm that it is safe, accessible, and doable before dark. Clouds can roll in anytime, but skies are usually clearest in the morning. That means you need rain gear *and* sunscreen, regardless of the current weather. Don't forget a big water bottle and some

Lauterbrunnen Valley: West Side Story

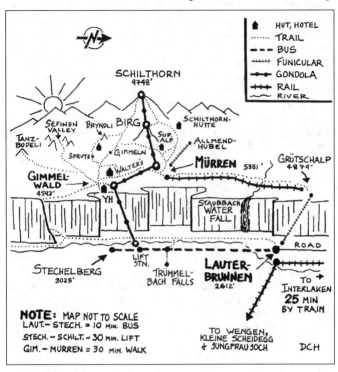

munchies. Refer to maps (within this chapter) as you read about the following hikes.

▲▲▲**The Schilthorn: Hikes, Lifts, and a 10,000-Foot Breakfast**—
The Schilthornbahn carries skiers, hikers, and sightseers effortlessly to the 10,000-foot summit of the Schilthorn, where the Piz Gloria station awaits with a solar-powered revolving restaurant, shop, and panorama terrace. Linger on top. Piz Gloria has a free "touristorama" film room with a multi-screen slide show and explosive highlights from the James Bond thriller that featured the Schilthorn *(On Her Majesty's Secret Service;* if it's not running, press the 007 button on the column in the middle of the room).

Watch hang gliders set up, psych up, and take off, flying 30 minutes with the birds to distant Interlaken. Walk along the ridge out back. This is a great place for a photo of the "mountain-climber you." For another cheap thrill, ask the gondola attendant to crank down the window (easiest on the Mürren–Birg section). Then stick your head out the window...and you're hang gliding.

The early-bird and afternoon-special **gondola tickets** (60 SF round-trip, before 9:00 or after 15:30) take you from Gimmelwald to the Schilthorn and back at a discount (normal rate-80 SF, or 94 SF from the Stechelberg car park; parking-2 SF/2 hrs, 6 SF/day). These same discounted fares are available all day long in the shoulder season (roughly May and Oct). Ask the Schilthorn station for a gondola souvenir decal (Schilthornbahn station in Stechelberg tel. 033-856-2141). For breakfast at 10,000 feet, there's no à la carte—only a fixed meal for 15 SF (rolls and hot chocolate or coffee) or 22.50 SF (add egg, ham, and Champagne; breakfast served 8:00–11:00). If you're going for breakfast before 9:00, consider an early-bird-plus-breakfast combo-ticket to save a few francs (73 SF round-trip from Gimmelwald, 84 SF from Stechelberg). Ask for more hot drinks if necessary. If you're not revolving, ask them to turn it on.

Lifts go twice hourly, and the ride (including 2 transfers) to the Schilthorn takes 30 minutes. Watch the altitude meter in the gondola. (The Gimmelwald–Schilthorn hike is free if you don't mind a 5,000-foot altitude gain.) You can ride up to the Schilthorn and hike down, but it's tough (weather can change; wear good shoes). Youth hostelers scream down the ice fields on plastic-bag sleds from the Schilthorn mountaintop. (English-speaking doctor in Lauterbrunnen.)

Just below Birg is **Schilthornhütte.** Drop in for soup, cocoa, or a coffee schnapps. You can spend the night in the hut's crude loft (dorm bed with breakfast-35 SF, 20 SF more for dinner, open July–Sept Fri-Sun, Dec–April daily, tel. 033-855-5053, schilthornhuette@muerren.ch).

Hard-core hikers could enjoy the **hike** from Birg to Gimmelwald (from Schilthorn summit, ride cable car halfway down, get off at Birg, and hike down from there; buy the round-trip excursion early-bird fare—which is cheaper than the Gimmelwald–Schilthorn–Birg ticket—and decide at Birg if you want to hike or ride down). The most interesting trail from Birg to Gimmelwald is the high one via Grauseeli Lake and Wasenegg Ridge to Brünli, then down to Spielbodenalp and the Sprutz waterfall. Warning: This trail is quite steep and slippery in places and can take four to six hours. Locals take their kindergartners on this hike, but it can seem dangerous to Americans unused to alpine hikes. Do not attempt this hike in snow—which you might find at this altitude even in the peak of summer. From the Birg lift, hike toward the Schilthorn, taking your first left down to the little, newly made Grauseeli Lake. From the lake, a gravelly trail leads down rough switchbacks (including a stretch where the path narrows and you can hang onto a guide cable against the cliff face) until it levels out. When you see a rock painted with arrows pointing to Mürren and Rotstockhütte, follow the path to Rotstockhütte, traversing the cow-grazed mountainside. Follow Wasenegg Ridge left and down along the barbed-wire fence to Brünli. (For maximum thrills, stay on the ridge and climb all the way to the

Berner Oberland

NOTE: THIS BIRD'S-EYE VIEW LOOKS SOUTH...

EIGER 13026'   MÖNCH 13449'   JUNGFRAU 13642'   SCHILTHORN 9748'

JUNGFRAUJOCH

TUNNEL

GREAT HIKE

KLEINE SCHEIDEGG 6762'

GIMMELWALD 4593'

BIRG 8791'

W. ALP

MÜRREN 5381'

STECHELBERG 3025'

NICE WALK

GRINDELWALD 3393'

MÄNNLICHEN 7317'

GRUND

GRÜTSCHALP 4879'

TO FIRST

WENGEN 4180'

LAUTERBRUNNEN 2612'

ISENFLUH

WILDERSWIL 1916'

SCHYNIGE PLATTE 6454'

ISELTWALD

SPIEZ

TO LUZERN

LAKE BRIENZ

BRIENZ

BALLENBERG

E.   W.

INTERLAKEN 1860'

LAKE THUN

TO BERN

Legend	
+++ PRIVATE RAIL - EURAIL NOT VALID	--- BUS
+++ OTHER RAIL - EURAIL VALID	•••• BOAT
o—o MTN. LIFTS	••••• TRAIL

NOT TO SCALE!

DCH

knobby little summit, where you'll enjoy an incredible 360-degree view and a chance to sign your name on the register stored in the little wooden box.) A steep trail winds directly down from Brünli toward Gimmelwald and soon hits a bigger, easy trail. The trail bends right (just before the popular restaurant/mountain hut at Spielbodenalp), leading to Sprutz. Walk under the Sprutz waterfall, then follow a steep, wooded trail that will deposit you in a meadow of flowers at the top side of Gimmelwald.

▲▲**North Face Trail from Mürren**—For a pleasant two-hour hike (4 miles, from 6,385 feet to 5,375 feet), ride the Allmendhubel funicular up from Mürren (7.40 SF, cheaper than Schilthorn, good restaurant at top). From there, follow the well-promoted and well-described route circling around to Mürren (or cut off near the end down to Gimmelwald). You'll enjoy great views, flowery meadows, mountain huts, and a dozen information boards along the way describing the climbing history of the great peaks around you.

Alpine Lifts in the Berner Oberland

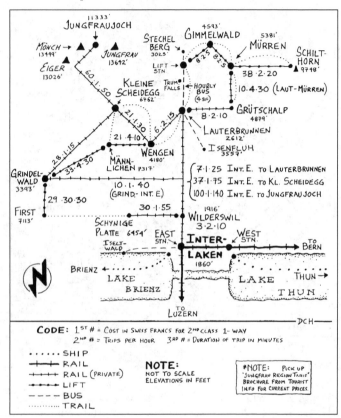

▲▲▲**The Männlichen-Kleine Scheidegg Hike**—This is my favorite easy alpine hike. It's entertaining all the way, with glorious Jungfrau, Eiger, and Mönch views. That's the Young Maiden being protected from the Ogre by the Monk. (Note that trails may be snowbound into June; ask about conditions at the lift stations or local TI. If the Männlichen lift is closed, take the train straight from Lauterbrunnen to Kleine Scheidegg.)

If the weather's good, descend from Gimmelwald bright and early to Stechelberg. From here, get to the Lauterbrunnen train station by post bus (3.80 SF, bus is synchronized to depart with the arrival of each lift) or by car (parking at the large multistoried pay lot behind the Lauterbrunnen station-2 SF/2 hrs, 9 SF/day). At Lauterbrunnen, buy a train ticket to Männlichen (28 SF one-way). Sit on the right side of the train for great waterfall views on your way up to Wengen. In Wengen, walk across town (buy a picnic but don't waste time here if it's sunny) and catch the Männlichen lift (departing every 15 min, beginning the first week of June) to the top of the ridge high above you.

From the Wengen-Männlichen lift station, turn left and hike uphill 20 minutes north to the little peak (Männlichen Gipfel) for that king- or queen-of-the-mountain feeling. Then take an easy hour's walk—facing spectacular alpine panorama views—to Kleine Scheidegg for a picnic or restaurant lunch. To start the hike, leave the Wengen-Männlichen lift station to the right. Walk past the second Männlichen lift station (this one leads to Grindelwald, the touristy town in the valley to your left). Ahead of you in the distance, left to right, are the north faces of the Eiger, Mönch, and Jungfrau; in the foreground is the Tschuggen peak, and just behind it, the Lauberhorn. This hike will take you around the left (east) side of this ridge. Simply follow the signs for Kleine (Kl.) Scheidegg, and you'll be there in about an hour—a little more for gawkers, picnickers, and photographers. You might have to tiptoe through streams of melted snow—or some small snow banks, even well into the summer—but the path is well marked, well maintained, and mostly level all the way to Kleine Scheidegg.

About 35 minutes into the hike, you'll reach a bunch of benches and a shelter with incredible unobstructed views of all three peaks—the perfect picnic spot. Fifteen minutes later on the left, you'll see the first sign of civilization: Restaurant Grindelwaldblick, offering a handy terrace lunch stop with tasty, hearty, and reasonable food (daily, closed Dec and May, see "Sleeping and Eating in Kleine Scheidegg," page 485). After 10 more minutes, you'll be at the Kleine Scheidegg train station, with plenty of other lunch options (including Bahnhof Buffet, see "Sleeping and Eating in Kleine Scheidegg," page 485).

From Kleine Scheidegg, you can catch the train to "the top of Europe" (see "Jungfraujoch," below). Or head downhill, riding the train or hiking (30 gorgeous min to Wengernalp station; 90 more steep min from there into the town of Wengen). The alpine views might be accompanied by the valley-filling mellow sound of Alp horns and distant avalanches.

If the weather turns bad or you run out of steam, catch the train early at the little Wengernalp station along the way. After Wengernalp, the trail to Wengen is steep and, though not dangerous, requires a good set of knees. Wengen is a good shopping town. (For accommodations, see "Sleeping in Wengen," page 483.) The boring final descent from Wengen to Lauterbrunnen is knee-killer steep—catch the train.

▲▲▲**Jungfraujoch**—The literal high point of any trip to the Swiss Alps is a train ride through the Eiger to the Jungfraujoch. At 11,300 feet, it's Europe's highest train station. The ride from Kleine Scheidegg takes about an hour (sit on right side for better views), including two five-minute stops at stations actually halfway up the notorious North

Face of the Eiger. You have time to look out windows and marvel at how people could climb the Eiger and how the Swiss built this train more than a hundred years ago. The second half of the ride takes you through a tunnel inside the Eiger (some newer trains run multi-lingual videos about the history of the train).

Once you reach the top, study the Jungfraujoch chart to see your options (many of them are weather-dependent). There's a restaurant, history exhibit, ice palace (a cavern with a gallery of ice statues), and a continuous 20-minute video. A tunnel leads outside, where you can ski (30 SF for gear and lift ticket), sled (free loaner discs with deposit), ride in a dog sled (6 SF, mornings only), or hike 45 minutes across the ice to Mönchsjochhütte (a mountain hut with a small restaurant). An elevator leads to the Sphinx observatory for the highest viewing point from which you can see Aletsch Glacier—Europe's longest, at nearly 11 miles—stretch to the south. Remember that your body isn't used to such high altitudes. Signs posted at the top remind you to take it easy.

The first trip of the day to Jungfraujoch is discounted; ask for a Good Morning Ticket and return from the top by noon (Nov–April you can get Good Morning rates for first or second train and stay after noon; train runs all year; round-trip fares to Jungfraujoch: from Kleine Scheidegg-normally 102 SF, 65 SF for first trip of day—about 8:02; from Lauterbrunnen-150 SF, 113 SF for first trip—about 7:08, confirm times and prices, discounts for Eurail/Eurail Selectpass and Swiss rail-pass holders, get leaflet on lifts at a local TI or call 033-828-7233, www.jungfrau.ch). For a trilingual weather forecast, call 033-828-7931; if it's cloudy, skip the trip.

▲▲Hike from Schynige Platte to First—The best day I've had hiking in the Berner Oberland was when I made the demanding six-hour ridge walk high above Lake Brienz on one side, with all that Jungfrau beauty on the other. Start at Wilderswil train station (just above Interlaken) and catch the little train up to Schynige Platte (6,560 feet). Walk through the flower display garden and into the wild alpine yonder. The high point is Faulhorn (8,790 feet, with its famous mountaintop hotel). Hike to a small gondola called "First" (7,110 feet), then descend to Grindelwald and catch a train back to your starting point, Wilderswil. Or, if you have a regional train pass (or no car but endless money), return to Gimmelwald via Lauterbrunnen from Grindelwald over Kleine Scheidegg. For an abbreviated ridge walk, consider the Panoramaweg, a short loop from Schynige Platte to Daub Peak.

▲Mountain Biking—Mountain biking is popular and accepted (as long as you stay on the clearly marked mountain-bike paths). A popular ride is the round-trip Mürren Loop that runs from Mürren to Gimmelwald, down the Sefinen Valley to Stechelberg, Lauterbrunnen (by funicular, bike costs same as person-7.80 SF), Grütschalp, and back to Mürren. You can rent bikes in Mürren (Stäger Sport, 25 SF/4 hrs, 35 SF/day, daily 9:00–17:00, closed May and Nov, across from TI/Sportzentrum, tel. 033-855-2355, www.staegersport.ch) or in Lauterbrunnen (Imboden Bike, 25 SF/4 hrs, 35 SF/day, full-suspension—reserve ahead—45 SF/half-day, 65 SF/full day, daily 8:00-18:30, tel. 033-855-2114).

You can also bike the Lauterbrunnen Valley from Lauterbrunnen to Interlaken. It's a gentle downhill ride via a peaceful bike path across the river from the road. Rent a bike at Lauterbrunnen (see above), bike to Interlaken, and return to Lauterbrunnen by train (to take bike on train, pay 3.30 SF extra from East station or 4.60 SF extra from West station). Or rent a bike at either Interlaken station, take the train to Lauterbrunnen, and ride back.

▲**More Hikes near Gimmelwald**—For a not-too-tough, three-hour walk (but there's a scary 20-minute stretch) with great Jungfrau views and some mountain farm action, ride the funicular from Mürren to Allmendhubel (6,344 feet) and walk to Marchegg, Saustal, and Grütschalp (a drop of about 1,500 feet), where you can catch the panorama train back to Mürren. An easier version is the lower Bergweg from Allmendhubel to Grütschalp via Winteregg. For an easy family stroll with grand views, walk from Mürren just above the train tracks to either Winteregg (40 min, restaurant, playground, train station) or Grütschalp (60 min, train station), then catch the panorama train back to Mürren. An easy, go-as-far-as-you-like trail from Gimmelwald is up the Sefinen Valley. Or you can wind from Gimmelwald down to Stechelberg (60 min).

You can get specifics at the Mürren TI. For a description of six diverse hikes on the west side of Lauterbrunnen, pick up the fine and free *Mürren-Schilthorn Hikes* brochure. This 3-D map of the Mürren mountainside makes a useful and attractive souvenir. For the other side of the valley, get the *Wandern Jungfraubahnen* brochure, also with a handy 3-D map of hiking trails (both brochures free, at stations, hotels, and TIs).

Rainy-Day Options

When it rains here, locals joke that they're washing the mountains. If clouds roll in, don't despair. They can roll out just as quickly, and there are plenty of good bad-weather options.

▲▲**Cloudy-Day Lauterbrunnen Valley Walk**—There are easy trails and pleasant walks along the floor of the Lauterbrunnen Valley. For a smell-the-cows-and-flowers lowland walk—ideal for a cloudy day, weary body, or tight budget—follow the riverside trail from Stechelberg's Schilthornbahn station for three miles to Lauterbrunnen's Staubbach Falls, near the town church (you can reverse the route, but it's a gradual uphill to Stechelberg). Detour to Trümmelbach Falls (below) en route. There's a fine, paved, car-free, riverside path all the way.

If you're staying in Gimmelwald: Take the lift down to Stechelberg (5 min), then walk to Lauterbrunnen, detouring to Trümmelbach Falls shortly after Stechelberg (15 min to falls, another 45 min to Lauter-brunnen). To return to Gimmelwald from Lauterbrunnen, take the funicular up to Grütschalp (10 min), then either walk (90 min to Gimmelwald) or take the panorama train (15 min) to Mürren. From Mürren, it's a downhill walk (30 min) to Gimmelwald. (This loop trip can be reversed.)

▲**Trümmelbach Falls**—If all the waterfalls have you intrigued, sneak a behind-the-scenes look at the valley's most powerful one, Trümmelbach Falls (10 SF, July–Aug daily 8:30–18:00, June 9:00–17:30, Easter–May and Sept–mid-Nov daily 9:00–17:00, closed mid-Nov–Easter, on Lauterbrunnen–Stechelberg road, take postal bus from Lauterbrunnen TI or Stechelberg gondola station, tel. 033-855-3232). You'll ride an elevator up through the mountain and climb through several caves (wet, with lots of stairs, and—for some—claustrophobic) to see the melt from the Eiger, Mönch, and Jungfrau grinding like God's band saw through the mountain at the rate of up to 5,200 gallons a second (that's 20,000 liters—nearly double the beer consumption at Oktoberfest). The upper area is the best; if your legs ache, skip the lower falls and ride down on the elevator.

Lauterbrunnen Folk Museum—The Heimatmuseum in Lauter-brunnen shows off the local folk culture (free if you're staying in the region, 2 SF if you're staying in Interlaken, 3 SF otherwise, mid-June–mid-Oct Tue, Thu, and Sat–Sun 14:00–17:00, closed off-season, just over bridge and below church at the far end of town, tel. 033-855-3586 or 033-855-1388).

Mürren Activities—This low-key alpine resort town offers a variety of rainy-day activities, from its shops to its slick *Sportzentrum* (sports center) with pools, steam baths, squash, and a fitness center (for details, see "Sleeping in Mürren," page 480). On Wednesday nights at 20:30 from June through August, Mürren's *Sportzentrum* hosts a lively free cultural night with alpenhorns, folk music, and local wine.

Interlaken Boat Trips—Consider taking a boat trip from Interlaken (see "Sights" in Interlaken, page 463).

▲▲**Swiss Open-Air Folk Museum at Ballenberg**—Across Lake Brienz from Interlaken, the Swiss Open-Air Museum of Vernacular Architecture, Country Life, and Crafts in the Bernese Oberland is a rich collection of traditional and historic farmhouses from every region of the country. Each house is carefully furnished, and many feature tradi-tional craftspeople at work. The sprawling 50-acre park, laid out roughly as a huge Swiss map, is a natural preserve providing a wonderful setting for this culture-on-a-lazy-Susan look at Switzerland.

The Thurgau house (#621) has an interesting wattle-and-daub (half-timbered construction) display, and house #331 has a fun bread museum. Visit the new chocolate shop. Use the 2 SF map/guide. The more expensive picture book is a better souvenir than guide (entry–16

SF, half-price after 16:00, houses open May–Oct daily 10:00–17:00, park stays open later, craft demonstration schedules are listed just inside entry, tel. 033-952-1030, www.ballenberg.ch).

A reasonable outdoor cafeteria is inside the west entrance, and fresh bread, sausage, mountain cheese, and other goodies are on sale in several houses. Picnic tables and grills with free firewood are scattered throughout the park.

The little wooden village of Brienzwiler (near the east entrance) is a museum in itself, with a lovely little church.

To get from Interlaken to Ballenberg: Take the train from Interlaken to Brienz (hrly, 30 min, 7.20 SF one-way from West station). From Brienz, catch a bus to Ballenberg (10 min, 3 SF one-way) or hike (45 min, slightly uphill). If you have the time, consider coming back by boat (Brienz boat dock next to train station, one-way to Interlaken-16 SF). Trains also run occasionally from Interlaken to Brienzwiler, a 20-min uphill walk to the museum (every 2 hrs, 30 min, 9.20 SF one-way from West station). A RailAway combo-ticket, available at either Interlaken station, includes transportation to and from Ballenberg and your admission (32 SF from West, 30.40 SF from East, add 9.40 SF to return by boat instead).

Mystery Park—This new theme park in Wilderswil (just south of Interlaken) ranks as a low sightseeing priority even in bad weather. The park has modest exhibits on six themes that explore the world's mysteries, from the construction of Stonehenge (with an impressive laser-light show that is the park's highlight) to the challenge of maintaining a space station on Mars (48 SF, daily 10:00–17:30, tel. 033-827-5757, www.mysterypark.ch). A free shuttle bus takes you to the park from Interlaken's East station every 20 minutes.

SLEEPING AND EATING

Sleeping in Gimmelwald
(4,593 feet, country code: 41)

To inhale the Alps and really hold it in, sleep high in Gimmelwald. Poor but pleasantly stuck in the past, the village has a creaky hotel, happy hostel, decent pension, a couple of B&Bs, and even a Web site (www.gimmelwald.ch). The only bad news is that the lift costs 7.80 SF each way to get there.

$$ Maria and Olle Eggimann rent two rooms—Gimmelwald's most comfortable—in their quirky but alpine-sleek chalet. Maria and Olle, who job-share the village's only teaching position and raise three kids of their own, offer visitors a rare and, for some, an almost too intimate peek at this community (D-110 SF, Db with kitchenette-180 SF for 2 or 3 people, optional breakfast-18 SF, no CC, last check-in 19:30, 3-night minimum for advance reservations; from gondola continue

SLEEP CODE

(1.40 SF = about $1, country code: 41)

Sleep Code: **S** = Single, **D** = Double/Twin, **T** = Triple, **Q** = Quad, **b** = bathroom, **s** = shower only, **no CC** = Credit Cards not accepted, **SE** = Speaks English, **NSE** = No English. Unless otherwise noted, credit cards are accepted, English is spoken, and breakfast is included.

To help you sort easily through these listings, I've divided the rooms into three categories, based on the price for a standard double room with bath:

$$$ **Higher Priced**—Most rooms 150 SF or more.
 $$ **Moderately Priced**—Most rooms between 90–150 SF.
  $ **Lower Priced**—Most rooms 90 SF or less.

At higher altitudes, many hotels, restaurants, and shops are closed between Easter and late May. Those traveling by car should note that you can't drive to Gimmelwald, Mürren, Wengen, Kleine Scheidegg, or Obersteinberg—but don't let that stop you from staying up in the mountains (park the car and zip up on a lift; see "Transportation Connections," below). Lauterbrunnen, Stechelberg, Isenfluh, and Interlaken are no problem for drivers.

straight for 200 yards along the town's only road, B&B on left, tel. 033-855-3575, oeggimann@bluewin.ch, SE fluently).

$$ Pension Restaurant Gimmelwald offers 13 basic rooms under low, creaky ceilings (D-110 SF, Db-130 SF, T-150 SF, Q-180 SF, 5 SF per person surcharge for 1-night stays). It also has sheetless backpacker beds (25–35 SF in small dorm rooms). The pension has a scenic terrace overlooking the Jungfrau and the hostel (below), and is the village's only restaurant, offering good meals (closed late Oct–Christmas and mid-April–mid-May, non-smoking rooms but restaurant can get smoky, 50 yards from gondola station; reserve by phone, plus obligatory reconfirmation by phone 2-3 days before arrival; tel. 033-855-1730, fax 033-855-1925, pensiongimmelwald@tcnet.ch, Liesi and Mäni).

$ Hotel Mittaghorn, the treasure of Gimmelwald, is run by Walter Mittler, a perfect Swiss gentleman. Walter's hotel is a classic, creaky, alpine-style place with memorable beds, ancient down comforters (short and fat; wear socks and drape the blanket over your feet), and a million-dollar view of the Jungfrau Alps. The loft has a dozen real beds, several sinks, down comforters, and a fire ladder out the back window. The hotel has one shower for 10 rooms (1 SF/5 min). Walter is careful not to let his place get too hectic or big, and he enjoys sensitive Back Door travelers. He runs the hotel with a little help from Rosemarie from the village.

To some, Hotel Mittaghorn is a fire waiting to happen, with a kitchen that would never pass code, lumpy beds, teeny towels, and minimal plumbing, run by an eccentric old grouch. These people enjoy Mürren, Interlaken, or Wengen, and that's where they should sleep. Be warned, you'll see more of my readers than locals here, but it's a fun crowd—an extended family (D-70–80 SF, T-100 SF, Q-125 SF, loft beds-25 SF, 6 SF surcharge per person for 1-night stays except in loft, all with breakfast, no CC, closed Nov–March, tel. 033-855-1658, www.ricksteves.com/mittaghorn). Reserve by telephone only, then reconfirm by phone the day before your arrival. Walter usually offers his guests a simple 15 SF dinner. Hotel Mittaghorn is at the top of Gimmelwald, a five-minute climb up the steps from the village intersection.

$ Mountain Hostel is a beehive of activity, as clean as its guests, cheap, and friendly. Phone ahead, or to secure one of its 50 dorm beds the same day, call after 9:30 and leave your name. The hostel has low ceilings, a self-service kitchen, a mini-grocery, a free pool table, and healthy plumbing. It's mostly a college-age crowd; families and older travelers will probably feel more comfortable elsewhere. Petra Brunner has lined the porch with flowers. This relaxed hostel survives with the help of its guests. Read the signs (please clean the kitchen), respect Petra's rules, and leave it tidier than you found it. The place is one of those rare spots where a congenial atmosphere spontaneously combusts, and spaghetti becomes communal as it cooks (20 SF per bed in 6- to 15-bed rooms, sheets included, showers-1 SF, no breakfast, hostel membership not required, no CC, Internet access-12 SF/hour, laundry-5 SF/load, 20 yards from lift station, tel. & fax 033-855-1704, www.mountainhostel.com, mountainhostel@tcnet.ch).

$ Esther's Guesthouse, overlooking the main intersection of the village, is like an upscale mini-hostel with five clean, basic, and comfortable rooms sharing two bathrooms and a great kitchen (S-40 SF, D-80–95 SF, T-100–120 SF, Q-150 SF, no CC, 2-night stays preferred, make your own breakfast or pay 12 SF and Esther will make it for you, non-smoking, tel. 033-855-5488, fax 033-855-5492, www.esthersguesthouse.ch, info@esthersguesthouse.ch, some English spoken).

$ Schlaf im Stroh (Sleep in Straw) offers exactly that, in an actual barn. After the cows head for higher ground in the summer, the friendly von Allmen family hoses out their barn and fills it with straw and budget travelers. Blankets are free, but bring your own sheet, sleep sack, or sleeping bag. No beds, no bunks, no mattresses, no kidding (21 SF, 10 SF for kids up to 10, thereafter kids pay their age plus 1 SF, no CC, includes breakfast and a modern bathroom, showers-2 SF, open mid-June–mid-Oct, depending on grass and snow levels, almost never full; from lift, continue straight through intersection, barn marked 1995 on right, run by Esther with same contact info as above).

Eating in Gimmelwald

Pension Gimmelwald, the only restaurant in town, serves a hearty breakfast buffet for 13.50 SF, fine lunches, and good dinners (10–20 SF), featuring cheese fondue, a tasty *Rösti*, local organic produce, homemade pies, and spherical brownies (daily 7:30–23:00). The hostel has a decent members' kitchen, but serves no food. Hotel Mittaghorn serves dinner only to its guests (15 SF). Consider packing in a picnic meal from the larger towns. If you need a few groceries and want to skip the hike to Mürren, you can buy the essentials—noodles, spaghetti sauce, and candy bars—at the Mountain Hostel's reception desk.

The local farmers sell their produce. Esther (at the main intersection of the village) sells cheese, sausage, bread, and Gimmelwald's best yogurt—but only until the cows go up in June.

Sleeping in Mürren
(5,381 feet, country code: 41)

Mürren—pleasant as an alpine resort can be—is traffic-free and filled with bakeries, cafés, souvenirs, old-timers with walking sticks, GE employees enjoying incentive trips, and Japanese tourists making movies of each other with a Fujichrome backdrop. Its chalets are prefab-rustic. Sitting on a ledge 2,000 feet above the Lauterbrunnen Valley, surrounded by a fortissimo chorus of mountains, the town has all the comforts of home (for a price) without the pretentiousness of more famous resorts. With help from a gondola, train, and funicular, hiking options are endless from Mürren. Mürren has an ATM (by the Co-op grocery), and there are lockers at both the train and gondola stations (located a 10-min walk apart, on opposite ends of town).

Mürren's **TI** can help you find a room, give hiking advice, and change money (July–Sept Mon–Fri 9:00–12:00 & 13:00–18:30, Thu until 20:30, Sat 13:00–18:30, Sun 13:00–17:30, less off-season, above the village, follow signs to Sportzentrum, tel. 033-856-8686, www.wengen-muerren.ch). The slick **Sportzentrum** (sports center) that houses the TI offers a world of indoor activities (13 SF to use pool and whirlpool; 8 SF for Gimmelwald, Lauterbrunnen, and Interlaken hotel guests; free for guests at most Mürren hotels—ask your hotelier for a voucher, pool open Mon–Sat 14:00–18:45, Thu until 20:15, closed Sun, May, and Nov–mid-Dec).

You can rent **mountain bikes** and hiking boots at Stäger Sport (bikes-25 SF/4 hrs, 35 SF/day, boots-12 SF/day, daily 9:00–17:00, closed May and Nov, across from TI/Sportzentrum, tel. 033-855-2355,

urren

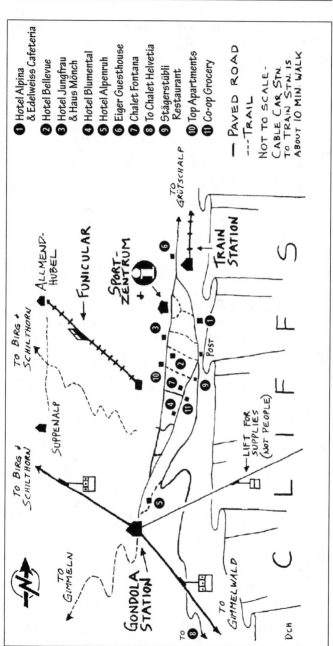

1 Hotel Alpina
& Edelweiss Cafeteria
2 Hotel Bellevue
3 Hotel Jungfrau
& Haus Mönch
4 Hotel Blumental
5 Hotel Alpenruh
6 Eiger Guesthouse
7 Chalet Fontana
8 To Chalet Helvetia
9 Stägerstübli
Restaurant
10 Top Apartments
11 Co-op Grocery

— PAVED ROAD
--TRAIL
NOT TO SCALE-
CABLE CAR STN.
TO TRAIN STN. IS
ABOUT 10 MIN. WALK

www.staegersport.ch). You can use the **Internet** at the TI (see above, 5 SF/20 min) or at Eiger Guesthouse (12 SF/hr, daily 8:00–23:00, tel. 033-856-5460, across from train station). Top Apartments will do your **laundry** by request (25 SF per load, unreliable hours: Mon–Sat 9:00–11:00 & 15:00–17:00, closed Sun, behind and across from Hotel Bellevue, look for blue triangle, call first to drop off in morning, tel. 033-855-3706).

Prices for accommodations are often higher during the ski season. Many hotels and restaurants close in spring, roughly from Easter to late May, and any time between late September and mid-December.

$$$ Hotel Alpina is a simple, modern place with 24 comfortable rooms and a concrete feeling—a good thing, given its cliff-edge position (Sb-75–95 SF, Db-140–170 SF, Tb-180–210 SF, Qb-210–240 SF with awesome Jungfrau views and balconies, 4–5 person apartments-250–300 SF, exit left from station, walk 2 min downhill, tel. 033-855-1361, fax 033-855-1049, www.muerren.ch/alpina, alpina@muerren.ch, Taugwalder family).

$$$ Hotel Bellevue has a homey lounge, great view terrace, hunter-themed Jägerstübli restaurant, and 17 good rooms at fair rates, most with balconies and views. The more expensive rooms are newly renovated and larger (Sb-95–125 SF, Db-170–210 SF, Internet access, tel. 033-855-1401, fax 033-855-1490, www.muerren.ch/bellevue, bellevue-crystal@bluewin.ch, run by friendly and hardworking Ruth and Othmar Suter).

$$$ Hotel Jungfrau offers 29 modern and comfortable rooms (Sb-95–110 SF, Db-190–210 SF with view, Sb-90–110 SF, Db-170–200 SF without, elevator, near TI/Sportzentrum, tel. 033-855-4545, fax 033-855-4549, www.hoteljungfrau.ch, mail@hoteljungfrau.ch).

$$$ Hotel Blumental has 16 older but nicely furnished rooms and a fun, woodsy game/TV lounge (Sb-75–80 SF, Db-150–170 SF, non-smoking rooms but smoky lobby, attached restaurant, tel. 033-855-1826, fax 033-855-3686, www.muerren.ch/blumental, blumental @muerren.ch, von Allmen family).

$$$ Hotel Alpenruh is yuppie-rustic and overpriced, but it's the only hotel in Mürren open year-round. The 26 comfortable rooms come with views and some balconies (Sb-105–140 SF, Db-180–260 SF, Tb-225–315 SF, prices vary with season, elevator, attached restaurant, free sauna, tanning bed-10 SF/20 min, free vouchers for breakfast atop Schilthorn, atop Allmendhubel, or at hotel, 10 yards from gondola station, tel. 033-856-8800, fax 033-856-8888, www.muerren.ch/alpenruh, alpenruh@schilthorn.ch).

$$ Eiger Guesthouse offers 14 good budget rooms. This is a friendly, creaky, easygoing home away from home (S-60–65 SF, Sb-80–85 SF, D-100–110 SF, Db-130–140 SF, 39–45 SF beds in 2- and 4-bunk rooms, with sheets and breakfast, Internet access, closed Nov and for one month after Easter, across from train station, tel. 033-856-5460, fax 033-856-5461, www.muerren.ch/eigerguesthouse, eigerguesthouse @muerren.ch, well run by Scotsman Alan and Swiss Véronique). The restaurant serves good, reasonably priced dinners. Its poolroom—with public Internet access—is a popular local hangout.

$$ Haus Mönch, a basic, blocky lodge run by Hotel Jungfrau, offers 20 woodsy, well-worn but fine rooms, plus good Jungfrau views (Db-140–144 SF, Tb-180 SF, near TI and Sportzentrum, tel. 033-855-4545, fax 033-855-4549, www.hoteljungfrau.ch, mail@hoteljungfrau.ch).

$ Chalet Fontana, run by charming Englishwoman Denise Fussell, is a rare budget option in Mürren, with simple, crispy-clean, and comfortable rooms (35–45 SF per person in small doubles or triples with breakfast, 5 SF cheaper without breakfast, 1 apartment with kitchenette-50 SF per person, third and fourth person-10 SF each, no CC, closed Nov–April, across street from Stägerstübli restaurant in town center, tel. 033-855-4385, mobile 078-642-3485, chaletfontana @muerren.ch). If no one's home, check at the Ed Abegglen shop next door (tel. 033-855-1245, off-season only).

$ Chalet Helvetia, run by friendly Frau Hunziker, offers a homey, clean two-bedroom apartment with bathroom, kitchen, separate entrance, and balcony for 40 SF per person (up to 5 people, no breakfast, 2-night minimum preferred, higher price for 1-night stays, a few blocks below cable car station on path to Gimmelwald, look for red *Zimmer* sign on right, tel. 033-855-4169, mobile 079-234-7867, kurthunziker105 @msn.com).

Eating in Mürren

For a rare bit of ruggedness, eat at the **Stägerstübli** (15–30 SF lunches and dinners, daily 11:30–22:00). **Kandahar Snack Bar** has fun, creative, and inexpensive light meals; a good selection of coffees, teas, and pastries; and impressive views (take-out available, run by lively Canadian Lesley, daily 10:00–18:00, at the **Sportzentrum).** The reasonable **Edelweiss** self-serve restaurant wins the Best View award (daily 10:30–18:00, next to Hotel Alpina). The recommended **Eiger Guesthouse** and **Hotel Bellevue** also have good restaurants (see "Sleeping in Mürren," above). For picnic fixings, shop at **Co-op** (Mon–Fri 8:00–12:00 & 13:45–18:30, Sat until 16:00, closed Sun).

Sleeping in Wengen
(4,180 feet, country code: 41)

Wengen, a bigger, fancier Mürren on the other side of the valley, has plenty of grand hotels, many shops, tennis courts, mini-golf, and terrific views. Minor celebrities (such as Graham Greene) come here to disappear. This traffic-free resort is an easy train ride above Lauterbrunnen and halfway up to Kleine Scheidegg and Männlichen, and offers more activities for those needing distraction from the scenery. Hiking is better from Mürren and Gimmelwald. The **TI** is one block from the station; go up to the main drag, turn left, and look ahead on the left (June–Sept and Dec–mid-April daily 9:00–18:00; mid-April–May and Oct–Nov Mon–Fri 9:00–18:00, closed Sat–Sun; Internet access-5 SF/20 min; tel. 033-855-1414, www.wengen-muerren.ch).

Sleeping above the Station

$$$ Hotel Berghaus, in a quiet area a five-minute walk from the main street, offers 19 rooms above a fine restaurant specializing in fish (Sb-82-117 SF, Db-164-234 SF, 5 percent cheaper with this book and cash, elevator, guests can use pool at Park Hotel for free, call on phone at station hotel board for free pick-up, or walk up street across from Bernerhof Hotel, bear right and then left at fork, 200 yards more past church on the left, tel. 033-855-2151, fax 033-855-3820, www.wengen .com/hotel/berghaus, berghaus@wengen.com, Fontana family).

$$$ Hotel Schönegg is a centrally-located splurge, right on Wengen's main drag (Sb-100-110 SF, Db-200-220 SF; higher July-Aug: Sb-115-125 SF, Db-230-250 SF; non-smoking rooms, all rooms have balconies and great views, cozy family room with fireplace, Internet access, good restaurant with big terrace, look for big yellow hotel on main drag near TI, tel. 033-855-3422, fax 033-855-4233, www.hotel -schoenegg.ch, schoenegg@tcnet.ch, Herr und Frau Berthod).

$$$ Hotel Eiger, next to the train station, is older but clean (Sb-102-125 SF, Db-204-250 SF, all rooms have balconies, tel. 033-856-0505, fax 033-856-0506, www.eiger-wengen.ch, hotel@eiger-wengen.ch).

Sleeping below the Station

The first two listings are bright, cheery, family-friendly, and five minutes below the station: leave the station toward the Co-op store, turn right and go under the rail bridge, bear right (paved path) at the fork, and follow the road down and around.

$$ Bären Hotel, run by friendly Therese and Willy Brunner, offers 14 tidy rooms with perky, bright-orange bathrooms (Sb-60–90 SF, Db-120–160 SF, Tb-180–210 SF, dinner-20 SF more, family rooms, tel. 033-855-1419, fax 033-855-1525, www.baeren-wengen.ch, info @baeren-wengen.ch).

$$ Familienhotel Edelweiss has 25 bright rooms, lots of fun public spaces, a Christian emphasis, and a jittery Chihuahua named Speedy (Sb-65–75 SF, Db-130–150 SF, non-smoking, each room has balcony or TV, great family rooms, elevator, TV lounge, game room, meeting room, kids' playroom, tel. 033-855-2388, fax 033-855-4288, www.vch.ch/edelweiss, edelweiss@vch.ch, Bärtschi family).

$$ Clare and Andy's Chalet (Trogihalten) offers three rustic, low-ceilinged rooms (1-room studio: Sb-52 SF, Db-80 SF; 2-room suite:

Sb/Db-98 SF, Tb-131 SF, Qb-172 SF; 4-room flat: Tb-147 SF, Qb-176 SF, breakfast-15 SF, dinner by request-30 SF, 4-night minimum preferred, prices higher for shorter stays, no CC, all rooms with balconies, leave station to the left and follow paved path next to Bernerhof Hotel downhill, soon after path becomes gravel look ahead and to the right, tel. & fax 033-855-1712, http://home.sunrise.ch/aregez, regez.chalet.wengen@spectraweb.ch, Clare's English, Andy's Swiss).

Sleeping and Eating in Kleine Scheidegg
(6,762 feet, country code: 41)

Confirm price and availability before ascending. These two places also serve meals.

$$ Bahnhof Buffet invites you to sleep face-to-face with the Eiger (dorm bed-63 SF, D-156 SF, prices include breakfast and dinner, in the train station building, tel. 033-828-7828, fax 033-828-7830, www.bahnhof-scheidegg.ch).

$ Restaurant Grindelwaldblick, a 10-minute hike from the station, really gets you up into the mountains (38 SF for bed in 12-bed room, includes sheets, closed Nov and May, tel. 033-855-1374, fax 033-855-4205, www.grindelwaldblick.ch).

Sleeping in Stechelberg
(3,025 feet, country code: 41)

Stechelberg is the hamlet at the end of Lauterbrunnen Valley, at the base of the lift to Gimmelwald, Mürren, and the Schilthorn.

$$ Hotel Stechelberg, at road's end, is surrounded by waterfalls and vertical rock, with 20 comfortable, spacious, and quiet rooms and a lovely garden terrace (D-82–104 SF, Db-120–158 SF, T-147 SF, Tb-186 SF, Q-168 SF, Qb-234 SF, post bus stops here, tel. 033-855-2921, fax 033-855-4438, www.stechelberg.ch, hotel@stechelberg.ch).

$ Nelli Beer, renting three rooms in a quiet, scenic, and folksy setting, is your best Stechelberg option (S-35 SF, D-60 SF, 2-night minimum, no CC, over river behind Stechelberg post office at big *Zimmer* sign, get off post bus at post office, tel. 033-855-3930, some English spoken).

$ Naturfreundehaus Alpenhof is a homey, cozy alpine lodge for hikers. New owners Marc (English) and Diane (Australian) have made it a quiet and peaceful place to relax (64 beds, 4–8 people per coed room, 22 SF per bed, less for members, breakfast-9 SF extra, laundry-10 SF, no CC, tel. 033-855-1202, alpenhof@naturfreunde.ch). Behind Hotel Stechelberg (post bus stop), take the path to the right, passing the Hotel's terrace and flowerpots, and cross the river. It's the second house on the left.

Sleeping in Lauterbrunnen
(2,612 feet, country code: 41)

Lauterbrunnen—with a train station, funicular, bank, shops, and lots of hotels—is the valley's commercial center. This is the jumping-off point for Jungfrau and Schilthorn adventures. It's idyllic, in spite of the busy road and big buildings. Stop by the friendly **TI** to check the weather forecast, use the Internet (5 SF/20 min), and to buy any regional train or lift tickets you need (June–Aug Mon–Sat 10:00–12:00 & 15:00–18:30, Sun 15:00–18:30, less off-season, 1 block up from station, tel. 033-856-8568, www.wengen-muerren.ch). You can rent **mountain bikes** at Imboden Bike on the main street (25 SF/4 hrs, 35 SF/day, full-suspension—reserve ahead—45 SF/half-day, 65 SF/full day, daily 8:00-18:30, tel. 033-855-2114). The Valley Hostel on the main street also runs an **Internet café** (12 SF/hr) and a small **launderette** (10 SF/load, don't open dryer door until machine is finished or you'll have to pay another 5 SF to start it again; both daily 8:00–22:00, less Nov–April, tel. 033-855-2008).

$$ Hotel Staubbach, a big Old World place—one of the first hotels in the valley (1890)—is being lovingly restored by hardworking American Craig and his Swiss wife, Corinne. Its 30 plain, comfortable rooms are family-friendly, there's a kids' play area, and the parking is free. Many rooms have great views. They keep their prices down by providing room-cleaning only after every third night (S-50 SF, Ss-60 SF, Sb-90 SF, D-80 SF, Db-110 SF, figure 40 SF per person in family rooms sleeping up to 6, 10 SF extra per room for 1-night stays, elevator, 4 blocks up from station on the left, tel. 033-855-5454, fax 033-855-5484, www.staubbach.ch, hotel@staubbach.ch).

$ Valley Hostel is practical, friendly, and comfortable, offering inexpensive beds for quieter travelers of all ages, with a pleasant garden and the welcoming Abegglen family: Martha, Alfred, Stefan, and Fränzi (D with bunk beds-52 SF, twin D-60 SF, beds in larger family-friendly rooms-23 SF each, no breakfast but kitchen is available, no CC, most rooms have balconies, cheese fondue on request for guests 18:00–19:30 —16 SF per person, non-smoking, Internet access, laundry, 2 blocks up from train station, tel. & fax 033-855-2008, www.valleyhostel.ch, info@valleyhostel.ch).

$ Chalet im Rohr, a creaky, old, woody place, has oodles of character and 26 SF beds in big one- to four-bed rooms (2 SF discount after second night, no breakfast, common kitchen-0.50 SF per person, no CC, closed for 3 weeks after Easter, below church on main drag, tel. & fax 033-855-2182).

$ Matratzenlager Stocki is rustic and humble, with the cheapest beds in town (14 SF with sheets in easygoing little 30-bed coed dorm with kitchen, closed Nov–Dec; across river from station, go below station to parking and take last right before garage, walk on path and then turn left over bridge, walk up and to the right 200 yards; tel. 033-855-1754).

$ **Camping:** Two campgrounds just south of town provide 15–35 SF beds (in dorms and 2-, 4-, and 6-bed bungalows, no sheets, kitchen facilities, no CC, big English-speaking tour groups): **Mountain Holiday Park-Camping Jungfrau,** romantically situated beyond Staubbach Falls, is huge and well organized by Hans (tel. 033-856-2010, fax 033-856-2020, www.camping-jungfrau.ch). It also has fancier cabins (24 SF per person). **Schützenbach Retreat,** on the left just past Lauterbrunnen toward Stechelberg, is simpler (tel. 033-855-1268, www.schutzenbach -retreat.ch).

Eating in Lauterbrunnen

Hotel Restaurant Jungfrau, along the main street on the right-hand side, offers a wide range of specialities served by a friendly staff (daily 12:00–14:00 & 18:00–20:00, tel. 033-855-3434, run by Brigitte Melliger).

At **Hotel Restaurant Oberland,** the Nolan family takes pride in serving tasty meals (daily 11:30–16:00 & 17:30–21:00, tel. 033-855-1241).

Hotel Restaurant Schützen has fine food but impersonal staff (daily 7:15–22:30, tel. 033-855-3026).

Sleeping in Obersteinberg
(5,900 feet, country code: 41)

$ Here's a wild idea: **Mountain Hotel Obersteinberg** is a working alpine farm with cheese, cows, a mule shuttling up food once a day, and an American (Vickie) who fell in love with a mountain man. It's a 2.5-hour hike from either Stechelberg or Gimmelwald. They rent 12 primitive rooms and a bunch of loft beds. There's no shower, no hot water, and only meager solar-panel electricity. Candles light up the night, and you can take a hot-water bottle to bed if necessary (S-81 SF, D-162 SF, includes linen, sheetless dorm beds-64 SF, these prices include breakfast and dinner, without meals S-37 SF, D-73 SF, dorm beds-20 SF, closed Oct–May, tel. 033-855-2033). The place is filled with locals and Germans on weekends, but is all yours on weekdays. Why not hike there from Gimmelwald and leave the Alps a day later?

Sleeping in Isenfluh
(3,560 feet, country code: 41)

The tiny hamlet of Isenfluh is even smaller than Gimmelwald and offers better views.

$$ **Pension Waldrand** has a restaurant (including great fresh salads) and four reasonable rooms (Db-120–130 SF, Tb-150 SF, includes breakfast, hrly bus from Lauterbrunnen, tel. 033-855-1227, fax 033-855-1392, www.waldrand.com, hotel_waldrand@bluewin.ch).

Sleeping in Interlaken
(country code: 41)

I'd head for Gimmelwald, or at least Lauterbrunnen (20 min by train or car). Interlaken is not the Alps. But if you must stay...

$$$ Hotel Lotschberg, with a sun terrace and 21 wonderful rooms, is run by English-speaking Susi and Fritz and is the best real hotel value in town. Happy to dispense information, these gregarious folks pride themselves on a personal touch that sets them apart from other hotels. Fritz also organizes guided adventures (Sb-92–110 SF, Db-129–155 SF, big Db-162–190 SF, extra bed-25 SF, family deals, cheaper prices are for Nov–May, non-smoking, elevator, Internet access-14 SF/hr, laundry service-9 SF/load, bike rental, honeymoon/romance decoration-40 SF or 60 SF with champagne, discounted parasailing for guests if you "Fly with Fritz"; 3-min walk from West station: cross the square in front of Migros store, then take first right, and then first left, to General Guisanstrasse 31; tel. 033-822-2545, fax 033-822-2579, www .lotschberg.ch, hotel@lotschberg.ch).

$$ Sunny Days B&B, run by Dave (British) and Brigit (Swiss), has nine colorful, cheery rooms ideal for families. Reserve ahead—this popular place books up early (Sb-98–110 SF, Db-110–155 SF, extra adult in room-45 SF, each additional child under 16 costs 38 SF extra, discounts for longer stays Nov–March, great breakfast, Internet access-16 SF/hr, laundry service-18 SF/load; exit left out of West station and take first bridge to your left, after crossing bridges turn left on peaceful Helvetiastrasse and go 3 blocks to #29; tel. 033-822-8343, fax 033-823-8343, www.sunnydays.ch, mail@sunnydays.ch).

$$ Guest House Susi's B&B is Hotel Lotschberg's no-frills, cash-only annex, run by Fritz and Susi, offering nicely furnished, cozy rooms (Sb-72–90 SF, Db-98–125 SF, apartments with kitchenettes for 2 people-100 SF; for 4–5 people-180 SF, cheaper prices Nov–May, no CC, same phone and fax as Hotel Lotschberg above, www.bnb -interlaken.ch, susis@bnb-interlaken.ch).

$$ Hotel Aarburg offers 13 plain, peaceful rooms in a beautifully located but run-down old building a 10-minute walk from the West station (Sb-80 SF, Db-130 SF, next to launderette at Beatenbergstrasse 1, tel. 033-822-2615, fax 033-822-6397, hotel-aarburg@tcnet.ch).

$ Villa Margaretha, run by perky, English-speaking Frau Kunz-Joerin, offers the best cheap beds in town. It's a big Victorian house with a garden on a quiet residential street. Keep your room tidy and you'll have a friend for life (D-86 SF, T-129 SF, Q-172 SF, the 3 rooms share a big bathroom, 2-night minimum, apartment-156–162 SF with a 1-week minimum, closed Oct–April, no CC, no breakfast served but dishes and kitchenette available, lots of rules to abide by; walk up small street directly in front of West station's parking lot entrance, go 3 blocks and look to your right for Aarmühlestrasse 13, tel. 033-822-1813).

$ **Backpackers' Villa (Sonnenhof) Interlaken** is a creative guest house run by a Methodist church group. It's fun, youthful, and great for families, without the frat-party ambience of Balmer's (below). Rooms are comfortable and half come with Jungfrau-view balconies (D-88 SF, T-120 SF, Q-144 SF, dorm beds in 5- to 7-bed rooms with lockers and sheets-32 SF per person, 5 SF more per person for rooms with toilets and Jungfrau-view balconies, includes breakfast, kitchen, garden, movies, small game room, Internet access-10 SF/hr, laundry-10 SF/load, bike rental, no curfew, open all day, check-in 16:00–22:00, 10-min walk from either station, across big grassy field from TI, Alpenstrasse 16, tel. 033-826-7171, fax 033-826-7172, www.villa.ch, backpackers@villa.ch).

$ **Balmer's Herberge** is many people's idea of backpacker heaven. This Interlaken institution comes with movies, table tennis, a laun-derette (8 SF/load), bar, restaurant, swapping library, Internet access (20 SF/hr), tiny grocery, bike rental, currency exchange, excursions, a shut-tle-bus service (which meets important arriving trains), and a friendly, hardworking staff. This little Nebraska is home for those who miss their fraternity. It can be a mob scene, especially on summer weekends (dorm beds-24 SF, S-40 SF; D, T, or Q-30–34 SF per person, includes sheets and breakfast, non-smoking, open year-round, easy Internet reservations recommended 5 days in advance, Hauptstrasse 23, in Matten, 15-min walk from either Interlaken station, tel. 033-822-1961, fax 033-823-3261, www.balmers.com, balmers@tcnet.ch).

$ **Happy Inn Lodge** has 16 cheap rooms above a lively, noisy restaurant a five-minute walk from the West station (S-30–40 SF, D-60–80 SF, bunk in 4- to 8-bed dorms-24–30 SF, breakfast-8 SF, Rosenstrasse 17, tel. 033-822-3225, fax 033-822-3268, www.happyinn.com, info@happyinn.com).

TRANSPORTATION CONNECTIONS

If you plan to arrive at the Zürich Airport and want to head straight for Interlaken and the Alps, see the Zürich chapter. Train info: toll tel. 0900-300-3004.

From Interlaken by train to: Spiez (2/hr, 20 min), **Brienz** (hrly, 30 min), **Bern** (hrly, 50 min), **Zürich** and **Zürich Airport** (hrly, 2.25 hrs, most direct but some with transfer in Bern). While there are a few long trains from Interlaken, you'll generally connect from Bern.

By train from Bern to: Lausanne (hrly, 70 min), **Zürich** (hrly, 70 min), **Appenzell** (hrly, 4.25 hrs, transfers in Zürich and Gossau or Bern and Gossau, or 5 hrs, change in Luzern and Herisau), **Salzburg** (4/day, 8 hrs, transfers include Zürich), **Munich** (7/day, 5.5–6.5 hrs, transfers in Zürich or Mannheim), **Frankfurt** (hrly, 4.5 hrs, some direct, others transfer in Basel or Mannheim), **Paris** (4/day, 4.5 hrs).

To Gimmelwald from Interlaken

By public transportation: Take the train from the Interlaken East *(Ost)* station to Lauterbrunnen. From here you have two options.

1) The faster, easier way—best in bad weather or at the end of a long day with lots of luggage—is to ride the post bus from Lauterbrunnen station (3.80 SF, hrly bus departure coordinated with arrival of train, stop: Schilthornbahn) to Stechelberg and the base of the Schilthornbahn gondola station, where the gondola will whisk you in five thrilling minutes up to Gimmelwald.

2) The more scenic route is to catch the funicular to Mürren (across the street from the train station). Ride up to Grütschalp, where a special scenic train *(Panorama Fahrt)* will roll you along the cliff into Mürren (total trip from Lauterbrunnen to Mürren: 30 min). From there, either walk a paved 30 minutes downhill to Gimmelwald, or walk 10 minutes across Mürren to catch the gondola (costs 7.80 SF and once in Gimmelwald, you'll have a 2- to 5-min uphill hike to reach accommodations).

By car: You can drive to Lauterbrunnen and to Stechelberg, but not to Gimmelwald (park in Stechelberg, and take the gondola—see below) or to Mürren, Wengen, or Kleine Scheidegg (park in Lauterbrunnen and take the train/funicular). For drivers, the most direct route to Gimmelwald is via the gondola at Stechelberg. It's a 30-minute drive from Interlaken to the Stechelberg gondola station (parking lot: 2 SF/2 hrs, 6 SF/day). Gimmelwald is the first stop above Stechelberg on the Schilthorn gondola (7.80 SF, 2/hr at :25 and :55). Note that for a week in early May and from mid-November through early December, the Schilthornbahn is closed for servicing, so you'll have to park in Lauterbrunnen (lot behind station: 2 SF/2 hrs, 9 SF/day) and go up to Gimmelwald via Mürren (see option #2, above).

BERN AND MURTEN

Enjoy urban Switzerland at its best in the charming, compact capital of Bern. Ramble the ramparts of Murten, Switzerland's best-preserved medieval town, and resurrect the ruins of an ancient Roman capital in nearby Avenches.

Planning Your Time

On a quick trip, Bern and Murten—only a half-hour away from each other by car or train—are each worth a half-day.

If you like cute small towns (as I do), make Murten your home base. Otherwise choose busier Bern. Either is easily accessible by train.

Bern is a handy stop between the Berner Oberland (Germany's Black Forest) and Murten. If you're day-tripping, put your bag in a locker at the Bern station, spend a few hours taking my self-guided Introductory Town Walk (below) and visiting some museums, and catch a late-afternoon train to Murten—where you can spend the evening walking the walls and enjoying a lakeside dinner. In the morning, linger in Murten, or move on to Lake Geneva via the French Swiss countryside (see next chapter).

Bern

Stately but human, classy but fun, the Swiss capital gives you the most (maybe even the only) enjoyable look at urban Switzerland. Window-shopping and people-watching along the arcaded streets and lively market squares are Bern's top attractions, but there's more to this city. Enjoy Bern's fine museums, quaint-for-a-capital ambience, and sleepy mascot bears.

West Switzerland Overview

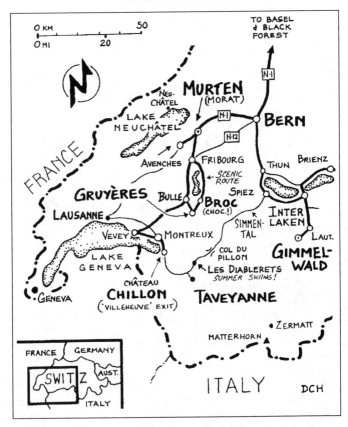

ORIENTATION

User-friendly Bern is packed into a peninsula bounded by the Aare River. The train station is located where the peninsula connects to the mainland. From there, a handy artery leads straight through the middle of town past most of the major sights to the tip of the peninsula (and, across a bridge, the bear pits).

Tourist Information

Start your visit at the TI inside the train station (June-Sept daily 9:00-20:30, Oct-May Mon-Sat 9:00-18:30, Sun 9:30-17:00, watch your bags, tel. 031-328-1212, www.bernetourism.ch). Pick up a 1 SF map of Bern (and maps for any other Swiss cities you'll be visiting) and a pile of other free brochures: general information booklet, museum guide, booklet on bus and walking tours, transit map, monthly "what's on" events guide, and informative leaflets on various sights. Ask about walking tours and the city sightseeing tour by raft on the Aare River (June–Sept). There's a second TI at the Bear Pits (June–Sept daily 9:00–18:00, March–May and Oct daily 10:00–16:00, Nov–Feb Fri–Sun 11:00–16:00, closed Mon–Thu).

Arrival in Bern

Bern's bustling station is easy to navigate. On the upper level, you'll find a **Migros** grocery store (daily 8:00–21:00), and a **pharmacy** (daily 6:30–22:00). Near the TI are **lockers** (4–5 SF) and **WCs** (2 SF).

From the station, it's a 30-minute downhill stroll through the heart of town to the Bear Pits and Rose Garden. For the most interesting route, see the Introductory Town Walk, below.

Getting around Bern

The city is walkable, though the trolley can come in handy. You could walk from the train station to the far end of town, then catch the made-for-tourists trolley #12 (a.k.a. the "Bearline") back to the station (buy cheapest ticket from machine at bus stop, 1.70 SF).

A standard single ticket costs 2.60 SF, a shorter trip runs 1.70 SF, and a full-day ticket is 9 SF.

Helpful Hints

Closed Day: Note that most of Bern's museums are closed on Monday.

Bike Rental: Free loaner city bikes are available from May to October in two locations: Bahnhofplatz (to the right as you exit the station) and Casinoplatz (2 blocks south of Clock Tower near Kirchenfeldbrücke; sometimes bikes are moved 4 blocks north to Kornhausplatz). Look for the *Bern rollt* kiosks. Leave your passport and a 20-SF deposit (daily 7:30–21:30). You can also rent bikes year-round at the train station baggage office (23 SF/half-day, 30 SF/full day).

INTRODUCTORY TOWN WALK

This orientation walk begins at the station and ends at the Bear Pits, at the far end of town.

Start your visit at the TI inside the train station. From the TI, cross the street, walk 50 yards, and turn left (around the church) onto Spitalgasse. As you walk, notice some of Bern's 11 historical **fountains,** such as the Bagpiper. The Reformation deprived the local artists of their most important patron, the Catholic Church. To compensate for their loss, the city of Bern commissioned these fountains in the middle of the

Introductory Bern Walk

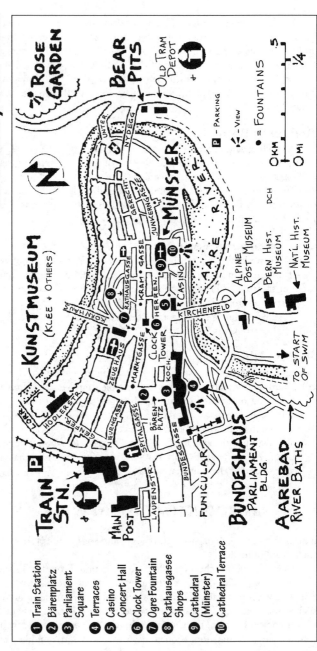

1 Train Station
2 Bärenplatz
3 Parliament Square
4 Terraces
5 Casino Concert Hall
6 Clock Tower
7 Ogre Fountain
8 Rathausgasse Shops
9 Cathedral (Münster)
10 Cathedral Terrace

16th century (the TI offers a "Fountain Walk" walking tour to explain them all).

Continue up Spitalgasse until you reach Bärenplatz. In summer, a daily market is held on this square. The biggest landmark, the **Prison Tower** (Käfigturm), used to be part of the city wall (built in 1256). Renovated 1641–1644, the tower served as a prison until 1897 (*Käfig* means "cage"). The windows on the right of the tower led to the cells. Later the tower was used as an archive.

As you face the Prison Tower, look to your left and find the controversial **fountain** by the Swiss surrealist artist Meret Oppenheim (1913–1985). This 1983 fountain, symbolizing growth and life, is supposed to demonstrate communication between an object of art and the beholder. It worked well . . . too well, in fact, as most citizens immediately communicated their dislike and wanted it destroyed. But Bern's politicians proved braver than expected, and the fountain still stands. Time has transformed the gray concrete column into a multicolored pillar decorated with moss, grass, and flowers. Also on your left, you'll see the **Dutch Tower.** Swiss soldiers were famous mercenaries who fought all over Europe. Returning from a battle in the Netherlands, the soldiers brought back the habit of smoking. But smoking was forbidden within the city walls of Bern—so they hid in this tower to smoke secretly.

Still facing the Prison Tower, on your right you'll find several good restaurants (see "Eating," page 501) and the **Parliament** building (Bundeshaus). You may see some high-powered legislators, but you wouldn't know it—everything looks very casual for a national capital.

Parliament Square (Bundesplatz) hosts a produce market on Tuesday and Saturday mornings, and it's the favorite spot for demonstrations.

Standing in front of the Parliament, check out the statuary. The woman on the top of the building represents political independence, the one on the left (under 1291) stands for freedom, and the one on the right (1848) symbolizes peace. The three big masks represent courage, wisdom, and strength—the virtues the population expects from their politicians to rule the country properly. For information on touring the Parliament, see "Sights," page 497.

Walk around behind the Parliament to the **terraces,** where you have a commanding view over the Aare River and the biggest swimming pool in Bern, the Marzilibad. On a clear day, you can see the peaks of the Eiger, Mönch, and Jungfrau (see Gimmelwald chapter)—and the far less imposing "mountain" of Bern, the Gurten. The Gurten is the city's favorite recreation spot, offering music festivals in summer and very modest skiing opportunities for the children in winter.

Heading back towards Kochergasse, you will come to the **Casino.** This building isn't for gamblers—it's the home of Bern's Symphony Orchestra (and the recommended Möwenpick restaurant; see "Eating," page 501).

Continue towards Marktgasse and stop at the **Zytglogge-turm.** This clock tower is Bern's most famous sight, and marks the first western gate to the city (1218–1256). The clock performs four minutes before each hour. Apparently, this nonevent was considered entertaining in 1530. To pass the time during the performance, read the TI's leaflet explaining what's so interesting about the fancy old clock. (Enthusiasts can tour the medieval mechanics daily at 16:30, 8 SF, 50 min, May–Oct, also at 11:30 July–Aug.)

Walk up Kornhausplatz past another fountain, the **Ogre** (*Chindlifresser,* literally "child-eater"). Two legends try to explain this gruesome sight. Either it is a folkloric representation of the Greek god Chronos, or a figure that was intended to scare children off the former city walls. The building behind on the left used to be the granary, and now houses the modern public library and the traditional Kornhauskeller restaurant (see "Eating," page 501).

Walk down Rathausgasse, with lots of arcaded shopping opportunities. There are over three miles of **arcades** in this tiny capital of 130,000 people. This is my kind of shopping town: Prices are so high there's no danger of buying (hours vary, but many shops open Mon–Fri 9:00–18:30, Thu later, Sat 8:00–16:00, closed Sun). Most shops are underneath the arcades, but don't miss the ones in the **cellars** that you can access only from the main road. Originally potatoes and coal were stored in these cellars, and later they were used for wine. The city was called "merry Bern" at this period in its history. People said that Bern was floating on wine, just as Venice was floating on water. The merry times ended when the French invaded and drank all the wine. The cellars were once again used for potatoes, and the city got a new nickname: "sad Bern." Napoleon's soldiers not only liberated Bern from its wine, but also from the tremendous treasury the city was known for. (It's said that the soldiers even kidnapped the bears from the bear pits.) Napoleon used this money to finance his Egyptian crusade.

As you stroll down Rathausgasse, you'll find an original shop on the left-hand side for toys and games, called the **Drachenäscht** (Dragon's nest, daily 9:00–18:30, Thu until 21:00). Farther on, turn right onto the tiny Schaalgässchen, which leads you to the fountain-filled Kramgasse, the main axis from the train station to the bear pit. Einstein fans will find his house at Kramgasse 49 (see description below).

Follow Kramgasse downhill until you reach the narrow Münstergässchen on your right, leading to Bern's **Cathedral,** the Münster, built in 1421. At 330 feet tall, the tower is the highest spire in Switzerland. The church was dedicated to St. Vincent of Zaragoza. During the Reformation, religious icons were destroyed by Protestants (an act called "iconoclasm"). This church's main portal is the only one that survived—probably because its theme is the Last Judgment, showing that no matter how rich you are or what rank you have in Church hierarchy, anyone can end up in Hell (an idea Protestants could support). Notice the humorous details in the representation of the condemned ones on the right (especially what the little green devil is doing to the sinful monk). For more on the cathedral, see "Sights," below.

Before you continue your walk, have a peek at the **Münster-plattform,** the terrace behind the Cathedral. Its construction began in 1334. To create it, all kinds of "recycled" stones from former buildings were used (archaeologists even unearthed some heads of statues that were victims of Reformation iconoclasts). Look down on the Aare and notice the security nets below you. The platform used to be the favorite place for suicides—to the terror of the people living below.

To get to the lower neighborhood (Matte) more safely, you can take the elevator at the eastern side of the platform (1 SF, Mon–Sat 6:00–20:30, Sun 7:00–20:30). But to get to the end of Bern's peninsula (and this tour), walk down Junkerngasse to the spot where Bern was founded in 1191 by Berchtold von Zähringer. Cross the bridge to reach the bear pits, the old tram depot (now a TI and multimedia show), and the path to the Rose Garden (for more on all of these, see below).

SIGHTS

Parliament (Bundeshaus)—You can tour Switzerland's imposing Parliament building (free 45-min tours up to 6 times daily Mon–Fri, usually in English at 14:00 as well as other times, tours are canceled if fewer than 5 people show up, must deposit passport before tour; no tours but you can watch when in session in March, June, mid-Sept–mid-Oct, and Dec; tel. 031-322-8522). Call the day before to confirm times of English tours.

▲**Cathedral**—The late-Gothic *Münster* is worth a look (April–Oct Tue–Sat 10:00–17:00, Sun 11:30–17:00, closed Mon; Nov–March Tue–Fri 10:00–12:00 & 14:00–16:00, Sat until 17:00, Sun 11:30–14:00, closed Mon, tel. 031-312-0462). Climb the spiral staircase 210 feet above the town for the view and the exercise (choose between two stairways: 312 or 354 steps). Elisabeth Bissig lives way up there, watching over the church, answering questions, and charging tourists 3 SF for the view.

Einstein's House—Einstein did much of his most important thinking while living in this house on the old town's main drag. It's just another house to me, but I guess everything's relative (3 SF, Tue–Fri 10:00–17:00, Sat 10:00–16:00, closed Sun–Mon and Dec–Jan, Kramgasse 49, tel. 031-312-0091).

▲**Bear Pits**—The symbol of Bern is the bear, and some lively ones frolic to the delight of locals and tourists alike in the big, barren, concrete pits *(Graben)* just over the river (April–Sept 8:00–18:00, Oct–March 9:00–16:00). You may see graffiti from the B.L.M. (Bear Liberation Movement), which, through its terrorist acts, has forced a reluctant city

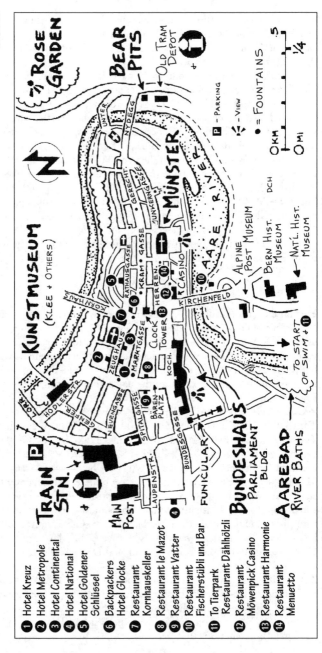

Bern

① Hotel Kreuz
② Hotel Metropole
③ Hotel Continental
④ Hotel National
⑤ Hotel Goldener
   Schlüssel
⑥ Backpackers
   Hotel Glocke
⑦ Restaurant
   Kornhauskeller
⑧ Restaurant le Mazot
⑨ Restaurant Vatter
⑩ Restaurant
   Fischerstübli und Bar
⑪ To Tierpark
   Restaurant Dählhölzli
⑫ Restaurant
   Möwenpick Casino
⑬ Restaurant Harmonie
⑭ Restaurant
   Menuetto

government to give the sad-eyed bears better living conditions.

Old Tram Depot—This depot, next to the Bear Pits, hosts a slick tourist center. Its excellent multi-media show, complete with an animated town model and marching Napoleonic-era soldiers, illustrates the history and wonders of Bern. Worth the time, the 20-minute show is more interesting than the bears (free, in English once hrly, June–Sept daily 9:00–18:00, March–May and Oct daily 10:00–16:00, Nov–Feb Fri–Sun 11:00–16:00, closed Mon–Thu). Up the pathway is the Rose Garden (Rosengarten), a restaurant offering basic, reasonably priced food and a great city view (March–Oct daily 9:00–22:00, tel. 031-331-3206).

▲▲The Berner Swim—For something to write home about, join the local merchants, students, and carp in a float down the Aare River. The Bernese, proud of their very clean river and their basic ruddiness, have a tradition—sort of a wet, urban paseo. On summer days, they hike upstream five to 30 minutes, then float back down to the excellent (and free) riverside baths and pools *(Aarebad)* just below the Parliament building. While the locals make it look easy, this is dangerous—the current is swift. If you miss the last pole, you're history. If a float down the river is a bit much, you're welcome to enjoy just the Aarebad, or you can try the other popular free pool, Lorrainebad (where the Aare flows much slower—a good spot for beginners). But if a taste of the river is not enough, try a popular day trip—rafting all the way from Thun to Bern (get details at TI).

▲▲Museum of Fine Arts (Kunstmuseum)—While it features 1,000 years of local art and some Impressionism, the real hit is its fabulous collection of Paul Klee's playful paintings. If you don't know Klee, I'd love to introduce you (7 SF, 1–11 SF extra for special exhibitions, no English inside but pick up free English map/brochure, Tue 10:00–21:00, Wed–Sun 10:00–17:00, closed Mon, 4 blocks north of station, Holdergasse 12, tel. 031-328-0944).

▲▲Kunsthalle—This museum, which hosts exhibitions of contemporary art, had its most famous moment in 1968. It was the first building that the Bulgarian-American artist Christo and his partner Jeanne-Claude wrapped—in 26,000 square feet of Polyethylene, fixed with 10,000 feet of nylon cord. To allow visitors to enter the exhibit, an entrance was cut out of the wrapping. The action lasted only six days, as the insurance company refused to cover the art collection during this time (6 SF, Tue 10:00–19:00, Wed–Sun 10:00–17:00, closed Mon, Helvetiaplatz 1, tel. 031-350-0040).

Other Bern Museums—Across the bridge from the Parliament building on Helvetiaplatz are several museums (Alpine, Berner History, Postal) that sound more interesting than they are (most open Tue–Sun 10:00–17:00, closed Mon, www.museen-bern.ch).

SLEEPING

$$$ **Hotel Kreuz,** with 100 rooms and a big lobby, is the most modern of these three business-class hotels. Enjoy the mod, airy atrium terraces (Sb-139–145 SF, Db-200–210 SF, Tb-230–240 SF; cheaper Fri–Sun: Sb-120–125 SF, Db-170–180 SF, Tb-200–210 SF, higher prices are for newer rooms, non-smoking rooms, elevator, free Internet access, laundry-7 SF/ load, Zeughausgasse 41, tel. 031-329-9595, fax 031-329-9596, www.hotelkreuz-bern.ch, info@hotelkreuz-bern.ch).

$$$ **Hotel Metropole,** across the street and run by the same company, has a small lobby and 59 less modern but homier rooms (Sb-136 SF, Db-195 SF, Tb-220 SF; cheaper Fri–Sun: Sb-115 SF, Db-170 SF, Tb-200 SF, non-smoking rooms, elevator plus a few stairs, Internet and laundry at Hotel Kreuz—see above, Zeughausgasse 26, tel. 031-311-5021, fax 031-312-1153, www.hotelmetropole.ch, info@hotelmetropole.ch).

$$$ **Hotel Continental,** a cheap annex of the nearby swanky Hotel Bern, has 40 slightly older rooms (Sb-140 SF, Db-200 SF, Tb-230 SF; cheaper Fri–Sun: Sb-115 SF, Db-160 SF, Tb-190 SF, elevator, Zeughausgasse 27, tel. 031-329-2121, fax 031-329-2199, www.hotel-continental.ch, continental@hotelbern.ch).

SLEEP CODE

(1.40 SF = about \$1, country code: 41)
Sleep Code: **S** = Single, **D** = Double/Twin, **T** = Triple, **Q** = Quad, **b** = bathroom, **s** = shower only, **no CC** = Credit Cards not accepted, **SE** = Speaks English, **NSE** = No English. Unless otherwise noted, credit cards are accepted, English is spoken, and breakfast is included.

To help you sort easily through these listings, I've divided the rooms into three categories, based on the price for a standard double room with bath:

$$$　**Higher Priced**—Most rooms 150 SF or more.
$$　**Moderately Priced**—Most rooms between 90–150 SF.
$　**Lower Priced**—Most rooms 90 SF or less.

Business-class hotels line Zeughausgasse, a quiet side street a few blocks in front of the station. The first three listings are Bern's best value, especially when rates drop on weekends. The rest of the recommended hotels are cheaper, but are generally significantly older and mustier, and a poorer value.

$$ Hotel National has 45 rooms with big windows and street noise—request a quiet room (S-60–80 SF, Sb-85–110 SF, D-100–110 SF, Db-130–150 SF, apartment-180–260 SF, extra bed-40 SF, elevator, free Internet access, Hirschengraben 24, tel. 031-381-1988, fax 031-381-6878, www.nationalbern.ch, info@nationalbern.ch).

$$ Hotel Goldener Schlüssel is an old, basic, comfortable, crank-'em-out hotel with 29 rooms in the center (S-88 SF, Sb-115 SF, D-125 SF, Db-155 SF, Tb-205 SF, extra bed-45 SF, elevator, Rathausgasse 72, tel. 031-311-0216, fax 031-311-5688, www.goldener-schluessel.ch).

$ Backpackers Hotel Glocke has dorm beds and a hotel with private rooms (dorms: 29 SF in 4- to 6-bed room, 39 SF in 2-bed room, sheets included, cheaper off-season; hotel: S-75 SF, D-120 SF, Db-160 SF, T-160 SF, Tb-200 SF, a few francs cheaper off-season and for longer stays, no breakfast but kitchen available, non-smoking, 1 flight of stairs then elevator, Internet access, laundry, kitchen, reception open 8:00–11:00 & 15:00–22:00, Rathausgasse 75, tel. 031-311-3771, fax 031-311-1008, www.bernbackpackers.com, info@bernbackpackers.com).

EATING

Between the Station and Bärenplatz

Aarbergergasse street is lined with a wide variety of restaurants, including **Gourmanderie Moléson** (serves Swiss specialties, closed Sun, #24); a pizzeria called **Pinocchio** (#6); and even an Argentinean steak house, **Churrasco** (#60). Locals flock to **Aarbergerhof,** nicknamed "Araber," serving traditional Swiss cuisine, as well as dishes from Asia and the Middle East (daily until 23:30, #40).

Around Bärenplatz

Restaurant Le Mazot is very cozy, with a huge selection of *Röstis,* fondues, raclettes, and other hearty Swiss meals (Bärenplatz 5, tel. 031-311-7088).

Restaurant Vatter is exclusively organic—mostly vegetarian, but with some meat options. The restaurant is connected with the organic produce store downstairs on Spitalgasse (closed Sun, Bärenplatz 2, tel. 031-312-5171).

Around Kornhausplatz

Kornhauskeller, decorated with coloful mural paintings, is a splurge in the cellar of the old granary, originally built to house the state's wine cellar (Mon–Sat 11:45–14:30 & 18:00–24:00, Sun 18:00–23:30, Kornhausplatz 18, tel. 031-327-7272).

Near the Cathedral

Möwenpick Casino is an upscale cafeteria with a big outdoor terrace underneath old chestnut trees (Mon–Sat 11:00–23:00, Sun 11:00–22:00, Herrengasse 25, tel. 031-328-0320). In the same building, you can find a picturesque wine cellar, the **Cavino** (Mon–Sat 11:00–23:00, closed Sun).

Restaurant Harmonie, owned by the Gyger family since 1915, is one of the oldest and most traditional places in the old town. It offers filling Swiss cuisine and is the favorite lunch spot for Swiss politicians (closed Sat–Sun, Hotelgasse 3, tel. 031-311-3840).

Menuetto is a chic veggie place, with delectable, imaginative dishes and lots of choices (25 SF and up). Daily specials can drop as low as 13 SF (Mon–Sat 11:15–14:15 & 17:30–22:00, closed Sun, Münstergasse 47).

At the Aare River

Restaurant Fischerstübli und Bar, specializing in fish, is the perfect place to be on a hot summer day (daily, on weekends only in the afternoon, Gerberngasse 41, tel. 031-311-5367)

Tierpark Restaurant Dählhölzli is probably the most popular family hangout on a sunny day. The huge outdoor terrace is divided into a full-service restaurant (marked with tablecloths) and a cheaper self-service section. Next to it is the Dählhölzli Zoo, where children can ride ponies and pet all kinds of animals while parents rest. Before you sit down, check if the chair is dry—this is also a favorite stop for the Aare swimmers to warm up with a cup of coffee. Don't be surprised to find guests in their swimsuits and waiters who gracefully accept wet bills (daily, Dalmaziquai 151a, tel. 031-351-1894).

TRANSPORTATION CONNECTIONS

By train to: Murten (hrly, 30 min, most transfer in Kerzers), **Lausanne** (2/hr, 70 min), **Interlaken** (hrly, 50 min), **Zürich** (2/hr, 70 min), **Fribourg** in Switzerland (2/hr, 30 min), **Freiburg** in Germany (at least hrly, 2 hrs, some direct, some with transfer in Basel), **Munich** (4/day, 5.5 hrs), **Frankfurt** (hrly, 4.5 hrs), **Paris** (4/day, 4.5 hrs). Train info: toll tel. 0900-300-3004.

Murten

The finest medieval ramparts in Switzerland surround the 5,000 people of Murten (Morat, if you're speaking French). We're on the linguistic cusp of Switzerland: 25 percent of Murten speaks French; a few miles to the south and west, nearly everyone does. This is the heart of the fertile Three Lakes Region (lakes Biel, Neuchâtel, and Murten)—also called the "vegetable garden of Switzerland" for its soil, which yields more than 60 varieties of produce.

Murten is a totally charming mini-Bern with surprisingly lively streets, the middle one nicely arcaded with breezy outdoor cafés and elegant shops (many closed Mon). Its castle is romantically set, overlooking the Murtensee lake and the rolling vineyards of gentle Mount Vully in the distance. Spend a night here and have dinner with a local Vully wine, light white or rosé. Murten is touristic, but seems to be enjoyed mostly by its own people. Nearby Avenches, with its Roman ruins, glows at sunset.

Throughout the town, you'll run into rusty metal walls. These are pieces of a huge monolith (by French architect Jean Nouvel) that rose out of the lake during Expo.02, the Swiss national exposition hosted by Murten two years ago. You can find a miniature reconstruction of the monolith in the Minigolf Snack Bar at the boat dock.

ORIENTATION

Tourist Information

Murten's **TI** is just inside the city walls at the eastern end of town (opposite end from station; May–Sept Mon–Fri 9:00–12:00 & 14:00–18:00, Sat 10:00–14:00, July–Aug also Sun 10:00–14:00, shorter hours and closed weekends Oct-April, Französische Kirchgasse 6, tel. 026-670-5112, www.murtentourismus.ch). Get a free map and ask about sights, biking, and boat trips. They offer a free town walk every Saturday in July and August (ask at TI for current schedule).

Arrival in Murten

By Train: To reach the town from the station (a 5-min walk), exit to the right, take the first left and walk up Bahnhofstrasse, then turn right through the town gate. You'll run right into Hotel Murtenhof.

By Car: Parking in Murten is medieval. Ask at your hotel. If you have a dashboard clock, you can try the blue spots near Hotel Ringmauer, but there are large free lots just outside either gate. Walk into Murten. It's a tiny town.

Helpful Hints

You can rent **bikes** at the train station ticket counters (23 SF/half-day, 30 SF/full day, daily 6:30–20:45). The **post office** is across the street from the station. Murten has no launderette. For **Internet** access, try A&A Computer (12 SF/hr, Mon–Fri 9:00–12:00 & 14:00–22:00, Sat 9:00–17:00, closed Sun, behind station at Engelhardstrasse 6, tel. 026-670-0520). You can't miss the **Co-op supermarket** (with a cafeteria) between the station and the center (Mon–Thu 8:00–19:00, Fri 8:00–20:00, Sat 7:30-16:00, closed Sun).

SIGHTS

Rampart Ramble—Murten's only required sightseeing is to scramble the ramparts (free, open daily, closed at night, easy stairway access near Hotel Ringmauer on south side of town, away from lake). Notice the old town clock reconstructed in the base of the tower (behind Hotel Ringmauer) and be glad you have a watch. Step out of the city wall on Törliplatz and turn around. From here you can see the different stages of the wall's construction. The first phase was built with large river stones, some arranged in a neat fish-bone pattern. Later the town ran out of money, and the next stage shows pebbles and rubble mixed with some kind of concrete. And finally, when the town prospered again, they finished the wall with cut sandstone. From here you can walk along the moat on Stadtgraben and admire the blooming gardens. They belong to the *Burgers*—the old noble families of Murten. At several places, you can see cannonballs still stuck in the city wall.

Lake Activities—To get down to the lazy lakefront, find the access at Rathausstrasse 17 (1 block from Hotel Murtenhof) and veer right halfway down the steps, by the benches. The lakefront offers a lovely promenade, mini-golf, and swimming.

Take a **one-hour cruise** (15.60 SF, 6/day May–Sept, 4/day Oct–April, call at least 2 hrs ahead to reserve off-season only, tel. 079-408-6635; TI can call for you and help with other boat questions). Consider a stop in the small town of Praz on the French-speaking shore. From there, you can hike through vineyards up Mount Vully, where a bench and fine lake and Alp views await.

For a **half-day or full-day cruise,** consider sailing on all three lakes of the region. Boats leave the town of Biel (an easy rail connection from Murten) daily at 9:50, cruise lake Biel, connect with canals to lakes Neuchâtel and Murten, and stop at several small medieval villages along the way. The boat arrives in Murten at 12:40, then turns around and heads back at 14:15, arriving in Biel at 18:00 (one-way-38 SF, round-trip-74 SF but a 64 SF "day card" covers the trip, get details from Murten TI or call BSG at tel. 032-329-8811, www.bielersee.ch).

Swimming Pool—The Olympic-size public swimming pool is next to the lake (5.50 SF, July–Aug 9:00–19:00, early summer and fall 9:30–19:00).

Biking—Expo.02 left the Three Lakes region with much-improved bike trails. Buy one of the excellent regional bike maps at a kiosk, rent a bike at the train station, and go for a lakeside ride. The TI and local bookstores sell a detailed map with biking and inline skating trails in this area. Ask for the excursion map by the Ministry for Topography (Bundesamt für Landestopographie; 19.80 SF, scale 1:75,000).

Near Murten

Avenches—This town, four miles south of Murten, was once Aventicum, the Roman capital of Helvetica. Back then, its population was 50,000. Today, it could barely fill the well-worn ruins of its 15,000-seat Roman amphitheater. You can tour the Roman museum (4 SF, April–Sept Tue–Sun 10:00–12:00 & 13:00–17:00, closed Mon, Oct–March Tue–Sun 14:00–17:00, closed Mon, near a dinky amphitheater in town center), but the best experience is some quiet time at sunset pondering the evocative Roman amphitheater and sanctuary in the fields, a half-mile walk out of town (free, always open).

Avenches, with a pleasant, small-French-town feel, is a quieter, less expensive place to stay than Murten. It also makes an easy day trip. The **TI** and the town are a seven-minute uphill walk from the station (Mon–Fri 8:00–12:00 & 13:30–17:30, Sat 9:00–12:30, closed Sun, tel. 026-676-9922, www.avenches.ch).

SLEEPING AND EATING

(1.40 SF = about $1, country code: 41)

When a price range is listed, prices vary with the season, type of room, or view.

Murten

$$$ Hotel Murtenhof, a worthwhile splurge, has 21 nicely appointed rooms—each a unique mix of old and new—and a lake view from its fine restaurant (Sb-110–165 SF, Db-140–260 SF, suites-280–410 SF, extra person-50 SF, elevator, parking-15 SF/day in garage or free on street, next to castle at Rathausgasse 1-3, tel. 026-672-9030, fax 026-672-9039, www.murtenhof.ch, info@murtenhof.ch). I eat on Hotel Murtenhof's terrace for their salad bar: 7.50 SF for a small plate, 15 SF for the big one. The small one, carefully stacked, holds plenty and comes with a sunset over the lake. The small plate is meant as a side dish, but, if you can handle the ridicule and don't mind being seated in back or outside, the big boss Theodore assured me you can eat one stacked high, and the waiters will even bring you a piece of bread and free water. The terrace is a good place to try the Vully wine—just point to the vineyards across the lake (restaurant open March–Nov Tue–Sun 11:00–23:00, closed Mon and Dec–Feb).

$$$ Hotel Krone offers 35 fine rooms at decent prices in a great location (Sb-100–135 SF, Db-170–200 SF, elevator, next door to Hotel Murtenhof at Rathausgasse 5, tel. 026-670-5252, fax 026-670-3610, hotel.krone.murten@bluewin.ch, Nyffeler family).

$$ Hotel Ringmauer (German for "ramparts") is friendly and characteristic, but noise can carry through its thin walls. Showers and toilets are within a dash of all 14 rooms (S-60 SF, D-110 SF, Db-120 SF, T-140 SF, Q-160 SF, attached restaurant, near town wall farthest from lake, Deutsche Kirchgasse 2, tel. 026-670-1101, fax 026-672-2083).

$$ Hotel Bahnhof, with indifferent management just across the street from the Murten train station, is a dead-last resort (S-70–80 SF, D-120 SF, Ds-135 SF, Bahnhofstrasse 14, tel. 026-670-2256, fax 026-672-1336, NSE).

Near Murten

$$ Hotel Bel Air is across the lake from Murten in lazy Praz, where hotel values are better. Bel Air has eight flowery, in-love-with-life rooms and balconies—many with breathtaking lake views (D-110 SF, T-165 SF, extra person-20 SF, cheaper for 3 nights or more, call ahead to arrange self-check-in if arriving on Thu, Route Principale 145, tel. 026-673-1414, www.bel-air-lac.ch). The hotel also runs a fine restaurant here (closed Thu), specializing in fish. While this is easy for drivers, train travelers will need to catch the boat from Murten (see above). They can depart Praz by boat weekday mornings at 8:15, or walk to the Sugiez train station (on the main Bern line) a half-mile away.

In and near Avenches

$ Friendly **Elisabeth Clement-Arnold** rents a room in her house (D-40 SF, breakfast Fri–Sun only-5 SF, no CC, bathroom is yours alone but down the hall, often nobody home until 19:00, reserve by e-mail, rue Centrale 5, tel. & fax 026-675-3031, eckadima@hotmail.com).

$ The Avenches **IYHF hostel,** the only hostel in the area, is a beauty. It's run by the Dhyaf family, has 4- to 10-bed rooms, and includes breakfast, a homey TV room, table tennis, a big backyard, and a very quiet setting near the Roman theater (32 SF for dorm bed in 4-bed room, 29 SF in 6- to 10-bed room, 36 SF per person for S or D and 34 SF per person for T when available, non-members pay 6 SF extra, office open 7:00–9:30 & 17:00–22:00, no curfew, 3 blocks from center at medieval *lavoir,* or laundry, Rue du Lavoir 5, tel. 026-675-2666, fax 026-675-2717, avenches@youthhostel.ch).

TRANSPORTATION CONNECTIONS

By train to: Avenches (hrly, 10 min), **Bern** (hrly, 30 min, most require a transfer in Kerzers), **Fribourg** in Switzerland (hrly, 30 min), **Lausanne** (hrly, 90 min, some direct, others require a transfer in Fribourg). Train info: toll tel. 0900-300-3004.

Route Tips for Drivers

Interlaken to Bern to Murten (50 miles): From Interlaken, catch the autobahn (direction: Spiez, Thun, Bern). After Spiez, the autobahn takes you directly to Bern. Circle the city on the autobahn, taking the fourth Bern exit, Neufeld Bern. Signs to *Zentrum* take you to Bern Bahnhof. Turn right just before the station into the Bahnhof Parkplatz (45-min meter parking outside, all-day lot inside, 2-4 SF/hr, depending on time of entry). You're just an escalator ride away from a great TI and Switzerland's compact, user-friendly capital. From the station, drive out of Bern following Lausanne signs, then follow the green signs to Neuchâtel and Murten. The autobahn ends 20 miles later in Murten (for parking, see "Arrival in Murten," above).

Murten to Lake Geneva (50 miles): The autobahn from Bern to Lausanne/Lake Geneva makes everything speedy. Murten and Avenches are 10 minutes off the autobahn. Broc, Bulle, and Gruyères are within sight of each other and the autobahn. It takes about an hour to drive from Murten to Montreux. The autobahn (direction: Simplon) takes you high above Montreux (pull off at great viewpoint rest stop) and Château de Chillon. For the castle, take the first exit east of the castle (Villeneuve). Signs direct you along the lake back to the castle.

LAKE GENEVA AND FRENCH SWITZERLAND

The southwest corner of Switzerland is predominantly French, *s'il vous plaît*, and, as you'll see, that means more than language. Lake Geneva (Lac Leman in French) is Switzerland's Riviera. Separating France and Switzerland, the lake is surrounded by Alps and lined with a collage of castles, museums, spas, resort towns, and vineyards. Its crowds, therefore, are understandable. This area is so beautiful that Charlie Chaplin and Idi Amin both chose it as their second home.

Skip the big, dull city of Geneva and make your home base in fun, breezy Lausanne. Explore the romantic Château de Chillon and stylishly syncopated Montreux. The French Swiss countryside offers up chocolates, Gruyère cheese, and a fine folk museum.

Planning Your Time

On a quick trip, you can get a good overview of the lake in a day or less. If you spent the night in Murten (see previous chapter) and you're in a hurry, make a beeline for Château de Chillon. Then head to Lausanne (maybe via a lazy boat cruise—see below) to take in some museums. With more time, explore some of the countryside options on your way to or from the lake (see "French Swiss Countryside," page 516).

Getting around Lake Geneva

Trains easily connect towns along Lake Geneva. Take the faster Direct trains if you're going between larger cities, such as Lausanne or Montreux, or the slower Régional or REV trains if you're heading for a smaller destination, such as Château de Chillon or Villeneuve (check the TV screens in the station for Direct, Régional, or REV to find the right train).

Boats carry visitors to all sights of importance. Daily boat trips (4/day in each direction May–Sept, less off-season) connect Château de

FRENCH PHRASES

Though many people in this part of Switzerland speak English, it's helpful to know some French phrases.

Good day.	**Bonjour.**	bohn-ZHOOR
Mrs.	**Madame**	mah-DAHM
Mr.	**Monsieur**	muhs-YUR
Please?	**S'il vous plaît?**	see voo play
Thank you.	**Merci.**	mehr-SEE
You're welcome.	**De rien.**	duh ree-AHN
Excuse me?	**Pardon?**	par-DOHN
Yes. / No.	**Oui. / Non.**	wee / nohn
Okay.	**D'accord.**	dah-KOR
Cheers!	**Santé!**	sahn-TAY
Goodbye.	**Au revoir.**	oh vwahr
women / men	**dames / hommes**	dahm / ohm
one / two / three	**un / deux / trois**	uhn / duh / twah
Do you speak English?	**Parlez-vous anglais?**	PAR-lay voo ahn-GLAY

Chillon with Montreux (10 min, 7.60 SF), Vevey (30 min, 10.20 SF), and Lausanne (90 min, 22 SF, first class costs about one-third more and gets you passage on the deck up top, where you should scramble for the first-come, first-served chairs; Eurailers sail free, but it uses up a flexi-day; tel. 021-614-6200, www.cgn.ch). The short cruise from Montreux to Château de Chillon is fun. The pretty town of Vevey gives you the most scenic 30-minute boat ride from Chillon and 60-minute ride from Lausanne, and makes an enjoyable destination.

Lausanne

This is the most interesting city on the lake, proudly dubbing itself the "Olympic Capital" (it's been home to the International Olympic Committee since 1915). Amble the serene lakefront promenade, stroll through the three-tiered colorful old town, explore the sculptures at Olympic Park, and visit its remarkable Museum of Art Brut. Take a peek at its Gothic cathedral and climb its tower for the view.

ORIENTATION

Tourist Information: Lausanne has two TIs, one in the train station (daily 9:00–19:00) and the other at the lakefront Ouchy metro stop (April–Sept daily 9:00–20:00, Oct–March daily 9:00–18:00; for both: tel. 021-613-7321, www.lausanne-tourisme.ch). Ask if there are free concerts at the cathedral and any walking tours in English (10 SF, tours offered May–Sept Mon–Sat usually at 10:00 and 15:00, subject to availability of English-speaking guide, meet in front of Town Hall at place de la Palud, tel. 021-321-7766).

Worth considering for two-day visits, the **Lausanne Card** covers city transit and offers significant discounts on some museums, including the recommended Olympic Museum, Collection de l'Art Brut, and City Museum (15 SF/2 calendar days, sold at TI, costs virtually the same as two 24-hour transit passes plus offers discounts).

Helpful Hints

The **launderette** closest to the train station is Quick-Wash (Wed–Mon 8:30–20:30, Sat–Sun 9:00–20:30, boulevard de Grancy 44, at corner with Passage de Montriond, below train station). For **Internet** access, try Quanta (8 SF/hr, daily 9:00–24:00, across street from train station and above McDonald's at place de la Gare 4) or Cyberland (8 SF/hr, daily 9:00–24:00, rue du Grand Pont 10, near Hôtel Régina). **Bike rental** is available at the train station baggage office (23 SF/half-day, 30 SF/full day).

Getting around Lausanne

You'll want a map to navigate this city, which is steeper than it is big. A five-stop funicular-metro connects the lakefront (called Ouchy; OO-shee) with the train station (CFF) and the upper part of Lausanne (called *vieille ville,* or *centre ville).* The cost is 2.40 SF (tickets good for 1 hr on buses, too; the cheaper 1.50 SF ticket is good for only 3 bus stops or 2 metro stops; 1 stop from station to *vieille ville* costs only 1.30 SF). You can walk, but everyone uses the metro. Buy tickets from the window or at the ticket machines (machines don't give change). The metro is across the street from the train station. If you're coming from the dock at Ouchy, angle left from the boats to reach the metro (TI there). For buses, buy tickets before boarding from the white-and-yellow machine at the bus stop. The 24-hour pass, which covers both the metro and the bus, is a good deal if you take three trips or more (7.20 SF). Don't believe the locals who assure you that your Eurailpass is good on public transportation in Lausanne—it isn't.

SIGHTS

Lausanne's Old City *(Vieille Ville)*

The vertical old city is laced with shopping streets, modern structures, and the elegant cathedral. From the top metro stop, walk under the viaduct, then wander left uphill along pedestrian streets to the cathedral.

Cathedral—This is a purely peaceful place with unusual stained-glass windows—all done by local artists in the 1920s, except for the 13th-century rose window—and a 225-step tower view (cathedral open April–Sept Mon–Fri 7:00-19:00, Sat–Sun 8:00–19:00, Oct–March until 17:30; tower and welcome center open April–Sept Mon–Sat 8:30–11:45 & 13:30–18:00, Sun 14:00–18:00, Oct–March until 17:00, last tower entry 30 min before closing time, 2 SF to climb tower).

City History Museum—This museum traces life in Lausanne from Roman times to the present with many fun interactive displays and CD-ROM demos. It's notable for its 1:200-scale model of Lausanne in the 17th century, accompanied by an audiovisual presentation (4 SF, free first Sat of every month, open Tue–Thu 11:00–18:00, Fri–Sun 11:00–17:00, closed Mon, English audioguide-4 SF, 4 place de la Cathédrale, tel. 021-331-0353). The museum is right next to the cathedral and viewpoint terrace.

Collection de l'Art Brut—This brilliantly displayed, thought-provoking collection comprises art produced by untrained artists, many labeled by society as criminal or insane. Enjoy the unbridled creativity and read about the artists (6 SF, Tue–Sun 11:00–18:00, closed Mon except July–Aug; bus #3 from station, stop Beaulieu; or bus #2 from Bel Air—near Hôtel Régina—stop Jomini; follow signs to Palais de Beaulieu, Avenue des Bergières 11, tel. 021-315-2570, www.artbrut.ch).

Lausanne's Waterfront

▲**Olympic Park and Museum**—This beautiful park and high-tech museum celebrate the colorful history of the games. Enjoy the park's Olympic flame (in front of museum), athletic monuments, and lake views for free (take escalator to top, ask in museum for free brochure explaining sculptures, and wander back down to lake).

The expensive but excellent museum (14 SF) is great for Olympics buffs—or for those of us who just watch every two years. The ground floor traces the history of the games (including some ancient Greek artifacts) and displays a century's worth of ceremonial torches. Upstairs you'll find medals from each Olympiad (pick your favorite) and explanations and equipment of various Olympic events (find Carl Lewis' shoes from L.A. in 1984, the Michael Jordan–signed basketball from the 1992 Barcelona "Dream Team," and Cathy Freeman's shoes from the 2000 Sydney games). Up top are a swanky restaurant and lakeview terrace. In the basement, you'll find a 3-D theater and an extensive film archive of thrilling moments in the history of the games—your choice of two mini-documentaries about any Olympiad event or ceremony are included with your ticket (14 SF, assemble 9 other tourists to get group rate of 10 SF per person, good English explanations, more in-depth English audioguide-3 SF, May–Sept daily 9:00–18:00, Thu until 20:00, Oct–April closed Mon, from Ouchy metro stop turn left and walk 5 min to Quai d'Ouchy 1, tel. 021-621-6511, www.olympic.org).

Vineyard Strolls—Picturesque vineyards abound along the lake near Lausanne. Consider a 5–10-minute train ride to Chexbres or Grandvaux and walk through the villages toward Lutry for stunning views of Lake Geneva. From Lutry, hop the train back to Lausanne (hrly, 8 min).

SLEEPING

$$$ **Hôtel Mirabeau,** a Best Western, offers 74 spiffy business-class rooms. If you want a touch of luxury in this expensive city, it's a decent splurge, a five-minute walk from the station (Sb-160–235 SF, Db-215–320 SF, 10 percent off these rates if you mention this book when you reserve and show it when you pay, suites and family rooms also available, non-smoking rooms, air-con in pricier rooms, elevator, park-

SLEEP CODE

(1.40 SF = about $1, country code: 41)

Sleep Code: **S** = Single, **D** = Double/Twin, **T** = Triple, **Q** = Quad, **b** = bathroom, **s** = shower only, **no CC** = Credit Cards not accepted, **SE** = Speaks English, **NSE** = No English. Unless otherwise noted, credit cards are accepted, English is spoken, and breakfast is included.

To help you sort easily through these listings, I've divided the rooms into three categories, based on the price for a standard double room with bath:

$$$ **Higher Priced**—Most rooms 200 SF or more.
$$ **Moderately Priced**—Most rooms between 120–200 SF.
$ **Lower Priced**—Most rooms 120 SF or less.

Lausanne hotels are expensive. Price ranges depend on season, room location, and view. The Régina, Voyageurs, and Raisin are in the *vieille ville,* and the rest are closer to the station. Breakfast is included unless otherwise noted.

ing-19 SF/day in garage, 12 SF/day on street, turn right out of station and walk 2 blocks to Avenue de la Gare 31, tel. 021-341-4243, fax 021-341-4242, www.mirabeau.ch, reservation@mirabeau.ch).

$$ Hôtel Régina, on a pedestrian street near a quaint square in the old town, is a find: 36 comfy, newly remodeled rooms, hospitable hosts, and a great location. Energetic Michel and Dora provide loads of sightseeing information (Sb-128–138 SF, Db-168–178 SF, third person-40 SF, suites-165–325 SF depending on number of people, cheaper in winter, non-smoking rooms, a few stairs then elevator, free Internet access, free parking 18:00–8:00, Rue Grand Saint-Jean 18, tel. 021-320-2441, fax 021-320-2529, www.hotel-regina.ch, info@hotel-regina.ch). Take the metro up to the last stop, use the pedestrian bridge, cross Rue du Grand Pont, and walk up Rue Pichard, turning right on the first street.

$$ Hôtel Elite, run by the Zufferey family, is on a quiet, leafy, residential street just above the Gare metro stop. Its 33 rooms are pleasant, modern, and slightly musty (Sb-125–180 SF, Db-170–240 SF, Tb-200–255 SF, 4-person suite with balcony and kitchen-350 SF, non-smoking rooms, elevator; from station bear left across street and go uphill around McDonald's, take first right to Avenue Sainte-Luce 1, tel. 021-320-2361, fax 021-320-3963, www.elite-lausanne.ch, info@elite-lausanne.ch).

$$ Hotel des Voyageurs has 33 predictable rooms across the street from Hôtel Régina (listed above). Part of the Comfort chain, it's a lesser value, without the Régina's charm but in an equally good location (Sb-108–180 SF, Db-150–230 SF, Tb-180–270 SF, non-smoking rooms, elevator, Rue Grand Saint-Jean 19, tel. 021-319-9111, fax 021-319-9112, www.voyageurs.ch, voyageurshotel@compuserve.com).

$ Hôtel du Raisin, an old, old, Old World dive with dingy, faded furnishings, has 12 rooms in a great but noisy location on a popular square in the old town (S-55 SF, Ss-60–70 SF, D-110 SF, Ds-120 SF, attached restaurant with sidewalk café, Place de la Palud 19, tel. & fax 021-312-2756, NSE).

$ Jeunotel, clean and affordable, has concrete walls and cell-block rooms. You know it's not a minimum-security prison because they give you a key (dorm bed-39 SF, S-60 SF, Sb-86 SF, D-96, Db-112 SF, T-117, cheaper with hostel membership, any age welcome, easy parking, Chemin du Bois-de-Vaux 36, tel. 021-626-0222, fax 021-626-0226, www.jeunotel.ch). Take the metro to Ouchy, then bus #2 to the Bois-de-Vaux stop (you'll see signs for the hotel, a block away).

EATING

The lakeside **Ouchy district** is the place to relax. It offers new squares with fountains, parks, playgrounds, promenades, and many crêperies, brasseries, and restaurants.

All of the following places are at the top of Lausanne, in the old city:

Café du Grütli offers typical Swiss cuisine on a cute little terrace near Place de la Palud (Mon–Fri 11:30–14:30 & 18:00–23:00, Sat until 18:00, closed Sun, Rue de la Mercerie 4, tel. 021-312-9493).

Le Bleu Lézard has great French cuisine with typical French ambience and a young clientele (daily 7:00–24:00, until later weekends, good Sunday brunch, Rue Enning 10, tel. 021-321-3830).

Les Brasseurs is a brewery with a restaurant, bar, and great ambience (Mon–Sat 11:00–24:00, until later weekends, Sun from 17:00, Rue Centrale 4, tel. 021-351-1424).

Vinothèque Louis is primarily a wine bar, where you can taste 40 different wines and order appetizers. To make your choice easier, they classify the wines by their character and label them accordingly. The top floor has the expensive Restaurant Gastronomique, the bottom floor has the *vinothèque* and bistro with good, reasonable food. There's also a big, modern terrace (daily 11:30–23:00, from top metro stop take elevator down to Place de l'Europe 9, tel. 021-213-0300).

TRANSPORTATION CONNECTIONS

By train to: Montreux (2/hr, 20 min on Direct train), **Château de Chillon** (hrly, 35 min on REV train), **Murten** (hrly, 90 min, change in Fribourg, Neuchâtel, or Payerne), **Geneva** (3/hr, 40 min), **Bern** (2/hr, 70 min), **Basel** (hrly, 2 hrs, change in Bern or Biel), **Milan** (6/day, 3.25-4 hrs). Train info: toll tel. 0900-300-3004.

Château de Chillon

This medieval castle, set wistfully at the edge of Lake Geneva, is a ▲▲▲ joy. Remarkably well-preserved, it has never been damaged or destroyed—always inhabited, always maintained. The Savoy family (their seal is the skinny red cross on the towers) enlarged it to its current state in the 13th century, when this was a prime location—at a crossroads of a major trade route from England and France to Rome.

Château de Chillon (shee-yon) was the Savoys' fortress and residence, with four big halls (a major status symbol) and impractically large lakeview windows (their powerful navy could defend against possible attack from the water). When the Bernese invaded in 1536, the castle was conquered in just two days, and the new governor made Château de Chillon his residence (and a Counter-Reformation prison). Inspired by the Revolution in Paris, the French-speaking people on Lake Geneva finally kicked out their German-speaking Bernese oppressors in 1798. The castle became—and remains—the property of the Canton of Vaud. It has been used as an armory, a warehouse, a prison, a hospital, and a tourist attraction. Rousseau's writings first drew attention to the castle, inspiring visits by Romantics such as Lord Byron and Victor Hugo, plus other notables including Dickens, Goethe, and Hemingway.

Follow the free English brochure from one fascinating room to the next. Enjoy the castle's tingly views, dank prison, battle-scarred weapons, simple Swiss-style mobile furniture, and 700-year-old toilets (rooms #15 and #22). Bonivard's Prison (#7) is named for a renegade Savoy who was tortured here for five years (lashed to the fifth column from the entrance). When the Romantic poet Lord Byron came to visit, Bonivard's story inspired him to write *The Prisoner of Chillon*, which vividly recounts a prisoner's dark and solitary life ("And mine has been the fate of those / To whom the goodly earth and air / Are bann'd, and barr'd—forbidden fare," full text available in the gift shop). You can still see where Byron scratched his name in a column (third from entrance, covered by glass). The chapel (#18) uses projectors to simulate the original frescoes. Models in room #24 explain the construction of the castle. Remember the grand views from the lakeside windows? Notice the small slits facing the road on the land side (#25)—more practical for defense. The 130-step climb to the top of the keep (#32) isn't worth the time or sweat. Stroll the patrol ramparts, then curl up on a windowsill to enjoy the lake.

Cost, Hours, and Information: 9 SF, April–Sept daily 9:00–18:00, shorter hours off-season, easy parking, tel. 021-966-8910, www.chillon.ch.

Getting to Château de Chillon: The castle sits at the eastern tip of Lake Geneva, about 20 miles east of Lausanne (and about a mile east of Montreux).

From Lausanne, you can connect to the castle using a combination of various methods: train, bus, boat, and hike. The hourly REV train (direction Villeneuve, 35 min, 10.40 SF) takes you directly to the station at Veytaux-Chillon, a few minutes' walk along the lake (ideal for picnicking) from the castle. The faster and more frequent Direct train whisks you to Montreux (2/hr, 20 min, 9.80 SF); from the Montreux station, cross Avenue des Alpes and go down the stairs. Cross the street and find the blue bus stop on your right, where you can hop bus #1 to Château de Chillon (2.80 SF, direction Villeneuve, stop Chillon; buy tickets at bus stop or from machine on board). You can also hike the one mile from Montreux to the Château de Chillon.

To return to Lausanne, simply reverse the directions (catch the train from the Veytaux-Chillon station back to Lausanne—trains leave hrly at :07—or bus from Château de Chillon to Montreux-2.80 SF, direction Vevey, stop Escaliers de la Gare, climb up to the station to train the rest of the way to Lausanne).

A slower but more scenic route is by boat between the Château de Chillon and Montreux or Vevey, connecting to Lausanne with trains.

For a longer trip, sail all the way between the Château de Chillon and Lausanne, one-way (90 min) or, for true *See*farers, round-trip (see "Getting around Lake Geneva," page 508).

Montreux

This expensive resort has a famous jazz festival each July. The lakeside promenade takes you along parks, palm trees, crêperies, ice-cream stands, and modern sculptures. In the center, meet the statue of Freddie Mercury, who had strong bonds with Montreux. His band, Queen, bought the local Mountain Recording Studios in 1978.

The Montreux **TI** (Mon–Fri 9:00–18:00, Sat–Sun 10:00–17:00, tel. 021-962-8484) has a list of moderate rooms in the center, including **Hôtel-Restaurant du Pont** (Sb-70 SF, Db-130 SF, good spaghetti, Rue du Pont 12, tel. 021-963-2249, hoteldupont@hotmail.com, NSE). The **hostel** is on the lake, a 10-minute stroll north of the Château de Chillon (dorm bed-30 SF, D-76 SF, nonmembers pay extra, Passage de l'Auberge 8, tel. 021-963-4934, fax 021-963-2729, montreux@youthhostel.ch).

If you're driving from Montreux to Lausanne, consider visiting the **Corniche de Lavaux.** This rugged, sometimes frightening, Swiss Wine Road swerves through picturesque towns and the stingy vineyards that produce Lake Geneva's tasty but expensive wine (including Mont-sur-Rolle and St-Saphorin). From Montreux, go west along the lake through Vevey, following blue signs to Lausanne along the waterfront and taking the Moudon/Chexbres exit. Be sure to explore some of the smaller roads. **Hikers** can take the boat to Cully and explore on foot from there.

French Swiss Countryside

The sublime French Swiss countryside is sprinkled with crystal-clear lakes, tasty chocolates, smelly cheese, and sleepy cows. If you're traveling between Murten, Lausanne, and Interlaken (see map on page 492), take time for a few of the countryside's sights, tastes, and smells.

Getting around the Countryside

Cross-country buses use Fribourg and Bulle as hubs: **Bulle–Gruyères** (2/day, 15 min) and **Fribourg-Bulle** (hrly, 30 min). The train is the best bet between Bulle and Gruyères (hrly, 7 min).

SIGHTS

Caillers Chocolate Factory—The Caillers factory, churning out chocolate in the town of Broc, welcomes visitors with a hygienic peek through a window, a 15-minute movie, and free melt-in-your-hands samples (free, Mon 13:30–16:00, Tue–Fri 9:00–11:00 & 13:30–16:00, closed Sat–Sun, closed Nov–March, follow signs to Nestlé and Broc Fabrique, groups of 4 or more should call a day in advance to reserve, tel. 026-921-5151). Broc town is just the sleepy, sweet-smelling home of the chocolate makers. It has a small, very typical hotel, **Auberge des Montagnards** (D-70 SF, great view of Gruyères, elegant dining room, tel. 026-921-1526, fax 026-921-1576). From Bulle, trains run hourly to Broc (10 min).

▲▲**Musée Gruèrien**—Somehow, the unassuming little town of Bulle built a refreshing, cheery folk museum that manages to teach you all about life in these parts and leave you feeling very good (5 SF, free English guidebook, Tue–Sat 10:00–12:00 & 14:00–17:00, Sun 14:00–17:00, closed Mon, tel. 026-912-7260). When it's over, the guide reminds you, "The Golden Book of Visitors awaits your signature and comments. Don't you think this museum deserves another visit? Thank you!"

▲**Gruyères**—This ultratouristy town, famous for its cheese, fills its fortified hilltop like a bouquet. Its ramparts are a park, and the ancient buildings serve tourists. The castle is mediocre, but do make a short stop for the setting. Minimize your walk by driving up to the second parking lot. Hotels here are expensive. For a spooky, offbeat contrast to idyllic Gruyères, consider the town's **H. R. Giger Museum**—dedicated to the Swiss artist who designed the monsters in the *Alien* movies. The museum, not for the faint of heart, shares those movies' dark aesthetic (10 SF, daily 10:00–18:00, tel. 026-921-2200).

▲▲**Gruyère Fromageries**—There are two very different cheese-making exhibits to choose from. Five miles above Gruyères, a dark and smoky 17th-century farmhouse in Moléson gives a fun look at the old and smelly craft (3 SF, mid-May–mid-Oct daily 9:30–22:00, closed mid-Oct-mid-May, cheese actually being made at 9:45 and 14:45, TI tel. 026-921-1030, www.fromagerie.fr.st). Closer, slicker, and modern, the cheese-production center at the foot of Gruyères town (follow *Fromagerie* signs) opens its doors to tourists with a continuous English audiovisual presentation (5 SF, daily 9:00–19:00, www.lamaisondugruyere.ch). The cute cheese shop in the modern center has lunches and picnic goodies (closed 12:00-13:30).

Glacier des Diablerets—For a grand alpine trip to the tip of a 10,000-foot peak, take the three-part lift from Reusch or Col du Pillon. The trip takes about 90 minutes and costs 50 SF. Stay for lunch. From the top, you can see the Matterhorn and a bit of Mont Blanc, the Alps' highest peak. This is a good chance to do some summer skiing (normally expensive and a major headache). A lift ticket and rental skis, poles, boots, and coat cost about 65 SF. The slopes close at 14:00 during the summer, and at 17:00 from October through April.

The base of the lift is a two-hour drive from Murten or Gimmelwald. Your best public-transportation bet is to catch an early train to

Diablerets with a transfer in Aigle. Then bus to Col du Pillon (7/day) and take the cable car to the top (last departure at 16:00). For more ski information, call 024-492-3377.

▲▲**Taveyanne**—This remote hamlet is a huddle of log cabins used by cowherds in the summer. The hamlet's old bar is a restaurant serving a tiny community of vacationers and hikers. Taveyanne is two miles off the main road between Col de la Croix and Villars. A small sign points down a tiny road to a jumble of huts and snoozing cows stranded at 5,000 feet. The inn is **Refuge de Taveyanne** (from 1882), where the Seibenthal family serves meals in a prizewinning rustic setting with no electricity, low ceilings, and a huge charred fireplace. Consider sleeping in their primitive loft (12 SF, no CC, 5 mattresses, access by a ladder outside, bathroom outside, closed Tue except July–Aug, closed Nov–April, tel. 024-498-1947). It's a fine opportunity to really get to know prizewinning cows.

APPENZELL

Welcome to cowbell country. In moo-mellow and storybook-friendly Appenzell, you'll find the warm, intimate side of the land of staggering, icy Alps. Savor Appenzell's cozy, small-town ambience.

Appenzell is Switzerland's most traditional region...and the butt of humor because of it. Entire villages meet in town squares to vote (an event featured on most postcard racks). Until 1989, the women of Appenzell couldn't vote on local issues. (But lately, the region has become more progressive. In 2000, its schools were the first to make English—rather than French—mandatory.)

A gentle beauty blankets the region overlooked by the 8,200-foot peak Säntis. As you travel, you'll enjoy an ever-changing parade of finely carved chalets, traditional villages, and cows moaning, "milk me." While farmers' bikini-clad daughters make hay, old ladies walk the steep roads with scythes, looking as if they just pushed the Grim Reaper down the hill. When locals are asked about Appenzell cheese, they clench their fists as they answer, "It's the best." (It is, without any doubt, the smelliest.)

If you're here in late August or early September, there's a good chance you'll get in on (or at least have your road blocked by) the ceremonial procession of flower-bedecked cows and whistling herders in traditional, formal outfits. The festive march down from the high pastures is a spontaneous move by the herding families, and when they finally do burst into town (a slow-motion Swiss Pamplona), the people become children again, running into the streets.

Planning Your Time

Appenzell's charms are subtle, prices are high, and the public transportation is limited. For many on a fast trip with no car, the area is not worth the trouble. But by car, it's a breeze.

Ideally, Appenzell is an interesting way for drivers to connect Austria and Bavaria with the Berner Oberland (Switzerland's Jungfrau

Appenzell Region

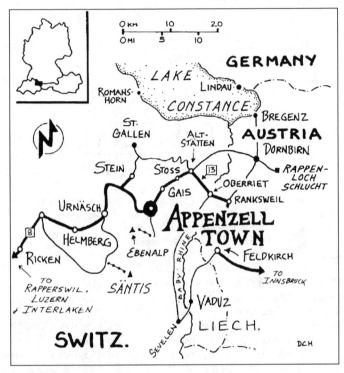

region). Drive in from Tirol in time to get up the lift to Ebenalp (for the most memorable overnight), descend the next morning and spend the day sampling the charms of Appenzell town, and get to the Interlaken area that night.

Getting around Appenzell

Those with a car have the region by the tail. Those without wheels will need more time and patience. The center of the Appenzell region is Appenzell town. A train connects Appenzell with Wasserauen (hrly except 2/hr in rush hour, 20 min) and Herisau (same train, opposite direction, 40 min), from which bigger trains depart hourly for St. Gallen (20 min) and Luzern (2 hrs). The Herisau train also stops at Urnäsch (20 min). Regional buses connect towns several times a day; for schedules, check with the TI or the post office. Appenzell's shuttle service, PubliCar, takes passengers to locations—such as Stein—not serviced by buses. To reserve, inquire at the TI or call 0800-553-060 (toll free) and ask for an English-speaking operator.

SIGHTS

Appenzell Town—In this traditional town, kids play "barn" instead of "house" while Mom and Dad watch yodeling on TV. The town center is a painfully cute pedestrian zone that delights tourists born to shop. The **TI** is on the main street (Hauptgasse 4, May–mid-Oct Mon–Fri 9:00–12:00 & 13:30–18:00, Sat–Sun 10:00–12:00 & 14:00–17:00; mid-Oct–April Mon–Fri 9:00–12:00 & 14:00–17:00, Sat–Sun 14:00–17:00; tel. 071-788-9641). The **post office** is in front of the train station. Don't bother looking for a launderette. You can access the **Internet** at the library (Tue–Wed 14:00–17:00, Thu 14:00–16:00, Fri 17:00–20:00, Sat 9:30–11:30, closed Sun) and rent bikes at the train station (23 SF/half-day, 30 SF/full day). The Appenzell Card (22 SF/1 day, 42 SF/3 days, 68 SF/5 days, purchase at TI) covers trains, lifts, and some museums in the region. This can be a good deal if you're visiting the Appenzeller Folk Museum and going round-trip to Ebenalp in a single day. Otherwise, skip it.

▲**Folk Music**—Folk-music concerts take place every Thursday (mid-June–mid-Oct) at 18:30 in the city hall. You can also sometimes find live music at local restaurants—ask at the TI.

▲**Appenzeller Folk Museum**—The folk museum next to the TI provides an excellent look at the local cow culture. Ride the elevator to the sixth floor and work your way down through traditional costumes, living rooms, art, and crafts (5 SF, April–Oct daily 10:00–12:00 & 14:00–17:00, Nov–March Tue–Sun 14:00–17:00, closed Mon, ask to borrow English handbook).

Bike to the Rhine—To experience this area on two wheels, rent a bike at the station and glide about two hours down into the Rhine Valley to the town of Alstätten. From there, take the single-car train back up the hill to Appenzell (details at TI).

▲▲**Ebenalp**—This cliff-hanging hut is a thin-air alternative to Appenzell town. Ride the lift from Wasserauen, five miles south of Appenzell town, to Ebenalp (5,380 feet). On the way up (left side), you'll get a sneak preview of

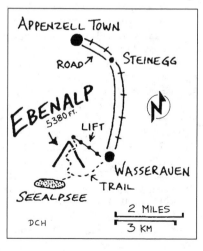

Ebenalp

Ebenalp's cave church and the cliffside boardwalk that leads to the guest house. From the top, you'll enjoy a sweeping view all the way to Lake Constance (Bodensee).

Leaving the lift, take a 12-minute hike through a prehistoric cave (slippery and dimly lit—hold the railing and you'll come to daylight), past a hermit's home (a tiny museum, always open) and the 400-year-old Wildkirchi cave church (hermit monks lived there 1658–1853), to a 170-year-old guest house built precariously into the cliff. Originally housing farmers, goats, and cows, the hut evolved into a guest house for pilgrims coming to the monks for spiritual guidance. Today, Berggasthaus Aescher welcomes tourists, offering cheap dorm beds and hot, hearty plates of *Rösti* (traditional hash browns with Alp cheese, see "Sleeping and Eating High in Ebenalp," page 523).

The region is a hit with hikers who make the circuit of mountain hotels. There are 24 hotels, each a day's hike apart. All originated as alpine farms. Of these, Berggasthaus Aescher is the oldest and smallest.

From Ebenalp's sunny cliff perch, you can almost hear the cows munching on the far side of the valley. Only the parasailors, like neon jellyfish, tag your world as 21st century. In the distance, nestled below Säntis Peak, is the Seealpsee. The one-hour hike down to the lake is steep but pleasurable (take left at first fork below guest house).

The Ebenalp lift runs about twice hourly until 19:00 in July and August, 18:00 in June and September, and 17:30 in spring and fall (18 SF up, 24 SF round-trip, free and reportedly safe parking at lift, free hiking brochure, closed for 2 weeks in both Nov and May for maintenance, tel. 071-799-1212, www.ebenalp.ch).

▲**Stein**—The town of Stein has the Appenzell Showcase Cheese Dairy (Schaukäserei, March–Oct daily 9:00–19:00, Nov–Feb daily 9:00–18:00, cheese-making normally 9:00–14:00, tel. 071-368-5070). It's fast, free, smelly, and well-explained in a 15-minute English video and the free English brochure (with cheese recipes). The lady at the cheese counter loves to cut it so you can sample it. They also have yogurt and cheap boxes of cold iced tea for sale. The restaurant serves powerful cheese specialties. Stein's great folk moo-seum *(Volkskunde)* is next door. This cow-culture museum, with old-fashioned cheese-making demonstrations, peasant houses, fascinating embroidering machinery, cow art, and folk-craft demonstrations, is not worth the 7 SF if you've seen the similar museum in Appenzell (Mon 13:30–17:00, Tue–Sat 10:00–12:00 & 13:30–17:00, Sun 10:00–17:00, Nov–March no demos but you can still see museum, tel. 071-368-5056). Without a car, the only way to get to Stein is by PubliCar (see "Getting around Appenzell," above).

▲**Urnäsch**—This appealing one-street town has Europe's cutest museum. The Appenzeller Museum, on the town square, brings this region's folk customs to life. Warm and homey, it's a happy little honeycomb of Appenzeller culture (5 SF, April–Oct daily 13:30–17:00,

Nov–March open only if you call ahead, winter entry fee-20 SF for groups smaller than 10, guided tour-20 SF plus entry, good English description brochure, tel. 071-364-2322).

SLEEPING AND EATING

Sleeping and Eating High in Ebenalp

There's no reason to sleep in Appenzell town. The Ebenalp lift, across from the tiny Wasserauen train station, is a few minutes' drive (or a 20-min train ride) south.

$$ Berg Gasthaus Ebenalp sits atop the mountains just above the lift. Its newly refurbished rooms are booked long in advance on Saturdays, but are empty otherwise (dorm beds with comforter-30 SF, D-104 SF, includes breakfast, coin-op shower, tel. 071-799-1194, Sutter family).

$$ From Wasserauen, you can hike up the private road to **Berggasthaus Seealpsee,** on the idyllic alpine lake Seealpsee (loft dorm beds with sheets-27 SF, S-50 SF, D-100 SF, includes breakfast, showers-2 SF, tel. 071-799-1140, fax 071-799-1820, www.seealpsee.ch, Dörig family).

$ Berggasthaus Aescher promises a memorable experience. The 170-year-old house has only rainwater and no shower. Friday and Saturday nights sometimes have great live music, but are often crowded and noisy, with up to 40 people, and parties going into the wee hours. Monday through Thursday, you'll normally get a small woody dorm to yourself. The hut is actually built into the cliffside; its back wall is the rock. From the toilet, you can study this alpine architecture. Sip your coffee on the deck, sheltered from drips from the gnarly overhang 100 feet above. The guest book goes back to 1940, there's a fun drawer filled with an alpine percussion section, and the piano in the comfortable dining/living room was brought in by helicopter. For a great 45-minute predinner hike, check out the goats. Take the high trail toward the lake and circle clockwise back up the peak to the lift and down the way you originally came. Claudia can show you the rock-climbing charts (dorm beds-32 SF, comes with comforter, breakfast-12 SF, dinner-14-22 SF, no CC, no towels or showers available, closed Nov–April, 12 min by steep trail below top of lift, tel. 071-799-1142, www.aescher-ai.ch, info@aescher-ai.ch, run by Claudia and Beny Knechtle-Wyss, their 5 children: Bernhardt-age 19, Reto-18, Lukas-15, Lilian-14, Dominik-12, 3 pigs, 12 goats, 4 donkeys, 14 rabbits, and a dog).

Sleeping in the Town of Appenzell

The town is small but touristy. Hotels are good and central. The *Zimmer* are six blocks from the center.

$$$ Hotel Adler, above a delicious café/bakery (daily 7:30–19:30, closed Wed Nov–June) in a fine location, offers two kinds of rooms:

SLEEP CODE

(1.40 SF = about $1, country code: 41)
Sleep Code: **S** = Single, **D** = Double/Twin, **T** = Triple, **Q** = Quad, **b** = bathroom, **s** = shower only, **no CC** = Credit Cards not accepted, **SE** = Speaks English, **NSE** = No English. Unless otherwise noted, credit cards are accepted, English is spoken, and breakfast is included.

To help you sort easily through these listings, I've divided the rooms into three categories, based on the price for a standard double room with bath:

$$$ **Higher Priced**—Most rooms 100 SF or more.
$$ **Moderately Priced**—Most rooms between 50–100 SF.
$ **Lower Priced**—Most rooms 50 SF or less.

newly refurbished, traditional Appenzeller or modern. Helpful Franz Leu, proud to be an Appenzeller, has turned the halls and traditional rooms of his hotel into a museum of regional art and culture (Sb-80–105 SF, Db-170–190 SF, suite-260–280 SF, elevator, between TI and bridge on Adlerplatz, tel. 071-787-1389, fax 071-787-1365, www .adlerhotel.ch).

$$$ Restaurant Hotel Traube (not Hotel Restaurant Taube), two blocks from the TI, is another comfortable hotel, with seven tastefully decorated rooms above a fine restaurant (Sb-85–110 SF, Db-150–180 SF, Marktgasse 7, tel. 071-787-1407, fax 071-787-2419, www.hotel -traube.ch, info@hotel-traube.ch).

$$ Zimmer: To experience a pleasant Swiss suburban neighborhood, consider the following: **Haus Lydia,** a six-room, Appenzell-style home filled with tourist information and a woodsy folk atmosphere, is on the edge of town and includes a garden and a powerful mountain view. Its crisp, newly renovated rooms are a fine value if you have a car or don't mind a 20-minute walk from the center (Sb-58 SF, Db-90 SF, great breakfast; east of town over bridge, past Mercedes-Esso station, take next right and go 600 yards, Eggerstanden Strasse 53, tel. 071-787-4233, fax 071-367-2170, www.hauslydia.ch, friendly Frau Mock-Inauen); she also rents a roomy apartment by the week (Db-61–88 SF). **Gastezimmer Koller-Rempfler** is a family-friendly, traditional, five-room place several blocks before Haus Lydia (Db-85–95 SF, Tb-115–120 SF, 5 SF less for 3-night stays, no CC, Eggerstanden Strasse 9, tel. 071-787-2117, niklauskoller@hotmail.com, NSE).

Eating in the Town of Appenzell

The Appenzeller beer is famous, good, and about the only thing cheap in the region. Ideally, eat dinner up in Ebenalp at **Berggasthaus Aescher,** even if you're staying in Appenzell town (see "Sleeping High in Ebenalp," page 523; last lift down at 19:00 in summer, earlier off-season).

In Appenzell, many good restaurants cluster around Lands-gemeindeplatz, where residents gather the last Sunday of each April to vote on local issues by show of hands. (The rest of the year, it's a parking lot.) The first four restaurants are within a block of this town square, just a few blocks up Hauptgasse from the TI (away from the bridge). All restaurants are open daily from about 8:00 to 24:00 unless otherwise noted.

For pleasant dining indoors or out, consider **Restaurant Hotel Traube** (closed Mon, see "Sleeping in the Town of Appenzell," page 523). **Hotel Appenzell** serves fine Swiss-style vegetarian meals in an elegant setting (at corner of square closest to TI, tel. 071-788-1515). For a more traditional Appenzeller atmosphere, join locals playing cards at **Restaurant Marktplatz** (closed Thu–Fri, on small parking lot across from Landsgemeindeplatz fountain, tel. 071-787-1204) and **Gasthaus Hof** (next to Hotel Appenzell, tel. 071-787-2210). If the weather's nice or you just feel like a walk, **Gasthaus Freudenberg** has reasonable meals and great views over Appenzell from outdoor tables (closed Wed and Nov, about a 15-min walk south from center, go under train station, turn right and follow the road next to the tracks until it jogs left, head up the street and continue straight to gravel path up the hill, tel. 071-787-1240).

TRANSPORTATION CONNECTIONS

From Appenzell town by train to: Zürich (2/hr, 2.25 hrs, transfer in Gossau or St. Gallen), **Bern** (hrly, 3.25 hrs, transfer in Gossau), **Interlaken** (hrly, 4.5 hrs, 2 transfers including Gossau or St. Gallen and Zürich or Bern), **Lausanne** (2/hr, 5 hrs, transfer in Gossau or St. Gallen), **Munich** (3/day, 4.5 hrs, transfer in St. Gallen).

Route Tips for Drivers

Hall to Appenzell (130 miles): From the Austria/Switzerland border town of Feldkirch, it's an easy, scenic drive through Altstätten and Gais to Appenzell. At the Swiss border, a gas station, or a post office, you must buy an annual road-use permit for 40 SF (or €30) to drive on the Swiss autobahn system (anyone without this tax sticker is likely to be fined).

From picturesque Altstätten, wind up a steep mountain pass and your world becomes a miniature train set. The Stoss railroad station, straddling the summit of the pass, has glorious views. Park here, cross to the chapel, and walk through the meadow—past munching cows—to the monument that celebrates an Appenzeller victory over Hapsburg Austria. From this spectacular spot, you can see the Rhine Valley, Liechtenstein, and Austrian Alps—and feast on a memorable picnic.

Side-Trip through Liechtenstein: If you must see the tiny and touristy country of Liechtenstein, take this 30-minute detour: From Feldkirch, drive south on E77 (follow FL signs) and go through Schaan to Vaduz, the capital. Park near the city hall, post office, and TI. Passports can be stamped (for 2 SF) in the TI (tel. from Switzerland 00423/232-1443). Liechtenstein's banks (open until 16:30) sell Swiss francs at uniform and acceptable rates. The prince looks down on his four-by-12-mile country from his castle, a 20-minute hike above Vaduz (castle closed to visitors but offers a fine view; catch trail from Café Berg). To leave, cross the Rhine at Rotenboden, immediately get on the autobahn and drive north from Sevelen to the Oberriet exit, and check another country off your list.

Appenzell to Interlaken/Gimmelwald (120 miles): It's a three-hour drive from Appenzell to Ballenberg (Swiss Open-Air Museum) and another hour from there to the Gimmelwald lift. Head out of Appenzell town following signs to Herisau/Wattwil. A few scenic miles out of town, in Stein, *Schaukäserei* signs direct you to the big, modern cheese dairy. From there, head for Wattwil. Drive through Ricken into the town of Rapperswil. Once you're in Rapperswil, follow the green signs to Gotthard/Zürich over the long bridge, then continue southward, following signs to Einsiedeln and Gotthard. You'll go through the town of Schwyz, the historic core of Switzerland that gave its name to the country.

From Brunnen, one of the busiest, most impressive, and expensive-to-build roads in Switzerland wings you along the Urnersee. It's dangerously scenic, so stop at the parking place after the first tunnel (on right, opposite Stoos turnoff), where you can enjoy the view and a rare Turkish toilet. Follow signs to Gotthard through Flüelen, then autobahn for Luzern, vanishing into a long tunnel that should make you feel a little better about your 40 SF autobahn sticker. Exit at the Stans-Nord exit (signs to Interlaken). Go along the Alpnachersee south toward Sarnen. Continue past Sarnensee to Brienzwiler before Brienz. A sign at Brienzwiler will direct you to the Ballenberg Freilicht (Swiss Open-Air Museum)/Ballenberg Ost. You can park here, but I prefer the west entrance, a few minutes down the road near Brienz.

From Brienzwiler, take the autobahn to Interlaken along the south side of Lake Brienz. Cruise through the old resort town, down Interlaken's main street. From the Ost Bahnhof (east train station), drive past the cow field with a great Eiger-Jungfrau view on your left and grand old hotels, the TI, post office, and banks on your right, to the West Bahnhof (west train station) at the opposite end of town. If stopping in Interlaken, park there. Otherwise, follow signs to Lauterbrunnen. Gimmelwald is a 30-minute drive and a five-minute gondola ride away.

APPENDIX

Let's Talk Telephones

For specifics on Germany, Austria, and Switzerland, see "Telephones" in this book's introduction.

Making Calls within a European Country: About half of all European countries use area codes (like we do); the other half use a direct-dial system without area codes.

To make calls within a country that uses a direct-dial system (Belgium, the Czech Republic, Denmark, France, Italy, Portugal, Norway, Spain, and Switzerland), you dial the same number whether you're calling across the country or across the street.

In countries that use area codes (such as Austria, Britain, Finland, Germany, Ireland, Netherlands, and Sweden), you dial the local number when calling within a city, and you add the area code if calling long-distance within the country.

Making International Calls: You always start with the international access code (011 if you're calling from the United States or Canada, or 00 from anywhere in Europe), then dial the country code of the country you're calling (see chart below).

What you dial next depends on the phone system of the country you're calling. If the country uses area codes, drop the initial 0 of the area code, then dial the rest of the number.

Countries that use direct-dial systems (no area codes) vary in how they're accessed internationally by phone. For instance, if you're making an international call to the Czech Republic, Denmark, Italy, Norway, Portugal, or Spain, simply dial the international access code, country code, and phone number. But if you're calling Belgium, France, or Switzerland, drop the initial 0 of the phone number.

European Calling Chart

Just smile and dial, using this key:
AC = Area Code, LN = Local Number.

European Country	Calling long distance within ...	Calling from the U.S.A./ Canada to ...	Calling from a European country to ...
Austria	AC + LN	011 + 43 + AC (without the initial zero) + LN	00 + 43 + AC (without the initial zero) + LN
Belgium	LN	011 + 32 + LN (without initial zero)	00 + 32 + LN (without initial zero)
Britain	AC + LN	011 + 44 + AC (without initial zero) + LN	00 + 44 + AC (without initial zero) + LN
Czech Republic	LN	011 + 420 + LN	00 + 420 + LN
Denmark	LN	011 + 45 + LN	00 + 45 + LN
Estonia	LN	011 + 372 + LN	00 + 372 + LN
Finland	AC + LN	011 + 358 + AC (without initial zero) + LN	00 + 358 + AC (without initial zero) + LN
France	LN	011 + 33 + LN (without initial zero)	00 + 33 + LN (without initial zero)
Germany	AC + LN	011 + 49 + AC (without initial zero) + LN	00 + 49 + AC (without initial zero) + LN
Gibraltar	LN	011 + 350 + LN	00 + 350 + LN From Spain: 9567 + LN
Greece	LN	011 + 30 + LN	00 + 30 + LN

European Country	Calling long distance within ...	Calling from the U.S.A./ Canada to ...	Calling from a European country to ...
Ireland	AC + LN	011 + 353 + AC (without initial zero) + LN	00 + 353 + AC (without initial zero) + LN
Italy	LN	011 + 39 + LN	00 + 39 + LN
Morocco	LN	011 + 212 + LN (without initial zero)	00 + 212 + LN (without initial zero)
Netherlands	AC + LN	011 + 31 + AC (without initial zero) + LN	00 + 31 + AC (without initial zero) + LN
Norway	LN	011 + 47 + LN	00 + 47 + LN
Portugal	LN	011 + 351 + LN	00 + 351 + LN
Spain	LN	011 + 34 + LN	00 + 34 + LN
Sweden	AC + LN	011 + 46 + AC (without initial zero) + LN	00 + 46 + AC (without initial zero) + LN
Switzerland	LN	011 + 41 + LN (without initial zero)	00 + 41 + LN (without initial zero)
Turkey	AC (if no initial zero is included, add one) + LN	011 + 90 + AC (without initial zero) + LN	00 + 90 + AC (without initial zero) + LN

- The instructions above apply whether you're calling a fixed phone or cell phone.

- The international access codes (the first numbers you dial when making an international call) are 011 if you're calling from the U.S.A./Canada, or 00 if you're calling from anywhere in Europe.

- To call the U.S.A. or Canada from Europe, dial 00, then 1 (the country code for the U.S.A. and Canada), then the area code and number. In short, 00 + 1 + AC + LN = Hi, Mom!

International Access Codes

When dialing direct, first dial the international access code of the country you're calling from. For the United States and Canada, it's 011. All European countries use 00 as their international access code.

Country Codes

After you've dialed the international access code, dial the code of the country you're calling.

Austria—43	Ireland—353
Belgium—32	Italy—39
Britain—44	Morocco—212
Canada—1	Netherlands—31
Croatia—385	Norway—47
Czech Rep—420	Poland—48
Denmark—45	Portugal—351
Estonia—372	Slovenia—386
Finland—358	Spain—34
France—33	Sweden—46
Germany—49	Switzerland—41
Gibraltar—350	Turkey—90
Greece—30	U.S.A.—1

Directory Assistance

• Austria: national—16, international—08, train info—051717
• Germany: national—11833, international—11834,
train info—01805/996-633
• German tourist offices: local code, then 19433
• Switzerland: national—111, international—191,
train info—0900/300-300
• Swiss info for Germany/Austria: 192

U.S. Embassies

Austria, in Vienna: Marriott Building 4th floor, Gartenbaupromenade 2, tel. 01/313-390, www.usembassy.at
Germany, in Berlin: Clayallee 170, tel. 030/832-9233, www.usembassy.de
Switzerland, in Bern: Jubilaeumsstrasse 93, tel. 031-357-7234, www.us-embassy.ch

Festivals and Public Holidays

For specifics, contact the National Tourist Offices (listed in this book's Introduction) and check these Web sites: www.whatsonwhen.com, www.whatsgoingon.com, and www.festivals.com. Vienna and Salzburg have music festivals nearly every month.

2004

JANUARY

S	M	T	W	T	F	S
				1	2	3
4	5	6	7	8	9	10
11	12	13	14	15	16	17
18	19	20	21	22	23	24
25	26	27	28	29	30	31

FEBRUARY

S	M	T	W	T	F	S
1	2	3	4	5	6	7
8	9	10	11	12	13	14
15	16	17	18	19	20	21
22	23	24	25	26	27	28
29						

MARCH

S	M	T	W	T	F	S
	1	2	3	4	5	6
7	8	9	10	11	12	13
14	15	16	17	18	19	20
21	22	23	24	25	26	27
28	29	30	31			

APRIL

S	M	T	W	T	F	S
				1	2	3
4	5	6	7	8	9	10
11	12	13	14	15	16	17
18	19	20	21	22	23	24
25	26	27	28	29	30	

MAY

S	M	T	W	T	F	S
						1
2	3	4	5	6	7	8
9	10	11	12	13	14	15
16	17	18	19	20	21	22
$^{23}/_{30}$ $^{24}/_{31}$	25	26	27	28	29	

JUNE

S	M	T	W	T	F	S
		1	2	3	4	5
6	7	8	9	10	11	12
13	14	15	16	17	18	19
20	21	22	23	24	25	26
27	28	29	30			

JULY

S	M	T	W	T	F	S
				1	2	3
4	5	6	7	8	9	10
11	12	13	14	15	16	17
18	19	20	21	22	23	24
25	26	27	28	29	30	31

AUGUST

S	M	T	W	T	F	S
1	2	3	4	5	6	7
8	9	10	11	12	13	14
15	16	17	18	19	20	21
22	23	24	25	26	27	28
29	30	31				

SEPTEMBER

S	M	T	W	T	F	S
			1	2	3	4
5	6	7	8	9	10	11
12	13	14	15	16	17	18
19	20	21	22	23	24	25
26	27	28	29	30		

OCTOBER

S	M	T	W	T	F	S
					1	2
3	4	5	6	7	8	9
10	11	12	13	14	15	16
17	18	19	20	21	22	23
$^{24}/_{31}$	25	26	27	28	29	30

NOVEMBER

S	M	T	W	T	F	S
	1	2	3	4	5	6
7	8	9	10	11	12	13
14	15	16	17	18	19	20
21	22	23	24	25	26	27
28	29	30				

DECEMBER

S	M	T	W	T	F	S
			1	2	3	4
5	6	7	8	9	10	11
12	13	14	15	16	17	18
19	20	21	22	23	24	25
26	27	28	29	30	31	

Jan	Perchtenlaufen (winter festival, parades)
	Tirol & Salzburg, Austria
Jan–Feb	Fasching (carnival season, balls, parades)
	Austria, Germany
Easter	Easter Festival
	Salzburg
May	May Day (on 1st) with maypole dances
	Austria, Germany
	Vienna Festival of Arts and Music
June	Frankfurt Summertime Festival (arts)
	Master Draught (play, procession, festival)
	Rothenburg, Germany
Late June	Midsummer Eve Celebrations
	Austria

July	Salzburg Festival (music)
	Montreux International Jazz Festival
Aug 1	Swiss National Day, with parades and fireworks
Sept–Oct	Oktoberfest (starts third weekend, runs 16 days)
	Munich
	Berlin Festwochen (arts festival)
	Imperial City Festival (costumes, parade, fireworks on second weekend)
	Rothenburg, Germany
Oct	Berlin Jazz Festival
Nov	St. Martin's Day Celebrations (feasts)
	Austria, Bavaria
	Onion Market Fair
	Bern, Switzerland
Dec	St. Nicholas Day parades, Austria
	L'Escalade (folk festival, parades)
	Geneva, Switzerland
	Christmas Fairs
	Austria, Germany, Switzerland

Climate

First line, average daily low; second line, average daily high; third line, days of no rain.

J	F	M	A	M	J	J	A	S	O	N	D

AUSTRIA • Vienna

J	F	M	A	M	J	J	A	S	O	N	D
25°	28°	30°	42°	50°	56°	60°	59°	53°	44°	37°	30°
34°	38°	47°	58°	67°	73°	76°	75°	68°	56°	45°	37°
16	17	18	17	18	16	18	18	20	18	16	16

GERMANY • Berlin

J	F	M	A	M	J	J	A	S	O	N	D
26°	26°	31°	39°	47°	53°	57°	56°	50°	42°	36°	29°
35°	37°	46°	56°	66°	72°	75°	74°	68°	56°	45°	38°
14	13	19	17	19	17	17	17	18	17	14	16

GERMANY • Munich

J	F	M	A	M	J	J	A	S	O	N	D
23°	23°	30°	38°	45°	51°	55°	54°	48°	40°	33°	26°
35°	38°	48°	56°	64°	70°	74°	73°	67°	56°	44°	36°
15	12	18	15	16	13	15	15	17	18	15	16

SWITZERLAND • Bern

J	F	M	A	M	J	J	A	S	O	N	D
29°	30°	36°	42°	49°	55°	58°	58°	53°	44°	37°	31°
38°	42°	51°	59°	66°	73°	77°	76°	69°	58°	47°	40°
20	19	22	21	20	19	22	20	20	21	19	21

Numbers and Stumblers

• Europeans write a few of their numbers differently than we do.
1 = 1 , 4 = 4 , 7 = 7 . Learn the difference or miss your train.
• In Europe, dates appear as day/month/year, so Christmas is
25/12/04.
• Commas are decimal points and decimals commas. A dollar and a
half is $1,50, and there are 5.280 feet in a mile.
• When counting with fingers, start with your thumb. If you hold up
your first finger to request one item, you'll probably get two.
• What Americans call the second floor of a building is the first floor in
Europe.
• Europeans keep the left "lane" open for passing on escalators and
moving sidewalks. Keep to the right.

Temperature Conversion

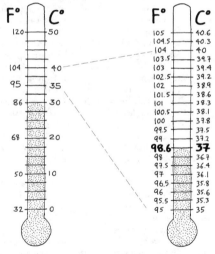

FOR WEATHER   FOR HEALTH

Metric Conversion (approximate)

1 inch = 25 millimeters   32 degrees F = 0 degrees C
1 foot = 0.3 meter   82 degrees F = about 28 degrees C
1 yard = 0.9 meter   1 ounce = 28 grams
1 mile = 1.6 kilometers   1 kilogram = 2.2 pounds
1 centimeter = 0.4 inch   1 quart = 0.95 liter
1 meter = 39.4 inches   1 square yard = 0.8 square meter
1 kilometer = .62 mile   1 acre = 0.4 hectare

Basic German Survival Phrases

English	German	Phonetics
Good day.	**Guten Tag.**	**goo**-ten tahg
Do you speak English?	**Sprechen Sie Englisch?**	**shprekh**-en zee **eng**-lish
Yes. / No.	**Ja. / Nein.**	yah / nīn
I (don't) understand.	**Ich verstehe (nicht).**	ikh fehr-**shtay**-heh (nikht)
Please.	**Bitte.**	**bit**-teh
Thank you.	**Danke.**	**dahng**-keh
I'm sorry.	**Es tut mir leid.**	es toot meer līt
Excuse me.	**Entschuldigung.**	ent-**shool**-dee-goong
(No) problem.	**(Kein) Problem.**	(kīn) proh-**blaym**
(Very) good.	**(Sehr) gut.**	(zehr) goot
Goodbye.	**Auf Wiedersehen.**	owf **vee**-der-zayn
one / two	**eins / zwei**	īns / tsvī
three / four	**drei / vier**	drī / feer
five / six	**fünf / sechs**	fewnf / zex
seven / eight	**sieben / acht**	zee-ben / ahkht
nine / ten	**neun / zehn**	noyn / tsayn
How much is it?	**Wieviel kostet das?**	**vee**-feel **kos**-tet dahs
Write it?	**Schreiben?**	**shrī**-ben
Is it free?	**Ist es umsonst?**	ist es oom-**zohnst**
Included?	**Inklusive?**	in-kloo-**see**-veh
Where can I	**Wo kann ich**	voh kahn ikh
buy / find...?	**kaufen / finden...?**	**kow**-fen / **fin**-den
I'd like /	**Ich hätte gern /**	ikh **het**-teh gehrn
We'd like...	**Wir hätten gern...**	veer **het**-ten gehrn
...a room.	**...ein Zimmer.**	īn **tsim**-mer
...the bill.	**...die Rechnung.**	dee **rekh**-noong
...a ticket to ___.	**...eine Fahrkarte nach ___.**	ī-neh **far**-kar-teh nahkh
Is it possible?	**Ist es möglich?**	ist es **mur**-glikh
Where is...?	**Wo ist..?**	voh ist
...the train station	**...der Bahnhof**	dehr **bahn**-hohf
...the bus station	**...der Busbahnhof**	dehr **boos**-bahn-hof
...tourist information	**...das Touristen-informationsbüro**	dahs too-ris-ten-in-for-maht-see-**ohns**-bew-roh
...toilet	**...die Toilette**	dee toh-**leh**-teh
men	**herren**	**hehr**-ren
women	**damen**	**dah**-men
left / right	**links / rechts**	links / rekhts
straight	**geradeaus**	geh-rah-deh-**ows**
When is this open / closed?	**Um wieviel Uhr ist hier geöffnet / geschlossen?**	oom **vee**-feel oor ist heer geh-**urf**-net / geh-**shlos**-sen
At what time?	**Um wieviel Uhr?**	oom **vee**-feel oor
Just a moment.	**Moment.**	moh-**ment**
now / soon / later	**jetzt / bald / später**	yetzt / bahld / **shpay**-ter
today / tomorrow	**heute / morgen**	**hoy**-teh / **mor**-gen

When using the phonetics, pronounce ī as the long i sound in "light."

Road Scholar Feedback for GERMANY, AUSTRIA & SWITZERLAND 2004

We're all in the same travelers' school of hard knocks. Your feedback helps us improve this guidebook for future travelers. Please fill this out (or use the online version at www.ricksteves.com/feedback), attach more info or any tips/favorite discoveries if you like, and send it to us. As thanks for your help, we'll send you our quarterly travel newsletter free for one year. Thanks! Rick

Of the recommended accommodations/restaurants used, which was:

Best _____

     Why? _____

Worst _____

     Why? _____

Of the sights/experiences/destinations recommended by this book, which was:

Most overrated _____

     Why? _____

Most underrated _____

     Why? _____

Best ways to improve this book:

_____

_____

I'd like a free newsletter subscription:

_____ Yes   _____ No   _____ Already on list

_____
Name

_____
Address

_____
City, State, Zip

_____
E-mail Address

Please send to: ETBD, Box 2009, Edmonds, WA 98020

Faxing Your Hotel Reservation

Use this handy form for your fax or find it online at
www.ricksteves.com/reservation. Photocopy and fax away.

One-Page Fax

To: _____ @ _____
         hotel   fax

From: _____ @ _____
          name   fax

Today's date: ___ /_____ /___
               day   month year

Dear Hotel _____,

Please make this reservation for me:

Name: _____

Total # of people: _____   # of rooms: _____   # of nights: _____

Arriving: ___ /_____ /___   My time of arrival (24-hr clock): _____
           day month year   (I will telephone if I will be late)

Departing: ___ /_____ /___
            day month year

Room(s): Single___ Double___ Twin___ Triple___ Quad___

With: Toilet___ Shower___ Bath___ Sink only___

Special needs: View___ Quiet___ Cheapest___ Ground Floor___

Credit card: Visa___ MasterCard___ American Express___

Card #: _____

Expiration date:_____

Name on card: _____

You may charge me for the first night as a deposit. Please fax, e-mail, or mail
me confirmation of my reservation, along with the type of room
reserved, the price, and whether the price includes breakfast. Please also
inform me of your cancellation policy. Thank you.

_____
Signature

_____
Name

_____
Address

_____
City   State   Zip Code   Country

_____
E-mail Address

INDEX

RICK STEVES

RICK STEVES is on a mission: to help make European travel accessible and meaningful for Americans. Rick has spent 100 days every year since 1973 exploring Europe. He's researched and written 24 travel guidebooks. He writes and hosts the public television series *Rick Steves Europe*, now in its seventh season. With the help of his hardworking staff of 60 at Europe through the Back Door, Rick organizes and leads tours of Europe and offers an information-packed Web site (www.ricksteves.com). Rick, his wife (and favorite travel partner) Anne, and their two teenage children, Andy and Jackie, call Edmonds, just north of Seattle, home.

FREE-SPIRITED TOURS FROM

Rick Steves

Small Groups
Great Guides
Guaranteed Prices
No Grumps

**Best of Europe ■ Eastern Europe ■ Turkey
Italy ■ Village Italy ■ South Italy ■ Britain
Ireland ■ France ■ Heart of France
South of France ■ Spain/Portugal
Germany/Austria/Switzerland
Scandinavia ■ London ■ Paris ■ Rome
Venice ■ Florence ■ Prague ■ Barcelona**

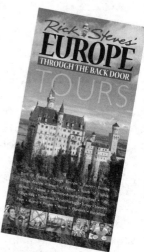

Looking for a one, two, or three-week tour that's run in the Rick Steves style?
Check out Rick Steves' educational, experiential tours of Europe.

Rick's tours are an excellent value compared to "mainstream" tours. Here's a taste of what you'll get...

■ **Small groups:** With just 24-28 travelers, you'll go where typical groups of 40-50 can only dream.

■ **Big buses:** You'll travel in a full-size 40-50 seat bus, with plenty of empty seats for you to spread out and be comfortable.

■ **Great guides:** Our guides are hand-picked by Rick Steves for their wealth of knowledge and giddy enthusiasm for Europe.

■ **No tips or kickbacks:** To keep your guide and driver 100% focused on giving you the best travel experience, we pay them good salaries—and prohibit them from taking tips and merchant kickbacks.

■ **All sightseeing:** Your price includes all group sightseeing, with no hidden charges.

■ **Central hotels:** You'll stay in Rick's favorite small, characteristic, locally-run hotels in the center of each city, within walking distance of the sights you came to see.

■ **Peace of mind:** Your tour price is guaranteed for 2004; deposits are 100% refundable for two weeks; we include prorated trip interruption/cancellation coverage; single travelers don't need to pay an extra supplement; you can easily save a seat online at www.ricksteves.com.

Interested? Visit **www.ricksteves.com** or call (425) 771-8303 for a free copy of Rick Steves' 2004 Tour Catalog!

Rick Steves' Europe Through the Back Door
130 Fourth Avenue North, PO Box 2009, Edmonds, WA 98020 USA
Phone: (425) 771-8303 ■ Fax: (425) 771-0833 ■ www.ricksteves.com

Free, fresh travel tips, all year long.

Visit **www.ricksteves.com**
to get Rick's free
64-page newsletter... and more!

Rick Steves

COUNTRY GUIDES 2004

Best of Europe
Best of Eastern Europe
France
Germany, Austria & Switzerland
Great Britain
Ireland
Italy
Scandinavia
Spain & Portugal

CITY GUIDES 2004

Amsterdam, Bruges & Brussels
Florence & Tuscany
London
Paris
Provence & The French Riviera
Rome
Venice

MORE EUROPE FROM RICK STEVES

Europe 101
Europe Through the Back Door 2004
Mona Winks
Postcards from Europe

More Savvy. More Surprising. More Fun.

PHRASE BOOKS & DICTIONARIES

French, Italian & German
French
German
Italian
Portuguese
Spanish

VHS RICK STEVES' EUROPE

The Best of Ireland
Bulgaria, Eastern Turkey, Slovenia
    & Croatia
The Heart of Italy
London & Paris
Prague, Amsterdam & the Swiss Alps
Romantic Germany & Berlin
Rome, Caesar's Rome, Sicily
South England, Heart of England & Scotland
Southwest Germany & Portugal
Travel Skills Special
Venice & Veneto 2003

DVD RICK STEVES' EUROPE

Rick Steves' Europe
    All Thirty Shows 2000-2003
Britain & Ireland
Exotic Europe
Germany, the Swiss Alps
    & Travel Skills
Italy

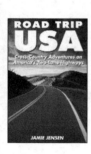